MECKLENBURG-
LOWER
POMERANIA

Rostock

Schwerin

BRANDENBURG

Berlin

Potsdam

Magdeburg

SAXONY-ANHALT

EASTERN
GERMANY

Leipzig

Erfurt

Dresden

THURINGIA

SAXONY

Nürnberg

BAVARIA

Munich

D0428780

EYEWITNESS TRAVEL
GERMANY

EYEWITNESS TRAVEL

GERMANY

MAIN CONTRIBUTORS: JOANNA EGERT-ROMANOWSKA
AND MAŁGORZATA OMILANOWSKA

LONDON, NEW YORK,
MELBOURNE, MUNICH AND DELHI
www.dk.com

PRODUCED BY Wydwnictwo Wiedza i Życie, Warsaw
CONTRIBUTORS Małgorzata Omilanowska, Marek Stańczyk,
Tomasz Torbus, Hanna Köster, Teresa Czerniewicz-Umer
CARTOGRAPHERS Kartographie Huber (Munich),
Magdalena Polak, Dariusz Romanowski
PHOTOGRAPHERS Adam Hajder, Dorota and Mariusz Jarymowiczowie,
Wojciech Mędrzak, Tomasz Myśluk, Paweł Wójcik
ILLUSTRATORS Lena Maminajszwili, Paweł Marczak,
Andrzej Wielgosz, Bohdan Wróblewski, Magdalena Żmudzińska DTP
DESIGNERS Paweł Pasternak, Paweł Kamiński
EDITORS Teresa Czerniewicz-Umer, Joanna Egert-Romanowska
PRODUCTION Anna Kożurno-Królikowska
DESIGNERS Ewa Roguska, Piotr Kiedrowski
Dorling Kindersley Limited
EDITORS Sylvia Goulding, Irene Lyford
TRANSLATORS Magda Hannay, Ian Wisniewski
DTP DESIGNERS Jason Little, Conrad Van Dyk
PRODUCTION Marie Ingledew

Printed and bound by Vivar Printing Sdn Bhd, Malaysia

First American Edition 2001
12 13 14 15 10 9 8 7 6 5 4 3 2 1

Published in the United States by Dorling Kindersley Limited,
80 Strand London WCR2 0RL, UK

Reprinted with revisions 2003, 2004, 2005, 2006, 2007, 2008, 2010, 2012
Copyright © 2001, 2012 Dorling Kindersley Limited, London

ISSN 1542-1554

ISBN 978-0-75668-559-1

Front cover main image:
Ramsau in Bavaria, Germany

THROUGHOUT THIS BOOK, FLOORS ARE REFERRED TO IN ACCORDANCE WITH
EUROPEAN USAGE, I.E., THE "FIRST FLOOR" IS THE FLOOR ABOVE GROUND LEVEL.

MIX
Paper from
responsible sources
FSC
www.fsc.org   FSC™ C018179

The information in this
Dorling Kindersley Travel Guide is checked regularly.
Every effort has been made to ensure that this book is as up-to-date
as possible at the time of going to press. Some details, however, such
as telephone numbers, opening hours, prices, gallery hanging
arrangements and travel information are liable to change. The
publishers cannot accept responsibility for any consequences arising
from the use of this book, nor for any material on third party
websites, and cannot guarantee that any website address in this book
will be a suitable source of travel information. We value the views
and suggestions of our readers very highly. Please write to: Publisher,
DK Eyewitness Travel Guides, Dorling Kindersley, 80 Strand, London
WC2R 0RL, UK, or email: travelguides@dk.com.

◁ Church in Bavaria nestled at the foothills of the Alps

CONTENTS

INTRODUCING GERMANY

Heraldic shield over the entrance
to the Nuremberg town hall

BERLIN AREA BY AREA

EASTERN GERMANY

Picturesque landscape in Mecklenburg

Statue of a dancing figure, Stadtmuseum in Munich (see p214)

Mainz Cathedral
(see pp350–51)

HOW TO USE THIS GUIDE

This guide will help you to get the most out of a visit to Germany, providing expert recommendations as well as thoroughly researched practical information. The first section, *Introducing Germany*, locates the country geographically and provides an invaluable historical and cultural context. Succeeding sections describe

the main sights and attractions of the different regions and major cities. Feature spreads, with maps and photographs, focus on important sights. Information on accommodation and restaurants is provided in *Travellers' Needs*, while the *Survival Guide* has useful tips on everything you need to know from money to getting around.

BERLIN

This section is divided into two parts: East and West. Sights outside the centre are described in the section *Around Berlin*. All sights are numbered and plotted on a map of the region. Detailed information for each sight is given in numerical order to make it easy to locate within the chapter.

Sights at a Glance describes, by category, buildings in a particular area: Historic Streets and Buildings, Museums and Galleries, Churches, Parks and Gardens.

2 Street-by-Street Map *gives a bird's-eye view of each sightseeing area described in the section.*

Stars indicate the sights that no visitor should miss.

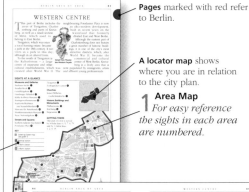

Pages marked with red refer to Berlin.

A locator map shows where you are in relation to the city plan.

1 Area Map *For easy reference the sights in each area are numbered.*

A suggested route for a walk is marked with a broken red line.

3 Detailed Information *All the sights of Berlin are described individually. Addresses, telephone numbers, opening hours, admission charges and information on how to get there are given for each sight. The key to symbols is shown on the back flap.*

1 Introduction
The landscape, history and character of each region are described, showing how the area has changed through the ages. It also outlines the sights on offer for visitors.

GERMANY AREA BY AREA
In this guide, Germany is divided into 13 areas, each of which is covered in a separate section. The most interesting cities, towns, villages and sights in the area are marked on the Area Map.

2 Regional Map
This shows the main roads and the general topography of the area. All sights are numbered, and there are also details on how to get there.

Boxes contain additional information about sights.

Colour coding at the edge of every page makes it easy to find each particular region.

3 Detailed Information
All major towns, places of interest and other tourist sights are listed in order and numbered according to the Regional Map. Each entry contains information on important sights.

A Visitors' Checklist for each of the main sights provides practical information to help you plan your visit.

4 Major Sights
At least two pages are dedicated to each major sight. Historic buildings are dissected in order to show their interiors. Interesting towns or town centres have street maps with the main sights indicated and described.

INTRODUCING GERMANY

DISCOVERING GERMANY

Germany is a country of marked contrasts and this is nowhere more apparent than in its geographic diversity. Modern cities of glass and steel sit only a few minutes-drive from ancient forests populated with ruined castles. From the windswept coasts of the northern part of the

Sculpture on a Berlin bridge

country to the alpine splendour of the southern states, Germany's natural beauty is multi-faceted. The same is true at the cultural level, where many regional differences can be seen in the architecture, dress and food. Visitors are certain to be impressed with the variety that Germany has to offer.

The imposing steel and glass dome of the Reichstag in Berlin

BERLIN

- **Checkpoint Charlie and the Kaiser-Wihelm-Gedächtnis-Kirche**
- **The Reichstag and Unter den Linden**
- **Shopping at KaDeWe**

In terms of its museums, other cultural attractions, architecture and shopping, Berlin is on a par with Paris, London and New York. **Checkpoint Charlie** (*see p80*) and the **Kaiser-Wilhelm-Gedächtnis-Kirche** (*see p86*) are two of Berlin's most famous memorials to the aftermath of World War II and are not to be missed. As the political epicentre of Germany, Berlin hosts a variety of diplomatic visitors throughout the year and provides a home to the country's parliament, the Bundestag, in the renovated **Reichstag** (*see p93*) building. A stroll along **Unter den Linden** (*see pp66–7*)

boulevard reveals a host of architectural and historical landmarks. Shopping opportunities abound, not least at **KaDeWe** (*see pp106–7*), one of the largest and most exclusively stocked shopping centres in Europe.

BRANDENBURG

- **Spreewald Biosphere Preserve**
- **Potsdam's royal splendour**
- **Schloss Sanssouci**

The federal state of Brandenburg is located in eastern Germany and surrounds the vibrant city of Berlin. The region has long been the country asylum for weary Berliners and it is well-known for its crystal-clear lakes and waterways, broad expanses of country-side, verdant tree-lined roads, fruit orchards and unspoilt natural scenery. Its sleepy villages and cultural attractions are

historically significant and the UNESCO protected **Spreewald Biosphere Preserve** (*see p141*) is geographically and culturally unique in Europe. Here you can punt between the island farmsteads of the area. The regional capital and former garrison town, **Potsdam** (*see pp134–5*), is one of Europe's most magnificent royal cities, filled with baroque architectural wonders commissioned by the Prussian kings, like **Schloss Sanssouci** (*see pp136–9*).

SAXONY-ANHALT

- **Historic Magdeburg**
- **Lutherstadt Wittenberg**
- **Wörlitz Park**

Located close to the geographic centre of Germany is the Eastern German state of Saxony-Anhalt. Few other German regions offer a similar variety of historical tourist

Schloss Sanssouci in Potsdam, Brandenburg

◁ Grapevines stretching as far as the eye can see in the North Rhine-Palatinate

A bridge over one of the many waterways in Wörlitz Park

attractions in such a small area. Prehistoric, medieval, Reformation and Renaissance sights are all within close visiting distance and often within the same towns. In **Magdeburg** *(see p152)*, the Monastery of Our Lady and the Cathedral are typical of the Gothic architecture found in the area. Saxony Anhalt is the birthplace of the Reformation with Martin Luther's hometown of Eisleben and the city of **Wittenberg** *(see pp154–5)* where he first posted his 95 propositions. The region also has some beautiful rural areas with a number of parks and gardens, most notably **Wörlitz Park** *(see pp156–7)*, which is well worth a visit.

SAXONY

- **Meissen porcelain**
- **Erzgebirge mountain region**
- **Dresden's restored grandeur**

Divided by the river Elbe, Saxony is considered Germany's gateway to the East with borders to both Poland and the Czech Republic. Saxony is also known for its unique craft traditions, the most famous of which is porcelain from **Meissen** *(see p167)*. The **Sächsische Silberstraße** *(see p166)*, which runs through the old silver mining route in the Erzgebirge mountains,

offers delightful scenery, while the beautiful buildings of **Dresden** *(see pp168–77)* continue to enchant. The city was all but destroyed in the war, but much has been done to restore it to its former glory.

A tree-lined hiking trail in the Thuringian Forest

THURINGIA

- **Thuringian Forest**
- **The mighty Wartburg**
- **Weimar's literary culture**

Thuringia is one of the least known regions of Germany, but should not be missed. Home to several natural reserves encompassing extensive walking trails in the **Thuringian Forest** *(see pp190–91)*, it is one of Germany's top destinations for hiking enthusiasts. In **Eisenach** *(see pp186–7)*, the Wartburg fortress dominates

the city – Wagner immortalized it in his opera *Tannhäuser* and Martin Luther translated the New Testament into German here. The city of **Weimar** *(see pp194–5)*, meanwhile, offers a glimpse into the lives of German authors Goethe and Schiller, who resided in this UNESCO heritage site, famous for its classical architecture.

MUNICH

- **Museums and architecture**
- **Hofbräuhaus Beer Hall**
- **Home to Oktoberfest**

"Munich nestles between art and beer like a village between hills," wrote Heinrich Heine some 150 years ago. Munich has much more to offer than just great beer, however. Composed of five central districts, the city manages to marry old Bavarian tradition with a vibrant modern life. The **Marienplatz** *(see pp210–11)* in the city's old town is a prime jumping-off point for seeing the city's beautiful architecture and numerous museums. There is a diverse music scene and a plethora of excellent restaurants. Visitors will also want to visit the renowned **Hofbräuhaus** *(see p215)* beer hall to experience Munich at its most traditional, and, from mid-September, the city hosts the world-famous **Oktoberfest** *(see p227)*, the biggest folk and beer fair in Europe.

Revellers enjoying beer and music at the annual Oktoberfest

BAVARIA

- **Fairytale castles**
- **German alpine heartland**
- **Medieval towns**

Bavaria is Germany's top tourist destination due to its mix of urban and rural landscapes. To the south, nestled among hills and lakes, is the eccentric King Ludwig II's 18th-century **Schloss Neuschwanstein** *(see pp282–3)*. The castle was built according to Ludwig's particular tastes in the style of a medieval fairytale castle. **Berchtesgadener Land** *(see pp276–7)* is a region of impressively spectacular alpine scenery, while to the east there are tranquil river valleys, miles of forest and an abundance of lakes. Besides the magnificent display of natural wonders is a multitude of well-preserved medieval Bavarian towns. **Rothenburg ob der Tauber** *(see pp262–3)* is foremost among these with its tiny cobbled alleyways, gabled houses and towers that form a picturesque skyline.

BADEN-WURTTEMBERG

- **Stuttgart and Heidelberg**
- **Black Forest spa towns**
- **The Bodensee (Lake Constance)**

Pristine and stately, **Stuttgart** *(see pp308–13)* is the regional capital with many parks and beer gardens to enjoy despite the high concentration of industry. However, **Heidelberg** *(see pp296–9)* is by far the most picturesque town in the region, with its mix of medieval and Baroque architecture. Baden Wurttemberg's **Black Forest** *(see pp326–7)* is renowned internationally for its spas, with elegant and exclusive **Baden-Baden** *(see p301)* topping this list. **The Bodensee** *(see pp320–21)*, or Lake Constance as it is more

The Bodensee (Lake Constance) from the Altes Schloss in Meersburg

commonly known, is on the border with Switzerland and is a favoured weekend spot, especially for sailing and caravanning enthusiasts.

RHINELAND-PALATINATE AND SAARLAND

- **Palatinate and Mosel wine regions**
- **Saarbrücken's varied architecture**
- **Trier's Porta Nigra**

These two regions bordering France account for much of Germany's wine production. These wines are best sampled by following the **Deutsche Weinstraße** *(see p347)* driving route where there are also many beautiful castles to be seen along the way *(see pp354–5)*. With a history of changing nationality, both states share a wonderful cultural mix unlike anywhere

A sun-drenched vineyard in the Mosel Valley

else in Germany. This is most apparent in **Saarbrücken** *(see p344)* which was ruled in turn by the Celts, Romans and Franks. The city's resulting range of architecture is now its main attraction. The region's Roman heritage is evident in many cities, particularly in **Trier** *(see pp340–43)*, with its Porta Nigra, the oldest defensive structure in Germany.

HESSE

- **The picturesque Waldecker Land**
- **Bustling Frankfurt**
- **Historic Wiesbaden**

Hesse lies at the heart of western Germany and is home to the beautiful **Waldecker Land** *(see pp366–7)*, which is full of wooded hills ideal for long rambles and cycling tours. At the heart of Hesse is **Frankfurt** *(see pp374–9)*, Germany's ultramodern financial city which has some of Europe's tallest skyscrapers. The banking district's glass and steel architecture is a famous post-card skyline but only a few minutes' walk away is the lovely Römerberg square and the banks of the river Main with its fascinating Museum Mile. In contrast to Frankfurt, many of Hesse's other cities are full of history, and none more so than **Wiesbaden** *(see pp372–3)* with its spa town heritage.

NORTH-RHINE WESTPHALIA

- **Gothic cathedral of Cologne**
- **Düsseldorf: fashion capital**
- **Modern culture in Dortmund and Essen**

North Rhine-Westphalia is the most densely populated federal state in Germany. The city of **Köln (Cologne)** *(see pp398–403)* with its famous Gothic cathedral, Roman ruins and enchanting old city is better known as a tourist destination than the state capital of **Düsseldorf** *(see pp392–3)*, but the latter has excellent shops. Once the centre of the German mining industry and steel production, the Ruhr area, incorporating **Dortmund** *(see p376)* and **Essen** *(see p376)*, is now renowned for its thriving arts scene.

Fischmarkt in Köln, overlooked by the Groß St Martin church

LOWER SAXONY, HAMBURG AND BREMEN

- **Pristine Hannover**
- **Windswept East Frisian Islands**
- **City-states of Hamburg and Bremen**

The regional capital of Lower Saxony, **Hannover** *(see pp444–5)*, is well known as a trade fair city, but it has much more to offer. There are several parks, the magnificent Baroque Herrenhäuser Gardens and the unusual town hall, built

on more than 6,000 beech pillars with Neo-Gothic and Secessionist detail. To the north are the seven **East Frisian Islands** *(see p428)* which line up like pearls on a string just off the North Sea coast. They are popular holiday destinations and home to a unique ecosystem. The city-states of **Hamburg** *(see pp434–8)* and **Bremen** *(see pp430–33)* are located in this region. Being port cities, both Hamburg and Bremen have a strong international flavour, seen in the diversity of shops and restaurants. In Bremen, the Bremen Town Musicians monument is a must-see if you have read the famous Grimm fairytale.

SCHLESWIG-HOLSTEIN

- **Sandy beaches on Sylt**
- **Flensburg's waterfront**
- **Gothic architecture in Lübeck**

Schleswig-Holstein is the most northerly-situated state of Germany and possesses a distinct Nordic feel. With long stretches of coastline and the rugged sandy beaches of the North Frisian Islands, most particularly **Sylt** *(see p459)*, this region makes an attractive holiday destination, especially for families. **Flensburg** *(see p459)* was once a trading centre with 200 ships; today there are some beautiful walks to be had around the harbour. **Lübeck** *(see pp462–5)* was the most important town in the area at

Bremen's most famous residents, the Bremen Town Musicians

the end of the Middle Ages and many of its superb Gothic buildings remain.

MECKLENBURG-LOWER POMERANIA

- **Hanseatic city Rostock**
- **State capital Schwerin**
- **Rugged Rügen**

The Mecklenburg-Lower Pomeranian region is full of towns with verdant, tree-lined avenues. Its Hanseatic towns, in particular **Rostock** *(see p476)*, are filled with richly decorated townhouses, cathedrals, abbeys and town halls. Over 800 years old, it is the largest town in the region, but it is the smaller **Schwerin** *(see pp470–71)* that is the state capital. It is home to one of the most beautiful Neo-Renaissance castles in Germany. The stretches of Baltic coastline here are unspoilt natural attractions and the island of **Rügen** *(see pp478–9)* boasts miles of untouched sandy beaches.

The picturesque harbour in Flensburg

Putting Germany on the Map

Located in the centre of Europe, between the North and Baltic Seas and the Alps, Germany covers an area of nearly 360,000 sq km (139,000 sq miles). Its neighbouring countries are Poland and the Czech Republic to the east, Austria and Switzerland to the south, France, Belgium, Luxembourg and Holland to the west, and Denmark to the north. The capital is Berlin. Its largest river is the Rhine. Germany is inhabited by over 81 million people.

KEY

- – · National border
- ✈ Airport
- ▬ Motorway
- ▬ Major road
- — Railway
- ⛴ Ferry terminal
- ---- Ferry route

0 km		100
0 miles		100

Baltic Sea

Słupsk

Rostock
E22
A20
E55
E251

Lübeck
E26
E55
E28
Szczecin

Braunschweig
(Brunswick)
E30

Bird's-eye view of Baldern Castle

BERLIN
E30

E30
Poznań

Magdeburg
E51

M **A** **N** **Y**

Cottbus

Zielona Góra
P O L A N D

Halle
Leipzig
14
E49 E51

Dresden

E36

Wrocław
E40

Erfurt
E40

Chemnitz
E52

Liberec

Wałbrzych

E55

E48

Pilsen

Nürnberg
E50

**C Z E C H
R E P U B L I C**

E56

E45

E53

E52

München
(Munich)
E552

E593
E52
Salzburg
E45

A U S T R I A

Aerial view of the old town of Neumarkt

Germany: Region by Region

The Federal Republic of Germany is made up of
16 states. Bremen is the smallest state, with
around 700,000 inhabitants; North Rhine-
Westphalia is the most densely populated
state, with 18 million inhabitants. The
largest state, Bavaria, covers an
area of 70,531 sq km
(27,232 sq miles).
Berlin, Bremen and
Hamburg are
self-governing
city-states.

HOW TO GET THERE

Germany has an excellent
transport system. There are 14
international airports with flights
to all parts of the world; a
comprehensive network of
toll-free motorways that make
travelling by car easy and fast;
and an efficient railway system,
with high-speed InterCity
Express (ICE) link between
major cities.

KEY

✈ Airport

🚉 Railway

━━━ Motorway

━━━ Major road

| 0 km | 100 |
| 0 miles | 100 |

BERLIN

Reinickendorf · Pankow · Wedding · Weissensee · Tiergarten · Prenzlauer Berg · Charlottenburg · Mitte · Friedrichshain · Wilmersdorf · Kreuzberg · Schöneberg · Treptow · Tempelhof · Neukölln · Steglitz

0 km 3
0 miles 3

AREA COLOURS

- Berlin

Eastern Germany

- Brandenburg
- Saxony
- Saxony-Anhalt
- Thuringia

Southern Germany

- Munich
- Bavaria
- Baden-Württemberg

Western Germany

- Rhineland-Palatinate & Saarland
- Hesse
- North Rhine-Westphalia

Northern Germany

- Hamburg, Bremen, Lower Saxony
- Schleswig-Holstein
- Mecklenburg-Lower Pomerania

A PORTRAIT OF GERMANY

*G*ermany is a wealthy country, whose people are generally regarded as hard-working, determined and efficient. This view stems from the country's industrial might and the smooth functioning of its economy, but it overlooks other important aspects of Germany. These include its important contributions to art and culture, its breathtaking scenery and excellent tourist facilities.

Contemporary Germany is far removed from the traditional, stereotyped view of the country. In the last 60 years, it has developed into a multi-ethnic, multi-cultural melting pot. Over 7 million of Germany's inhabitants are immigrants; the majority of these are Turks, with more recent guest workers arriving from the former Yugoslavia, Italy and Greece. In the city of Stuttgart, every third inhabitant is a foreigner; in Frankfurt it is one in four. Hamburg has more mosques than any other city in Europe and, in some schools in Berlin, German children are in the minority. Almost every town has a selection of Italian, Chinese, Greek and Turkish restaurants and cafés, testifying to the multi-ethnicity of its population.

The colourful Bavarian coat of arms

HISTORY AND ROMANCE

For many, the river Rhine epitomizes tourist Germany, particularly the romantic stretch between Mainz and Cologne. The country has far more than this to offer in the way of scenery, however. There is the ever-changing Baltic coastline, the sandy islands of the North Sea, the lakes of Mecklenburg, lonely castles perched on crags in Baden and Thuringia, mountain ranges including the Alps, the vast Bodensee lake, medieval cities and fairy-tale villages. Not all of the latter are original, as countless towns were destroyed by bombs during World War II, but many have been meticulously rebuilt to the original plans, and now it is difficult to tell the difference between the old and the new.

Verdant Alpine meadow against a backdrop of majestic, snowy peaks

◁ Alter Flecken – Freudenberg's quarter of traditional-style houses

Procession during the Plärrer Fest, a beer festival in Augsburg

TRADITIONS

Today's German nation has evolved over the past thousand years, mainly from various Germanic tribes, notably the Franks, Saxons, Swabians and Bavarians. Traditions and dialects have developed within regional ethnic groups that emerged as a result of historical alliances. There is no such thing as a single German tradition. Even the assumption that Germany is a country of beer-drinkers is belied by the large numbers of wine-lovers. These groups, along with consumers of stronger beverages, have given Germany a high position in the world league table for alcohol use. Nevertheless, drunks are rarely seen in Germany.

Bavarian scene on a beer glass

Various ethnic groups in the country are ascribed different characteristics. The people of Mecklenburg, for example, are seen as introspective, while Swabians are regarded as thrifty; the Saxons are seen as disciplined and cunning, while Bavarians are typified as a people bound by rustic traditions, quick to quarrel and fight. Indeed, one of the most pop-

A Bavarian dressed in regional costume

ular Bavarian men's folk-dances ends with them slapping each other in the face. Bavaria, of course, is home to the traditional Oktoberfest, a beer festival that brings millions of people to Munich every year from virtually all over the world.

The people of the Rhineland have a reputation for enjoying life. Their favourite season is the Carnival period, and they spend practically the entire year preparing for this week-long event. It begins on the last Thursday before Lent, with "town soldiers", helped by the huge crowds, storming the town hall. The town councillors surrender and power passes to the masked revellers. On the Monday, the Carnival proceeds through the thronged streets of the towns on the Rhine, and the pubs are busy until the end of Shrovetide.

Carnival is rooted in ancient rituals marking the banishment of winter. This custom was most common in the south of Germany, but it also reached the Rhineland, the Palatinate and Hessen. When the German government moved back to Berlin from Bonn in the Rhineland in 1999, attempts were made to establish Carnival in the new capital, but it never really took root.

ART AND CULTURE

Germany is a land of sagas and legends that tell of woodland spirits, beautiful princesses, magicians and sirens such as the Lorelei. These legends have had a strong influence on German art. An example is the German epic poem, the *Nibelungenlied*, which was written around 1200 on the basis of old legends. This poem was the inspiration for Richard Wagner's cycle of operas, *The Ring of the Nibelungen*, as well as for a trilogy of plays by Christian Friedrich Hebbel and a film by Fritz Lang.

Germans have won eight Nobel Prizes for Literature. The most recent prizewinner was Günter Grass, whose *Tin Drum* brought him world renown. More recently a film adaptation of the book was made by Volker Schlöndorff, which won the Golden Palm at the Cannes Film Festival. After a relatively stagnant period, the German film industry became revitalized around 1995 with a number of hits, albeit only at the national level. German cinemas are now always full and traditional cinemas are increasingly being replaced by multiplexes.

Germans read widely, even in today's age of television and the internet. Every year 70,000 new books are published in Germany and eight times that many titles are on sale. Germany is second only to the United States in the number of books published annually, while the number of bookshops per square kilometre is the highest in the world. The same applies to museums and art galleries.

Germany has over 2,000 national, provincial and local history museums,

The historical Frohnauer hammer forge near Annaberg in Saxony

as well as numerous church museums, folk museums and former royal palaces. This variety and choice owes much to the fact that, in the past, local dukes acquired collections of art in order to impress others and to demonstrate their wealth. The Bavarian dukes also built up extensive collections of machines, artisans' tools, musical instruments and minerals. As early as the 16th century, Munich was an international centre of the arts and the Grünes Gewölbe in 17th-century Dresden was one of the largest treasuries for storing fine art in Europe. Of the many art galleries to be found throughout Germany, the finest are in Cologne, Frankfurt, Stuttgart, Munich and Berlin.

Lorelei overlooking the Rhine

Music also flourishes in Germany. Most large cities have their own symphony orchestra and opera company and every year some 100 regional and local music festivals take place. Musical comedies are especially popular.

The imposing Schönburg Castle, near Oberwesel on the Rhine

SOCIETY AND POLITICS

The scars of World War II are more evident in Eastern Germany, although they are gradually disappearing there, too. Görlitz, Bautzen, Leipzig and Weimar have now acquired a splendour that was previously hidden behind the grim façade of East Germany. The mental, social and political scars of the war and subsequent division of Germany have, however, left deeper scars. Although reunification took place on 3 October 1990, unity among the people themselves has been longer in

The Reichstag building, where the *Bundestag* sessions are held

coming. East Germans are the poor relations: the region has high unemployment rates and its people tend to regard their western counterparts as arrogant and self-assured. The latter, for their part, claim that the inhabitants of the "new states" are jealous and ungrateful despite the billions of marks and euros that have been poured into the region to equalize living standards.

Germany has almost always been divided regionally into states with fluctuating borders. The present-day states were, for the most part, created after 1945 while those in East Germany were not created until forty years later. In all cases, old territorial and historical ties were taken into account. That is the reason for their evocative names, such as the "Free State of Bavaria" or the "Free State of Saxony".

There are now 16 federal states, or provinces. North Rhine-Westphalia, Baden-Wurttemberg and Bavaria are the largest and are like economically powerful countries. At the other end of the scale, the tiny province of Saarland has only 1.1 million inhabitants, while the Free Hanseatic City of Bremen has fewer than 700,000. The former East German states are also relatively small but all play an important role in the *Bundesrat*, or Federal Council, where they are instrumental in enacting legislation. All laws, apart from those relating to the Federation as a whole, such as defence or foreign policy, require the agreement of the *Bundesrat*, which is made up from current local governments. Depending on the number of inhabitants, each federal state has from four to six votes.

The skyline of Frankfurt am Main, reminiscent of New York

A government with a majority in the *Bundestag* (parliament) cannot always count on support in the *Bundesrat*, even if it has a majority there. Each state looks after its own interests and often makes alliances with other states to achieve its own aims, without regard for party loyalty. The complex working of German federalism is based on the compromises that this system requires.

Bathers on the sandy beaches of Norddeich

DAILY LIFE

The traditional image of German women used to be summed up in the "three Ks": *Küche, Kinder, Kirche* (kitchen, children, church). As in other Western European countries, however, this stereotype no longer holds true. Although cookery is fashionable and there are countless TV cookery programmes starring celebrity chefs, for everyday meals, ready-prepared dishes are eaten, either at the work canteen or from the supermarket. The German birthrate is declining, while the anti-authoritarian model of education that was introduced in the 1960s has to some extent relieved parents of many of the more onerous duties of child-rearing. As a result, many young people show little respect for their elders. The churches, for their part, are usually empty. Although the largest churches (Catholic and Protestant) have many adherents, the vast majority are not practising believers and limit themselves to payment of church dues.

Participant in a parade marking the Reunification celebrations

Germans speak of themselves as a high-performance society *(Leistungsgesellschaft)*, which gives the highest rewards to those who devote almost all their energies to their careers. As a result, stress is often a factor in people's lives, from schooldays onwards. In Germany today there are increasing numbers of people who live alone. Single-person households are most common in the cities and even young people regard their careers as of paramount importance. Large numbers say that they are not interested in having a family.

Nevertheless, Germans enjoy mass events such as public holidays and popular festivals. The country has the highest number of public holidays in Europe and German workers have the longest annual holidays. Its citizens are Europe's most enthusiastic travellers, each year spending over 35 million euros on foreign holidays. When they return there is a tendency to long for the southern climes they have just visited – perhaps this explains why restaurants offering Mediterranean food are so popular.

The Bodensee, a popular tourist destination

Flora and Fauna

Black-headed gull

Germany is a vast country whose varied geography has given rise to a great diversity of flora and fauna. It is famous for its forests, many of mixed deciduous trees, including oak, beech and birch. Around 31 per cent of the country is forested.

The Alpine regions have a rich variety of wild flowers, with meadow species a particular feature in spring and summer. On the northern peat moors, heaths and heathers are common. Germany is home to a wide range of wildlife, including wild boar, lynx and marmots. Many valuable wildlife areas have now been placed under protection.

GERMAN WILDLIFE

The fauna of Germany is typical of central Europe, with a variety of woodland, wetland and Alpine birds. Of the larger mammals, visitors are most likely to see deer, squirrels and foxes. Small populations of rarer species such as lynx and European beaver exist, but these are threatened with extinction.

Alpine raven

COASTAL REGIONS

Germany's coasts vary considerably: the North Sea coast is predominantly flat with drained land, dikes and islands; the Baltic Sea coast is hillier with sandy inlets and cliffs. Together with differences in tides and temperature, these variations determine the variety of species found along coastal regions.

LAKES

Most of Germany's lakes are grouped in the northern part of the country, mainly in the Mecklenburg region, where they are divided from the south by the mountain ranges, rifts and valleys of the Central Uplands. However, the largest lake in Germany – the Bodensee (Lake Constance) – is situated in the south, on the border with Austria and Switzerland.

Cross-leaved heath *is a species of heath that is commonly found growing on the moors and peat bogs and in the damp coastal forests of northern Germany.*

Yellow floating heart *grows in shallow, fertile water. Its habitats are disappearing but it still survives in the Rhine basin and on the lower Elbe.*

Sea lavender *is one of the salt-tolerant species that grow along Germany's North Sea coast.*

Yellow flag *is a protected species of iris that is found amongst reeds and in damp woodlands, particularly in older, mixed species forests.*

Sea holly *is a beautiful thistle-like plant with an amethyst hue. It is commonly found growing in sand dunes.*

The white water lily, *with its elegant floating flowers and lush foliage, adorns lakes and reservoirs.*

Wild boars *are mammals of the pig family, living in boggy forests. They feed mainly on acorns, beechnuts and the small animals that live in the ground cover of the forest.*

Deer *live in leafy and mixed forests and are one of the most common mammals seen in Germany.*

Marmots *live on vegetation growing in the high Alpine meadows. Rodents of the squirrel family, they sleep in burrows at night and whistle loudly when anxious.*

Lynx *are distinguished by small tufts of hair on the tips of their ears. These mammals are becoming ever rarer.*

UPLANDS

Upland landscapes dominate the southern part of Germany, including Bavaria. Here, the climate is mild, and forests cover nearly a third of the region. In this picturesque and popular part of the country, winter-sports centres and spa resorts are common.

MOUNTAINS

Mountain ranges in Germany vary both in age and in height above sea level. Older, not very high mountains covered with forests predominate. The Bavarian Alps are higher and more recent. Here sub-alpine plants grow, with alpine plants at higher altitudes.

Beech *is one of the commonest trees found in Germany's forests of mixed deciduous species.*

Gentian, *with its intensely blue trumpet-like flowers, is one of the most impressive plants to be seen in the Alps. It is pollinated by bumblebees.*

Holly, *the symbol of Christmas with its glossy leaves and scarlet berries, is found in forests of beech or beech and fir in the west of the country.*

Edelweiss *is a small flowering plant with flat, white flowers and grey-green woolly leaves. It grows high up in the Alps.*

Hepatica *is a protected plant in Germany. It blooms in early spring and the seeds of the blue, star-like flowers are distributed by ants.*

Rhododendron hirsutum *is a low, dense variety of rhododendron, one of a group of plants that grow at sub-Alpine levels.*

German Literature

The first known examples of written German date from the 8th century. German literature flourished in the Renaissance, although it was mainly later writers who entered the world's canon of great literature. Goethe and Schiller, who wrote many of their most famous works in the *Sturm und Drang* (Storm and Stress) era, in the late 18th century, count among the greatest. Germany also produced many dramatists, poets and novelists in the 19th and 20th centuries. German writers have won eight Nobel Prizes for literature, awarded to Nelly Sachs, Thomas Mann, Heinrich Böll and Günter Grass among others.

Schleswig-Holstein

Gotthold Ephraim Lessing
(1729–81), the most famous German writer of the Age of Enlightenment, wrote dramas such as Nathan the Wise, *reviews of plays performed in Hamburg as well as essays on literary and cultural theory.*

Lower Saxony, Hamburg, Bremen

North Rhine-Westphalia

Erich Maria Remarque
(1898–1970) emigrated from Germany in 1931. His pacifist writings, including All Quiet on the Western Front *and* L'Arc de Triomphe, *brought him acclaim around the world.*

Hesse

The Brothers Grimm,
Jacob Ludwig Karl (1785–1863) and Wilhelm Karl (1786–1859), were university professors and philologists, but better known as collectors and publishers of some of the world's favourite fairy-tales.

Rhineland-Palatinate & Saarland

Baden-Wurttemberg

Friedrich Schiller
(1759–1805) wrote about the concept of individual freedom in his great dramas, such as The Robbers *and* Wallenstein. *He also wrote ballads and songs, including* Ode to Joy.

0 km   75

0 miles   75

Thomas Mann *(1875 1955) was awarded the Nobel Prize in 1929. The best-known of his novels is* Buddenbrooks, *which chronicles the life of a Lübeck family.*

Gerhart Haupt-mann *(1862–1946), dramatist, novelist and winner of the Nobel Prize in 1912, lived and worked mainly in Silesia. The Weavers is his most famous drama.*

Mecklenburg-Lower Pomerania

Theodor Fontane *(1819–98) was born in Neuruppin, and his literary activities were chiefly connected with Brandenburg. He was the author of realistic novels such as* Effi Briest, *and he wrote excellent theatre reviews.*

Berlin

Saxony-Anhalt

Brandenburg

Bertolt Brecht *(1898–1956), the great dramatist, poet and director, wrote* The Threepenny Opera, *and was a co-founder of the Berliner Ensemble theatre company.*

Saxony

Thuringia

Karl May *(1842–1912) was known around the world as the author of travel books but his great popularity stems from a cycle of stories featuring the Indian chief* Winnetou, *which he wrote in Radebeul.*

Bavaria

Johann Wolfgang von Goethe *(1749–1832) was the most highly acclaimed German poet and writer of the* Sturm und Drang *period. Born in Frankfurt, he spent most of his life in Weimar. His most famous work is* Faust.

Lion Feuchtwanger *(1884–1958) lived in Munich until his opposition to the National Socialists forced him to emigrate in 1933. He wrote in exile, alluding to contemporary events in his historical novels.*

Munich

Music in Germany

German composers have made an enormous contribution to the world's cultural heritage. Many great musical geniuses were born and worked here, including Johann Sebastian Bach and Ludwig van Beethoven. Today their work, and that of other German composers, continues to be performed to enthusiastic new generations of music-lovers in concert halls and opera houses around the world. In Germany, their work is celebrated regularly at hugely popular music festivals.

Richard Strauss

Renowned composer, Johann Sebastian Bach (1685–1750)

EARLY MUSIC

During the early Middle Ages, music evolved in the courts and monasteries of Europe. The basis of sacred music was the Gregorian chant, which was introduced by Pope Gregory I in the late 6th century. An influential role in medieval court music was played by roving poets (*Minnesänger*), who sang love verses to a lute accompaniment. From the 14th century, German singing guilds known as *Meistersinger* emerged. Unlike the *Minnesänger*, these artistes adopted a settled lifestyle. In the succeeding centuries, both vocal and instrumental music continued to evolve, with many new forms appearing.

In the second half of the 17th century, interest in organ music developed and organ schools were established in many towns. One of the best

was in Nuremberg. This was directed by Johann Pachelbel (c.1653–1706), who worked in Vienna, Stuttgart, Erfurt and Nuremberg as a church organist. He is best known for his organ work *Canon*, a set of variations on a theme.

The first German opera, *Dafne*, was composed by Heinrich Schütz (1585–1672). Completed in 1627, the opera has unfortunately been lost.

THE 18TH CENTURY

A huge flowering of musical talent took place in Germany during the 18th century, when divisions both in German politics and religion led to the development of several important artistic and cultural centres. The most renowned figure in

Georg Friedrich Händel (1685–1759)

German music in the 18th century was undoubtedly Johann Sebastian Bach who, until 1717, was associated with the Weimar court. From 1723 until his death, he was associated with Leipzig, where he was the choir master at the church of St Thomas. Bach's output as a composer is vast and embraces most of the musical forms known at that time. His Passions are today performed in many countries during Holy Week, and his Brandenburg Concertos are among his most frequently performed works. His sons – Wilhelm Friedemann, Carl Philipp Emanuel, Johann Christoph Friedrich and Johann Christian – also became acclaimed composers and made significant contributions to German classical music.

Georg Friedrich Händel was another great composer of late Baroque music. Before forging a prestigious career in England, he began as the cathedral organist in Halle, from where he transferred to the opera house in Hamburg. A friend of Händel and another important composer, Georg Philipp Telemann (1681– 1767) was employed as conductor at many German courts. His work includes chamber music, operas and church music.

MUSIC FESTIVALS

The Bach festival in Leipzig's Church of St Thomas

Germany is a country of musical festivals, which are usually held in the summer and early autumn. Among the most popular are the festivals dedicated to the works of a single composer, such as Wagner in Bayreuth, Bach in various cities of Thuringia, Handel in Halle and Beethoven in Bonn. Apart from these specialized festivals, opera festivals with a broader repertoire are also popular. These include the outdoor opera festival in Berlin and the Sommerfestspiele in Xanten.

Son of a court musician and arguably the greatest figure in classical music, Ludwig van Beethoven (1770–1827) was born in Bonn, although he worked mainly in Vienna. Among his best-known works are his nine symphonies, as well as piano and violin concertos, two masses, various chamber works and the opera *Fidelio*.

The life of this great composer, is shrouded in legend. Succeeding generations have been fascinated not just by his music, but also by the fact that he began to lose his hearing at the age of 30. During his final years, when totally deaf, he composed from memory.

Statue of Ludwig van Beethoven

THE 19TH CENTURY

Romanticism brought about the flowering of opera in Germany. One of the leading creators in this tradition was the composer Ernst Theodor Amadeus Hoffmann (1776–1822), whose opera *Undine* was staged for the first time in 1816 in Berlin. Carl Maria von Weber (1786–1826) rose to prominence following the success of his opera *Der Freischütz*, which was the first opera in the German Romantic tradition. Another

Composer Felix Mendelssohn-Bartholdy (1809–47)

major figure from this time was Felix Mendelssohn-Bartholdy, whose "Wedding March" from *A Midsummer Night's Dream* accompanies wedding celebrations around the world. As well as this famous piece of music, however, Mendelssohn left a legacy that includes five symphonies, piano music, chamber music and oratorios. In 1843, Mendelssohn founded Germany's first musical conservatory, in Leipzig.

The master of chamber music was Robert Schumann (1810–56), a poet and composer whose miniature works for piano, violin sonatas and song cycles all remain popular. The Hungarian composer Franz Liszt, who worked in Weimar from 1848 to 1861, also made a significant contribution to the evolution of German music.

In the second half of the 19th century, Richard Wagner was the major influence on German opera. During his early years, he composed traditional operas such as *Tannhäuser*. He later developed his own creative synthesis, integrating lyrics with the music. This found its finest expression in his Ring cycle, which was based on medieval sagas.

Wagner's ideas about musical theatre, including his use of *leitmotifs* (recurring phrases), were adopted by Richard Strauss (1864–1949), who composed many operas, symphonies and songs. The first bars of his symphonic poem *Zarathustra* became a guiding musical motif in Stanley Kubrick's 1968 film *2001: A Space Odyssey*. Johannes Brahms (1833–97) composed in traditional forms and was

Richard Wagner (1813–83)

Composer and pianist Johannes Brahms (1833–97)

unsympathetic to the progressive ideas of Wagner and Liszt. From 1872 to 1875, Brahms was the musical director of the *Gesellschaft der Musikfreunde* (Society of Friends of Music).

THE 20TH CENTURY

During the 20th century, many contemporary composers continued the traditions of the earlier masters. One renowned figure was Paul Hindemith (1895–1963), whose work includes opera, ballet and concertos. His music was banned by the Nazis in 1933 and Hindemith emigrated to the USA in 1939.

Another important figure in German musical life was Carl Orff (1895–1982) whose best-known work is the oratorio *Carmina Burana*, based on 13th-century Latin and German poems found in a Benedictine monastery in Bavaria. The Austrian composer Arnold Schönberg (1874–1951) lived in Berlin during the 1920s and exerted great influence on German music.

Among the most important composers living and working in Germany today, mention should be made of Hans Werner Henze, Dieter Schnebel, Helmut Lachenmann, Moritz Eggert and Jörg Widmann.

German Painting

The diversity in German painting has its roots in the political and religious divisions that existed in the country in the past. The Old Masters working in the north, for example, were more likely to be influenced by the Netherlandish school, while artists working in the south leaned towards Italian styles. German art reached the peak of its individuality during the late-Gothic, late-Baroque and Expressionist periods – all periods when one of the chief characteristics of artistic style was strength of expression.

Emil Nolde *(1867–1956), one of Germany's foremost Expressionists, painted landscapes of his native region. Pictured above is his* North Friesian Landscape.

Schleswig-Holstein

Master Francke *(14th–15th century) was the leading representative of the North German Late-Gothic style, working in Hamburg c.1410–24. He painted religious scenes and his works include* St Thomas's Altar, *of which this is a detail.*

Bremen, Hamburg and Lower Saxony

North Rhine-Westphalia

Hesse

Rhineland-Palatinate and Saarland

Peter von Cornelius *(1783–1867) joined the Nazarenes during the anti-academic rebellion. He later became director of the academy in Dusseldorf and others. He painted the picture* The Wise and Foolish Maidens *at that time.*

Baden-Wurttemberg

Adam Elsheimer *(1578–1610) was born in Frankfurt am Main but spent most of his life in Rome. His poignant landscapes, such as* The Flight to Egypt *shown here, greatly influenced the development of 17th-century painting.*

Caspar David Friedrich
(1774–1840) was one of the most prominent exponents of Romanticism. He created poignant images, such as this Traveller above the Sea of Clouds, *in which Man contemplates the power of Nature as created by God.*

Mecklenburg-Lower Pomerania

Max Liebermann
(1847–1935) is considered one of the leading representatives of Impressionism. His Man with Parrots *was painted during his association with the Berlin Secession.*

Berlin

Saxony-Anhalt   *Brandenburg*

Lionel Feininger
(1871–1956) was born in the USA but spent much of his life in Germany. He lectured at the Bauhaus and painted Cubist-inspired scenes of architectural subjects, such as this Gelmeroda IX.

Saxony

Thuringia

Albrecht Dürer *(1471–1528) is one of the best-known German painters. This great master of the Renaissance period was also an outstanding engraver and art-historian. His* Paumgärtners' Altar *was made for St Catherine's Church in Nuremberg.*

Bavaria

Munich

Wilhelm Leibl *(1844–1900) painted this scene of women praying in a village church in Bavaria,* Three Women in a Church, *which is regarded as one of the outstanding works of German Realism.*

0 kilometres   80

0 miles   80

Castles in Germany

In a number of German regions, medieval castles are among the most characteristic features of the landscape. Some have survived only in the form of picturesque ruins, but many others, refurbished and modernized over the years, continue to be the main residence for the families for whom they were built. The most impressive grouping of great fortresses is to be found along the banks of the Mosel and the central Rhine, while, in the Münster area, you will see the most beautiful moated castles to have survived in the lowlands.

Crest from the castle portal in Gotha

The Great Knights' Hall, where knights ate, drank and entertained, was a feature of every castle.

The 15th-century Michaelskapelle

Marburg Castle *is one of the best-preserved fortresses in Hesse. At its core is a 12th-century building, but the castle's current appearance is the result of work carried out between the 14th and 16th centuries (see p369).*

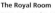
The Royal Room was an apartment specially designated for the use of important guests.

The Wartburg *in Eisenach is one of the most important monuments in Thuringia, not only because of its excellently preserved architecture but also for its association with Martin Luther (see pp186–7).*

Heidelberg Castle *has survived as a picturesque ruin. A Gothic-Renaissance structure of imposing proportions, it continues to captivate with its commanding position and fascinating architecture (see pp298–9).*

Gardens were laid out in the 19th century in an area between the castle walls and the site of the farm buildings.

Raesfeld *is one of the most beautiful castles in Münsterland, a region of Westphalia that is renowned for its historic moated castles. The castle was extended in the mid-17th century for Alexandra II von Velen (see p388).*

19TH-CENTURY CASTLES

In the 19th century, many ruined castles in Germany were rebuilt in a wave of nostalgia for the Middle Ages. A number of completely new castles were built, which were modelled on medieval designs.

The Schwerin castle, *built on an island, has a 16th-century chapel, but the rest, dating from 1843–57, was inspired by the French castles along the river Loire (see p470)*

Lichtenstein castle *owes its fame to the novel* Lichtenstein *by Wilhelm Hauff and its beauty to the Romantic-style remodelling that was carried out in 1840–41 (see p315).*

Evangelical Chapel

The main entrance to the castle leads through a gate house – here in the form of a tower.

Wernigerode's *castle dominates the entire city. Despite later extensions, it has retained a late-Gothic tower, a beautiful staircase dating from 1495 and some valuable furnishings (see p146).*

BURG HOHENZOLLERN

The family seat of the Hohenzollern family, Burg Hohenzollern in Hechingen, is set on a clifftop in the Swabian Jura. The first building was established here in the 13th century and rebuilt many times over the years. The current medieval appearance is the result of work that was carried out in 1850–67 in the spirit of romantic historicism *(see p314)*.

Burg Eltz, *set high above the Mosel, is one of the most beautiful castles in Germany. Built between the 12th and 16th centuries, it has survived with very few alterations (see p345).*

German Scientists and Inventors

Germany is popularly regarded as a nation of practical people, so it is hardly surprising that the history books abound with the names of Germans who have made important contributions to technological progress and the development of science. They include Johann Gutenberg (c.1400–68), who invented printing with movable type, and Karl Benz (1844–1929) and Gottlieb Daimler (1834–1900) who developed the first petrol-driven car. In terms of Nobel Prize winners alone (and not counting those who received the prize for achievements in other fields), there is currently a total of 69 Germans. One of the most illustrious of these is physicist Albert Einstein (1879–1955).

1791 Alexander von Humboldt, a naturalist and geographer, discovers the presence of carbon dioxide in the air

c.1600 Johann Schult invents the dental mirror.

1645 Athanasius Kircher constructs the magic lantern – the first projector

1671 Gottfried Wilhelm Leibniz, philosopher and mathematician, is known for his important philosophical works and his (disputed) claim to have invented differential calculus

c.1707 Johann F Böttger produces the first European porcelain

1718 Jacob Leupold constructs the first decimal scale

1747 Andreas Marggraf succeeds in extracting sugar crystals from sugar beet

1600	1650	1700	1750

1600	1650	1700	1750

1669 Hennig Brand discovers phosphorus

1694 Rudolph Jacob Camerarius discovers the existence of gender in plants, and explains the role of stamens and pollen in fertilization

1781 Martin H Klaproth, chemist, discovers uranium

1740 Johann Pott, porcelain pioneer, discovers manganese

1609, 1619 Johannes Kepler discovers the principal laws of planetary movement

1650 Otto von Guericke, researching air pressure and electrostatic phenomena, develops the vacuum pump

1745 Ewald G Kleist invents the first electric condenser

GERMAN PHILOSOPHERS

German intellectuals have played a major role in the history of philosophy. Gottfried Leibniz (1646–1716), for example, was one of the most renowned exponents of modern rationalism. At the turn of the 18th and 19th centuries, Germany was a fertile source of new ideas, with the work of philosophers such as Immanuel Kant and G W Friedrich Hegel. Karl Marx and Friedrich Engels expounded materialism, while Friedrich Nietzsche developed his cultural and human philosophy. Martin Heidegger and Karl Jaspers were leading existentialists.

Georg Wilhelm Friedrich Hegel (1770–1831)

1813 Karl Freiherr von Drais invents the first two-wheeled vehicle – a kind of bicycle

1874 Otto Lilienthal constructs the first glider for engineless flights

1989 Wolfgang Paul and Hans Dehmelt receive the Nobel prize for research into nuclear and molecular physics and for their work in the 1950s developing the "Paul trap" – a device for capturing ions

1991 Erwin Neher and Bert Sakmann receive the Nobel prize for research into defining the process of communication between cells

1876 Nikolaus Otto invents the internal combustion engine

1987 Georg Bednorz and Karl A Müller receive the Nobel prize for discovering high temperature super-conductivity in metal oxides

1831 Justus von Liebig develops a new method of chemical analysis

1841 Julius Mayer formulates the principle of conservation of energy

1882 Robert Koch discovers the tuberculosis bacillus (Nobel prize in 1905)

1922 The Nobel Prize is awarded to Albert Einstein, who developed the theory of relativity

1999 Günter Blobel is awarded the Nobel prize for discovering the process that determines the direction of movement and the location of proteins within cells

1865 Rudolf J E Clausius formulates the second law of thermo-dynamics

1850	1900	1950	2000

1850	1900	1950	2000

1885 Karl Benz and Gottlieb Daimler construct the first petrol driven car

1963 Nobel Prize awarded to Karl Ziegler for his work on industrial production of polymers

1886 Heinrich Hertz discovers radio waves

1918 Nobel Prize awarded to Max K Planck who founded the principles of quantum theory

1944 Nobel Prize awarded to Otto Hahn for discovery (with Lise Meitner) of the process of nuclear fission

1903 Arthur Korn demonstrates how to transmit a photograph from a distance

1866 Ernest W Siemens develops the dynamo

1938 Ernst Ruska and Max Knoll construct the first electron microscope

1850 Wilhelm Bauer constructs a submarine

1841 Christian Schönbein discovers ozone

1941 Konrad Zuse constructs the Z3 calculator – the first digital "computer"

1826 Georg S Ohm shows that the ratio of a steady current to voltage is a constant

1901 Nobel Prize awarded to Wilhelm C Röntgen, for his discovery of X-rays and their uses

German Beer

Hop flower cones

Although fine wines are produced in Germany, beer is unquestionably the country's favourite alcoholic drink. Germans drink an average of 100 litres of beer annually and Bavarians lead the world in consumption, drinking an average of 215 litres each per annum. Beer is drunk on every occasion, but it tastes best in the summer when it is poured straight from a barrel at one of the numerous festivals or public holidays.

The mass *is a tankard that is used to serve beer in Bavaria. It holds a litre, but waitresses are used to carrying eight or nine such tankards at a time.*

GERMAN BREWERIES

In Germany most towns and the larger villages have a brewery. The country's oldest brewery, established in 1040, is the Weihenstephan Benedictine monastery in Freising, which is believed to be the oldest working brewery in the world. Many large breweries and consortiums produce beer that is known throughout the world, but beers produced by small operators, which are available only in a few regional pubs, are in no way inferior. When visiting Germany, do try the produce of small local breweries as well as the beer produced by the giants, such as Paulaner and Löwenbrau.

Historic brewing facilities in Freising (see p251)

Logo of the famous Munich brewery, Paulaner

STYLES OF BEER

One of the most popular styles of beer is *Pils* (short for *Pilsener*) a light, bottom-fermented beer of the lager type. Of the seasonal beers, it is worth trying spring beers such as *Maibock* or *Doppelbock*, and in autumn the strong beer that is brewed especially for the Oktoberfest. In the lower Rhine valley, *Altbier* is still produced; this is a top-fermented beer, prepared by traditional methods. In the south, *Weizenbier*, a wheat beer, is also produced. The Berlin version, *Berliner Weisse* (white beer), is served with fruit juice. Dark beers, such as *Dunkel* and *Schwarzbier*, also enjoy great popularity. Breweries have their own specialities. In Bamberg, they produce *Rauchbier*, which has a light smokiness; in Kulmbach it is *Eisbock*, which gains its thicker consistency through a freezing process.

Wheat beer, Berliner Weisse

Seasonal autumn beer, Bock

DRINKING BEER

In Germany, beer is served with a head. Pouring lager from a barrel is supposed to take about 10 minutes, so the head sinks to the regulation level and has a thick consistency. A small beer is normally 0.3 litre, a large one 0.5 litre. In Bavaria, however, a large beer is served in a *Mass*, a tankard holding 1 litre. When travelling in Germany, order the brew of the local brewery, ideally in a *Bierkeller* or *Bierstube* (pub) and, in summer, in a *Biergarten* (beer garden). The largest gardens are in Bavaria – Munich's *Hirschgarten* caters for 8,000 beer drinkers. The Oktoberfest, which is celebrated each year in Munich *(see p227)*, is the largest beer festival in the world.

The largest pub in the world, created during the Oktoberfest

HOW BEER IS BREWED

The method of brewing beer that is now virtually standard dates from the 19th century, when Czech brewers first produced bottom-fermented beers at lower temperatures. The method was perfected by Gabriel Sedlmayr. Each brewery has its secrets, but the initial stages of production are the same.

A climbing plant, hops are trained to grow up special supports

Mashing vat

Barley and hops

1 *The main ingredients in the production of beer are barley, hops and crystal-clear water. Other grains, including wheat and rice, can also be used — for example Weizenbier is made from wheat rather than barley. The first stage of brewing is malting, when the grains are soaked and left to germinate. After a few days, these are dried and then milled.*

2 *The milled barley is mixed with warm water and placed in a copper mashing vat. During the mashing process, the starches in the grain turn into fermentable sugars. The mash is then filtered to separate out a liquid, known as the wort, from the mash.*

3 *The wort is put into a copper vessel with the hops and then cooked. Depending on the amount of hops added, the beer will be more or less bitter. Traditionally the hops are added to the vessel by hand, in carefully measured proportions. Sometimes, however, they are added, as required, during the cooking process.*

4 *The wort is filtered again, cooled and combined with yeast. Fermentation then takes place. At temperatures above 20° C (68° F), the liquid reaches "top fermentation", which takes 3–5 days. "Bottom fermentation", where the temperature is below 12° C (54° F), takes 7–10 days.*

5 *The young beer produced by fermentation is left to rest in special containers that enable a higher pressure to be maintained. During this resting stage, which can last from a couple of weeks to a year or even longer, the beer matures. The effect of resting the beer is to make it stronger. Resting takes place in metal or traditional wooden barrels.*

6 *The mature beer, which is ready to be sold, is then transferred to bottles or cans and pasteurized. This process removes micro-organisms that threaten the quality of the beer.*

Traditional wooden barrels containing resting beer

Sport in Germany

Sport has long enjoyed a significant role in German life both for active participants and spectators. The country regularly produces world champions in a variety of activities, including football, tennis and motor racing. Excellent facilities exist throughout the country for taking part in sporting activities, including sailing, swimming, climbing and skiing as well as in field- or track-based events. Southern Germany plays host to a variety of winter sports and competitions.

The German Open in Hamburger Rothenbaum

FOOTBALL

The largest sports organization in the country, the German Football Association has over 6 million registered members in some 25,000 clubs. The national team has won the World Cup three times – in 1954, 1974 and 1990 – and the European Cup in 1972, 1980 and 1996.

One of the outstanding figures in German football is Franz Beckenbauer, who was a member of the team that won the European Cup in 1972 and the World Cup in 1974. He trained the team that took second place in the 1986 World Cup and first place in 1990. Beckenbauer was twice named the best footballer in Europe.

The best-known club is Bayern München, which has won the German Cup a record 21 times. Matches between teams in the elite *Bundesliga* enjoy a great following. League matches are held on Saturday afternoons while European Cup games are usually held on Wednesday evenings. The club teams include a significant number of professionals from abroad. The 2006 World Cup was held in Germany.

Competing in Hamburg's annual Deutsches Spring Derby

SHOW-JUMPING AND EQUESTRIAN EVENTS

Show-jumping is another sport at which Germany excels. Since it was introduced to the Olympic Games in 1912, German riders have won 32 gold, 18 silver and 21 bronze medals. Major equestrian events are held in Hamburg and Aachen in June. Hamburg's Derby Week is popular with racing fans.

LAWN TENNIS

The German Tennis Association is the largest in the world with over 2 million members, belonging to some 10,200 clubs. From the mid-1980s, Germany became one of the world's most successful tennis nations thanks to some outstanding players. In 1985, aged 18, Boris Becker was the youngest player to win the Wimbledon championships. He repeated his achievement in 1986 and 1989 and was runner-up to fellow-German Michael Stich in 1991. From 1987–91 Steffi Graf was ranked number one among the world's female tennis players.

ATHLETICS

During the Cold War period, East and West German athletes competed against each other for the glory of their rival political systems as much as for the love of their sport. The extraordinary achievements of the East German athletes during that time have since been tarnished by revelations of systematic drug abuse. Since reunification, some athletes have managed to maintain their reputations, but the majority have not.

Germany's most important event, the Internationales Stadionfest (DKB-ISTAF), is held each year in Berlin, as the climax of the season.

Bundesliga football match (Hertha BSC Berlin v FC Bayern München)

FORMULA ONE

Back in the 1930s, motor-racing was dominated by the famous "Silver Arrows", made by Mercedes-Benz. Formula One has been a decidedly German discipline since its beginnings in 1950. In all the events there have always been at least three German drivers taking part. The German Formula One Grand Prix is held each July at the Hockenheim-Ring, near Heidelberg. In most years there is a second Grand Prix at the Nürburgring circuit close to the Belgian border. This is dubbed the European Grand Prix or the Luxembourg Grand Prix.

Germany's leading Formula One driver, Michael Schumacher, won the World Championship in 1994 and 1995 and every year from 2000 to 2004.

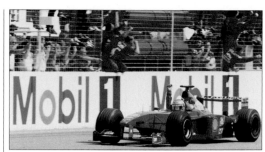

The Hockenheim race track near Heidelberg

Markus Eberle during the slalom in Ofterschwang in the Allgäu

SKIING

Since 1953, the last week of December and the first week of January have been dominated by the Four Ski Jumps Championship for ski jumpers. This classic event, which is held in Oberstdorf and Garmisch-Partenkirchen in Germany, as well as in Innsbruck and Bischofshofen in Austria, attracts several thousand spectators and millions of television viewers. German athletes have gained first place in this competition 15 times over the years.

As well as in the German Alps, which have the most popular ski resorts, excellent conditions exist for downhill and cross-country skiing in the less glamorous and less expensive Black Forest and the Harz Mountains.

CYCLING

Cycling enjoys a great following in Germany. The Tour de France is broadcast simultaneously by two television stations, and ever-increasing numbers of people are taking part in the sport, both for pleasure and competitively. Success on the cycle track has long been a German tradition, but Jan Ullrich exceeded all expectations when he won gold in the long distance and silver in a time trial at the Sydney Olympics in 2000.

SAILING

Kieler Woche is the most important regatta in the world, according to Paul Henderson, the President of the International Sailing Federation. On 1 September 1881, five officers of the Emperor's navy held a yachting race in the Bay of Kiel, as it was then called. The following year 20 yachts competed while thousands of spectators watched from the shore. The championship went on to become an international event, which gained in prestige as the Emperor took part in each race from 1894 until 1914.

Today it is traditional for the president of the German Federal Republic to formally open the regatta (in the last week of June) in which thousands of yachts from many countries take part.

SWIMMING

Swimming, more than any other sport in Germany, has seen a decline in success since reunification and the subsequent cessation of competition between East and West. At the 1988 Olympics in Seoul, for example, Kristin Otto won 6 gold medals. In 2000, the reunified German team returned from Sydney having gained only three bronze medals. Two figures who rose to the top in the past are Michael Gross, who was a member of the West German team, and Franziska van Almsick, a member of the East German team.

Franziska von Almsick during the German Swimming Championships

GERMANY THROUGH THE YEAR

Germans love to have fun and this is evident from the huge number of light-hearted events that are held throughout the year. Virtually every town has a calendar of festivals and fairs. These include folk festivals connected with local traditions – for example celebrating the asparagus or grape harvest.

A festival mascot

Many towns preserve the tradition of an annual fair – or *Jahrmarkt* – known in Westphalia as *Kirmes* and in Bavaria as *Dult*. Germany is also known for its music and film festivals, which attract an international audience, as well as for organizing major international trade fairs, such as the annual Frankfurt Book Fair.

Witches participating in the Walpurgisnacht celebrations in Thale

SPRING

Spring is an idyllic time to arrive in Germany. In the high mountains, conditions are still ideal for skiing, while in the valleys everything is already in bloom. In April and May the first spring fairs and festivals are held. Spring is also time for the traditional solemn observance of Easter and its associated celebrations. May Day, which is also International Labour Day, is marked both by traditional festivities and, in some cities, by demonstrations.

MARCH

Sommergewinn *(3 weekends before Easter)* Eisenach. The largest folk festival in Thuringia, linked with a fair.
CeBIT *(beginning of March)* Hanover. International trade fairs dedicated to information technology, telecommunications and automation.
Easter During Holy Week, Passion concerts are held throughout the country and colourful church services take place, particularly in

rural Catholic areas. On Easter Sunday, in cities in the Luzyce region, horse races and a gala take place.
Leipziger Buchmesse *(mid–March)* Leipzig. International book fair, with antiquarian books.

APRIL

Thüringer Bach-Wochen *(April)* Celebration of the life and works of Johann Sebastian Bach with concerts and lectures: held in Arnstadt, Eisenach, Erfurt, Gotha, Mühlhausen and Weimar.
Hannover Messe *(2nd half of April)* Hanover. International industrial trade fairs.

The International Dixieland Festival, held annually in Dresden in May

Hamburger Dom *(April, August and November)* Hamburg. The largest folk festival in northern Germany, held three times a year.
Walpurgisnacht *(30 April/ 1 May)*. On the witches' sabbath, witches gather on Brocken Mountain and in several other places in the Harz mountains.
Kurzfilmtage *(end April/ beginning of May)*. Oberhausen. The International Festival of Short Films has been held here since 1955.

MAY

Maibaumaufstellen *(1 May)*. In Bavarian villages, maypoles are decorated with highly ornamental wreaths.
Rhein in Flammen *(May–September)* Festivals with firework displays, in towns in the Rhine Valley.
Hafengeburtstag *(8–10 May)* Hamburg. A huge festival with fireworks, regatta and a parade of sailing boats.
Ruhrfestspiele *(May–June)* Recklinghausen. Cultural festival with a number of concerts and performances.
International Dixieland Festival *(2nd week of May)* Dresden. A traditional jazz festival has been held here since 1971.
Blutritt *(Friday after Ascension)* Weingarten. A horseback procession carrying religious relics around the town – held here for 450 years,
Leineweber Markt *(end of May)* Bielefeld. Street theatre, jazz and folk concerts.

SUMMER

In Germany the summer is a time of great open-air festivals and other outdoor events and activities. Nearly every town and village has its festival with a parade, street shows, concerts and fairs. In many places there are colourful illuminations and firework displays. Banquets and knights' tournaments are held in historic castles, while concert series are organized in palaces and castles with the tourist particularly in mind. In June, a number of classical music festivals take place, while July is a popular month for water-related festivals.

Yacht race during the annual Kieler Woche regatta in Kiel

JUNE

Bachfest Leipzig *(early June)* Leipzig. International music competition dedicated to Johann Sebastian Bach.
Internationales Stadionfest (DKB-ISTAF), *(2nd Sunday in June)* Berlin. The largest athletics event of the season.
Luther's Wedding *(second weekend in June)* Wittenberg. A celebration of the marriage of Martin Luther to Katharina von Bora with music and a parade.
Spreewaldfest *(June)* Spreewald. Festivals are held throughout the summer in Lübben and other villages.
Fronleichnam. Observed in Catholic majority states. Processions in towns in Bavaria and in Cologne.

A wedding couple during the Landshuter Hochzeit festival

Christopher Street Day *(mid-June)*. Gay and lesbian parades held in many cities, including Berlin and Köln.
Kieler Woche *(3rd week in June)* Kiel. Huge regatta with concerts and fairs.
Open-Air-Saison *(4th week in June, beginning of July)* Berlin. Opera festival held on outdoor stages.
Schützenfest *(June)* marks the traditional start of the hunting season. Celebrated in many north German cities.

JULY

Landshuter Hochzeit *(every 4th summer: next in 2013)* Landshut. Re-enactment of the wedding feast of Georg, son of Duke Ludwig the Rich and Polish Princess Jadwiga. Costumed wedding procession and medieval tournament.
Lights of Cologne *(early July)* Cologne. Very popular, big fireworks event.
Schwörmontag *(penultimate Monday)* Ulm. Folk festival with a parade by the Danube.
Kinderzeche *(3rd Monday)* Dinkelsbühl. Ten-day folk festival commemorating the events of the Thirty Years' War (1618–48).
Richard-Wagner-Festspiele *(last week July/August)* Bayreuth. Festival dedicated to the works of Richard Wagner.
Wikingerfest *(even years)* Schleswig. Historical festival with costumed participants, tournaments and regattas.
Machseefest *(late July)* Hannover. Summer outdoor carnival on the shores of Lake Machsee.

AUGUST

Zissel *(beginning of August)* Kassel. Picturesque folk festival with parades, markets and concerts.
Mainfest. Frankfurt am Main. Feast of the river Main.
Gäubodenfest *(mid-August)* Straubing. Folk festival with a market and beer tasting.
Weindorf *(end August)* Stuttgart. Huge wine festival with wines served along with typical Swabian cuisine.

Performance of *Tannhäuser* at Richard-Wagner-Festspiele, Bayreuth

AUTUMN

Autumn is an extremely popular time for tourism in Germany, especially September and early October when many cities, including Berlin and Munich, organize cultural events and important festivals. The autumn is also the time when the most significant trade fairs and great sporting events take place. At this time, also, conditions in the mountains and countryside continue to be ideal for outdoor activities such as walking and cycling.

SEPTEMBER

Berliner Festwochen, Berlin. Lasting all month, this is a major series of cultural events, opera performances, exhibitions and various literary events.
Beethovenfestival, Bonn. A musical festival celebrating the works of Beethoven in the city where he was born.
Heilbronner Herbst *(1st Saturday)* Heilbronn. Popular wine festival, which also includes parades and firework displays.
Popkomm *(mid-September)* Berlin. One of the world's biggest music industry conferences, which also features public performances by up-and-coming bands and DJs.
Berlin-Marathon *(mid-late September)* Berlin. Marathon

Pumpkin race during Dorffest

through the streets of the city centre, taking in several notable landmarks, with runners in various age groups and the participation of the disabled in wheelchairs.
Oktoberfest *(last two weeks of September)* Munich. World-famous beer festival held over 16 days, beginning with a parade through the city's streets. Ceremonial removal of the bung from a new barrel of beer that has been brewed for the festival.
Plärrer *(May and September)* Augsburg. Two-week festival held twice a year, considered one of the most important in Swabia.

Dorffest im Spreewald *(end of September)* Lehde. Folk festival.
Cannstatter Wasen *(end September/beginning October)* Stuttgart. The second largest beer festival in the world.

OCTOBER

Tag der Deutschen Einheit *(3 October)*. National holiday, established after re-unification. Concerts, parades and meetings.
Frankfurter Buchmesse *(2nd week in October)* Frankfurt am Main. The world's largest book fair, which attracts publishers from around the world and also features talks by authors.
Freimarkt *(mid-October)* Bremen. Two-week folk festival beginning with a procession.
Liszt-Tage Weimar. Celebration of the life and work of Franz Liszt, with concerts at which world-class musicians are invited to perform.
Colmansfest *(2nd Sunday)* Schwangau. Religious festival featuring hundreds of horses and decorated carriages.
Kasseler Musiktage *(end of October)* Kassel. One of Europe's longest-established classical music festivals.

NOVEMBER

Weinfest *(1st weekend in November)* Cochem. Festival celebrating the removal of the bung from the first barrel of young Mosel wine.
Martinsfest *(11 November)*. St Martin's Day is celebrated in northern Baden and the Rhineland with fairs and the essential roast goose. In the Rhine Valley, St Martin's Day signifies the beginning of the Carnival season.
Internationales Film-festival *(2nd week in November)* Mannheim-Heidelberg. Annual festival of short, documentary and educational films.

The International Book Fair in Frankfurt am Main

Berlinale – the grand festival of world cinema

WINTER

December is synonymous with Christmas festivities. Every city has fairs where you can buy Christmas-tree decorations, delicacies and presents. In December, shops have longer opening hours and the skiing season begins in the Alps. January and February are a time for parties and balls (the Carnival season), with enjoyment reaching a peak in the last few days of the season. Then the fun continues all weekend from Thursday, reaching a height on *Rosenmontag* then diminishing on the last Tuesday of Carnival.

DECEMBER

Christkindelsmarkt and **Weihnachtsmarkt**. Christmas fairs are held from the

The famous Christmas market in the city of Nuremberg

beginning of the month until Christmas Eve. The most beautiful are in Baden-Wurttemberg and in Bavaria, while the most renowned is held in Nuremberg.
Christmas *(25/26 December)*. Traditionally celebrated throughout Germany. A Christmas tree is considered essential, together with presents and delicacies.
New Year's Eve *(31 December)*. The New Year is greeted at balls, opera galas, in restaurants, clubs, private houses and in the streets and squares of city centres.

JANUARY

Four Ski Jumps Tournament *(begins 1 January)*. Renowned tournament for ski-jumping held annually in Garmisch-Partenkirchen.
Sechs-Tage-Rennen *(early January)* Berlin. Spectacular cycle races with associated events, held in Berlin Velodrome.
Grüne Woche *(2nd week)* Berlin. International trade fairs dedicated to agriculture, animal breeding and the food processing industry. Producers from all over the world offer specialities from their own national cuisines.

FEBRUARY

Berlinale–Internationale Filmfestspiele *(2nd and 3rd weeks)* Berlin. International film festival in which major stars participate.

Fastnacht, also known as **Fasnet**, **Fasching** or **Karneval** (Shrovetide). Carnival is celebrated enthusiastically in virtually every region of Germany. The most interesting events are held in the Rhine Valley, and particularly in Cologne. *Karneval am Rhein*, which marks the lasts three days of the Carnival, begins on the Thursday of the week before Ash Wednesday with a women's parade, known as *Weiberfastnacht*. On the Monday there is a superb costume parade, known as *Rosenmontagsumzug*.

Costumed revellers on the streets of Cologne during Carnival

PUBLIC HOLIDAYS

Neujahr *New Year* (1 Jan).

Hl. Dreikönige *Three Kings* (6 Jan. Bavaria, Baden-Wurttemberg, Saxony-Anhalt).

Karfreitag *Good Friday*.

Ostern *Easter*.

Maifeiertag/Tag der Arbeit *Labour Day*.

Christi Himmelfahrt *Ascension*.

Pfingsten *Pentecost*.

Fronleichnam *Corpus Christi* (Bavaria, Baden-Wurttemberg, Hesse, North Rhine Valley-Westphalia, Rhine Valley-Palatinate and Saar).

Mariä Himmelfahrt *Assumption of the BVM* (15 Aug: Bavaria, Saar).

Nationalfeiertag *Reunification of Germany Day* (3 Oct).

Allerheiligen *All Saints* (1 Nov: Bavaria, Baden-Wurttemberg, North Rhine Valley-Westphalia, Rhine Valley-Palatinate).

Weihnachten *Christmas* (25/26 Dec).

The German Climate

Germany lies in a temperate climatic zone. In the north of the country, with marine influences predominating, summers tend to be quite cold and winters mild, with relatively high rainfall. In the eastern part of the country, however, the climate is more continental and this produces harsher winters and hotter summers. Germany's highest rainfall and the lowest temperatures are recorded in the Alps.

SCHLESWIG-HOLSTEIN

Average daily maximum temperature

Average daily minimum temperature

Average daily amount of sunshine

Average monthly rainfall

°C (F)				
	2.2 (36)	10.5 (51)	20 (68)	13 (55)
0	-2 (28)	3 (37)	12 (54)	7 (45)
☀	1.3 hrs	5.5 hrs	7 hrs	3 hrs
☂	80 mm	55 mm	92 mm	90 mm
month	Jan	Apr	Jul	Oct

BREMEN, HAMBURG, LOWER SAXONY

°C (F)				
	3.2 (38)	12.5 (55)	22 (72)	14 (57)
0	-2 (28)	3.5 (38)	12 (54)	6 (43)
☀	1.3 hrs	5 hrs	6 hrs	3 hrs
☂	56 mm	48 mm	69 mm	55 mm
month	Jan	Apr	Jul	Oct

NORTH RHINE-WESTPHALIA

°C (F)				
	4.5 (40)	14 (57)	23 (73)	15 (59)
0	-1 (30)	3.6 (38)	12.5 (55)	6 (43)
☀	1.5 hrs	5 hrs	6.5 hrs	3.7 hrs
☂	62 mm	54 mm	84 mm	55 mm
month	Jan	Apr	Jul	Oct

HESSE

°C (F)				
	3 (37)	14 (57)	24 (75)	14 (57)
0	-2 (28)	4 (39)	13 (55)	6 (43)
☀	1.3 hrs	5 hrs	7.4 hrs	3.3 hrs
☂	44 mm	51 mm	63 mm	50 mm
month	Jan	Apr	Jul	Oct

RHINELAND-PALAT-INATE, SAARLAND

°C (F)				
	3 (37)	13 (55)	23 (73)	14 (57)
0	-1.5 (29)	4 (39)	12 (54)	7 (45)
☀	1.3 hrs	5 hrs	7 hrs	3 hrs
☂	60 mm	53 mm	69 mm	65 mm
month	Jan	Apr	Jul	Oct

BADEN WURTTEMBERG

°C (F)				
	4 (39)	14 (57)	23 (73)	15 (59)
0	-1 (30)	5 (41)	13 (55)	7 (45)
☀	1.7 hrs	5 hrs	8 hrs	4 hrs
☂	60 mm	80 mm	95 mm	66 mm
month	Jan	Apr	Jul	Oct

Flensbu
Schles
Har
Bremen
Nienb
Hanov
Münster
Paderborn
Göttin
Dortmund
Düsseldorf
Kasse
Cologne
Siegen
Aachen
Bonn
Marburg
Koblenz
Frankfurt am Main
Mainz
Würzb
Trier
Mannheim
Saarbrücken
Heidelberg
Karlsruhe
Stuttg
U
Freiburg im Breisgau
Konsta

0 km   100

0 miles   100

MECKLENBURG-LOWER POMERANIA

°C (F)	Jan	Apr	Jul	Oct
high	3 (37)	10 (50)	21 (70)	12.5 (55)
low	-2 (28)	4 (39)	14 (57)	7.5 (46)
☀ hrs	1.5	5.5	7.5	3.5
☂ mm	40	42	72	50

BRANDENBURG

°C (F)	Jan	Apr	Jul	Oct
high	2 (36)	13 (55)	24 (75)	14 (57)
low	-3 (27)	3.5 (38)	13 (55)	6 (43)
☀ hrs	1.5	5.5	7.5	3.7
☂ mm	44	44	52	35

BERLIN

°C (F)	Jan	Apr	Jul	Oct
high	2 (36)	13 (55)	24 (75)	13 (55)
low	-4 (25)	4 (39)	13 (55)	3 (41)
☀ hrs	1.9	6.4	8.1	4.1
☂ mm	43	41	70	47

SAXONY-ANHALT

°C (F)	Jan	Apr	Jul	Oct
high	2.4 (36)	13 (55)	23 (73)	14 (57)
low	-3 (27)	3.5 (58)	12 (54)	6 (43)
☀ hrs	1.5	5	7	3.5
☂ mm	33	40	48	29

SAXONY

°C (F)	Jan	Apr	Jul	Oct
high	1.5 (35)	12 (54)	22 (72)	13 (55)
low	-4 (39)	3 (37)	12 (54)	6 (43)
☀ hrs	2	4.5	6.6	4
☂ mm	42	55	76	47

BAVARIA

°C (F)	Jan	Apr	Jul	Oct
high	2 (36)	14 (57)	23 (73)	13 (55)
low	-4 (25)	3 (37)	12 (54)	3 (37)
☀ hrs	1.5	5	7.5	4
☂ mm	46	47	69	45

THURINGIA

°C (F)	Jan	Apr	Jul	Oct
high	1.5 (35)	12 (54)	22 (72)	13 (55)
low	-3.5 (26)	3 (37)	12 (54)	5 (41)
☀ hrs	1.7	5	7	4
☂ mm	24.5	45	46	33

MUNICH

°C (F)	Jan	Apr	Jul	Oct
high	1 (34)	13 (55)	23 (73)	13 (55)
low	-6 (43)	3 (37)	12 (54)	4 (39)
☀ hrs	2.2	6	7.7	4.6
☂ mm	59	62	140	67

Map labels: Bergen, Rostock, Wismar, Güstrow, Neubrandenburg, Wittenberge, Neuruppin, Stendal, BERLIN, Brandenburg, Potsdam, Frankfurt am Oder, Luckenwalde, Magdeburg, Dessau, Lutherstadt Wittenberg, Cottbus, Halle, Leipzig, Dresden, Erfurt, Weimar, Altenburg, Chemnitz, Plauen, Hof, Bamberg, Nuremberg, Regensburg, Neuburg, Passau, Augsburg, MUNICH, Garmisch-Partenkirchen

THE HISTORY OF GERMANY

Germany is a country of cultural and religious contrasts Regional differences in culture, language and traditions arose from the historical division of the country into many small states. Such differences have been further accentuated by the recent experience of generations of Germans who, until 1990, grew up under two conflicting social systems: capitalism and communism.

EARLY HISTORY

In the 1st millennium BC, the basins of the Rhine, Danube and Main rivers were settled by Celts, who had been largely displaced by Germanic tribes by the 2nd century BC. In the 1st century BC the Roman legions waged wars with the Germans, and conquered the territories west of the Rhine. The settlements they founded there later developed into towns like Trier, Mainz, Cologne and Xanten. The Romans made numerous attempts to conquer the eastern regions between the Rhine and the Elbe rivers. They eventually reached the Elbe at the end of the 1st century BC, but the Germans, under the leadership of Arminius, also known as Germanus, defeated the Roman armies in the Teutoburg Forest in AD 9, and so ended their presence in this region. A system of fortifications, or *limes*, built in the 2nd century along the course of the Danube and the Rhine, divided the region into two: *Germania Romana*, the Roman province, and *Germania Libra*, free Germany. The free German tribes,

Heinrich I, from the house of Liudolf

notably the Goths, often entered into alliances with the Romans. In the 5th century, however, they took advantage of Rome's weakness to appropriate parts of the empire for themselves.

EARLY MIDDLE AGES

After the collapse of the Roman Empire, the area between the Rhine and the Elbe was ruled by the Franks, who gradually converted to Christianity from the 6th century. One of the most important figures in this process was the 8th-century missionary, St Boniface. When Charlemagne was crowned Emperor in 800, the territory of present-day Germany became part of the Frankish Empire. The Empire was partitioned by the Treaty of Verdun in 843, with the eastern part going to Ludwig the German. In the 10th century the kingdom, which was made up of numerous tribal states, passed to the house of Liudolf. Otto I, son of Heinrich I and the first king from this Saxon family, was crowned Emperor in 962 after several political and military victories, in particular his defeat of the Magyars.

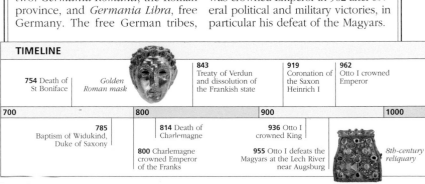

TIMELINE

754 Death of St Boniface

Golden Roman mask

843 Treaty of Verdun and dissolution of the Frankish state

919 Coronation of the Saxon Heinrich I

962 Otto I crowned Emperor

700 — 800 900 1000

785 Baptism of Widukind, Duke of Saxony

814 Death of Charlemagne

800 Charlemagne crowned Emperor of the Franks

936 Otto I crowned King

955 Otto I defeats the Magyars at the Lech River near Augsburg

8th-century reliquary

◁ **Germany's Awakening, a patriotic 19th-century work by Christian Köhler**

CONSOLIDATING POWER

With Otto being crowned emperor, the dynasty of the Saxon house of Liudolf acceded to power. It gave the country three further rulers – Otto II, Otto III and Heinrich II. In the year 925 Otto I annexed Lotharingia (present-day Lorraine). On the eastern frontier he created two "marks", the Nordmark and the Ostmark, as buffer states designed to

Stained-glass window in Augsburg cathedral

subjugate the Slav-populated regions east of the Oder River. After Heinrich II's death, the house of the Salian Franks took the imperial throne and used their authority to limit the power of the local feudal dukes.

THE INVESTITURE CONTROVERSY

In the 11th century the empire came into conflict with the papacy. Matters came to a head in the so-called "investiture controversy". Pope Gregory VII asserted the church's right to appoint bishops. Emperor Heinrich IV meanwhile, who had been relying on the support of the clergy he had appointed, called his bishops together and asked the Pope to step down. Pope Gregory VII excommunicated Heinrich.

The dukes of Saxony used the opportunity to appoint a king in opposition to Heinrich, and the Pope attempted to intervene in the dispute. Heinrich IV saw himself forced to march to Canossa in Italy, where the Pope had sought refuge, in order to stop his empire from falling apart. Doing penance in this way forced the Pope to withdraw his excommunication. However, the dispute did not end there, but continued for several years, finally ending with the Signing of the Concordat of Worms in 1122.

Enamelled Romanesque medallion, dating from c.1150

HOHENSTAUFENS AND WELFS

After the Salian dynasty died out in 1125 and the brief reign of Lothar III of the Saxon dynasty, another long drawn-out conflict broke out, between the houses of Hohenstaufen and Welf (known in Italian as Ghibellines and Guelphs). Imperial power went to the Hohenstaufens, while the greatest political victories were scored by Friedrich I Barbarossa (meaning "red beard"). He intended gradually to break up his subject principalities and to rule them under a feudal system. The 12th century also saw further expansion eastwards and northwards into areas inhabited by the northwestern Slavic tribes. From the start of the 13th

12th-century reliquary from the Welf family vaults

TIMELINE

11th-century reliquary cross

Portable altar from the vaults of the Welfs

1027 Coronation of Konrad II, first Emperor of the Salians

1074 Beginning of Investiture Struggle

1077 Heinrich IV does penance at Canossa

1122 The Concordat of Worms

1138 Coronation of Konrad III, first Hohenstaufen Emperor

1155 Coronation of Friedrich I Barbarossa as Emperor

1000	1050	1100	1150

century Barbarossa also conquered territories occupied by the Baltic peoples and the Estonians, which involved armed expeditions by the North German cities and orders of knights.

Friedrich II, crowned Emperor in 1220, was also King of Sicily and his Italian interests brought further conflict with the papacy. Ultimately his policies brought about the collapse of imperial power. After his death in 1250, his successor was unable to find any support, which led to the period known as the Great Interregnum.

Emperor Rudolf I of Habsburg

THE INTERREGNUM

The fall of the Hohenstaufens marked the end of the old imperial system. The absence of an overall ruler led to a breakdown in law and order, and resulted in the rise of the *Raubritter* (robber-barons). To protect their common interests, the trading cities set up alliances. The collapse of imperial power, and the decline in the power of the dukes thus gradually led to an increase in the power of the German cities.

From the beginning the imperial throne had been elective, with dukes electing the emperor from the male members of the dynasty. There was also no capital city, as the emperors moved from one city to another, thus spreading the costs of maintaining the imperial court among different duchies. In the

13th century a system evolved by which only seven elector-dukes had the right to elect the emperor. These were the Margrave of Brandenburg, the Elector of Palatine (or the Bavarian dukes), the Duke of Saxony, the King of Bohemia and the Archbishops of Trier, Cologne and Mainz. Starting with Rudolf I of Habsburg, who was elected king of Germany in 1273, until 1438 the kings came from the rival houses of Habsburg, Wittelsbach and Luxemburg. After 1312, the same houses also competed for the title of Emperor. The most outstanding of the 14th-century rulers of Germany was Karl IV of Luxemburg, who resided permanently in Prague. In 1338 the electors had rejected the requirement for the Pope to confirm election results. In 1356 Karl IV issued the "Golden Bull" which underlined the federal nature of the state, and clarified the rules for electing its leader.

A "Minneteppich" – part of a medieval tapestry, depicting a variety of human traits and a griffin, the mythical beast

1200	1250	1300	1350

1250 Beginning of the Great Interregnum

1312 Heinrich VII crowned Emperor

Silver coin from 1369

1273 End of the Great Interregnum and coronation of Rudolf I

1348 Prague University founded

1356 Golden Bull issued

1386 Heidelberg University founded

The Hanseatic League

The German Hanseatic League, or Hanse, was only one of many guilds of traders or cities that existed in the Middle Ages, but its important historical role made it one of the best known. Established in the 13th century, it reached its peak in the 14th century and declined again in the 16th century. Over 160 cities, primarily the trading cities of northern Germany, but also including Baltic ports as far afield as Visby, Riga and Tallinn, joined the League. It exercised total control over trade from the Baltic in the east to England in the west. The Hanseatic cities were among the wealthiest in Europe, and crafts and the arts flourished there.

Madonna of the Roses
*15th-century painting
by Stefan Lochner of
the Cologne School.*

The Wise and Foolish Maidens
*The flowering of art in the Hanseatic cities
brought about works such as this portal of
Magdeburg Cathedral.*

**Hanse ships,
loaded with
merchandise,
entering the
harbour**

**Revenue
officials
awaiting the
cargo**

**Crucifix in
Lübeck
Cathedral**
*This crucifix is
one of only few
painted wood-
carvings made
by Bernt Notke
of Lübeck that
have survived
until today.*

**Round
wooden
cranes**
with swivel-
ling arms were
used to
unload ships.
One example
still survives in
Lüneburg.

Cogs
*Cogs – heavy, flat-bottomed sailing
ships with limited manoeuvrability – were
fishermen's and merchants' boats or navy
vessels in the North Sea and the Baltic
from the 12th to the 14th centuries.*

Panoramic view of Lübeck
The vast port town of Lübeck was the largest Hanseatic city. This 15th-century woodcut shows a view of the city with its numerous church spires.

Harbour officials in their offices

The Leichter was a harbour boat used to carry cargo from the ships to the warehouses.

Hamburg merchants

Russian merchants, recognizable by their distinctive clothing, are engrossed in intense negotiations.

THE PORT OF HAMBURG

Hamburg, along with Bremen, Lübeck and Gdansk, was one of the leading Hanseatic cities. In the 14th century, it was the main centre for trade between the North Sea and the Baltic. This miniature, showing the port of Hamburg, dates from the 15th century.

THE HANSEATIC CITIES

In the major Hanseatic cities, the most prominent buildings grew up around the *Markt* (market square) and along the streets that led to the port. The market square would contain the *Rathaus* (town hall), with its multifunctional interiors, and the equally splendid banqueting halls and ballrooms, such as the Gürzenich in Cologne. The main cathedrals in the cities were dedicated either to St Mary or St Nicholas. The gabled residential houses had narrow façades with distinctive portals. The townscape of the port areas was dominated by granaries, warehouses and numerous cranes. The cities were all enclosed and protected by solid fortifications.

The town hall in Brunswick, *with its open upper arcades and statues of the Welfs, is one of the finest surviving Hanseatic secular buildings.*

The Kröpeliner Tor *in Rostock* (see p476) *is one of 22 towers on the defensive walls around the medieval city centre.*

Jan Hus being burned at the stake

THE HUSSITE WARS AND THE HABSBURG DYNASTY

The last king and emperor of the house of Luxemburg, Sigismund, brought an end to the "Great Schism" in the Western church that had persisted since 1378. The Council of Constance, which he called in 1414, led to the election of a single, rather than two rival popes. However, new religious controversy was provoked by the death sentence for heresy passed in 1415 on Jan Hus, a religious reformer from Bohemia. The ensuing Hussite Wars ravaged the northern and western regions of Germany.

From 1482 the imperial crown went to the Habsburgs, who retained it

Title page of the first German edition of the Bible

until 1740. Attempts at political reform in the second half of the 15th century failed. The most ambitious reformer was Maximilian I. He called an Imperial Tribunal in 1495 which set about transferring part of the king's authority to the judiciary; however, it did not result in any great practical changes, although it gave slightly more power to the *Reichstag*, the imperial parliament

THE REFORMATION

Germany entered the 16th century as a country simmering with social conflict, gradually becoming steeped in the ideas of humanism, thanks to the writings of Erasmus of Rotterdam and others. The rise of Martin Luther, who in 1517 nailed his 95 Theses to the door of the Castle Church in Wittenberg, and who opposed the trade in

Lion-shaped water jug (1540)

indulgences conducted by the clergy, set the Reformation in motion *(see pp126–7)*. The idea of ecclesiastical reform propounded by Luther gained a growing following. His supporters included princes who hoped to profit from the secularization of church property, as well as other social classes that simply saw an opportunity to improve their lot. In 1519 Maximilian I died, and Karl V was elected to succeed him. Karl's interests were focused on Spain and the Netherlands, and he was unable to prevent the spread of Lutheranism.

TIMELINE

Maximilian I

1400		1450		1500	
1419–36 Hussite Wars		**c.1450** The first printing press		**1517** Luther's Theses and the start of the Reformation	**1540** The first stock exchanges are set up in Augsburg and Nürnberg
1414–18 Council of Constance	**1438** Coronation of Albrecht II, first Emperor of the House of Habsburg		**1495** Edict banning the waging of private wars	**1522** The Knights' War	**1524–25** The Peasants' War

Urban life in Germany in the early 16th century, in a painting by Jörg Breu the Elder (c.1475 1537)

The unrest led to rebellions such as the Knights' War of 1522 and the Peasants' War of 1524, and these were followed by continuous religious conflict. In 1530 the Protestants set up the League of Schmalkalden, which was finally broken up by the Emperor in the war of 1546–7. These basically religious clashes ultimately led to the division of Germany into a northern Protestant part and a Catholic south, a situation that was sanctioned in 1555 by the Peace of Augsburg. This established the principle of *cuius regio, eius religio*, which meant that each ruler had the right to decide on the faith of the region, and the only option left for anyone of a different persuasion was to move elsewhere.

THE THIRTY YEARS' WAR

The second half of the 16th century was relatively stable for Germany, despite the religious conflicts. However, the influ- ence of the Counter-Reformation in the early 17th century ended this stability. The Protestant Union and Catholic League were established in 1608 and 1609 respectively. Unrest in Prague, where the states with a Protestant majority opposed the election of the Catholic Ferdinand II as king of Bohemia, began the Thirty Years' War. This religious war quickly spread throughout Germany, and also drew in Denmark, Spain, Sweden and France. Much of the country and many towns were laid waste, and vast numbers of people died. Finally, in 1648, the German states, France and Sweden signed the Peace of Westphalia in Münster, resulting in major losses of territory for Germany, mainly in the north. A new political system emerged, with the German princes enjoying complete political independence, under a weakened emperor and pope. The second half of the 17th century was marked by the rebuilding of towns and the hard work of restoring the ruined economic infrastructure.

A scene in the Thirty Years' War, in a painting by Wilhelm von Diez

16th-century tile, depicting a falconer

Monument to the Great Elector, Friedrich Wilhelm I

1546 Schmalkalden War begins

1550

1555 Religious Peace of Augsburg

1600

1608 Foundation of the Protestant Union

1609 Establishment of the Catholic League

1618 Thirty Years' War breaks out

1640 Accession to the Brandenburg throne by Friedrich Wilhelm I

1650

1648 Peace of Westphalia ends the Thirty Years' War

Goethe in the Roman Campagna by Johann H. W. Tischbein (1787)

ABSOLUTISM AND THE RISE OF PRUSSIA

In the second half of the 17th century and throughout the 18th century, Germany was a loose federation of small, politically weak states in the west, and much more powerful states in the east and the south – Saxony, which was ruled by the house of Wettin, and Bavaria, ruled by the Wittelsbachs. However, the rising star was the state of Brandenburg, ruled by the house of Hohenzollern, which from 1657 also ruled Prussia. In 1701 the Elector Friedrich III crowned himself King of Prussia (as Friedrich I), and subsequently the name "Prussia" was applied to all areas ruled by the house of Hohenzollern. During the 18th century Prussia became the greatest rival to Habsburg Austria. In 1740, Friedrich II, also known as Frederick the Great, was crowned King of Prussia. Under his rule, Berlin became a major European city and a centre of the Enlightenment. In 1740–42, in the Seven Years' War, Frederick the Great took Silesia from the Habsburgs without major losses. In 1772 he took part in the first partition of Poland.

In the second half of the 18th century Germany produced a succession of great poets and playwrights – figures such as Gotthold Ephraim Lessing, Friedrich Schiller and Johann Wolfgang von Goethe.

Portrait of Frederick the Great as successor to the throne

THE NAPOLEONIC WARS, RESTORATION AND REVOLUTION

From 1793 onwards the German states were involved in the Napoleonic Wars. After France's occupation of the lands west of the Rhine, a territorial reform was carried out by the Reichsdeputations Hauptschluss in 1803. This resulted in the secularization of most church property, and the total of 289 states and free cities was reduced to 112 larger states. States that gained from this supported Napoleon in his defeat of Austria in the war of 1805–7. In 1806 the Holy Roman Empire of German Nations was dissolved, and Bavaria, Saxony and Wurttemberg were given the status of kingdoms. Napoleon defeated Prussia at Jena and the country was occupied by France.

TIMELINE

1700	1730	1760	1790

1701 The first king of Prussia is crowned

1702–14 Germany joins the War of Spanish Succession

1740–42 The Silesian War

Leopold Hermann von Boyen, Prussian army general

1813 Battle of the Nations at Leipzig

1710 Meißen porcelain factory opened

1700 Academy of Sciences founded in Berlin

1756–63 The Seven Years' War

1740 Frederick the Great crowned King of Prussia

1803 Territorial reform of the German states

1806 Dissolution of the Empire

1814–15 The Congress of Vienna

The tide turned for Germany at the Battle of Leipzig in 1813, when Russia, Austria and Prussia defeated the French. After Napoleon's final defeat at Waterloo in 1815, the Congress of Vienna established a German Confederation under Austrian control. Its supreme body was the Bundestag (federal parliament), which met at Frankfurt am Main.

Victory Report at the Battle of Leipzig by Johann Peter Krafft (1839)

Vase with portrait of Kaiser Wilhelm II

The wars of liberation against Napoleon had led to a growth in nationalism and democratic awareness, as well as a desire for unification. In 1848 the March Revolution broke out in Berlin. Its main driving force was the urban middle class, but the revolt was finally put down by Prussian troops in 1849.

In the 1820s and 1830s, Germany underwent rapid industrialization, and the establishment of the Zollverein (customs union) in 1834 marked the first step towards a united Germany. Uniting Germany was the main goal of the Prussian premier Otto von Bismarck. Prussia's victories over Austria in 1866 and France in 1871 resulted in the proclamation of a German Empire on 18 January 1871.

THE SECOND REICH

The Second Reich was a federation of 25 states, and its first Chancellor was Otto von Bismarck. The unification of Germany led to a widespread confrontation between the state and the Catholic Church (known as the "Kulturkampf"). The economy, however, flourished, due to the boom in industry, in particular mining, metallurgy, electrical and chemical engineering. This led to the rise of a workers' movement, inspired by the ideas of Karl Marx. In 1875 the workers' parties united and formed the Social Democratic Party of Germany (SPD). Although the party was banned between 1878 and 1890, it rapidly gained support, and a system of social welfare for workers was gradually introduced.

At the beginning of the 20th century, Germany was a powerful state with overseas colonies. Imperialist tendencies grew, and increased tensions in European politics, particularly in the Balkans, led inevitably to war.

Fighting on the Barricades in May 1848, a fanciful picture of the revolution in Berlin by Julius Scholz

1834 German Customs Union (Zollverein) is established	1848 The Communist Manifesto is published	1871 Proclamation of the German Empire with Prussian king as Emperor Wilhelm I	1898 Construction of the German navy begins
	1848–49 The March Revolution		
1820	**1850**	**1880**	**1910**
	1844 Silesian weavers' uprising	1870–71 Franco-Prussian War	1890 Fall of Bismarck
Neo-Gothic chalice designed by K.F. Schinkel		1866 Prussian-Austrian War	Abandoned, *bas-relief* by Ernst Barlach

Bismarck's Germany

The establishment of a Reich headed by the King of Prussia on 18 January 1871 ensured Prussia's prominent role over the following decades. The Chancellor was the Prussian Prime Minister Otto von Bismarck. Thanks to large reparations paid by France and a favourable economic situation, the economy flourished throughout the Reich. This in turn fostered the development of science and culture. The cities grew rapidly, and the housing shortage led to the development of huge *Mietskasernen*, blocks of apartments for renting.

GERMANY IN 1871

■ *The Second German Reich*

Kaiser Wilhelm I
Mosaics, depicting a procession of members of the house of Hohenzollern, decorate the vestibule of the Kaiser-Wilhelm Gedächtnichskirche (memorial church) in Berlin.

The Kaiser's Family Taking a Walk in Sanssouci Park
"Happy family" portraits such as this one were often painted for propaganda purposes.

The Reichstag
The monumental Reichstag (parliament building), was built in the centre of the capital, Berlin, by the architect Paul Wallot.

Members of
Parliament

Heads of the
federal states

A Steel Mill in Königshütte
Germany's economic progress was achieved through a high degree of industrialization. Adolf von Menzel's painting depicts a steel mill in Königshütte, Upper Silesia.

Officer's helmet
The characteristic spiked helmet worn by German soldiers was known as a Pickelhaube.

Ludwig II of Bavaria
The federal states, which made up the Reich, enjoyed complete autonomy. Their rulers, however, for instance King Ludwig II of Bavaria, patron of Richard Wagner and builder of "fantastic" castles and palaces, had little real political influence.

The Kaiser's wife, Augusta Victoria

Mourning dress
was worn by the women and black ribbons by the men as a mark of respect for the two previous Kaisers who had died in 1888 – the father and grandfather of Wilhelm II.

Wilhelm, the heir to the throne

The Diplomatic Corps

Otto von Bismarck

Kaiser Wilhelm II

INAUGURATION OF THE REICHSTAG
This vast canvas by Anton von Werner (1893) shows the opening ceremony for the Reichstag after the coronation of Kaiser Wilhelm II on 25 June 1888 in the Kaiser's Palace in Berlin. The painter depicts the moment when the Kaiser delivers his speech.

Otto von Bismarck
Originating from a Pomeranian family of Junkers, the Prussian Premier and Chancellor of the Reich was one of the most prominent political figures of his time.

WORLD WAR I

When Germany entered World War I in 1914, the Kaiser's generals hoped for a quick victory, but their invasion of France was halted on the Marne. The war dragged on for the next four years, devastating much of Europe, and ending in Germany's defeat. The Allied offensive in the summer of 1918 forced Germany to the negotiating table – it also led to the November revolution in Germany. Within days the state monarchs were toppled from power, Kaiser Wilhelm II abdicated, and on 9 November 1918 a republic was proclaimed. The form of government had not been decided, and at first the political advantage was held by the socialists. But the Workers' Uprising in Berlin in 1919 was defeated.

Ein Volk, ein Reich, ein Führer!

Propaganda poster for Adolf Hitler

THE WEIMAR REPUBLIC

The Treaty of Versailles of 1919 imposed many unfavourable conditions on Germany. The country lost a great deal of her territory, mainly to Poland, France and Lithuania, and she was obliged to pay huge reparations, undergo partial demilitarization and limit arms production.

During the Weimar Republic, Germany was riddled with instability. The economy collapsed under the heavy burden of reparation payments and the onset of hyperinflation. Constant changes of government failed to stabilize the political situation, which led to the rise both of left-wing revolutionaries and of right-wing nationalists, and to a general dissatisfaction with the country's status after the humiliating Treaty of Versailles. It is perhaps remarkable that at this time German culture flourished.

DURCH LICHT ZUR NACHT

Cover of a Socialist magazine attacking the book-burning

However, this was not sufficient to stave off the political disaster that led to the rise of the Nazi Party (the NSDAP or National Socialist German Workers' Party).

THE THIRD REICH

Adolf Hitler was appointed Chancellor by President Hindenburg on 30 January 1933 and immediately started to get rid of potential opponents. A fire that burned down the Reichstag served as a pretext for persecuting the communists,

A Berlin synagogue burning during Kristallnacht, 1938

TIMELINE

1914 World War I breaks out

BLONDE VENUS

Poster of Marlene Dietrich

1915

9 Nov 1918 Declaration of the Republic

1919 Signing of the Treaty of Versailles

1920

1921 Adolf Hitler becomes leader of the NSDAP

1923 Hitler's Putsch in Munich

1925 Hitler writes *Mein Kampf*

1925

1926 Germany accepted in League of Nations

1926 Hitler Youth set up

while in April 1933 a boycott of Jewish businesses began. Trade unions were banned, as were all parties apart from the Nazis. Books by "impure" authors were burned, and the work of "degenerate" artists was exhibited as a warning, marking the start of the persecution of artists and scientists, many of whom decided to emigrate. At the same time, Hitler attempted to present to the world a face of openness and success, particularly with the Berlin Olympics of 1936. Germany broke almost all the demilitarization conditions of the Versailles Treaty. The growth in arms production brought with it an improved economic situation, increasing Hitler's popularity. All his opponents who had not managed to emigrate were either killed or sent to concentration camps.

In 1935 the Nuremberg Laws were passed, which officially sanctioned the persecution of Jews. During the *Kristallnacht* (crystal night) of 9 November 1938, synagogues throughout Germany were burned and Jewish shops and homes were looted, resulting in streets littered with broken glass. Hitler's plans to conquer Europe were realized in March 1938, with the "Anschluss" (annexation) of Austria, then in 1939 German forces occupied Czechoslovakia. After obtaining peace guarantees from the USSR, Germany invaded Poland on 1 September 1939, thus starting World War II.

Pieta, sculpture by Käthe Kollwitz (1937–8)

The centre of Dresden after Allied carpet-bombing

WORLD WAR II

The first two years of World War II were marked by one victory after another for the German Army, which managed to occupy half of Europe. Great Britain was the only country that succeeded in fending off Hitler. In 1941 the Wehrmacht occupied large swathes of the Soviet Union. Terror and genocide were instigated in all occupied territories. The decision to exterminate all Jews in Europe was taken at the Wannsee Conference in Berlin in January 1942. Attempts to oppose Hitler in Germany were crushed. The course of the war did not change until 1943, when on 31 January Germany suffered a major defeat in the Battle of Stalingrad.

The Allied landings in Normandy and the creation of the second front helped bring the war to an end. When Soviet forces reached Berlin in 1945 the city lay in ruins and the populace was starving. During five and a half years, 55 million people had lost their lives.

Nazi war criminals on trial at Nuremberg

THE AFTERMATH OF WORLD WAR II

Germany's unconditional surrender was signed on 8 May 1945, ending the bloodiest war in human history. Peace negotiations began which were to shape the new face of Europe for decades to come. In fact, discussions on Germany's future had already taken place at the Tehran and Yalta Conferences, where the leaders of the Big Three Powers met. But it was not until the Potsdam Conference that the terms were finally agreed.

Germany lost large parts of its territory to the east, displacing the German population there. It was decided to demilitarize Germany. The four Allied powers – the USA, the USSR, Britain and France – divided Germany into zones of occupation which they would rule until democratic structures were in place. The main perpetrators of war crimes were tried in Nuremberg and sentenced to death. Unfortunately, tensions increased between the Western powers and the Soviet Union, rapidly escalating in the "Cold War", which was largely played out in occupied Germany. In

The Berlin Airlift in 1948–9

1948 the three western zones introduced a new currency, which led the Soviets to blockade the western part of Berlin. Thanks to the Berlin Airlift, which supplied the population with food and fuel, the blockade was abandoned. On 23 May 1949 the Federal Republic (Bundesrepublik) of Germany was established in the three western zones, and on 7 October 1949 the German Democratic Republic (DDR) was set up in the Soviet zone. West Berlin, as it was then known, became an enclave inside East Germany.

GERMANY 1949–90

■ *Federal Republic*

□ *DDR*

GERMANY DIVIDED

The German Democratic Republic was democratic only in name. It became one of the satellites of the Soviet Union, and as the westernmost outpost of the Eastern Bloc it was subject to great restrictions. Attempted

Graffiti-covered section of the Berlin Wall

TIMELINE

1945	1950	1955	1960	1965	1970	1975	198

4–11 Feb 1945 Yalta Conference **8 May** Germany capitulates

24 Jun 1948 Blockade of West Berlin starts

1949 Federal Republic and DDR established

17 Jun 1953 Workers' uprising in East Berlin

1955 Federal Republic and German Democratic Republic gain sovereignty

Konrad Adenauer

13 Aug 1961 Building of the Berlin Wall

1968 Student riots

1972 Official relations established between East and West Germany; Munich Olympics

1973 West and East Germany accepted into UN

The Trabant, a trademark of East German industry

1982 Helmut Kohl becomes German Chancellor

Reunification ceremony outside the Reichstag in Berlin in 1990

Eastern Bloc. Democratic changes in Poland set off a chain reaction. In 1989, people started to flee the German Democratic Republic en masse via its embassy in Prague and across the Austro-Hungarian border. Then, on 9 November 1989, the Berlin Wall fell due to protests in the East, and East Germans were free to leave. When, only three weeks later, Chancellor Helmut Kohl presented a ten-point plan for German reunification, few believed that it would happen, but the country was officially reunified on 3 October 1990. Since then, Germany has been undergoing a process of integration.

protests, such as the Workers' Uprising of 17 June 1953 in Berlin, were ruthlessly suppressed. For many people the only solution was to leave the country. As the exodus of skilled workers to the West continued, on 13 August 1961 a wall with barbed wire was built to contain them. Many attempts to cross the frontier between the two Germanies ended in death. A highly efficient apparatus was set up in East Germany to watch over citizens' activities by the infamous Stasi secret police.

The first Chancellor of the Federal Republic of Germany, Konrad Adenauer, had Germany's integration into Western Europe as his main objective. Thanks to aid under the Marshall Plan, the economy rapidly recovered. Willy Brandt, first elected as Chancellor in 1969, pursued a policy of openness to the East, and recognized the German Democratic Republic.

REUNIFICATION

German reunification was made possible by a number of political events, in particular those going on in Eastern Europe. The Soviet premier Gorbachev's policy of *glasnost* led to the loosening of political constraints throughout the

Crowds visiting the giant Expo 2000 exhibition in Hannover

3 Oct 1990 Reunification of Germany		Helmut Kohl and Richard von Weizsäcker at the reunification ceremony	2002 Floods cause havoc across Germany		2011 Germany hosts the FIFA Women's World Cup		
1985	**1990**	**1995**	**2000**	**2005**	**2010**	**2015**	**2020**

8 Nov 1989 Fall of the Berlin Wall

1994 Withdrawal of last Russian military units from Berlin

1998 Gerhard Schröder becomes Chancellor

2000 Expo 2000 World Fair in Hannover

2005 Angela Merkel is the first female chancellor in a "Grand Coalition" government

2006 Germany hosts FIFA World Cup

2005 Ceremonial reopening of the reconstructed Frauenkirche in Dresden, a symbol of East-West efforts

BERLIN
AREA BY AREA

Berlin at a Glance

Since the reunification of Germany in 1990, Berlin has become an increasingly popular destination for visitors. The following pages provide a useful guide to places of interest both in the town centre and the outskirts, including historic monuments such as Nikolaikirche *(see p80)*, museums, modern developments, such as the Potsdamer Platz, as well as places of recreation and amusement, such as the Botanical Gardens *(see p104)*. In the guide, we have divided central Berlin into two parts (east and west); these, however, do not correspond with the city's former partition into East and West Berlin.

LOCATOR MAP

The Tiergarten *was once a royal hunting estate but, after 1818, it was converted into a landscaped park by Peter Joseph Lenné* (see p87) *with lakes and streams.*

WESTERN CENTRE

The Gemäldegalerie (see pp90–91) *houses an exceptional collection of European masters, including Hans Holbein's* Portrait of George Gisze (1532).

The Kaiser-Wilhelm-Gedächtnis-Kirche *was almost totally destroyed by bombs during World War II. A new annex was built in 1963 to a design by Egon Eiermann* (see p86).

◁ **Aerial view of Berlin**

The Reichstag *is a vast, Neo-Renaissance building, designed in 1884 by Paul Wallot. It now features an elliptical dome, which was designed in the 1990s by Sir Norman Foster (see p93).*

The Pergamonmuseum *owes its name to the magnificent Zeus Altar from Pergamon, which stands in the main hall. Built between 1912 and 1930, the museum houses rich collections of Greek, Roman and Asian art (see pp76–7).*

EASTERN CENTRE

0 metres 400

0 yards 400

The imposing *Neo-Classical Brandenburg Gate stands at the end of Unter den Linden. It is crowned with a 6-m (20-ft) high sculpture of the Roman Quadriga driven by Victoria, the goddess of victory (see p69).*

The Jüdisches Museum *(Jewish Museum) is housed in a building designed by Daniel Libeskind. It features a symbolic projection of a broken Star of David (see p80).*

EASTERN CENTRE

This part of Berlin is the historic centre of the city, and includes the Mitte district and parts of Kreuzberg. Its beginnings date back to the 13th century when two

Relief on Schadow-Haus

settlements were established on the banks of the river Spree. One was the former Cölln, situated on an island, and the other its twin settlement, Berlin. Berlin's first church, the Nikolaikirche, survives to this day.

This part of the city features most of its historic buildings, which are located mainly along Unter den Linden. It also includes Museuminsel, the location of the vast Berliner Dom as well as of the impressive collection of museums that gives the island its name. These include the Pergamonmuseum.

During the city's partition, Mitte belonged to East Berlin while Kreuzberg was in West Berlin.

SIGHTS AT A GLANCE

Museums and Galleries
Alte Nationalgalerie ⑲
Altes Museum ⑰
Bodemuseum ㉑
Checkpoint Charlie ㉘
DDR Museum ⑮
Deutsches Technikmuseum
Berlin ㉛
Jüdisches Museum ㉙
Märkisches Museum ㉗
Neues Museum ⑱
Pergamonmuseum ⑳
Topographie des Terrors ㉚
Zeughaus ⑧

Streets and Squares
Alexanderplatz ㉔
Bebelplatz ③
Nikolaiviertel ㉖
Schlossplatz ⑭
Unter den Linden ⑤

Churches
Berliner Dom ⑯
Deutscher Dom ⑫
Französischer Dom ⑩
Friedrichswerdersche
Kirche ⑨
Marienkirche ㉒
St Hedwigs-
Kathedrale ④

Historic Buildings and Monuments
Brandenburger
Tor ①
Fernsehturm ㉕

Holocaust Denkmal ②
Humboldt-Universität ⓪
Konzerthaus ⑪
Neue Wache ⑦
Rotes Rathaus ㉓
Schlossbrücke ⑬

GETTING THERE
This part of Berlin is served by S-Bahn 1, 2, 3, 5, 7, 9, 75 and U-Bahn 2, 5 & 6. Busses 100 & 200 run along Unter den Linden and Karl-Liebknecht-Strasse.

KEY

▪ Street-by-Street map
See pp68–9

▪ Street-by-Street map
See pp74–5

🚉 Railway station

Ⓢ S Bahn station

Ⓤ U-Bahn station

0 metres   400
0 yards   400

◁ *Personification of History* adorning the monument of Friedrich Schiller

Street-by-Street: Around Bebelplatz

Eagle from Altes Palais

The section of Unter den Linden between Schlossbrücke and Friedrichstrasse is one of the most attractive areas in central Berlin. As well as some magnificent Baroque and Neo-Classical buildings, many of them designed by famous architects, there are also some restored palaces that are now used as public buildings. Of particular interest is the beautiful Baroque building of the Zeughaus (the former Arsenal), which now houses the German History Museum.

Neue Wache
Now serving as a memorial to all victims of war and dictatorship, this monument was designed by Karl Friedrich Schinkel **7**

Humboldt University
The university courtyard teems with life all year round. Second-hand book-sellers set up their stalls in front of the gate **6**

0 metres		100
0 yards		100

Unter den Linden
Replanted with four rows of lime trees in 1946, this is one of the most famous streets in Berlin **5**

CHARLOTTENSTRASSE

UNIVERSITÄTSSTRASSE

UNTER DEN LINDEN

BEBEL–PLATZ

Branden-burg Gate

Altes Palais

Staatsbibliothek
Designed by Ernst von Ihne and constructed between 1903 and 1914, this impressive building houses part of the State Library collection.

KEY
– – – Suggested route

For hotels and restaurants in this region see pp488–90 and pp526–8

★ **Zeughaus (Deutsches Historisches Museum)**
Minerva, goddess of wisdom, decorates this beautiful Baroque building, which has a wing designed by I M Pei ❽

LOCATOR MAP
See Street Finder, maps 1, 4 & 5

Staatsoper
Unter den
Linden

★ **Friedrichswerdersche Kirche**
In this Neo-Gothic church, designed by Karl Friedrich Schinkel, is a museum devoted to the great architect ❾

Rotes
Rathaus

Kronprinzenpalais
A magnificent portal from the dismantled Bauakademie building can be found the rear of the palace.

HINTER DER KATH. KIRCHE

St-Hedwigs-Kathedrale
Bas-reliefs (1837) by Theodore Wilhelm Achtermann adorn the cathedral's supports ❹

STAR SIGHTS

★ Friedrichswerdersche
Kirche

★ Zeughaus

Brandenburger Tor ❶
Brandenburg Gate

Pariser Platz. **Map** 4 A2, 15 A3.
Ⓢ & Ⓤ *Brandenburger Tor.* 🚌 *100.*

The Brandenburg Gate is the quintessential symbol of Berlin. A magnificent Neo-Classical structure, modelled on the Athenian Propylaea (the entrance to the Acropolis), it was constructed between 1788 and 1791. Its sculptured decorations were completed in 1795. A pair of pavilions, once used by guards and customs officers, frames its powerful Doric colonnade and entablature. The bas-reliefs depict scenes from Greek mythology and the whole structure is crowned by Johann Gottfried Schadow's famous sculpture, *Quadriga*. In 1806, during the French occupation, the sculpture was dismantled, on Napoleon's orders, and taken to Paris. On its triumphal return in 1814, it was declared a symbol of victory, and the goddess received a staff bearing the Prussian eagle and an iron cross adorned with a laurel wreath.

Throughout its history, the Brandenburg Gate has borne witness to many of Berlin's important events. Located in East Berlin, the gate was restored between 1956 and 1958, when the damaged *Quadriga* was rebuilt in West Berlin. Over the next 40 years it stood watch over the divided city, until 1989, when the first section of the Berlin Wall came down.

Frieze and sculpture, *Quadriga*, on the Brandenburg Gate

Holocaust Denkmal ②

Map 4 A2. ⑤ & Ⓤ *Brandenburger Tor.* 🚌 *100, 200, M85.*

Translated as "Memorial to the Murdered Jews of Europe", Germany's national Holocaust memorial was designed by American architect Peter Eisenman. Completed in 2005 after years of debate, it is made up of a large field with dark grey steles of various heights that symbolise the six million Jews and others murdered by the Nazis in concentration camps between 1933 and 1945.

Visitors can walk their own route through the slabs, and there is an information centre underneath the memorial.

Bebelplatz ③

Map 4 C2. ⑤ & Ⓤ *Friedrichstraße.* 🚌 *100, 200, TXL.*

Bebelplatz was intended to be the focal point of the Forum Fridericianum – an area designed to mirror the

Relief on the façade of the Staatsoper (Opera House), Bebelplatz

grandeur of ancient Rome. Although the plans were only partly implemented, many important buildings were eventually erected here.

In 1933, the square was the scene of the infamous book-burning act organized by the Nazis. Some 25,000 books, written by authors considered to be enemies of the Third Reich, were burned. Today, a monument in the square commemorates this dramatic event.

The façade of St-Hedwigs-Kathedrale, with beautiful bas-relief sculptures

St-Hedwigs-Kathedrale ④
St Hedwig's Cathedral

Bebelplatz. **Map** 4 C2. **Tel** *(030) 203 48 10.* ⑤ & Ⓤ *Friedrichstraße.* 🚌 *100, 147, 200, TXL.* ⏺ *10am–5pm Mon–Fri, 10am–4:30pm Sat, 1pm–5pm Sun & holy days.*

This huge church is the Catholic Cathedral of the Roman Archdiocese of Berlin. The initial design was similar to the Roman Pantheon. Construction began in 1747, although work continued on and off until 1887.

It was damaged during World War II and rebuilt between 1952 and 1963. The building received a reinforced concrete dome and its interior was refurbished in a modern style. The crypt contains bishops' tombs and a 16th-century Madonna.

Unter den Linden ⑤

Map 1 F4, 4 A2, B2, C2, 5 D2. ⑤ & Ⓤ *Brandenburger Tor.* 🚌 *100, 200, TXL.*

One of the most famous streets in Berlin, Unter den Linden starts at Schlossplatz and runs down to Pariser Platz and the Brandenburg Gate. It was once the route to the royal hunting grounds, which were later transformed into the Tiergarten.

In the 17th century, the street was planted with lime trees, to which it owes its name. Although the original trees were removed around 1658, four rows of limes were planted in 1820.

During the 18th century, Unter den Linden became the main street of the westward-growing city and gradually came to be lined with

WILHELM AND ALEXANDER VON HUMBOLDT

The Humboldt brothers rank among the most distinguished Berlin citizens. Wilhelm (1767–1835) was a lawyer and politician on whose initiative the Berlin University (later renamed Humboldt University) was founded in 1810. At the university, he conducted studies in comparative and historical linguistics. His brother Alexander (1769–1859), a professor at the university, researched natural science, including meteorology, oceanography and agricultural science.

Alexander von Humboldt

prestigious buildings, which have been restored in the years following World War II.

Since the reunification of Germany in 1990, Unter den Linden has acquired several cafés and restaurants, as well as many smart shops. The street has also become the venue for interesting outdoor events. It is usually crowded with tourists and students browsing the book-stalls around the Humboldt Universität and the Staats-bibliothek (State Library).

Humboldt Universität **6**

Humboldt University

Unter den Linden 6. **Map** 4 C2. **Ⓢ** & **Ⓤ** Friedrichstraße. ▦ 100, 200, TXI.

The university building was constructed in 1753 for Prince Heinrich of Prussia. The overall design of the palace, with its main block and the courtyard enclosed within two wings, has been extended many times. Two marble statues by Paul Otto (1883) stand at the entrance; these represent Wilhelm and Alexander von Humboldt.

Many famous scientists have worked at the university, including physicians Rudolf Virchow and Robert Koch and physicists Max Planck and Albert Einstein. Among its graduates are Heinrich Heine, Karl Marx and Friedrich Engels.

After World War II, the university was in the Russian sector and the difficulties encountered by the students of the western zone led to the establishment in 1948 of the Freie Universität.

Neue Wache **7**

Unter den Linden 4. **Map** 7 A3, 16 E2. **Ⓢ** Hackescher Markt. ▦ 100, 200, TXL. ◻ 10am–6pm daily.

Designed by Karl Friedrich Schinkel and built between 1816 and 1818, this monu-ment is considered to be one of the finest examples of Neo-Classical architecture i n Berlin. The front of the monument is dominated by a huge Doric portico with a frieze made up of bas-reliefs depicting goddesses of victory.

In 1930–31 the building was turned into a monument to soldiers killed in World War I. Following its restoration in 1960, Neue Wache became the Memorial to the Victims of Fascism and Militarism. It was rededicated in 1993 to the memory of all victims of war and dictatorship. Inside is an eternal flame and a granite slab over the ashes of an unknown soldier, a resistance fighter and a concentration camp prisoner. In the roof opening is a copy of the sculpture *Mother with her Dead Son*, by Berlin artist Käthe Kollwitz.

Zeughaus **8**

Unter den Linden 2. **Map** 7 B3, 16 F3 (20 30 40). **Ⓢ** Hackescher Markt. ▦ 100, 200, TXL. **New wing** ◻ 10am–6pm daily.

This former arsenal was built in the Baroque style in 1706 under the guidance of Johann Arnold Nering, Martin Grünberg, Andreas Schlüter and Jean de Bodt. A magnificent structure, its wings surround an inner courtyard. Its exterior is decorated with Schlüter's sculptures, which include masks of dying warriors.

Princesses Luise and Friederike in the Schinkel-Museum

Home to the German History Museum since 1952, it was renovated in 2005. A modern, glass and steel wing, designed by architect I M Pei, now houses temporary exhibits, and there is an extensive exhibition on German history.

Friedrichswerder-sche Kirche (Schin-kel-Museum) **9**

Werderscher Markt. **Map** 5 D2. **Tel** (030) 2090 5577. **Ⓤ** & **Ⓢ** Fried-richstrasse. ▦ 100, 147, 248. ◻ 10am–6pm daily.

The first Neo-Gothic church to be built in Berlin, this small, single-nave structure with its twin-tower façade was designed by Karl Friedrich Schinkel and built between 1824 and 1830.

Schinkel's original interior was largely destroyed in World War II. Following its reconstruction, the church was con-verted to a museum. It currently houses the Nationalgalerie's permanent sculpture exhibi-tion. Highlights include a model of the famous sculpture by Johann Gottfried Schadow, depicting the princesses Fried-erike and Luise (later Queen of Prussia).

Part of the façade of the Zeughaus on Unter den Linden

Side elevation of the Französischer Dom, built for Huguenot refugees

Französischer Dom ⑩
French Cathedral

Gendarmenmarkt 5. **Map** 4 C2. *Tel (030) 206 49 922/3.* **U** *Stadtmitte or Französische Straße.* **Museum** ☐ *noon–5pm Tue–Sat, 11am–5pm Sun.* ⬛ **Church** ☐ *noon–5pm Tue–Sun.* ✝ *Sun 10am.*

Although the two churches standing on opposite sides of Schauspielhaus seem i dentical, their only common feature is their matching front towers. The French cathedral was built for the Huguenot community, who found refuge in protestant Berlin following their expulsion from France after the revocation of the Edict of Nantes in 1598. The modest church, built between 1701 and 1705 by Louis Cayart and Abraham Quesnay, was modelled on the Huguenot church in Charenton, France, which was destroyed in 1688. The interior features a late-Baroque organ from 1754.

The structure is dominated by a massive, cylindrical tower, which is encircled by Corinthian porticos at its base. The tower and porticos were designed by Carl von Gontard and added around 1785. It houses the Huguenot Museum, which charts the history of the Huguenot community in France and Brandenburg.

A viewing platform (temporarily closed), which is 40 m (131 ft) above the ground, is the city's highest historic observation platform and offers stunning views of Berlin's skyline.

Konzerthaus ⑪
Concert Hall

Gendarmenmarkt 2. **Map** 4 C2. *Tel (030) 203 09 21 01.* **U** *Stadtmitte.*

A late Neo-Classical jewel, this magnificent theatre building, known until recently as the Schauspielhaus, is one of the greatest achievements of Berlin's best-known architect, Karl Friedrich Schinkel. It was built between 1818 and 1821 around the ruins of Langhan's National Theatre, destroyed by fire in 1817. The portico columns were retained in the new design. Following bomb damage in World War II, it was reconstructed as a concert hall and the exterior was restored to its former glory. The Konzerthaus is now home to the Berlin Symphony Orchestra.

The whole building is decorated with sculptures alluding to drama and music. The façade, which includes a huge Ionic portico with a set of stairs, is crowned with a sculpture of Apollo riding a chariot pulled by griffins.

In front of the theatre stands a shining white marble statue of Friedrich Schiller, which was sculpted by Reinhold Begas and erected in 1869. Removed by the Nazis during the 1930s, the monument was returned

Interior of the Konzerthaus, formerly the Schauspielhaus

to its rightful place in 1988. The statue is mounted on a high pedestal surrounded by allegorical figures representing Lyric Poetry, Drama, Philosophy and History.

Deutscher Dom ⑫
German Cathedral

Gendarmenmarkt 1. **Map** 4 C3. *Tel (030) 227 30431.* **U** *Stadtmitte or Französische Straße.* **Exhibition** ☐ *10am–6pm Tue–Sun (to 7pm May–Sep).*

The cathedral at the southern end of the square is an old German Protestant-Reformed church. Based on a five-petal shape, it was designed by Martin Grünberg and built in 1708 by Giovanni Simonetti. In 1785 it acquired a dome-covered tower identical to that of the French cathedral.

Burned down in 1945, it was rebuilt in 1993, with its interior adapted as exhibition space. On display is the popular "Fragen an die Deutsche Geschichte" ("Questions on German History"), which was formerly on show in the Reichstag building.

Sculpture from Deutscher Dom

Schlossbrücke ⑬

Map 5 D2. ⓢ *Hackescher Markt.* 🚌 *100, 200, TXL.*

This is one of the city's most beautiful bridges, connecting Schlossplatz with Unter den Linden. It was built in 1824 to a design by Karl Friedrich Schinkel. Statues were added to the top of the bridge's sparkling red-granite pillars in 1853. These figures, made of white Carrara marble, were also created by Schinkel. The statues depict tableaux from Greek mythology, such as Iris, Nike and Athena, training and looking after their favourite young warriors. The elaborate wrought-iron balustrade is decorated with intertwined sea creatures.

The surviving Stadtschloss portal fronting a government building

Schlossplatz ⓐ

Map 5 D2. Ⓢ *Hackescher Markt.*
🚌 *100, 147, 200, TXL.*

This square was once the site of a huge residential complex known as Stadtschloss (City Castle). Built in 1451, it served as the main residence of the Brandenburg Electors. It was transformed from a castle to a palace in the mid-16th century when Elector Friedrich III (later King Friedrich I) ordered its reconstruction in the Baroque style. The main seat of the Hohenzollern family for almost 500 years until the end of the monarchy, the palace was partly burned during World War II but was provisionally restored and used as a museum.

In 1950–51, despite protests, the palace was demolished and the square was renamed Marx-Engels-Platz under the GDR.

Now all that remains is the triumphal-arch portal that once adorned the façade on the Lustgarten side. This is now incorporated into the wall of the former government building, the Staatsratsgebäude, which was erected in 1964 on the square's south side. The building's decor features the remaining original sculptures, including the magnificent atlantes by the famous Dresden sculptor, Balthasar Permoser. Their inclusion was due to their propaganda value: it was from the balcony of the portal that in 1918 Karl Liebknecht proclaimed the birth of the Socialist Republic.

In 1989 the square reverted to its original name and a former GDR government building was torn down. A palace-like building, the Humboldt-Forum, will be an international and cultural centre when complete in 2018.

DDR Museum ⓑ

Karl-Liebknecht Str. 1. **Map** 5 D2.
***Tel** (030) 847 123 731.* Ⓢ & Ⓤ
Alexanderplatz. 🚌 *100, 200, TXL.* ⏱
10am–8pm Mon–Sun (to 10pm Sat).

This small, privately-run museum provides a fascinating, interactive insight into daily life in the former East Germany. Visit a reconstructed apartment and take a simulated ride in an old Trabant car through a concrete housing estate.

Berliner Dom ⓒ

Am Lustgarten. **Map** 5 D1. **Tel** (030) 20 26 91 36. Ⓢ *Hackescher Markt.* 🚌 *100, 200, TXL* ⏱ *Apr–Sep. 9am–8pm Mon–Sat, noon–8pm Sun, Oct–Mar: 9am–7pm Mon–Sat, noon–7pm Sun.* 📷 ✚ *10am, 6pm Sun.*

The original Berliner Dom was based on a modest Baroque design by Johann Boumann. Built between 1747 and 1750, the cathedral included the original crypt of the Hohenzollern family, one of the largest of its kind in Europe. The present Neo-Baroque structure is the work of Julius Raschdorff and dates from 1894 to 1905. Following severe World War II damage, the cathedral has been restored in a simplified form. The Hohenzollern memorial chapel, which adjoined the northern walls, has been dismantled.

The Neo-Baroque interior of the Berliner Dom

BERLIN'S BRIDGES

Despite wartime damage, Berlin's bridges are still well worth seeing. The Spree river and the city's canals have some fine, exemplary architecture on their banks, while many of the bridges were designed and decorated by famous architects and sculptors. Probably the most renowned bridge is the Schlossbrücke designed by Karl Friedrich Schinkel. Further south along the Kupfergrabenkanal, the Schleusenbrücke, dating from c.1914, is decorated with reliefs of the early history of the city's bridges and sluices. The next bridge, heading south, is the Jungfernbrücke (1798), which is the last drawbridge in Berlin. The next bridge along is the Gertraudenbrücke. Where Friedrichstrasse crosses the Spree river is the Weidendammer Brücke, built originally in 1695–7 and subsequently rebuilt in 1923, with an eagle motif adorning its balustrade. On the Spree near the Regierungsviertel is the magnificent Moltkebrücke (1886–91). The bridge is guarded by a huge griffin wielding a shield adorned with the Prussian eagle, while cherubs dressed in a military fashion hold up lamps. On the arches of the bridges are portraits of leaders, designed by Karl Begas.

Ornamental feature of a bear on the Liebknechtbrücke

Street-by-Street: Museum Island

The long island that nestles in the tributaries of the
Spree river is the cradle of Berlin's history. It was here
that the first settlements appeared at the beginning of the
13th century: Cölln is mentioned in documents dating
back to 1237, and its twin settlement, Berlin, is mentioned
a few years later, in 1244. The island's character was
transformed by the construction of the Brandenburg
Electors' palace, which served as their residence from
1470. Although it was razed to the ground in 1950, some
interesting buildings on the north side of the island have
survived, including the Berliner Dom (Berlin Cathedral)
and the impressive collection of
museums that give the
island its name,
Museuminsel.

LOCATOR MAP
See Street Finder, maps 4 & 5

Bode Museum
*A rounded corner of the
building, crowned with
a dome, provides a
magnificent end-piece to
the tip of the island* **㉑**

★ Pergamonmuseum
*The museum is famous
for its reconstruction of
fragments of ancient
towns, as well as the
original friezes from
the Pergamon altar* **⑳**

AM KUPFER-GRABEN

Neues Museum
*This museum houses
exhibitions on
antiquities and ancient
Egyptian art following
renovations completed
in 2009* **⑱**

Alte Nationalgalerie
*The equestrian statue of
King Friedrich Wilhelm IV
in front of the building is
the work of Alexander
Calandrelli* **⑲**

KEY

– – – Suggested route

For hotels and restaurants in this region see pp488–90 and pp526–8

★ Altes Museum
The corners of the central building feature the figures of Castor and Pollux, heroes of Greek mythology ⓱

Lustgarten
A 70-ton granite bowl, the biggest in the world, was placed in the garden in 1828.

LUSTGARTEN

BODESTRASSE

STAR SIGHTS

★ Pergamonmuseum

★ Altes Museum

Altes Museum ⓱
Old Museum

Am Lustgarten (Bodestraße 1–3).
Map 5 D1. **Tel** (030) 20 90 55 77.
Ⓢ Hackescher Markt. 🚌 100, 200,
TXL. 🕙 10am–6pm Mon–Wed &
Fri–Sun, 10am–10pm Thu. 🎧

Designed by Karl Friedrich Schinkel, this museum building is one of the world's most beautiful Neo-Classical structures, with an impressive 87-m (285-ft) high portico supported by 18 Ionic columns. Officially opened in 1830, the museum was purpose-built to house the royal collection of art and antiquities.

Following World War II, the building was used only for temporary exhibitions. It now houses the Antikensammlung, with a magnificent collection of Greek, Roman and Etruscan antiquities.

Neues Muscum ⓲
New Museum

Bodestraße 1–3. **Map** 5 D1.
Ⓢ Hackescher Markt or
Friedrichstraße. 🚌 100, 200,
TXL. 🚊 M1, M4, M5.
🕙 10am–6pm Tue–Sun,
10am–10pm Thu. 🎧

The Neues Museum was built on Museum Island between 1841 and 1855 to a design by Friedrich August Stüler. Until World War II, it housed a collection of antiquities, mainly ancient Egyptian art. The rooms in the museum building were decorated specifically to complement the exhibitions they contained, while wall paintings by Wilhelm von Kaulbach depicted key events in world history. The building was damaged in 1945 and the museum closed. It reopened in October 2009 after reconstruction and once again houses the Egyptian Museum as well as the Museum of Pre-history and Early History.

Many sculptures, sarcophagi, murals and architectural fragments of various eras are on display, including the famous bust of Nefertiti. Most popular is the collection from 19th-century archaeological digs by Richard Lepsius and Johann Ludwig Burckhardt at Tell al-Amarna, Egypt. Tell al-Amarna was the capital founded by Pharaoh Amenhotep IV in the 14th century BC. In a break with tradition, Amenhotep and his wife, Nefertiti, are depicted in a more naturalistic manner.

Alte Nationalgalerie ⓳
Old National Gallery

Bodestraße 1–3. **Map** 5 D1.
Tel (030) 20 90 55 77.
Ⓢ Hackescher Markt. 🚌 100,
200, TXL. 🚊 M1, M4, M5.
🕙 10am–6pm Tue–Sun, 10am–
10pm Thu.

The old Nationalgalerie building, designed by Friedrich August Stüler, was erected between 1866 and 1876. It was originally intended to house the collection of modern art that had been on display in the Akademie der Künste (Art Academy). After World War II, however, the collection was split up into several sections and part of it was shown in West Berlin, where the Neue Nationalgalerie was specifically erected for this purpose *(see p88)*. This building was then renamed Alte Nationalgalerie.

Following the reunification of Germany, the modern art collections were merged again. Two new exhibition halls now show paintings from the German Romantic era, including work by Caspar David Friedrich and Karl Friedrich Schinkel. The famous 19th-century marble sculpture of the two Prussian princesses by Johann Gottfried Schadow is also on display, as is a significant collection of works by Adolph Menzel, including his most famous painting, *The Balcony Room*.

Pericles' Head

Pergamonmuseum ⑳

The Pergamonmuseum was built between 1912
and 1930 to a design by Alfred Messels and
Ludwig Hoffmann. It houses one of the most
famous collections of antiquities in Europe and
owes its name to the famous Pergamon Altar,
which takes pride of place in the main hall. The
three independent collections – the Museum of
Antiquities (Greek and Roman), the Museum of
Near Eastern Antiquities and the Museum of
Islamic Art – are the result of intensive archaeological excavations by German expeditions to the
Near and Middle East at the end of the 19th and
beginning of the 20th century.

★ **Pergamon Altar** *(170 BC)*
*This scene, featuring the goddess
Athena, appears on the large
frieze illustrating a battle between
the gods and the giants.*

Roman Mosaic
*(3rd or 4th century AD)
This ancient mosaic was
found at Jerash, Jordan.
A second part of it is in
the collection of the Stark
Museum of Art, Texas.*

Non-exhibition
rooms

First
floor

The Goddesss Athena
*This enchanting Hellenistic
sculpture of the goddess
Athena is one of many
displayed in the museum.*

Ground floor

Main
entrance

Assyrian Palace
*Parts of this beauti-
fully reconstructed
palace interior,
from the ancient
kingdom of Assyria,
date from the 12th
century BC.*

Aleppo Zimmer
(c.1603)
This magnificent panelled room comes from a merchant's house in the Syrian city of Aleppo.

VISITORS' CHECKLIST

Bodestraße 1–3 (entrance from Am Kupfergraben). **Map** 4 C1, 5 D1. **Tel** (030) 20 90 55 77. Ⓢ *Friedrichstraße or Hackescher Markt.* 🚌 *100, 200, TXL.* ☐ *10am–6pm daily (to 10pm Thu).* ⚫ *1 Jan, Tue after Easter and Pentecost, 24, 25, 31 Dec.* 🚫 🚻 ♿ 🚹 📷 *without flash.* www.smb.museum.de

GALLERY GUIDE

The central section of the ground floor houses reconstructions of ancient monumental structures, while the left wing is devoted to the Antiquities of Greece and Rome. The right wing houses the Museum of Near Eastern Antiquities; the first floor of the right wing houses the Museum of Islamic Art.

Façade of the Mshatta Palace *(AD 744)*
This fragment is from the southern façade of the Jordanian Mshatta Palace, presented to Wilhelm II by Sultan Abdul Hamid of Ottoman in 1903.

★ **Market Gate from Miletus** *(c.120 AD)*
Measuring over 16 m (52 ft) in height, this gate opened onto the southern market of Miletus, a Roman town in Asia Minor.

★ **Ishtar Gate from Babylon**
(6th century BC)
Original glazed bricks decorate both the huge Ishtar gate and the impressive Processional Way that leads up to it.

STAR EXHIBITS

★ Ishtar Gate from Babylon

★ Market Gate from Miletus

★ Pergamon Altar

KEY

☐ Antiquities (Antikensammlung)

☐ Near Eastern antiquities (Vorderasiatisches Museum)

☐ Islamic art (Museum für Islamische Kunst)

☐ Non-exhibition rooms

The Bodemuseum designed by Ernst von Ihne

Bodemuseum ㉑

Monbijoubrücke (Bodestraße 1–3).
Map 4 C1. **Tel** (030) 20 90 56 01.
Ⓢ Hackescher Markt or Friedrichstraße.
☐ 10am–6pm daily (to 10pm Thu).
🚋 M1, M4, M5, 12.

The fourth museum building on Museuminsel was constructed between 1897 and 1904. It was designed by Ernst von Ihne to fit the wedge-shaped northwestern end of the island. The interior was designed with the help of an art historian, Wilhelm von Bode, who was the director of the Berlin state museums at the time.

The museum displayed a rather mixed collection that included some old masters. Its original name, Kaiser Friedrich Museum, was changed after World War II. Following the reassembling of the Berlin collections, all the paintings were rehoused in the Kulturforum (see pp84–5), while the Egyptian art and the papyrus collection were moved to the Ägyptisches Museum (Egyptian Museum) at the Neues Museum (see p75).

Following its refurbishment, the building once again houses a collection of over 50,000 coins, plus medals and Byzantine art. It is also home to an extensive collection of sculptures, which includes the works of Tilman Riemenschneider, Donatello, Gianlorenzo Bernini and Antonio Canova. A copy of the magnificent equestrian statue of the Great Elector, Friedrich Wilhelm, by Andreas Schlüter, has also taken its place in the old hall.

Marienkirche ㉒

Karl-Liebknecht-Straße 8. **Map** 5 E1.
Tel (030) 242 44 67. Ⓢ Hackescher
Markt. 🚌 100, 200, TXL. ☐ Apr–
Oct: 10am–9pm daily; Nov–Mar:
10am–6pm daily. ✝ 10:30am Sun.

St Mary's Church, or the Marienkirche, was first established as a parish church in the second half of the 13th century. Started around 1280, construction was completed early in the 14th century. During reconstruction works in 1380, following a fire, the church was altered slightly, but its overall shape changed only in the 15th century when it acquired the front tower. In 1790, the tower was crowned with a dome, designed by Carl Gotthard Langhans, which includes both Baroque and Neo-Gothic elements.

The Marienkirche was once hemmed in by buildings, but today it stands alone in the shadow of the Fernsehturm (Television Tower). The early Gothic hall design and the

Baroque altar in the Marienkirche, designed by Andreas Krüger

lavish decorative touches make this church one of the most interesting in Berlin. An alabaster pulpit by Andreas Schlüter, dating from 1703, is decorated with bas-reliefs of St John the Baptist and the personifications of the Virtues.

The Baroque main altar was designed by Andreas Krüger around 1762. The paintings with which it is adorned include three works by Christian Bernhard Rode.

A Gothic font, dating from 1437, is supported by three black dragons and decorated with the figures of Jesus Christ, Mary and the Apostles.

Rotes Rathaus ㉓
Red Town Hall

Rathausstraße 15. **Map** 5 E2.
Ⓤ & Ⓢ Alexanderplatz. Ⓤ Klosterstraße, 🚌 TXL, 248.

This impressive structure is Berlin's main town hall. Its predecessor was a much more modest structure that, by the end of the 19th century, was inadequate to meet the needs of the growing metropolis.

The present building was designed by Hermann Friedrich Waesemann, and the construction works went on from 1861 until 1869. The architect took his main inspiration from Italian Renaissance municipal buildings, but the tower is reminiscent of Laon cathedral in France. The walls are made from red brick and it was this, rather than the political orientation of the mayors, that gave the town hall its name.

The whole building has a continuous frieze known as the "stone chronicle", which was added in 1879. The frieze features scenes and figures from the city's history and traces the development of its economy and science.

The Rotes Rathaus was severely damaged during World War II but, following its reconstruction between 1951 and 1958, it became the seat of the East Berlin authorities. The West Berlin magistrate was housed in the

Fernsehturm ㉕

The television tower, called by the locals *Telespargel*, or toothpick, remains to this day the city's tallest structure at 368 m (1,207 ft). It is also the second-tallest structure in Europe. The tower was built in 1969 to a design by a team of architects including Fritz Dieter and Günter Franke, with the help of Swedish experts. However, the idea for the tower originated much earlier from Hermann Henselmann (creator of the Karl-Marx-Allee development) in the Socialist-Realist style.

The television antenna is visible all over Berlin.

Transmitter aerial

The metal sphere is covered with steel cladding.

View from the Tower
On a clear day the viewing platform offers a full view of Berlin. Visibility can reach up to 40 km (25 miles).

Concrete structure rising to 250 m (820 ft)

The concrete shaft contains two elevators that carry passengers to the café and viewing platform.

Tele-Café
One of the attractions of the tower is the revolving café. A full rotation takes about half an hour, so it is possible to get a bird's-eye view of the whole city while sipping a cup of coffee.

The monumental, red-brick town hall, known as the Rotes Rathaus

Schöneberg town hall (*see p103*). Following the reunification of Germany in 1990, the Rotes Rathaus became the centre of authority, housing the offices of the mayor and the Berlin cabinet.

The forecourt sculptures by Fritz Kremer, which depict Berliners helping to rebuild the city, were added in 1958.

Alexanderplatz ㉒

Map 5 E1, F1. ⓤ & ⓢ *Alexanderplatz.* 🚌 100, 200, TXL.

Alexanderplatz, or "Alex" as it is called locally, has a long history, although it would be hard now to find any visible traces of the past. Once known as Ochsenmarkt (oxen market), it was the site of a cattle and wool market. It was later renamed after Tsar Alexander I who visited Berlin in 1805. At that time, the square boasted a magnificent monumental colonnade, which was designed by Carl von Gontard.

In time, houses and shops sprang up around the square and a market hall and urban train line were built nearby.

"Alex" became one of the city's busiest spots. Its frenzied atmosphere was captured by Alfred Döblin (1878–1957) in his novel *Berlin Alexanderplatz*.

In 1929, attempts were made to develop the square, though only two office buildings were added – the Alexanderhaus and the Berolinahaus, both by Peter Behrens.

World War II erased most of the square's buildings and they were replaced by characterless 1960s edifices, including the Park Inn Hotel (formerly Hotel Stadt Berlin) and the Fernsehturm. However, the area has been redeveloped and is home to several shopping plazas and cinemas, as well as open-air markets during the holidays.

Riverside buildings of the Nikolaiviertel

Nikolaiviertel ㉖

Map 5 E2. **U** & **S** Alexanderplatz.
U Klosterstraße. 100, 147, 200, 248, M48.

This small area on the bank of the Spree is a favourite place for both Berliners and tourists. Some of Berlin's oldest houses stood here until they were destroyed in World War II. The redevelopment of the area, which was carried out by the GDR government between 1979 and 1987, was an interesting attempt to recreate a medieval town. Now, with the exception of one or two restored buildings, the Nikolaiviertel consists entirely of newly built replicas of historic buildings.

The **Nikolaikirche** was destroyed by bombing in 1945 and rebuilt in 1987. All that remains of the original structure, which was probably built around 1230, is the base of the two-tower façade of the present church, which dates from around 1300.

The only Baroque building in Nikolaiviertel to escape damage during World War II was the **Knoblauchhaus**, a small townhouse built in 1759 for the Knoblauch family. The current appearance of the building is the result of work carried out in 1835 when the façade was given a Neo-Classical look.

Ephraim-Palais was built in 1766 for Nathan Veitel Heinrich Ephraim, Frederick the Great's mint master and court jeweller. Parts of the original structure, which were saved from demolition, were used in the reconstruction.

Märkisches Museum ㉗

Am Köllnischen Park 5. **Map** 5 F2.
Tel (030) 30 86 62 15. **U** Märkisches Museum. **S** Jannowitzbrücke. 147, 265. ◯ 10am–6pm Tue, Thu–Sun, noon–8pm Wed. (free 1st Wed of month). Presentation of mechanical instruments 3pm Sun.

Built between 1901 and 1908, this complex of red brick buildings was inspired by the brick-Gothic style popular in the Brandenburg region. The museum, founded in 1874, is dedicated to the cultural history of Berlin from the first settlements to today. The department "Berliner Kunst" (art), for example, presents a remarkable collection of paintings, sculpture, textiles, faiences, glass and porcelain. The main hall features the original Gothic portal from the sculpture *Quadriga*, which once crowned the Brandenburg Gate *(see p69)*. A further collection is devoted to the Berlin theatre from 1730 to 1933. One of the galleries houses some old-time mechanical musical instruments.

Checkpoint Charlie ㉘

Friedrichstraße 43–45. **Map** 4 C4.
Tel (030) 253 72 50. **U** Kochstraße. M29. **Haus am Checkpoint Charlie** ◯ 9am–10pm daily.

The name of this notorious border crossing between the American and Soviet sectors comes from the word that signifies the letter C in the international phonetic alphabet: Alpha, Bravo, Charlie.

Between 1961 and 1990, Checkpoint Charlie was the only crossing for foreigners between East and West Berlin. It came to represent a symbol of both freedom and separation for the many East Germans trying to escape Soviet communism.

Today, a single watchtower is all that remains. Next to it is a museum – **Haus am Checkpoint Charlie**. Its rich collection details the years of the Cold War in Berlin.

Jüdisches Museum ㉙

Lindenstraße 14. **Map** 4 C5.
Tel (030) 25 99 33 00. **U** Hallesches Tor or Kochstraße. M29, M41, 265. ◯ 10am–10pm Mon, 10am–8pm Tue–Sun.

The building housing the city's Jewish Museum is an exciting and imaginative example of 20th-century architecture. Designed by a Polish-Jewish architect based in the United States, Daniel Libeskind, the plan, shape, style, and

The exterior of the Märkisches Museum, echoing a medieval monastery

interior and exterior arrangement of the building are part of a profoundly complicated philosophical programme. The museum's architecture itself is intended to convey something of the tragic history of the millions of Jews who perished in the Holocaust. For example, the zig-zag layout recalls a torn Star of David.

The interior arrangement is dominated by a gigantic empty crack, which cuts a swathe through the building. Several corridors lead to a windowless Holocaust tower.

The collection focuses on Jewish history and art. Also on display are artifacts that were once part of everyday Jewish life in Berlin.

The museum is accessible only through an underground passageway in the former Berlin-Museum building next door.

The austere, steel-clad walls of the Jüdisches Museum

Topographie des Terrors ⅗

Stresemannstraße 110 (enter on Niederkirchner Straße). **Map** 4 B4. *Tel (030) 25 45 09 50. Ⓢ & Ⓤ Potsdamer Platz, Anhalter Bahnhof. M29. ◯ May–Sep: 10am–8pm daily; Oct–Apr: 10am–6pm daily.*

During the Third Reich, Prinz-Albrecht-Straße was probably the most frightening address in Berlin: here, three of the most terrifying Nazi political departments had their headquarters. The Neo-Classical Prinz-Albrecht palace,

which stood at Wilhelmstraße No. 102, became the headquarters of Reinhard Heydrich and the Third Reich's security service. The school of arts and crafts at Prinz-Albrecht-Straße No. 8 was occupied by the head of the Gestapo, Heinrich Müller, while the Hotel Prinz Albrecht at No. 9 became the headquarters of the Schutzstaffel or SS.

After World War II, the buildings were pulled down. In 1987, however, in cellars that were once used as torture cells, an exhibition documenting Nazi crimes was mounted. In 2010, a documentation centre opened in the grounds.

Exhibition documenting Nazi crimes at the Topographie des Terrors

Deutsches Technikmuseum Berlin ㉛

Trebbiner Straße 9. **Map** 4 A5. *Tel (030) 90 25 40. Ⓤ Gleisdreieck. 140. ◯ 9am–5:30pm Tue–Fri, 10am–6pm Sat & Sun.* & 🔄

The Technical Museum was first established in 1982 with the intention of grouping more than 100 smaller, specialized collections under one roof. The current collection is arranged on the site of the former trade hall, the size of which allows many of the

museum's exhibits, such as locomotives, water towers and storerooms, to be displayed full-size and in their original condition.

Of particular interest in the collection are the dozens of locomotives and railway carriages from different eras, as well as vintage cars. There are also exhibitions dedicated to flying, the history of paper manufacture, printing, weaving, electro-technology and computer technology. There are also two windmills, a brewery and an old forge. The section called Spectrum is especially popular with children as it allows them to try the "hands-on" experiments. One hall is dedicated to the display of aircraft and aircraft engines.

A special attraction of the Technical Museum is the Historical Brewery, which opened in 1995. The building was once used by the brewery Tucker Bräu for storing beer, but it was destroyed in World War II. Decades later, the brewery was rebuilt on four levels. Some visitors claim they can smell roasted malt.

One of dozens of locomotives displayed in the Deutsches Technikmuseum

WESTERN CENTRE

This part of Berlin includes the areas of Tiergarten, Charlottenburg and parts of Kreuzberg, as well as a small section of Mitte, which used to belong to East Berlin.

Tiergarten, which was once a royal hunting estate, became a park in the 18th century. It survives as a park to this day, although in an altered form.

To the south of Tiergarten is the Kulturforum – a large centre of museums and other cultural establishments, which was created after World War II. The neighbouring Potsdamer Platz is now an ultra-modern development, built in recent years on the wasteland that formerly divided East and West Berlin.

Although the eastern part of Charlottenburg does not feature a great number of historic buildings, it is one of the city's most attractive districts, which, after World War II, became the commercial and cultural centre of West Berlin. Kreuzberg is a lively area that is now populated by immigrants, artists and affluent young professionals.

Detail from Theater des Westens façade

SIGHTS AT A GLANCE

Museums and Galleries
Bauhaus-Archiv **7**
Bendlerblock **8**
Gemäldegalerie **9**
Hamburger Bahnhof **18**
Käthe-Kollwitz-Museum **3**
Kunstgewerbemuseum **12**
Kupferstichkabinett
   und Kunstbibliothek **10**
Museum für Naturkunde **19**
Musikinstrumenten-Museum **14**
Neue Nationalgalerie **11**
Regierungsviertel **17**

Streets and Squares
Kurfürstendamm (Ku'damm) **2**
Potsdamer Platz **15**

KEY

◾ Street-by-Street map
   See pp84–5

🚉 Railway station

Ⓢ S-Bahn station

Ⓤ U-Bahn station

Tiergarten **5**
Zoologischer Garten **4**

Churches
Kaiser-Wilhelm-
   Gedächtniskirche **1**

Historic Buildings and Monuments
Philharmonie **13**
Reichstag **16**
Siegessäule **6**

GETTING THERE
This part of town is served by S-Bahn lines 3, 5, 7, 9, 75 and by U-Bahn lines 1, 2, 9, 55.

◁ **Mosaic in Kaiser-Wilhelm-Gedächtniskirche depicting a herald bearing the Prussian royal insignia**

Street-by-Street: Kulturforum

Sculpture by Henry Moore

The idea of creating a new cultural centre in West Berlin was first mooted in 1956. The first building to go up was the Berlin Philharmonic concert hall, built from 1960 to 1963 to an innovative design by Hans Scharoun. Most other elements of the Kulturforum were realized between 1961 and 1987, and came from such famous architects as Ludwig Mies van der Rohe. The area is now a major cultural centre that attracts millions of visitors every year.

★ **Kunstgewerbe-museum**
Among the collection at the Museum of Arts and Crafts you can see this intricately carved silver and ivory tankard, made in an Augsburg workshop around 1640 **12**

Kupferstichkabinett
The large collection of prints and drawings owned by this gallery includes this portrait of Albrecht Dürer's mother **10**

★ **Gemäldegalerie**
Among the most important works of the old masters exhibited in this gallery of fine art is this Madonna in Church *by Jan van Eyck (c.1425)* **9**

Kunstbibliothek
The Art Library boasts a rich collection of books, graphic art and drawings.

REICHPIETSCHUFER

LANDWEHRKANAL

STAR SIGHTS

★ Gemäldegalerie

★ Kunstgewerbe-museum

★ Philharmonie

KEY

– – – Suggested route

Neue Nationalgalerie
Sculptures by Henry Moore and Alexander Calder stand outside this streamlined building, designed by Ludwig Mies van der Rohe **11**

★ **Philharmonie**
*Its exterior covered
in a layer of golden
aluminium, the
Berlin Philhar-
monic concert hall
is known all over
the world for its
superb acoustics* **13**

LOCATOR MAP
See Street Finder maps 1 & 3

Musikinstrumenten-Museum
*This harpsichord is part of a collection
of musical instruments dating from
the 16th to the 20th century* **14**

St-Matthäus-Kirche
*This 19th-century church
stands out among the
modern buildings of
the Kulturforum.*

SCHAROUNSTRASSE

POTSDAMER STRASSE

MATTHÄIKIRCH
PLATZ

ISMUNDSTRASSE

POTSDAMER STRASSE

0 metres   50

0 yards   50

Neue Staatsbibliothek
*Hans Scharoun designed this
public lending and research
library built in 1978.*

Kaiser-Wilhelm-Gedächtnis-Kirche ❶

This church-monument is one of Berlin's most famous landmarks. The vast Neo-Romanesque church was designed by Franz Schwechten. It was consecrated in 1895 and destroyed by bombs in 1943. After the war the ruins were removed, leaving only the front tower, at the base of which the Gedenkhalle (Memorial Hall) is situated. This hall documents the church's history and contains some original ceiling mosaics, marble reliefs and liturgical objects. In 1963, Egon Eiermann designed a new octagonal church in blue glass and a new freestanding bell tower.

VISITORS' CHECKLIST

Breitscheidplatz. **Map** 2 B4.
Tel (030) 218 50 23.
Ⓢ & Ⓤ *Zoologischer Garten*
or Ⓤ *Kurfürstendamm.*
🚌 *100, 200, X-9.* ⬜ **Church**
9am–7pm daily. **Gedenkhalle**
10am–4pm Mon–Sat. 🕐 *10am*
& 6pm Sun. 📷 **www.**
gedaechtniskirche-berlin.de

Tower Ruins
The damaged roof of the former church has become one of the best-known symbols of Berlin.

Tower Clock

★ **Kaiser's Mosaic**
Kaiser Heinrich I, seated on his throne, is depicted in this elaborate mosaic.

Figure of Christ
This vast sculpture by Hermann Schaper once decorated the church altar. It survived World War II damage.

Main entrance

Main Altar
The massive figure of Christ on the Cross is the work of Karl Hemmeter.

STAR SIGHTS

★ Kaiser's Mosaic

Ku'damm ❷

Plan 2 A5, 2 B4. **U** *Kurfürsten-damm.* 🚌 *109, 110, X10, M19, M29, M46.*

The eastern area of the Charlottenburg region, around the boulevard known as Kur-fürstendamm (the Ku'damm), was developed in the 19th century. Luxurious buildings were constructed along the Ku'damm, while the areas of Breitscheidplatz and Witten-bergplatz filled up with hotels and department stores. After World War II, with the old cen-tre (Mitte) situated in East Ber-lin, Charlottenburg became the centre of West Berlin. After the war the area was transformed into the heart of West Berlin, with dozens of new company headquarters and trade centres being built. It is now Berlin's main shopping street.

***Mother and Child*,** from the Käthe-Kollwitz-Museum

Käthe-Kollwitz-Museum ❸

Fasanenstraße 24. **Map** 2 A5. *Tel (030) 882 52 10.* **U** *Uhlandstraße or Kurfürstendamm.* 🚌 *109, 110, X10, M19, M29, 249.* ⏰ *11am–6pm daily.* 🌐 🏠 www.kaethe-kollwitz.de

This small private museum provides a unique oppor-tunity to become acquainted with the work of Käthe Kollwitz (1867–1945). Born in Königsberg, the artist settled in Berlin where she married a doctor who worked in Prenz-lauer Berg, a working-class district. Her drawings and sculptures portrayed the social

A tranquil area within the Tiergarten

problems of the poor, as well as human suffering.

This museum displays the work of Käthe Kollwitz and includes posters, drawings and sculptures as well as documents, such as letters and photographs.

Zoologischer Garten ❹
Zoological Garden

Hardenbergplatz 8 / Budapester Str. 34. **Map** 2 B3, C3, 2 B4, C4. *Tel (030) 25 40 10.* Ⓢ & **U** *Zoolo-gischer Garten.* 🚌 *M46, X9, X10, X34, 100, 109, 149, 200, 245, 249.* ⏰ *spring & summer: 9am–6.30pm, autumn: 9am–5:30pm, winter: 9am–4:30pm.* 🏠 www.zoo-berlin.de

The zoological garden is actually part of the Tiergarten and dates from 1844, making this one of the oldest zoos in Germany. The main attraction is its family of polar bears. A monkey house contains a family of gorillas, and there is a specially dark-ened pavilion for observ-ing nocturnal animals. A glazed wall in the hippo-potamus pool enables visitors to observe these enormous animals moving through the water. The large aquarium contains sharks, piranhas and unusual animals from coral reefs. There is also a huge terrarium with an over-grown jungle that is home to a group of crocodiles. Just to the west of the zoological garden on Jebensstraße is the **Newton-Sammlung**. This gallery houses photographs by Helmut Newton.

Tiergarten ❺

Map 2 C3, 3 D3, E3, F3. Ⓢ *Tiergarten or Bellevue.* 🚌 *100, 187, 341.*

Once a forest used as the Elector's hunting reserve, the Tiergarten was transformed into a landscaped park by Peter Joseph Lenné in the 1830s. A Triumphal Avenue, lined with statues of the country's rulers and statesmen, was built in the eastern section at the end of the 19th century.

World War II inflicted huge damage, but replanting has restored the Tiergarten and its avenues are bordered with statues of figures such as Johann Wolfgang von Goethe and Richard Wagner.

Near the lake and the Land-wehrkanal are memorials to Karl Liebknecht and Rosa Luxemburg, the leaders of the Spartakus movement who were assassinated in 1918.

Siegessäule ❻
Triumphal Column

Großer Stern. **Map** 3 D2. **U** *Hansaplatz.* Ⓢ *Bellevue.* 🚌 *100, 187, 106.* ⏰ *Apr–Oct: 9:30am–6.30pm Mon–Fri, 9:30am–7pm Sat & Sun; Nov–Mar: 10am–5pm Mon Fri, 10am–5:30pm Sat & Sun.*

This column, based on a design by Johann Heinrich Strack, was built to com-memorate victory in the Prusso-Danish war of 1864. After further Prussian victo-ries in wars against Austria (1866) and France (1871), a gilded figure representing Victory, known as the "Goldelse", was added to the top. It originally stood in front of the Reichstag building but was moved to its present location by the Nazi government in 1938. The base is decorated with bas-reliefs commemorating battles, while higher up a mosaic frieze depicts the founding of the German Empire in 1871. An observa-tion terrace offers magnificent views.

Siegessäule (Triumphal Column)

The captivating, streamlined buildings of the Bauhaus-Archiv

Bauhaus-Archiv **●**

Klingelhöferstraße 14. **Map** 3 D4, E4. **Tel** (030) 254 00 20. **U** Nollendorfplatz. 🚌 100, 187, M29. 🕐 10am–5pm Wed–Mon. 🖼 **Library** 9am–1pm Mon–Fri. 🛗 www.bauhaus.de

The Bauhaus school of art, started by Walter Gropius in 1919, was one of the most influential art institutions of the 20th century. Originally based in Weimar, it inspired many artists and architects. Staff and students included Mies van der Rohe, Paul Klee and Wassily Kandinsky. The school moved to Berlin in 1932 from Dessau, but was closed by the Nazis in 1933.

After the war, the Bauhaus-Archiv was relocated to Darmstadt. In 1964 Walter Gropius designed a building to house the collection but, in 1971, the archive was moved to Berlin and the design was adapted to the new site. As Gropius had died in 1969, Alexander Cvijanovic took over the project. Built between 1976 and 1979 the gleaming white building with its glass-panelled gables houses the archive, library and exhibition halls.

Bendlerblock (Gedenkstätte Deutscher Widerstand) **●**

Stauffenbergstraße 13–14. **Map** 3 E4, F4. **Tel** (030) 26 99 50 00. **U** Mendelssohn-Bartholdy-Park. 🚌 M29, M48. 🕐 9am–6pm Mon–Fri (to 8pm Thu), 10am–6pm Sat & Sun. ⬤ 1 Jan, 24, 25 & 31 Dec.

The collection of buildings known as the Bendlerblock was built during the Third Reich as an extension to the

German State Naval Offices. During World War II they were the headquarters of the Wehrmacht (German Army). It was here that a group of officers planned their assassination attempt on Hitler on 20 July 1944. When the attempt led by Claus Schenk von Stauffenberg failed, he and his fellow conspirators were arrested and death sentences passed. Stauffenberg, Friedrich Olbricht, Werner von Haeften, and Ritter Mertz von Quirnheim were shot in the Bendlerblock courtyard. A monument commemorating this event, designed by Richard Scheibe in 1953, stands where the executions were carried out.

On the upper floor of the building there is an exhibition which documents the history of the German anti-Nazi movements.

Gemäldegalerie **●**

See pp90–91.

Kupferstichkabinett und Kunstbibliothek **●**

Matthäikirchplatz 8. **Map** 3 F3. **Tel** (030) 266 20 02. **S** & **U** Potsdamer Platz or **U** Mendelssohn-Bartholdy-Park. 🚌 M48, M85, 200, M29, M41. **Kupferstichkabinett: Exhibitions** 10am–6pm Tue–Fri, 11am–6pm Sat & Sun. **Studio gallery** 9am–4pm Tue–Fri. **Kunstbibliothek: Exhibits** 10am–6pm Tue–Fri, 11am–6pm Sat & Sun. **Library** 2–8pm Mon, 9am–8pm Tue–Fri. 🖼 🛗 🚫

The print collections of galleries in the former East and West Berlin were united in 1994 in the Kupferstichkabinett (Print Gallery), whose

collection includes around 2,000 engraver's plates, over 520,000 prints and 80,000 drawings and watercolours.

The **Kunstbibliothek** (Art Library) is not only a library with a range of publications about the arts; it is also a museum with an extensive collection of posters, advertisements and other practical forms of design.

Munch's lithograph Girl on a Beach, Kupferstichkabinett

Neue Nationalgalerie **⓫**

Potsdamer Straße 50. **Map** 3 F4. **Tel** (030) 266 26 51. **U** & **S** Potsdamer Platz or **U** Mendelssohn-Bartholdy-Park. 🚌 M48, M85, 200, M29, M41. 🕐 10am–6pm Tue & Wed, Fri; 10am–10pm Thu, 11am–6pm Sat & Sun. 🖼 🛗

After World War II, when this magnificent collection of modern art ended up in West Berlin, the commission to design a suitable building to house it was given to Mies van der Rohe. The result is a striking building with a flat steel roof over a glass hall, which is supported only by six slender interior struts.

The collection comprises largely 20th-century art, but begins with artists of the late 19th century, such as Edvard Munch. German art is well represented: as well as the Bauhaus movement, the gallery shows works by exponents of a crass realism, such

Karl Schmidt-Rottluff's *Farm in Daugart* (1910), Neue Nationalgalerie

as Otto Dix. The most celebrated artists of other European countries are included, as are examples of post World War II art.

Kunstgewerbe-museum 🄬

Tiergarten-Str. 6. **Map** 3 F3.
Tel *(030) 266 2902.* Ⓢ *Potsdamer Platz.* Ⓤ *Potsdamer Platz or Mendelssohn-Bartholdy-Park.* 🚌 *100, 123, 148, 200, M29, M11.* 🚇 *for renovation 2012–2013.* 📷 ♿ ⌀

This museum holds a rich collection embracing many genres of craft and decorative art, from the early Middle Ages to the modern day. Goldwork is especially well represented, as are metal items from the Middle Ages. Among the most valuable exhibits is a collection of medieval goldwork from the church treasures of Enger and the Guelph treasury from

Brunswick. The museum also takes great pride in its collection of late Gothic and Renaissance silver from the civic treasury in the town of Lüneberg. In addition, there are fine examples of Italian majolica, and 18th- and 19th-century German, French and Italian glass, porcelain and furniture.

Philharmonie 🄭
Philharmonic and Chamber Music Hall

Herbert-von-Karajan-Straße 1.
Map 3 F3. ***Tel*** *(030) 25 48 80.*
Ⓢ & Ⓤ *Potsdamer Platz or* Ⓤ *Mendelssohn-Bartholdy-Park.* 🚌 *200, M29 M11.*

Home to one of the most renowned orchestras in Europe, this unusual building is among the finest postwar architectural achievements in

Europe. Built between 1960 and 1963 to a design by Hans Scharoun, the Philharmonie pioneered a new concept for concert hall interiors, with a podium occupying the central section of the pentagonal hall, around which are galleries for the public. The exterior is reminiscent of a circus tent. The gilded exterior was added between 1978 and 1981.

Between the years 1984 to 1987 the Kammermusiksaal, which was designed by Edgar Wisniewski on the basis of sketches by Scharoun, was added to the Philharmonie. This building consolidates the aesthetics of the earlier structure by featuring a central multi-sided space covered by a fanciful tent-like roof

Musikinstrumenten-Museum 🄮

Tiergartenstraße 1. **Map** 1 D5.
Tel *(030) 25 48 10.* Ⓢ & Ⓤ *Potsdamer Platz.* 🚌 *200.*
🕐 *9am–5pm Tue–Fri (to 10pm Thu), 10am–5pm Sat & Sun.*
Wurlitzer Organ demonstration *noon, first Sat of the month.* 📷 ♿

Behind the Philharmonie, in a small building designed by Edgar Wisniewski and Hans Scharoun between 1979 and 1984, the fascinating Museum of Musical Instruments houses a collection dating from 1888. Intriguing displays trace the development of each instrument from the 16th century to the present day. Most spectacular of all is a working Wurlitzer cinema organ dating from 1929. Saturday demonstrations of its impressive sounds attract enthusiastic crowds. There is also an archive and a library.

The tent-like gilded exterior of the Philharmonie and Kammermusiksaal

Gemäldegalerie 9

The Gemäldegalerie collection is exceptional in the consistently high quality of its paintings. Unlike those in other collections, they were chosen by specialists who, from the end of the 18th century, systematically acquired pictures to represent all the major European schools. Originally displayed in the Altes Museum building *(see p75),* the paintings achieved independent status in 1904 when they were moved to what is now the Bodemuseum *(see p78).* After the division of Berlin in 1945, part of the collection was kept in the Bodemuseum, while the majority ended up in the Dahlem Museum *(see p104).* Following reunification, and with the building of a new home as part of the Kulturforum development, this unique collection has finally been united again.

Woman in a Bonnet by Rogier van der Weyden

★ **Cupid Victorious** *(1602)*
Inspired by Virgil's Omnia vincit Amor, *Caravaggio depicted a playful god trampling over the symbols of Culture, Fame, Knowledge and Power.*

Madonna with Child and Angels *(c.1477)*
A frequent subject of Sandro Botticelli, the Madonna and Child are depicted surrounded by angels holding lilies to symbolize purity.

Circular lobby leading to the galleries

Birth of Christ *(c.1480)*
This beautiful religious painting is one of the few surviving paintings on wood by Martin Schongauer.

Portrait of Hieronymus Holzschuher *(1526)*
Albrecht Dürer painted this affectionate portrait of his friend, who was the mayor of Nuremberg.

Main entrance

The Glass of Wine
(1661/62)
Jan Vermeer's carefully composed picture of a young woman drinking wine with a young man gently hints at the relationship developing between them.

VISITORS' CHECKLIST

Matthäikirchplatz. **Map** 3 F3.
Tel (030) 266 42 30 40.
Ⓢ & Ⓤ Potsdamer Platz. Ⓤ
Mendelssohn-Bartholdy-Park. 🚌
M29, M41, 200. ◯ 10am–6pm
Tue, Wed, Fri–Sun; 10am–10pm
Thu. ● first Tue after Easter and
Whitsun, 1 May, 24, 25 & 31
Dec. 🖼 🍽 🎒 🚻 ♿ 🚫 📷
www.smb.museum.de

Love in the French Theatre
This picture has a companion piece called Love in the Italian Theatre. *Both by French painter, Joan Antoine Watteau (1684–1721).*

★ Portrait of Hendrickje Stoffels (1656–57)
Rembrandt's portrait of his lover, Hendrickje Stoffels, is typical of his work in the way it focuses on the subject and ignores the background.

KEY

- 🟦 13th–16th-century German painting
- 🟦 14th–16th-century Dutch and French painting
- ⬜ 17th-century Flemish and Dutch painting
- 🟦 18th-century French, English and German painting
- ⬜ 17th–18th-century Italian painting, 17th-century German, French and Spanish painting
- 🟦 13th–16th-century Italian painting
- 🟦 16th–18th-century miniatures

GALLERY GUIDE

The main gallery contains over 900 masterpieces grouped by period and country of origin. These are complemented by around 400 works in the gallery on the lower floor.

★ Netherlandish Proverbs *(1559)*
Pieter Brueghel managed to illustrate more than 100 proverbs in this painting.

STAR EXHIBITS

- ★ Cupid Victorious
- ★ Netherlandish Proverbs
- ★ Portrait of Hendrickje Stoffels

Potsdamer Platz ⓯

In the short space of a few years a modern financial and business district sprang up on the vast empty wasteland surrounding the Potsdamer Platz. It boasts splendid constructions designed by Renzo Piano, Arata Isozaki and Helmut Jahn. As well as office blocks, the area has many public buildings, including cinemas and a theatre, as well as a huge shopping centre – the Arkaden, plus luxury hotels, restaurants and several bars.

The Beisheim Center has a mix of exclusive apartments and international hotels.

The Sony Center

POTSDAMER PLATZ

ENTLASTUNGSSTRASSE

LANDWEHRKANAL

The Sony Tower, *designed by Helmut Jahn, is the most modern building in Potsdamer Platz and is curved on one side and flat on the other.*

This office building, which is the tallest in Potsdamer Platz, was designed by the architects Kollhoff & Timmermann Partnership.

Arkaden, opened in autumn 1998, immediately became one of the city's favourite shopping centres.

Theater am Potsdamer Platz, designed by Italian architect Renzo Piano, hosts musicals throughout the year and is the main location for Berlinale, the annual film festival.

The Debis House, *designed by Italian architect Renzo Piano.*

| 0 metres | 100 |
| 0 yards | 100 |

For hotels and restaurants in this region see pp488–90 and pp526–8

The Reichstag, crowned by a dome designed by Sir Norman Foster

Reichstag ⑯

Platz der Republik. **Map** 1 E4, 4 A1, A2. **Tel** (030) 22 73 21 52. Ⓤ Bundestag. Ⓢ Brandenburger Tor. ▦ 100, M85. **Dome** ◯ by appointment only. **Assembly Hall** ◯ Apr–Oct: 9am–6pm Mon–Fri, 9am–5pm Sat–Sun. Nov–Mar: 9am–5pm Mon–Fri, 10am–4pm Sat & Sun.

Built to house the German Parliament, the Reichstag was constructed between 1884 and 1894 to a New Renaissance design by Paul Wallot.

In February 1933, a fire destroyed the main hall, and the impending world war delayed rebuilding work for decades. Between 1957 and 1972, the reconstructed Reichstag was the meeting-place for the lower house of the German Parliament as well as a spectacular backdrop for festivals and rock concerts.

After German reunification in 1990, the Reichstag was the first meeting place of a newly elected Bundestag. The most recent update, by Sir Norman Foster, transformed the Reichstag into a meeting hall.

Regierungsviertel ⑰
Government Quarter

Map 1 D3, D4 ,E3, E4; 4, 4 A1, A2. Ⓤ Bundestag. Ⓢ Brandenburger Tor. ▦ 100, M85.

Located in the bend of the river Spree, the new government quarter was built between 1993 and 2003

to accomodate the relocation of the German government from Bonn in 1999.

Most of the buildings offer limited access to the public, however, several art and political exhibitions are open daily and art and architecture tours run at weekends.

Hamburger Bahnhof ⑱

Invalidenstraße 50/51. **Map** 1 D2, B2. **Tel** (030) 397 834-11. Ⓤ Zinnowitzer straße. Ⓢ Hauptbahnhof. ▦ M41, TXL, 120, 123, 147, 245. ▦ M6, M8, 12. ◯ 10am–6pm Tue–Fri, 11am–8pm Sat, 11am–6pm Sun. ● Mon, 24 & 31 Dec. ⚿ ▦ ◪

This museum is situated in a Neo-Renaissance building, formerly the Hamburg Railway station, which dates from 1847. It stood vacant after World War II but, following refurbishment by Josef Paul Kleihues, it was opened to the public in 1996. The neon installation surrounding the façade is the work of Dan Flavin. The museum houses a magnificent collection of contemporary art, including the work of Erich Marx and, from 2004, the world-renowned Flick collection. The result is one of the

**Jeff and Ilona (1991),
Hamburger Bahnhof**

best modern art museums to be found in Europe, which features not only art, but also film, video, music and design.

Museum für Naturkunde ⑲
Natural History Museum

Invalidenstraße 43. **Map** 1 E2. **Tel** (030) 20 93 85 91. Ⓤ Naturkunde-museum. ▦ 147, 245. ▦ M6, M8, 12. ◯ 9:30am–5pm Tue–Fri, 10am–6pm Sat & Sun. ● 24, 25 & 31 Dec. ◪

Occupying a purpose-built Neo-Renaissance building constructed between 1883 and 1889, this is one of the biggest natural history museums in the world, with a collection containing over 60 million exhibits. Although it has undergone several periods of extension and renovation, it has maintained its unique old-fashioned atmosphere.

The highlight of the museum is the world's largest dinosaur skeleton, which is housed in the glass-covered courtyard. The colossal brachiosaurus measures 23 m (75 ft) long and 12 m (39 ft) high. It was discovered in Tanzania, in 1909, by a German fossil-hunting expedition.

The adjacent rooms feature collections of colourful shells and butterflies, as well as stuffed birds and mammals. A favourite with children is Bobby the Gorilla, who lived in Berlin Zoo from 1928 until 1935. The museum also boasts an impressive collection of minerals and meteorites.

**Brachiosaurus skeleton in the
Museum für Naturkunde**

FURTHER AFIELD

Berlin is a huge city with a unique character that has been shaped by the events in its history. Until 1920 the city consisted only of the districts that now comprise mainly Mitte, Tiergarten, Wedding, Prenzlauer Berg, Friedrichshain and Kreuzberg. At that time the city was surrounded by satellite towns and villages that had been evolving independently over many centuries.

In 1920, as part of great administrative reform, seven towns, 59 parishes and 27 country estates were incorporated into the city, thus creating an entirely new city covering nearly 900 sq km (350 sq miles), with a population of 3.8 million. This metropolis extended to small towns of medieval origin, such as Spandau, as well as to private manor houses and palaces, towns and smart suburban districts. Although the 20th century has changed the face of many of these places, their unique characters have remained undiminished. Because of this diversity, a trip to Berlin is like exploring many different towns simultaneously.

Detail from Schloss Charlottenburg

SIGHTS AT A GLANCE

Museums and Galleries
Anne Frank Zentrum ⑬
Brecht-Haus ⑫
Brohan-Museum ❶
Brücke-Museum ㉕
Gedenkstätte Berlin-
　Hohenschönhausen ⑯
Gedenkstätte Plötzensee ❾
Langhansbau ❹
Sammlung Berggruen ❷
Stasi Museum ⑰

Places of Interest
Old Flughafen Tempelhof ⑳
Klein Glienicke ㉙
Köpenick ⑱
Museumszentrum Dahlem ㉓
Nikolskoe ㉘

Olympiastadion ❼
Pfaueninsel ㉗
Prenzlauer Berg ⑭
Strandbad Wannsee ㉖

Streets, Squares and Parks
Karl-Marx-Allee ⑮
Schlosspark ❸
Treptower Park ⑲
Victoriapark ㉑

Historic Buildings and Monuments
Jagdschloss Grunewald ㉔
Messegelände ❻
Neue Synagoge ⑪

Rathaus Schöneberg ㉒
Schloss Charlottenburg ❺
Schloss Tegel ❿
Zitadelle Spandau ❽

KEY

▇	Central Berlin
▢	Outskirts of Berlin
✈	Airport
▬	Motorway
▬	Main road
═	Secondary road
—	Railway line

0 metres　　400
0 yards　　400

MAP OF GREATER BERLIN

◁ Façade of Schloss Charlottenburg

Pablo Picasso's *Woman in a Hat* (1939), Sammlung Berggruen

The museum opened in what was once the west pavilion of the barracks, using the space freed up by moving the Antikensammlung to Museum Island *(see p74).* The exhibition halls were modified according to the designs of Hilmer and Sattler, who also designed the layout of the Gemäldegalerie.

The Sammlung Berggruen is well known for its large collection of paintings, drawings and gouaches by Pablo Picasso. In addition to these, the museum displays more than 20 works by Paul Klee and paintings by other major artists – Matisse, Braque and Cézanne. The exhibition is supplemented by some excellent sculptures, particularly those of Henri Laurens and Alberto Giacometti.

Bröhan-Museum ❶

Schlossstraße 1a. *Tel (030) 32 69 06 00.* Ⓤ *Richard-Wagner-Platz & Sophie-Charlotte-Platz.* Ⓢ *Westend.* 🚌 109, M45. ⏰ 10am–6pm Tue–Sun. ◉ 24 & 31 Dec. 🅰 (free 1st Wed).

Located in a late-Neo-Classical building is this interesting, small museum. The collection was amassed by Karl H Bröhan who, from 1966, collected works of art from the Art Nouveau (Jugendstil or Secessionist) and Art Deco styles. The paintings of artists who were particularly connected with the Berlin Secessionist movement are especially well represented. Alongside the paintings are fine examples of other media and crafts including furniture, ceramics, glassware, silverwork and textiles.

Each of the main halls features an individual artist, often employing an array of media. There is also a display of furniture by Hector Guimard, Eugène Gaillard, Henri van de Velde and Joseph Hoffmann, glasswork by Emile Gallé, and porcelain from the best European manufacturers.

Sammlung Berggruen ❷

Schlossstraße 1. *Tel (030) 326 95 815.* Ⓤ *Richard-Wagner-Platz & Sophie-Charlotte-Platz.* Ⓢ *Westend.* 🚌 109, 309, M45. ⏰ 10am–6pm Tue–Sun. 🅰 (free 4pm–8pm Thu.) 🅿 ♿

Heinz Berggruen assembled this tasteful collection of art dating from the late 19th and first half of the 20th century. Born and educated in Berlin, he emigrated to the US in 1936, spent most of his life in Paris, but finally entrusted his collection "Picasso and his Time" to the city of his birth.

Schlosspark ❸
Palace Park

Luisenplatz (Schloss Charlottenburg). Ⓤ *Richard-Wagner-Platz & Sophie-Charlotte-Platz.* Ⓢ *Westend.* 🚌 109, 309, M45. **Neuer Pavillon** *Tel (030) 32 09 14 43.* **Mausoleum** *Tel (030) 32 09 14 46.* ⏰ Apr–Oct: 10am–6pm Tue–Sun, Nov–Mar: noon–4pm. **Belvedere** *Tel (030) 32 09 14 45.* ⏰ Apr–Oct: 10am–6pm Tue–Sun; Nov–Mar: noon–4pm Tue–Sun.

This extensive royal park surrounding Schloss Charlottenburg is a favourite place for Berliners to stroll. The park is largely the result of work carried out after World War II, when 18th-century prints were used to help reconstruct the layout of the original grounds. Just behind Schloss Charlottenburg

French-style garden in the Schloss Charlottenburg park

is a French-style Baroque garden, constructed to a strict geometrical design with a vibrant patchwork of flower beds, carefully trimmed shrubs and ornate fountains adorned with replicas of antique sculptures. Beyond the curved carp lake is a less formal English-style landscaped park, the original layout of which was created between 1819 and 1828 under the direction of the renowned royal gardener, Peter Joseph Lenné.

Designed by Karl Friedrich Schinkel and completed in 1825, the Neo-Classical **Neuer Pavillon** is a charming two-storey building with rooms ranged around a central staircase. A cast-iron balcony encircles the entire structure.

The **Mausoleum** in which Queen Luise, wife of Friedrich Wilhelm III, was laid to rest, was designed by Karl Friedrich Schinkel in the style of a Doric portico-fronted temple. After the death of the king in 1840, the mausoleum was refurbished to create room for his tomb. The tombs of the king's second wife and those of Kaiser Wilhelm I and his wife were added later.

Built as a summerhouse for Friedrich Wilhelm II, with a mixture of Baroque and Neo-Classical elements, the **Belvedere** now houses the Royal Porcelain Collection, with pieces ranging from the Rococo period up to late Biedermeier.

Langhansbau ❹

Luisenplatz (Schloss Charlottenburg). **Tel** (030) 32 67 48 40. Ⓤ Richard-Wagner-Platz. 🚌 109, 309, M45. 🕐 9am–5pm Tue–Fri, 10am–5pm Sat & Sun. ♿ 📷

This Neo-Classical pavilion was designed by Carl Gotthard Langhans and added to the orangery wing of the Schloss Charlottenburg (see pp98–9) between 1787 and 1791. It was originally used as the court theatre and for many years housed a museum which documents cultures and civilizations

from the Stone Age up to medieval times. The collection is now housed in the reconstructed Neues Museum on Museum Island (see p75).

Schloss Charlottenburg ❺

See pp98–9.

The Funkturm (radio tower) in Berlin's Messegelände

Messegelände ❻

Hammarskjöldplatz. Ⓢ Messe Nord/ICC. Ⓤ Kaiserdamm. 🚌 139, 218, X49.

The pavilions of the vast exhibition and trade halls south of Hammarskjöldplatz cover more than 160,000 sq m (1,700,000 sq ft). The original

exhibition halls were built before World War I, but nothing of these buildings remains. The oldest part is the Funkturm and the pavilions surrounding it. The building at the front (Ehrenhalle) was built in 1936 to a design by Richard Ermisch, and is one of the few surviving buildings in Berlin designed in a Fascist architectural style.

The straight motorway at the rear of the halls is the famous Avus, the first German autobahn, built in 1921. At one point adapted as a car-racing track, it now forms part of the autobahn system.

Olympiastadion ❼

Olympischer Platz. 🅱 & Ⓤ Olympia-Stadion. **Tel** (030) 30 68 81 00. 🕐 late Mar–May: 9am–7pm daily; Jun–mid-Sep: 9am–8pm daily, mid-Sep–late Oct: 9–7pm daily, Nov–late Mar: 9am–4pm daily. ♿ 📷 **www**.olympiastadion-berlin.de

Olympiastadion, originally known as Reichssportfeld, was built for the 1936 Olympic Games in Berlin. It was designed by Werner March in the Nazi architectural style and was inspired by the architecture of ancient Rome. To the west of the stadium lie the Maifeld and what is now called the Waldbühne. The former is an enormous assembly ground surrounded by grandstands and fronted by the Glockenturm, a 77 m (250 ft) tower, while the latter is an open-air amphitheatre. A four-year high-tech modernization project on the stadium was completed in 2004. It now features a sweeping, illuminated roof.

Newly modernized and ever impressive Olympiastadion

Schloss Charlottenburg 🟎

Detail from the main gate

The palace in Charlottenburg was intended as a summer home for Sophie Charlotte, the wife of Elector Friedrich III. Construction began in 1695 to a design by Johann Arnold Nering. Johann Eosander von Göthe enlarged the palace between 1701 and 1713, adding the orangery wing. Further extensions were undertaken between 1740 and 1746 by Frederick the Great (Friedrich II) who added the new wing.

The palace was restored to its former elegance after World War II and its richly decorated interiors are unequalled in Berlin.

GALLERY GUIDE
The ground floor of the main building can only be visited by guided tour. The upper floor and the Neuer Flügel can be visited independently.

First floor

Ground floor

★ Porzellankabinett
This exquisite mirrored gallery has walls lined from top to bottom with a fine display of Japanese and Chinese porcelain.

Schlosskapelle
Only the pulpit in the court chapel is original. All the remaining furniture and fittings, including the splendid royal box, are reconstructions.

Monument to the Great Elector

Main entrance

Palace Façade
The central section of the palace, decorated with Corinthian pilasters and topped with a decorative cornice, is the oldest part of the building. It is the work of Johann Arnold Nering.

Fortuna
This sculpture by Richard Scheibe crowns the palace, replacing the original statue destroyed during World War II.

VISITORS' CHECKLIST

Luisenplatz. **Altes Schloss (Nering-Eosanderbau)** *Tel (030) 32 09 11.* **U** *Richard-Wagner-Platz & Sophie-Charlotte-Platz.* **S** *Westend.* 🚌 *109, M45, 309.* ⏰ *9am–5pm Tue–Sun.* 📷 *(compulsory on ground floor only).* 🎧 **Neuer Flügel (Knobelsdorff-Flügel)** *Tel (030) 32 09 442.* ⏰ *Apr–Oct: 10am–6pm Wed–Mon; Nov–Mar: 10am–5pm Wed–Mon.* 🎧

KEY

- ☐ Official reception rooms
- ☐ Sophie-Charlotte's apartments
- ☐ Neuer Flügel or Knobelsdorff-Flügel exhibition space
- ☐ Friedrich Wilhelm II's apartments
- ☐ Mecklenburg apartments
- ☐ Friedrich Wilhelm IV's apartments
- ☐ Friedrich Wilhelm II's apartments
- ☐ Frederick the Great's apartments
- ☐ Non-exhibition space

Ahnengalerie
This long gallery, lined with huge oil paintings and decorated with oak-panelling, was completed in 1713.

Weisser Saal

Goldene Galerie

Frederick the Great's Apartments
Located in the new wing, these elegant living quarters feature the king's exquisite furniture.

STAR SIGHTS

★ Gersaint's Shop Sign

★ Porzellankabinett

★ Gersaint's Shop Sign (1720)
An avid collector of French painting, Frederick the Great bought this and seven other fine canvases by Antoine Watteau for his collection.

Hohenzollern coat of arms above the main gate of Spandau's citadel

Spandau ❽

Zitadelle Spandau Am Juliusturm
64. *Tel (030) 354 94 40.* Ⓤ
Zitadelle. 🚌 *X33.* ⏰ *10am–5pm
daily.* 🌐 **www**.zitadelle-spandau.de

Spandau is one of the oldest
towns within the area of
greater Berlin, and it has
managed to retain its own
distinctive character. Although
the town of Spandau was only
granted a charter in 1232,
evidence of the earliest
settlement here dates back to
the 8th century.

The area was spared the
worst of the World War II
bombing, so there are still
some interesting sights to visit.
The heart of the town is a
network of medieval streets
with a picturesque market
square and a number of the
original timber-framed houses.
In the north of Spandau,
sections of the town wall
dating from the 15th century
are still standing.

In the centre of town is the
magnificent Gothic St-Nikolai-
Kirche, dating from the 15th
century. The church holds
many valuable ecclesiastical
furnishings, such as a
splendid Renaissance stone
altar from the end of the 16th
century, a Baroque pulpit
from around 1700 that came
from a royal palace in Potsdam, a Gothic baptismal font
and many epitaphs.

A castle was first built on
the site of the Zitadelle
Spandau (citadel) in the 12th
century, but today only the
36 m (120 ft) Juliusturm
(tower) remains. In 1560 the
building of a fort was begun

here, to a design by Francesco
Chiaramella da Gandino. It
took 30 years to complete and
most of the work was supervised by architect Rochus Graf
von Lynar. Although the
citadel had a jail, the town's
most infamous resident,
Rudolf Hess, was incarcerated
a short distance away in a
military prison after the 1946
Nuremberg trials. In 1987,
when the former deputy
leader of the Nazi party died,
the prison was torn down.

Gedenkstätte Plötzensee ❾
Plötzensee Memorial

Hüttigpfad 16. *Tel (030) 26 99 50 00.*
Ⓤ *Jakob-Kaiser-Platz, then* 🚌 *123,
126.* ⏰ *Mar–Oct: 9am–5pm;
Nov–Feb: 9am–4pm.*

A narrow street leads from
Saatwinkler Damm to the site
where nearly 2,500 people
convicted of crimes against

**Memorial to concentration camp
victims at Gedenkstätte Plötzensee**

the Third Reich were hanged.
The Gedenkstätte Plötzensee
is a simple memorial in a
brick hut, which still retains
the iron hooks from which
the victims were suspended.

Claus Schenk von Stauffenberg and the other main
figures in the assassination
attempt against Hitler on 20
July 1944 were executed in
the Bendlerblock *(see p88),*
but the rest of the conspirators were executed here
at the Plötzensee prison.

Count Helmut James von
Moltke, one of the leaders of
the German resistance movement, was also killed here.
He was responsible for organizing the Kreisauer Kreis –
a political movement that
gathered and united German
opposition to Hitler.

Schloss Tegel ❿

Adelheidallee 19–21. *Tel (030) 434
31 56.* Ⓤ *Alt Tegel.* 🚌 *124, 133,
222.* ⏰ *May–Sep: 10am, 11am,
3pm, 4pm.* 📷 *compulsory.*

Schloss Tegel is one of the
most interesting palace
complexes in Berlin. The site
was occupied in the 16th
century by a manor house. In
the second half of the 17th
century, this was rebuilt into a
hunting lodge for the Elector
Friedrich Wilhelm. In 1766
the ownership of the property
passed to the Humboldt
family and, between 1820 and
1824, Karl Friedrich Schinkel
thoroughly rebuilt the palace,
giving it its current style.

Decorating the elevations
on the top floor of the towers
are tiled bas-reliefs designed
by Christian Daniel Rauch,
depicting the ancient wind
gods. Some of Schinkel's
marvellous interiors have
survived, along with several
items from what was once a
large collection of sculptures.
The palace is still privately
owned by descendants of the
Humboldt family, but guided
tours are offered on Mondays.

It is also worth visiting the
park in which the palace
stands. On the western limits
of the park lies the Humboldt
family tomb, also designed by
Schinkel. The tomb contains a

For hotels and restaurants in this region see pp488–90 and pp526–8

The elegant Neo-Classical façade of Schloss Tegel

copy of a splendid sculpture by Bertel Thorwaldsen. The original piece stands inside the Schloss Tegel.

The Neue Synagoge with its splendidly reconstructed dome

Neue Synagoge ⓫
New Synagogue

Oranienburger Straße 30. **Tel** (030) 880 28 300. Ⓢ Oranienburger Straße. 🚋 M1, M6. ◯ daily. 🖼 🚫

Construction of the New Synagogue, begun in 1859 by architect Eduard Knoblauch, was completed in 1866. The design was a response to the asymmetrical shape of the plot of land, with a narrow façade flanked by a pair of towers and crowned with a dome containing a round vestibule.

With its gilded dome, this was Berlin's largest synagogue until it was partially destroyed during the infamous *Kristallnacht* in 1938. The building was damaged further by Allied bombing in 1943 and was eventually demolished in 1958.

Reconstruction began in 1988 and was completed in 1995. Public exhibitions by the Centrum Judaicum are held in the front of the building.

Brecht-Weigel-Gedenkstätte ⓬
Brecht-Weigel Memorial

Chausseestraße 125. **Tel** (030) 200 57 18 44. 🚇 Naturkunde Museum or Oranienburger Tor. 🚌 340. 🚋 M6, 12. 📷 compulsory. Every half hour (every hour on Sun). 10am–3:30pm Tue, 10am–11:30pm Wed, Fri, 10am–6:30pm Thu, 10am–3:30pm Sat, 11am–6pm Sun. ⬤ Mon, public holidays. 🖼

Playwright Bertolt Brecht was associated with Berlin from 1920, but emigrated in 1933. After the war, his left-wing views made him an attractive potential resident of the newly created German socialist state. Lured by the promise of his own theatre, he returned to Berlin in 1948 with his wife, the actress Helene Weigel.

In 1953, Brecht moved into Chausseestraße 125 and lived there until his death in 1956. His wife founded an archive of his work, which is located on the second floor.

Bertolt Brecht's study in his former apartment

Anne Frank Zentrum ⓭

Rosenthalerstraße 39. **Tel** (030) 288 86 56 00. 🚇 Weinmeistertraße. Ⓢ Hackescher Markt. ◯ 10am–6pm Tue–Sun. 🖼 www.annefrank.de

Anne Frank's short life and her diary are at the heart of this interactive exhibition, which connects history to the present day. Visitors are encouraged to reflect on their own views through listening to young people from Berlin discussing the issues that occupied Anne Frank, such as identity, values, war and discrimination.

Prenzlauer Berg ⓮

Sammlung Industrielle Gestaltung Kulturbrauerei entrance, Knaackstraße 97. **Tel** (030) 473 77 79 40 🚇 Senefelderplatz or Eberswalder straße. ◯ phone ahead to check.

Towards the end of the 19th century, this was one of the most impoverished, densely populated districts of Berlin, which became a centre for anti-Communist opposition.

After 1989, however, artists, professionals and students began to gather here from all parts of Germany and Europe, creating a colourful, vibrant community.

Schönhauser Allee is the main thoroughfare of Prenzlauer Berg. A former old brewery was transformed into the "Kulturbrauerei", a centre for cultural events. It also houses a museum – **Sammlung Industrielle Gestaltung** – with a collection of industrial designs from East Germany.

Heading along Sredzkistraße you reach Husemannstraße. This beautifully renovated street complete with shops and inns gives the impression of Berlin around the year 1900. Amid the greenery around Belforter Straße is a water tower built in the mid-19th century. Near-by, on Schönhauser Allee, there is an old Jewish cemetery dating from 1827. Among those buried here is the renowned painter Max Liebermann.

Fragment of Socialist Realist decoration from Karl-Marx-Allee

Karl-Marx-Allee ⓯

Map 5 F1. **U** *Strausberger Platz or Weberwiese.*

The section of Karl-Marx-Allee between Strausberger Platz and Frankfurter Tor is effectively a huge open-air museum of Socialist Realist architecture. The route to the east was named Stalinallee in 1949 and chosen as the site for the showpiece of the new German Democratic Republic. The avenue was widened to 90 m (300 ft) and, over the next ten years, huge residential tower blocks and a row of shops were built. The designers, led by Hermann Henselmann, succeeded in combining three sets of architectural guidelines. They used the Soviet wedding cake style according to the precept: "nationalistic in form but socialist in content", and linked the whole work to Berlin's own traditions. Hence there are motifs taken from famous Berlin architects Schinkel and Gontard, as well as from the renowned Meissen porcelain.

The buildings on this street, renamed Karl-Marx-Allee in 1961, are now considered historic monuments.

Gedenkstätte Berlin-Hohen-schönhausen ⓰

Genslerstraße 66. **Tel** *(030) 9860 82 30.* **Ⓢ** *Landsberger Allee, then* **🚋** *M5, M6.* **🚌** *256.* **◯** *11am–3pm Mon–Fri, 10am–4pm Sat & Sun. English tour 2:30pm daily, public tours 2pm Sat.* 📷

This museum was established in 1995 within the former Stasi detention centre. The

building was part of a huge complex built in 1938. In May 1945, the occupying Russian authorities created a special transit camp here, in which they interned war criminals and anyone under political suspicion. From 1946 the buildings were refashioned into the custody area for the KGB; in 1951, it was given over to the Stasi.

The prisoners' cells and interrogation rooms are on view, two of which have no windows and are lined with rubber. Housed in the cellars was the "submarine" – a series of cells without daylight to which the most "dangerous" suspects were brought.

Forschungs- und Gedenkstätte Normannenstraße (Stasi-Museum) ⓱

Ruschestraße 103 (Haus 1). **Tel** *(030) 553 68 54.* **U** *Magdalenenstraße.* **◯** *11am–6pm Mon–Fri, 2–6pm Sat–Sun.* 📷 **www**.stasimuseum.de

Under the German Democratic Republic, this huge complex of buildings at Ruschestrasse housed the Ministry of the Interior. It was here that the infamous Stasi (GDR secret service) had its

Office of the infamous Stasi chief Erich Mielke at the Stasi Museum

headquarters. The Stasi's "achievements" in infiltrating its own community were without equal in the Eastern block.

Since 1990 one of the buildings has housed a museum that displays photographs and documents depicting the activities of the Stasi. Here, you can see a model of the headquarters, and equipment that was used for bugging and spying on citizens suspected of holding unfavourable political views. You can also walk around the office of infamous Stasi chief Erich Mielke.

Köpenick ⓲

Ⓢ *Spindlersfeld, then* **🚌** *167 or* **Ⓢ** *Köpenick, then* **🚌** *164, 167.* **🚋** *27, 60, 61, 62, 68.* **Kunstgewerbemuseum** *Schloss Köpenick, Schlossinsel.* **Tel** *(030) 6566 17 49.* **◯** *10am–5pm Thu–Sun.*

Köpenick is much older than Berlin. In the 9th century AD, this island contained a fortified settlement known as Kopanica. In about 1240 a castle was built on the island, around which a town began to evolve. Craftsmen settled here and, after 1685, a large colony of Huguenots also settled.

In the 19th century Köpenick recreated itself as an industrial town. Despite wartime devastation it has retained its historic character and, though there are no longer any 13th-century churches, it is worth strolling around the old town. By the old market square and in the neighbouring streets, modest houses have survived that recall the 18th century, alongside buildings from the end of the 19th century.

At Alt Köpenick No. 21 is a vast brick town hall built in the style of the Brandenburg Neo-Renaissance. In 1906, a famous swindle took place here and the event became the inspiration for a popular comedy by Carl Zuckmayer, *The Captain from Köpenick.*

Köpenick's greatest attraction is a three-storey Baroque palace, built between 1677 and

A reconstructed drawing room from 1548 in the Kunstgewerbemuseum

1681 for the heir to the throne Friedrich (later King Friedrich I), to a design by the Dutch architect Rutger van Langfield. In 2003, the **Kunstgewerbemuseum** (*see p88*) opened a suite of Renaissance and Baroque rooms to the public in the Köpenick Palace.

Gigantic wreath commemorating the Red Army in Treptower Park

Treptower Park ⓲

Archenhold-Sternwarte, Alt-Treptow. Ⓢ Treptower Park. 🚌 166, 167, 265. **Archenhold Sternwarte** *Tel* (030) 536 06 37 19. 📷 compulsory; 2–4:30pm Wed–Sun. **www**.sdtp.de

The vast park in Treptow was laid out in the 1860s on the initiative and design of Johann Gustav Meyer. In 1919 it was where revolutionaries Karl Liebknecht, Wilhelm Pieck and Rosa Luxemburg assembled 150,000 striking workers.

The park is best known for the colossal monument to the Red Army. Built between 1946 and 1949, it stands on the grave of 5,000 Soviet soldiers killed in the battle for Berlin in 1945. The gateway, which leads to the mausoleum, is marked by a vast granite sculpture of a grieving Russian Motherland surrounded by statues of Red Army soldiers.

In the farthest section of the park is the astronomical observatory, **Archenhold Sternwarte**, which was built for a decorative arts exhibition in 1896. Given a permanent site in 1909, the observatory was used by Albert Einstein for a lecture on the Theory of Relativity in 1915. It is also home to the longest reflecting telescope in the world (21 m or 70 ft), and a small planetarium.

Beyond Treptower Park lies another park, Plänterwald.

Old Flughafen Tempelhof ⓳

Platz der Luftbrücke. Ⓤ Platz der Luftbrücke. 🚌 104, 184.

Tempelhof was once Germany's largest airport. Built in 1923, the structure is typical of Third Reich architecture. Additions to the original structure were completed in 1939.

In 1951, a monument was added in front of the airport. Designed by Edward Ludwig, it commemorates the airlifts of the Berlin Blockade. The names of those who lost their lives appear on the plinth.

After a long public debate, Tempelhof was decommissoned as a functioning airport in 2008. It has been turned into a public park and exhibition venue.

Viktoriapark ⓴

Ⓤ Platz der Luftbrücke. 🚌 104, 140.

This rambling park, with several artificial waterfalls, short trails and a small hill, was designed by Hermann Mächtig and built between 1884 and 1894. The Neo-Gothic Memorial to the Wars of Liberation at the summit of the hill is the work of Karl Friedrich Schinkel and was constructed between 1817 and 1821. The monument commemorates the Prussian victory against Napoleon's army in the Wars of Liberation. The monument's cast-iron tower is well ornamented.

In the niches of the lower section are 12 allegorical figures by Christian Daniel Rauch, Friedrich Tieck and Ludwig Wichmann. Each figure symbolizes a battle and is linked to a historic figure – either a military leader or a member of the royal family.

Rathaus Schöneberg ㉒

Schöneberg Town Hall

John-F-Kennedy-Platz. Ⓤ Rathaus Schöneberg.

The Schöneberg town hall is a gigantic building with an imposing tower, which was built between 1911 and 1914. From 1948 to 1990 it was used as the main town hall of West Berlin, and it was outside here, on 26 June 1963, that US President John F Kennedy gave his famous speech. More than 300,000 Berliners assembled to hear the young president say "*Ich bin ein Berliner*" – "I am a Berliner", intended as an expression of solidarity from the democratic world to a city defending its right to freedom.

While Kennedy's meaning was undoubtedly clear, pedants were quick to point out that what he actually said was "I am a small doughnut".

Japanese woodcut from the Museum für Ostasiatische Kunst

Museumszentrum Dahlem ㉓

Lansstraße 8, Dahlem. *Tel (830) 14 38.* Ⓤ *Dahlem Dorf.* 🚌 *X111, X83.* **Museum für Asiatische Kunst (Museum of Asian Art), Museum Europäischer Kulturen (Museum of European Cultures), Ethnologisches Museum (Museum of Mankind)** ◯ *10am–6pm Tue–Fri, 11am–6pm Sat & Sun.* 📷 **www**.smb.spk-berlin.de

Dahlem's first museums were built between 1914 and 1923, but the district was confirmed as a major cultural and education centre after World War II with the establishment of the Freie Universität and completion of the museum complex. With many of Berlin's collections fragmented, a miscellany of art and artifacts was put on display here. In the 1960s the museums were extended and the Museumszentrum was created to rival East Berlin's Museum Island.

German reunification in 1990 meant that the collections could once again be reunited and reorganized. Paintings were moved to the Kulturforum *(see pp84–5),* and sculptures to the Bode-museum *see p78).*

Three museums are now housed at Dahlem: the Ethnologisches Museum, which focuses on pre-industrial societies from around the world; the Museum für Asiatische Kunst, one of the largest musems of Asian art in the world and the Museum Europäischer Kultures.

Highlights include bronzes from Benin and gold Inca jewellery at the Museum of Mankind and Japanese woodcuts from Chinese Turkestan at the Museum of Asian Art. The Exhibition of Native North American Cultures, part of the Museum of Mankind, opened in 1999, includes a collection of 600 ceremonial objects.

Jagdschloss Grunewald ㉔

Am Grunewaldsee 29. *Tel (030) 813 35 97.* 🚌 *115, X10.* ◯ *Apr–Oct: 10am–6pm Tue–Sun; Nov–Mar: tours only, 11am, 1pm, 3pm Sat & Sun.* 📷 **www**.spsg.de

Jagdschloss Grunewald is one of the oldest surviving civic buildings in Berlin. Built for the Elector Joachim II in 1542, it was rebuilt around 1700 in a Baroque style.

In this small palace on the edge of the Grunewaldsee is Berlin's only surviving Renaissance hall, which currently houses a collection of paintings that includes a range of canvases by Rubens and van Dyck, among others.

In the east wing is the small Waldmuseum, which has a collection of illustrations depicting forest life and the history of forestry. Opposite the Jagdschloss, a hunting museum (Jagdmuseum) houses a collection of historic weapons and equipment.

Brücke-Museum ㉕

Bussardsteig 9, Dahlem. *Tel (030) 831 20 29.* 🚌 *115.* ◯ *11am–5pm Wed–Mon.* **www**.bruecke-museum.de

This elegant Functionalist building hosts a collection of German Expressionist painting linked to the Die Brücke group. It is based on almost 80 works by Schmidt-Rottluff bequeathed to the town of Dahlem in 1964. In addition to other works of art contemporary to Die Brücke, there are paintings from the later creative periods of these artists, as well as works of other closely associated artists. Nearby lie the foundation's headquarters, established in the former studio of the sculptor Bernhard Heliger.

Strandbad Wannsee ㉖

Wannseebadweg. Ⓢ *Nikolassee.* 🚌 *112, 218.*

The vast lake Wannsee, on the edge of Grunewald, is a popular destination for Berliners seeking recreation. The most developed part is the southeastern corner where there are yachting marinas and harbours. Further north is one of the largest inland beaches in Europe, Strandbad Wannsee, which was developed between 1929 and 1930 by the construction of shops, cafés and changing rooms on man-made terraces. It is also pleasant to walk around Schwanenwerder island, with its many elegant villas.

Boarding point for lake cruises on the Wannsee

The Schloss Pfaueninsel designed by Johann Brendel

Pfaueninsel ㉗

Pfaueninsel. **Tel** *(030) 805 86 830.*
Ⓢ *Wannsee, then take* 🚌 *218.*
🚢 *Schloss Pfaueninsel.* ☐ *Apr–Oct·*
10am–5pm Tue–Sun. 🎦

This picturesque island, named for the peacocks that inhabit it, is now a nature reserve, reached by ferry across the Havel river. It was laid out in 1795 according to a design by Johann August Eyserbeck. Its final form, which you see today, is the work of the landscape architect Peter Joseph Lenné.

One of the most interesting sights on the island is the small romantic palace of **Schloss Pfaueninsel**. Dating from 1794, it was designed by Johann Gottlieb Brendel for Friedrich Wilhelm II and his mistress Wilhelmine Encke (the future Countess Lichtenau). The palace was built of wood, with a façade fashioned in the form of a ruined medieval castle. The cast-iron bridge that links the towers was built in 1807. The palace is open to the public in the summer months, when you can see the 18th- and 19th-century furnishings.

Other sights worth visiting include **Jakobsbrunnen** (James's Well), which was built to resemble an ancient ruin. Towards the northeast corner of the island is the **Luisentempel** in the form of a Greek temple. Its sandstone portico was relocated to the island from the mausoleum in Schlosspark Charlottenburg *(see pp98–9)* in 1829. Nearby is a stone commemorating Johannes Kunckel, an alchemist who lived on

Pfaueninsel in the 17th century. During his quest to discover how to make gold, he discovered a method of producing ruby-coloured glass. Near the **Aviary**, home to multicoloured parrots and pheasants, is a tall fountain that was designed by Martin Friedrich Rabe in 1824.

Nikolskoe ㉘

Nikolskoer Weg. Ⓢ *Wannsee, then take* 🚌 *316.*

Across the river from Pfaueninsel (Peacock Island) is Nikolskoe. Here you'll find the Blockhaus Nikolskoe, a Russian-style *dacha* (country house) that was built in 1819 for the future Tsar Nicholas I and his wife, the daughter of King Friedrich Wilhelm III.

The house was built by the German military architect Captain Snethlage, who was responsible for the Alexandrowka estate in Potsdam

Guests on the terrace of the Blockhaus Nikolskoe in summer

(see p134). Following a fire in 1985, the *dacha* was reconstructed. It currently houses a restaurant.

Close by is the church of St Peter and Paul, which was built between 1834 and 1837, to a design by Friedrich August Stüler. The body of the church is completed by a tower crowned by an onion-shaped dome, reflecting the style of Russian Orthodox sacral architecture.

Klein Glienicke ㉙

Königstr. 36. 🚌 *316.* **Tel** *(0331) 96 94 200.* ☐ *Apr–Oct: 10am–6pm Tue–Sun; Nov–Mar: 10am–5pm Sat & Sun.* 🎦

The palace in the palace-park of Klein Glienicke was built in 1825 according to a design by Karl Friedrich Schinkel for Prince Karl of Prussia. The charming parkin which it is located was created by Peter Joseph Lenné. Beyond the Neo-Classical palace extends an irregular cluster of buildings, grouped around a courtyard, including a pergola and staff cottages. Passing by the palace, you approach the **Coach House**, also designed by Schinkel and now housing a restaurant. Nearby are an orangery and greenhouses designed by Ludwig Persius. Also by Persius is the **Klosterhof**, a mock monastery with pavilions, on whose walls are many Byzantine and Romanesque architectural elements from Italy. Towards the lake is the **Grosse Neugierde**, a circular pavilion based on the Athenian monument to Lysikrates from the 4th century BC. From here there are beautiful views across the Havel river and **Glienicker Brücke** (known under the East German regime as the bridge of unity). The border with West Berlin ran across this bridge where, during the Cold War, the exchange of spies was conducted.

Karl Friedrich Schinkel's Neo-Classical Schloss Klein Glienicke

SHOPPING IN BERLIN

With a shopping centre in every district, each selling a variety of merchandise, Berlin is a place where almost anything can be bought, so long as you know where to shop. The most popular areas are Kurfürstendamm and Friedrichstrasse, but the smaller shops in Wedding, Friedrichshain, Schöneberg and the Tiergarten are also worth a visit. Small boutiques selling flamboyant Berlin-style clothes crop up in unexpected courtyards, while the top fashion houses offer the latest in European elegance. Early on Saturday morning is often the best time to visit the city's various markets, the most popular of which – with their colourful stalls full of hats, bags and belts – can be found on Museum Island and near the Tiergarten. The Galeries Lafayette, KaDeWe and any of the city's numerous bookshops all make ideal venues for a pleasant afternoon's window shopping.

A shop-floor display in the lobby of KaDeWe

PRACTICAL INFORMATION

The majority of shops are open Monday to Saturday from 10am to 8pm. Before Christmas, many shops are open on Sundays. Some smaller stores do not accept credit cards, so be sure to have some cash.

DEPARTMENT STORES AND SHOPPING CENTRES

The **Alexa Centre**, a large shopping mall located at Alexanderplatz, houses most of the major fashion chains. Kaufhaus Des Westens, better known as **KaDeWe** at Wittenbergplatz, is undoubtedly the biggest and the best department store in Berlin, while **Galeries Lafay-ette** on Friedrichstrasse is nothing less than a slice of Paris in the heart of Berlin. Perfumes, domestic accessories and clothing attract an enormous clientele.

Another very popular store is **Wertheim** on the Ku'damm. Although the outfits sold here are less haute couture than at Galeries Lafayette, there is still an enormous choice and the top-floor restaurant offers excellent views over the city.

One of the newest shopping centres is the **Potsdamer Platz Arkaden**, which is a very popular meeting place. On a slightly smaller scale is **Das Schloss** in Steglitz, and the **Gesundbrunnencenter** is the biggest shopping passage in Berlin with stalls full of bargains. **Europa-Center** is the most visually stunning with its beautiful sculpted fountains.

FASHION

The Ku'damm and Friedrich-strasse areas play host to all the best known high street names and department stores, as well as most of the top fashion houses in Berlin. **Escada** is one of the best known of the German designers, but Berlin also has a wealth of young designers and their lines are mainly to be seen in the northern part of the Mitte area. **NIX**, for example, offers timeless clothes made from heavy, dark fabrics, while **Department Store Quartier 206** sells everything from evening dresses to casual wear and accessories. It offers only top international designer wear and many unique pieces. An exciting designer is **Antonia Goy**, who creates stunning dresses and accessories for women.

For men's fashions, once again the Ku'damm area is the

The spacious Wertheim department store on Kurfürstendamm

Store front of German fashion house Escada

place to look. **Patrick Hellmann** is certainly worth a visit with its wide choice of the best designer labels around.

ANTIQUES

The antiques trade in Berlin is booming, and there are many markets and galleries opening all the time. Berlin's most prestigious auction house is **Galerie Bassenge**, while **ART 1900** and **Zeitlos** on Suarez-straße offer trinkets and knick-knacks from various periods. Many Berliners spend their Saturday and Sunday mornings at flea markets browsing the stalls. In particular, the **Antik & Trödelmarkt am Ostbahnhof** is considered one of the best places to pick up bargains.

FOOD PRODUCTS

All manner of foods and wine are available in Berlin, and they make excellent gifts and souvenirs. Kaffee und Kuchen (coffee and cakes) is a strong German tradition, so why not head to **Buchwald** and purchase one of their delicious cakes to take home. You will also find that bakeries all over the city sell traditional *Berliners* (doughnuts) along with a good value range of delicious pastries and breads.

Wine fans will love **Viniculture**, which offers one of the best selections of German wine around or, if you've become a fan of local meats, pick from a bewildering range of organic sausages at **Fleischerei Bachhuber**.

Berlin also plays host to a number of food markets. The **Winterfeldmarkt** is probably the most popular, but the **Wochenmarkt** on Wittenberg-platz also has a particularly loyal following.

SEASONAL SALES

Twice a year (January and July) all the shops in Berlin empty their shelves in the end of season *Schlussverkauf*. Goods bought in a sale are officially non-returnable, though sometimes you may find you are able to negotiate with the shop assistant.

A number of shops sell "second season" items – these are new, but they were stocked for the previous season and as such are generously reduced in price and make great bargain buys.

The central "glass cone" of the Galeries Lafayette department store

ENTERTAINMENT IN BERLIN

With so much on offer, from classical drama and cabaret to variety theatre and an eclectic nightclub scene, it is possible to indulge just about any taste in Berlin. During the summer months many bars and restaurants set up outdoor tables and the areas around Unter den Linden, the Kurfürstendamm, Kreuzberg and Prenzlauer Berg in particular, seem to turn into one large social arena. The city really comes into its own at night, when its clubs, all-night cafés and cocktail bars give you the chance to dance till dawn. The city has many night-life centres, each with a slightly different character. Prenzlauer Berg is the best choice for mainstream bars, cafés and clubs, while Friedrich-shain has a vibrant subculture, and Schöneberg has a lively gay scene. The Mitte district in the Eastern Centre offers a true mixture with its opera house and classical theatre surrounded by lively and sleek bars. On a Sunday, a quiet trip down the river or along the canals offers a pleasant way to unwind.

Flute player in costume

The Berlin Philharmonic Orchestra

PRACTICAL INFORMATION

There are so many things going on in Berlin that it can be difficult to find what you are looking for. Listings magazines like *Tip* or *Zitty* are invaluable aids and offer the widest range of suggestions. Information on festivals, sports events, cinema programmes, theatre schedules, cabarets and concerts can be found on the following websites: www.berlinonline.de and www.berlin.de.

For visitors who have just arrived in town, however, and have not made it yet to an Internet café or a kiosk, the chances are the local bar or your hotel foyer has leaflets on the wall to point you in the right direction. There are also lots of posters around town telling you what is on offer. *EXBERLINER* magazine has listings in English, and it should be available at most kiosks.

Tickets for events should generally be bought in advance, though last-minute tickets are often available from **Hekticket Theaterkassen**. The disabled, pensioners and students with the appropriate ID are often entitled to discounted tickets. All major venues will provide good wheelchair access.

CLASSICAL MUSIC

The Berlin Philharmonic Orchestra is one of the world's finest orchestras and it performs regularly at the beautiful **Philharmonie**, with its awe-inspiring architecture and fantastic acoustics. Chamber orchestras perform in the smaller **Kammermusiksaal** attached to the bigger hall. **Konzerthaus Berlin**, formally known as the Schauspielhaus, is another important venue for classical music having been magnificently restored after World War II.

Opera lovers will find themselves well catered for in Berlin as there are three major opera houses. The **Staatsoper Unter den Linden's** impressive, yet conservative repertoire includes traditional German classics and Italian opera, while the **Komische Oper** is known for its broad range of lighter opera and, because its operas frequently have a long run, there are

Prokofiev's *The Love of Three Oranges* staged at the Komische Oper

Traditional jazz music at Berlin's Jazzfest

often last-minute tickets available. The **Deutsche Oper** on Bismarckstrasse is housed in a somewhat plainer building than the other opera venues, but it boasts performances ranging from Mozart to Wagner.

MUSIC FESTIVALS

The **Berliner Festwochen** takes place throughout the month of September and top orchestras and performers come from all over the world to put on classical music concerts around the city.

Also in September, pop fans will love **Berliner Clubnacht**, which offers an opportunity to dance on 60 floors in 44 Berlin clubs.

Jazzfest Berlin takes place in July and tends to attract lovers of more traditional styles of jazz, but it also focuses on the more experimental and innovative styles of the genre in its accompanying Total Music Meeting.

ROCK, POP & JAZZ

Whether it is a major event by a world-famous band or a small-scale evening of jazz improvisation, you need not look too far to find what you want. The biggest concerts tend to take place in sports halls and stadiums, like **O₂ World** and the **Olympiastadion** *(see p97)*, whilst smaller venues like **Privatclub** and **SO 36** play host to the best new talent in popular music. In addition, a lot of the action tends to take place in the city's many bars, discos and

clubs or, if you are looking for particularly atmospheric concerts, you might try those put on at the **Passionskirche**, a converted church in Kreuzberg.

Jazz clubs abound in Berlin, as the style remains very popular amongst locals. The **A-Trane** and **b-flat** are classical jazz bars where you can listen to small bands just about every night of the week, and **Quasimodo** is renowned for its schedule of local and touring jazz, soul and world music performers.

Apart from the typical classical jazz clubs, jazz can also be heard in many of the city's smaller bars, like **Schlot**. If it is a mixture of soul, rap and jazz you want to listen to, then head for

the **Junction Bar** in Kreuzberg. The small bebop jazz club in Kreuzberg is a good choice for meeting locals, and the **Badenscher Hof Jazzclub** is always a good bet.

WORLD MUSIC

Berlin is home to a wide variety of world music. The Haus der Kulturen der Welt organizes all kinds of concerts at its own **Café Global** and **Kulturbrauerei** has become the main venue for world-class artists.

Latin American discos are becoming ever more popular and **Havanna** in Schöneberg is one of the city's best.

Irish music is also well represented in Berlin's pubs – **Wild at Heart** is very popular, although it does not play Irish music all the time.

Rosa's Dance Co. at the "Tanz" dance festival, organized by the Hebbel Am Ufer (HAU)

CLASSICAL AND MODERN DANCE

There are three major ballet groups in Berlin and they work within Berlin's opera houses. The Komische Oper has a modern repertoire, whilst the Staatsoper Unter den Linden focuses on more classical work.

The **Hebbel Am Ufer (HAU)** stages avant-garde pieces and welcomes troupes from all over the world and also organizes the dance festival "Tanz" every August. The seating at all three theatres is rather limited, so you need to book well in advance.

Tanzfabrik, based on Möckernstrasse in Kreuzberg, is an excellent stage for all kinds of modern dance and it also organizes dance workshops as well as popular body-work courses.

One of the many concerts at Berlin's annual Popkomm festival

NIGHTLIFE

Among its many artistic claims, Berlin is also the techno capital of Europe, with over a million devotees celebrating the genre at a number of annual festivals.

One of the best clubs for techno lovers is **Tresor**, situated in a former power plant. The best DJs in town can be heard here.

Columbia Club is a concert venue featuring touring rock bands, so the look and style of the place changes with each performance.

If it is a good old-fashioned disco you are looking for, with happy tunes and a little less techno, the **Far Out** is the place to go.

There is also a new generation of clubs offering a sleek combination of restaurant, lounge, dance floor and event centre. Each night there is a different, often themed, party, or simply a relaxed lounge occasion. The top two locations are **40seconds**, set in an old high-rise with a great view of the night-lit city, and the exclusive **Spindler + Klatt**. Other clubs, such as **Felix**, welcome a well-to-do clientele to contemporary pop music. By contrast, **White Trash** and **Café Moskau** attract a more alternative, hip and young urban crowd.

During the summer, you can dance to pop music in the open air at **Golgatha** in Kreuzberg's Viktoriapark.

Delicious Doughnuts is one of the best places in town for ambient, house and acid-jazz, while lovers of soul and reggae should head for the lively **Hoppetosse Boat Bar**. For anyone looking for something a little more intimate, the romantic atmosphere of **Sophienclub** might be worth investigating.

Those who enjoy dancing should head for **Ballhaus** in Mitte, which offers a different style each evening – either salsa, tango, swing, cha-cha or disco.

The city also has a vibrant gay and lesbian scene. **SchwuZ**, **Berghain** and **Ackerkeller** are among the best gay venues in Berlin.

The reconstructed medieval settlement at the Museumdorf Düppel

SPECTATOR SPORTS

As a rule, Berlin's sports teams tend to be among the country's best, and rank highly in each of their respective leagues. Hertha BSC's football matches take place in the **Olympiastadion** and Alba Berlin's basketball games are on at the **O₂ Arena**. For international events it is usually best to book in advance.

Lovers of horse racing have two tracks to choose from in Berlin. **Trabrennbahn** in Mariendorf is open all year and the races held here are strictly commercial. **Galopprennbahn Hoppegarten**, on the other hand, has a much more friendly, approachable feel.

CHILDREN'S ACTIVITIES

People of all ages are catered for in Berlin, and children are no exception. **Visit Berlin** can offer details of special children's discounts for many different activities. The

Flamingos in the beautiful Zoologischer Garten

Zoologischer Garten is very popular, with its playgrounds and many animal enclosures. Small children will love the **Kinderbauernhof Görlitzer Bauernhof**, which has a collection of domestic animals. In addition, Berlin's museums are well set up for children. The **Deutsches Technikmuseum** *(see p81)* allows children to take part in all kinds of experiments, while the **Ethnologisches Museum** prepares special exhibitions for children. A visit to the **Museumsdorf Düppel** is an excellent way to show a child life in a medieval village and the **Puppentheatermuseum** offers a chance for children to take part in minor performances.

Another option is one of the city's many lively circuses, such as **Circus Cabuwazi**, or, if it is sport that your child enjoys, it is possible to swim in many rivers, lakes and, of course, swimming pools (the **Berliner Bäderbetriebe** hotline offers useful information). Also, each district has its own ice-skating rink, but the **Eisstadion Berlin Wilmersdorf** is by far the best, whilst **FEZ Wuhlheide** offers a special daily programme for kids.

The Story of Berlin is a fun way to experience the history of Berlin in a multimedia exhibit, and the **Berliner Gruselkabinett** (Room of Fear) is suitably scary.

The **Zeiss-Planetarium** or the **Planetarium am Insulaner** offer kids the opportunity to explore the universe in a fun, yet educational, way.

DIRECTORY

PRACTICAL INFORMATION

Hekticket Theaterkassen
Hardenbergstraße 29d.
Map 2 B4.
Karl Liebknechtstraße 12.
Map 5 D1.
Tel 230 99 30.
www.hekticket.de

CLASSICAL MUSIC

Deutsche Oper
Bismarckstraße 34–37.
Tel 34 38 43 43.

Philharmonie & Kammermusiksaal
Herbert-von-Karajan-Str. 1.
Map 3 F3.
Tel 25 48 89 99.

Komische Oper
Behrenstraße 55–57.
Map 1 F4.
Tel 47 99 74 00.

Konzerthaus Berlin
Gendarmenmarkt 2.
Map 4 C2.
Tel 203 09 21 01/02.

Staatsoper Unter den Linden
Temporarily at Schiller-theater, Bismarckstraße 110.
Tel 20 35 44 38.

MUSIC FESTIVALS

Berliner Festspiele
Schaperstraße 4.
Map 2 B5.
Tel 25 48 90.

Jazzfest Berlin
Schaperstraße 24.
Tel 25 48 90.

Berliner Clubnacht
www.berlin-clubnacht.de

ROCK, POP & JAZZ

A-trane
Pestalozzistraße 105.
Map 2 A3.
Tel 313 25 50.

b-flat
Rosenthaler Straße 13.
Map 5 D4.
Tel 283 31 23.

Badenscher Hof Jazzclub
Badensche Straße 29.
Tel 861 00 80.

Junction Bar
Gniesenaustraße 18.
Tel 694 66 02.

Passionskirche
Marheineckeplatz.
Tel 69 40 12 41.

Quasimodo
Kanststr. 12a. **Map** 2 B4.
Tel 312 80 86.

Schlot
Chausseestraße 18 (enter via Schlegelstraße).
Tel 448 21 60.

SO 36
Oranienstraße 190.
Tel 61 40 13 06.

WORLD MUSIC

Café Global
John-Foster-Dulles-Allee 10.
Map 3 F2.
Tel 39 78 71 75.

Havanna
Hauptstraße 30.
Tel 784 8565.

Kulturbrauerei
Schönhauser Allee 36,
Prenzlaverberg.
Tel 44 35 260.

Tempodrom
Möckernstr. 10. **Map** 4 B4.
Tel 695 33 885.

Wild at Heart
Wiener Stra. 20, Kreuzberg.
Tel 610 74701.

CLASSICAL AND MODERN DANCE

Hebbel Am Ufer
Hau Eins, Zwei and Drei
Stresemannstraße 29
Hallesches Ufer 32
Tempelhofer Ufer 10.
Map 4 B5.
Tel 259 00 40.

Tanzfabrik
Möckernstraße 68.
Tel 786 58 61.

NIGHTLIFE

Ackerkeller
Bergstraße 68.
Tel 364 61356.

Ballhaus
Auguststraße 24, Mitte.
Tel 282 92 95.

Berghain
Am Wriezener Bahnhof,
Frederichshain.
Tel 364 61356.

Café Moskau
Karl-Marx-Allee.
Tel 24 63 16 26.

Columbia Club
Columbiadamm 9–11,
Kreuzberg.

Delicious Doughnuts
Rosenthaler Straße 9.
Map 5 D1.
Tel 28 09 92 74.

Far Out Club
Joachimstalerstraße 15.
Map 2 B5.
Tel 32 00 07 23.

Felix
Behrenstr. 72. **Map** 4 A2.
Tel 301 117 152.

40seconds
Potsdamer Str. 58.
Tel 89 06 42 41.

Golgatha
Dudenstraße 48–64.
Tel 785 24 53.

Hoppetosse
Eichenstraße 4.
Tel 533 203 40.

SchwuZ
Mehringdamm 61.
Tel 629 0880.

Sophienclub
Sophienstraße 6.
Tel 282 45 52

Spindler + Klatt
Köpenicker Str. 16–17.
Map 5 F3
Tel 319 88 1860.

Tresor
Köpenicker Str. 59–73.
Tel 24 72 49 82.

White Trash
Schönhauser Allee 167.
Tel 50 34 86 68.

SPECTATOR SPORTS

Galopprennbahn Hoppegarten
Goetheallee 1.
Tel (03342) 389 30.

O$_2$ World
Mühlenstraße 12–30/
O$_2$-Platz-1.
Tel 20 60 70 80.

Olympiastadion
Olympischer Platz.
Tel 306 88 100.

Trabrennbahn
Mariendorfer Damm 222,
Tempelhof.
Tel 740 12 12.

CHILDREN'S ACTIVITIES

Visit Berlin Berlin Tourist Information
Tel (030) 25 00 25.
www.visitberlin.de

Berliner Bäderbetriebe
Tel (01803) 10 20 20.

Berliner Grusselkabinett
Schöneberger Straße 23a.
Tel 26 55 55 46.

Circus Cabuwazi
Four locations.
Tel (030) 611 92 75.
www.cabuwazi.de

Deutsches Technikmuseum
Trebbiner Straße 9.
Tel 90 25 40.

Eisstadion Berlin Wilmersdorf
Fritz-Wildung-Straße 9.
Tel 824 10 12.

Ethnologisches Museum
Lansstraße 8.
Tel 83 01 438.

FEZ Wuhlheide
An der Wuhlheide 197,
Köpenick.
Tel 53 07 10

Kinderbauernhof Görlitzer Bauernhof
Wiener Straße 59b.
Tel 611 74 24.

Museumsdorf Düppel
Clauertstraße 11.
Tel 802 66 71.

Planetarium am Insulaner
Munsterdamm 90.
Tel 790 09 30.

Puppentheater-museum
Karl-Marx-Straße 135.
Tel 687 81 32.

The Story of Berlin
Kurfürstendamm 207–208. *Tel* 88 72 01 00.

Zeiss-Planetarium
Prenzlauer Allee 80.
Tel 42 18 45 12.

Zoologischer Garten
Hardenbergplatz 9,
Charlottenburg.
Tel 25 40 10.

Theatre and Cinema

Berlin can lay many claims to being a centre for artistic greatness, but possibly its most valid claims lie in the areas of theatre and cinema. Berlin has been the capital of German cinema since brothers Emil and Max Skladanowsky showed a series of short films to a spellbound German public in 1896. By 1918 there were already some 251 cinemas in Berlin and by 1925, the number of people involved in the film industry was nearly 50,000. At the same time, Berlin was fast becoming a landmark in European theatre thanks mainly to Reinhardt and Brecht. During the years of Nazi rule, many theatre people were killed or forced to emigrate as the stage became a propaganda machine, but after World War II a revival spread through Berlin's theatres. The popularity of theatre and cinema continues today, perpetuated by the annual Film Festival.

A Berlin International Film Festival poster from 1960

TICKET AND PRICE INFORMATION

Tickets for both cinema and theatre are usually reasonably priced in Berlin, but there are a few tips which are useful to remember if you are planning to visit either.

Students and senior citizens do not always receive a discount at the cinema, but often Tuesday or Wednesday is declared Cinema Day, when some tickets are €1–2 cheaper. It is worth knowing that most ticket offices do not accept credit cards, so take cash.

For theatres, it is usually possible to pre-book tickets at least two weeks before a performance. You can buy them directly from the box office of the theatre, online or by telephone. Independent ticket vendors usually charge a commission of between 15 and 22 per cent.

Hekticket Theaterkassen specializes in last-minute tickets, so check with them on the day for special deals.

MAJOR STAGES

The **Deutsches Theater** and its small hall **Kammerspiele** on Schumannstrasse are top-class theatres and offer a varied repertoire of productions. At **Volksbühne** you can see interesting performances of classical plays in modern settings and new plays by young authors.

The **Berliner Ensemble** (or BE for short) was once managed by Bertolt Brecht and Heiner Müller. The spectacles created by these two are still performed today.

Other major venues include the **Maxim Gorki Theater**, the **Renaissance-Theater** and the **Schaubühne**.

ALTERNATIVE THEATRE

There are a number of alternative theatres in Berlin. The three-theatre company **Hebbel am Ufer (HAU)** is devoted to avant-garde

theatre and considered the city's best alternative stage. The smaller boulevard theatres like **Theater am Kurfürstendamm** offer different, and somewhat lighter programmes.

Other notable venues include **Bat-Studiotheater** and the **Kleines Theater**.

MUSICALS, REVIEWS AND CABARETS

There are three main musical theatres in Berlin, in addition to the many small venues which fit musicals into their more general repertoire. **Friedrichstadtpalast** and **Admiralspalast**, in the eastern part of the city, stage many of the new major shows, while the **Theater des Westens** in Charlottenburg tends to be more traditional. In addition to these is the **Theater am Potsdamer Platz**, a modern theatre which was established in the newly built Potsdamer Platz in 1999 and shows recent musical hits.

As for cabaret, there are probably as many acts in Berlin today as there were in the 1920s. **Distel**, in Friedrichstrasse, continues its success from GDR times, and **Die Stachelschweine** celebrates its popularity in western Berlin.

Other great venues for lively musicals, reviews and cabarets include **Bar jeder Vernunft**, **Chamäleon Variété**, **Scheinbar**, **Wintergarten Variété** and **Wühlmäuse**.

BIG SCREENS AND BIG FILMS

After the fall of the Berlin Wall, many multiplex cinemas were built, the biggest being the **CinemaxX Potsdamer Platz** and the **Cinestar Sony Center**,

The retro façade of Friedrichstadtpalast in the east of Berlin

which show films in the original language. In most cinemas, mainstream Anglo-American movies tend to be dubbed rather than subtitled.

For a breathtaking experience, try the **IMAX** at the Sony Centre, with its huge 3-D screen.

STUDIO CINEMA

There are plenty of small studio cinemas scattered across town which show a number of new independent films. **Hackesche Höfe Kino** or **Central**, situated near Hackescher Markt, offer a pleasant break from city life and have bars of their own.

The **Arsenal**, on Potsdamer Platz, shows German film classics; if you are interested in original language films, Berlin has various options. **Cinéma Paris** in Charlottenburg is the place to go for French films, while the **Odeon** in Schöneberg specializes in English and American films.

OPEN-AIR CINEMA

Open-air cinemas start operating as soon as the weather allows. The biggest is **Waldbühne** – a concert hall that seats an audience of 20,000. Others can be found in Hasenheide, Künstler Haus Bethanien garden in Friedrichshain or at Potsdamer Platz. The films shown are a mixture of new releases and old classics, and showings tend to start at around 9pm.

DIRECTORY

TICKET AND PRICE INFORMATION

Hekticket Theaterkassen
Hardenbergstraße 29d.
Map 2 B4. **Tel** 230 99 30.
www.hekticket.de

MAJOR STAGES

Berliner Ensemble
Bertolt-Brecht-Platz 1.
Map 1 F3. **Tel** 28 408
155. www.berliner-ensemble.de

Deutsches Theater
Schumannstraße 13.
Map 1 F3.
Tel 28 44 12 25.
www.deutschestheater.de

Kammerspiele
Schumannstraße 13a.
Map 1 F3.
Tel 28 44 12 22.
www.deutschestheater.de

Maxim-Gorki Theater
Am Festungsgraben 2.
Map 4 C2. **Tel** 20 22 11
29. www.gorki.de

Renaissance-Theater
Hardenbergstraße 6.
Map 2 A3.
Tel 312 42 02. www.
renaissance-theater.de

Schaubühne am Lehniner Platz
Kurfürstendamm 153.
Tel 89 00 20.
www.schaubuehne.de.

Volksbühne
Rosa-Luxemburg-Platz.
Tel 240 655.

ALTERNATIVE THEATRE

Bat-Studiotheater
Belforter Straße 15.
Tel 755 41 7777.
www.bat-berlin.de

Kleines Theater
Südwestkorso 64
Tel 821 20 21.
www.kleines-theater-de

Hebbel am Ufer (HAU)
Hallesches Ufer 32.
Tel 25 90 04 27.

Theater am Kurfürstendamm
Kurfürstendamm 206.
Map 2 A5.
Tel 88 59 11 88.

MUSICALS, REVIEWS AND CABARETS

Admiralspalast
Friedrichstrasse 101.
Map 4 C1.
Tel 47 99 74 99.
www.admiralspalast.de

Bar jeder Vernunft
Schaperstraße 24.
Map 2 B5. **Tel** 883 15 82.

Chamäleon Variété
Rosenthaler Straße 40–41.
Map 5 D4. **Tel** 4000 590.
www.chamaeleonberlin.
de.

Distel
Friedrichstraße 101.
Map 1 F3.
Tel 204 47 04.

Friedrichstadt-palast
Friedrichstraße 107.
Map 1 F3. **Tel** 23 26 23
26. www.friedrichstadt
palast.de

Scheinbar
Monumentenstraße 9.
Tel 704 55 99.

Stachelschweine
Europa-Center.
Map 2 C4. **Tel** 261 47
95. www.die-stachel
schweine.de

Theater am Potsdamer Platz
Marlene-Dietrich-Platz 1.
Map 4 A3.
Tel 259 244 555.
www.stage-
entertainment.de.

Theater des Westens
Kantstraße 12.
Tel 259 244 555.
www.stage-
entertainment.de

Tipi-das Zelt am Kanzleramt
Tiergarten, Große
Querallee. **Map** 1 D4.
Tel (01803) 27 93 58.
www.tipi-am-kanzleramt.
de

Wintergarten Variété
Potsdamer Straße 96.
Map 3 F4.
Tel 25 00 88 88.
www.wintergarten-
variete.de

Wühlmäuse
Pommernallee 2–4.
Tel 306 73011.
www.wuehlmaeuse.de

BIG SCREENS AND BIG FILMS

CinemaxX Potsdamer Platz
Potsdamer Straße 1–19.
Map 4 A3.
Tel (0180) 524 63 62 99.
www.cinemaxx.de

Cinestar Sony Center & Imax
Potsdamer Straße 4.
Map 4 A3.
Tel 01805 118811

STUDIO CINEMA

Arsenal
Potsdamer Straße 2.
Map 4 A3.
Tel 26 95 51 00.

Central
Rosenthaler Straße 39.
Map 5 D1.
Tel 28 59 99 73.

Cinéma Paris
Kurfürstendamm 211.
Tel 881 31 19.

Hackescher Höfe Kino
Rosenthaler Straße 40–41.
Map 5 D1.
Tel 283 46 03.

Odeon
Hauptstraße 115.
Tel 78 70 40 19.

OPEN-AIR CINEMA

Waldbühne
Glockenturmstraße 1.
Tel 74 73 75 00.

BERLIN STREET FINDER

Map references given for historic buildings, hotels, restaurants, bars, shops and entertainment venues refer to the maps included in this section of the guidebook. The key map below shows the area of Berlin covered by the Street Finder. The maps include all major sightseeing areas, historic attractions, railway stations, bus stations, U-Bahn stations and the suburban stations of the S-Bahn. The names of the streets and squares in the index and maps are given in German. The word Straße (or STRASSE, Str) indicates a street, Allee an avenue, Platz a square, Brücke a bridge and Bahnhof a railway station.

KEY

■ Major sight	🚌 Bus terminus	⊠ Post office
■ Place of interest	🚊 Tram stop	═ Railway line
■ Other building	🅿 Parking	─ Pedestrian-only street
Ⓢ S-Bahn station	✚ Hospital with emergency dept.	
Ⓤ U-Bahn station	🚓 Police station	**SCALE OF MAPS 1–5**
🚉 Railway station	✝ Church	
🚌 Bus stop	✡ Synagogue	0 metres 250

0 yards 250

1:15 000

EASTERN GERMANY

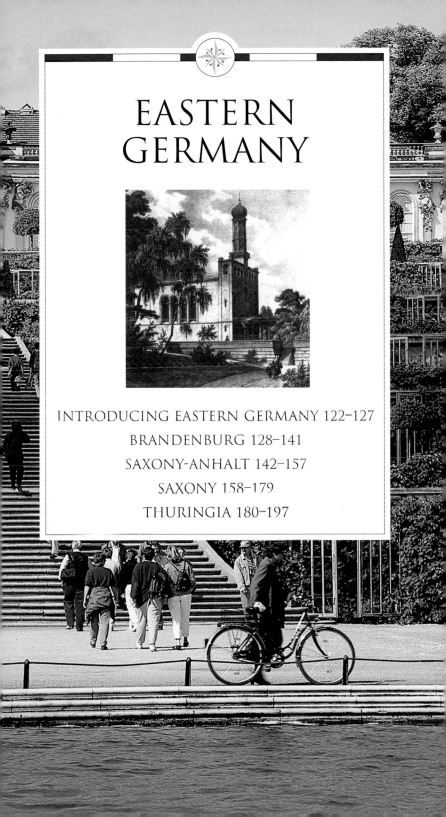

Eastern Germany at a Glance

The eastern region of Germany is immensely rich in tourist attractions. The imposing valley of the Elbe River, the beautiful lake district of Lower Brandenburg, attractive trails in the Harz Mountains of Saxony-Anhalt, the Thuringian Forest as well as the Erzgebirge and the Lusatian Mountains in Saxony all invite the visitor with their dramatic scenery and excellent recreational facilities.

Eastern Germany is rich in historic sights, too, ranging from the Baroque residences of Potsdam in Brandenburg to the grand architecture of Dresden and Leipzig in Saxony and the important cultural centre of Weimar in Thuringia. The most rewarding destinations in the region are featured here.

The Magdeburg Reiter, *in the market square, is the copy of one of Thuringia's most famous sights. The identity of the rider is not certain.*

Naumburg Dom *is a huge, well preserved Gothic cathedral (see pp150–51), one of Germany's greatest buildings. Splendid statues of its founders, Ekkehart and Uta, adorn the walls of the presbytery.*

Erfurt Dom *dominates the townscape. A massive Gothic structure, the cathedral's three towers were built on the Romanesque foundations of an earlier church.*

SAXONY-ANHALT
(see pp142–57)

THURINGIA
(see pp180–97)

Weimar, *with its picturesque market square (see pp194–5) and historic buildings, was an important cultural centre for many centuries. Friedrich Schiller, Johann Wolfgang von Goethe and Johann Sebastian Bach all lived here.*

◁ Schloss Sanssouci, Potsdam

Sanssouci *in Potsdam* (see pp136–7), *the enchanting Baroque summer residence built for Prussia's King Frederick the Great, stands on the site of former gardens and vineyards.*

LOCATOR MAP

Schloss Wörlitz *is surrounded by a romantic landscaped park* (see pp156–7) *criss-crossed by a network of waterways open to pleasure boats.*

BRANDENBURG
(see pp128–41)

The Völkerschlachtdenkmal in Leipzig (see pp162–3) *was erected to celebrate the centenary of the battle fought by Prussia, Austria, Russia and Sweden against Napoleon's army in 1813.*

SAXONY
(see pp158–79)

The Zwinger in Dresden (see pp174–5), *Saxony's glorious palace and a Baroque jewel, was immaculately restored to its original glory after World War II destruction.*

Meissen Porcelain

Until the early 18th century the only porcelain known in Europe was that imported from the Far East, and the Chinese jealously guarded the secrets of its production. Finally, in 1707, Johann Friedrich Böttger and Ehrenfried Walther von Tschirnhaus succeeded in developing a recipe which made it possible to produce genuine porcelain. A factory was set up in Meissen, and from 1713 it began to export its products to the entire European continent. Its first famous designers were Johann Joachim Kändler and Johann Gregor Höroldt.

Figurine by J. J. Kändler

The Porcelain Museum, *opened in 1906, holds exhibitions and demonstrations illustrating the various stages in the manufacture of porcelain. The museum also runs courses on porcelain-making.*

BÖTTGER STONEWARE

Johann Friedrich Böttger's first success in recreating Chinese ceramics came in 1707 when, with the assistance of Ehrenfried Walther von Tschirnhaus, he managed to produce stoneware almost identical to that produced in Yi Hsing. The stoneware was dark, varying in colour from red to brown.

These plates and bowls *are typical examples of Böttger stoneware; its plain and simple lines were modelled on Far-Eastern designs.*

The dark colour of the dishes is due to the use of red clays.

The "Yellow Lion" design, *dating from c.1728, was used to decorate the first Meissen service.*

Imari tree

The "Yellow Lion" was in reality a tiger.

FAR-EASTERN MOTIFS

Until the 17th century the only porcelain known in Europe came from the Far East, and the first items made from Saxon hard porcelain were initially strongly influenced by the Asian products. In Meissen, Chinese figurines and dishes were copied, adapting "European" shapes, but using Japanese or Chinese motifs for decoration. Special designs were created to adorn the services intended for the royal court. The oldest among these include the "Yellow Lion" and the "Red Dragon". New designs, inspired by European art, began to appear after 1738, and gradually replaced the Asian patterns.

PRODUCTION PROCESS

The process of porcelain production has not changed significantly over the centuries. The formula for "hard-paste" porcelain contains kaolin, quartz and feldspar. Each product is dried and fired, with glazed products being fired twice. The decoration can be applied before or after the glazing process. Hand-painted and gilded items are the most expensive.

Demonstration of the intricate art of hand-painting porcelain at the Meissen factory

TABLEWARE

In the second half of the 18th and in the 19th centuries, porcelain manufacturers developed their own designs. This proved so popular that some remain in production to this day. The best-known Meißen designs are the "vine-leaves" and the "onion" patterns, first introduced in the 18th century. Customers can thus still replace items in the services which have graced their family tables for generations.

This coffee pot and cup is decorated with the cobalt "onion" pattern, depicting stylized pomegranate fruits.

FINE-ART MOTIFS

A new type of decoration, which became popular in the second half of the 18th century, involved the accurate copying of famous paintings or etchings onto a vase, a pot or a plate. This type of decoration proved particularly popular during the Classicist period.

Decorator copying an etching onto a vessel

Vase decorated with a miniature of a painting by Antoine Watteau

SERVICES AND FIGURINES

Several outstanding sculptors and painters were employed in the Meißsen porcelain manufacture to design unique services and figurines for the royal courts. The most famous among them are the services designed by Johann Joachim Kändler. He also created sets of figurines to adorn dining tables, vases and censers (containers for burning incense) for decorating the home, and large religious compositions for churches.

"Swan" Service Tureen

Figurine of August III

Europa, a figure from the "Four Continents" series, designed by J. J. Kändler

MARKS ON MEISSEN PORCELAIN

All porcelain manufacturers mark their products with their own symbols. The symbols are generally applied under the glaze, at the bottom of the piece. The Meissen factory initially used marks that imitated Japanese or Chinese writing; later, for a short time, letters were used, and from 1724 blue trademarks in the shape of crossed swords became the standard mark. The last three symbols below identify the respective court for which each piece of porcelain was produced.

Königliche Porzellan-Fabrik, trademark used in 1723

Königliche Porzellan-Manufaktur, trademark used in 1723–4

Trademarks used from 1724

Augustus Rex, the initials of King August

Königliche Hof-Küche

Königliche Hof-Conditorei Warschau

Luther and the Reformation

Coat of arms

In 1517, on the eve of All Souls' Day (31 October), Martin Luther nailed his 95 "theses" to the doors of the castle church in Wittenberg, condemning the practice of indulgences. His subsequent pronouncements, in which he criticized many aspects of the Church's teaching, made him the "father" of the Reformation movement in Germany and other countries. Luther's teaching gained the support of many of the princes, who in 1531 formed the Schmalkalden Union and started to introduce a new administration to the Church. This led to religious wars which finally ended with the Augsburg Peace Treaty, signed in 1555, which confirmed the religious division of Germany.

The Bible, *translated into German by Luther, was first published in one volume in 1534. One year later an illustrated, two-volume luxury version was published in Augsburg.*

The Schlosskapelle *in Hartenfels Castle, in Torgau (see p164), was built in 1543–4 and consecrated by Martin Luther. It is generally considered to be the first church built specifically for the Lutheran community.*

The baptism of a child is performed by Philipp Melanchthon.

The Last Supper, at the centre of the altar, stresses the importance attached by Lutherans to the sacrament of communion. The figures of the Apostles are portraits of the main church reformers.

Martin Luther, *the great theologian and religious reformer, initiator of Church reform and founder of Lutheranism, is depicted in this portrait by Lucas Cranach the Elder (1520).*

This group of faithful, listening to the sermon, includes members of Luther's family.

Luther's Room (Lutherstube), *shown here, is part of Luther's House in Wittenberg (see p154). The famous reformer lived here with his wife and family.*

Cup Bearer Serving at the Table is the title of a portrait by Lucas Cranach the Younger.

Philipp Melanchthon, *an associate of Luther's and the co-founder of Lutheranism, initiated a great educational reform. He was also known as* praeceptor Germaniae, *Germany's teacher.*

REFORMATION ALTAR

The main altar of St Mary's Church in Wittenberg *(see pp154–5)* is one of the most important works of art of the Reformation period. The central picture was painted by Lucas Cranach the Elder (c.1539), the wings by his son, Lucas Cranach the Younger, before 1547.

Protestant confession is taken by Johannes Bugenhagen.

Sermon preached by Martin Luther, who points to the figure of the crucified Christ.

Katharina von Bora, *a former nun, became Martin Luther's wife in 1525. She lies buried in the Marienkirche in Torgau (see p164), in a tomb which survives to this day.*

BRANDENBURG

T*he province of Brandenburg is a lowland region criss-crossed by a dense network of rivers, canals and lakes. Quiet in part, it is also crossed by some of the main tourist routes to Berlin. Its most popular attractions are the historic sights of its capital city, Potsdam, and the Spreewald, where all day can be spent boating on the waterways of the Lusatian forests and villages.*

In early medieval times, the area that was to become present-day Brandenburg was the scene of violent conflict between various Germanic tribes. The latter conquered the region, and in 1157 created the margravate of Brandenburg. Its first ruler was Albrecht der Bär (Albert the Bear), from the house of Ascan. From 1415, Brandenburg was ruled by the Hohenzollern dynasty. It was quick to embrace the Reformation, which was officially adopted here as early as 1538. In 1618, Brandenburg merged with the duchy of Prussia through personal union. The region became entangled in the Thirty Years' War and suffered devastating losses; depopulated and plundered, it took Brandenburg many years to rise from the ashes. In 1701, the Great Elector, Frederick III, crowned himself King Frederick I, and the whole region now assumed the name of Prussia.

While Berlin remained the seat of power and a strong industrial and cultural centre, 18th-century Potsdam also played an important role: it was, after all, the favourite haunt of Frederick the Great. Other towns in the region were less significant – Brandenburg was, and still is, a fairly rural region. Reunification in 1990, however, has opened up the newly created land to Berliners and tourists alike.

Travellers in Brandenburg will encounter ancient tree-lined avenues that stretch to the horizon. The Spreewald, Brandenburg's lake district, is an oasis of tranquillity, ideal for boating and cycling. Brandenburg also has grand castles in Oranienburg, Branitz just outside Cottbus and Rheinsberg, Gothic churches and monasteries in Lehnin and Chorin and the towns of Brandenburg/Havel and Potsdam.

Baroque palace in Rheinsberg, on the shores of the Grienericksee

◁ A picturesque corner in the Babelsberg Palace in Potsdam

Exploring Brandenburg

Brandenburg is ideally suited for gentle exploration by bicycle or car, and its proximity to Berlin allows the visitor to make a one-day excursion to the capital. A whole day should be allocated for visiting Potsdam and the castle of Sanssouci, and another day for a boat trip in the Spreewald. A visit to Cottbus can be combined with an excursion to Frankfurt an der Oder. The best time for a visit to Chorin is the summer when concerts are held there in the ruined monastery.

SEE ALSO

• *Where to Stay* pp490–91
• *Where to Eat* pp528–30

Cecilienhof, the summer residence of the Hohenzollern family in Potsdam

Schloss Branitz in Cottbus

KEY

▬	Motorway
▬	Major road
▬	Minor road
▬	Main railway
▬	Minor railway
▬	International border
▬	Regional border

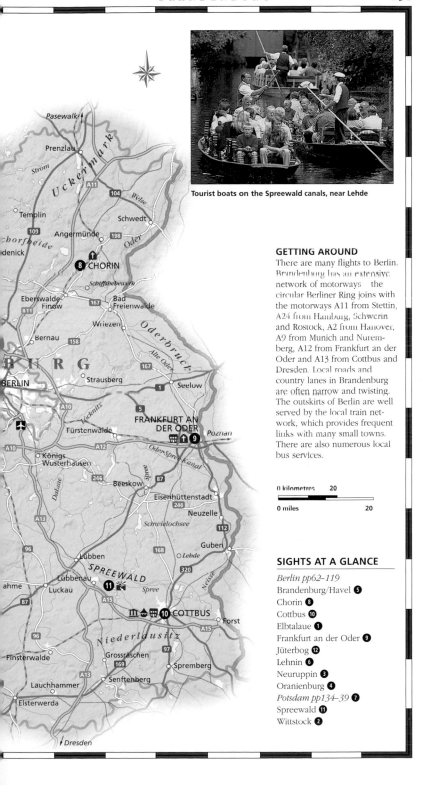

Tourist boats on the Spreewald canals, near Lehde

GETTING AROUND

There are many flights to Berlin. Brandenburg has an extensive network of motorways – the circular Berliner Ring joins with the motorways A11 from Stettin, A24 from Hamburg, Schwerin and Rostock, A2 from Hanover, A9 from Munich and Nuremberg, A12 from Frankfurt an der Oder and A13 from Cottbus and Dresden. Local roads and country lanes in Brandenburg are often narrow and twisting. The outskirts of Berlin are well served by the local train network, which provides frequent links with many small towns. There are also numerous local bus services.

0 kilometres   20

0 miles   20

SIGHTS AT A GLANCE

Elbtalaue ❶

Road map D2. 🚉 *to Wittenberge or Bad Wilsnack.* 🛈 *Am Markt 5, Bad Wilsnack (038791-26 20).* **www**.bad-wilsnack.de

The Elbe valley in the western part of Prignitz is an area of gentle rolling hills and unspoiled nature. Storks, increasingly rare in Germany, still nest here. When travelling around this parkland it is worth stopping at **Pritzwalk** to admire the late-Gothic Nikolaikirche (St Nicholas church). Another place of interest is **Perleberg** with its picturesque market square featuring an original 1515 timber-frame building, a sandstone statue of the knight Roland (1546), now standing by the 1850 Town Hall, and the town's star attraction – the 15th-century Gothic Jakobskirche (church of St Jacob).

Bad Wilsnack owes its fame to the discovery of the therapeutic properties of the iron oxide-rich mud found in the surrounding marshes. Already known in medieval times, the town was an important place of pilgrimage. After a church fire, in 1384, three hosts displaying the blood of Christ were found untouched on the altar. The Gothic **Nikolaikirche** (church of St Nicholas), which survives to this day, was built soon after for the pilgrims.

Plattenburg Castle, in a scenic situation on an island, is also worth a visit. Combining late-Gothic and Renaissance architecture, it is used as a venue for concerts.

Chapel of the Holy Sepulchre in Heiligengrabe, near Wittstock

Wittstock ❷

Road map E2. 🏠 *13,700.* 🚌 🛈 *Walter-Shulz-Pl. 1, Wittstock/Dosse (03394-43 34 42).* **www**.wittstock.de.

The small town of Wittstock was first awarded its municipal status in 1284. From the 13th century to the Reformation, Wittstock was the see of the Havelberg bishops. Although much of the town was destroyed, the original city walls remained almost completely intact, with one surviving gate – the **Gröper Tor**. All that remains of the former bishop's castle is the gate tower, which now houses a small museum. The town's star attraction is the Gothic **Marienkirche** with its late-Gothic reredos depicting the crowning of St Mary. It originated in the wood carving workshop of Claus Berg, probably after 1532. Other interesting features include the 1516 sacrarium and the late-Renaissance pulpit.

Environs
Ten km (6 miles) to the west lies **Heiligengrabe**, with its Gothic Cistercian Abbey. One of its many highlights is the 1512 **Chapel of the Holy Sepulchre** with an intricately sculpted gable and some charming timber-frame cloister buildings.

Neuruppin ❸

Road map E2. 🏠 *27,300.* 🚌 🛈 *Karl-Marx-Str. 1 (03391-454 60).* **www**.neuruppin.de.

The town of Neuruppin, in a scenic location on the shores of a large lake, the Ruppiner See, is mainly Neo-Classical in style, having been rebuilt to the design of Bernhard Matthias Brasch after the great fire of 1787. The only older buildings are the Gothic post-Dominican church and two small hospital chapels. Neuruppin is the birthplace of the architect **Karl Friedrich Schinkel** and the novelist **Theodor Fontane** *(see p27).*

Environs
The beautifully restored palace of **Rheinsberg**, 25 km (16 miles) to the north, was converted from 16th-century Renaissance castle in 1734–7. In 1734–40 it was the residence of the Crown Prince, who later became Frederick the Great, King of Prussia. Some 30 km (19 miles) northeast of Rheinsberg is the National Socialist concentration camp **Ravensbrück**, for women and children. It is now a place of remembrance.

Schinkel monument

Oranienburg ❹

Road map E3. 🏠 *30,000.* 🚉 🚌 🛈 *Bernauer Str. 52 (033 01-70 48 33).* **www**.tourismus-or.de.

The star attraction of the town is **Schloss Oranienburg,** the Baroque residence built for Louisa Henrietta von

The Gothic-Renaissance Plattenburg Castle, in the Elbtalaue

Nassau-Oranien, wife of the Great Elector Friedrich Wilhelm. Designed by Johann Gregor Memhardt and Michael Matthias Smids, it was built in 1651–5 and later extended to reach its present H-shape.

🏛 **Schloss Oranienburg**
Schlossplatz 1. *Tel (03301) 53 74 37.*
◯ *Apr–Oct: 10am–6pm Tue–Sun;*
Nov–Mar: 10am–5pm Sat & Sun.

Baroque palace in Caputh, north of Lehnin

Environs

Sachsenhausen, which is located northeast of Oranienburg, is now a place of remembrance and a museum. Opened in 1936 by the National Socialists, this concentration camp claimed the lives of 100,000 inmates.

🏛 **Sachsenhausen**
Tel (03301) 20 00. ◯ *mid-Mar mid-Oct: 8:30am–6pm daily; mid-Oct–mid-Mar. 8.30am–4.30pm daily.*
www.gedenkstaette-sachsenhausen.de

Brandenburg/ Havel ❺

Road map C3. 👥 *87,700.* 🚉 🚌
ℹ *Neustädtischer Markt 3 (03381-796 360).* 🎭 *Havelfestspiele (Jun).*
www.stadt-brandenburg.de

Brandenburg is the oldest town of the region. It was settled by Slavs as early as the 6th century, and a mission episcopate was established here in 948. Scenically sited on the Havel River, it has preserved historic centres on three islands, despite wartime destruction. The oldest island is the **Dominsel**, with its

Romanesque **Dom St Peter und St Paul**. This cathedral was constructed from 1165 to the mid-13th century. In the 14th century it was raised and given new vaultings. It contains numerous valuable Gothic objects, including the **"Czech" altar** (c.1375), the present main altar (from Lehnin, 1518) and the sacrarium of the same year. The most valuable treasures are on display in the **Dommuseum**.

Other sights worth visiting are the huge, 15th-century **Katharinenkirche** built by Hinrich Brunsberg, the **Gotthardkirche**, in the Altstadt ("old town"), with its Romanesque façade and Gothic interior, the Gothic Rathaus (Town Hall), with a statue of Roland from 1474, and the **Stadtmuseum**, a museum of local history.

🏛 **Dommuseum**
Burghof 10. *Tel (03381) 211 2221.*
◯ *10am–5pm daily, 12:30–5pm Sun.* 🎟 www.brandenburg-dom.de

🏛 **Stadtmuseum**
Ritterstr. 96. *Tel (03381) 58 45 01.*
◯ *9am–5pm Tue–Fri, 10am–5pm Sat & Sun.* 🎟

Lehnin ❻

Road map E3. 👥 *3,100.* 🚌
ℹ *Markgrafenplatz (03382 704 480).*

Visitors mainly come to see the huge Klosterkirche (abbey) founded for the Cistercian order of Otto I, son of Albert the Bear. The church was built from the late 12th to the late 13th century, originally in Romanesque, then in early-Gothic style. Following the dissolution of the monastery, in 1542, the buildings fell into disrepair, but much of the abbey has survived.

⛪ **Klosterkirche**
Klosterkirchplatz. *Tel (03382) 76 80 10.* ◯ *Apr–Oct: 10am–4pm Mon–Fri, 10am–5pm Sat, 1–5pm Sun; Nov–Mar: 10:30am–3:30pm Mon–Sat, 1–4pm Sun.*
www.klosterkirche-lehnin.de

Environs

Caputh, situated 23 km (14 miles) to the north, has an early-Baroque **Palace** built during the second half of the 17th century, as summer residence for the wives of the Great Electors. The interior has many original features.

The Gothic "Czech" altar in the Dom St Peter und St Paul in Brandenburg

Potsdam ❼

An independent city close to Berlin, Potsdam, with over 150,000 inhabitants, is also the capital of Brandenburg. The first documented reference to Potsdam dates back to AD 993; it was later granted municipal rights in 1317. The town blossomed during the times of the Great Electors and then again in the 18th century. Potsdam suffered very badly during World War II, particularly on the night of 14–15 April 1945 when Allied planes bombed the town centre.

A sculpture on display in Park Sanssouci

Sightseeing in Potsdam

Potsdam remains one of Germany's most attractive towns. Tourists flock to see the magnificent royal summer residence, Schloss Sanssouci, to stroll around Neuer Garten (new garden) with its Marmorpalais (marble palace) and Cecilienhof, to visit the old city centre and the Russian colony of Alexandrowka, to be entertained in the film studios of Babelsberg and to take a walk around the parks of Schloss Babelsberg.

⚓ Cecilienhof

Am Neuen Garten (Neuer Garten). *Tel* (0331) 969 42 44. ⟮⟯ 695.
⬡ Apr–Oct: 10am–6pm Tue–Sun; Nov–Mar: 10am–5pm Tue–Sun.
The Cecilienhof residence played a brief but important role in history, when it served as the venue for the 1945

Potsdam Conference (*see p139*). Built between 1913 and 1917, the palace is the most recent of all Hohenzollern dynasty buildings. Designed by Paul Schultze-Naumburg in the style of an English country manor, Cecilienhof is a sprawling, asymmetrical, timber-frame building with inner courtyards and irregular breaks.

The palace remained a residence of the Hohenzollern family after they had lost the crown – the family stayed in Potsdam until February 1945. Today the palace is a hotel, where visitors interested in history are able to relax amid green shrubs. The large, scenic park

remains open to the public even when the rooms used during the Potsdam Conference are closed to visitors.

⚓ Marmorpalais

Am Neuen Garten (Neuer Garten). *Tel* (0331) 969 42 46. ⟮⟯ 695.
⬡ Apr: 10am–6pm Sat & Sun; May–Oct: 10am–6pm Tue–Sun.
This small palace, situated on the edge of the lake, is a beautiful example of early Neo-Classical architecture. The palace is named after the Silesian marble used on its façade. The main part of it was built between 1787 and 1791 by Carl von Gontard to a design and under the direction of Carl Gotthard Langhans, on the initiative of King Friedrich Wilhelm II.

🏠 Alexandrowka

Russische Kolonie Allee/Puschkinallee.
🚋 92, 95. ⟮⟯ 603, 609, 638, 639.
A visit to Alexandrowka takes the visitor into the world of Pushkin's fairy tales. Wooden log cabins with intricate carvings, set in their own gardens, create a charming residential estate. They were constructed in 1826 under the direction of the German architect Snethlage, for twelve singers of a Russian choir that was established in 1812.

🏠 Holländisches Viertel

Friedrich-Ebert-Str, Kurfürstenstr., Hebbelstr., Gutenbergstr.
⟮⟯ 138, 601–604, 606–612.
🚋 92, 95.
Just as amazing as the Russian colony of Alexandrowka is the Holländisches Viertel (Dutch quarter), part of a Baroque town built in the middle of Germany. Dutch workers arrived in Potsdam in the early 18th century and, between 1733 and 1742,

A view of the Baroque Dutch district known as Holländisches Viertel

For hotels and restaurants in this region see pp490–92 and pp528–30

a settlement was built for them on the orders of Friedrich Wilhelm I to plans by Johann Boumann the Elder. It comprised 134 gabled houses arranged in four groups. The houses were built from small red bricks and finished with stone and plaster details.

⛪ Nikolaikirche

Alter Markt. *Tel* (0331) 270 86 02.
🚌 601, 603, 692, 694,
🚋 91, 92, 93, 95, 96, 99.
🕐 Apr–Oct: 9am–7pm daily; Nov–Mar: 9am–5pm daily.

This imposing church built in the late Neo-Classical style, is indisputably the most beautiful church in Potsdam. It was

The Nikolaikirche, with its dome resting on a colonnaded wall

built on the site of an earlier, Baroque church, which burned down in 1795. It was designed during 1828–30 by Karl Friedrich Schinkel and the building work was supervised by Ludwig Persius. The interior decoration and furnishings of the church date from the 1850s, but were mostly based on the earlier designs by Schinkel.

🏛 Marstall

Breitestr. 1a. *Tel* (0331) 271 81 12.
🖼 🚌 601, 603, 692, 694. 🚋 91, 92, 93, 95, 96, 98. 🕐 10am–6pm daily.

This long Baroque pavilion, once used as royal stables, is the only remaining building of a royal residence. It was constructed in 1714 and currently houses a film museum devoted to the history and work of the nearby Babelsberg Film Studio.

🏛 Bildergalerie

Zur Historischen Mühle. *Tel* (0331) 969 41 81. 🚌 612, 614, 695.
🕐 15 May–15 Oct: 10am–5pm Tue–Sun. 🖼

Baroque paintings once owned by Frederick the Great, including Caravaggio's *Doubting Thomas*, Guido

Reni's *Cleopatra's Death*, as well as paintings by Rubens and van Dyck, are on show in the picture gallery situated next to Schloss Sanssouci.

Caravaggio's *Doubting Thomas*, on show in the Bildergalerie

POTSDAM

0 metres 750
0 yards 750

Key to Symbols see back flap

Park Sanssouci

The enormous Park Sanssouci, which occupies an area of 287 hectares (700 acres), is one of the most beautiful palace complexes in Europe. The first building to be constructed on the site was Schloss Sanssouci, built as the summer palace of Frederick the Great. It was erected in 1747, on the site of a former orchard. Over the years, Park Sanssouci was expanded considerably and other palaces and pavilions added. To enjoy the park fully, allow at least a whole day.

Flower-filled urn, Park Sanssouci

Communs
Situated next to a pretty courtyard, this building has an unusually elegant character. It is now used to house palace staff.

★ Neues Palais
Constructed between 1763 and 1769, the monumental building of the Neues Palais is crowned by a massive dome.

Römische Bäder
Shaded by pergolas overgrown with greenery, the Roman baths include a Renaissance-style villa.

0 metres	200
0 yards	200

STAR SIGHTS

★ Neues Palais

★ Schloss Sanssouci

Schloss Charlottenhof
This Neo-Classical palace gained its name from Charlotte von Gentzkow, the former owner of the land on which the palace was built.

Lustgarten
The extensive parkland is made up of several gardens. The Lustgarten (pleasure garden) is nearest to the Orangerie.

VISITORS' CHECKLIST

An Der Orangerie 1.
Tel (0331) 969 42 02.
606, 695. Apr–Oct: 10am–6pm, Nov–Mar: 10am–5pm. Mon. (free access to park). www.spsg.de

Orangerie
This large Neo-Renaissance palace was built in the mid-19th century to house foreign royalty and other guests.

Neue Kammern
Once the orangerie of the Sanssouci Palace, this Rococo pavilion was later rebuilt as a guest house.

★ **Schloss Sanssouci**
A beautifully terraced vineyard creates a grand approach to Schloss Sanssouci, the oldest building in the complex.

Bildergalerie
Built between 1755 and 1764, this is Germany's oldest purpose-built museum building. The Baroque pavilion houses an art gallery.

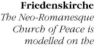

Friedenskirche
The Neo-Romanesque Church of Peace is modelled on the Basilica of San Clemente in Rome.

Chinesisches Teehaus
An exhibition of exquisite Oriental porcelain is housed in the small, Rococo-style Chinese Tea House.

Paintings in the music room, in Schloss Sanssouci

♣ Schloss Sanssouci

Zur Historischen Mühle. *Tel (0331)
969 40.* ◯ Apr–Oct: 10am–6pm Tue–
Sun; Nov–Mar: 10am–5pm Tue–Sun.
Damenflügel ◯ May–Oct:
10am–6pm Sat & Sun. **Schlossküche**
◯ Apr–Oct: 10am–6pm Tue–Sun. 🖼

This Rococo palace was built
in 1745–7 by Georg Wenzeslaus von Knobelsdorff to sketches by Frederick the Great.
Knobelsdorff and Johann
August Nahl designed the interior. *Sanssouci* ("carefree")
was the perfect name for
the enchanting castle. The
Damenflügel, the castle's west
wing which was added in
1840 to house ladies and
gentlemen of the court, and
the Schlossküche (castle
kitchen) can also be visited.

♣ Schloss Neue Kammern

Zur Historischen Mühle (Lustgarten).
Tel (0331) 969 42 06. ◯ Apr:
10am– 6pm Wed–Mon; May–
Oct: 10am–6pm Tue–Sun. 🖼
obligatory. 🖼

The Neue Kammern (new
chambers) adjoin Schloss
Sanssouci in the west, like the
Bildergalerie in the east. As
part of this ensemble it was
originally built in 1747 as an
orangery, to a design by
Georg Wenzeslaus von
Knobelsdorff who gave it its
elegant Baroque forms. The
building has an attractive roof
with sloping ends and sides.
In 1777 Frederick the Great
ordered the building to be
transformed into guest accommodation. The architect,
Georg Christian Unger, left
the exterior of the orangery
largely untouched but
converted the interior into

sumptuous suites and four
elegant halls. The Rococo
décor has been maintained,
similar to that of other palaces
and pavilions of Sanssouci.

🏛 Orangerieschloss

Maulbeerallee. (Nordischer Garten).
Tel (0331) 969 42 80. ◯ Apr: 10am–
6pm Sat & Sun; May–Oct: 10am–
6pm Tue–Sun; **viewing terrace**
◯ Apr–May: 10am–5pm Sat & Sun;
May–Oct 10am–5pm Tue–Sun.

Above the park towers the
Orangerie, designed in Italian
Renaissance style and
crowned by a
colonnade. It was
built to house
guests, not
plants, and
served as
guest resi-
dence for Tsar
Nicolas and his wife,
King Friedrich Wilhelm
IV's sister. The
Orangerie was
constructed in
1852–60 for the king
by Friedrich August
Stüler, with the final
design partly based on plans
by Ludwig Persius. Modelled
on the Regia Hall in the Vati-
can, the rooms were grouped
around the Raphael Hall and
decorated with replicas of this
great Italian master's works.
The observation terrace offers
a good view over Potsdam.

🏛 Chinesisches Teehaus

Ökonomieweg (Rehgarten).
Tel (0331) 969 42 22. ◯ 15 May–
15 Oct: 10am–5pm Tue–Sun.

The lustrous, gilded pavilion
that can be seen glistening
between the trees from a

**Figure on the roof of
Chinesisches Teehaus**

distance is the Chinese Teahouse. Chinese art was very
popular during the Rococo
period – people wore
Chinese silk, wallpapered
their rooms with Chinese
designs, lacquered their
furniture, drank tea from
Chinese porcelain and built
Chinese pavilions in their
gardens. The one in Sans-
souci was built in 1754–56 to
a design by Johann Gottfried
Büring. Circular in shape, it
has a centrally located main
hall surrounded by three
studies. Between these are
pretty *trompe l'oeil* porticos.
The structure is covered with
a tent roof and topped with a
lantern. Gilded ornaments,
columns and Chinese figures
surround the pavilion.
Originally a tea room and
summer dining house, it
houses today a collection of
18th-century porcelain.

🏛 Römische Bäder

Lenné-Str. (Park Charlottenhof).
Tel (0331) 969 42 25. 📠 606.
📠 91. ◯ May–Oct: 10am–
6pm Tue–Sun.

The Roman baths, situated by
the edge of a lake, form a
picturesque group of pavilions
which served as accommodation for the king's guests.
They were designed in
1829–40 by Karl Friedrich
Schinkel, with the help
of Ludwig Persius. The
gardener's house
at the front stands
next to a low,
asymmetrical
tower, built in the
style of an Italian
Renaissance
villa. In the back-
ground, to the left,
extends the former bathing
pavilion, which is currently
used for temporary exhibitions. The pavilions are
grouped around a garden
planted with colourful shrubs
and vegetables.

♣ Schloss Charlottenhof

Geschwister-Scholl-Str. (Park
Charlottenhof). *Tel (0331) 969 42
02.* 📠 91. ◯ May–Oct: 10am–5pm
Tue–Sun. 🖼 obligatory.

This small Neo-Classical palace stands at the southern
end of Park Sanssouci, known
as Park Charlottenhof. Built in

1826–9 for the heir to the throne, the future King Friedrich Wilhelm IV, this small, single-storey building was designed by Karl Friedrich Schinkel in the style of a Roman villa. Some of the wall paintings, designed by Schinkel in the so-called Pompeiian style, are still in place. There is also a collection of Italian engravings. The most interesting part of the interior is the Humboldt Room. The palace is surrounded by a landscaped park designed by Peter Joseph Lenné.

♣ Neues Palais

Am Neuen Palais. *Tel (0331) 969 42 02.* ☐ *Apr–Oct: 10am–6pm Wed–Mon, Nov–Mar: 9am–5pm Wed–Mon.* 🚫 ☐ *obligatory.*

One of Germany's most beautiful palaces, this imposing Baroque structure, on the main avenue in Park Sanssouci, was built for Frederick the Great to initial plans by Georg Wenzeslaus von Knobelsdorff in 1750. Its construction, to designs by Johan Gottfried Büring, Jean Laurent Le Geay and Carl von Gontard, was delayed until 1763–9, after the Seven Years' War. The vast, three-wing structure comprises over 200 richly adorned rooms and has many interesting sculptures. The south wing houses the kings' quarters.

The impressive Marble Hall in the Baroque Neues Palais

THE POTSDAM CONFERENCE

Towards the end of World War II, the leaders of the Allies – Winston Churchill, Franklin Roosevelt, and Joseph Stalin – met in Schloss Cecilienhof in Potsdam. The aim of this conference, which lasted from 17 July until 2 August 1945, was to resolve the problems arising at the end of the war. The main participants changed, however, before it was concluded. Churchill was replaced by newly-elected Clement Attlee, and Harry S. Truman took over after President Roosevelt died. The conference set up the occupation zones, the demilitarization and monitoring of Germany, the punishment of war criminals and the reparations. It also revised the German borders. These decisions established the political balance of power in Europe, which continued for 45 years.

Attlee, Truman and Stalin in Potsdam

♣ Schloss Babelsberg

Park Babelsberg 10. *Tel (0331) 969 42 50.* ⬤ *closed until 2013.*

Built in 1833–5 for Prince Wilhelm (Kaiser Wilhelm I), by Karl Friedrich Schinkel, this extravagant castle ranks as one of his finest works. An irregular building with many towers and bay windows, built in the spirit of English Neo-Gothic, with allusions to Windsor Castle and Tudor style, it now holds the Museum of Pre-History.

⚏ Filmpark Babelsberg

Großbeerenstr. *Tel (0331) 721 27 38.* ☐ *15 Apr–31 Oct: 10am–6pm daily.* 🖼 www.filmpark.de

This amazing film park was laid out on the site where Germany's first films were produced in 1912. From 1917 the studio belonged to Universum-Film-AG (UFA), which produced some of the most famous films of the silent era, including Fritz Lang's *Metropolis* and some films with Greta Garbo. The *Blue Angel*, with Marlene Dietrich, was also shot at Babelsberg, but subsequently, the studios were used to film Nazi propaganda. The studio is still operational, and the public can admire some of the old sets, the creation of special effects and stuntmen in action.

⚏ Einsteinturm

Albert-Einstein-Str. ☐ *visits daily from Oct–Mar by arrangement with the Urania Society (0331 291 741).* 🚌 *694.*

This tower, built in 1920–21 by Erich Mendelssohn, is one of the finest examples of German Expressionist architecture. Its fantasy forms were to demonstrate the qualities of reinforced concrete to spectacular effect. However, the cost of formwork, assembled by boat builders, limited the use of the material to the first storey, while the upper floors are plastered brickwork.

Chorin ❽

Road map E2. 🏰 510. 🚉 *Kloster Chorin, Amt 11A.* **Tel** *(033366) 703 77.* ⬚ *Apr–Oct: 9am–6pm daily; Nov–Mar: 9am–4pm daily.* 🎫 🎵 *Choriner Musiksommer.*

On the edge of the vast **Schorfheide** forest, which has been listed as a World Biosphere Reserve by UNESCO, stands one of Brandenburg's most beautiful Gothic buildings – the Cistercian **Kloster** (abbey) of Chorin. The Cistercians arrived here in 1258, but work on the present Gothic abbey did not start until 1270. The church is a triple-nave, transeptial basilica, with a magnificent façade. Preserved to this day are two wings of the monastic quarters plus several domestic buildings. Following the dissolution of the monastery in 1542, the entire complex fell into disrepair. Today the church, deprived of its traditional furnishings, is used as a venue for classical concerts. The park established by Peter Joseph Lenné is conducive to pleasant strolls.

Environs
For visitors to Niederfinow, the giant **Schiffshebewerk** (bargelift) is a definite must. This wonder of technology was designed for lifting and lowering ships from one canal to another. Commissioned in 1934, it is 60 m (197 ft) tall and capable of lifting barges laden with 1,000 tonnes or more.

Portal of the St Marienkirche in Frankfurt an der Oder

Frankfurt an der Oder ❾

Road map F3. 🏰 87,900. 🚉 🚌 ℹ️ *Karl-Marx-Str. 1. (0335-32 52 16).* 🎵 *Frankfurter Musikfesttage (Mar); Hansefest (Jul); Kleist-Tage (Oct).*

Frankfurt, on the banks of the river Oder, was granted municipal rights in 1253, prospered in the 13th century and joined the Hanseatic league in 1368. In 1945, the right bank was ceded to Poland and is now known as Słubice.
Viadrina University, founded in 1506, was reopened in 1991 and now educates both German and Polish students. The town's most famous resident was the playwright and writer Heinrich von Kleist who was born here in 1777.

The Gothic **Rathaus** (town hall) in the centre escaped destruction in World War II and now houses an art gallery. The main church, **Marienkirche** (church of St Mary), is a vast, five-nave Gothic hall which has stood in ruins since 1945. Some of the Gothic furnishings were rescued and can now be seen in **St Gertraud** (church of St Gertrude) which dates back to 1368. The main altar from 1489 and the huge, 5m- (16ft) -tall candelabrum from 1376 are particularly valuable. Another Gothic church, originally built for the Franciscans in 1270, has been transformed into the **C.P.E. Bach Konzerthalle** (concert hall), named after Carl Philipp Emmanuel Bach, son of Johann Sebastian.

Environs
Neuzelle, 36 km (23 miles) to the south, has a magnificent former Cistercian Abbey, with an impressive Baroque relief façade.

Cottbus ❿

Road map F3. 🏰 121,000. 🚉 *Bahnhofstr.* 🚌 ℹ️ *Berliner Platz 6. (0355-754 20);* **www**.cottbus.de 🎵 *Karnevalsumzug (Feb); Cottbuser Musik-Herbst (Oct).*

Tourists rarely visit Cottbus, despite the many attractions offered by the town. Its enchanting town square is surrounded by impressive Baroque buildings. The house

The Baroque Schloss Branitz in Cottbus

at No. 24 is the quaint Löwen-apotheke (lion's pharmacy), which now houses a small pharmaceutical museum, the **Brandenburgisches Apothekenmuseum**, with displays of historical interiors. Nearby, the Gothic **Ober-kirche St Nikolai** features an unusual original late-Gothic mesh vaulting. Another interesting Gothic structure, the **Wendenkirche** (Sorbian church), is a former Francis-can church, from the 14th–15th centuries.

Other attractions of the town include the remains of the medieval city walls with three preserved towers. Perhaps the most attractive building in Cottbus is the **Staatstheater** (state theatre) designed in Jugendstil (Art Nouveau style) by Bernhard Sehring and built in 1908.

The **Wendisches Museum** is devoted to the culture of the Sorbs which is experiencing a revival *(see p181)*.

Schloss Branitz is a late-Baroque palace, originally built in the 18th century, at the southeastern edge of town. It became the residence of Prince Hermann von Pückler-Muskau in 1845, who had its interior redesigned by Gottfried Semper. Today, the palace houses the **Fürst-Pückler-Museum**, which exhibits paintings by Karl Blechen, a local artist from Cottbus. The star attraction of the palace is its **Park**, which was designed by Prince Pückler-Muskau himself. This vast landscaped garden includes a lake with an island on which stands a grass-covered mock-Egyptian earth pyramid containing the tomb of the extravagant and eccen-tric Prince.

🏛 **Schloss Branitz and Fürst-Pückler-Museum**
Kastanienalle 11. *Tel (0355) 751 50.*
⬜ *Apr–Oct: 10am–6pm daily, Nov–Mar: 11am–5pm; Tue–Sun.* 📷

🏛 **Wendisches Museum**
Mühlenstr. 12. *Tel (0355) 79 49 30.*
⬜ *10am–5pm Tue–Fri, 1–5pm Sat & Sun and bank holidays.*

🏛 **Brandenburgisches Apothekenmuseum**
Altmark 24. *Tel (0355) 239 97.* ⬜ *visits possible with guide 11am–2pm Tue–Fri; 2pm & 3pm Sat & Sun.* 📷

Boats and canoes in the Spreewald, near Lübben

Spreewald ⓫

Road map F3. 🚉 *Lübben.* ℹ *Raddusch, Lindenstr. 1 (035433-722 99), Lübbenau, Ehm-Welk-Str. 15 (03542-36 68).* 🚉 📷 *Spreewaldfest in Lübbenau (Jul) and Lübben (Sep).* **www**.spreewald.de

Designated as one of the World Biosphere Reserves, this marshy region, criss-crossed by hundreds of small rivers and canals, attracts large numbers of tourists each year. An all-day trip by **Kahn** (boat) or canoe, which is best started in **Lübben** or **Lübbenau**, can prove to be an unfor-gettable experience. The splendour of nature, numerous water birds and the endless chain of small restaurants which serve meals straight from the jetty, ensure an exciting day for the visitor. Do not miss the local speciality, pickled gherkins.

Lübben has an original Gothic church and a Baroque palace, rebuilt in the 19th century. Lüb-benau features a small Baroque church and the Neo-Classical house of the von Lynar family. In **Lehde** the small open-air museum and the private collection of the **Bauernhaus- und Gurken-museum** – the only gherkin museum in Germany – are highly recommended.

Environs

Luckau, 18 km (11 miles) west of Lübben, has a lovely town square, surrounded by attractive Baroque houses with stucco façades, and the ornamented, 14th-century Gothic Nikolaikirche.

Jüterbog ⓬

Road map E3. 🚶 *13,000.* 🚉 🚌 ℹ *Markt 21 (03372-46 31 13).*

Jüterbog is a small, pictur-esque town featuring many Gothic structures including some well-preserved sections of three city walls with gates and towers, dating back to the 15th century. It also boasts a beautiful town hall with arcades and three churches. **Nikolaikirche** (church of St Nicholas), the largest of them, is a magnificent hall church, with a twin-tower façade, built in several stages. The so-called New Sacristy features a set of medieval wall paintings, while the naves contain many Gothic furnishings.

Statue on Jüterbog town hall

Environs

Five km (3 miles) to the north of Jüterbog stands **Kloster Zinna**, a former Cistercian Abbey with an early-Gothic stone church. It features 16th-century stained-glass windows depicting the saints Bernhard and Benedikt.

The early-Gothic ex-Cistercian Kloster Zinna, near Jüterbog

SAXONY-ANHALT

The scenic Harz mountains, a popular recreation area with fascinating rock formations and pleasant walks, are the best known attraction of Saxony-Anhalt. Yet this state also boasts a number of interesting towns, such as Lutherstadt Wittenberg and Magdeburg, steeped in history and blessed with magnificent historic remains, which range from Romanesque churches and abbeys to medieval castles.

This province consists of the areas of the former Duchy of Anhalt and the Prussian province of Saxony, that part of the Kingdom of Saxony which was incorporated into Prussia after the Congress of Vienna (1815) as punishment for supporting Napoleon.

The landscape in this region is highly varied. Its northern part, the Altmark, is a largely flat area of farmland and heath. The gentle hills of the Harz Mountains in the southwest, although not especially high (their highest peak, the Brocken, rises to only 1142 m/3747 ft), are picturesque and fairly well provided with tourist facilities. The eastern, flat part of the region is more industrialized. It also includes two very important towns: the small town of Wittenberg, where Martin Luther proclaimed his theses in 1517, thus launching the Reformation, and Dessau, the former capital of the Duchy of Anhalt and from 1925 to 1932 the seat of the Bauhaus Art School. The southern part of the province, with its interesting and varied landscape, features one of the land's most impressive historic buildings – the gigantic Naumburg Cathedral.

After World War II Saxony-Anhalt was occupied by the Soviets, and in 1949 it was incorporated into the GDR. It underwent major industrial development, mainly due to lignite mining. The state of Saxony-Anhalt was first created in 1947, only to be abolished five years later. It was finally re-established as a federal state in 1990, with Magdeburg as its capital.

Timber-frame houses in Quedlinburg

◁ Family house near the small town of Halberstadt

Exploring Saxony–Anhalt

Touring Saxony-Anhalt can be an
unforgettable experience, especially for
admirers of Romanesque art, as this
region abounds in churches and
abbeys of that period. A visit to
Wörlitz provides the opportunity to
see one of Germany's most beautiful
landscaped gardens. Nature lovers, hill-
walkers and, in the winter, cross-country
skiers should include a few days in the
romantic Harz Mountains in their schedule.
An added attraction here is a ride on the
narrow-gauge railway drawn by a steam
engine which, today as in years gone by,
still links some of the most interesting
places of the region.

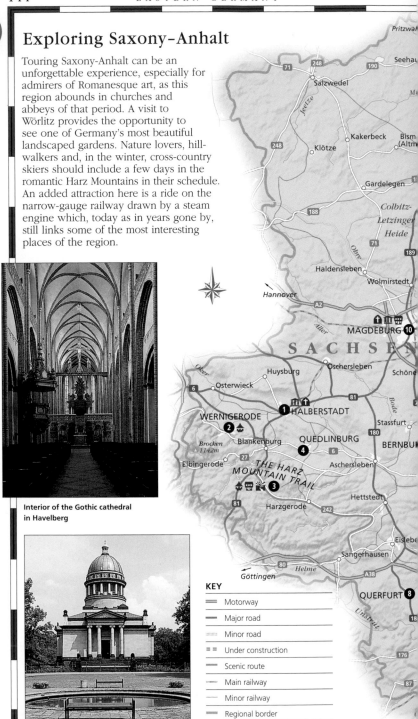

**Interior of the Gothic cathedral
in Havelberg**

Zoo-Park in Dessau

KEY

▬▬	Motorway
▬▬	Major road
═══	Minor road
▬ ▬	Under construction
▬▬	Scenic route
▬▬	Main railway
▬▬	Minor railway
▬▬	Regional border
△	Summit

Map labels: Pritzwal, Seehau, Salzwedel, Kakerbeck, Bism (Altm, Klötze, Gardelegen, Colbitz-Letzinger Heide, Haldensleben, Wolmirstedt, Hannover, MAGDEBURG 10, SACHSE, Huysburg, Oschersleben, Schöne, Osterwieck, WERNIGERODE 2, HALBERSTADT 1, Brocken 1142m, Blankenburg, QUEDLINBURG 4, Stassfurt, BERNBU, Elbingerode, THE HARZ MOUNTAIN TRAIL 3, Aschersleben, Hettstedt, Harzgerode, Eisleb, Sangerhausen, Göttingen, Helme, QUERFURT 8

ELBERG **12**

TENDAL

13 TANGERMÜNDE
  Jerichow

  Genthin

Potsdam

N H A L T

Zerbst
  Rosslau   Coswig
                              15 LUTHERSTADT
16 ♦   WITTENBERG
🏛 ♦ WÖRLITZ
DESSAU **14** PARK
            Oranienbaum
Köthen

  Wolfen

    Ritterfeld

6 HALLE

  Leipzig

7 MERSEBURG

Weissenfels

AUMBURG

  Zeitz

Gera

Listening to a summer water concert, in Wörlitz Park

GETTING AROUND

The A2 motorway from Hanover to Berlin runs through Magdeburg to the northern part of the region. Another motorway, the A9 which links Berlin and Munich, provides easy access to Dessau and Halle, which is also served by the recently constructed A14 motorway from Leipzig to Magdeburg. Other major and minor roads, well signposted, provide access to smaller towns and villages. Larger towns are easily accessed by rail or local bus services. In the Harz Mountains the narrow-gauge train is an alternative form of transport.

0 km		15
0 miles		15

SEE ALSO

SIGHTS AT A GLANCE

Interior of the Gothic Cathedral of Halberstadt

Halberstadt ➊

Road map D3. 🏔 *42,000.* 🚉 🚌
ℹ *Hinter dem Rathause 6 (03941-55 18 15).* **www**.halberstadt.de

Halberstadt enjoys a picturesque location in the foothills of the Harz Mountains. Its history goes back to the 9th century, when it became a seat of a mission episcopate. Once an important town, Halberstadt had 80 per cent of its buildings destroyed during World War II. Fortunately, many of its beautiful historic buildings have been restored to their former glory.

The vast **St Stephans Dom** is the fourth successive church built on the same site. Construction began in the 13th century and the church was consecrated in 1491. The two-tower transeptial basilica ranks as one of the most beautiful pure Gothic forms in Germany. Its oldest part is the 12th-century font. Also notable are the Romanesque Crucifixion group (c.1220), set above the choir screen, and several examples of Gothic sculpture. Stained-glass windows from around 1330 have survived in the Marian Chapel, and 15th-century windows can be found along the cloisters and in the presbytery.

The adjoining chapter buildings contain one of Germany's richest cathedral treasures – the **Domschatz**, with precious 12th-century tapestries, numerous sculptures and liturgical vessels.

Other interesting churches to have survived in the old town district include the Romanesque 12th-century **Liebfrauenkirche** and the Gothic **Marktkirche St. Martini** with a statue of Roland, symbolizing the freedom of the city. Remaining timber-frame houses can be seen in Gröper- and Taubenstrasse.

Romanesque Crucifixion group in the Dom, Halberstadt

> 🏛 **Domschatz**
> *Tel* 03941 24237.
> ◯ call for times.
> ✔ obligatory.

Environs
An original 12th-century Benedictine church stands in Huysburg, 11 km (7 miles) to the northwest.

Wernigerode ➋

Road map D3. 🏔 *36,000.* 🚉 🚌
ℹ *Marktplatz 10 (03943-55 37 835).*
🎭 *Rathausfest (Jun); Schlossfestspiele (Jul & Aug).* **www**.wernigerode.de

Wernigerode is attractively situated at a confluence of two rivers. Timber-frame houses lean across its steep, winding streets, and a massive castle rises above the town. The **Harzquerbahn**, a narrow-gauge railway which links the small towns and villages in the Harz Mountains, between Wernigerode and Nordhausen, provides another popular tourist attraction. The Brockenbahn runs between Wernigerode and the Brocken mountain.

Strolling around the Old Town it is well worth stepping into St John's Church, featuring a Romanesque west tower. It contains some late-Gothic features, including the font and the altar. The variety of ornaments adorning the houses in Wernigerode is truly staggering. Particularly interesting are the houses along **Breite Straße**, the town's main shopping street which is closed to traffic.

♙ Schloss Wernigerode
Am Schloss 1. *Tel* 03943-55 30 30.
◯ May–Oct: 10am–6pm; Nov–Apr: 10am–5pm Tue–Fri; 10am–6pm Sat & Sun. 🖼
The fairy-tale castle, spiked with towers, was created during the years 1861–83 on the site of an older fortress. Now a museum, it houses the Stolberg-Wernigerode family art collection. The castle ramparts afford a fantastic view of the town and the nearby Harz mountains.

Environs
The small town of **Osterwieck**, 22 km (14 miles) to the north, has over 400 timber-frame buildings, dating mainly from the 16th and 17th centuries.

The romantic façade of Schloss Wernigerode, now a museum

The Harz Mountain Trail ❸

The tourist trail across the Harz Mountains leads through charming historic towns and villages, as well as past the other attractions of the region including some fascinating caves and unusual rock formations.

The Rübeland Caves ①
Rübeland's main attractions are the Hermannshöhle and Baumannshöhle, two caves with amazing stalactites and stalagmites.

Blankenburg ②
This charming mountain town is overlooked by an 18th-century castle. The Teufels-mauer, a spectacular 4-km (2-mile) long sandstone cliff, attracts many climbers.

Thale ③
Many mountain walks start in Thale, including one to the Hexentanzplatz, a platform suspended above a cliff, from where witches fly to Sabbath celebrations in the Walpurgis Night.

Harzgerode ⑦
The town has charming timber-frame houses in the Old Town, and a 16th-century castle.

Burg Falkenstein ⑥
This huge castle, built in the 12th century and extended many times, is now a museum. From the castle, the visitor can enjoy a splendid view over the surrounding Harz Mountains.

Gernrode ④
The star attraction in this town is the 10th-century church of St Cyriacus. Its interior is devoid of ornaments, yet enchantingly pure in form.

Ballenstedt ⑤
The former home of the von Anhalt-Bemburg family enchants visitors to this day with its imaginative design, including the Baroque castle set in a park.

KEY

▬▬	Tour route
▬▬	Other road
═══	Scenic route
☀	Viewpoint

0 km 2
0 miles 2

The Renaissance portal of
Quedlinburg Schloss

Quedlinburg ❹

Road map D3. 🏛 *26,000*. 🚉 🚌
ℹ️ *Markt 2 (03946-90 56 24 and
90 56 25)*. 🎭 *Musiksommer (Jun–Sep)*.

The rise of the small town of
Quedlinburg was closely
connected with its convent,
established in 936 by Emperor
Otto I and his mother, St
Mathilde. On the hill above
the town stands the vast
Romanesque structure of the
Stiftskirche St Servatius
(Collegiate Church of St
Servatius), built between 1017
and 1129. Its old crypt, the
Huysburg, which belonged to
the previous church, features
Romanesque wall paintings
and contains tombs of the
prioresses and of the Emperor
Henry and his wife Mathilde.

An exhibition of treasures is
shown in the arms of the
transept, including the
Romanesque reliquary of St
Servatius and the remaining
fragments of the 12th-century
Knüpfteppich (tapestry). The
Quedlinburg Schloss,
a Renaissance palace sur-
rounded by gardens, occupies
the other side of the hill.

Both Old and New Town of
Quedlinburg have valuable
examples of timber-frame
architecture. The buildings
date from various times – the
modest house at **Wordgasse
3**, from around 1400, is the
oldest surviving timber-frame
building in Germany. Also
noteworthy are the numerous
churches, including the 10th-
century **Norbertinenkirche**,
the **Wippertikirche** with its
early-Romanesque crypt, and
the 15th century, late-Gothic
Marktkirche St Benedicti.

Bernburg ❺

Road map D4. 🏛 *36,000*. 🚉 🚌
ℹ️ *Lindenplatz 9 (03471 346 9311)*.
🎭 *Walpurgisnacht (May)*.
www.bernberg.de

Once the capital of one of
Anhalt's Duchies, Bernburg
enjoys a picturesque location
on the banks of the Saale River.
It has a **Bergstadt** (upper town)
and a **Talstadt** (lower town),
and its attractions include the

Gothic parish churches and the
town square with its Baroque
buildings. The most important
historic building is the **Bernburg Schloss**, a castle built on a
rock. It owes its present
appearance to refurbishments
(1540–70), yet many features of
this multi-wing structure are
much older, including the
12th-century Romanesque
chapels and Gothic towers.

Burg Giebichenstein, in Halle, with
the Arts and Crafts College

Halle ❻

Road map D4. 🏛 *232,300*. 🚉 🚌
ℹ️ *Marktplatz 13 (0345 122 99 84)*.
🎭 *Händel-Festspiele (Jun); Hallesche
Musiktage (Nov)*. **www**.halle.de

Halle is an old town with a
rich history in commerce and
trade, its wealth founded on
the production and sale of
salt. Later, the town was
turned into a centre for the

Burg Giebichenstein, in Halle, with
the Arts and Crafts College

The impressive Bernburg Schloss, built on a rock

Renaissance residence in Merseburg

chemical industry. Halle has preserved most of its historic heritage. On the **Marktplatz** (town square) stands an interesting church, **Unser Lieben Frauen** (Our Lady), whose late-Gothic main body (1530–54) was positioned between two pairs of towers that had remained intact from previous Romanesque churches. Nearby is the **Roter Turm** (Red Tower), an 84-m (276 ft) tall belfry, built in 1418–1506. The house at Nikolaistraße 5, the birthplace of Georg Friedrich Händel, now houses a small museum, the **Händel-Haus**. In Domplatz stands the early-Gothic **Dom**, built in 1280–1331 by the Dominicans and restored between 1525 and 1530 in Renaissance style, and elevated to the rank of cathedral. Inside there is an interesting pulpit dating from 1525, and the statues of saints situated by Peter Schroh's pillars.

Halle has some other medieval churches, including the late-Gothic **Moritzkirche** built in the latter part of the 14th century. It is also worth visiting the **Kunststiftung des Landes Sachen-Anhalt**, housed in the refurbished Citadel building known as **Moritzburg** and built during 1484-1503. On the outskirts of town stands **Burg Giebichenstein**, the former castle residence of the Magdeburg bishops. The upper part of the castle remains in ruins, while the lower part houses an Arts & Crafts College.

> **⌂ Kunststiftung des Landes Sachen-Anhalt**
> Friedemann-Bach-Platz 5. **Tel** (0345) 21 25 90. ☐ 10am–6pm Tue–Sun. 🎟 free last Sun of month.

Merseburg ❼

Road map D4. 🏠 40,000. 🚊 🚌
ℹ Burgstr. 5 (03461-21 41 70)
🎭 Schlossfest (Jun).
www.merseburg.de

The first sight visitors see as they arrive in Merseburg is the **Domburg** – a vast complex of buildings spiked with towers, consisting of a cathedral and residences. The cathedral is not uniform in style; it includes some Romanesque elements (the eastern section and twin towers in the west) erected in the 11th and 12th centuries, and the late-Gothic triple-nave main body, which was built in 1510–17. All that remains of the older, early-Romanesque structure is the crypt, underneath the presbytery. The cathedral contains remarkable Gothic and Renaissance features, as well as numerous sarcophagi of bishops, such as that of Thilo von Troth (1470). The chapter buildings house a library with precious manuscripts, including the **Merseburg Bible** (c. 1200). Adjacent to the cathedral is a three-wing Renaissance-style **Schloss**. Magnificent portals and an attractive oriel in the castle's west wing are noteworthy.

Querfurt ❽

Road map D4. 🏠 11,000. 🚌
ℹ Markt 14 (034771-237 99) 🎭
Brunnenfest (Jun). **www**.querfurt.de

The narrow streets of Querfurt are crammed with timber-frame houses, and the giant **Schloss** towers over the town square with its Renaissance town hall. The castle's present form is the result of Renaissance refurbishments, but it maintains many Romanesque features, such as the 11th-century donjon (keep), known as **Dicker Heinrich** (Fat Henry) and a 12th-century church. Also worth seeing is the burial chapel, the Baroque **Fürstenhaus** (ducal house) and a small museum, situated in the former armoury and granary.

Naumburg ❾

Road map D4. 🏠 30,500. 🚊 🚌
ℹ Markt 12 (03445-27 31 25).
www.naumburg-tourismus.de
🎭 Hussiten-Kirsch-Fest (Jun).

The town's star attraction is the **Dom** (cathedral of Saints Peter and Paul see pp150–51). There is a late-Gothic **Rathaus** (town hall), restored in Renaissance style, and the main square is surrounded by quaint houses. Further attractions include the **Marientor** gate (1455–6) with the puppet theatre, and the Gothic **Stadtkirche St. Wenzel** (Church of St Wenceslas). The latter has two paintings by Lucas Cranach the Elder as well as the 18th-century organ that Johann Sebastian Bach played on. Friedrich Nietzsche, the philosopher, spent his childhood at No. 18 Weingarten, now a small museum.

Gothic stone retable of the main altar in Naumburg Dom

Naumburg Dom

The impressive Cathedral of Saints Peter and Paul in Naumburg is one of the finest Gothic structures in Germany. The present cathedral is the second to be built on the same site; only a section of the eastern crypt survived of the earlier Romanesque church. Construction started before 1213, with the earliest parts including the late-Romanesque east choir, the transept and the main body. The early-Gothic west choir was built in the mid-13th century, the newer Gothic east choir c.1330. The northeast towers date from the 15th century, the southwest towers from 1894.

West choir

Stained-glass Windows in the Presbytery
The stained-glass windows depict scenes of the apostles of virtue and sin. Some sections are original 13th-century work, but two were completed in the 19th century.

★ Founders' Statues
The statues of Margrave Ekkehard and his wife, Uta, are true masterpieces – the artist succeeded marvellously in capturing the beauty and sensitivity of his subjects.

★ Portal of the West Reading Room
The Gothic twin portal depicts the Crucifixion, a moving and highly expressive group sculpture by the brilliant "Naumburger Meister" whose identity remains unknown.

STAR FEATURES

★ Founders' Statues

★ Portal of the West Reading Room

★ Main Portal

Pulpit
*The richly orna-
mented pulpit
basket, from 1466,
and the adjoining
stairs have been
renovated.*

VISITORS' CHECKLIST

Domplatz 16–17. **Tel** (03445)
23 01 10. ☐ Mar–Oct:
9am–6pm Mon–Sat, noon–6pm
Sun; Nov–Feb: 10am–4pm
Mon–Sat, noon–4pm Sun.

St Mary's Altar
*This late-Gothic triptych (c.1510) depicts the Virgin
Mary with the Infant, framed by Saints Barbara
and Catherine, with the Apostles in the wings.*

**Sarcophagus
of Bishop
Dietrich II**

**East
choir**

East Choir Altar
*This Gothic altar
features the Virgin Mary
with the Infant Jesus,
surrounded by the
figures of the saints.*

The Main Altar,
built in the mid-
14th-century, is a
stone retable depict-
ing the Crucifixion
with the saints which
was transferred
from another altar.

★ Main Portal
*The late-Romanesque, 13th-century
portal is decorated on the left side
with eagles. The tympanum features
Christ in a mandorla (almond-
shaped area) supported by angels.*

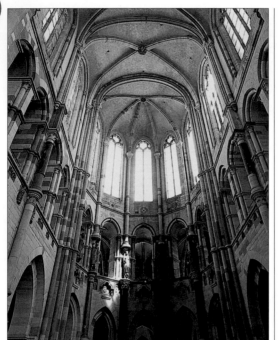

Interior of the Gothic presbytery in the Magdeburg Dom

Magdeburg ⑩

Road map D3. 🏛 *235,000.* 🚆 🚌
🛈 *Ernst-Reuter-Allee 12 (0391-838 0405).* 🎭 *Jazzfestival (Jun), Klassik-Open Air (Jul).* **www**.magdeburg-tourist.de

The large-scale development of Magdeburg, today the capital of Saxony-Anhalt and a port on the river Elbe, began in the 10th century when Emperor Otto I established his main residence here. In medieval times the town became a political and cultural centre. Following the abolition of the archbishopric and the destruction wrought by the Thirty Years' War, it lost its political importance. About 80 per cent was destroyed during World War II, but it is still worth a visit since many historic buildings have been reconstructed in the Old Town.

🏛 Dom St Mauritius und St Katharina
Domplatz. Tel (0391) 541 04 36. ⏲ *May–Sep: 10am–6pm; Apr & Oct: 10am–5pm; Nov–Mar: 10am–4pm.*
The vast Magdeburg cathedral is one of the most important Gothic churches in Germany. Its construction, which started in 1209 on the site of an earlier Romanesque church, was completed in 1520, although much of it was built by the mid-14th century. The result is a lofty, aisled basilica with transept, cloisters, a ring of chapels surrounding the presbytery and a vast twin-tower façade. The cathedral has several magnificent, original sculptures. Other notable features include the tomb of Emperor Otto I, as well as the 12th-century bronze tomb plaques of archbishops Friedrich von Wettin and Wichmann. The memorial for the dead of World War I is the work of Ernst Barlach, dating from 1929. Visitors to the cathedral may notice several elements that were preserved from ancient structures and have been incorporated into the walls or used as ornaments inside the building.

🏛 Kulturhistorisches Museum
Otto-von-Guericke-Str. 68–73.
Tel *(0391) 540 35 01.* ⏲ *10am–5pm Tue–Sun.* 🖼
This museum contains works of art, archaeological finds and historic documents of the town. Its most valuable exhibit is the Magdeburger Reiter (Magdeburg Rider), a sculpture dating from around 1240 of an unknown ruler on a horse (probably Otto I).

🔒 Kloster Unser Lieben Frauen
Regierungsstr. 4–6.
Kunstmuseum Tel *(0391) 56 50 20.* ⏲ *10am–5pm Tue–Sun.* 🖼
This Austere Romanesque church, Magdeburg's oldest building, was built for the Norbertine order during the second half of the 11th and the early 12th centuries. Stripped of all its ornaments, it now serves as a concert hall. The adjacent Romanesque abbey is a museum with medieval and modern sculptures (Barlach, Rodin).

🏠 Halle an der Buttergasse
Alter Markt. Weinkeller Buttergasse.
The basement of a late-Romanesque market hall from c.1200 was rediscovered in 1948, and is used today as a wine cellar.

🏛 Rathaus
Alter Markt.
The present Baroque town hall, built in 1691–8 on the site of an earlier, late-Romanesque town hall, was restored after World War II.

🔒 Pfarrkirche St Johannis
Am Johannisberg 1.
Viewing tower
Tel *(0391) 59 34 50.* ⏲ *Mar–Oct: 10am–6pm Tue–Sun; Nov–Feb: 10–5pm.* 🖼
Near the market square is the Gothic church of St John, destroyed during World War II and later rebuilt. In 1524 Martin Luther preached here. Today it is used as a concert hall.

Kloster Unser Lieben Frauen in Magdeburg

Stendal ⓫

Road map D3. 🏠 *39,600.*
🚌 🚆 ℹ️ *Kornmarkt 8 (03931-65 11 90).* 🎭 *Rolandfest (early Jul).*
www.stendal.de

In medieval times Stendal was one of the richest towns of the Brandenburg margravate, and its most valuable historical remains date from that period. The late-Gothic **St Nikolai** cathedral was built in 1423–67, on the foundations of a Romanesque Augustinian church. Its star attractions are 15th-century stained-glass windows in the presbytery and the transept.

The late-Gothic, 15th-century church **St Marien** (St Mary) has some original Gothic elements, and the oldest parts of the **Rathaus** (town hall) date back to the 14th century. Other attractions include the remains of the town walls, with a beautiful tower, **Uenglinger Torturm.**

Gothic traceries of the cloisters in the Dom, Havelberg

Havelberg ⓬

Road map D3. 🏠 *7,000.* 🚆 ℹ️
Uferstr. 1. (039387-79 091).
www.havelberg.de

Havelberg played an important role in the Christianization of this region, with a mission episcopate established here as early as the mid-10th century. The present cathedral – **Dom St Marien** – was built in 1150–70, and although redesigned in the early 14th century, it nevertheless maintained its Romanesque character. Its most interesting

Back of the Gothic Rathaus In the market square in Tangermünde

features include huge stone candelabra taken from the former reading room, dating back to around 1300, and the present reading room, which is decorated with reliefs carved in the workshop of the Parler family, in Prague, between 1396 and 1411.

Tangermünde ⓭

Road map D3. 🏠 *10,000.* 🚆 🚌
ℹ️ *Markt 2 (039322-223 93).*
www.tourismus-tangermuende.de

Situated at the confluence of the Tanger and Elbe rivers, this town grew rapidly during medieval times. For centuries it remained the seat of the Brandenburg margraves, and King Charles IV chose it as his second residence. The town joined the Hanseatic League, and grew in status thanks to its trade links.

The **Rathaus** (town hall) has timber-frame architecture and houses the municipal museum.

The only remains of the old castle are its main tower and the **Kanzlei** (chancellery). In 1377, King Charles IV brought the Augustinian monks to town and had the **St Stephanskirche** (church of St Stephen) built for them. Construction continued until the end of the 15th century. This magnificent, late-Gothic hall church with transept and cloister contains interesting features: a 1624 organ made in the

Hamburg workshop of Hans Scherer the Younger, the 1619 pulpit created by Christopher Dehne and a font dating from 1508, the work of Heinrich Mente.

The east wing of the beautiful Gothic **Rathaus** (town hall) dates back to 1430 and is the work of Heinrich Brunsberg, its richly ornamented spire being typical of his work. The west wing with its arcades was added around 1480, and the external stairs date from the 19th century.

Tangermünde has retained some remains of the city walls, dating from around 1300 and including a magnificent late-Gothic gate, the **Neustädter Tor**, whose tall, cylindrical tower has intricate, lacy ceramic ornaments.

🏛️ **Rathaus (Stadtgeschichtliches Museum)**
Am Markt **Tel** *(039322) 42 153.*
🕐 *10am–5pm Tue–Sun.*

Environs
A Romanesque **Klosterkirche** (abbey) in Jerichow, 10 km (6 miles) north of Tangermünde, is the earliest brick structure of the region. It was built in the 1150s, for Norbertine monks. The west towers were completed during the 15th century. Its austere, triple-nave vaulted interior is impressive. There are also many remains of the former abbey.

Interior of the former Norbertinenkirche, in Jerichow, north of Tangermünde

Dessau ⑭

Road map E3. 🏛 *84,400.* 🚆 🚌
ℹ️ *Zerbster Str. 2c (0340-204 14 42).*
🎭 *Kurt-Weill-Fest (late Feb–Mar),*
Elbmusikfest (Jun). **www**.dessau.de

Dessau, once a magnificent city and the capital of the duchy of Anhalt-Dessau, is less attractive today, yet it has some excellent historic sights. In the town centre are some interesting Baroque churches and the **Johannbau**, the remains of a Renaissance ducal residence.

Dessau is also known for the **Bauhaus** complex. Built in 1925 to a design by Walter Gropius, it is the home of the famous art school, which moved here from Weimar. The **Bauhausmuseum** is housed in one of its wings. Nearby, in Friedrich-Ebert-Allee, five of the so-called **Meisterhäuser** – master houses for the Art College professors – have survived World War II. The houses of Lyonel Feininger and Paul Klee are open to the public. Wassily Kandinsky was also a former resident. The **Korn-haus**, on Elballee, restored in 1996, contains a restaurant, café and dance hall.

Many splendid residences set in landscaped gardens were built in 18th- and 19th-century Dessau. In the town centre stands a Neo-Classical palace, **Schloss Georgium**, built in 1780 to a design by Friedrich Wilhelm von Erd-mannsdorff. Today it houses a collection of old masters, including works by Rubens, Hals and Cranach.

🏛 **Bauhausmuseum**
Gropiusallee 38. *Tel (0340) 65 080.*
◻ *10am–6pm daily.* 🖼

⚜ **Schloss Georgium**
Puschkinallee 100. *Tel (0340) 61 38
74.* ◻ *10am–5pm Tue–Sun.* 🖼

Environs
Haldeburg, which is situated on the outskirts of Dessau, has a Neo-Gothic hunting lodge built in 1782–3, and Mosigkau boasts **Schloss Mosigkau**, Princess Anna Wilhelmina's Baroque resi-dence, designed by Christian Friedrich Damm. It contains some excellent examples of 17th-century painting.

In **Oranienbaum**, 12 km (7 miles) east of Dessau, stands a late-17th-century, early-Baroque palace that was built for Princess Henrietta Katharine of Orange by the Dutch architect Cornelius Ryckwaert.

⚜ **Schloss Mosigkau**
Knobelsdorffallee 2. *Tel (0340) 50
255 721.* ◻ *Apr, Oct: 10am–5pm
Sat & Sun; May–Sep: 10am–6pm
Tue–Sun.* ⬤ *Dec–Mar.* 🎨 🖼

Lutherstadt Wittenberg ⑮

Road map E3. 🏛 *55,000.* 🚆 🚌
ℹ️ *Schlossplatz 2 (03491-41 48 48).*
🎭 *Wittenberger Stadtfest & Luthers
Hochzeit (Jun).*
www.wittenberg.de

This small town, named after its most famous resident, Martin Luther, enjoys a scenic position on the banks of the Elbe River. Its main development took place during the 16th century, under the Great Elector, Frederick the Wise. Witten-berg became the capital of the Reformation thanks to the work of Martin Luther and Philipp Melanchthon, and as such it attracts many visitors. Another famous resident of that period was the painter Lucas Cranach the Elder.

⚜ **Schloss Wittenberg**
Schlossplatz. **Museum für Naturkunde und Völkerkunde** (Museum of Natural History and Ethnography) *Tel (03491) 43 34
920.* ◻ *9am–5pm Tue–Sun.* 🖼
Built for Frederick the Wise in 1489–1525, the castle was greatly altered during recon-struction following fire and wartime damage. A museum is housed in the west wing.

The tomb of Frederick the Wise, in Schlosskirche

🏛 **Schlosskirche**
Schlossplatz. *Tel (03491) 40 25 85.*
◻ *May–Oct: 10am–6pm Mon–Sat,
11:30–6pm Sun; Nov–Apr:10am–
4pm Mon–Sat, 11:30am–4pm Sun.*

Built after 1497, this church was made famous by Martin Luther, who allegedly posted his theses on its door in 1517. The original door no longer exists, but the church con-tains many interesting tombs, including that of Frederick the Wise, created in 1527 in the workshop of Hans Vischer, as well as modest tombs of Mar-tin Luther and Melanchthon.

Schloss Georgium in Dessau

For hotels and restaurants in this region see pp492–4 and pp530–32

was built between the 13th and 15th centuries. Luther was married to Katharina von Bora in this church where he also preached, and six of their children were baptised. Inside there is a magnificent Reformation altar (constructed in 1547), the work of father and son Cranach, as well as interesting tombs and epitaphs.

Melanchthonhaus

Collegienstr. 60. **Tel** *(03491) 40 32 79.* ☐ *Apr–Oct: 10am–6pm daily; Nov–Mar: 10am–5pm Tue–Sun.* 🎟
This museum is devoted to Luther's closest ally, Philipp Schwarzerd, generally known as Melanchthon

Lutherhaus

Collegienstr. 54. **Tel** *(03491) 42 030.* ☐ *same as Melanchthonhaus.* 🎟
The museum, which is in the former residence of Martin Luther and his family, also chronicles the work of Lucas Cranach the Elder. It has a large number of documents relating to the Reformation and Luther's translation of the Bible.

The market square with Baroque fountain, in Lutherstadt Wittenberg

Cranachhaus

Markt 4. **Tel** *(03491) 420 19 11.* ☐ *10am–5pm Mon–Sat (from 1pm Sun).* ☐ *Nov–Apr: Mon.*
This beautiful, early 16th-century Renaissance house once belonged to Lucas Cranach the Elder and was the birthplace of his son, Lucas Cranach the Younger. His studio was located at No. 1 Schlossstraße.

Rathaus

Markt 26. ☐ *10am–5pm Tue–Sun.*
The Renaissance town hall was built in 1523–35, and later twice extended in the 16th century. In its forecourt are two 19th-century monuments: to Martin Luther by Gottfried Schadow and to Philipp Melanchthon by Friedrich Drake.

Marienkirche

Kirchplatz. **Tel** *(03491) 40 44 15.* ☐ *Easter–Oct: 10am–6pm daily (Sun from 11:30am); Nov–Easter: 10am–5pm daily (Sun from 11:30am).*
The Gothic church of St Mary with its twin-tower façade

LUTHERSTADT WITTENBERG TOWN CENTRE

| 0 metres | 500 |
| 0 yards | 500 |

Neues Rathaus

Stadtpark

BERLINER STRASSE

PFAFFENGASSE

JURISTENSTRASSE

BÜRGERMEISTERSTRASSE

ARSENAL PLATZ

MAUERSTRASSE

Stadtpark

LUTHERSTRASSE

COSWIGER STRASSE

JUDENSTRASSE

Rathaus ④

Marienkirche ⑤

SCHLOSSSTRASSE

Schlosskirche ①②

Schloss Wittenberg

Markt

ALTSTADT

③ Cranachhaus

FLEISCHERSTRASSE

NEUSTRASSE

WALLSTRASSE

COLLEGIENSTRASSE

MITTELSTRASSE

TEUENGASSE

WEBERSTRASSE

HALLESCHE STRASSE

Sportplatz

AM STADTGRABEN

Melanchthonhaus ⑥ ⑦

Lutherhaus

Hauptbahnhof 500m (550 yards)

WESERSTRASSE

Key to Symbols *see back flap*

Wörlitz Park ⓰

Wörlitz is a charming, English-style landscaped garden, the first of its kind in continental Europe. It was established in stages, commencing in 1764, for Prince Leopold III, Frederick Franz of Anhalt-Dessau. Many famous gardeners worked in Wörlitz, including Johann Christian Neumark and Johann Leopold Ludwig Schoch, as well as the architect Friedrich Wilhelm von Erdmannsdorff. The country house (1769–1773), the first building in the Classical style in Germany, houses a valuable collection of sculpture, furniture and paintings. Another interesting collection, including Swiss glass pictures, can be admired in the Gotisches Haus.

Floratempel
Modelled on an ancient temple with columns, this Neo-Classical temple served as a music pavilion.

★ Gotisches Haus
This house, built in stages, is one of the earliest examples of German Neo-Gothic style. On display inside is a unique collection of Swiss glass pictures.

Rousseau-Insel, lined with poplars, was modelled on Ermenonville, the island where the French philosopher was first buried.

Rosen-Insel
Rose island was created as one of several artificial islands in the part of the garden designed by Johann Christian Neumark.

Gondolas on the Lake
Romantic gondolas wait by the jetties to take tourists across the lake.

Lake Concert
Classical concerts are held on Wörlitz Lake in the evening during the summer season. The audience is all afloat in boats.

VISITORS' CHECKLIST

🚌 🅿 ℹ️ *Förstergasse 26 (34905 310 09); www.woerlitz-information.de*
Schloss ⬜ *Apr & Oct: 11am–5pm Tue–Fri; 10am–5pm Sat & Sun.* 🚫 ♿

Amalien-Insel
In keeping with the fashion of the day, this artificial island, on Großes Walloch lake, has a grotto, which provides a cool resting place.

The Pantheon, built in 1795–6, houses a collection of antique sculptures.

0 metres	500
0 yards	500

Pantheon

WEIDEN-HEGER

Herderinsel *Großes Walloch* *Amalien-Insel*

NEUE ANLAGEN

agoge

Wörlitzer See
The largest of the three lakes, which are all joined by canals, this is prettiest when the water lilies are in bloom.

Stein (Rock Island) is a working artificial volcano modelled on Mount Vesuvius in Italy.

Stein

★ **Synagogue**
Built in 1790 and modelled on the Vesta Temple in Rome, the synagogue was gutted by the National Socialists in 1938 and now shows a Jewish history exhibit.

STAR FEATURES

★ Gotisches Haus

★ Synagogue

SAXONY

*S*axony has a long history and is rich in historic sites. Its capital city, Dresden, ranks among the most beautiful and interesting towns in Germany, despite the devastation it suffered during World War II. The region also boasts the enchanting Erzgebirge Mountains and the glorious scenery of "Saxon Switzerland", where the mighty Elbe river runs amid fantastic rock formations.

In the 10th century, Emperor Otto I created an eastern border province (margravate) in the area presently known as Saxony. It quickly grew in size as it expanded into neighbouring territories inhabited by the Polabian Slavs. It was divided and part became the Meissen Margravate, ruled by the powerful house of Wettin from 1089. This dynasty's political power increased when it acquired the Saxon Electorate in 1423; subsequently the entire region under their rule became known as "Saxony".

From 1697 until 1763 Saxony was united with Poland, and the Saxon Great Electors, Frederick Augustus the Strong and his son Frederick Augustus II, were also kings of Poland. During this period Saxony flourished, and Dresden became a major centre of the arts and culture until the Seven Years' War (1756–63) put an end to the region's prosperity. In 1806, Saxony declared itself on the side of Napoleon, and the Great Elector acquired the title of King. But Saxony paid a heavy price for supporting Napoleon – following the Congress of Vienna (1815), the kingdom lost the northern half of its territory to Prussia, and in 1871 it was incorporated into the German Empire.

At the end of World War II Saxony was in the Soviet-occupied zone and became part of the GDR in 1949. Since 1990 it has been a state in the Federal Republic of Germany. Saxony is densely populated and in some parts heavily industrialized, but it also has many interesting and unspoiled towns.

The scenic Bastei rocks in Saxon Switzerland

◁ **Kriebstein Castle, overlooking the Zschopau river**

Exploring Saxony

When travelling in Saxony, a visit to Dresden is a must. Visitors should set aside several days to explore its historic sights and magnificent museums. Dresden is also a convenient base for excursions to the attractive landscapes of the Sächsische Schweiz ("Saxon Switzerland") and further afield – to Bautzen, Görlitz and Zittau, or to the Erzgebirge Mountains, towards Freiberg and Chemnitz. Another town worth visiting, at least for a day, is Leipzig with its historic sights, cultural events, trade fairs and exhibitions.

The Old Town of Bautzen, situated high above the banks of the Spree River

SIGHTS AT A GLANCE

SEE ALSO

- *Where to Stay* pp494–5

- *Where to Eat* pp532–4

For additional map symbols *see back flap*

The giant castle and cathedral complex in Meissen

GETTING AROUND

Leipzig and Dresden both have airports, as well as excellent train and road connections with the rest of Germany. The A6 motorway runs west from Görlitz, through Dresden and Chemnitz; the A13 links Dresden with Berlin, and the A14 with Leipzig. Other roads, national and regional, are clearly sign-posted, and all the towns described in this guide can also be reached by local buses.

Saddle horses grazing on paddocks near Kamenz

Young musicians in the Barockgarten, in Großsedlitz, near Dresden

KEY	
═══	Motorway
▬▬	Major road
═══	Minor road
▬▬	Scenic route
▬•▬	Main railway
───	Minor railway
▬▬	International border
▬▬	Country border
△	Summit

Leipzig ❶

Granted town status in 1165, Leipzig is not only one of Germany's leading commercial towns, but also a centre of culture and learning, with a university founded in 1409. An important centre for the German publishing and book trade, it is the home of the Deutsche Bücherei, the German national library established in 1912. During the various trade fairs, such as the Book Fair in spring, it receives a great number of visitors, and it has much to offer in terms of entertainment, including concerts by the renowned Gewandhaus symphony orchestra and the Thomanerchor boys' choir, which boasts Johann Sebastian Bach as a past choirmaster.

Lofty interior of the Neo-Classical Nikolaikirche

Exploring Leipzig

Most of the interesting sights can be found in the old town encircled by the Ring road, which includes Europe's biggest railway station, the **Hauptbahnhof**, built in 1902–15 to a design by William Lossow and Max Hans Kühne. The heart of musical Leipzig beats in the eastern part of the old town, around Augustusplatz. Here stands the **Neues Gewandhaus** (built 1977– 81) and the **Opernhaus** (built 1959– 60). The University Tower nearby is being redesigned.

In Nikolaikirchhof stands the **Nikolaikirche** (church of St Nicholas). The present church was built during the 16th century, although the lower sections of its north tower date from the 12th century. It has Neo-Classical furnishings. The **Alte Handelsbörse** (old stock exchange) in Naschmarkt is

an early-Baroque building, designed by Johann Georg Starcke. Built in 1678–87 and reconstructed almost from the ground after World War II, it is now a concert hall. In front of the building stands a monument (1903) to Goethe showing him as a student.

In the market square, near the beautiful Renaissance town hall, is the **Alte Waage**, the old municipal weigh-house, a Renaissance work by Hieronymus Lotter. It was built in 1555 and reconstructed in 1964 following damage in World War II.

The area to the south of the town square is taken up by a block of trade fair buildings. The most interesting are the beautifully restored **Specks Hof** (Reichestraße/Nikolai-straße), the oldest arcade in Leipzig with three enclosed courts built between 1908 and 1929, and **Mädlerpassage**, built in 1912–14, a Modernist commercial building with a three-tier passageway connecting Grimmaische Straße and Naschmarkt. Beneath it is the **Auerbachs Keller**, magnificent, 16th-century vaults, immortalized by Goethe in *Faust* and featuring a room that bears his name. The **Commerzbank** (Klostergasse/Thomasgasse) and the **Riquet Café**, a fine Viennese-style coffee house, are attractive Art Nouveau buildings.

Lovers of Johann Sebastian Bach's music will wish to visit **Thomaskirche**, the magnificent late-Gothic church of St Thomas,

built in 1482–96, where Bach was the choirmaster from 1723. It now contains the composer's tomb. Worth noting are the beautiful Renaissance galleries built by Hieronymus Lotter, in 1570. The famous Thomanerchor choir still sings at services on Friday evenings and Saturday afternoons, and organ concerts are held in the churches of St Thomas and St Nicholas during the summer months. Bach is also commemorated with a monument in front of the church (1908). Nearby, the **Bosehaus**, a Baroque 17th-century building, is the home of the Bachmuseum, devoted to the composer.

🏛 Grassimuseum

Johannisplatz 5–11.
Museum für Völkerkunde
Tel (0341) 97 31 900.
Museum für Angewandte Kunst
Tel (0341) 22 29 100.
Museum für Musikinstrumente
Tel (0341) 97 30 750. **www.**
grassimuseum.de ☐ *Library and museum shop with workshops and lectures. Exhibitions 10am–6pm Tue–Sun.*

The Grassimuseum is one of Germany's greatest museum complexes, housing three fascinating collections: the Museum für Völkerkunde (ethnography) with exhibits from around the world; the Museum für Musikinstrumente (musical instruments) with a magnificent collection, including the world's oldest surviving clavichord, and the Museum für Angewandte (decorative arts) with its stunning gold and ivory ornaments, as well as the valuable town treasury.

The early-Baroque pavilion of the Alte Handelsbörse, the old stock exchange

Elder, Martin Schongauer and Caspar David Friedrich, as well as other magnificent European paintings. There are canvases by Jan van Eyck, Rubens, Frans Hals, Tintoretto and sculptures by Balthasar Permoser, Antonio Canova and Auguste Rodin.

🔒 Russische Kirche

Philipp-Rosenthal-Str. 51a.
Tel *(0341) 878 14 53.* 🕐 *10am–5pm daily (to 4pm in winter).*
The Russian Orthodox Church of St Alexius was built in 1912–13 to commemorate the 22,000 Russian soldiers who died in 1813, in the Battle of the Nations. The architect, Vladimir Pokrowski, based his design on the churches of Novgorod in Russia.

🏛 Völkerschlachtdenkmal

Prager Str. ***Tel*** *(0341) 241 68 70.*
🕐 *Apr–Oct: 10am–6pm daily, Nov–Mar: 10am–4pm daily.* 🎫
This giant, Teutonic-style monument is the work of architect Bruno Schmitz. Completed for the centenary of the 1813 Battle of the Nations, which pitched the combined Prussian, Austrian and Russian armies against Napoleon, it now houses a small museum.

VISITORS' CHECKLIST

Road map E4. 🏘 *493,000.*
✈ *Flughafen Leipzig–Halle.*
🚉 *Willy-Brandt-Platz.*
Tel *(0341) 224 11 55 & 22 40.*
ℹ *Richard-Wagner-Str. 1 (0341-710 42 60).* 🎭 *Leipziger Buchmesse (Mar); Leipziger Orgelsommer (Jul–Aug); Inter-nationaler Johann-Sebastian-Bach Wettbewerb (Jul); Leipziger Jazztage (Oct).* **www**.leipzig.de

🏛 Altes Rathaus

Markt 1. ***Tel*** *(0341) 261 77 60.*
Museum für Geschichte der Stadt Leipzig 🕐 *10am– 6pm Tue–Sun.*
The grand Renaissance town hall, built in 1556 to a design by Hieronymus Lotter, is now the home of the municipal museum. One room is devoted to Felix Mendelssohn-Bartholdy, who conducted the symphony orchestra from 1835 until his death in 1847.

🏛 Bacharchive und Bachmuseum

Thomaskirchhof 15–16. ***Tel*** *(0341) 913 72 202.* 🕐 *10am–6pm daily.*
This museum houses archives and documents relating to the life and works of the composer J. S. Bach.

The Russische Kirche, a pastiche of the churches in Novgorod

🏛 Deutsches Buch- und Schriftmuseum

Deutscher Platz 1. ***Tel*** *(0341) 227 13 24.* 🕐 *9am–4pm Mon–Sat.*
This museum is devoted to the history of German literature. It contains rare manuscripts and old prints.

🏛 Museum der Bildenden Künste

Katharinenstr. 10 (Sachsenplatz).
Tel *(0341) 216 999 20.* 🕐 *10am–6pm Tue & Thu–Sun, noon–8pm Wed.*
This museum has an excellent collection of German masters, including Lucas Cranach the

LEIPZIG CITY CENTRE

Alte Handelsbörse ④
Altes Rathaus ⑥
Alte Waage ⑤
Gewandhaus ②
Mädlerpassage ⑦
Nikolaikirche ③
Opernhaus ①
Thomaskirche ⑧

0 metres 200
0 yards 200

Key to Symbols *see back flap*

Doorway of Schloss Hartenfels, with its coat of arms, in Torgau

Torgau ❷

Road map E3. 🏛 23,000. 🚉 🚌
ℹ *Markt 1 (03421-70 140).* 📷
Torgauer Auszugsfest (May).
www.torgau.eu

This small town, with its scenic location on the Elbe, was once the favourite residence of the Saxon Electors. Its main square is surrounded by attractive houses of various styles, in particular Renaissance. The Renaissance **Rathaus** (town hall), built in 1561–77, has a lovely semicircular oriel. Other old town attractions include the **Marienkirche**, a late-Gothic church with an extended Romanesque west section. The interior has many original features, including a painting by Lucas Cranach the Elder, *The Fourteen Helpers*, and the tomb of Luther's wife, Katharina von Bora, who died in Torgau.

The main historic building in Torgau is the Renaissance **Schloss Hartenfels**, built on the site of a 10th-century castle. Its courtyard is surrounded by clusters of residential wings, including the late-Gothic Albrechtspalast built in 1470–85, the Johann-Friedrich-Bau (1533–6) with its beautiful external spiral staircase and the early-Baroque west wing (1616–23). The **Schlosskapelle** (castle chapel), which was consecrated by Martin Luther in 1544, is considered to be one of the oldest churches built for Protestants.

Muldetal ❸

Road map E4.

Several magnificent old castles nestle in the scenic hills at the confluence of two rivers – the Zwickauer Mulde and the Freiberger Mulde. In the small town of **Colditz**, with its timber-frame houses, lovely Renaissance town hall and Gothic church of St Egidien, stands a huge Gothic castle built in 1578–91 on the site of an 11th-century castle. During World War II it was a famous prisoner-of-war camp known as Oflag IVC.

In **Rochlitz**, 11 km (7 miles) south of Colditz, stands another large castle, built in stages from the 12th to the 16th centuries. Travelling further south you will encounter other castles: the **Wechselburg**, a reconstructed Baroque castle featuring a late-Romanesque collegiate church, as well as the Renaissance castle in **Rochsburg**. In the neighbouring Zschopau valley stands the magnificent, oval **Burg Kriebstein**, built in stages and completed in the late 14th century. This fortress houses a small museum and concert hall, and medieval music concerts are held here during the summer.

Zwickau ❹

Road map E4.
🏛 120,000. 🚉 🚌
ℹ *Hauptstr. 6 (0375-27 13 240).* 📷 *Robert-Schumann-Tage (Jun); TrabiTreffen (Jun).*
www.zwickau.de

An old commercial town, Zwickau flourished in the 15th and 16th centuries. Today it is known for the Trabant cars that were produced here during the GDR era. Almost all the town's attractions can be found in the old town, on the banks of the

Zwickauer Mulde river. The most important historic building in the town is the **Dom St Marien** (cathedral of St Mary), a magnificent late-Gothic hall-church built 1453–1537. Preserved to this day are its original main altar dating from 1479, the work of Michael Wolgemut, the grand architectural Holy Tomb of Michael Heuffner, dating from 1507, as well as a Renaissance font and a pulpit of 1538, both by Paul Speck.

Also worth visiting in the old town are the **Old Pharmacy**, the **Schumann-Haus**, the composer's birthplace (1810), and the Renaissance **Gewandhaus** (cloth house), once the seat of the Drapers' Guild and now a theatre and museum.

Chemnitz ❺

Road map E4. 🏛 260,000. 🚉
Georgstr. 🚌 *Markt.* ℹ *Markt 1 (0371-690 680/ 0371-19 433).*
www.chemnitz-tourismus.de

After World War II, when 90 per cent of its buildings had been reduced to rubble, the town was rebuilt in the

Gate of the Renaissance pulpit in the Dom St Marien, in Zwickau

Lew Kerbel's monument to Karl Marx at the Stadthalle in Chemnitz

Socialist-Realist style and renamed Karl-Marx-Stadt. Only a handful of historic buildings escaped destruction. The most interesting is the **Schlosskirche**, the former Benedictine abbey church St Maria, built at the turn of the 15th and 16th centuries.

Sights in the town centre include the reconstructed **Altes Rathaus** (old town hall), the Gothic **Roter Turm** (red tower) and remains of fortifications. In the main square is the reconstructed Baroque **Siegertsches Haus**, originally built in 1737–41 to a design by Johann Christoph Naumann. The new town centre is dominated by the vast **Stadthalle** (city hall) with Lew Kerbel's 1971 monument to Karl Marx. The **König-Albert-Kunstsammlungen** has a museum of natural history and a fine arts collection, including works by Karl Schmidt-Rottluff.

🏛 **Kunstsammlungen Chemnitz**
Theaterplatz 1. *Tel (0371) 488 44 24.* ◻ *11am–6pm Tue–Sun.* **Bibliothek** *1–6pm Wed.* 🏷

Augustusburg ➏

Road map E4. 🏠 *5,000* 🚌 **ℹ**
Marienberger Str. 24 (037291-395 50).
Schloss ◻ *Apr–Oct: 9:30am–6pm daily, Nov–Mar: 10am–5pm daily.*
www.augustusburg.de

The small town is insignificant compared with the vast palace complex bearing the

same name. The best way to get there is by cable car, from Erdmannsdorf. This Renaissance hunting palace was built for the Great Elector, Augustus, in 1567–72, on the site of the former Schloss Schellenberg, which had been destroyed by fire. Constructed under Hieronymus Lotter and Erhard van der Meer, it is a symmetrical, square building with towered pavilions at each corner, joined by galleries, gates and a chapel to the east, with an altar by Lucas Cranach the Younger. Today the palace houses several museums devoted to motorcycles, coaches and hunting.

Sächsische Silberstraße ➐

See pp166–7.

Freiberg ➑

Road map F4. 🏠 *15,000.* 🚌 🚌
ℹ *Burgstr. 1 (03731-419 5190)*
🎭 *Bergstadtfest (Jun), Silbermann-Tage (Sep).* **www**.freiberg.de

Development of this mining town was due to the discovery of silver deposits, and Freiberg was granted town status in 1186. It escaped World War II with remarkably little damage.

Today its attractions include the reconstructed old town and many historic buildings, the gem among them being the **Dom St Marien** (cathedral). This late-Gothic hall-church, erected at the end of the 15th century, features a

magnificent main portal, the Goldene Pforte, dating from 1225–30. Inside are many original items, such as a tulip-shaped pulpit (1505), two Baroque organs by Gottfried Silbermann and many sculptures and epitaphs.

When visiting nearby Untermarkt, it is worth going to the **Stadt-und Bergbaumuseum** (municipal and mining museum) which explains the history of mining in the area, as well as the collection of minerals at the **Mineralien-und Lagerstätten sammlung der Bergakademie**.

Otto of Meissen, founder of Freiberg

A stroll along the winding streets will take the visitor to **Obermarkt**, where the 15th-century Gothic town hall, a fountain with the statue of the town's founder and attractive houses can be seen.

⛪ **Dom St Marien**
Untermarkt 1. **Goldene Pforte**
Tel (03731) 225 98. 🚗 *May–Oct: 10am–noon, 2–5pm daily; Nov–Apr: 11am–noon, 2–4pm daily.* **Organ presentation** *11:30am Sun.*

🏛 **Stadt-und Bergbau-museum**
Am Dom 1. *Tel (03731) 202 50.*
◻ *10am–5pm Tue–Sun.* 🏷

⛪ **Mineralien-und Lagerstättensammlung der Bergakademie**
Brennhausgasse 14. *Tel (03731) 39 22 64.* ◻ *9am–noon & 1–4pm Wed–Fri, 9am–4pm Sat.*

Façade of the Renaissance Schloss Augustusburg

Sächsische Silberstraße ❼

The Saxon silver route, through the Erzgebirge (mineral ore mountains), takes the visitor to some of the most interesting and scenic places of the region. Silver was mined here from the 12th century, and mining traditions have been preserved to this day. Small towns entice visitors with their interesting parish churches, former mining settlements, museums and disused mines.

Schneeberg ①
A small mining town, which to this day cultivates its art and crafts traditions, Schneeberg is also famous for the St Wolfgangkirche, with an altar masterpiece by Lucas Cranach the Elder.

Annaberg-Buchholz ③
Although the town enjoyed only a brief spell of prosperity in the 16th century, its church from that period, St Annen, ranks among the most beautiful examples of late-Gothic architecture in Saxony.

Oberwiesenthal ②
This important wintersports resort, close to the Czech border and at the foot of the Fichtelberg, offers a ski-jump, downhill ski runs and toboggan runs.

0 km   5

0 miles   5

Marienberg ⑥
This small town, with its wonderful Renaissance town hall, is known mainly for the production of furniture.

KEY

- ▬ Suggested route
- ═ Other road
- ▬ Scenic route
- – · State boundary
- ❄ Viewpoint

Greifensteine ⑤
Fantastic, craggy rock formations in the north of the region, shaped like an amphitheatre, attract rock-climbers and hill-walkers.

Frohnau ④
The biggest attraction of this town is its old forge, featuring the Frohnauer Hammer, a huge original hammer that remained in use until 1904.

TIPS FOR DRIVERS

Length of the route: 55 km (34 miles).
Stopping points: inns and restaurants in every town.

Meissen 9

Road map 4E. 36,000.
Markt 3 (03521-419 40).
Stadt- und Weinfest (Sep).
www.stadt-meissen.de

Meissen is famous for its porcelain manufacture. Its history began in 929, when Henry I made it the bridge-head for his expansion to the east, into Slav territories. In 966 Meissen became the capital of the newly estab-lished Meissen Margravate, and in 968 a bishopric.

This town has retained much of its charm. In the town square is the late Gothic **Rathaus** (town hall), built in 1472–8, some beautiful Renaissance houses and the **Frauenkirche**, a late-Gothic, 15th-century church boasting the world's oldest porcelain carillon, which was hung here in 1929. It is also worth taking a stroll to St Afra's church, built in the 13th century for the Augustian monks.

♦ Albrechtsburg
Domplatz 1. **Tel** (03521) 47 070.
Mar–Oct: 10am–6pm daily,
Nov–Feb: 10am–5pm daily.
24, 25, 31 Dec.
The Albrechtsburg is a vast, fortified hilltop complex with a cathedral and an Elector's palace. The latter was built in 1471–89 for the Wettin brothers, Ernst and Albrecht. Designed by Arnold von West-falen, its special feature is the magnificent external spiral staircase. From 1710 the palace was used as a porcelain fac-tory. It was restored to its

The Baroque hunting lodge in Moritzburg

former glory in 1864. Huge wall paintings of this period, showing historical scenes, are the work of Wilhelm Römann. The cathedral church of St John the Evangelist and St Donat, built from the mid-13th century to the early 15th century, has some splendid early Gothic sculptures, an altar by Lucas Cranach the Elder in the Georgskapelle and ducal tombs in the Fürstenkapelle.

♦ Staatliche Porzellan-Manufaktur
Talstraße 9. **Tel** (03521) 46 87 00.
May–Oct: 9am–6pm daily; Nov–Apr:
9am–5pm daily. **www**.meissen.com
The first porcelain factory in Europe was set up in 1710 in the castle and moved to its present premises in 1865. Documents relating to the history of the factory and many interesting examples of its products are on display in the exhibition rooms. Guided tours and demonstrations take the visitor through all the stages of the porcelain manu-facturing process.

Moritzburg 10

Road map 4E. Schlossallee 3b
(035207-85 40). Kammermusikfes-
tival (Aug); Fischzug (Oct)

The first hunting lodge in this marshy region was built in the mid-16th century, for Moritz of Saxony. The present **Schloss Moritzburg** is the result of extensive alterations ordered by Augustus the Strong, directed by Matthäus Daniel Pöppelmann, and carried out in 1723–26. The result is a square building, with four cylindrical corner towers. Much of the interior has survived, including period furnishings and hunting trophies.

Also open to visitors is the 17th-century castle chapel decorated with splendid stucco ornaments. Augustus the Strong ordered the marshes to be drained, and the newly availa-ble land to be transformed into landscaped gardens and lakes. The **Fasanenschlösschen** (little pheasant castle) in the eastern part of the gardens features several interesting Rococo interiors, and also houses a zoological exhibition.

At the end of World War II, the German artist Käthe Koll-witz spent the last years of her life in Moritzburg. The house in which she lived and worked is now the **Käthe-Kollwitz-Gedenkstätte**.

♦ Schloss Moritzburg
Tel (035207) 8730. Feb–Mar:
10am–4pm Sat & Sun; Apr–Oct:
10am–5:30pm daily; Nov–Dec:
10am–4pm Tue–Sun.

♦ Fasanenschlösschen
as above. compulsory.

The late-Gothic Rathaus in Meissen

For hotels and restaurants in this region see pp494–5 and pp532–4

Dresden ⑪

One of Germany's most beautiful cities, Dresden first gained its pre-eminence in the year 1485, when the Albertine Wettins decided to establish their residence here. The town blossomed during the 18th century when it became a cultural centre and acquired many magnificent buildings. Almost all of these, however, were completely destroyed during the night of 13/14 February 1945, when British and American air forces mounted a vast carpet-bombing raid on the city. Today, meticulous restoration work is in progress to return the historic city centre to its former glory, now with renewed effort because of the damage caused by flooding in 2002.

Statue of the Saxon King Johann, in front of the Sächsische Staatsoper

Newly renovated Frauenkirche

🏛 Sächsische Staatsoper

Theaterplatz 2. **Tel** *(0351) 49 110.* **Tours Tel** *(0351) 79 66 305.*
The imposing, Neo-Renaissance building of the Saxon state opera is one of Dresden's landmarks. It is also known as Semperoper after its creator, the famous architect Gottfried Semper, who designed it twice: the first building, erected in 1838–41, burned down in 1869, the second one was completed in 1878. Reconstruction after World War II dragged on until 1985. The opera house was the venue for many world premieres, including *Tannhäuser* and *The Flying Dutchman* by Richard Wagner, as well as many works by Richard Strauss.

In front of the opera, in Theaterplatz, is a monument to the Saxon King Johann, by Johannes Schilling.

🏛 Schinkelwache

Theaterplatz. **Box office** ℹ
Tel *(0351) 49 11 705.* ◯ *10am–6pm Mon–Fri, 10am–1pm Sat & Sun.*
This small Neo-Classical building, with its sophisticated lines and its immaculate proportions, is the work of the famous Berlin architect, Karl Friedrich Schinkel. It was built between 1830 and 1832.

🛐 Hofkirche

Theaterplatz. (Entrance on Schlossplatz). ◯ *daily.*
This monumental Baroque royal church has served as the Catholic Dom (cathedral church) of the Dresden-Meißen Diocese since 1980. The presence of this Catholic church in staunchly Protestant Saxony was dictated by political necessity: in his struggle for the Polish crown, the Elector, Augustus the Strong, was forced to convert to Catholicism. The church was designed by an Italian architect, Gaetano Chiaveri, and built in 1738–51.

The church's interior has two-tier passageways which run from the main nave to the side naves. Rebuilt after World War II, it features a magnificent Rococo pulpit by Balthasar Permoser, a painting by Anton Raphael Mengus entitled *Assumption* in the main altar, and the vast organ – the last work of Gottfried Silbermann.

🛐 Frauenkirche

An der Frauenkirche. **Tel** *(0351) 65 60 656.* ◯ *10am–noon, 1pm–6pm daily.*
This giant church, designed by Georg Bähr and built in 1726–43, has been restored to its former glory. Once again, the shining, giant dome dominates the city's skyline. Completely destroyed in 1945 by Allied bombing, its shell survived intact, only to collapse later. Reconstruction began in 1993 and is now complete. Notable features include an elegant cupola and, inside, a colourful dome.

🏛 Residenzschloss

Taschenberg 2. **Grünes Gewölbe Tel** *(0351) 49 142 000.* ◯ *10am–6pm Wed–Mon.* **Hausmann-sturm** ◯ *10am–6pm Wed–Mon.*
This former residence of the

Façade of a wing of the Residenz-schloss, with *sgraffito* decoration

Wetting family was built in stages from the late 15th to the 17th centuries. It is now restored and houses some of the most beautiful art collections in East Germany, including the world famous Grünes Gewölbe (Green Vaults), a vast collection of royal jewels, gems and table decorations. The Hausmann-sturm, which is a tall tower, affords a great view of the Dresden skyline.

🏛 Fürstenzug
Augustusstr.

Langer Gang (long walk) is a long building, erected in 1586–91, which connects the castle with the Johanneum. The elegant façade facing the courtyard is decorated with *sgraffito* and has shady arcades supported by slim columns. It provided an excellent backdrop for tournaments and parades. The wall facing the street features the so-called Fürstenzug (procession of dukes) – a magnificent, 102 m (111 yd)-long frieze depicting the procession of many Saxon rulers. The frieze was originally created by Wilhelm Walther in 1872–6 using the *sgraffito* technique, but it was replaced in 1907 by 24,000 Meissen porcelain tiles

🏛 Verkehrsmuseum (Johanneum)
Augustusstr. 1. **Tel** (0351) 86 440. ⬜ 10am–5pm Tue–Sun.

This late 16th-century Renaissance building, originally designed as royal stables by Paul Buchner, was refurbished in the mid-18th century and housed first a gallery of paintings, later an armoury and a porcelain collection. Since 1956 it has been a museum of transport, with old trams, locomotives, a collection of vintage cars and models of famous German ships.

Fragment of the Fürstenzug, outside Langer Gang

DRESDEN CITY CENTRE

Albertinum ⑩
Brühlsche Terrasse ⑨
Frauenkirche ⑧
Fürstenzug ⑥
Goldener Reiter ⑮
Hofkirche ④
Japanisches Palais ⑯
Johanneum ⑦
Kreuzkirche ⑫
Museum f. Sächs. Volkskunst ⑭
Neues Rathaus ⑬
Residenzschloss ⑤
Sächsische Staatsoper ②
Schinkelwache ③
Stadtmuseum Dresden ⑪
Zwinger ①

0 metres 100
0 yards 100

Key to Symbols see back flap

⊞ Brühlsche Terrasse
Brühlsche Terrasse.

Once part of the town's fortifications, this attractive terrace subsequently lost its military importance and was transformed into magnificent gardens by the diplomat and patron of arts Heinrich von Brühl, after whom it is named. Offering splendid views over the River Elbe, it was known as "the balcony of Europe". There are several great buildings on the terraces – the first one, seen from Schlossplatz, is the Neo-Renaissance **Landtag** (parliament building); next to it is a small Neo-Baroque building, the **Secundogenitur** library built for the second generation of Brühls, now a popular café; this is followed by the **Kunstakademie** (art academy), known as Zitronenpresse (lemon squeezer) because of its ribbed glass dome. Among the statues and monuments on the terrace are works by the sculptor Ernst Rietschel, the architect Gottfried Semper and the painter Caspar David Friedrich.

⊞ Albertinum
Brühlsche Terrasse. **Tel** *(0351) 491 45 90. Galerie Neue Meister.*
⏻ *10am–6pm Tue–Sun.*
www.skd-dresden.de

Originally a royal arsenal, the Albertinum was rebuilt in its current Neo-Renaissance style in the 1880s by Carl Adolf Canzler. Forty years earlier, Bernhard von Lindenau had donated his considerable fortune to the city to set up a collection of contemporary art, which was then displayed in the Albertinum. Today, the building houses two magnificent collections. That of the **Galerie Neue Meister**, which

Two Women on Tahiti, Paul Gauguin, 1892, in the Albertinum

was established in the mid-19th century, contains paintings from the 19th and 20th centuries, including works by the German Impressionists Lovis Corinth and Max Liebermann, landscapes by Caspar David Friedrich, canvases by the Nazarine group of painters and works by European masters such as Edgar Degas, Paul Gauguin, Vincent van Gogh, Édouard Manet and Claude Monet.

The Albertinum's other collection, the **Skulpturensammlung**, is a small collection of sculptures, including remarkable late Baroque and early Rococo works by Balthasar Permoser.

🔓 Kreuzkirche
An der Kreuzkirche 6.
Tel *(0351) 439 39 20.*
⏻ *Summer: 10am–6pm Mon–Fri; winter: 10am–4pm Mon–Fri.*
Tower *10am–5pm daily.*

The present Baroque/Neo-Classical church was built in 1764–92 to a design by Johann Georg Schmidt. To commemorate the shelling in World War II, the interior has not been fully restored. The Cross of Nails from the ruins of Coventry Cathedral in England creates a powerful symbolic link between the two countries.

⊞ Goldener Reiter
Neustädter Markt.

The **Neustadt** (new town), on the right bank of the Elbe, lost much of its former glory through destruction in World War II. Visitors may therefore be surprised to come across this glistening, gilded equestrian statue of Augustus the Strong in the middle of a square, at the end of the plane tree-lined Hauptstraße. The monument, which was erected in 1736, is the work of Jean Joseph Vinache, court sculptor to Augustus.

The Goldener Reiter in the new town

⊞ Neues Rathaus
Dr.-Külz-Ring.

The giant Neo-Renaissance new town hall, in the southwest of the old town, was erected in 1905–1910. Its round tower (70 m/230 ft), crowned with a gilded statue of Hercules, offers a good view of the old city centre. In the foyer is a large model of the city as planned for 2015.

🏛 Museum für Sächsische Volkskunst (Jägerhof)
Köpckestr. 1. **Tel** *(0351) 49 14 20 00.*
⏻ *10am–6pm Tue–Sun.*

This Renaissance hunting lodge on the north bank of

Secundogenitur library on Brühlsche Terrasse

◁ **Schloss Moritzburg, near Dresden**

the Elbe was built between 1568 and 1613. Its west wing – the only part that escaped destruction – now houses a museum of ethnography with collections of Saxon culture and traditions, especially from the Erzgebirge Mountains.

🏛 Japanisches Palais

Palaisplatz II. *Tel (0351) 81 44 08 41.* **Museum für Völkerkunde** (Museum of Ethnography) ☐ *10am–6pm Tue–Sun.* **Landesmuseum für Vorgeschichte** (State Museum of Prehistory) ☐ *10am–6pm Tue–Sun.* **Senckenberg Naturhistorische Sammlungen** ☐ *10am–6pm Tue–Sun.*
Originally the Dutch Palais, this three-wing structure was built in 1715. It was extended in 1729–31, by Zacharias Longuelune, for Augustus the Strong's Japanese porcelain collection, at which time the palace changed its name. For years the palace served as a library; today it holds spectacular exhibitions run by the above-mentioned museums.

🏺 Pfunds Molkerei

Bautzner Str. 79. *Tel (0351) 80 80 80.* ☐ *10am–6pm Mon–Sat, 10am–3pm Sun.*
In the 19th-century part of the Neustadt, with its many bars, galleries, pubs and fringe theatres, stands this old dairy founded by Paul Pfund. Its interior is lined with dazzling, multi-coloured tiles, showing Neo-Renaissance motifs relating to the dairy's products. Today there is a shop which offers hundreds of dairy products, as well as a small bar, where visitors can sample the specialities.

🏛 Kraszewski-Museum

Nordstr. 28. *Tel (0351) 804 44 50.* ☐ *1–6pm Wed–Sun.*
This small museum is devoted to the life of the Polish writer

The Baroque Schloss Pillnitz, Augustus the Strong's summer residence

Józef Ignacy Kraszewski who, having escaped arrest in Warsaw, settled in Dresden in 1853. Inspired by the town's history, several of his novels (for example *Hrabina Cosel, Brühl*) are set during the time of Augustus the Strong.

🌳 Großer Garten

City centre.
The history of this great garden goes back to the 17th century, although it has been redesigned several times since. At the park's centre stands an early Baroque palace built in 1678–83 to a design by Johann Georg Starcke. A miniature railway takes visitors to Carolasee, a boating lake. It also stops at the botanical gardens in the northwest section of the park, and at the zoo. The Mosaikbrunnen (mosaic fountain) nearby was designed by Hans Poelzig and built in 1926.

🏛 Blaues Wunder

Loschwitz/Blasewitzer Brücke.
The suspension bridge which spans the River Elbe in the eastern part of the town is painted blue and nicknamed "blue wonder". Built in 1891–3, its main span is 141.5 m (464 ft) long. The bridge leads to Loschwitz, a neighbourhood in a picturesque location amidst hills, which has many attractive villas and small palaces built in the 19th century.

🏛 Schloss Pillnitz

Tel (0351) 261 30. **Kunstgewerbemuseum Bergpalais** ☐ *May–Oct: 10am–6pm Tue–Sun.* **Wasserpalais** ☐ *May–Oct: 10am–6pm Wed–Mon.*
This charming summer residence, on the banks of the Elbe, was built in 1720–23 by Augustus the Strong and designed by Matthäus Daniel Pöppelmann. There are two parallel palaces: the Bergpalais (mountain palace) and the Wasserpalais (water palace); the latter can be reached by stairs directly from the river jetty. Between 1818 and 1826 the two palaces were joined by a third one, the Neues Palais. Today the Bergpalais houses a fascinating museum of decorative art. The main attraction, however, is the park, laid out in English and Chinese styles, with an orangery and pavilions.

🏛 Karl-May-Museum

Radebeul. Karl-May-Str. 5. *Tel (0351) 837 30 10.* ☐ *Mar–Oct: 9am–6pm; Nov–Feb: 10am–4pm Tue–Sun.* ● *1 Jan, 24, 25, 31 Dec.*
Radebeul, 5 km (3 miles) northwest of Dresden, is much visited by the fans of Winnetou, a fictional Indian chief, and his friend Old Shatterhand. A museum is devoted to the life and work of the author, Karl May, who lived and died in Radebeul. It also displays May's large collection of Native American costumes and other items.

The suspension bridge across the Elbe River, nicknamed "Blaues Wunder"

For hotels and restaurants in this region see pp494–5 and pp532–4

The Zwinger

The most famous building in Dresden is the Zwinger, a beautiful Baroque structure. Its name means 'intermural', and it was built in the space between the former town fortifications. Commissioned by Augustus the Strong, it was constructed in 1709–32 to a design by Matthäus Daniel Pöppelmann, with the help of the sculptor Balthasar Permoser. Its spacious courtyard, once used to stage tournaments, festivals and firework displays, is completely surrounded by galleries into which are set pavilions and gates. Today it houses several art collections.

Mathematisch-Physikalischer Salon
A valuable collection of scientific instruments, clocks, sextants and globes, including a 13th-century Arabic globe of the sky. The salon is closed until early 2013.

Kronentor
This gate owes its name (crown gate) to the crown positioned on top of its dome.

Main entrance

Allegorical figures
crown the balustrades.

★ Porzellansammlung
The porcelain collection holds Japanese and Chinese pieces but its centrepiece is a collection of Meissen porcelain, including parts of the stunning Swan Service made for Heinrich Brühl, to a design by Joachim Kaendler.

Glockenspielpavillon
Once known as Stadtpavillon (town pavilion), the name of this building was changed to carillon pavilion when it acquired a carillon with Meissen porcelain bells, in 1924–36.

Wallpavillon
A stunning marriage of archi-tecture and sculp-ture, this Baroque masterpiece is crowned by a statue of Hercules, symbol-izing the Elector, Augustus the Strong.

VISITORS' CHECKLIST

Sophienstraße/Ostra-Allee/Theat-erplatz. **Porzellansammlung Tel** (0351) 491 42000. ☐ 10am–6pm Tue–Sun. **Mathematisch-Physikalischer Salon Tel** 491 42000. ● for renovation until 2013. **Rüstkammer Tel** 491 42000. ☐ 10am–6pm Tue–Sun. 🖥 **www**.skd.museum

★ Nymphenbad
This fountain features tritons and nymphs, sculptures, and grottoes, which were popular in the Baroque era.

Courtyard

Galerie Alte Meister
This gallery of old masters occupies the wing which was added by Gottfried Semper (see pp176–7).

★ Rüstkammer
Exhibited in the armoury are magnificent arms, with the best examples dating from the 16th century, including a suit of armour made for Erik XIV by Eliseus Libaerts in 1562–4.

STAR FEATURES

★ Nymphenbad

★ Porzellansammlung

★ Rüstkammer

Gemäldegalerie Alte Meister

The Dresden gallery of old masters contains what is considered to be one of Europe's finest art collections. Its core consists of the canvases collected by the Wettin family from the 16th century, but the majority of exhibits were purchased at the order of King Augustus II the Strong and his son Augustus III. It was during that time that the gallery was moved to its own premises – first to the Johanneum and later to its present home in the Zwinger, built by Gottfried Semper in 1847–55.

2nd floor

1st floor

Feast of Love (c.1717)
The so-called fête galante is one of many splendid paintings by Antoine Watteau, depicting a flirtatious group in a park.

Ground floor

Madonna and Infant Triptych (1437)
This superb small triptych depicting The Virgin Mary with the Holy Infant, St Catherine and the Archangel St Michael, is one of very few works signed by its creator, Jan van Eyck.

Girl Reading a Letter
(c.1659) This exquisite painting, of a lone woman by the window reading a letter, is among the finest works by Jan Vermeer van Delft.

Main entrance

★ **Self-Portrait with Saskia**
(c.1635) This magnificent painting depicting Rembrandt with his wife, Saskia, is considered by some to be a representation of the Prodigal Son of the Bible.

GALLERY GUIDE

The ground floor has works by Canaletto; the 1st floor has German paintings and 15th to 18th-century European works, and the 2nd floor has 18th-century and Spanish pastels, paintings and miniatures.

Portrait of a Man (c.1633)
This highly expressive portrait, by Diego Rodríguez de Silva y Velázquez, remained unfinished, yet it still captivates with its powerful imagery.

VISITORS' CHECKLIST

Theaterplatz 1. **Tel** (0351) 491 42000. ☐ 10am–6pm Tue–Sun.
🚻🅿🖼📷 www.skd.museum

Tribute Money (c.1516)
Titian depicts the theme of this popular New Testament parable in an unusual way, zooming in on the figures of Christ and a Pharisee who shows him a coin.

Dresden landscapes and portraits

Miniatures

Sleeping Venus (c.1508–10)
This famous nude was probably painted by Giorgione, but when he died of the plague in 1510, his friend, Titian, completed the work.

KEY

- 15th–17th-century Italian painting
- 15th–16th-century German painting
- Canaletto and scenes of Dresden
- 17th-century Dutch and Flemish painting
- 17th-century French painting
- Spanish painting
- 18th-century Italian and French painting
- German, Czech, Austrian, English and Swiss painting
- Non-exhibition space

Tapestry room

Underground vaults

★ **Sistine Madonna** (1512/13)
This enchanting picture of the Madonna and Child by Raphael owes its name to St Sixtus's church in Piacenza, for which Pope Julius II had commissioned it.

STAR EXHIBITS

★ Self-Portrait with Saskia

★ Sistine Madonna

Market square with Renaissance Rathaus (town hall) in Pirna

Pirna ⑫

Road map F4. 38,000.
Am Markt 7 (03501-55 64 47).
www.pirna.de
Stadtfest (Jun).

In the old town, on the banks of the River Elbe, Pirna has preserved an amazingly regular, chequerboard pattern of streets. Time has been kind to the many historic buildings in this town. Its greatest attraction is the **Marienkirche**, a late-Gothic hall-church with fanciful vaulting designed by Peter Ulrich von Pirna and painted by Jobst Dorndorff, in 1545–6. Inside, an original late-Gothic font and a Renaissance main altar can be seen.

Other interesting buildings are the mid-16th century **Rathaus** (town hall) with its Gothic portals, the beautiful houses in the town square and the ex-Dominican, Gothic church of St Heinrich. **Schloss Sonnenstein**, extended during the 17th and 18th centuries, towers above the old town.

Environs

10 km (6 miles) southwest of Pirna is the picturesque **Schloss Weesenstein**, much altered from its Gothic origins until the 19th century. It houses a small museum with an interesting collection of wallpapers.

⚜ **Museum Schloss Weesenstein**
Müglitztal, Am Schlossberg 1. **Tel** (035027) 6260. Apr–Oct: 9am–6pm; Nov–Mar: 10am–5pm Tue–Sun.

Sächsische Schweiz ⑬

Saxon Switzerland, the wonderfully wild region around the gorge cut into the Lusatian mountains by the River Elbe, features stunningly bizarre rock formations and several formidable castles. The best way to explore the area is on foot as many places are inaccessible to cars. Alternatively you can admire the spectacular scenery from a boat, on the Elbe.

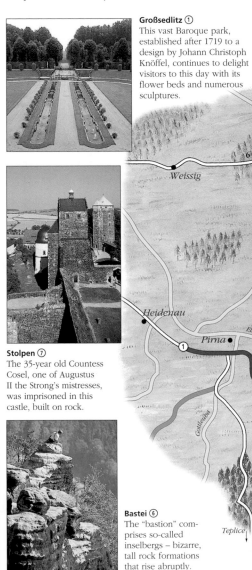

Großsedlitz ①
This vast Baroque park, established after 1719 to a design by Johann Christoph Knöffel, continues to delight visitors to this day with its flower beds and numerous sculptures.

Stolpen ⑦
The 35-year old Countess Cosel, one of Augustus II the Strong's mistresses, was imprisoned in this castle, built on rock.

Bastei ⑥
The "bastion" comprises so-called inselbergs – bizarre, tall rock formations that rise abruptly. Connected by footbridges, they offer splendid views.

Festung Königstein ②
This powerful fortress was built in the second half of the 16th century on the site of a medieval castle, and altered in subsequent centuries. Spectacular views have made it a popular tourist destination.

Lilienstein ③
This tall rock, which has to be climbed on foot, rewards the visitor with splendid views of Festung Königstein.

Burg Hohnstein ④
The castle, which holds within its walls a medieval building, is now a museum and one of Germany's largest youth hostels.

Bad Schandau ⑤
A small spa that is popular as a base for walking tours into the surrounding mountains. A small railway, the Kirnitzschtalbahn, takes visitors to a scenic waterfall, the Lichtenhainer Wasserfall.

Bautzen

Bischofswerda
6

Gr. Röder

⑦

rröhrsdorf

Polenz

LBSANDSTEIN-
GEBIRGE

⑤

⑥

③

Elba

2

②

④

Schmilka

ACHSISCHE SCHWEIZ

KEY
▬	Tour route
═	Road
▬	Scenic route
☀	Viewpoint

0 km   4
0 miles   4

TIPS FOR VISITORS

Length of tour: 41 km (25 miles).
Stopping places: inns and restaurants in every town.
Suggestions: walk from the railway at the Lichtenhainer Waterfalls to the Kuhstall (cow stable) and Barbarine needle rocks.

For additional map symbols *see back flap*

Gothic altar from 1513 in St Annen church, in Kamenz

Kamenz ⑭

Road map F4. 👤 16,800. 🚉 🚌 🛈
Pulsnitzer Str. 11 (03578 379 205). 🎭
Hutbergfest (May). **www**.kamenz.de

The best time for a visit to Kamenz is the end of May or June, when the rhododendrons that cover the Hutberg (294 m/965 ft high) are in flower. The poet, Gotthold Ephraim Lessing, was born in Kamenz in 1729. Although his house no longer exists, the **Lessingmuseum**, founded in 1929, is devoted to his work.

A great fire destroyed much of the town in 1842, but it spared the late-Gothic **St Marien** church, a four-nave 15th-century structure with Gothic altars and other interesting features. Equally noteworthy for their furnishings are the Gothic ex-Franciscan **St Annen** church and the unusual hall-church **Katechismuskirche**. Originally part of the town's fortification system, it has a row of loopholes on its upper storey. The old cemetery and the Gothic funereal church **Begräbniskirche St Just** are also worth a visit. As is the new **Museum der Westlausitz**, a museum of the local region.

🏛 **Lessingmuseum**
Lessingplatz 1–3. **Tel** (03578) 380 50. ⏲ 9am–5pm Tue–Fri, 1pm–5pm Sat & Sun.

Bautzen ⑮

Road map F4. 👤 44,000. 🚉 🚌
🛈 *Hauptmarkt 1 (03591-4 20 16).* 🎭
Vogelhochzeit (Jan); Lausitzer Fischwochen (Oct). **www**.bautzen.de

This town is scenically situated on a high rock overhanging the Spree River valley. Known mainly for its top-security jail for political prisoners during the GDR era, today it enchants visitors with its beautifully reconstructed old town. Many signs are bilingual, German and Sorbian, reflecting the fact that Bautzen is the cultural capital of the Sorbs. The winding streets with their original houses, the city walls, the curiously crooked **Reichenturm** tower and the Baroque town hall in the town square form a very attractive complex. It is also worth climbing the

Impressive Baroque entrance to the Domstift in Bautzen

15th-century **Alte Wasserkunst**, a tower that pumped Spree water up to the town. It is the symbol of Bautzen and offers splendid views.

The cathedral **Dom St Peter** is now used jointly by Catholics (choir) and Protestants (nave). The late-Gothic **Schloss Ortenburg** houses the **Sorbisches Museum**, devoted to Sorbian history and culture.

🏛 **Sorbisches Museum**
Ortenburg 3. **Tel** (03591) 42 403. ⏲ Apr–Oct: 10am–5pm Tue–Sun; Nov–Mar: 10am–4pm Tue–Sun.

Doorway of the Neo-Renaissance palace in Bad Muskau

Bad Muskau ⑯

Road map F4. 👤 4,170. 🚌
🛈 *Schlossstr. 6 (035771-504 92).*
www.badmuskau.de

Bad Muskau, a small town and spa, boasts one of Saxony's most beautiful parks, which has been included in the UNESCO Cultural Heritage list. It was created in 1815–45 by the writer Prince Hermann von Pückler-Muskau. The Neo-Renaissance palace at its centre was destroyed in World War II and reopened after reconstruction in 2008. The English-style landscaped park surrounding it, a nature reserve since 1952, is well worth visiting. Its main part, on the northern shores of the Lusatian Neisse River, is in Poland. A joint Polish-German programme has opened the entire area to visitors from both sides of the border.

Baroque Neptune fountain in Untermarkt, in Görlitz

Görlitz ⓱

Road map F4. 🏙 66,000. 🚇 🚌
ℹ️ *Obermarkt 32 (03581-475 70).*
🎭 *Kultursommer (May– Sep);
Sommertheater (Jul); Straßentheater
festival (Aug)* **www** goerlitz.de

This border town, whose eastern part, Zgorzelec, has belonged to Poland since 1945, boasts a long history. Its oldest records date back to 1071. Founded in 1210–20, the town flourished in the 15th and 16th centuries. In 1990 an extensive restoration plan was begun, and now visitors can see its historic buildings in their former glory.

The charming houses in **Obermarkt** (upper market), the Renaissance portals and decorations on houses in Brüderstraße and the fascinating **Untermarkt** (lower market), with its vast town hall complex, enchant everyone. The older wing of the town hall, the work of Wendel Roskopf, has an amazing external staircase with Renaissance ornaments, and winds around the statue of Justice.

One of the most remarkable churches is the imposing five-nave, 15th-century **Hauptstadtpfarrkirche St Peter und St Paul** whose Baroque furnishings are among the finest in Saxony. Also noteworthy is the **Oberkirche**, with an original Gothic main altar and 15th-century wall paintings in the side nave. One of Görlitz's curiosities is the **Heiliges Grab** (Holy tomb), built in 1481–1504, a group of three chapels that are replicas of churches in Jerusalem. Görlitz still has remains of its medieval town fortifications with original towers and gates, including the **Kaisertrutz**, a 15th-century barbican, extended in the 19th century and now home to the town's art collection.

Environs
The small town of **Ostritz**, 16 km (10 miles) to the south, has a charming original Cistercian abbey, St Marienthal (1230). Its red-and-white buildings are to this day inhabited by nuns, who show visitors around and serve food and home-brewed beer.

Zittau ⓲

Road map F4. 🏙 28,000. 🚇 🚌
ℹ️ *Markt 1 (03583-75 22 00).*
🎭 *Klosterfest (Ascension) (May); Fest am Dreiländereck (Jun); Stadtfest (Jul).*
www.zittau.eu

Zittau is an excellent starting point for excursions into the Zittau Mountains, a paradise for rock-climbers, walkers and nature lovers. The town itself is splendidly preserved, with many historic buildings, such as the beautiful, Baroque **Noacksches Haus** (Markt 2). The Neo-Renaissance **Rathaus** (town hall) was built in 1840–45, to a design by Carl Augustus Schramm. The **Johanniskirche**, by Karl Friedrich Schinkel, combines elements of Neo-Classical and Neo-Gothic styles and is an excellent example of Historicist architecture.

Environs
The charming spa town of **Oybin**, 9 km (6 miles) south of Zittau, can be reached by narrow-gauge railway. Its attractions include the hilltop ruins of a Gothic abbey, immortalized by Caspar David Friedrich. It is worth timing your visit for a Saturday evening in summer, when you can witness the procession of torch-bearing monks or listen to a concert.

Fountain with a statue of Roland, the French knight, in Zittau

THE SORBS

The Sorbs, also known as the Lusatians or Wends, are an indigenous Slav minority who live in the eastern regions of Saxony and Brandenburg. Their ancestors, the Lusatian Slavs, were conquered by Germans in the 10th century. Although condemned to extermination by the National Socialists, today they enjoy complete cultural autonomy. The revival of their language and traditions is apparent in the bilingual signs in towns.

THURINGIA

Thuringia is a beautiful state, with much to entice the visitor. The Thuringian Forest, in the south, is a highland area densely covered with spruce, beech and oak forests, inviting visitors to ramble along its enchanted trails, while the area's medieval abbeys, castles and charming small towns are popular destinations with those who are interested in art and history.

The Kingdom of Thuring, as it was known in the 5th century, was conquered by the Franks in the following century. The demise of the Thuringian land-graves, who had ruled here for hundreds of years, resulted in the outbreak of the Thuringian War of Secession. It ended in 1264, with most of Thuringia falling into the hands of the Wettin dynasty.

Split into several smaller principalities, the region lost its political might, but driven by the ambitions of many of its rulers, magnificent castles, churches and abbeys were built everywhere. Thanks to enlightened royal sponsors many towns became important cultural centres, such as 18th-century Weimar, whose residents at one time included Johann Wolfgang von Goethe, Friedrich Schiller, Johann Gottfried Herder and Christoph Martin Wieland.

After World War II, Thuringia was initially occupied by the US Army, but it soon passed into the Soviet sphere of influence, and in 1949 it became part of the GDR. In 1952 Thuringia lost its status as a federal state, but this was later restored in the reunited Federal Republic of Germany, in 1990.

The majority of tourist attractions can be found in the southern part of the state. The Thuringian Forest has many popular health resorts and wintersport centres, such as Oberhof. This highland area, cut with deep river gullies, is littered with medieval castles built on steep crags. Many of these are now no more than picturesque ruins, but others, such as the Wartburg, have been completely restored to their former glory, and today delight visitors with their magnificent interiors.

Schloss Belvedere, the royal summer residence in Weimar

◁ **A path through the beautiful Thüringer Wald (Thuringian Forest)**

Exploring Thuringia

A visit to Thuringia is most enjoyable in late
summer, when the magnificent forests of the Thuringian
Mountains are set ablaze with all the hues of red
and yellow as the leaves turn colour, or in spring
when verdant green cloaks the trees. Allow at
least one day to explore Erfurt, the state's
capital city, with a further two days in
Weimar. Eisenach, with its
magnificent Wartburg castle,
is also a must.

Street vendor selling hand-
painted Easter eggs in Erfurt

SIGHTS AT A GLANCE

Altenburg ⑭
*Eisenach-Wartburg
pp186–7* ❶
Erfurt pp192–3 ❽
Gera ⑬
Gotha ❻
Heiligenstadt ❷
Jena ❿
Kyffhäuser Mountains ❺
Mühlhausen ❸
Rudolstadt ⑪
Saalfeld ⑫
Sondershausen ❹
Weimar pp194–5 ❾

Walks

Thüringer Wald
(Thuringian Forest) ❼

4

243 Nordhausen

Eichsfeld Bleicherode

Göttingen

A38 Leinefelde

❷ ⊞ 🏠
HEILIGENSTADT

⊞ 🏚
SONDERSHAUSEN ❹

Hainle

247

249

Greus

Hainich

249 ❸ ⊞ 🏠 MÜHLHAUSEN

Bad
Tennstedt

Bad
Langensalza *Unstrut*

T H Ü

7 🏛 🏚 🏠
EISENACH
❶

84

247

Bad Hersfeld

A4

Wutha-Farnroda

❻ GOTHA
🏛 🏚

7

Drei Gleiche

88 Friedrichroda

Werra *THÜRINGER* Arns

Bad Liebenstein

❼ 📽 *WA*

Schmalkalden Oberhof

Ilmena

19 Zella-Mehlis

Meiningen A71 Suhl

19

89

4

Hildburghausen

Schweinfurt *Werra*

Petersburg fortress in Erfurt

For additional map symbols *see back flap*

SEE ALSO

- *Where to Stay* pp496–7
- *Where to Eat* pp534–6

The fields near Meiningen, in the Thuringian Forest

GETTING AROUND

Erfurt has an airport. The A4 motorway running through Thuringia links Gera with Jena, Weimar, Erfurt, Gotha and Eisenach. Other towns can be reached by local roads, which are clearly sign-posted. When touring the Thuringian Forest it is well worth following one of the marked tourist routes, such as Klassikerstraße (the route of the classics) or Porzellanstraße (porcelain street).

0 km   15

0 miles   15

KEY

▬▬	Motorway
▬	Major road
▭▭	Minor road
▬╌	Main railway
──	Minor railway
▬	Regional border

The Renaissance town hall in Gotha

Eisenach – Wartburg ❶

The mighty fortress towering above the town is the legendary castle which was probably founded by Ludwig the Jumper, in the late 11th century. Reputedly, it was the setting for the singing contest immortalized by Wagner in his opera *Tannhäuser*. Between 1211 and 1228 the castle was the home of Saint Elizabeth of Thuringia, and from 4 May 1521 until March 1522 Martin Luther found refuge here while he translated the New Testament into German. Major reconstruction in the 19th century gave the castle its old-time romantic character.

Festsaal
The impressive and ornate Festival Hall extends over the entire length and width of the Romanesque Palas. Today, it is the venue for a number of events.

★ Elisabethkemenate
The mosaics adorning the walls of St Elizabeth's rooms illustrate the story of the saint's life. They were designed by August Oetken and placed in 1902–06.

Landgrafenzimmer
In 1854 the landgraves' chambers in the oldest part of the castle, the Palas, were decorated with paintings depicting the castle's history, by Moritz von Schwind.

Bergfried
This vast, square tower crowned with a cross is the work of 19th-century restorers.

STAR FEATURES

★ Elisabethkemenate

★ Lutherstube

For hotels and restaurants in this region see pp496–7 and pp534–6

Vogtei
In 1872 this building acquired an original oriel window (c.1475), brought here from the Harsdörffersches House in Nuremberg.

★ Lutherstube
The room where Martin Luther lived and worked for ten months is very plainly furnished and has simple wood-panelling on the walls.

Entrance gate

Neue Kemenate
The so-called "new chambers" were added during the mid-19th century. Today they house an art collection with beautiful sculptures from Tilman Riemenschneider's workshop.

VISITORS' CHECKLIST

Road map C/D4. 🏠 44,000. 🚉
🚌 🛈 Markt 9 (03691-79 23-0).
🎭 Thüringer Bachwochen (Mar–Apr). **Wartburg Tel** (03691) 25 00; www.wartburg-eisenach.de
📷 guided tours Apr–Oct: 8.30am–5pm daily (gate closes 8pm); Nov–Mar: 9am–3:30pm daily (gate closes 5pm).

Exploring Eisenach
The town, at the foot of the castle hill, was founded in the middle of the 12th century and played an important political role in medieval times. There are interesting remains of fortifications, dating from the late 12th century, which include a Romanesque gate, the Nikolaitor. The Nikolaikirche nearby, also Romanesque in style, once belonged to the Benedictine Sisters. In the market square is a 16th-century town hall, and in Lutherplatz stands the house where Martin Luther once lived; it is now a small museum of his work.

🏛 Predigerkirche
Predigerplatz 4.
Tel (03691) 78 46 78.
📷 11am–5pm Tue–Sun. ♿
This church, built in honour of Elisabeth von Thüringen shortly after she had been canonized, is part of the Thuringer Museum and has been used for changing exhibitions since 1899. It also houses a permanent exhibition, "Medieval Art in Thuringia".

🏛 Automobile Welt Eisenach
F. Naumanstr. 10. **Tel** (03691) 77 21 2
📷 11am–5pm Tue–Sun.
This car museum celebrates the local car manufacturing industry in Eisenach. Its collection includes old BMWs and Wartburgs.

🏛 Bachhaus
Frauenplan 21. **Tel** (03691) 7 93 40.
📷 10am–6pm daily. ♿
www.bachhaus.de
Johann Sebastian Bach, the famous composer, was born in Eisenach in 1685. His birthplace is now demolished, but this small museum nearby is devoted to his life and work.

The Bachhaus and museum, surrounded by a garden

Heiligenstadt ❷

Road map C4. 🏛 *17,500.* 🚉 🚌
ℹ *Wilhelmstr. 50 (03606-67 71 41).*
www.heilbad-heiligenstadt.de

This pleasant spa and health resort, well placed for visiting the gardens of Eichsfeld, is worth an extended stop. Heiligenstadt is the birthplace of Tilman Riemenschneider, an outstanding sculptor of the Gothic era; it is also the place where the poet and writer Heinrich Heine was baptized in 1825, at the age of 28.

Heiligenstadt has several churches worth visiting, including the Gothic **Pfarrkirche St Marien** with its original wall paintings dating from around 1500. Not far from the church stands the **Friedhofskapelle St Annen**, an octagonal Gothic cemetery chapel. The town's most interesting church, however, is the **Stiftskirche St Martin**, dating back to the 14th–15th centuries. It has a well-preserved Romanesque crypt and an amusing Gothic pulpit, made in the shape of a book-holding chorister.

Mühlhausen ❸

Road map D4. 🏛 *38,000.* 🚉 🚌
ℹ *Ratsstr. 20 (03601-40 47 70).*
🎭 *Mühlhauser Stadtkirmes (Aug).*
www.muehlhausen.de

Mühlhausen is one of Thuringia's older towns, with its earliest records dating back to AD 967. In medieval times it enjoyed the status of an imperial free town, which could explain why it became the centre of political activities during the 1525 Peasants'

Part of the well-preserved town walls surrounding Mühlhausen

War, led by Thomas Müntzer, a local clergyman. In 1975, on the 450th anniversary of the revolt, the town underwent restoration, and it delights visitors to this day with its beautifully preserved old town surrounded by **city walls**, including gates and towers, which have survived almost intact.

Mühlhausen's streets are lined with charming timber-frame houses. It is also worth stepping into one of the six Gothic churches in this area. The **Pfarrkirche Divi Blasii**, built for the Teutonic Knights, has 14th-century stained-glass windows in the presbytery. The ex-Franciscan **Barfüßerklosterkirche** (on the Kornmarkt) houses a museum devoted to the Peasants' War. The huge five-nave 14th-century **Marienkirche**, a hall-church, is one of Thuringia's largest sacral buildings. It has a magnificent main portal and late-Gothic altars. Another interesting historic structure is the **Rathaus** (town hall), in a narrow street between the old and the new town. This vast complex was enlarged several times, from medieval times until the 18th century.

Sondershausen ❹

Road map D4. 🏛 *23,000.* 🚌
ℹ *Markt 9 (03632-78 81 11).*
🎭 *Residenzfest (Jun),
Schlossfestspiele (Jul).*
www.sondershausen.de

Sondershausen was the capital city of the small principality of Schwarzburg-Sondershausen. The town's main attraction is the **Schloss** (ducal palace), a sprawling building built in stages from the 16th to the 19th century. The palace features some interesting original interiors. Particularly noteworthy are the **Am Wendelstein** rooms, decorated with 17th-century stucco ornaments, as well as the Neo-Classical Liebhabertheater (connoisseurs' theatre, c.1835) and the Baroque Riesensaal (giants' hall), a ballroom with 16 enormous statues of ancient gods. When strolling around the palace gardens it is worth looking at the **Karussell**, an octagonal building dating from 1700.

The most interesting Neo-Classical building complex in town can be found around **Marktplatz** (market square).

Environs

In the **Hainleite** hills, 4.5 km (3 miles) south of Sondershausen, stands the Jagdschloss Zum Possen, once an 18th-century hunting lodge, now an inn. The timber-frame observation tower nearby, dating from 1781, affords beautiful views of the district. **Nordhausen**, situated 20 km (12 miles) to the north, is worth visiting for its attractive timber-frame houses and its 14th-century cathedral, Dom zum Heiligen Kreuz, with a Romanesque crypt.

The extensive façade of the ducal palace in Sondershausen

For hotels and restaurants in this region see pp496–7 and pp534–6

Monument to Wilhelm I in the Kyffhäuser Mountains

Kyffhäuser Mountains ❺

Road map D4. ▮ *Bad Franken-hausen, Anger 14 (034671•71 717).*

This small mountain range, which runs along the border between Thuringia and Saxony-Anhalt, is not only picturesque but also shrouded in legends and associated with important historic events.

According to one legend, the Emperor Frederick I Barbarossa found his final resting place in one of the caves. Allegedly, he did not drown during the Crusades, as historic records would have us believe, but is waiting here, in the company of six knights. As soon as his beard is long enough to wind three times around the table, it is said, he will return to save Germany from oppression. On the site of the former imperial palace now stands a giant monument with a figure of Barbarossa and an equestrian statue of Emperor Wilhelm I – the work of Bruno Schmitz, erected in 1891–6.

A small health resort, **Bad Frankenhausen**, nestles at the foot of the mountains. It has a number of Gothic churches and a Renaissance palace, now home to a small museum. Nearby, on the **Schlachtberg** (slaughter mountain), the decisive battle in the Peasants' War took place. Today there is a circular pavilion with a vast panoramic picture of the battle, painted in 1971–5.

Gotha ❻

Road map D4. ▮ *48,000.* ▮ ▮
▮ *Hauptmarkt 33 (03621-50 78 57 12).* ▮ *Gothardusfest (May).*
www.gotha.de

From 1640 the old commercial town of Gotha was the capital of Saxe-Gotha and later of Saxe-Coburg-Gotha Duchy, the dynasty from which Prince Albert, Queen Victoria's husband, descended. The vast ducal palace, **Schloss Friedenstein**, built in 1643–55, towers above the city. This mighty rectangular structure was the first Baroque building in Thuringia. Particularly noteworthy are the ballroom, the palace chapel with the ducal sarcophagi in the crypt and the court theatre, built in 1683. The palace museum houses an art collection including works by famous artists such as Peter Paul Rubens, Anton van Dyck, Frans Hals and Jan van Goyen. The palace garden is also worth a visit. To the south of the palace stands a Neo-Renaissance building, which was purpose-built for the ducal art collection. Now it houses the **Museum der Natur**, a natural history museum. The Renaissance town hall (1567–77) in the old town is surrounded by a number of interesting houses.

Gotha played an important role in the German workers' movement: the Socialist Workers' Party (today's SPD), was founded here in 1875. The conference hall has been reconstructed and houses the **Gedenkstätte der Deutschen Arbeiterbewegung** (memorial to the German workers' movement).

⛫ **Schloss Friedenstein**
Tel 03621 8234 51. ▯ May–Oct: 10am–5pm Tue–Sun; Nov–Apr: 10am–4pm Tue–Sun.

🏛 **Gedenkstätte der Deutschen Arbeiterbewegung**
Am Tivoli 3. **Tel** (03621) 70 41 27. ▯ only by prior arrangement.

Doorway of the Renaissance town hall on the Hauptmarkt, in Gotha

Thüringer Wald (Thuringian Forest) ❼

Narrow, winding roads lead through the mountains, which are densely covered with spruce forests. Small towns, charming spas and wintersports resorts nestle in the valleys, while the ruins of once fearsome castles occupy the hilltops. This is prime walking country, and Gotha is the best starting point for a walking holiday. For a longer hike, stop in Ilmenau, and from there follow the upward trail marked G, to a hunters' shelter and a foresters' lodge.

Friedrichroda ①
The Neo-Gothic Reinhardsbrunn castle in Friedrichroda was the place where Queen Victoria met her fiancé, Prince Albert von Sachsen-Coburg-Gotha, in 1840.

Drei Gleichen ⑨
This name, meaning "three of the same", refers to three castles – Mühlburg and Burg Gleichen have stood in ruins for centuries, but the third castle, Wachsenburg, has survived and now serves as a hotel.

Arnstadt ⑧
This picturesque town, once the home of Johann Sebastian Bach, features a town hall in the Mannerist style, dating from the late 16th century. Other places of interest are an early-Gothic church and a Baroque palace which is now home to a wax museum.

TIPS FOR WALKERS

Length: 150 km (90 miles).
Stopping places: inns and restaurants in every town.
Suggestions: walk along the Goethe-Wanderweg trail, from Ilmenau. Train journey by Thüringerwaldbahn, from Gotha via Friedrichroda to Tabarz.

Trusetal ②

The magnificent waterfall in Trusetal, the work of human hands, was built in the mid-19th century. Another site worth visiting is the nearby Marienglashöhle in Friedrichroda, an unusual crystal grotto.

Schmalkalden ③

This charming little town, packed with timber-frame houses, attracts visitors to the Wilhelmsburg, its Renaissance palace, and to Neue Hütte, an interesting old smelting plant dating from 1835.

0 km   75

0 miles   75

Oberhof ④

This is a popular winter-sports resort, with excellent ski-jumps. In the summer it is worth visiting the Rennsteiggarten, the town's botanical gardens with a vast collection of alpine plants.

Suhl ⑤

Famous from the 16th century as a centre of arms manufacture, Suhl's history can today be gleaned in the local Waffen-museum (armaments museum).

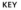

Ilmenau ⑥

This small university town, teeming with life, is the starting point of the so-called Goethe-Wanderweg, a walking trail leading to all the places where the famous poet once stayed.

Paulinzelle ⑦

The 12th-century Romanesque abbey, now in ruins, was once a home for Benedictine monks, but it was later abandoned during the Reformation.

KEY

▬	Suggested route
=	Other road
▬	Scenic route
✵	Viewpoint

Erfurt ❽

The Thuringian capital, Erfurt, is also the oldest town in the region – its earliest historic records date from AD729, and in AD742 a bishopric was founded here. As an important trading post between east and west, the town grew quickly. Erfurt University was founded in 1392; it became a stronghold for radical thought, and Martin Luther was one of its pupils. Until the 17th century, Erfurt was famous for its red dyes extracted from the madder root; in the 18th century the town became a horticultural centre, and to this day it hosts an impressive garden show in one of Germany's largest parks.

Picturesque half-timbered houses, lining the Krämerbrücke

Exploring Erfurt

The town, on the banks of the river Gera, is dominated by two hills. On the higher one, **Petersberg**, stands a huge fortress surrounding a Romanesque church, while the lower **Domberg** has two churches, the **Dom St Marien** and the **St Severi-kirche**. From the Domplatz, at the foot of the hill, a row of narrow streets leads to Fischmarkt. If you cross the river here, you will get to Erfurt's old commercial district and its market square, the Anger.

🔓 Dom St Marien

Domberg. *Tel (0361) 646 12 65.*
◻ *Apr–Oct: 9am–6pm Mon–Sat,*
1–6pm Sun; Nov–Mar: 10am–5pm
Mon–Sat, 1–5pm Sun. 🖼

The wide stairs leading from Domplatz to the main entrance of the cathedral provide a good view over the 14th-century Gothic presbytery, which is supported by a massive vaulted substructure, known as the Kavaten. The main body of the cathedral dates from the 15th century, but its huge towers are the remains of an earlier Romanesque building.

Maria Gloriosa, a huge bell 2.5 m (8 ft) in diameter, hangs in the centre tower. Cast by Gerhard Wou in 1497, it is one of the largest bells in the world. The church interior has well preserved Gothic decorations and rich furnishings. Particularly valuable are the 14th- and 15th-century stained-glass windows, the Gothic stalls (c.1370) and

Rich furnishings in the Gothic interior of Dom St Marien

Wolfram, a Romanesque bronze candelabra, (c.1160), shaped like a man.

🔓 St Severi-Kirche

Domberg. *Tel (0361) 57 69 60.*
◻ *Apr–Oct: 9am–6pm Mon–Sat,*
1–6pm Sun; Nov–Mar: 10am–5pm
Mon–Sat, 1–5pm Sun.

This five-nave Gothic hall-church, next to the cathedral, dates from the late 13th and early 14th century. Inside it has the Gothic sarcophagus of St Severus, from about 1365, a huge font of 1467 and interesting Gothic altars.

▥ Fischmarkt

This small market square, with its Neo-Gothic town hall (1870–74), is surrounded by houses dating from various periods, including the 16th-century Renaissance buildings **Zum Breiten Herd** (No. 13, To the Wide Hearth) and **Zum Roten Ochsen** (No. 7, To the Red Ox). On the streets off the market square are three Gothic churches: Michaeliskirche, opposite the ruins of the late-Gothic university buildings, the twin-nave Allerheiligenkirche (late 13th to early 14th century), and the ex-Dominican Predigerkirche.

▥ Krämerbrücke

The "merchant bridge" which spans the River Gera is one of Erfurt's most interesting structures. The present stone bridge was built around 1325. It is lined by 32 houses with shops, dating mainly from the 17th to 19th centuries, which replaced its 60 original medieval houses. On its eastern viaduct stands Ägidienkirche, a 14th-century Gothic church.

🔓 Augustinerkloster–Augustinerkirche

Augustinerstr. 10. *Tel (0361) 576 60 10.* 🔲 *10am–4pm daily.* 🖼
This early Gothic church was built for Augustinian monks at the end of the 13th century. Particularly noteworthy are its original Gothic stained-glass windows. In the neighbouring monastery, the reconstructed cell where Martin Luther lived as a monk can be admired.

Fischmarkt, surrounded by houses from various periods

VISITORS' CHECKLIST

Road map D4. 200,000.
Flughafenstraße 4 (0361-65
60). Am Bahnhofsplatz.
Bürgermeister-Wagner-
Straße. Benediktsplatz 1
(0361-66400). Krämerbrück-
enfest (Jun), Weinfest (Aug),
Petersbergfest (Sep), Christmas
market (Dec). www.erfurt.de

🏛 Stadtmuseum

Johannesstr. 169. **Tel** (0361) 655 56
51. ◻ 10am–6pm Tue–Sun.
Erfurt's history museum is
housed in a beautiful, late-
Renaissance building called
Zum Stockfisch (To the Dried
Cod), built in 1607.

🏯 Anger

Now pedestrianized, this is a
market square and Erfurt's
main shopping street, lined
with attractive 19th-century
mansions and commercial
premises. There are two
Gothic churches: **Kaufmanns-
kirche** and **Reglerkirche**,
with a huge Gothic altar
dating from around 1470. At
Nos. 37 and 38 there is the
Dacherödensches Haus, a
complex of beautiful Renaissance buildings.

🏛 Angermuseum

Anger 18. **Tel** (0361) 55 45 615.
◻ 10am–6pm Tue–Sun.
Barfüßerkirche Barfüßerstr. 20
Tel (0361) 55 45 615. ◻ Mar–Nov:
10am–6pm Tue–Sun.
The museum, housed in a
Baroque building, has a
collection of decorative and
sacred arts including paintings
by Lucas Cranach the Elder,
and 19th- and 20th century
German works. One of its
rooms is decorated with
Expressionist murals (1923–4)
by Erich Heckel. The
medieval section is in the
presbytery of the **Barfüßerkirche**, a former Franciscan
church that was destroyed
during World War II.

🏛 EGA and Gartenbaumuseum

Cyriaksburg, Gothaer Str. 38. **Tel**
(0361) 223 22 0. ◻ 10am 4pm
daily (to 8pm May–Oct). **Museum
Tel** (0361) 22 39 90. ◻ 10am–6pm
Tue–Sun. Jan & Feb.
On the hill around Erfurt's
ruined castle (c.1480) are the
grounds of the International
Garden Show (*Erfurter
Gartenausstellung*). As well
as exhibition halls, show gardens and a butterfly house,
there is a museum of horticul-
ture and beekeeping.

Environs

Molsdorf, 10 km (6 miles) to
the southeast, has a lovely
16th-century Baroque palace
set in landscaped parkland,
with a museum.

ERFURT CITY CENTRE

Anger ⑦
Angermuseum ⑧
Augustinerkirche ⑤
Dom St. Marien ①
Fischmarkt ③
Krämerbrücke ④
St Severi-Kirche ②
Stadtmuseum ⑥

0 m   300
0 yards   300

Key to Symbols *see back flap*

Gartenbaumuseum
MOLSDORF
Airport
3 km (2 miles)

Hauptbahnhof
250m (275 yards)

Weimar ❾

Had it not been for the enlightened sponsorship of its rulers, Weimar would have become just another residential town in Thuringia. The town flourished, particularly under Duke Carl Augustus and his wife Anna Amalia, when Goethe, Schiller and Herder lived here. Famous 19th- and 20th-century residents included Franz Liszt, Richard Strauss, Friedrich Nietzsche and many distinguished writers and artists associated with the Bauhaus School, which was founded here in 1919. It also gave its name to the Weimar Republic, the democratic German State, lasting from World War I to 1933.

Exploring Weimar

Weimar is relatively small and most of its tourist attractions are near the town centre, on the left bank of the Ilm River. In the north of the centre are the Neues Museum and the Stadtmuseum (municipal museum). Many interesting buildings can be found around Theaterplatz, from where you proceed towards the Markt to visit the ducal palace. In the south of the centre are the former homes of Goethe and Liszt.

🏛 Neues Museum

Weimarplatz 5. **Tel** (03643) 545 400.
⭕ Apr–Oct: 11am–6pm Tue–Sun; Nov–Mar: 11am–4pm Tue–Sun.
This Neo-Renaissance building, once the Landesmuseum (regional museum), was transformed into a gallery in 1999. It displays changing exhibits of modern art, with an emphasis on colour.

🏛 Stadtmuseum

Karl-Liebknecht-Str. 5–9.
Tel (03643) 826 00.
⭕ 11am–5pm Tue–Sun.
This museum is devoted to the history of Weimar, but it also holds an interesting natural history collection. It is housed in a Neo-Classical house, which was built in the late 18th century for the publisher Justin Bertuch.

St Peter und St Paul, also known as the Herderkirche

🎭 Deutsches Nationaltheater

Theaterplatz 2. **Tel** (03643) 75 50.
The present Neo-Classical building, built in 1906–7 to a design by Heilmann & Littmann, is the third theatre to stand on this site. Famous conductors who worked here include Franz Liszt and Richard Strauss, and it was also the venue for the world premiere of Wagner's *Lohengrin*. In 1919 the National Congress sat in the Nationaltheater and passed the new constitution for the Weimar Republic. In front of the theatre is a monument to Goethe (who founded the theatre) and Schiller, by the sculptor Ernst Rietschel (1857).

The Stadtschloss in Burgplatz, with its tall Renaissance tower

🏛 Bauhaus-Museum

Theaterplatz. **Tel** (03643) 545 400.
⭕ 10am–6pm daily. 📷
This museum is devoted to the famous art school, which was founded in Weimar in 1919, moved to Dessau in 1925 (see p154) and later, in 1933, to Berlin (see p88).

🏛 Wittumspalais

Theaterplatz.
Tel (03643) 545 401. ⭕ Apr–Oct: 10am–6pm Wed–Mon; Nov–Mar: 10am–4pm Wed–Mon. 📷
The Dowager Duchess Anna Amalia lived in this Baroque palace, designed by Johann Gottfried Schlegel and built in 1767–9. Visitors can admire fine interiors and mementoes of the Enlightenment figure Christoph-Martin Wieland.

🏛 Schillerhaus

Schillerstr. 12.
Tel (03643) 545 401. ⭕ Apr–Sep: 9am–6pm Tue–Fri & Sun, 9am–7pm Sat; Oct: 9am–6pm Tue–Sun; Nov–Mar: 9am–4pm Tue–Sun. 📷
The museum is in the house where Friedrich Schiller wrote *Wilhelm Tell* (1804) and spent the last years of his life.

🛐 St Peter und St Paul

Herderplatz. **Tel** (03643) 85 15 18.
⭕ Apr–Oct: 10am–6pm Mon–Fri, 10am–noon & 2–4pm Sat; Nov–Mar: 11am–noon & 2–4pm daily.
This late-Gothic hall-church has Baroque furnishings and an original altar painted by the Cranachs. It is also known as the Herderkirche, after the poet who preached here.

🏛 Kirms-Krackow-Haus

Jakobstr. 10. **Tel** (03643) 545 401.
⭕ Apr–Oct: 10am–6pm Tue–Sun.
⚫ Nov–Apr. 📷
This Renaissance house, which was extended in the late 18th century, illustrates how people lived in Goethe's time.

♙ Stadtschloss

Burgplatz 4. **Schlossmuseum**
Tel (03643) 54 59 60. ⭕ Apr–Oct: 10am–6pm Tue–Sun; Nov–Mar: 10am–4pm Tue–Sun. 📷
This vast ducal castle was re-built in the Neo-Classical style for Duke Carl August. It has original interiors and fine paintings from the Weimar Art School, and a gallery devoted to Lucas Cranach.

Picturesque Baroque summer residence known as Schloss Belvedere

VISITORS' CHECKLIST

Road map D4. 🏛 62,000. 🚉
Schopenhauerstr. 🚌 *Washing-
tonstr.* ℹ *Markt 10 (03643-74
50).* **www**.weimar-tourist.de 🌐
*Thüringer Bach-Wochen (Mar),
Spiegelzelt (May/Jun), Kunstfest
(Aug/Sep), Fest an Goethes
Geburtstag 28 Aug), Liszt-Tage
(Oct), Zwiebelmarkt (Oct).*

♠ Herzogin-Anna-Amalia Bibliothek

Platz der Demokratie 4.
***Tel** (03643) 54 52 00.* ⏱ *9:30am–
2:30pm Tue–Sun.*
This former Mannerist palace,
also known as Grünes Schloss
(green castle), became the
duchess' library in 1761–6.
Its oval Rococo interior is
one of the finest of its type
in Europe.

♠ Schloss Belvedere

***Tel** (03643) 545 400.* ⏱ *Apr–Oct:
10am–6pm Tue–Sun.* 🌐
This ducal summer residence,
which was built between
1724 and 1732 in Belvedere
Park, has a fine collection of
decorative art from the Rococo
period and a wonderful park.

🏛 Goethes Wohnhaus and National Museum

Frauenplan 1. ***Tel** (03643) 54 53 00.*
⏱ *Apr–Oct: 9am–6pm, Nov–Mar:
9am–4pm.* ⬤ *Mon.* 🌐
This house was presented to
Goethe by the Duke Carl
Augustus. Here the writer
wrote his most famous work,
Faust. Today the museum
shows items associated with
Goethe and other Enlighten-
ment poets from Weimar.

♣ Goethes Gartenhaus

Park an der Ilm. ⏱ *Apr–Oct:
10am–6pm Wed–Mon; Nov–Mar:
10am–4pm Wed–Mon.* 🌐
Goethe's first home in Weimar,
this small villa is in the pleasant
park alongside the River Ilm
which Goethe helped design.

🎹 Liszt Museum

Marienstr. 17. ***Tel** (03643) 54 54 01.*
⏱ *Apr–Dec: 10am–6pm Tue–Sun.*
⬤ *Jan–Mar.* 🌐
Franz Liszt lived here in
1869–86, while he composed
the *Hungarian Rhapsody.* His
apartment and the room in
which he worked have been
preserved to this day.

Environs

Buchenwald, 8 km (5 miles)
north of Weimar, was the site
of a concentration camp set
up by the Nazis. During the
period 1937 to 1945, over
54,000 people were killed
here. It is now a place of
remembrance, a museum and
a documentation centre.

🏛 Buchenwald

***Tel** (03643) 430 100.*
⏱ *Apr–Oct: 10am–6pm Tue–Sun;
Nov–Mar: 10am–4pm Tue–Sun.*

WEIMAR CITY CENTRE

Bauhaus-Museum ③
Deutsches
    Nationaltheater ②
Goethe-Museum ⑩
Grünes Schloss ⑨
Krims-Krackow-Haus ⑦
St Peter und St Paul ⑥
Schillerhaus ⑤
Stadtschloss ⑧
Stadtmuseum ①
Wittumspalais ④

0 m   300
0 yards   300

Key to Symbols *see back flap*

The modest Gothic town hall on Marktplatz, in Jena

Jena 🔟

Road map D4. 🏛 *100,000*. 🚉 🚌
ℹ️ *Markt 16 (03641-49 80 50).* 🎭
Altstadtfest (Sep). **www**.jena.de

Jena is famous for the world-renowned Carl-Zeiss–Jena Optical Works and its university, founded in 1558. One of the most important schools in Germany, its former tutors included Schiller, Fichte and Hegel. The oldest university building is the **Collegium Jenense**. The main building was built by Theodor Fischer in 1905–8. The complex includes a 120-m (394-ft) cylindrical tower block, completed in 1972 and known as the "phallus Jenensis".

In the town's main square, Marktplatz, stands the late-Gothic **Rathaus** (town hall), dating from the early 15th century. Once every hour, a figure known as the Schnapphans tries to catch a ball, a symbol of the human soul. The Gothic church of **St. Michael** nearby was built in the 15th and the 16th centuries. The **Stadtmusem Alte Göhre** has an interesting collection of regional history. In Unterer Markt the **Romantikerhaus** is worth a visit; formerly the home of Johann Gottlieb Fichte, it now houses a museum devoted to the Romantic period.

Also worth visiting are the fascinating **Optisches Museum** on the history of the Carl Zeiss Works and the **Zeiss-Planetarium**, the world's oldest of its type. In the north is the **Goethe-Gedenkstätte**, a museum devoted to Goethe's work as poet, politician and scientist.

🏛 **Stadtmuseum Göhre**
Markt 7. **Tel** *(03641) 498 261.*
⏰ *10am–5pm Tue–Sun,
3–10pm Thu.*

🏛 **Romantikerhaus**
Unterer Markt 12A. **Tel** *(03641) 49
82 49.* ⏰ *10am–5pm Tue–Sun.*

🏛 **Optisches Museum**
Carl-Zeiss-Platz 12. **Tel** *(03641) 44
31 65.* ⏰ *10am–4:30pm Tue–Fri,
11am–5pm Sat.*

Historical Zeiss-Workshop 🎟️
11:30am Sat.

Environs
Dornburg, 12 km (8 miles) to the northeast, has three palaces: the Altes Schloss, a Gothic castle transformed in the Renaissance; the Renaissanceschloss (1539–47) and the charming Rokoko-schloss (1736–41).

Rudolstadt 1️⃣1️⃣

Road map D4. 🏛 *28,000*. 🚉 🚌
ℹ️ *Marktstr. 57 (03672-48 64 40).*
🎭 *Tanz-und Folk Fest (Jul).*
www.rudolstadt.de

Although Rudolstadt has the Gothic-Renaissance St Andreas church, a fascinating 16th-century town hall and some historic houses, tourists come here mainly to see majestic **Schloss Heidecksburg**, a vast palace perched on a hill. Its present form is mainly the result of reconstruction work carried out in the mid-18th century by Johann Christoph Knöffel and Gottfried Heinrich Krone. Inside are some beauti-

Baroque Schloss Heidecksburg towering over Rudolstadt

fully arranged Rococo state rooms. The museum also has a splendid porcelain collection, a gallery of paintings and the so-called Schiller's Room. From the castle there are fantastic views of the Schwarza valley.

♦ **Schloss Heidecksburg**
Schlossbezirk 1. **Tel** *(03672) 42 900.*
⏰ *Apr–Oct: 10am–6pm Tue–Sun;
Nov–Mar: 10am–5pm Tue–Sun.*

Entrance gate to the 11th-century Schloss Ranis, near Saalfeld

Saalfeld 1️⃣2️⃣

Road map D4. 🏛 *34,000*. 🚉 🚌
ℹ️ *Am Markt 6 (03671-339 50).*
🎭 *Zunftmarkt (Jun).*

Saalfeld flourished in the 14th–16th centuries. From 1680 it was the seat of the Duchy of Sachsen–Saalfeld, and the magnificent Baroque **Schloss**, built between 1676 and 1720, dates from this period. The former palace chapel, now used as a concert hall, is particularly noteworthy. Also worth visiting is the **Johanniskirche**, a late-Gothic hall-church with interesting furnishings, a valuable Gothic Holy Tomb and the sculpted life-size figure of John the Baptist, carved by Hans Gottwalt, a student of Tilman Riemenschneider.

Another interesting building in Saalfeld is the early-Renaissance **Rathaus** (town hall), built in 1529–37. The town also has well preserved medieval town fortifications with gates and towers. In the southern part of the town stands the **Hoher Schwarm**, ruins of a 13th-century Gothic castle. In Garnsdorf, on the outskirts of Saalfeld, are the **Feengrotten**, grottoes created by both natural and human activity. From the mid-16th century until 1846 alum slate was mined in this cave, called "Jeremiasglück" (Jeremiah's good fortune). It was finally closed due to humidity, but the dripping water has created some astonishingly colourful stalagmites and stalactites.

�${}$ **Feengrotten Grottoneum**
Feengrottenweg 2. *Tel (03671) 550 40.* ◯ *Apr–Oct: 9.30am–5pm daily, Nov–Mar: 10:30am–3:30pm daily, Jan: 10:30am–3:30pm daily.*

Environs

From Saalfeld it is worth taking a trip to the Hohenwarte-Talsperre, an artificial lake and paradise for watersports enthusiasts. **Burg Ranis**, a scenic hill-top castle, was probably built in the 11th century for an emperor. Later it became the seat of the Thuringian landgraves, Meißen margraves and the counts of Schwarzburg. Now it houses a museum of the region's natural history.

Gera ⑬

Road map D4. 👥 *121,000.* 🚉 🚌
🛈 *Heinrich Str. 35 (0365-830 44 80).* 🎭 *International Open Air Theatre Festival (Jun), Geraer Höhlerfest (Sep).*

The second largest town in Thuringia, Gera is not impressive at first sight, but it has many attractions, including a picturesque **Rathaus** (town hall) whose oldest, Renaissance part dates from 1573–6. The Geraer Elleblon, on the right-hand side of the entrance, is a unit of measurement equal to 57 cm (22 in). A short distance from the market square, in Nikolaiberg, you will find the **Salvatorkirche**. This Baroque church got its Secession-style interior in 1903, after a fire. The theatre (1900–02) was designed in the same style, by

Picturesque Altenburg Castle complex

Heinrich Seeling. The Küchengarten (kitchen garden) surrounds the ruins of **Schloss Osterstein** of which only the Baroque orangerie remains. It now houses the **Kunstsammlung**, with paintings by Lucas Cranach the Elder, Max Liebermann and others.

Otto Dix, a leading artist of the *Neue Sachlichkeit*, was born in Gera, and his birthplace has been turned into the **Otto-Dix-Haus**.

🌿${}$ **Kunstsammlung**
Küchengartenallee 4.
Tel (0365) 838 42 30.
◯ *11am–6pm Tue–Sun.*

🏛${}$ **Otto-Dix-Haus**
Mohrenplatz 4. *Tel (0365) 832 49 27.* ◯ *11am–6pm Tue–Sun.*

The multi-coloured Renaissance doorway of the Rathaus in Gera

Altenburg ⑭

Road map E4. 👥 *45,000.*
🚉 🚌 🛈 *Moritzstr. 21 (03447-55 18 38).* 🎭 *Prinzenraubfest (Jul); Altstadtfest (Aug).*
www.altenburg-tourismus.de

In Germany, Altenburg is known as "Skatstadt", the town of skat, a traditional and very popular card game. Altenburg also has some fascinating historic remains. The **Schloss** (ducal castle), which towers over the old town, has a 10th-century tower, reconstructed mainly in the Baroque style. Today the castle houses the **Spielkartenmuseum** (museum of playing cards). The late-Gothic castle church is also worth seeing. It has rich Baroque furnishings and an organ which was played by the composer Bach. Next to the castle gardens is the **Lindenau-Museum**, with Augustus von Lindenau's collection of 16th–20th century paintings and sculptures, including works by Simone Martini, Fra Angelico, Auguste Rodin, Ernst Barlach and Max Liebermann. The old town, at the foot of the hill, has a beautiful Renaissance town hall with an enormous octagonal tower. In Brühl Platz is a fountain and the figures of skat players, as well as the Baroque **Seckendorffsche Palais** and the Renaissance chancellery.

🏛${}$ **Schloss und Spielkartenmuseum**
Schloss 2–4. *Tel (03447) 51 27 12.*
◯ *10am–5pm Tue–Sun.*

🏛${}$ **Lindenau-Museum**
Gabelentzstraße 5. *Tel (03447) 895 53.* ◯ *noon–6pm Tue–Fri, 10am–6pm Sat, Sun.*

SOUTHERN GERMANY

Southern Germany at a Glance

The southern regions of Germany, with their wealth of natural beauty, historic sights and folk culture, are particularly attractive to tourists. This part of the country includes two *Länder*: Bavaria, famous for its Alps, beer and the fairytale castle of Ludwig II at Neuschwanstein, and Baden-Württemberg, whose highlights include the Bodensee lake, Heidelberg and taking a trip on the scenic Schwarzwaldbahn railway line between Offenburg and Villingen.

LOCATOR MAP

Würzburg Residenz
Set in a magnificent park on the eastern outskirts of the town, this imposing bishop's palace was built between 1720 and 1744, to a design by Balthasar Neumann. The palace is constructed in a U-shape, with a central pavilion flanked by four two-storey courts.

BADEN-
WURTTEMBERG
(see pp288–327)

Heidelberg Castle *is one of Germany's finest examples of a Gothic-Renaissance fortress. Its origins go back to the 13th century, but new buildings sprang up around the inner courtyard during the 16th century as the castle gained importance as a royal residence.*

Maulbronn Abbey,
founded in the heart of the Stromberg region in 1147, is one of the best-preserved abbeys in Europe. It was established by Cistercian monks with the bequest of a knight named Walter von Lomersheim and provides a graphic account of the austere life led by the monks.

Vierzehnheiligen Church, *built in 1743–72 to a design by Balthasar Neumann, is one of the most famous examples of South German Rococo. The monumental "Altar of Mercy" (Gnadenaltar) includes statues of the Fourteen Saints of the Intercession, to whom the church is dedicated.*

BAVARIA
(see pp238–87)

Nördlingen Town Hall *was built in the 14th century, but its present form dates from the early 17th century. Prisoners used to be held in a space beneath the external stone stairway. By the wooden entrance is a wall carving of a medieval fool bearing a German inscription that translates as "Now there are two of us."*

Neuschwanstein Castle *is one of the three castles built for the Bavarian King Ludwig II (1845–86), involving enormous effort and expenditure. Standing on a high rock, overlooking a lake, the castle was the fulfilment of the King's vision, which was greatly inspired by the operas of Wagner.*

The Frauenkirche *in Munich was completed in 1488 and features two 99-m (325-ft) high towers crowned with copper domes. The church is one of the largest in southern Germany.*

The Baroque in Southern Germany

Because of religious conflicts and the Thirty Years' War (1618–48), the Baroque style did not flourish in Germany until the 18th century. Then it did so most lavishly in the southern, Catholic regions of the country. Here, influenced by Italian architecture, the Baroque reached new heights of flamboyance: the impressive spaciousness of religious buildings provided the setting for dynamic compositions in sculpture, fine stuccowork and vividly coloured *trompe l'oeil* paintings. Southern Germany's major artists of the 18th century included Balthasar Neumann, François Cuvilliés and the Asam brothers.

The main altar in Rohr, *which was created by Egid Quirin Asam in 1723, is in the form of a proscenium (stage) with wings. The sculptural group depicts the Assumption of the Virgin Mary into Heaven.*

Ceiling frescos *were a basic element of the Baroque interior. This example by Johann Baptist Zimmermann in the Wieskirche in Steingaden, presents a glowing vision of the afterlife.*

Galleries with curved balustrades add vitality to the interior.

Figures of saints *clad in flowing, dynamic robes and standing in curving, asymmetrical poses, complement the rich iconography and complex composition of the altars.*

Light plays a vital role in enlivening the interior decoration.

18th-century *monasteries in southern Germany, like this one in Ottobeuren with its imposing stairway, are reminiscent of royal residences.*

Late Baroque church *façades, such as that of the Theatinerkirche in Munich, have a "rippled" design that creates an unusual effect of light and shadow.*

Vaults with fine painting and exquisite stuccowork round off the architectural elements.

The monstrance in Passau *is a fine example of the art of 18th-century goldsmiths, who created these receptacles for the consecrated Host.*

BAROQUE RESIDENCES

South German Baroque was not limited solely to religious architecture. As well as the magnificent monasteries and pilgrimage churches, it was also the inspiration for the impressive residences that were built by abbots as well as by bishops. As in the rest of Europe, these were modelled on the French royal palace in Versailles with its imposing grandeur, striking interiors and breathtaking gardens.

The Baroque vestibule *in the Neues Schloss in Schleißheim (see pp264–5) is decorated with exquisite stuccowork and frescos.*

Schloss Nymphenburg *was a summer residence of the rulers of Bavaria. It has a grand driveway and a park (see pp224–5).*

BAROQUE INTERIORS

Although they may seem over-elaborate, the late Baroque interiors of southern German churches are carefully-planned compositions intended to have a powerful effect. Their magnificent combination of architecture, sculpture and painting, and often organ music, resulted in "Gesamtkunstwerk" – a homogenous work that combines all the arts.

The pulpit and other furnishings are designed to blend harmoniously with the decoration.

Stuccowork *fills every interior space that is not decorated with paintings. Sometimes gilded, sometimes white, it may depict complex scenes or, in some cases, be adorned with ornamental designs.*

Schloss Favorite *is a small palace that forms part of a huge Baroque-style residence in Ludwigsburg (see pp306–7).*

The German Alps

Part of Germany extends into a fairly moderate section of the Alps, Europe's highest mountain range. They stretch from the Bodensee (Lake Constance) to Berchtesgaden. A section of the northern calcareous Alps belonging to the Eastern Alps of Allgäu, Bavaria and Salzburg falls within Germany. The mountains are a holidaymaker's paradise all year round. In the summer mountain walks can be enjoyed, with well-marked trails, as well as climbing, hang-gliding and paragliding; in the winter skiing is possible in superbly equipped resorts.

Alpine Chough

Alpine meadows *are rich pasture lands, providing premium quality hay. They are also home to a rich variety of wildflowers.*

Mountain streams *have, over the years, cut a path through the rocks to create picturesque ravines. One of the most beautiful is this one at Wimbachklamm.*

Mountain peaks with their breath-taking jagged rocks.

Local architecture blends happily into the landscape.

THE ALPINE LAKES

A melting glacier created many lakes in Bavaria. Their clear, unpolluted waters attract all kinds of watersports enthusiasts, while the picturesque surroundings are equally popular with other recreational users.

The Königssee, with its crystal-clear waters, is located high in the Berchtesgaden National Park.

The Watzmann is Germany's second highest peak.

Schwarzeck

Steinplatte

Reit im Winkl

Schlierse

Oberaudorf

The Zugspitze, *at 2,962m (9,700 ft), is the highest peak in all of Germany.*

ALPINE FLORA AND FAUNA

Alpine vegetation varies according to height above sea level. On the lower slopes are mixed deciduous forests. Higher up are Alpine forests, generally coniferous. Above the tree line, dwarf mountain pine grow and higher still are stretches of high-altitude meadows. Beyond this is bare rock. Wild goats are found above the tree line and chamois in the foothills.

The Alpine ibex *lives only in the Italian and Swiss Alps. This wild goat with long, backward-curving horns is a rare sight.*

The mouflon *is a wild sheep with large horns. It is also found in Corsica and Sardinia.*

Alpine rock jasmine *forms carpets of colour on the mountain slopes.*

The Alpine pasqueflower *is a white variant of the species that tolerates the harsh soil and climatic conditions of its Alpine habitat.*

The peacock butterfly *is a common Eurasian species that has adapted successfully to the harsh Alpine environment.*

Alpine thrift, *with its round heads of pink and purple flowers, is a delightful sight.*

Tegernsee

Walchensee is overlooked by one of the largest hydroelectric power stations in Germany.

Garmisch-Partenkirchen is one of the venues of the annual Four Ski Jumps competition.

Kochelsee

Alpspitze

The Zugspitze is the highest peak in Germany.

MUNICH

The capital of Bavaria, Munich is sometimes called "Germany's secret capital". Lying right at the heart of Europe, the city rapidly overshadowed once powerful neighbours, such as Ingolstadt, Augsburg and Nuremberg, to become southern Germany's main metropolis. With its vibrant cosmopolitan atmosphere, fine buildings, museums and shops, it is one of the country's most popular tourist destinations.

The citizens of Munich have been known for centuries for their love of the arts. The masterpieces that were created here during the Baroque and Rococo periods were equal to Italian and French works.

In the 19th century, the town's development continued along Neo-Classical lines, gaining for it the name of "Athens on Isar". Just how appropriate the name is can be seen when strolling along Ludwigstrasse or Königsplatz or visiting the Glyptothek, which houses Ludwig I's collection of Greek and Roman sculptures.

In the late 19th century the Munich Academy of Fine Arts was amongst Europe's best art schools. Not many cities have as great a choice of world-class theatres, operas and museums as can be found here in Munich.

But it is not only art that gives Munich its unique charm. The country's biggest folk festival, the Oktoberfest, is held each year in Theresienwiese, where visitors to the town can join in the revelries or just sit and watch, ordering a plate of sauerkraut with sausages and washing it down with some of the excellent Bavarian beer.

When planning a shopping trip to Munich visitors can be sure that its shops are equal to those of Paris and Milan, not only in the breadth of their range but also in terms of their prices.

The town is also one of Germany's main centres of high-tech and media industries. Many TV stations and film studios, as well as over 300 book and newspaper publishers, have their main offices in Munich.

The Neo-Gothic Rathaus in Marienplatz, Munich's central square

◁ Interior of the Baroque Asamkirche, built between 1733 and 1746 by the Asam brothers

Exploring Munich

Munich, the capital of Bavaria, is exceptionally rich in interesting museums, churches and historic sights. This urban conurbation of about 1.3 million inhabitants increasingly swallows up the neighbouring areas. Many tourist attractions are located outside the town centre but, thanks to excellent public transport, it is easy to visit them. It is worth taking a trip to Nymphenburg to visit the famous palace and gardens there. Another interesting excursion is a stroll along Leopoldstraße or Theresienwiese, where the huge, annual Oktoberfest is held.

GETTING THERE

Munich is an important railway junction and has its own international airport. It also has motorway connections with all the major towns and cities in Germany.

The distinctive towers of Munich's skyline

STAR SIGHTS

Churches
Asamkirche ⑥
Bürgersaal ①
Dreifaltigkeitskirche ③
Frauenkirche ④
Ludwigskirche ㉒
Michaelskirche ②
Theatinerkirche (St Cajetan) ⑯

Buildings
Altes Rathaus ⑩
Bayerische Staatsbibliothek ㉑
Feldherrnhalle ⑮
Neues Rathaus ⑪
Propyläen ㉙
Residenz (pp216–17) ⑭
Schloss Nymphenburg (pp224–5) ㉛
Villa Stuck ㉟

Museums and Galleries
Alte Pinakothek (pp222–3) ㉕
Archäologische Staatssammlung ⑳

Bayerisches Nationalmuseum ⑱
Deutsches Jagd- und Fischereimuseum ⑤
Deutsches Museum (pp228–9) ㉞
Glyptothek ㉗
Haus der Kunst ⑰
Jüdisches Zentrum Jakobsplatz ⑧
Lenbachhaus ㉚
Museum Brandhorst ㉓
Neue Pinakothek ㉔
Pinakothek der Moderne ㉖
Schack-Galerie ⑲
Staatliche Antiken-sammlungen ㉘
Stadtmuseum ⑦
Völkerkundemuseum ⑫

Other Attractions
Bavaria-Filmstadt ㊱
Englischer Garten ㉝
Hofbräuhaus ⑬
Olympiapark ㉜
Theresienwiese ㊲
Viktualienmarkt ⑨

KEY

▨	Street-by-Street map *pp210–11*
P	Parking
ⓗ	Tourist information
⊠	Post office
🚖	Taxi-rank
✝	Church, cathedral, chapel
Ⓢ	S-Bahn
Ⓤ	U-Bahn

SEE ALSO
• *Where to Stay* pp497–9
• *Where to Eat* pp536–8

LOCATOR MAP

MUNICH

ENGLISCHER GARTEN

GREATER MUNICH

Television Tower in Olympiapark

0 metres 400

0 yards 400

Street-by-Street: Around Marienplatz

In medieval times, Marienplatz was Munich's salt- and corn-market. The origins of Munich itself lie with a handful of monks who built their abbey here, giving the place its name (from the word for 'monks') and its heraldic arms. In 1175 town status was officially bestowed on Munich and in 1180 the town was allocated to the Wittelsbachs, who soon established a residence here. During the Reformation, Munich became a bastion of Catholicism and an important centre of the Counter-Reformation. Its magnificent churches, the Altes Rathaus (old town hall) and the Residenz all bear witness to that era.

Karlstor
Known as the Karl's Gate, the west entrance to the old town was part of the medieval fortifications. It was given its present name in 1791, in honour of Elector Karl Theodore.

Augustinerbräu
The oldest and most celebrated brewery in Munich was founded by Augustinian monks in 1328. It currently occupies two 19th-century houses with picturesque façades.

★ Bürgersaal
Bürgersaal was built in 1709–10 for a Marian congregation (followers of the Virgin Mary), as a place of meeting and worship. It includes an upper and lower church. Rupert Mayer, an opponent of Nazism, is buried in the crypt. He was beatified in 1987 ❶

| 0 metres | 50 |
| 0 yards | 50 |

Michaelskirche
The interior of St Michael's Church is surprisingly large. The massive barrel vaulting over the nave is the second largest after St Peter's Basilica in Rome ❷

STAR SIGHTS

★ Altes Rathaus

★ Bürgersaal

★ Frauenkirche

★ Neues Rathaus

KEY
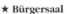 Suggested route

For hotels and restaurants in this region see pp497–9 and pp536–8

Deutsches Jagd- und Fischereimuseum
A huge collection of hunting and fishing exhibits is housed in the Augustinerkirche. The deconsecrated church, which has an ornate Rococo interior, once belonged to the Augustinian order **5**

LOCATOR MAP

★ Frauenkirche
Partially demolished in 1944–45, this imposing church, with its landmark dome-topped towers, has been rebuilt along Gothic lines **4**

★ Neues Rathaus
The ornate façade of the new town hall includes figures from Bavarian legend and history. The bronze statue at the top is the "Münchner Kindl" – a character that features in the city's heraldic arms **10**

St Mary's Column

ISTRASSE

BEN

KAUFINGERSTRASSE

ROSENSTRASSE

DIENETSTR

MARIEN PLATZ

RINDERMARKT

Isartor

Vikthalichmaikt

★ Altes Rathaus
The old town hall was remodelled in its original 15th-century style in the late 19th century. It was rebuilt again after World War II. It now houses a collection of historic toys **9**

Interior of the Bürgersaal, featuring original 19th-century frescoes

Bürgersaal ❶

Neuhauser Straße 14. **Map** 1 F4.
Tel (089) 219 97 20.
Ⓤ or Ⓢ *Karlsplatz.* 🚋 *18, 19, 20, 21, 27.* **Lower church hall**
◯ *8:30am–7pm daily.* **Upper church hall** ◯ *10:30am–noon daily.*

This church belonging to the Marian congregation was designed by Giovanni Antonio Viscardi and built by Johann Georg Ettenhofer in 1709–10. (The Marian congregation, founded in 1563, is linked to the Jesuit order.)

The church was damaged during World War II, but still features original frescos. In the oratory is a figure of the *Guardian Angel* by Ignaz Günther (1770), a fine example of south-Bavarian Rococo. Rupert Mayer, parish priest during World War II and Munich's leading opponent of Nazism, is buried in the crypt.

Michaelskirche ❷
St Michael's Church

Neuhauser Straße 52. **Map** 2 A4.
Ⓤ or Ⓢ *Karlsplatz.* 🚋 *18, 19, 20, 21, 27.* ◯ *8am–7pm Tue–Thu & Sat; 10am–7pm Mon & Fri; 7am–10:15pm daily in Jun.*

The monumental St Michael's Church was built by Duke Wilhelm V for the Jesuits who

arrived here in 1559. The foundation stone was laid in 1585 and initial building work on the first church, which was smaller than the present one, commenced in 1588. However, the tower in front of the presbytery collapsed, demolishing a large part of the building. A transept and new presbytery were added to the remaining part of the building and the church – which was the first Jesuit church in northern Europe – was consecrated in 1597. The

Statue of St Michael at the entrance to Michaelskirche

interior of Michaelskirche is awe-inspiring, with its wide, well-proportioned nave, three pairs of shallow chapels on either side, a short transept and an elongated presbytery. It is not certain who was the architect of the project, but it is believed that Wolfgang Müller created the main body of the church and Wendel Dietrich the Mannerist façade. Later extensions are thought to be the work of a Dutch architect, Friedrich Sustris.

In the church crypt, which is open to the public, are the tombs of many members of the Wittelsbach dynasty, including King Ludwig II.

Dreifaltigkeits-kirche ❸
Holy Trinity Church

Pacellistraße 6. **Map** 2 A3. 🚋 *19.*
◯ *8am–4pm Mon–Wed, Fri–Sun; noon–4pm Thu.*

The Baroque church of the Holy Trinity is one of the few historic buildings in the city that avoided bomb damage in World War II. The church was built as a votive gift from the city's aristocracy and clergy in the hope of averting the dangers threatened by the War of the Spanish Succession (1702–14). The foundation stone was laid in 1711 and the church was consecrated seven years later. The royal architect, Giovanni Antonio Viscardi, assisted by Enrico Zucalli and Georg Ettenhofer, created a building that is one of the most beautiful examples of Italian Baroque in Munich. The church's original features include the dome fresco by Cosmas Damian Asam, *The Adoration of the Trinity*.

Frauenkirche ❹

Frauenplatz 1. **Map** 2 B4. Ⓤ or Ⓢ Karlsplatz & Marienplatz. 🚋 19. **Church** 🕐 7am–7pm Sat–Thu, 7am–6pm Fri. **Tower** 🕐 Apr–Oct. 10am–5pm Mon–Sat (7am–8:30pm Thu). 🌑 Sun & holidays.

The site of the Frauenkirche was originally occupied by a Marian chapel, built in the 13th century. Some two hundred years later, Prince Sigismund ordered a new, much bigger church to be built on the site. Its architects were Jörg von Halspach and Lukas Rottaler. The Frauenkirche was completed in 1488, though the distinctive copper onion-domes were not added to its towers until 1525. The church is one of southern Germany's biggest Gothic structures, which can accommodate a congregation of about 2,000.

A triple-nave hall with no transept features rows of side chapels, a gallery surrounding the choir and a monumental western tower. The whole huge structure measures over 100 m (330 ft) in length and almost 40 m (130 ft) wide.

The church treasures that escaped destruction during World War II include a Marian painting, dating from around 1500, by Jan Polak; the altar of St Andrew in St Sebastian's chapel, with statues by Meister von Rabenden and paintings by Jan Polak, dating from 1510; and the monumental tomb of Emperor Ludwig IV of Bavaria, the work of Hans Krumpper (1619–22).

Carving on main Frauenkirche portal

Deutsches Jagd- und Fischerei- museum ❺

German Museum of Hunting and Fishing

Neuhauser Straße 2. **Map** 2 A4. **Tel** (089) 22 05 22. Ⓤ or Ⓢ Marienplatz. 🚋 18, 19, 20, 21, 27. 🕐 9:30am–5pm Mon–Wed, Fri–Sun, 9:30am–9pm Thu. 📷

Immediately adjacent to St Michael's Church is the Augustinerkloster, the former Augustinian church, which now houses the Museum of Hunting and Fishing. The original building dates from around 1300 (the first Augustinian monks arrived here in 1294). It was rebuilt in the mid-15th century and then remodelled in the Baroque style in 1620–21. The church was deconsecrated in 1803.

Since 1966, the building's ornate Rococo interior has housed a very interesting museum, with a collection of weapons dating from the Renaissance, Baroque and Rococo periods, as well as hunting trophies and related paintings, prints and

Pulpit in the Rococo-style Asamkirche

dioramas. Artists represented in the museum's collection include several great names such as Rubens, Snyders and Antonio Pisanello.

Asamkirche ❻

Asams' Church

Sendlinger Straße 32. **Map** 2 A5. Ⓤ Sendlinger Tor. 🚋 16, 17, 18, 27. 🚌 52, 152. 🕐 8am–6pm daily. ✝ 5pm Mon, Tue, Thu, 8:30am Wed, 6pm Sat, 10am Sun. 📷 noon Sat (7 May–24 Sep).

Officially known as St Johann-Nepomuk, this gem of Rococo architecture stands in Sendlingerstrasse and is part of a complex built by the Asam brothers in the mid-18th century. In 1729–30, the sculptor and stuccoist Egid Quirin Asam acquired two properties that he intended to convert into a family home for himself. He subsequently acquired a plot adjacent to these properties, where he wished to build a church devoted to the newly canonized St Nepomuk, a Bohemian monk who had drowned in the Danube. Above the entrance to the church is a statue of the saint.

At the same time, Cosmas Damian, the brother of Egid Quirin Asam, bought a plot on which he built the presbytery. The church building adjoins the residential house of Egid Quirin. The two buildings were joined by a corridor and from one of his bedroom windows the artist could see the main altar.

In this small but unique church, the Asam brothers achieved a rare and striking unity of style. In the dimly lit interior, with its dynamically shaped single nave, no surface is left unembellished. The eye is drawn to the altar, which features a sculpted group of the Holy Trinity.

A Wilhelm von Kaulbach painting (1847) in the Stadtmuseum

Stadtmuseum ❼
Town Museum

St Jakobsplatz 1. **Map** 2 A5.
Tel (089) 23 32 23 70. **U** or
S Marienplatz. **U** Sendlinger Tor.
◯ 10am–6pm Tue–Sun. 🖼️ 🖥️

A few steps away from the Viktualienmarkt, on St Jakobsplatz, stands the Town Museum. Its rich collection has been housed since 1880 in the former arsenal building, which was built in 1491–93 by Lucas Rottaler. It is one of Munich's most fascinating museums, with exhibits such as *Typisch München!* (Typical Munich!) illustrating the everyday lives of the city's citizens from the Middle Ages to the present day.

Its greatest treasures are the famous ten dancing Moors by Erasmus Grasser (1480), carved in lime wood and originally numbering 18. Also on the ground floor, in the Waffenhalle, is a splendid collection of arms. Other displays include furniture (in styles ranging from Baroque to Art Deco), photographs, film, brewing equipment and musical instruments. There is also a large and fascinating doll collection, which includes a variety of original puppets, and a collection of paintings and prints.

The museum regularly stages special exhibitions. A cinema, the *Filmmuseum*, puts on nightly showings of English-language films.

Jüdisches Zentrum Jakobsplatz ❽
Jewish Centre Jakobsplatz

St Jakobsplatz 16. **Map** 2 A5.
U or **S** Marienplatz. **Tel** 23 39 60
96. ◯ Jewish Museum: 10am–6pm
Tue–Sun. 🖼️ **www**.juedisches-
museum-muenchen.de

The Jewish Museum, the Jewish Community Centre of Munich and Upper Bavaria, and the main synagogue, Ohel Jakob, together constitute a prestigious modern centre for Munich's Jewish community.

The museum is housed in a cube-shaped building. Three floors of exhibitions, plus a library and a learning centre, all provide extensive information on Jewish culture and history and highlight important aspects of contemporary Jewish life.

The synagogue, also cube-shaped, is crowned by a light-flooded roof. The community centre contains the administrative department, the rabbinate, conference rooms, a kindergarden, a public full-time school, a youth and arts centre and a kosher restaurant.

Viktualienmarkt ❾

Peterplatz-Frauenstraße. **Map** 2 B5.
U or **S** Marienplatz. 🚌 52.

Right at the heart of the city is the Viktualienmarkt, a large square that has been the city's main marketplace for the last 200 years. Apart from stalls selling vegetables and fruit brought in daily

Colourfully laden market stalls in Munich's Viktualienmarkt

from suburban orchards or village gardens, the local beer garden provides a welcome retreat for a beer or snack.

One of the features of the square is a statue of a famous Munich actor and comedian, Karl Valentin (1882–1948).

An impressive view over the market can be enjoyed from the tower of Peterskirche (St Peter's Church), which stands alongside the square.

Signs of the Zodiac adorning the clock face on the Altes Rathaus

Altes Rathaus ❿
Old Town Hall

Marienplatz 15. **Map** 2 B4. **U** or
S Marienplatz. ◯ to visitors.
Spielzeugmuseum Tel (089) 29
40 01. ◯ 10am–5:30pm daily. 🖼️
www.spielzeugmuseum-muenchen.de

Munich's old town hall stands in the eastern part of Marienplatz, immediately next to the new town hall. The original building, which has been remodelled several times, was built in 1470–75 by Jörg von Halspach, who also designed the Marian church.

The building's present Neo-Gothic look is the result of remodelling work carried out between 1877 and 1934, when the nearby dual carriageway ring road was being built.

The interior of the building, which was restored following World War II bomb damage, features the Dance Hall with a wooden cradle vault. It is adorned with an old frieze featuring 87 (originally 96) heraldic arms painted by Ulrich Füetrer in 1478, and a further seven carved by Erasmus Grasser in 1477. The figures standing by the walls are copies of the famous dancing Moors, whose originals by Erasmus

Grasser (1480) are kept in the Town Museum (Stadtmuseum).

The lofty tower rising above the old city gate (Talbrucktor) was remade in 1975 based on pictures dating from 1493. Since 1983, the tower has housed the toy collection of the Spielzeugmuseum.

Neues Rathaus ⓫
New Town Hall

Marienplatz. **Map** 2 B4. **Tel** (089) 233 00. Ⓤ or Ⓢ *Marienplatz.*
⬭ **Town Hall and Tower:** May–Oct: 10am–7pm daily; Nov–Apr: 10am–5pm Mon–Fri. ● Sat & Sun. 🔔 ⬭ **Carillons.** Mai–Oct: 11am, noon, 5pm daily; Nov–Feb: 11am, noon.

The Neo-Gothic new town hall standing in Marienplatz was built by Georg Hauberrisser in 1867–1909. Its 100-m (330-ft) high façade features a fascinating set of statues depicting Bavarian dukes, kings and electors, saints, mythical and allegorical figures as well as a variety of gargoyles inspired by medieval bestiaries. The central façade features an 80 m (260-ft) high clock tower, known as Glockenspiele. Each day, at 11am and 5pm, the bells ring out a carillon, while mechanical knights fight a tournament and a crowd dances. The latter is a reenactment of the first coopers' dance, which was held in 1517 to boost the morale of citizens when the town was beset by the plague. Other mechanical figures appear in the windows on the seventh floor in the

Statue on façade of Neues Rathaus

evenings (9:30pm in summer, 7:30pm in winter). These are flanked by figures of the town guardsman carrying a lantern and the Guardian Angel blessing a Munich child, the *"Münchner Kindl"*.

Richly decorated entrance to the Völkerkundemuseum

Völkerkunde-museum ⓬
State Museum of Ethnography

Maximilianstraße 42. **Map** 2 D4. **Tel** (089) 210 136 100. 🚋 19.
⬭ 9:30am–5:30pm, Tue–Sun. 📷

On the opposite side of the ring road from the Maximilianeum (the Upper Bavaria Government building) is the State Museum of Ethnography. Built in 1858–65, to a design by F. Riedel, its façade is decorated with eight figures personifying the virtues of the Bavarian people: patriotism, diligence, magnanimity, piety, loyalty, justice, courage and wisdom. Originally intended to house the Bavarian National Museum (now in Prinzregentenstraße), the building has been home to the State Museum of Ethnography since 1925. It is the second largest (after Berlin) ethnographic museum in Germany.

The origins of the museum's collection go back to 1782, when curios taken from the treasures of various Bavarian rulers were exhibited in a gallery in the gardens of the residence. Attention began to focus on ethnography after expansion of the collection in 1868. The museum currently houses some 300,000 exhibits depicting the art and culture of non-European nations, with a particular emphasis on the Far East (China and Japan), South America and Eastern and Central Africa. The collection is presented in a series of changing exhibitions.

Hofbräuhaus ⓭

Platzl 9. **Map** 2 C4. **Tel** (089) 22 16 76. Ⓤ or Ⓢ *Marienplatz.* ⬭ 9am–11:30pm daily. **www**.hofbraeuhaus.de

The Hofbräuhaus is the most popular beer hall in Munich and a great tourist attraction. Established as a court brewery in 1589 by Wilhelm V, it was originally housed in Alter Hof, but moved to Platzl in 1654. In 1830 permission was granted to build an inn where beer could be sold to the public.

The Neo-Renaissance form of the building dates from 1896. The Schwemme, on the ground floor, is a large hall with painted ceiling and room for about 1,000 guests. The Festsall, on the first floor, has a barrel-shaped vault and can accommodate 1,300 guests.

In a courtyard, surrounded by chestnut trees, is the beer garden, which is always very popular during the summer.

Guests enjoying a drink in the beer garden of the Hofbräuhaus

Residenz ⑭

Necklace dating from 1557

This former residence of Bavarian kings has housed a museum since 1920. Over the years, the original Wittelsbachs' castle, which had stood on the site since the 14th century, was gradually extended. Major work in the 17th century included new surroundings for the Brunnenhof and the construction of buildings around the imperial courtyard, Hofkapelle and Reiche Kapelle. Königsbau and Festsaalbau were added in the first half of the 19th century. The Renaissance façade includes two magnificent portals and features a statue of the Holy Virgin as Patroness of Bavaria (Patrona Boiariae).

Hofkapelle
This imposing chapel, dating from the early 17th century, was modelled on St Michael's Church. Vault decorations date from 1614.

Reiche Kapelle
This was the private chapel of Maximilian I. Though smaller than the Residenz's other chapel, it is richly furnished.

Grottenhof
In the eastern section of this courtyard is this grotto lined with crystal, coloured shells and tufa.

★ **Nibelungensäle**
Built by Leo von Klenze, Königsbau features five Halls of the Nibelungs. The rooms owe their name to the wall paintings, which depict scenes from the famous German medieval epic Nibelungenlied.

★ Cuvilliés-Theater

Built in 1751–55, this masterpiece of theatre architecture was designed by François Cuvilliés, and is considered to be Europe's finest surviving Rococo theatre. The world premiere of Mozart's Idomeneo was staged in the theatre on 29 January 1781.

★ Schatzkammer V

Room V's collection includes items such as the Bavarian crown insignia and a sword belonging to Duke Christoph of Bavaria.

Entrance

Nationaltheater

Schatzkammer

Besides royal insignia, liturgical vessels and various everyday objects, the treasure house contains some unusual gold and jewellery items. The star attraction of Room III is this small equestrian statue of St George, the work (1586–97) of Friedrich Sustris.

STAR SIGHTS

★ Cuvilliés-Theater

★ Nibelungensäle

★ Schatzkammer V

Feldherrnhalle

Odeonsplatz. **Map** 2 B3.
U *Odeonsplatz.* 🚋 *19.* 🚌 *100.*
⭘ *daily.*

Until 1816, the site of this
monumental building was
occupied by a Gothic town
gate – Schwabinger Tor. In
the early 19th century, however, when Kings Maximilian
I Joseph and Ludwig I
decided to expand Munich
northwards and westwards,
their chief architect, Leo von
Klenze, ordered the gate to
be pulled down, as it stood in
the way of the prestigious
thoroughfare (Ludwigstrasse)
that he intended to build.

Built in 1841–44, the Feldherrnhalle was designed by
Friedrich von Gärtner, who
modelled it on the Loggia dei
Lanzi in Florence. Intended as
a monument to the heroes of
Bavaria, the interior contains
statues of two great military
leaders, Johann Tilly and
Karl Philipp von Wrede by
Ludwig Schwanthaler.

The central carved
composition devoted to
the heroes of the 1870–71
Franco-Prussian War is
much newer, dating from
1882. It was designed by
Ferdinand von Miller.

The Feldherrnhalle
was the scene of Hitler's
unsuccessful "Beer-hall
Putsch", after which
he was arrested.
This resulted in the
loggia acquiring
a certain cult
status in Nazi
propaganda.

HITLER AND THE FELDHERRNHALLE

On the evening of 8 November 1923, Adolf Hitler
announced the start of the "people's revolution" in the
Bürgerbräukeller and ordered the takeover of the central
districts of Munich. On 9 November a march of some 2,000
people acting on his orders was stopped by a police
cordon outside the Feldherrnhalle in Residenzstraße. Four
policemen and 16 of Hitler's supporters were shot. The
marchers were dispersed, and Hitler fled to Uffing am
Starnberger See,
but was arrested
and imprisoned.
When Hitler
finally came to
power in 1933,
he turned what
became known
as the Hitler-
Putsch into a
central element
of the Nazi cult.

**The accused in the trial against the
participants in the Hitler-Putsch of 1923**

Theatinerkirche
(St Cajetan) ⑯
St Cajetan's Church

Theatinerstraße 22. **Map** 2 B3.
U or **S** *Marienplatz.* 🚋 *19.*
⭘ *7am– 7pm daily.*

In Odeonsplatz, next to Feldherrnhalle, stands one of the
most magnificent churches
in Munich, St Cajetan's
Church. When Henrietta
Adelaide of Savoy
presented the Elector
Ferdinand with his long-
awaited heir, Maximilian,
the happy parents vowed
to build an abbey in
commemoration.
The project was
given to an
Italian architect,
Agostino Baralli,

who based his design on St
Andrea della Valle, in Rome.

Although construction work
on the church ended in 1690,
the façade – designed by
François de Cuvilliés – was
not completed until 1765–68.
The interior of the church is
adorned with stuccos by
Giovanni Antonio Viscardi
and furnished in rich Baroque
style. Its twin towers and
copper dome are dominant
features on the Munich skyline.

Haus der Kunst ⑰
Arts House

Prinzregentenstraße 1.
Map 3 D2. *Tel* (089) 21 12 71 13.
🚌 *100.* ⭘ *10am–8pm daily,
10am–10pm Thu.*

Built between 1933 and 1937,
the Neo-Classical building is
the work of a Nazi architect,
Paul Ludwig Trost. It opened
its doors in 1937 with a display
of propaganda art, which was
proclaimed by the Nazis as
"truly German".

Since 1945 the building has
become a dynamic centre of
modern art that is famous for
its temporary exhibitions.

Its central hall, the former
Ehrenhalle (Hall of Honour),
which was subdivided into
smaller spaces, was reopened
in stages, each stage accompanied by a special exhibition. In
2006 the hall once again
became the centre of the
building and is used as a

Pediment on the gable of Theatinerkirche, with copper dome behind

space for events and temporary installations. In the foyer is a permanent exhibition documenting the history of the building.

In 2002 the National Collection of Modern and Contemporary Arts, which was housed in the west wing, moved to the Pinakothek der Moderne (see p221).

Bayerisches Nationalmuseum ⓲
Bavarian National Museum

Prinzregentenstraße 3. **Map** 3 E3. **Tel** (089) 211 24 01. 🚋 17. 🚌 100. 🕙 10am–5pm Tue–Wed, Fri–Sun, 10am–8pm Thu. 🚫 Mon. **www.bayerisches-nationalmuseum.de**

The Bavarian National Museum was founded in 1855 by King Maximilian II. Between 1894 and 1900 it acquired a new building in Prinzregentenstrasse, designed by Gabriel von Seidel; this building alone is worth a closer look. The complex structure consists of wings representing various architectural styles, while the ground floor features halls that are built in styles that are appropriate to their exhibits. This means that the visitor can see Romanesque and Gothic art in Neo-Romanesque and Neo-Gothic rooms, Renaissance art in Neo-Renaissance rooms and Baroque in Neo-Baroque rooms. The individual rooms have been arranged in subject groups, with paintings and sculptures supplemented by superb collections of decorative art and everyday objects, including furniture. The exhibits include a beautiful sculpture of the Madonna by Tilman Riemenschneider.

The first-floor collections are arranged thematically and include German porcelain,

Conrad Meit's *Judith* (1515), Bavarian National Museum

clocks, glass paintings, ivory carvings, textiles and gold items. Particularly interesting is a collection of small oil sketches, painted by artists when designing some large-scale compositions, such as an altar or a ceiling painting.

A special annex houses the Bollert Collection, which contains sculptures from the late-Gothic period.

Schack-Galerie

Poster advertising an exhibition at the Schack-Galerie

Schack-Galerie ⓳

Prinzregentenstraße 9. **Map** 3 E3. **Tel** (089) 23 80 52 24. 🕙 10am–6pm Wed–Sun. 🚌 100. 🚋 17. 🏛

The magnificent collection of German paintings on display in this gallery come from the private collection of Adolf Friedrich von Schack. They are housed in this elegant building built in 1907 by Max Littmann for use by the Prussian Legation.

As Schack's main interest was in 19th-century painting, the gallery features works that represent the Romantic period, including Leo von Klenze and Carl Spitzweg, as well as witty, fairy-tale works by Moritz von Schwind. Particularly notable are his *Morning*, *In the Woods* and *Rübezahl* – in which the mythical Guardian of the Riesengebirge Mountains wanders through an enchanted

forest. Late 19th-century painters are represented by Franz von Lenbach, Anselm Feuerbach and, above all, by Arnold Böcklin. Böcklin's Romantic works, which are full of symbolism, include *Villa on the Coast* and *Man Scaring a Deer*. The gallery has a large collection of landscapes, including interesting sun-soaked Italian scenes by German masters, as well as a valuable collection of paintings devoted to historic themes.

Archäologische Staatssammlung ⓴
Prehistory Museum

Lerchenfeldstraße 2. **Map** 3 E2. **Tel** (089) 211 24 02. 🚋 17. 🚌 100. 🕙 9:30am–6pm Tue–Sat, 9:30am–8pm Sun. 🏛 🚫 **www.archaeologie-bayern.de**

Immediately adjacent to the Bavarian National Museum is the Prehistory Museum, which was founded in 1885 by King Ludwig II. Since 1976 this spacious building has housed a rich collection of artifacts from various parts of Bavaria. The oldest items in the collection date from the Palaeolithic era while later exhibits illustrate the region's early history. The collection includes Bronze Age, Roman and early Medieval treasures.

A 3rd-century mosaic floor from a Roman villa, on display in the Prehistory Museum

Bayerische Staatsbibliothek ㉑
Bavarian National Library

Ludwigstraße 16. **Map** 2 C1, C2.
Tel (089) 286 38 23 22. **U** *Odeon, Universität.* ☐ *8am–noon daily.*
☒ *(telephone bookings required).*
www.bsb-muenchen.de

The monumental Bavarian national library was designed by Friedrich von Gärtner, who took over, in 1827, from Leo von Klenze as the main architect on the prestigious Ludwigstrasse project – commissioned by King Ludwig I. Gärtner was also responsible for the Feldherrnhalle, Siegestor, St Ludwig's Church, and the University building.

This massive structure, in a style reminiscent of the Italian Renaissance, was erected between 1832 and 1843. Its external staircase is adorned with the seated figures of Thucydides, Hippocrates, Homer and Aristotle, by Ludwig von Schwanthaler.

Equally impressive are the stairs leading to the main rooms, which are modelled on the Scala dei Gianti of the Doge Palace in Venice. With its collection of 5 million volumes, the library is on a par with the Berlin Staats-bibliothek *(see p68)* as the biggest in Germany.

A statue of Hippocrates at the Bavarian National Library

The imposing twin-tower façade of Munich's Ludwigskirche

Ludwigskirche ㉒
St Ludwig's Church

Ludwigstraße 20. **Map** 2 C1.
U *Universität.* ☐ *7:30am–8pm daily.*

Inspired by the Romanesque churches of Lombardy, Friedrich von Gärtner built this monumental basilica between 1829 and 1844.

The vast interior features magnificent frescos designed by the main exponent of the Nazarene style, Peter von Cornelius, and painted by his associates. Von Cornelius himself painted the massive choir fresco, *The Last Judgement*. One of the biggest in the world, it rivals in size Michelangelo's *Last Judgement*.

Museum Brandhorst ㉓

Theresienstr. 35a. **Map** 2 B2.
Tel (089) 23 80 53 45. **U**
Köningsplatz. ▦ *100, 154.* ☷
27.☐ *10am–6pm Tue–Sun,*
10am–8pm Thu. ▨
www.museum-brandhorst.de

Museum Brandhorst features the modern and contempo-rary art of the Udo and Anette Brandhorst collection. It com-prises over 700 works, includ-ing more than 60 works by Cy Twombly, and an impres-sively large collection of Andy Warhol's works. Other artists

represented include Joseph Beuys, Damien Hirst, Jean-Michel Basquiat, Sigmar Polke and Mike Kelley.

Original editions of over a hundred books illustrated by Picasso are also on display.

Neue Pinakothek ㉔
The New Pinakothek

Barerstraße 29. **Map** 2 A1. *Tel (089) 23 80 51 95.* **U** *Theresienstraße.*
☷ *2.* ▦ *27.* ☐ *10am–6pm Thu–Mon, 10am–8pm Wed.* ▨
www.neue-pinakothek.de

This building, designed by architect Alexander von Branca from 1975–1981, features a representative collection of German works. This includes Neo-Classicism through Romanticism, the "Nazarenes", German and Austrian Biedermeier, Realism, Historicism, Impressionism, Pointillism and Secession paintings.

It also includes works by renowned French Realists, Impressionists, Post-Impres-sionists and Symbolists, purchased in 1909–11, when the gallery's director was the art historian Hugo von Tschudi.

The space between the Old and New Pinakothek is a sculpture park that features a work by Henry Moore.

Goya's *Marquesa de Caballero* in the Neue Pinakothek

Alte Pinakothek ㉕
The Old Pinakothek

See pp222–3.

Façade of the Glyptothek, with its central column portico

Pinakothek der Moderne 26

Barer Straße 40. **Map** 2 A2.
Tel *(089) 23 80 53 60.* Ⓤ *König-splatz.* 🚋 *53.* 🚊 *27.* ◯ *10am–6pm Tue–Wed & Fri–Sun, 10am–8pm Thu.*
📷 ♿ 🅿
www.pinakothek-der-moderne.de

Designed by the German architect Stephan Braunfels, this gallery was built to complement the collections in the Alte and Neue Pinakotheks nearby. The modern building brings together the worlds of art, design, graphics, jewellery and architecture under one roof.

Highlights of the collection include Cubist works by Picasso and Georges Braque, and paintings by Matisse, Giorgio De Chirico and Max Beckmann. Pop Art, Minimal Art and Photorealism are also represented. The design exhibition is outstanding.

Glyptothek 27

Glyptotheca

Königsplatz 3. **Map** 1 F2.
Tel *(089) 28 61 00.* Ⓤ *Königsplatz.* ◯ *10am–5pm Tue–Sun, 10am–8pm Thu.*

The Königsplatz complex, including Glyptothek and Propylaeum, was the work of Leo von Klenze. It was built in 1816–34 to house Ludwig I's collection of Greek and Roman sculptures and was the first public museum to be devoted to a single art discipline.

The most famous pieces in the museum's collection are the ancient statue of a young man, *Apollo of Terentia* (560 BC), the tomb stele of Mnesareta (380 BC) and sculptures from the front of the Aphaia temple of Aegina.

Staatliche Antiken-sammlungen 28

The National Collection of Antiquities

Königsplatz 1. **Map** 1 F2. ***Tel*** *(089) 59 98 88 30.* Ⓤ *Königsplatz.* ◯ *10am–5pm Tue–Sun, 10am–8pm Wed.* 📷

Built in 1838–48 by Georg Friedrich Ziebland, this building is on the south side of the Königsplatz. Since 1967, it has housed one of the world's finest collections of antique vases from the 5th and 6th centuries BC. There are also many other master-pieces of Greek, Roman and Etruscan ornamental art, jewellery and small statues. Among the famous exhibits is a golden Greek necklace from the 4th century BC.

Propyläen 29

Königsplatz. **Map** 1 F2. Ⓤ *Königsplatz.*

Derived from the Propylaea to the Athenian Acropolis, this magnificent Neo-Classical structure stands at the end of Brienner Strasse and is visible from as far as Karolinenplatz. Built by Leo von Klenze in 1846–62, its austere form, featuring Doric porticos, provides an excellent final touch to the composition of Königsplatz by linking together the National Collection of Antiquities and the Glyptotheca.

The Propyläen is also a symbolic gateway to the new parts of the city. It was funded by the private foundation of King Ludwig I, although built after his abdication.

The carved decorations depict scenes from the Greek War of Liberation against Turkey (1821–29), led by King Otto I, son of Ludwig I.

Lenbachhaus 30

Luisenstraße 33. **Map** 1 F2, ***Tel*** *(089) 23 33 20 00.* Ⓤ *Königsplatz.* 🚫 *for renovations until 2013.* www.lenbachhaus.de
Kunstbau ◯ *10am–10pm Tue–Sun.*

This Italian-style villa was built between 1887 and 1891 by Gabriel von Seidl for painter Franz von Lenbach.

Since 1929, it has housed the Municipal Art Gallery. As well as masterpieces such as *Portrait of a Man* by Jan Polak (c.1500), it also has the world's biggest collection of works by the *Der Blaue Reiter* (The Blue Rider) artists. Kandinsky was a leading proponent of this movement.

The Kunstbau, part of Lenbachhaus, is in a subway station under Königsplatz. It features temporary exhibitions.

Fountain in the beautiful front garden of the Lenbachhaus

Alte Pinakothek ㉕

Construction work on the Alte Pinakothek, one of the world's most famous art galleries, began in 1826 and was completed 10 years later. Leo von Klenze designed the Italian-Renaissance-style building. The history of princely collections goes back to the Renaissance period, when Wilhelm IV the Steadfast (ruled 1508–50) decided to adorn his residence with historic paintings. His successors were equally keen art collectors and, by the 18th century, an outstanding collection of 14th- to 18th-century paintings had been amassed.

St Luke Painting the Madonna (c.1484)
This is one of the most frequently copied masterpieces by the Dutch painter Roger van der Weyden.

★ Four Apostles (1526)
These two panels were painted by Albrecht Dürer, a founding figure of the German school of art. They were acquired in 1627 by Maximilian I from the town of Nuremberg.

Emperor Charles V (1548)
This portrait was painted by the Venetian artist Titian during the Emperor's visit to the Reich's Parliament in Augsburg.

Main entrance

Adoration of the Magi (1504)
The depiction of the adoration is just one small part of the most important altarpiece by Hans Holbein the Elder.

KEY

- ☐ Flemish and Dutch paintings
- ☐ German paintings
- ☐ Italian paintings
- ☐ French paintings
- ☐ Spanish paintings
- ☐ Temporary exhibitions
- ☐ Non-exhibition space

STAR EXHIBITS

★ Descent from the Cross

★ Four Apostles

★ Land of Cockaigne

Rape of the Daughters of Leukippos (1618)
A highlight of the museum is the Rubens collection, which includes his depiction of the abduction of Hilaeria and Phoibe by Castor and Pollux.

VISITORS' CHECKLIST

Barer Straße 27. **Road map** 2
A1. **Tel** (089) 23 80 52 16.
Ⓤ Königsplatz. 🚌 53. 🚋 27.
🕙 10am–6pm Wed–Sun, 10am–
8pm Tue. 🎫 (admission free to
children under 8.) 🅿🛗♿☐📷
www.alte-pinakothek.de

GALLERY GUIDE
The ground-floor rooms of the gallery are devoted to the works of German old masters dating from the 16th and 17th centuries. On the first floor are works by Dutch, Flemish, French, German, Italian and Spanish artists.

First floor

★ **Descent from the Cross** (1633)
Rembrandt's dramatic vision of the Saviour's sacrifice emotively depicts Christ's passion.

Disrobing of Christ (c.1583–84)
The gallery's small but interesting collection of Spanish paintings includes this work by El Greco, one of his three most important compositions.

★ **Land of Cockaigne** (1567)
In this vividly detailed painting by Pieter Brueghel the Elder, the Flemish artist depicts the mythical land of plenty. The work is an ironic condemnation of gluttony and laziness, themes that are depicted in its many humorous scenes.

Ground floor

Schloss Nymphenburg ③

One of Europe's most beautiful palaces, Schloss Nymphenburg grew up around an Italianate villa built in 1663–64 for the Electress Henriette-Adelaide to a design by Agostino Barelli. The palace was dedicated to the pastoral goddess Flora and her nymphs, hence the name. Several additions were made over the years, including four pavilions. These were designed by Joseph Effner and Enrico Zuccalli who directed works from 1715. Built to the side of the original villa, these were connected by arcaded passageways.

Porcelain parrot in front of the factory

★ Gallery of Beauties
Portraits of royal favourites include this one of Helene Sedlmayr, a 17-year-old girl from Munich.

Entrance to Schloss Nymphenburg
Seen in this view are the original Italianate villa and two of the side pavilions that were added later.

Marstallmuseum
The former stables house a collection of carriages that once belonged to Bavarian rulers. They include the magnificent carriages of Ludwig II.

Porcelain Factory
Established in 1747 by Franz Anton Bustelli and transferred to Nymphenburg in 1761, this is one of the oldest porcelain factories in Europe.

KEY

— — — Suggested route

STAR SIGHTS

★ Amalienburg

★ Festsaal

★ Gallery of Beauties

★ Amalienburg
The interior of this hunting lodge in the Schlosspark is a superb example of Rococo style by François Cuvilliés.

VISITORS' CHECKLIST

Tel (089) 17 90 80.
🇺 *Rotkreuzplatz.* 🚊 *12, 17.*
🕐 *Apr–15 Oct: 9am–6pm daily;
16 Oct–Mar: 10am–4pm daily.* 📷

Magdalenenklause
After a lifetime of revels, Maximilian Emanuel commissioned a hermitage where he could pray and meditate. It was completed in 1725.

Badenburg

Pagodenburg

Museum Mensch und Natur
This museum is devoted to geology and human biology.

Lackkabinett
This small 17th-century cabinet owes its name to its panels of black and red Chinese lacquer.

Botanical Garden
A collection of botanical specimens, including many rare plants, is featured in this fascinating garden.

★ Festsaal (Steinernen Saal)
Featuring decorations devoted to the goddess Flora, this vast Rococo ballroom is the work of father and son Johann Baptist and Franz Zimmermann.

View from the platform of the television tower in Olympiapark

Olympiapark **②**

Tel *(089) 30 67 24 14.* **U** *Olympiazentrum.* 🚋 *20, 21.* 🚌 *173.* **Television tower** ☐ *9am–midnight daily.* 📷

Built for the 1972 Olympic Games, this vast sports stadium can be spotted from almost anywhere in Munich, as it is the site of a 290-m (950-ft) high television tower, the Olympiaturm. The entire complex was designed by Germany's leading architects, Behnisch and Partners.

The stadium has three main facilities: the Olympic Stadium, which seats 62,000 spectators, the Olympic Hall and the Swimming Hall. In what is one of the most original constructions of 20th-century German architecture, all three are covered by a vast transparent canopy, stretched between a series of tall masts to form an irregular tent.

The stadium includes many other facilities, such as an indoor skating rink, a cycle racing track and tennis courts.

The sports complex is located beside the park's artificial lake.

Apart from sporting events, the Olympiapark hosts many popular events, including fireworks displays and regular open-air rock and pop concerts in the summer months.

Next to the park are the BMW Museum and BMW Welt, featuring the world's largest permanent BMW collection.

Englischer Garten **③**

U *Giselastraße.* 🚌 *54.*

The idea of creating this garden, which would be open to all the inhabitants of Munich and not only to its aristocracy, came from Count von Rumford, an American-born chemist and physicist who lived in Bavaria from 1784. As the region's Minister of War, he was responsible for reorganizing the Bavarian army. His idea of creating a garden of this size – the garden covers an area of 5 sq km (1,235 acres) – right in the centre of a large city, was quite unique in Germany. In 1789, taking advantage of his influential position, he persuaded Karl Theodor to put his plans into action.

The project leader was Friedrich Ludwig von Sckell. He was brought to Munich from Schwetzingen by the Elector to create the garden on an area of former marshland.

Opened in 1808, the Karl-Theodor-Park is today known simply as the Englischer Garten (English Garden). It is a popular place for long walks, jogging or just lying on the grass in the cool shade of a spreading old tree.

There are some interesting old buildings in the park, such as the Monopteros, a Neo-Classical temple by Leo von Klenze (1837), and the Chinese Tower (1789–90), which is similar to the pagoda in London's Kew Gardens. The Tower stands in one of the park's beer gardens.

It is also worth dropping in to the Japanese Teahouse, where the gentle art of tea brewing is demonstrated.

Deutsches Museum **④**

See pp228–9.

Franz von Stuck's *Die Sünde*, on display in the Villa Stuck

Villa Stuck **⑤**

Prinzregentenstraße 60. **Tel** *(089) 45 55 51 0.* 🚋 *18.* 🚌 *100.* ☐ *11am–6pm Tue–Sun.* 📷

This villa was the home of the famous painter Franz von Stuck, the co-founder of the Munich Secession school of painting. As well as numerous portraits, nudes and sculptures, Von Stuck was the creator of many mythological and allegorical scenes, all painted in dark colours

Chinese Tower in the Englischer Garten

Submarine used in the film *Das Boot*, displayed in Bavaria-Filmstadt

and full of eroticism. These include eight variations (1893) on the theme of sin. His *Amazon* (1897) stands in front of the villa.

Franz von Stuck built the villa in 1897–98, to his own design, decorating it with his own paintings and sculptures. Since 1968, it has housed a museum. A permanent exhibition of Stuck's work is displayed in the magnificent music room on the ground floor, while the second-floor rooms are used for temporary exhibitions devoted mainly to early 20th-century art.

Bavaria-Filmstadt 36

Bavariafilmplatz 7. **Tel** (089) 64 99 20 00. 🚊 25. ⏰ mid-Apr–Oct: 9am–4pm daily; Nov: 10am–3pm daily. 🎬 only, in English at 1pm daily. 🌐 www.filmstadt.de

Commonly known as Hollywood on Isar, this vast site in the southern suburb of Geiselgasteig covers an area of over 3.5 sq km (865 acres).

Since 1919 the world's greatest cinema stars have worked here, including Orson Welles and Billy Wilder. The British film director Alfred Hitchcock made his first films here (*The Pleasure Garden*, 1925 and *The Mountain Eagle*, 1926). Elizabeth Taylor, Gina Lollobrigida and Romy Schneider have all stood in front of the cameras here.

Strolling visitors to the site will often come across some well-known characters who have appeared in films such as *E.T.* or *The Neverending Story*, which were filmed here. The sets of other films made here, including *Enemy*

Mine and *Cabaret*, can also be seen. You can also peep into the submarine that was reconstructed for Wolfgang Petersen's classic film *Das Boot* (1981) – the film follows the voyage of one such boat during World War II. The Bullyversum (named after "Bully" Herbig, a German comedian, actor and director) is an interactive 3-D adventure.

VIP tours of the Filmstadt include fascinating demonstrations of many technical film-making tricks and techniques. A special attraction is the cinema called Showscan, whose seats move according to the story on the screen, giving visitors the sensation of a trip through the universe or of flying through the tunnels of an old silver mine.

Theresienwiese 37

Theresienhöhe. **U** Theresienwiese. 🎪 Oktoberfest (Sep–Oct).

For most of the year this is simply a vast oval meadow encircled by the Bavariaring. Theresienwiese comes into its own once a year, however, during the Oktoberfest. Then it turns into a gigantic, boisterous beer-drinking venue, with stalls, marquees, funfair and loud music.

Towering above the meadow is a monumental 18-m (59-ft) high statue, symbol of the state of Bavaria. Made in 1844–50, the statue is the work of Ludwig Schwanthaler. It incorporates an internal staircase leading to the figure's head, where there is a viewing platform.

Just behind the statue is the Ruhmeshalle, a Neo-Classical building surrounded by a colonnade. Designed by Leo von Klenze and built in 1843–53, the building contains numerous busts of eminent Bavarians.

Bavaria statue in Theresienwiese

OKTOBERFEST

Munich's Oktoberfest is one of the biggest folk fairs in Europe. In 1810 the site on which it is held was the venue for a horse race, held to celebrate the marriage of Ludwig (later King of Bavaria) and Thérèse von Saxe-Hildburghausen. A few years later it became the venue for an autumn fair that has grown into an enormous event over the years. Chief amongst the attractions is beer, drunk in vast quantities, in marquees erected by the breweries. The festival starts in late

Revellers at the annual Oktoberfest in Theresienwiese

September with a huge procession through the town and the ceremonial opening of the first barrel of beer. It finishes, 16 days later, on the first Sunday of October.

Deutsches Museum ③④

The Deutsches Museum, one of the oldest and largest museum of technology and engineering in the world, draws over 1.4 million visitors each year. It was founded in 1903 by Oskar von Miller, an engineer. The building in which it is housed, located on the Museum Island, was designed by Gabriel von Seidl in 1925. The collections cover most aspects of technology, from its history to its greatest achievements. The museum also houses one of the world's largest libraries of technology.

Exterior of the Museum
The building combines Neo-Baroque, Neo-Classical and modern elements.

Decorative Arts
This plate with the portrait of a lady from Ludwig I's "gallery of beauty" is an example of reproduction techniques applied to porcelain. The ceramics section illustrates the development of faience, stoneware and porcelain.

Second floor

First floor

★ Physics
Galileo's workshop features a large collection of the scientific equipment used by the famous astronomer and physicist to establish the basic laws of mechanics.

★ Pharmaceutics
Among the exhibits in this recently created section is a model of a human cell magnified 350,000 times and graphically illustrating how it functions.

Main entrance

Ground floor

MUSEUM GUIDE

The museum's 20,000 exhibits are displayed over seven floors. While those on the lower floors include heavy vehicles and sections on chemistry, physics, scientific instruments and aeronautics, those on the middle floors relate to the decorative arts. The upper floors are devoted to astronomy, computers and microelectronics.

Sixth floor

Fifth floor

Fourth floor

Third floor

VISITORS' CHECKLIST

Museumsinsel 1. **Tel** 21 791.
U *Fraunhoferstr.* **S** *Isartor.*
17, 18. 131.
9am–5pm daily. (children under 6 free). by arrangement (21 79 252).
www.deutsches-museum.de

Telecommunications
The Philips camera of 1967 was one of the first colour television cameras in the world.

KEY

	Design and Technology
	Centre for New Technology
	Kids' Kingdom
	Physics and Chemistry
	Musical Instruments
	Decorative Arts
	Time, Weights and Measures
	Automation, Microelectronics and Telecommunications
	Astronomy
	Agriculture and Geodesy
	Miscellaneous

★ Musical Instruments
The keyboard instruments room contains the earliest southern German organ and a 17th-century inlaid harpsichord.

Kids' Kingdom
This is an area where children between the ages of 3 and 8 can learn about science and technology in a fun and imaginative way. There are many exciting exhibits, including a giant guitar, a fire engine and an electric light cinema.

STAR EXHIBITS

- ★ Musical Instruments
- ★ Pharmaceutics
- ★ Physics

For hotels and restaurants in this region see pp497–9 and pp536–8

SHOPPING IN MUNICH

Munich often claims to be Germany's richest and most sophisticated city, and so when it comes to shopping you are sure not to be disappointed. The key shopping areas are dotted around the centre of the city. You can conveniently walk around the pedestrianized central area, with numerous options for taking

Accessories from Slips

a break for lunch or a coffee. Not to be missed is the visual and gourmet treat of the Viktualienmarkt food market, the classic department store Ludwig Beck and some of the smaller speciality stores tucked away in side streets. In the less commercial shopping streets, stores tend to open late morning or in the afternoon only.

MAIN SHOPPING AREAS

Munich's key luxury shopping street is Maximilianstraße and those streets connected to it, Theatinerstraße, Brienner-straße and Residenzstraße. Here you will find all the top international brands and jewellery stores. For more affordable shops head to the central pedestrianized area between Kaufingerstraße, Neuhauserstraße and Marienplatz. Here you will find family stores, large chains, mid-market fashion, souvenirs and department stores. For less conventional areas with small specialist boutiques and local designers seek out the Glockenbach-viertel around Hans-Sachs Straße, or streets radiating out from Gärtnerplatz, home to the Art Nouveau State Theatre and relaxed cafés. Schwabing is the young Bohemian area with a variety of casualwear and jeanswear stores, plus fashion boutiques and plenty of laid-back bistros and coffee bars.

DEPARTMENT STORES AND SHOPPING CENTRES

The most famous department store in Munich is **Ludwig Beck**, which has a particularly impressive Christmas decorations department in December. **Galeria Kaufhof** is another large national department store chain offering several floors of goods. Shopping Centres (*Einkaufspassagen*) are also aplenty. **Fünf Höfe** ("the five courtyards") is central and upmarket. It sits between Theatiner, Maffei, Kardinal-Faulhaber and Salvator streets and mixes shopping, art and culture with cafés including a great restaurant/café attached to the Kunsthalle art museum. Munich has three other large shopping malls. **Olympia-Einkaufszentrum** (OEZ) is vast with over 140 stores on two levels. **Perlacher** shopping mall (PEP) has over 110 stores. The **Riem Arcaden** is home to the largest branch of H&M, a huge Lego store, C&A and Ludwig Beck Fashion.

Pedestrianized shopping area in central Munich

FASHION

Munich has a wide variety of shops for clothes and accessories. Try the following boutiques to find Munich-style chic. **Theresa** has the best choice of designer fashion and accessories, while **Trachten Angermaier** sells Bavarian folk costumes, including dirndls, and **Off & Co** in Schwabing has fashion items for men and women. Hohenzollern-straße in Schwabing is a good place to shop for youthful street fashion and trainers. For traditional Bavarian Loden costumes take a look in **Lodenfrey**.

CHILDREN'S SHOPS

Munich is a stylish and expensive city and parents love to dress their children accordingly. This means there are some good shopping opportunities for kids' clothing and toys, mainly in the department stores and C&A. A large central store for

The exclusive shopping centre, Fünf Höfe

One of the city's regularly held flea markets

mother, baby and toys is **Schlichting**, as well as **Thierchen Kindermode** for original handmade clothing. **Noemi & Friends** is a kids' beauty salon cum accessories shop, a haven for little and big girls. **Die Puppenstube** is also good for old-fashioned toys and gifts.

FLEA MARKETS

Flea markets are popular, especially at the weekends. Most take place on Saturday, some every two weeks and most only from spring to late autumn. The key ones around Munich are **Zenith Flohmarkt** and **Antik Palast**

flea market at Lilienthalallee, every weekend, and **Floh-markt Riem**, the largest flea market in Bavaria, at the trade show grounds.

FOOD SHOPPING

Viktualienmarkt *(see p214)* is a huge produce market, selling fruit, vegetables, spices, meat, poultry, fish, preserves and flowers. It is a feast for all the senses and a permanent fixture – open daily. *Bio* is the German word for organic and Germans have always been enthusiastic about organic produce. **Basic Bio** is a good organic supermarket in the city centre. For a selection of gourmet treats head to **Dallmayr** or

Käfer, the city's top delicatessens, while butchers' shops sell the famous Bavarian white sausages.

CHRISTMAS MARKET

Munich holds a traditional Christmas market *(Christkindlmarkt)* from the first week of Advent until Christmas Eve. The market is a great tourist attraction and special trips are organized from all over Europe. Wooden stalls sell a huge variety of handcrafted decorations, in particular wooden mangers and tree decorations, all delicately carved, in addition to candles, ornaments, food and mulled wine.

Christkindlmarkt, Munich's Christmas market

DIRECTORY

DEPARTMENT STORES AND SHOPPING CENTRES

Galeria Kaufhof
Kaufingerstraße 1–5. **Map** 2 B4. **Tel** (089) 231851.
www.galeria-kaufhof.de

Ludwig Beck
Marienplatz 11.
Map 2 B4.
Tel (089) 236910.
www.ludwigbeck.de

Fünf Höfe
Theatinerstraße. **Map** 2 B4.
www.fuenfhoefe.de

Olympia Einkaufszentrum
Hanauer Straße 68.
www.olympia-einkaufszentrum.de

Perlacher Einkaufs-passage (PEP)
Thomas-Dehler-Straße 12.
www.einkaufscenter-neuperlach.de

Riem Arcaden
Willy-Brandt-Platz 5.
www.riem-arcaden.de

FASHION

Lodenfrey
Maffeistraße 7.
Map 2 B4.
www.lodenfrey.com

Off & Co
Belgradstraße 1.
www.offandco.com

Trachten Angermaier
Rosental 11 and
Landsberger Str. 101–103.
www.trachten-angermaier.de

Theresa
Maffeistraße 3. **Map** 2 B4.
www.mytheresa.com

CHILDREN'S SHOPS

Die Puppenstube
Luisenstraße 68.
Tel (089) 2723267.

Noemi & Friends
Marktstraße 13, Schwabing.
www.noemiandfriends.de

Schlichting
Weinstraße 8. **Map** 2 B4.
www.schlichting.de

Thierchen Kindermode
Hans-Sachs-Straße 15.
www.thierchen.net

FLEA MARKETS

Antik Palast
Lilienthalallee 29.
www.antikpalast-muenchen.de

Flohmarkt Riem
Am Messeturm.
Tel (089) 960 51632.
www.flohmarkt-riem.com

Zenith Flohmarkt
Lilienthalallee. **Tel** 0173 683 5152. www.flohmarkt-freimann.de

FOOD SHOPPING

Basic Bio
Westenriederstraße 35.
Map 2 B4. **Tel** (089) 242 0890. www.basic-ag.de

Dallmayr
Dienerstraße 14–15. **Map** 2 B4. www.dallmayr.de

Käfer
Prinzregentenstraße 73.
www.feinkost-kaefer.de

Viktualienmarkt
Petersplatz-Frauenstraße.
Map 2 B4.

ENTERTAINMENT IN MUNICH

Munich is best known for the Oktoberfest, the Olympic grounds and Hofbräuhaus, but it also has an international reputation as a city of culture. There are 56 theatres, three large orchestras and one opera house. Munich has the rich and the powerful of its past to thank for creating and preserving

Bird from Munich Zoo

its many splendid venues. This cultured metropolis on the Isar caters to all tastes, from traditional to modern, whether in theatre, music or film. There are several festivals during the year, as well as various sporting events, when the city comes alive, attracting visitors from all over the world.

ENTERTAINMENT GUIDES AND TICKETS

Munich Found is the best events magazine and the **Tourist Board** has com pre-hensive listings of events happening all over Munich. Also, check the Thursday edition of *Süddeutsche Zeitung* and the daily *Münchner Merkur.*

You can book tickets direct from box offices by phone or in person. There are also two **Zentraler Kartenverkauf** ticket kiosks in Marienplatz underground concourse, or use the **Abendzeitung Schalterhalle** (kiosk).

THEATRE, OPERA AND CLASSICAL MUSIC

State theatres are subsidized and so tickets are very reasonably priced. The Bavarian State Orchestra, Opera and Ballet all perform at the **Nationaltheater**. The **Deutsches Theater** offers musicals and shows, while the **Prinzregententheater** has the Bavarian State Opera and a concert hall. The Art

Nouveau **Staatstheater am Gärtnerplatz** (closed for renovation from May 2012) presents opera, ballet, operetta, musicals and the Symphony Orchestra. **Gasteig Culture Center** is a world-class concert hall, home to the Munich Philharmonic Orchestra. The city also hosts an opera festival in July.

MUSIC AND DANCE

The **Pasinger Fabrik** offers a good programme of jazz, chansons and café theatre. There are numerous dance events and dance clubs. Big name artists, such as James Blunt, Massive Attack and The Rolling Stones, tend to perform at the **Circus Krone Bau**, **Zenith Kulturhalle**, **Olympiahalle** and the **Olympic Stadium**.

FILM

As the centre of the German film industry Munich offers 76 cinemas, the **Bavaria Film Studios** and a college for film and television. Try the English tour of the studios daily at 1pm. The **Munich Film Festival**

in July boasts over 200 films on 15 screens, almost all of them German, European or world premieres.

FESTIVALS

Munich's most famous festival is the **Oktoberfest**. For the whole of September it takes over a dedicated fairground, Theresienwiese, with beer

Munich's world-famous Oktoberfest

tents, traditional Bavarian brass bands, people dressed in traditional Bavarian costume (*Trachten*), fairground rides and the famous iced gingerbread hearts, *Lebkuchen*. There is also the **Tollwood Festival** in July and December, which has music, food, a circus, performances in tents, family fun and a craft fair. Munich also celebrates the *Dult* on three occasions throughout the year. *Dult* is the old word for street fair or market and there are traditional stalls and merry-go-rounds. Carnival or *Fasching* is celebrated throughout Munich with parties, processions and dressing up, but it is not as important here as in other cities.

The imposing Nationaltheater on Max-Joseph-Platz

Munich's ultra-modern Allianz Arena

SPORT

Most Münchners love the outdoors. Many make regular trips to the not too distant Alps. Running, skiing, rollerblading, cycling, Nordic walking and football are all very popular. The English Garden in the city centre is a huge park where people rollerblade, cycle, run or just meet up with friends.

Munich has two football teams: FC Bayern and TSV 1860 München, also known as "the Lions" because they are sponsored by the Löwenbräu Munich brewery with a lion as its coat of arms. The **Allianz Arena** is the fantastic stadium built for the 2006 World Cup. It is an architectural marvel which lights up in various colours. For Bayern Munich merchandise head to the **FC Bayern Shop** in the Arena. The shop website gives details of other stores located at Central Station and the Hofbräuhaus.

Other key sporting events are the Bavarian International Tennis Championships (ATP tournament), the BMW International Golf Open and Munich Blade Night, Monday evenings from April to September, when rollerbladers take over the streets. Runners will enjoy the Media Marathon and also the Münchner Stadtlauf (city run). A sport unique to Munich is surfing on the River Isar at the weirs.

KIDS' ENTERTAINMENT

Children will love Kids' Kingdom – **Kinderreich** – in the Deutsches Museum. The area is designated for children and has giant interactive games and water games, plus a real fire engine. Adults can only enter with their kids. Several playgrounds can be found along the River Isar in the city centre, but the best is **Westpark Spielzone Ost**, which can be reached by the underground. The new **Sea Life Olympia-park** centre also provides an excellent outing, as does the zoo at **Tierpark Hellabrunn**.

Sea life exhibit at Olympiapark Munich

DIRECTORY

ENTERTAINMENT GUIDES AND TICKETS

Abendzeitung Schalterhalle
Sendlingerstr. 10. **Map 2** A5. **Tel** (089) 267024.

Munich Tourist Board
www.muenchen.de

Zentraler Kartenverkauf
Tel (0180) 54818181. www.muenchenticket.de

THEATRE, OPERA AND CLASSICAL MUSIC

Deutsches Theater
Schwanthalerstr. 13. **Map** 1 E4. **Tel** (089) 552 340.

Gasteig Culture Center
Rosenheimer Str. 5. **Tel** (089) 480980.

Nationaltheater
Max-Joseph-Platz. **Map** 2 B4. **Tel** (089) 21851920.

Prinzregenten-theater
Prinzregentenstr. 12. **Map** 3 D3. **Tel** (089) 21852899.

Staatstheater am Gärtnerplatz
Gärtnerplatz 3.
Tel (089) 202411.

MUSIC AND DANCE

Circus Krone Bau
Marsstraße 43. **Map** 1 E3. **Tel** (085) 545 8000. www.circus-krone.de

Olympiahalle and Olympic Stadium
Spiridon-Louis-Ring 21.
Tel (089) 54 818181 (tickets). www. olympiapark-muenchen.de

Pasinger Fabrik
August-Exter-Str. 1. (089) 82929079.

Zenith Kulturhalle
Lilienthalallee 29. www.zenith-die-kulturhalle.de

FILM

Bavaria Film Studios
www.filmstadt.de

Munich Film Festival
www.filmfest-muenchen.de

FESTIVALS

Oktoberfest
www.oktoberfest.de

Tollwood Festival
www.tollwood.de

SPORT

Allianz Arena
www.allianz-arena.de

FC Bayern Shop
www.shop.fcbayern.de

KIDS' ENTERTAINMENT

Kinderreich
Deutsches Museum, Museumsinsel 1. **Tel** (089) 21791. www.deutsches-museum.de

Westpark Spielzone Ost
Pressburger Straße.

Sea Life Olympiapark
Willi-Daume-Platz 1.
Tel (089) 45 00 00. www.sealifeeurope.com

Tierpark Hellabrunn
Tierparkstr. 30. **Tel** (089) 625 080. www.zoo-munich.de

MUNICH STREET FINDER

Map references given in this chapter for sights (and in the Munich hotel and restaurant listings at the back of the book) refer to the maps here. The key map below shows the area of Munich covered by the *Street* *Finder*. The maps include the major sightseeing areas, historic attractions, railway stations, bus stations, U-Bahn and S-Bahn stations and train stations. The word Straße (Str.) indicates a street, Platz a square, Brücke a bridge and Bahnhof a railway station.

KEY TO THE MUNICH STREET FINDER

■ Major sight	ℹ️ Tourist information	— Pedestrianized street
■ Place of interest	🅿️ Parking	
▫ Other building	✚ Hospital with casualty unit	**SCALE OF MAPS 1-3**
Ⓢ S-Bahn station	🚓 Police station	0 metres 200
Ⓤ U-Bahn station	✝ Church	
🚆 Railway station	⊠ Post office	0 yards 200
🚕 Taxi rank	═ Railway line	

BAVARIA

*B*avaria is the biggest federal state in the Federal Republic of Germany. It is made up of regions that, in the past, were either independent secular territories or bishoprics. It includes former free towns of the Holy Roman Empire, such as Nördlingen, Rothenburg ob der Tauber, Dinkelsbühl, Nuremberg and Augsburg, which lost their independence to Bavaria only in the early 19th century.

The area that is now known as Bavaria was inhabited in early times by Celts and Romans. The German Baiovarii, which gave the territory its name, arrived here during the 5th and 6th centuries. In the second half of the 6th century, the area was conquered by the Franks then, from 1180 until 1918, Bavaria was ruled by the Wittelsbach dynasty. During Medieval times, this split into the Upper Bavarian line (Straubing, Ingolstadt and Munich) and the Lower Bavarian line (Landshut). In 1505, separate provinces were once again combined into a single country. During the 16th and 17th centuries the duchy of Bavaria was the bulwark of Roman Catholicism within the Holy Roman Empire and during the reign of Maximilian I, Bavaria fought against the Protestant Union in the Thirty Years' War. For his loyalty to Rome, Maximilian I was rewarded in 1623 with the title of Elector, which meant that he could vote in elections for the Emperor. Following the fall of the Holy Roman Empire, Bavaria became a kingdom and remained as such until 1918.

Bavaria's turbulent history has left behind a rich architectural and cultural heritage. In addition to Roman antiquities, Baroque fortresses and fairy-tale castles, the region also has more than its share of glorious Alpine scenery, beer halls and colourful festivals, all of which make this one of the most popular parts of Germany for tourists. The capital, Munich, is a lively cosmopolitan city of wide boulevards and leafy squares with a wide choice of shops, restaurants, cinemas and theatres.

Girls dressed in national costume celebrating St Leonard's Festival

◁ Interior of the Abbey library, in Metten

Exploring Bavaria

Bavaria is a paradise for tourists. Its beautiful lakes attract lovers of water sports, while the mountainous regions of the Bavarian Forest offer the unspoiled charms of nature. The Alps, with their charming mountain hostels and numerous ski-lifts, provide endless possibilities for enjoyment. Towns and villages feature magnificent historic sights and the capital, Munich, combines the advantages of a lively metropolis with a peaceful atmosphere that is not often found in large cities.

The façade and central rotunda of Bayreuth's Eremitage

SIGHTS AT A GLANCE

Fulda
Erfurt
Bad Neustadt an der Saale
A7
A71
279
Sinn
Fränkische Saale
Hammelburg
Schweinfurt
Frankfurt
Werneck
A70
Regnitz
ASCHAFFENBURG ①
Karlstadt
19
Main
BAMBER
WÜRZBURG ⑥
POMMERSFELDE
Kitzingen
A3
Neustadt an der Aisch
Tauber
ROTHENBUR OB DER TAU
A7
13
A6
ANSBAC
Heilbronn
Gunzenhause
DINKELSBÜH ⑪
NÖRDLIN ⑫
25
Donauwör
16
Dilling der Do
Günzburg
Ulm
Ne
Neu-Ulm
AUGSBU
300
A7
Günz
LAND AM
Memmingen
A96
OTTOBEUR ㊺
Marktoberdorf
KEMPTEN ㊶
LINDAU
Bodensee
FÜSSEN
HOHENSCHWANGAU ㊵
㊷
Feldkirch
OBERSTDORF ㊸
Iller

0 km   30

0 miles   30

The beautiful riverside town of Passau

KEY

▬	Motorway
▬	Major road
▭	Minor road
= =	Under construction
▬▬	Main railway
——	Minor railway
▬▬	International border
▬	Regional border
△	Summit

SEE ALSO

- **Where to Stay** pp499–503
- **Where to Eat** pp538–42

Nuremberg's imposing Kaiserburg, overlooking the city

GETTING AROUND

Munich, Nuremberg and Augsburg are all served by
international airports, while fast train services operate
throughout the region. The main motorways are the A93
linking Saxony with Ratisbon, the A9 between Thuringia
and Munich, the A3 between Frankfurt and Passau and the
A8, which runs between Stuttgart and Salzburg.

Red sandstone exterior of Schloss Johannisburg, Aschaffenburg

Aschaffenburg ❶

Road map C5. 👥 67 000. 🚊
ℹ️ *Schlossplatz 1 (06021-39 58 00).*

Situated in Lower Franconia, Aschaffenburg enjoys a scenic position on the hilly right bank of the river Main. The town became the second seat of the Mainz bishops in the 13th century, the first being Mainz.

The northwest part of the old town features a majestic, red sandstone riverside castle, **Schloss Johannisburg**, which was once occupied by the Mainz bishops-electors.

The castle gallery holds a fine collection of European paintings, dating from the 15th to the 18th century. It includes works by Hans Baldung Grien and the most important collection of Lucas Cranach canvases in Europe. In the castle library are valuable medieval codices, such as the 10th-century *Book of Gospel Readings (Evangelarium)* from Fulda.

Occupying a scenic position above a vineyard a short distance to the northwest of the castle is Pompejanum. The Bavarian king Ludwig I was so fascinated with the discovery of Pompeii that he ordered a replica of the Castor and Pollux villa *(Casa di Castore e Polluce)* to be built. This he filled with his rich collection of antiquities.

After undergoing restoration work to repair war damage, the museum opened its doors to the public again in 1994.

🏰 **Schloss Johannisburg**
Schlossplatz 4. *Tel (06021) 38 65 70.* ⭕ *Apr–Sep: 9am–6pm Tue–Sun; Oct–Mar: 10am–4pm Tue–Sun.* 🎫

Pommersfelden ❷

Road map D5. ℹ️ *Hauptstraße 11 (09548-922 00).*

On the edge of the Steigerwald – a popular hiking area – is the small village of Pommersfelden, which is dominated by its magnificent Baroque palace, **Schloss Weißenstein**. The palace was commissioned by the Mainz Archbishop and Elector and the Prince-Bishop of Bamberg, Lothar Franz von Schönborn. It was built, in only five years (1711–16), to a design by the famous architect, Johann Dientzenhofer.

This masterpiece of secular Baroque architecture is worth visiting for several reasons. Particularly interesting is the three-storey-high ornamental ceiling by Johann Rudolf Byss. The most spectacular room is the Marble Hall, which features paintings by Michael Rottmayr. The well-preserved interior of the palace houses a gallery, a library, and a valuable collection of furniture. After visiting the palace, you can take a stroll around its gardens, which were

created by Maximilian von Welsch in 1715, in what was the then fashionable, geometric French style. It is now laid out in English-garden style.

🏰 **Schloss Weißenstein**
Tel (09548) 98180.
⭕ *Apr–Oct: 10am–5pm daily.*
⏱️ *every hour. (Short tour: 11:30am and 4:30pm.)* 🎫

Coburg ❸

Road map D5. 👥 *44,000.* 🚊
ℹ️ *Herrngasse 4 (09561-741 80).*

Former residence of the Wettin family, Coburg is situated on the bank of the river Itz. It is dominated by a massive fortress, the **Veste Coburg**, which is one of the largest in Germany. Coburg's origins go back to the 11th century, but its present-day appearance is mainly the result of remodelling that was carried out in the 16th and the 17th centuries.

The fortress consists of a number of buildings clustered around several courtyards and surrounded by a triple line of walls. The complex is now a museum, housing various collections, including prints and drawings, arms and armour.

In 1530, the fortress provided refuge to Martin Luther who, as an outlaw, hid here from April until October. The room in which he hid is

Ornate entrance to Coburg's Stadthaus

furnished with antique furniture and features a portrait of Luther, painted by Lucas Cranach the Younger.

Among the most important buildings in the old town are the late-Gothic church of St Maurice and a beautiful Renaissance college building that was founded by Prince Johann Casimir in 1605. On the opposite side of the market square is the town hall, originally built in 1577–79 and remodelled in the 18th century.

Further along is the town castle, **Schloss Ehrenburg**, which was built in the 16th century on the site of a dissolved Franciscan monastery. The castle burned down in 1693 and was subsequently rebuilt. The façade facing the square was remodelled by Karl Friedrich Schinkel in Neo-Gothic style.

The castle has some fine interiors, including the Baroque Riesensaal and Weisser Saal and a chapel with rich stucco decorations.

Interior of the monumental, Baroque Vierzehnheiligen church

⚑ Veste Coburg
Tel (09561) 87 979. ☐ *Apr–Oct: 9:30am–5pm Tue–Sun; Nov–Mar: 1–4pm Tue–Sun.* 🔲

⚑ Schloss Ehrenburg
Schlossplatz 1. *Tel* (09561) 808 832. ☐ *Apr–Sep: 9am–5pm Tue–Sun; Oct–Mar: 10am–3pm Tue–Sun.* 🔲 *every hour.* 🔲

Vierzehnheiligen ➍

Staffelstein. **Road map** D5. *Tel* (09571) 950 80. ☐ *Apr–Oct: 8am–7:30pm; Nov–Mar: 8am–6:30pm.* **www**.vierzehnheiligen.de

High above the river Main is Banz Abbey, a Benedictine monastery built in 1695 by Johann Leonhard and Leonhard Dientzenhofer. Opposite is the pilgrimage church of the Fourteen Saints of Intercession. The first chapel, built in the 16th century, became too small to accommodate the growing numbers of pilgrims so, in 1741, the foundation stone

was laid for the monumental new church, designed by Balthasar Neumann. Built in 1741–72, this is one of the most famous masterpieces of South German Baroque, with magnificent Rococo furnishings. The building is a cross-shaped basilica, with a monumental twin-tower façade.

The interior has an exceptionally dynamic style, achieved by combining the longitudinal and central planes: the three ovals laid along the main axis join with the two circles of the transept. The centrepiece of the nave is the "Altar of Mercy", which stands at the spot where, according to a 1519 legend, a shepherd had visions of Christ with the fourteen Saints of Intercession. The altar features statues of the fourteen saints, and are the work of F X Feuchtmayr and J G Üblher (1763). The rich stucco decorations and frescoes are the work of Giuseppe Appiani.

Fränkische Schweiz ➎

Road map D5.

The area popularly known as Franconian Switzerland (*Fränkische Schweiz*) covers the area between Nuremberg, Bamberg and Bayreuth. One of Germany's most beautiful tourist regions, it offers its visitors picturesque green meadows, magnificent highlands covered with cornfields, imposing castles perched on top of high rocks, fabulous dolomite rocks and deep caves with stalactites. Its towns and villages, with their charming inns and timber-frame houses, look like a setting for *Snow White and Seven Dwarfs*. The main routes across the area run alongside its rivers – the Wiesent, Leinleiter, Püttlach and Trubach. The Wiesent, which is ideal for canoeing, cuts across the region from east to west, joining the river Regnitz near the town of Forchheim. The town features many timber-frame houses, including the old town hall dating from the 14th to the 16th century. Near Forchheim, in **Ebermannstadt**, is a Marian church with a fine Madonna. The federal route B470

Madonna from Marienkapelle in Ebermannstadt

leads to the picturesque village of Tüchersfeld, which is built into the rocks. A good base for exploring this area is the village of Pottenstein. St Elizabeth of Thuringia is said to have stayed here in 1227. To the east of the castle is a cave with impressive stalactites.

Schloss Greifenstein in Heiligenstadt, in Fränkische Schweiz

Würzburg 6

The bombing raid on Würzburg on 16 March 1945 lasted for about 20 minutes and destroyed over 80 percent of the town's buildings. It seemed that Würzburg, which occupies a picturesque position on the banks of the river Main, had been erased from the face of the earth. Like Dresden, however, the town rose from the ashes and once again it enchants visitors with its rich heritage of historic sights. As well as being a popular tourist destination, Würzburg is also an important commercial and cultural centre for Lower Franconia and home of the excellent Franconian wine.

View over Würzburg, with Dom St Kilian in the foreground

⛩ Residenz
See pp246–7.

⛪ Dom St Kilian
Domplatz. ***Tel*** *(0931) 53 691.*
◯ *10am–5pm Mon– Sat, 1–6pm Sun and holidays.*
Next to the great cathedral churches of Mainz, Speyer and Worms, this is Germany's fourth largest Romanesque church. It was built in 1045–1188, its patron saint an Irish monk who came to Würzburg in AD 686.
　The church is a three-nave basilica with a transept and a twin-tower façade. Inside, the Romanesque main nave with its flat roof contrasts sharply with the Baroque stucco embellishments of the choir.
　In the north nave is an interesting group of bishops' tombs, including two that are the work of Tilman Riemenschneider. At the end of the north transept is a chapel, which was built by Balthasar Neumann for the bishops of the House of Schönborn.

⛪ Neumünster
St-Kilians-Platz.
Just north of the cathedral, the Neumünster church was built in the 11th century at the burial site of St Kilian and his fellow Irish martyrs, St Kolonat and St Totnan.
　The church's imposing Baroque dome and its red sandstone façade date from the 18th century. Featured in

The beautiful red sandstone façade of Neumünster-Kirche

the interior are numerous works of art, including a late 15th-century Madonna and the *Man of Sorrow* by the 15th-century German sculptor Tilman Riemenschneider. The north door leads to a lovely small courtyard; the remains of the cloister date from the Hohenstauf period. Under a lime tree is the resting place of a famous medieval minstrel Walther von der Vogelweide.
　A procession is held each year on St Kilian's day (8 July) when theological students carry the skulls of the martyrs, contained in a transparent box, from the west crypt to the cathedral where they are put on public display.

➕ Bürgerspital
Theaterstraße.
The Bürgerspital was founded in 1319 by Johann von Steren. Hospitals like this originally provided charitable care for the old as well as the infirm, and today this institution provides care for over one hundred elderly residents of Würzburg. It operates as a self-financing foundation, its main source of income being from vine-growing. Residents are given a quarter of a litre (½ pint) of an excellent home-produced wine each day, with double the ration on Sundays. Visitors can also sample various vintages.

➕ Juliusspital
Juliuspromenade. ***Tel*** *(0931) 393 14 00.* ◯ *Apr–mid-Nov: guided tours by appointment.*
Founded in 1576 by Julius Echter, Juliusspital was remodelled in the 17th and the 18th centuries. The Rococo pharmacy (1760–65) in the hospital arcades has survived intact and is well worth a visit.

⛩ Rathaus
Rueckermainstraße.
Würzburg's picturesque town hall was built in several stages. Begun in the 13th century, it was subsequently extended in the 15th and 16th centuries. Particularly noteworthy are the beautiful 16th-century paintings on the façade and the late-Renaissance tower, Roter Turm, which dates from around 1660.

An old crane near Alte Mainbrücke over the river Main

⊞ Alte Mainbrücke

Connecting the old town and Festung Marienberg, this beautiful bridge was built in 1473–1543. It is the oldest bridge over the Main.

⚓ Festung Marienberg

Fürstenbau-Museum
Tel (0931) 355 170. ◻ 16 Mar–Oct: 9am–6pm Tue–Sun. ● Nov–Mar. ⬜

Mainfränkisches Museum
Tel (0931) 205 940. ◻ Apr–Oct: 10am–5pm Tue–Sun; Nov–Mar: 10am–4pm Tue–Sun. ⬜

Burgführungen ⬜ 16 Mar–Oct: 11am, 2pm, 3pm, 4pm Tue–Fri, 10am, 11am, 1pm, 2pm, 3pm, 4pm Sat & Sun.

Built on the site of an old Celtic stronghold, the Marienberg Fortress towers above the town. In AD 707 a church was built here and, in 1201, work commenced on a fortress that served as the residence of the prince-bishops until 1719. Within its fortifications stands the first original donjon church dating from the 13th century, and the Renaissance-Baroque palace. The museum exhibits illustrate the 1,200-year history of the town. The former arsenal now houses the Franconian Museum with its valuable collection of sculptures by Tilman Riemenschneider.

VISITORS' CHECKLIST

Road map C5. 🏠 128,000. ✈ 7 km (4½ miles) west. 🚉 Hauptbahnhof. ℹ Falkenhaus am Markt (0931-372398). 🎭 Afrikafestival (May), Würzburger Weindorf (May/Jun), Mozartfest (Jun), Kilianifest (Jul), Bachtage (Nov–Dec).

⛪ Käppele

Mergentheimer Strasse.
Standing at the top of a hill at the southwestern end of the city, this twin-towered Baroque chapel is the work of Balthasar Neumann (1747–50). Its interior is lavishly decorated with beautiful wall paintings by Matthias Günther.

Festung Marienberg, built on a hill overlooking the river Main

WURZBURG CITY CENTRE

Hauptbahnhof

Flughafen
7 km (4.5 miles)

RÖNTGENRING
HAUGERRING
Congress Centrum
Friedensbrücke
GERBERSTR.
Juliuspital ⑤
Stift Haug
BERLINER PLATZ
DREIKRONENSTRASSE
JULIUSPROMENADE
HEINESTRASSE
THEATERSTR.
SEMMELSTR.
LUDWIGSTRASSE
KAPUZINERSTR.
RENNWEGER RING
Marienkapelle
SCHÖNBORNSTRASSE
EICHHORNSTR.
④ Bürgerspital
Mainfranken Theater Würzburg
Rathaus ⑥
MARKT
③ Neumünster
RENNWEG
MARTIN-LUTHER-STRASSE
⑦
DOMSTRASSE
② Dom St Kilian
① Residenz
Alte Mainbrücke
Domschatz
SCHÖNTALSTR.
BALTHASAR-NEUMANN-PROM.
OTTOSTRASSE
Festung Marienberg ⑧
SAALGASSE
Alte Universität
Hofgarten
FRIEDRICH-EBERT-RING
St Burkard
NEUBAUSTR.
SANDERSTRASSE
SANDERRING
LEISTENSTRASSE
OBERER MAINKAI
Main
MERGENTHEIMER STR.
Ludwigsbrücke
Käppele

0 metres 300
0 yards 300

Key to Symbols see back flap

Residenz in Würzburg

Sculpture from Residenz garden

This vast complex was commissioned by two prince-bishops, the brothers Johann Philipp Franz and Friedrich Karl von Schönborn. Its construction between 1720 and 1744 was supervised by several architects, including Johann Lukas von Hildebrandt and Maximilian von Welsch. However, the Residenz (which is on UNESCO's World Heritage list) is mainly associated with the architect Balthasar Neumann, who was responsible for the overall design.

Napoleon's bedroom

Main entrance

Martin-von-Wagner-Museum entrance

★ Treppenhaus
The work of the Venetian artist Giovanni Battista Tiepolo, the largest fresco in the world adorns the vault of the staircase.

Frankonia-Brunnen
This fountain, designed by Ferdinand von Miller, was constructed in the parade square in front of the Residenz. It was funded by donations from the inhabitants of Würzburg.

The Coat of Arms of the Patron
The richly carved coat of arms are by Johann Wolfgang von der Auwery and are the personal arms of Friedrich Karl von Schönborn, Prince-Bishop of Bamberg and Würzburg.

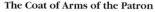

For hotels and restaurants in this region see pp499–503 and pp538–42

★ Kaisersaal

The centrepiece of the palace, the sumptuous emperor's chamber, testifies to the close relationship between Würzburg and the Holy Roman Empire. There are Tiepolo frescoes here too.

Garden Hall

This vast, low hall has Rococo stucco works by Antonio Bossi, dating from 1749. There is also a painting on the vaulting by Johan Zick dating from 1750, depicting The Feast of the Gods and Diana Resting.

Venetian Room

This room is named after three tapestries depicting the Venetian carnival. Further ornaments include decorative panels with paintings by Johann Thalhofer, a pupil of Rudolph Byss

★ Hofkirche

The church interior is richly decorated with paintings, sculptures and stucco ornaments. The side altars were designed by Johann Lukas von Hildebrandt and feature paintings by Giovanni Battista Tiepolo.

STAR SIGHTS

★ Hofkirche

★ Kaisersaal

★ Treppenhaus

Bamberg ●

Situated on seven hills like ancient Rome, Bamberg features a splendidly preserved old town, encircled by the branches of the river Regnitz. The town is famous not only for its exceptional artistic heritage but also for its excellent beer, produced by one of the nine breweries that operate here. Its long history goes back to AD 902, when the Babenberg family established their residence here. The town grew and prospered in the wake of the Thirty Years' War. In 1993, Bamberg became a UNESCO World Heritage Site.

Beautiful rose garden at the rear of the Neue Residenz

Exploring Bamberg

A good place to start sight seeing is the Domplatz, one of Germany's loveliest squares, with its magnificent cathedral church and the old bishop's palace. After visiting the Neue Residenz you can go down to the river, where you will find the water palace, Concordia. The old town is reached by crossing one of two bridges – Untere or Obere Brücke.

🔒 Dom

See pp250–51.

🏛 Alte Hofhaltung Historisches Museum

Domplatz 7. **Tel** (0951) 871 142.
⏰ May–Oct: 9am–5pm Tue–Sun.
📷

On the west side of Domplatz stands a magnificent portal, with statues of the imperial couple Heinrich II and Kunigunde. This is the gate to the former bishop's residence, built at the turn of the 15th and 16th centuries in place of an old fortress of Heinrich II. Within the building's wings is a pleasant courtyard. Inside is a museum that focuses on the history of the region.

🏛 Neue Residenz und Staatsgalerie

Domplatz 8. **Tel** (0951) 519 390.
⏰ Apr–Sep: 9am–6pm daily;
Oct–Mar: 10–4pm daily. 📷
www.schloesser-bayern.de
The Neue Residenz, with its richly decorated apartments and the Emperor's Room, was built in 1695–1704 and is the work of Johann Leonhard Dientzenhofer. Its walls are adorned with magnificent frescos painted by the Tyrolean artist Melchior Steidl. The walls and pillars feature

the Habsburg family tree, while 16 statues represent Emperors of the Holy Roman Empire. The Neue Residenz houses a collection of old German masters, including *The Flood* by Hans Baldung Grien and three canvases by Lucas Cranach the Elder.

🔒 Karmelitenkloster

Kreuzgang ⏰ 9–11.30am,
2:30–5:30pm daily.
The hospital-abbey complex of St Theodore was founded in the late 12th century by Bishop Eberhard. Since 1589 the church and abbey have belonged to the Carmelite order. The south tower and Romanesque portal are the remains of the massive 12th-century basilica. The interior of the church was redesigned in the late 17th and early 18th centuries so the altar is now situated at its western end, while the entrance is on the site of the previous presbytery. The layout of the cloisters on the south side of the church is typical of Cistercian designs.

♣ Wasserschloss Concordia

Concordiastrasse. ● to the public.
This magnificent Baroque palace, which enjoys a scenic position on the water's edge, was built for Counsellor Böttinger between 1716 and 1722, to a design by Johann Dientzenhofer. The building now houses a science institute.

🏛 Altes Rathaus

The Baroque lower bridge, Untere Brücke, provides a magnificent view over the upper bridge, Obere Brücke,

The Baroque palace Concordia on the bank of the river Regnitz

Picturesque fishermen's cottages in Klein-Venedig

VISITORS' CHECKLIST

Road map D5. 🏘 71,000. ✈
8 km (5 miles) to the southeast.
🏨 *Geyerswörthstraße 3 (0951-
297 62 00).* 🎭 *Calderon-
Festspiele (June), Sandkirchweih
(August).* **www**.bamberg.info

with its fabulous town hall. This originally Gothic seat of the municipal authorities was remodelled in 1744–56 by Jakob Michael Küchel. The half-timbered structure of the Rottmeisterhaus, which seems to be gliding over the waves of the river Regnitz, was added in 1688.

🏛 Klein-Venedig

"Little Venice" is a district of fishermen's cottages, their picturesque façades adorned with pots of geraniums. Visitors come here for a glass of Rauchbier – a local beer with a smoky flavour – while they enjoy the view.

🏛 Grüner Markt

With its historic houses and adjacent Maximilianplatz, Grüner Markt lies at the heart of the old town. It features the magnificent Baroque

St Martin's Church, built in 1686–91 by the Dientzenhofer brothers. Also notable is the late-Baroque St Catherine Hospital and Seminary, built by Balthasar Neumann, which now serves as the town hall.

🔓 Kirche St Michael

Fränkisches Brauereimuseum
Michaelsberg.
⏰ *Apr–Oct: 1–5pm Wed–Fri,
11am–5pm Sat & Sun.* 🈂
The Benedictine abbey that stood on this site was founded in 1015. The surviving church was built after 1121 and later remodelled in the 16th and 17th centuries. On the ceiling of the church, nicknamed the "Botanical Gardens", are paintings depicting almost 600 species of medicinal plants. The abbey's Baroque buildings date from the 17th and 18th centuries and are the work of Johann Dientzenhofer

and Balthasar Neumann. The abbey's brewery now houses a museum.

🏛 Schloss Seehof

Memmelsdorf. ***Tel*** *(0951) 409 570.*
⏰ *Apr–Oct: 9am–6pm Tue–Sun.*
⛔ *Nov–Mar.* 🈂 🈂
Built and designed by Antonio Petrini in 1686, this was originally the summer residence of the prince-bishops of Bamberg. The nine magnificent state rooms have been restored and are open to the public.

Façade of Schloss Seehof in Memmelsdorf

BAMBERG CITY CENTRE

Alte Hofhaltung ②
Altes Rathaus ⑥
Dom ①
Karmeliterkloster ⑤
Klein-Venedig ⑦
Neue Residenz
   und Staatsgalerie ③
Wasserschloss
   Concordia ⑤

0 metres   300
0 yards   300

Key to Symbols *see back flap*

Bamberg Cathedral

Bamberg's skyline is dominated by the cathedral of St Peter and St George, which combines the late Romanesque and early French-Gothic styles. It was founded in 1004 and consecrated in 1012, and again in 1237 after being demolished by fire and then rebuilt. This is a triple-nave basilica with two choirs, whose apses are flanked by two pairs of towers. The cloisters were built between 1399 and 1457, while the monumental sculptures adorning the portals date from the 13th century. The western choir holds the only papal grave in Germany, that of Pope Clement II, who had been the local bishop.

Sculpted figure of Ecclesia

Interior
The illuminated main nave features a graceful, early Gothic, cross-ribbed vault.

★ **Bamberger Reiter**
By the northwestern pillar of the eastern choir stands the famous equestrian statue of the "Bamberg Rider", dating from about 1230. Many scholars have puzzled over the identity of the rider, but the riddle remains unsolved.

St George's Choir

★ **Tomb of Heinrich II and Kunigunde**
This beautiful sarcophagus of the imperial couple is the work of Tilman Riemenschneider, completed in 1513.

Marien-pforte

Emperor's Cloak
The Diocesan Museum houses an exhibition of sacral art. It also features a collection of imperial vestments, including Heinrich II's blue cloak of stars.

St Peter's Choir

Hochaltar des Peterschores
The main altar of the west choir is adorned with sculptures depicting the Crucifixion (1648–49) by Justus Glesker.

★ **Marian Altar by Veit Stoß**
Veit Stoß was commissioned to create this altar by his son, Andrew Stoß, who was a Carmelite prior in Nürnberg at the time. After the victory of the Reformation in Nürnberg, however, he moved to Bamberg in 1543.

STAR SIGHTS

★ Bamberger Reiter

★ Marian Altar by Veit Stoß

★ Tomb of Heinrich II and Kunigunde

Marienpforte
This magnificent stonework adorns the main entrance. The tympanum features reliefs depicting scenes from the Last Judgement.

Bayreuth ❽

Lovers of German music associate this town with the composer Richard Wagner (1813–83), who took up residence here in 1872. Established in 1231, Bayreuth originally belonged to the family of Count von Andechs-Meran; in 1248 it passed to the Margraves of Nuremberg (von Zollern) and, since 1806, Franconian Bayreuth has belonged to Bavaria. The town flourished during the 17th and 18th centuries when it was the residence of the Margraves, particularly during the time of Margravine Wilhelmine, sister of the Prussian King Frederick the Great and wife of Margrave Frederick.

Extraordinary Baroque interior of the Markgräfliches Opernhaus

🖾 Markgräfliches Opernhaus
Opernstraße 14. **Tel** (0921) 759 69 22. ⬚ Apr–Sep: 9am–6pm daily; Oct–Mar: 10am–4pm daily. 🖾

One of the finest theatres in Europe, the Markgräfliches Opera House was built in the 1740s by Joseph Saint-Pierre. Its ornate Baroque interior was designed by Giuseppe Galli Bibiena and his son Carlo, who came from a famous Bolognese family of theatre architects.

⚜ Neues Schloss
Ludwigstraße 21. **Tel** (0921) 759 690. ⬚ Apr–Sep: 9am–6pm daily; Oct–Mar: 10am–4pm daily. 🖾

The Neues Schloss (New Castle) was commissioned by Margravine Wilhelmine and built by Joseph Saint-Pierre. The elongated, three-storey structure combines classical lines with a rustic ground floor. The Italian wing was added in 1759. To this day nearly all the rooms have retained their original

Baroque and Rococo decor. The park is arranged in a typically English style.

⛲ Villa Wahnfried
Richard-Wagner-Museum. Richard-Wagner-Straße 48. **Tel** (0921) 75 72 816. ⬚ Apr–Oct: 9am–5pm daily (to 8pm Tue & Thu); Nov–Mar: 10am–5pm daily. 🖾 ⬤ Easter Sunday.

On the northeast side of the castle garden is Villa Wahnfried. Built for Wagner by Carl Wölfel, the villa was destroyed during World War II but was restored in the 1970s. In the garden is Wagner's tomb and that of his wife Cosima, the daughter of Franz Liszt.

⛫ Franz-Liszt-Museum
Wahnfriedstraße 9. **Tel** (0921) 516 64 88. ⬚ Sep–Jun: 10am–noon, 2–5pm daily; Jul–Aug: 10am–5pm daily. 🖾

A short distance from Villa Wahnfried, at the junction of Wahnfriedstrasse and Lisztstrasse, stands the house in which Hungarian composer Franz Liszt died in 1886. It now houses a museum dedicated to the composer.

⛲ Eremitage
4 km (2.5 miles) northeast of town. **Tel** (0921) 759 69 37. ⬚ Apr–Sep: 9am–6pm daily, 1 Oct–15 Oct: 10am–4pm. ⬤ 16 Oct–Mar.

In 1715–18, following the example of the French king Louis XIV and the fashion among the nobility for playing at ascetism, Margrave Georg Wilhelm ordered the building of the Eremitage complex as a retreat. With its horseshoe-shaped orangery, the hermitage (or Altes Schloss) was given to Margravine Wilhelmine as a birthday present. She then set about transforming it into a pleasure palace.

Tomb of Wagner and his wife in the garden of Villa Wahnfried

RICHARD WAGNER (1813–1883)
The German composer is inseparably linked with Bayreuth, where he enjoyed his greatest artistic triumphs. His career, which did not run smoothly in early days, began in Magdeburg, Königsberg and Riga. From there he had to flee, via London to Paris, from his pursuing creditors. His reputation was firmly established by successful performances of his romantic operas *The Flying Dutchman* (1843) and *Tannhäuser* (1845) in Dresden. Wagner's long-time sponsor was the eccentric Bavarian king, Ludwig II. From 1872 Wagner lived in Bayreuth, where Festspielhaus was built specifically for the operas.

Bust of Wagner by Arno Breker (1939)

Festspielhaus, specially designed venue for the annual Wagner Festival

VISITORS' CHECKLIST

Road map D5. 🏠 75,000. ✈ 10 km (6 miles) to northeast. 🚉 Hauptbahnhof. 🚌 *Luitpoldplatz 9 (0921-885 88).* 🎵 *Musica Bayreuth (May), Fränkische Festwoche (May), Richard-Wagner-Festspiele (Jul–Aug), Bayreuther Barock (Sep).*

Festspielhaus

Festspielhugel. *Tel* (0921) 787 80. Sep–Oct:10am, 11am, 2pm, 3pm Tue–Sun; Nov–Apr 10am, 2pm Tue–Sun.

Each July and August, Wagner festivals are held in this theatre, which was built in 1872–75 to a design by Gottfried Semper. The world premiere of *The Ring of the Nibelung* was performed here in 1876.

Environs

Approximately 20 km (12 miles) to the northwest of Bayreuth is the town of **Kulmbach**. Famous for its countless breweries, the town hosts a big beer festival each year, in July and August. Its town hall has a beautiful, Rococo façade dating from 1752. From here you can walk to the castle hill to visit the Plassenburg Fortress, which has belonged to the Hohenzollern family since 1340. Until 1604, this was the seat of the von Brandenburg-Kulmbach Margraves. The vast structure was built in 1560-70. The gem in its crown is the Renaissance courtyard with arcades (Schöner Hof). The castle houses a vast collection of tin figurines, with some 30,000

items. In **Ködnitz**, to the southeast of Kulmbach, is the Upper Franconian Village School Museum. Based on the original school furnishings and various old photographs, the exhibition illustrates the teaching methods that were used in this region more than a hundred years ago.

Some 25 km (16 miles) from Bayreuth, in Sanspareil Park near Hollfeld, is the **Felsentheater** – an unusual 80-seat theatre set in a natural grotto.

Felsentheater, in a natural grotto in Sanspareil Park near Bayreuth

BAYREUTH CITY CENTRE

Franz-Liszt-Museum ④
Markgräfliches Opernhaus ①
Neues Schloss ②
Villa Wahnfried ③

Berching ⑨

Map D6. 👥 *7,500.* 🚆 *Petten-koferplatz 12 (08462-205 13).*

This charming little town, situated in the valley of the river Sulz, boasts a history that stretches back to the 9th century. To this day it retains the complete enclosure of its medieval city walls, including towers and gates with old oak doors. The most beautiful of the towers is the *Chinesische Turm* (the Chinese Tower).

The regional museum is well worth visiting, as are some of the local churches. These include an early Gothic church, Mariae Himmelfahrt, remodelled after 1756 by M Seybold and featuring some beautiful Rococo stucco ornaments. The Baroque St Lorenz, with its 13th century tower and original late-Gothic altar, is also noteworthy.

Amberg ⑩

Map D5. 👥 *43,000.* 🚆 *Hallplatz 2 (09621-102 39).*

Situated at the edge of the Franconian Jura, on the banks of the river Vils, Amberg owes its development to local iron ore deposits and the steel industry. The well-preserved, oval-shaped old town is still encircled by medieval walls. At the centre is an enchanting market square with the vast 15th-century late-Gothic hall-church, Pfarrkirche St Martin, and Gothic town hall (1356), both still with their original interiors.

Amberg was once the residential town of the Rhine palatines, whose Renaissance palace and chancellery have survived to the present day.

The symbol of Amberg is the Stadtbrille, the bridge spanning the river Vils, whose arches reflected in the river resemble a pair of spectacles – hence its nickname "the town's spectacles".

The late-Gothic main altar in St George's Church, Dinkelsbühl

Dinkelsbühl ⑪

Map D6. 👥 *11,000.* 🚆 🚌 *Altrathausplatz 14, (09851-902 440).* 🎭 *Kinderzeche (mid-Jul).*

This old Franconian town is one of the best-preserved medieval urban complexes in Germany. The walls surrounding the city include four towers – Wörnitzer, Nördlinger, Seringer and Rothenburger Tor – which are all almost intact. The residential district of the town consists

mainly of timber-framed houses. The finest example of these is the Deutsches Haus, which stands opposite St George's Church. Dating from the late 15th to the early 16th century, the house once belonged to the Drechsel-Deufstetten family and is now a hotel-restaurant.

The late-Gothic Church of St George is a triple-nave hall-church with no transept. Together with the presbytery, it forms one large interior crowned with magnificent network vaults. The most valuable items of the interior furnishings include the pulpit, the font – which dates from around 1500 – and the Crucifixion in the main altar, which is attributed to Michael Wolgemut. A fine view of the town can be obtained from the church tower.

In Turmgasse stands the Baroque palace of the Teutonic Order, built in 1760–64 by Mathias Binder.

Nördlingen ⑫

Map D6. 👥 *20,000.* 🚆 🚌 *Marktplatz 2 (09081-841 16).* 🎭 *Stabenfest (May), Nördlinger Pfingstmesse Scharlachrennen (Jun–Jul), Sommerfestspiele (Jul), Historisches Stadtmauerfest (every third year in Sep; next in 2013).*

The town is situated in the Ries Basin, which is an immense and well-preserved crater that was formed millions of years ago by a meteor strike.

During the Middle Ages Nördlingen was a free town of the Holy Roman Empire and an important trade centre. The fortification walls which surround the city, including fifteen towers (dating from the 14th to the 15th centuries) have survived almost intact to this day.

The late-Gothic church of St George was built by Nikolaus Eseler, who also built the St George Church in Dinkelsbühl. The church is a triple-nave hall-church with round pillars and network vaults. Its imposing west tower, known as the Daniel Tower, offers a magnificent

The symbol of Amberg is the bridge named "the town spectacles"

For hotels and restaurants in this region see pp499–503 and pp538–42

panoramic view of the town and its environs.

The St Salvator's Church features original Gothic altars and a portal that has the scene of the *Last Judgement* in the tympanum.

The former hospital of the Holy Spirit is now home to an interesting **Stadtmuseum**. The 14th-century town hall features a striking external stone stairway (1618).

Statue from the Tanzhaus façade

🏛 **Stadtmuseum**
Vordere Gerbergasse 1.
Tel (09081-273 82 30).
⬜ Mar–Oct: 1:30–4:00pm Tue–Sun.
📅 Nov–Feb: open only to guided tours (reserve a place in advance by telephone). ♿

Ansbach ⑬

Map D6. 🏙 40,000. 🚉
ℹ Johann-Sebastian-Bach-Platz 1 (0981-512 43 or 194 33. 📷
Ansbacher Frühlingsfest (May), Bach-Woche (every two years in Jul: the next one is in 2013), Ansbacher Rokokospiele (Jul), Heimatfest (Jul).

The town, situated west of Nuremberg, began its history in AD 748 with the foundation of a Benedictine Abbey by a man named Gumbert. A settlement called Onoldsbach, which sprang up nearby, is now called Ansbach. From 1460 until 1791 Ansbach was the home of the von Brandenburg-Ansbach Margraves and in 1791 it was incorporated into Prussia; after 1806 it passed into Bavaria. The Markgräfliche residence is

situated in the north-eastern part of the Old Town. Remodelled several times it is now a Baroque Neo-Classical structure. Its 27 original state apartments include the Mirror Room, Mirror Gallery, Dining Room and Audience Room. It now houses the Museum of Faience and Porcelain. The nearby Hofgarten has a 102-m (335-ft) long Orangery. It also houses a Kaspar Hauser Collection.

🏛 **Markgrafenmuseum**
Kaspar-Hauser-Platz 1.
Tel (0981) 977 50 56.
⬜ 10am–5pm Tue–Sun. ♿

🏛 **Markgräfliche Residenz "Ansbacher Fayence und Porzellan"**
Promenade 27. **Tel** (0981) 953 83 90. ⬜ Apr–Sep: 9am–6pm Tue–Sun; Oct–Mar: 10am–4pm Tue–Sun. 📷 hourly. ♿

Eichstätt ⑭

Map D6. 🏙 15,000. 🚉
ℹ Domplatz 8 (08421-600 1400).

Willibald, a close companion and compatriot of the Anglo-Saxon missionary Boniface, established a missionary-abbey (Eihstat) here. Soon afterwards Eichstätt became an episcopal town. In 1634 a fire ripped through the town, destroying four-fifths of its houses and four churches; after this the town was rebuilt in Baroque style.

Eichstätt is home to the country's only Catholic university, established in 1980. On the outskirts of town, on

Majestic Walhalla near Donaustauf

a hill overlooking the River Altmühl, stands the picturesque Willibald Castle, which until the 18th century was the residence of prince-bishops. Now it houses an interesting museum of artifacts from the Jurassic era, where visitors can see a very well preserved skeleton of *archaeopteryx*.

A new bishop's residence was built nearby from 1702 until 1768. Its west wing features a magnificent staircase and the Mirror Room, in which the works of Mauritio Pedetti, Johann Jakob Berg and Michael Franz are displayed.

Donaustauf ⑮

Walhalla. **Tel** (09403) 96 16 80.
⬜ Apr–Sep: 9am–5:45pm; Oct: 9am–4:45pm; Nov–Mar: 10am–11:45am & 1–3:45pm. 📷

In 1830–41 Leo von Klenze built the Walhalla *(see above)*. This monument to the national glory occupies a scenic location on the River Danube. The building stands on a raised terrace and has the form of a Neo-Classical columned temple (similar to the Parthenon in Athens). It is adorned with 121 marble busts of artists and scientists.

Orangery of the Markgräfliche residence, in Ansbach

Nürnberg (Nuremberg) ⑯

Situated on the river Pegnitz, Nuremberg is not only a paradise for lovers of its famous gingerbread and sausages but is also the symbol of Germany's history. The earliest records of the town, the second largest in Bavaria, date from 1050 when it was a trading settlement. From 1219 Nuremberg, a free town of the Holy Roman Empire, was an important centre of craft and commerce. Its most rapid development took place in the 15th and 16th centuries, when many prominent artists, craftsmen and intellectuals worked here, making Nuremberg one of the cultural centres of Europe.

Picturesque alley near Frauentor

Exploring Lorenzer Seite

The southern part of the old town, known as Lorenzer Seite, is separated from the northern part by the river Pegnitz and encircled to the south by the city walls. Many of the area's historic treasures were carefully reconstructed following severe bomb damage during World War II.

🚪 Frauentor

Frauentorgraben.
Frauentor is one of the most attractive gates into the old town. It is installed in the massive city walls that were constructed during the 15th and 16th centuries. The vast tower, Dicker Turm, was erected nearby in the 15th century. Königstor, a magnificent gate that once stood to the right of Dicker Turm, was dismantled in the 19th century. Beyond Frauentor are a number of alleys with half-timbered houses, shops and cafés, built after the war.

🔒 Marthakirche

Königstraße 74–78.
Dating from the 14th century, the small hospital church of St Martha is tucked between the surrounding houses. Though its interior is virtually devoid of furnishing, it features some magnificent Gothic stained-glass windows, which date from around 1390.

🏛 Mauthalle

Hallplatz 2.
The massive structure that dominates Königstrasse is a Gothic granary built in 1498–1502 by Hans Beheim the Elder. It originally housed the town's municipal scales and the customs office. In the 19th century, the building was converted into a department store and continues in that role today, following post-war reconstruction.

🏛 Germanisches Nationalmuseum

See pp260–61.

🔒 St Lorenz-Kirche

Lorenzer Platz.
The most important building in Nuremberg is the Gothic church of St Lorenz, whose basilica-style main body was built around 1270–1350. The vast hall presbytery was added much later, in 1439–77. On entering the church it is worth taking a look at the magnificent main

Flughafen
8 km (5 miles)

St-Johannis-
Friedhof

NEUTOR

WESTTORGRABEN

WESTTORMAUER

SPITTLERTORGRABEN

SCHLOTFEGERGASSE

LUDWIGSTRASSE

OTTOSTRASSE

KARL-GRILLENBERGER-STR

HINTERE

VORDERE LE

ENGELHARDSG

JAKOBSTRASSE

🚇 Weisser
Turm

DR. KURT

🅿

🚇 Plärrer

FRAUENTORMAUER

FRAUENTORGRA

| 0 metres | 300 |
| 0 yards | 300 |

Key to Symbols *see back flap*

SIGHTS AT A GLANCE

Panoramic view over the rooftops of Nuremberg

For hotels and restaurants in this region see pp499–503 and pp538–42

Impressive Mauthalle dominating Königstraße

portal, which is adorned with sculptures. In the main nave of the church, suspended from the ceiling above the altar, is a superb group sculpture, *Annunciation*, the work of Veit Stoß (1519). He was also the creator of the crucifix within the main altar and the magnificent statue of the Archangel Michael standing by the second pillar

the 1350 Gothic original. Diagonally across the square is the Nassauer Haus, a Gothic mansion whose lower storeys were built in the 14th century. The upper floors were added in the 15th century.

A short distance from the square, in Karolinenstraße, is a fine sculpture by Henry Moore.

Heilig-Geist-Spital

In the centre of town, on the banks of the river Pegnitz, stands the Hospital of the Holy Spirit. Founded in 1332, this is one of the largest hospitals built in the Middle Ages and features a lovely inner courtyard with wooden galleries. The wing that spans the river was built during extension works in 1488–1527. Lepers were kept at some distance from the other patients, in a separate half-timbered building that was specially erected for the purpose. From 1424 until 1796, the insignia of the Holy Roman Empire were kept here rather than in the castle.

The Heilig-Geist-Spital now houses an old-folks' home and a restaurant. The entrance to the building is on the northern side of the river.

of the main nave. There are also several Gothic altars and some magnificent 15th-century stained-glass windows (1493–95) by Adam Kraft. The pillars of the nave are adorned with a number of fascinating statues of the Apostles, dating from the late 14th century.

Lorenzer Platz

Overlooked by the church of St Lorenz, Lorenzer Platz is a popular meeting place for the citizens of Nuremberg and visitors alike. Outside the church is the Fountain of the Virtues, *Tugendbrunnen* (1589), with water cascading from the breasts of its seven Virtues. Nearby is a statue of St Lorenz, which is a copy of

Heilig-Geist-Spital reflected in the waters of the river Pegnitz

Exploring Nürnberg (Nuremberg)

Nuremberg was once an important publishing centre. Schedel's *Liber Chronicarum* was published here in 1493 and, in 1543 – following the town's official adoption of the Reformation in 1525 – *The Revolutions of the Celestial Spheres* by Copernicus was published. The Thirty Years' War ended the town's development but, during the 19th century, it became the focus for the Pan-German movement. In 1945–49 the town was the scene of the trials for war crimes of Nazi leaders.

Detail of *Schöner Brunnen*, in Hauptmarkt

🏛 Hauptmarkt

Each year the Hauptmarkt provides a picturesque setting for the town's famous Christkindlesmarkt, which goes on throughout Advent. At this famous market you can buy gingerbread, enjoy the taste of German sausages, warm yourself with a glass of red wine spiced with cloves and buy locally made souvenirs.

Nuremberg's star attraction is the Gothic *Schöner Brunnen* (Beautiful Fountain), which was probably erected around 1385 but replaced in the early 20th century with a replica. It consists of a 19-metre (62-ft) high, finely carved spire

standing at the centre of an octagonal pool. The pool is surrounded by a Renaissance grille that includes the famous golden ring: the local tradition is that if you turn the ring three times, your wishes will come true. The pool is adorned with the statues of philosophers, evangelists and church fathers, while the spire is decorated with the statues of Electors and of Jewish and Christian heroes. Features and details of the original fountain are kept in the **Germanisches National-museum** *(see pp260–61)*.

🏛 Frauenkirche

Hauptmarkt. ◯ *9am–6pm Mon–Sat, 12:30pm–7pm Sun.*
Commissioned by Emperor Charles IV, this Gothic hall-church dates from 1352–58. Over its richly decorated vestibule is the oriel of the west choir. Its gable contains a clock from Männleinlaufen, installed in 1509. Each day at noon the clock displays a procession of Electors paying homage to the Emperor. Also noteworthy is the Gothic altar *(Tucher Altar)*, which dates from 1445.

🏛 Rathaus

Rathausplatz.
The present town hall consists of several sections. Facing the Hauptmarkt is the oldest, Gothic part, built in 1332–40 and remodelled in the early 15th century. Behind, facing Rathausplatz, is the Renaissance part, built in 1616–22 by Jakob Wolff. Its magnificent portals are decorated with heraldic motifs. The courtyard features a fountain dating from 1557.

🏛 Spielzeugmuseum

Karlstraße 13–15. **Tel** *(0911) 231 31 64.* ◯ *10am–5pm Tue–Fri, 10am–6pm Sat & Sun.* ● *Good Friday, 24, 25, 26, 31 Dec.* 📷
This enchanting toy museum, established in 1971, houses a magnificent collection of tin soldiers and a huge collection of dolls and puppets. Its greatest attraction, however, is a collection of antique dolls' houses, filled with miniature furniture and equipment.

🏛 Kirche St Sebald

Winklerstraße 26. ◯ *year-round: 11am–6pm Sun; Jan–Mar: 9:30am–4pm Mon–Sat; Apr–May & Oct–Dec: 9:30am–6pm Mon–Sat; Jun–Sep: 9:30am–8pm Mon–Sat.*
The oldest of Nuremberg's churches, Kirche St Sebaldus was built in 1230–73 as a Romanesque, two-choir basilica. During remodelling in the 14th century, it was given two side naves and a soaring western hall-choir. The Gothic towers were completed in the late 15th century. At the centre of the presbytery is the magnificent tomb of St Sebald. This cast bronze structure was made by Peter Vischer the Elder. It houses a silver coffin (1397) containing relics of the saint. The church features some splendid carvings by Veit Stoß, including a magnificent statue of St Andrew (1505), which stands in the ambulatory around the presbytery, the Volckamersche Passion (1499) and the Crucifixion scene in the main altar (1520). Also noteworthy is the magnificent Gothic font and the Tucher family epitaph by Hans von Kulmbach (1513).

Heraldic arms adorning the tympanum of the town hall portal

For hotels and restaurants in this region see pp499–503 and pp538–42

The timber-frame building of the Dürerhaus

ALBRECHT DÜRER (1471–1528)

One of the most outstanding painters of the Renaissance era, Dürer was born in Nuremberg. He began his career as a goldsmith in his father's workshop, and learned painting at Michael Wolgemut's studio. He achieved fame not only as a painter, but also as a brilliant engraver and respected theoretician. He was a shrewd observer of the surrounding world and a sensitive artist, whose works are highly valued.

Dürer's self-portrait

🔒 Egidienkirche

Egidienplatz.

Egidienkirche is the only surviving Baroque church in Nuremberg. Its façade, built after the fire of 1696, hides a building containing elements of the previous Romanesque-Gothic Benedictine church. The older chapels, including the Euchariuskapelle, Tetzelkapellethe and Wolfgangkapelle, survive to this day.

♣ Kaiserburg

Kaiserburg-Museum. Innerer Burghof. **Tel** (0911) 200 95 40.
🕐 Apr–Sep: 9am–6pm daily; Oct–Mar: 10am–4pm daily. 🗓

The three castles that tower over Nuremberg include the central burgraves' castle, with the Free Reich's buildings to the east, and the Imperial castle (whose origins go back to the 12th century) to the west. When climbing up the Burgstrasse you will first reach the Fünfeckturm (Pentagonal Tower), which dates from 1040. The oldest building in town, it is an architectural relic of the von Zollern burgraves' castle. At its foot are the Kaiserstallung (Emperor's stables), which now houses a youth hostel.

A continued climb will bring you, on the left, to the courtyard of the imperial palace, which features a round tower (*Sinwellturm*) dating from the 12th century, and a deep well – the *Tiefe Brunnen*. Passing through the inner gate of the castle you will finally reach its heart, the residential building.

🏛 Albrecht Dürer-Haus

Albrecht-Dürer-Straße 39. **Tel** (0911) 231 25 68. 🕐 Jul–Sep & during Christkindlesmarkt: 10am–5pm daily, 10am–8pm Thu; Oct–Jun: 10am–5pm Tue–Sun, 10am–8pm Thu. 🗓 📷

Born in 1471 in a house on the corner of Burgerstrasse and Obere Schmiedgasse, the renowned artist and engraver Albrecht Dürer lived in this house from 1509 until his death in 1528. On the three-hundredth anniversary of his death, the building was bought by the town and many rooms have since been reconstructed. The ground-floor room now contains a printing press dating from Dürer's time. Copies of his pictures provide a useful insight into the work of this famous Nuremberg citizen.

🏛 St-Johannis-Friedhof

Am Johannisfriedhof.

The St John's Cemetery is one of the best preserved and most important in Europe. Since it was established in 1518, it has provided a resting place for many famous people, including Albrecht Dürer (No. 649), the sculptor Veit Stoß (No. 268), the goldsmith Wenzel Jamnitzer (No. 664) and the painter Anselm Feuerbach (No. 715).

The cemetery also contains a rich array of tombs from the 16th, 17th and 18th centuries.

🏛 Dokumentationszentrum Reichsparteitagsgelände

Bayernstr. 110. **Tel** (0911) 231 56 66. 🕐 9am–6pm Mon–Fri, 10am–6pm Sat & Sun.

The vast, unfinished building complex in the southern part of town dates from the Nazi era. Its construction began in 1933 and it was intended to be a venue for National Party gatherings. The building now houses a historical exhibition and archive.

The buildings of the Kaiserburg, towering over the town

Nuremberg: Germanisches Nationalmuseum

This museum, which was officially opened in 1852, was founded by a Franconian aristocrat named Hans von Aufsess. It houses a unique collection of antiquities from the German-speaking world. In 1945, towards the end of World War II, the buildings that had originally housed the museum were bombed. The architecture of the modern building, which was completed in 1993, cleverly incorporates the remaining fragments of a former Carthusian abbey. Among the most valuable items in the museum's collection are works by Tilman Riemenschneider, Konrad Witz, Lucas Cranach the Elder, Albrecht Altdorfer, Albrecht Dürer and Hans Baldung Grien.

Madonna with Child Crowned by Angels
This picture was painted by Hans Holbein the Elder (c.1465–1524) who created many festive altarpieces using warm colours.

★ **Archangel** (1516)
This enchanting wood-carving of the archangel Raphaël is one of many works produced by Veit Stoss after his return from Cracow.

Cloisters

Former Carthusian church

Ground floor

Brooch from Domagnano
This Ostrogothic buckle from the 5th century AD, shaped like an eagle, was discovered in the late 19th century in Domagnano, in San Marino. It probably belonged to a rich Ostrogothic aristocrat.

★ **Cover of the Codex Aureus**
The richly ornamented cover of the Codex Aureus, *also known as the Golden Gospel Book of Echternach, was produced in Trier in the 10th century.*

GALLERY GUIDE

The exhibits have been arranged in sections, ranging from prehistory to the Middle Ages, and are located on the ground and first floors. Twentieth-century art is on the second floor and the toy collection is housed separately.

VISITORS' CHECKLIST

Kartäusergasse 1 **Tel** *(0911) 133 10.* ◯ *10am–6pm Tue–Sun, until 9pm Wed.* ⬤ *Shrove Tue, 24, 25, 31 Dec.* 🎟 **www**.gnm.de

First floor

Library

Torquetum

Johannes Praetorius from Nuremberg produced this engraved copper device in 1568, designed to measure the positions of the stars.

Library

KEY

▢	Textiles and folk art
▢	Baroque arts and crafts
▢	Crafts and guilds
▢	Scientific instruments and pharmaceutical history
▢	Musical instruments and applied arts
▢	Middle Ages
▢	Arms and armour, garden sculpture
▢	Prehistory and early history
▢	Archive, prints and drawings, coins and medals
▢	Temporary exhibitions
▢	Non-exhibition space

★ Portrait of Michael Wolgemut (1516)

Albrecht Dürer painted this portrait of his predecessor and master, Wolgemut, 30 years after commencing work at his studio.

STAR SIGHTS

★ Cover of Codex Aureus

★ Portrait of Michael Wolgemut

★ Schlüsselfeld Vessel

★ Archangel

★ Schlüsselfeld Vessel

This beautiful silver-gold sailing ship, supported by a two-tailed mermaid, is an ornamental table vessel made in 1503 by an unidentified goldsmith from Nuremberg.

Street-by-Street: Rothenburg ob der Tauber ⓰

Eagle crest from the town hall

If you want to sample the atmosphere of the Middle Ages, visit Rothenburg on the river Tauber, whose origins go back to the 12th century. Rothenburg was granted the status of a free town within the Holy Roman Empire in 1274 but its major growth took place in the 15th century. During the Thirty Years' War (1618–48) the town, which fought on the Protestant side, was captured by the Emperor's army. Little has changed since that time and the city walls still surround Gothic cathedrals and an array of gabled houses.

Reichsstadtmuseum
The former Dominican abbey now houses a museum devoted to the town's history. The abbey kitchen – the oldest surviving kitchen in Germany – is also open to visitors.

Franziskanerkirche
In this Gothic church is a retable depicting The Stigmatization of St Francis, believed to be an early work by Tilman Riemenschneider.

★ St Jakobs Kirche
In the Gothic church of St Jakob (built between 1373 and 1464) is the superb Zwölfbotenaltar by Friedrich Herlin.

★ Mittelalterliches Kriminalmuseum
Many blood-curdling exhibits are on display at this museum, which houses a collection of instruments of torture and punishment.

VISITORS' CHECKLIST

Road map C5. 🏰 *12,000.* 🚉
🛈 *Marktplatz 2 (09861-404
800).* 🎭 *Meistertrunk (around
Whitsun), Reichsstadt-Festtage
(first weekend in Sep),
Weihnachtsmarkt (Dec).*
Topplerschlösschen
Tel (09861) 73 58.
🕐 *1–4pm Fri–Sun.* ⬤ *Nov.* 🌐

View from Burggarten

*The castle garden (Burggarten) is reached
through Burgtor, the tallest of the town's
gates. The garden, which during the
Middle Ages was the site of the
Hohenstaufen family castle,
provides a magnificent
view over the town
and the river
valley.*

Galgentor

*Galgentor, an old
execution place, is also
known as Würzburger
Tor, since it is the gate
leading to Würzburg.*

Rödertor

*The best preserved segments of
the old city walls are around the
Rödertor gate, which dates from
the late 14th century.*

KEY

— — — Suggested route

★ Rathaus

*The town hall con-
sists of the surviving
Gothic section with
a tower, and the
later Renaissance
structure with
Baroque arcades.*

STAR SIGHTS

★ Mittelalterliches
  Museum

★ Rathaus

★ St Jakobs Kirche

Andechs ⓲

Road map D7. ℹ *Andechser Straße 16 (08152-932 50).*

The village of Andechs, at the summit of the 700-m (2,300-ft) high Holy Mountain of the same name, is not only the destination of pilgrimages to the local church, but also of many less spiritual trips to the *Bräustüberl*, where visitors can refresh themselves with a glass or two of the excellent beer brewed by local monks.

The present triple-nave Gothic hall-church was built in 1420–25. Its Rococo interior dates from 1755. The lower tier of the main altar contains the famous *Miraculous Statue of the Mother of God* (1468), while the upper tier features the *Immaculata* by Hans Degler (1609). On selected feast days, holy relics are displayed on the altar gallery.

Ammersee near the Holy Mountain of Andechs

Landsberg am Lech ⓳

Road map D7. 🏠 *24,000.* 🚉 ℹ *Hauptplatz 152 (08191-12 82 46).*

The history of Landsberg goes back to 1160 when Henry the Lion built his castle here, on the right bank of the river Lech. During the 13th century, the surrounding settlement grew into a town, which soon became a major trading centre. Religious conflicts, culminating in the Thirty Years' War, put an end to the town's development but, in the late 17th century, the town once again became

an important commercial and cultural centre. Adolf Hitler wrote *Mein Kampf* here, while serving a prison term for his unsuccessful coup attempt in Munich.

At the heart of Landsberg is the Hauptplatz with its Baroque town hall and the intricately carved 14th-century tower, Schmalztor.

In Ludwigstrasse is the late-Gothic parish church, Stadtpfarrkirche Mariä Himmelfahrt, whose Baroque-style interior features a statue of the *Madonna and Child* by Hans Multscher. Bayertor, the original town gate, is in the eastern part of the old town.

The town's **Neues Stadtmuseum** is a useful source of information on local history.

> 🏛 **Neues Stadtmuseum**
> Von-Helfenstein-Gasse 426.
> **Tel** *(08191) 12 83 60.* 🕐 *2–5pm Tue–Sun, 10am–5pm Sat & Sun.* ♿

Dachau ⓴

Road map D6. 🏠 *35,000.* 🚉 ℹ *Konrad-Adenauer-Straße 1 (08131-75286 or 75287).*

For most people the name Dachau is inextricably linked with the concentration camp that was built here by the Nazis in 1933. Since 1965, the whole site has been designated as a memorial, **KZ-Gedenkstätte Dachau**, to the 32,000 prisoners who died there, with a permanent exhibition in the former domestic quarters of the camp.

Dachau is a beautiful town with many historic buildings. On the southwestern edge of the old town stands **Schloss Dachau**, summer residence of the Wittelsbachs. The palace that stands here today was created in the 18th century from the western wing of an earlier castle, the work of Joseph Effner.

In the early 19th century the castle housed a colony

Relief from the church façade in Landsberg

of artists who had tired of city life. They were known as *Gruppe Neu Dachau*. Even earlier, however, the beauty of the surrounding countryside had been discovered by the impressionist painter Max Lieber-mann (1847–1935). The **Dachauer Gemäldegalerie** contains works of art inspired by local scenery, including one by Liebermann.

> 🏛 **Dachauer Gemäldegalerie**
> Konrad-Adenauer-Straße 3.
> **Tel** *(08131) 56 75 16.* 🕐 *11am–5pm Tue–Fri, 1–5pm Sat & Sun.* ♿
>
> ⛪ **Schloss Dachau**
> Schlossstraße 2. **Tel** *(08131) 879 23.* 🕐 *Apr–Sep: 9am–6pm Tue–Sun; Oct–Mar: 10am–4pm Tue–Sun.* ♿
>
> ⚑ **KZ-Gedenkstätte Dachau**
> Alte Römerstraße 75. **Tel** *(08131) 66 99 70.* 🕐 *9am–5pm Tue–Sun.*

Schleißheim ㉑

Road map D6. Oberschleißheim.

Schleißheim is situated barely 14 km (9 miles) from Munich, making it within easy reach for an afternoon visit to its Baroque palace and park.

Surrounded by canals and now somewhat neglected, the park was established in the 17th and 18th centuries and includes three palaces. The modest **Altes Schloss** was

Baroque façade of the Wittelsbach palace, Schloss Dachau

built in 1623 for Prince Wilhelm V. Now it houses an exhibition of religious folk art.

Schloss Lustheim is a small, Baroque, hermitage-type palace, built in 1684–87 by Enrico Zucalli for the Elector Max Emanuel. As well as its beautiful interiors and stunning frescoes, it boasts a magnificent collection of Meissen porcelain, which is displayed in the **Museum Meißener Porzellan**.

The newest building is the **Neues Schloss**, designed by Enrico Zucalli. Work began in 1701 but was not completed until the second half of the 18th century. Despite wartime damage, it retains many original features. It now houses exhibits belonging to the Bavarian State Museum.

The imposing bulk of the Neues Schloss in Ingolstadt

🏛 **Altes Schloss**
Tel (089) 315 87 20.
⬜ *ds Neues Schloss.*

🏛 **Neues Schloss**
Tel (089) 315 87 20. ⬜ *Apr–Sep: 9am–6pm Tue–Sun; Oct–Mar: 10am–4pm Tue–Sun.* ● *Mon.*

🏛 **Schloss Lustheim**
Tel (089) 315 87 20. ⬜ *Apr–Sep: 9am–6pm Tue–Sun; Oct–Mar: 10am–4pm Tue–Sun.*

Museum Meißener Porzellan
Tel (089) 315 87 242.
⬜ *Apr–Sep: 9am–6pm Tue–Sun; Oct–Mar: 10am–4pm Tue–Sun.*

Freising ㉒

Road map D6. 🏙 40,000. 🚉
ℹ *Marienplatz 7 (08161-541 22).*

Situated on the banks of the river Isar is the old town of Freising. Its history is closely connected with St Korbinian, who founded the bishopric here in the early 8th century. Korbinian died around AD 725 and his remains still lie in the crypt of the Dom – the Cathedral Church of the Birth of the Virgin Mary and St Korbinian (1159–1205). This is a five-nave basilica, without transept, with an elongated choir and a massive twin-tower western façade. Its interior was remodelled in

Detail from Neues Schloss in Schleißheim

Baroque style by the Asam brothers, in 1724–25. The four-nave Romanesque crypt features a famous column, which is decorated with carvings of fantastic animals *(Bestiensäule)*. Nearby is the **Diözesanmuseum**, whose vast ecclesiastical collection includes two paintings by Rubens.

At the southwestern end of the old town stands a former monastery, Weihenstephan, which is home to the world's longest-established brewery.

🏛 **Diözesanmuseum**
Domberg 21 *Tel* (08161) 487 90.
⬜ *10am–5pm Tue–Sun.*

Ingolstadt ㉓

Road map D6. 🏙 115,000. 🚉
ℹ *Rathausplatz 2 (0841-305 30 30).*

Lying on the river Danube, this former seat of the Wittelsbach family features many important historic buildings dating from the

Middle Ages and the Renaissance and Baroque periods. Among the most outstanding is the Church of the Virgin Mary, a triple-nave hall structure with circular pillars, chapels and choir with an ambulatory. Inside is the original Gothic-Renaissance main altar dating from 1572.

Another notable building is the Neues Schloss, built between the 15th and 18th centuries, with its stately rooms and Gothic chapel. It now houses the **Bayerisches Armeemuseum**.

A true gem of Bavarian architecture is the **Church of St Maria Victoria**, the work of Cosmas Damian Asam.

The **Deutsches Medizinhistorisches Museum** exhibits medical instruments and has a garden with medicinal plants.

🏛 **Bayerisches Armeemuseum**
Neues Schloss, Paradeplatz 4.
Tel (0841) 937 70. ⬜ *9am–5:30pm Tue–Fri, 10am–5:30pm Sat & Sun.*

🏛 **Deutsches Medizinhistorisches Museum**
Anatomiestraße 18–20.
Tel (0841) 305 28 60. ⬜ *10am–5pm Tue–Sun.*

Striking Baroque interior of the Church of St Maria Victoria, Ingolstadt

Arcaded courtyard of Neuburg Castle

Neuburg an der Donau ②④

Road map D6. 🏠 25,000. 🚉
ℹ️ Ottheinrichplatz A118 (08431-552 40).

Perched on a promontory overlooking the river Danube, Neuburg is one of Bavaria's loveliest towns. During the Middle Ages, it changed hands frequently but was eventually ruled by Ottheinrich the Magnanimous, under whom the town grew and prospered on an unprecedented scale. He was the founder of the castle, built between 1534 and 1665, whose massive round towers still dominate the town. Its earliest part is the east wing. The courtyard, which is surrounded by arcades, features beautiful frescos by Hans Schroer. In the tower is a staircase adorned with paintings. The castle chapel, completed in 1543, is one of the oldest, purpose-built Protestant churches in Germany.

In Amalienstraße, leading down towards the town, stands the former Jesuits' College and the Court Church (Hofkirche). Work on the church began in the late 16th century and was completed in 1627. It was intended to be a Protestant church, but the ruling family converted back to Catholicism during its construction and it was taken over by the Jesuits who turned it into a counter-reformation

Marian church. The triple-nave hall-structure has an exquisite interior decorated in gold, white and grey.

Among many old buildings that survive in the town centre are the Graf-Veri-Haus and the Baron-von-Hartman-Haus in Herrenstrasse. To the east of town stands the Grünau Castle (Jagdschloss), built for Ottheinrich in 1530–55.

Environs

18 km (11 miles) to the south, Schrobenhausen is the birth-place of the painter Franz von Lenbach, who was born in 1836. A museum in Ulrich-Peisser-Gasse is devoted to his life and work. While there, it is worth visiting St Jacob's Church, to see the fine 15th-century wall painting there.

Heraldic crest on
Neuberg Castle

🏛 **Schlossmuseum Neuburg**
Residenzstraße 2.
Tel (08431) 88 97. 🕐 Apr–Sep: 9am–6pm Tue–Sun; Oct–Mar: 10am–4pm Tue–Sun. 📷

Landshut ②⑤

Road map E6. 🏠 57,000. 🚉
ℹ️ Altstadt 315 (0871-92 20 50).
📷 Fürstenhochzeit (every 4 years, next in 2013), Hofmusiktage (every 2 years, next in 2012), Frühjahrsdult (Apr–May), Bartlmädult (end Aug), Haferlmarkt (Sep).

The earliest records of Landshut date from 1150. One hundred years later this was already a town and the main

centre of power of the Dukes of Lower Bavaria. In 1475 the town was the scene of a lavish medieval wedding, when Duke Georg of the House of Wittelsbach married the Polish Princess Jadwiga. Since 1903 the town has held regular re-enactments of the wedding feast (Landshuter Fürstenhochzeit).

Landshut has preserved its medieval urban layout, with two wide parallel streets, Altstadt and Neustadt, with clusters of historic 15th–16th century buildings. Opposite the town hall in Alstadt is the **Stadtresidenz**, a town house modelled on the Palazzo del Tè in Mantua. Sometimes known as the "Italian House", this was the first Renaissance palace to be built in Germany.

The vast brick church of St Martin (1385–1500) is a triple-nave, narrow hall-church featuring a presbytery, network vaults (1459) and the tallest church tower in Bavaria.

Landshut is dominated by the fortified 13th–16th century **Burg Trausnitz**, featuring a medieval tower, a Renaissance palace (1568–78) and the **Kunst- und Wunderkammer** ("room of arts and wonder"), a branch of the Bayerisches Nationalmuseum (see p219).

Environs

From Landshut, it is worth taking a trip to Moosburg, situated 14 km (9 miles) to

Stained-glass window in Landshut depicting Duke Georg and Jadwiga

the west. Its early 13th-century Church of St Castulus features a 14-m (46-ft) high Marian altar by Hans Leinberger (1514).

♣ Burg Trausnitz & Kunst- und Wunderkammer
Tel (0871) 92 41 10. ☐ Apr–Sep: 9am–6pm daily; Oct–Mar: 10am–4:30pm.

♣ Stadtresidenz
Altstadt 79. *Tel* (0871) 92 41 10. ☐ Apr–Sep: 9am–6pm Tue–Sun; Oct–Mar: 10am–4pm Tue–Sun. ☐ obligatory. ☐ ● Mon.

Interior of St George's Chapel in Burg Trausnitz

Dingolfing ㉖

Road map E6. ☒ 15,400.
🛈 Im Bruckstadel, Fischerei 9 (08711) 32 71 00.

The main tourist attraction in this small town on the banks of the river Isar is its Gothic castle. Built in the 15th century by the Bavarian dukes, this vast edifice now houses the Regional Museum. It is also worth taking a stroll to see Pfarrkirche St Johannes, a late-Gothic brick building dating from the late 15th century. Although what remains of its furnishings are merely the poor remnants of its former glory, nevertheless the church is still considered one of the most beautiful Gothic buildings in Bavaria.

Environs
In Landau an der Isar, situated 13 km (8 miles) to the east of Dingolfing, stands the picturesque Baroque church of Mariä Himmelfahrt, dating from the first half of the 18th century. There is also an interesting small church, the Stein-felskirche (c.1700) inside a natural rock cave. In Arnstorf, 30 km (19 miles) to the east, is one of the few remaining Bavarian castles on water. Known as the Oberes Schloß, the castle was probably built in the 15th century and remodelled during the 17th and 18th centuries.

Straubing ㉗

Road map E6. ☒ 44,500. 🚉
🛈 Theresienplatz 20 (09421-19 433).
🎭 Agnes-Bernauer-Festspiel (July, every four years, next in 2015), Gäubodenvolksfest (August).

This market town enjoys a picturesque setting on the river Danube. The 60 m (200 ft) long Strassenmarkt, which consists of two squares, Theresienplatz and Ludwig-platz, is a part of the former trade route that led to Prague. The area is lined with historic buildings in Baroque, Neo-Classical and Secession styles.

At the centre of Strassen-markt stands the 14th-century municipal tower, which offers a splendid view over the towns of the Bavarian Forest. At Ludwigplatz 11 is the "Lion's Pharmacy", where the famous Biedermeier painter, Karl Spitzweg, worked as an apprentice in 1828–30.

Turning from Theresienplatz into Seminargasse or Jakobs-gasse, you will reach the monumental brick structure of the parish church of St Jakob (1400–1590). This triple-nave hall-church, crowned with a network vault, retains many original features, including stained-glass windows in the chapels of Maria-Hilf-Kapelle (1420) and St Bartholomew. The so-called Moses' Window in the Chapel of St Joseph was made in 1490 in Nuremberg, based on a sketch provided by Wilhelm Playdenwurff. In the Cobbler's Chapel (Schusterkapelle) hangs a painting of *Madonna and Child*, by Hans Holbein (c.1500). Overlooking the Danube is a 14th–15th century castle. The Agnes-Bernauer Festival, held every four years, takes place in the courtyard of the castle. The Gäubodenvolksfest is the second largest folk festival in Bavaria after the Munich Okto-berfest. The **Gäubodenmuseum** has a magnificent collection of Roman artifacts.

Environs
In the tiny village of Auf-hausen, 21 km (12 miles) to the west, is the beautiful late-Baroque pilgrimage church of Maria Schnee. Built by Johann Michael Fischer in 1736–51, it includes magnificent wall paintings by the Asam brothers and a statue of the Madonna. Commissioned by Duke Wilhelm V of Bavaria, the Gnadenmadonna is believed to pardon sins.

In Oberalteich, some 10 km (6 miles) to the east, is the beautiful church of St Peter and St Paul built in the early 17th century for the Benedictine order. Inside, an unusual hang-ing staircase leads to the galler-ies, while the vestibule is decorated with stucco orna-ments, depicting bird motifs.

In Windberg, 22 km (14 miles) east of Oberalteich, is a Romanesque Marian church whose main portal (c.1220) features an image of the Madonna in the tympanum.

🏛 Gäubodenmuseum
Fraunhoferstraße. *Tel* (09421) 974 110. ☐ 10am–4pm Tue–Sun.

Main altar in Ursulinenkirche, Straubing

Regensburg (Ratisbon) 28

The area of Regensburg was once a Celtic settlement and later a campsite of the Roman legions. The outline of the Roman camp is still visible around St Peter's Cathedral. In the early 6th century, Regensburg was the seat of the Agilolfa ruling family and, in AD 739, a monk named Boniface established a bishopric here. From AD 843, Regensburg was the seat of the Eastern Frankish ruler, Ludwig the German. From 1245 it was a free town of the Holy Roman Empire and throughout the Middle Ages remained South Germany's fastest growing commercial and cultural centre.

Picturesque Steinere Brücke leading to the old town of Regensburg

🏛 Steinerne Brücke

An outstanding example of medieval engineering, this 310-m (1,000-ft) long bridge over the Danube was built in 1135–46. It provides the best panoramic view of Regensburg. Near the bridge gate, Brückentor, stands an enormous salt warehouse topped with a vast five-storey roof.

🏛 Wurstküche (Wurstkuchel)

Thundorferstraße. ☐ *8am–7pm daily.*
Immediately behind the salt warehouse is the famous *Wurstküche* (sausage kitchen), which has probably occupied this site since as early as the 12th century and may have served as a canteen for the builders of the bridge. Its Regensburger sausages are definitely worth trying.

🏛 Altes Rathaus

Rathausplatz. ☑ *May–Sep: 3:15pm Mon–Sat.* **Reichstagsmuseum.** *Tel (0941) 507 34 40.* ☑ *(every 30 mins) Apr–Oct: 9:30am–noon, 1:30–4pm daily (English tours 3pm); Nov, Dec, Mar: 10am, 11:30am, 1:30pm, 3pm, 3:30pm daily; Jan & Feb: 10am, 11:30am, 1:30pm, 3pm daily.* ☑
In Rathausplatz stands an old 15th-century town hall with a 13th-century tower. It contains

a splendid, richly decorated hall – *Reichssaal* – where the Perpetual Imperial Diet (the first parliament of the Holy Roman Empire) sat between 1663 and 1806. Benches in the chamber were coloured to indicate who could sit where: for example, red benches for Electors. The adjoining new town hall dates from the late 17th–early 18th century.

Late-Gothic oriel on the side elevation of the Altes Rathaus

🔒 Dom St Peter

Domschatzmuseum
Krauterermarkt 3.
Tel (0941) 597 25 30. ☐ *Apr–Oct: 10am–5pm Tue–Sat, noon–5pm Sun; Dec–Mar: 10am–4pm Fri–Sat, noon–4pm Sun.* ● *Nov.* ☑
Towering above the city, on the site of the former Roman military camp, is the massive brick structure of St Peter's Cathedral. Built between 1250 and 1525, its imposing western towers were added only in 1859–69. The master architect, Ludwig, modelled his design for the building on French examples (the Rayonnant style). The stained-glass

SIGHTS AT A GLANCE

Alte Kapelle ⑤
Altes Rathaus ③
Dom St Peter ④
Schloss Thurn und Taxis ⑥
Steinerne Brücke ①
St Jakob Kirche ⑦
Wurstküche ②

For hotels and restaurants in this region see pp499–503 and pp538–42

19th-century spires on the Gothic St Peter's Cathedral

windows of the choir date from the early 14th century. The **Domschatzmuseum** has a collection of ecclesiastical vestments.

🏛 Alte Kapelle

Alter Kornmarkt.
The Old Chapel is really a Marian collegiate church. It stands on the foundations of an older, early Romanesque chapel dating from the Carolingian period. The building has been remodelled several times and contains some beautiful Rococo stuccoes by Anton Landes.

⛪ Schloss Thurn und Taxis

Emmeramsplatz 5. **Tel** (0941) 504 81 33. ☐ daily. 🎫 Apr–Oct: 11am, 1pm, 2pm, 3pm, 4pm, 5pm (also 10am Sat & Sun); Nov–Mar: 10am, 11am, 2pm, 3pm Sat & Sun. 🌐
In the south end of the town you will find the buildings and churches of the former St Emmeram Abbey, which have been

VISITORS' CHECKLIST

Road map D6. ✈ 142,000.
ℹ Altes Rathaus (0941 507 44 10). 🎪 Frühjahrsdult (Whitsun), Bach-Woche (Jun), Bayerisches Jazz-Weekend (Jul), Herbstdult (Aug–Sep), Christkindlmarkt & Domspatzen concerts (Dec).
www.regensburg.de

Enchanting Rococo interior of Alte Kapelle

the burial chapel. In 1998, the Bavarian State Museum opened a branch here, the Schatzkammer, which has valuable collections of decorative art

🏛 Baumburger Turm

Watmarkt.
Regensburg has many unique ancestral palaces dating from the 14th–15th centuries, with high towers modelled on Northern Italian architecture. Some 20 of the original 60 towers have survived. One of the most beautiful is the residential tower, Baumburger Turm. Nearby, at Watmarkt 5, stands the equally beautiful Goliathhaus, where Oskar Schindler lived for a time in 1945. A commemorative plaque has been placed at the rear of the building.

tastefully incorporated into the palace complex of the ducal family von Thurn und Taxis. These include a Gothic cloister dating from the 12th–14th centuries, a library with magnificent frescos by Cosmas Damian Asam and

Gothic portals of St Emmeram Abbey in Schloss Thurn und Taxis

Winter view of Gnadenkapelle complex, from Altötting

Altötting ㉙

Road map E6. 🏠 *11,000.*
ℹ️ *Kapellplatz 2a (08671-50 62 19).*
🚉 🕊️ *pilgrimages to Altötting (Whitsun).* **www**.altoetting.de

Altötting is renowned as the earliest destination of pilgrimages to the "Miraculous Statue" of the Virgin Mary (1330). The statue stands in the Wallfahrtskapelle St Maria, which consists of two parts. The central, octagonal chapel, **Gnadenkapelle** (c.AD 750) was once the baptistery. The external chapel was built in 1494 and the ambulatory in 1517. It also houses the so-called "Silver Prince", representing the miraculously cured son of the Prince-Elector, Karl Albrecht. Many Bavarian kings and princes wished to be buried here.

Nearby is the interesting Romanesque-Gothic church of St Philip and St Jacob (1228–30 and 1499–1520). Its Neo-Classical interior contains many tombstones, while a separate chapel, Tillykapelle, is the burial place of Johann Tserclaes von Tilly, a hero of the Thirty Years' War and the Emperor's general.

The **Schatzkammer** (Treasury) was housed in the former sacristy, but after Pope Benedict XVI turned it into a chapel in 2006 a new Schatzkammer and Wallfahrtsmuseum (Pilgrimage Museum) were built. The collection includes an exquisite example of French enamel and gold artwork, the *Goldenes Rössl* (Golden Steed), which dates from around 1400. Despite its name, the theme of this work is the Adoration of the Magi. It was commissioned

by Isobel of Bavaria as a New Year gift for her husband, Charles VI of France.

🏛 Neue Schatzkammer and Wallfahrtsmuseum
Kapellplatz 4. **Tel** *(08671) 924 2015.*
◯ *10am–4pm Tue–Sun.*
● *Nov–mid-Mar.* 📷

Walkway around Gnadenkapelle, in Altötting, filled with offerings

Burghausen ㉚

Road map E6. 🏠 *17,000.* ℹ️
Stadtplatz 112 (08677-88 71 40). 🚉

The very picturesque town of Burghausen is situated on the river Salzach. Towering over the town, the river and the lake is Burghausen Castle, a large castle complex built on a high ridge stretching for

1,100 m (1,200 yds). Work on the castle started in 1253, but most of the buildings were erected during the reign of King George the Rich and therefore have magnificent, late-Gothic forms. The king's wife, Jadwiga Jagiellon, whom he married in grand style in Landshut *(see p266)*, was later rejected by him and she spent her final days in the fortress of Burghausen.

The **Burg** consists of two main parts: the main castle, with tower, the residential quarters, the courtyard and domestic buildings; and the castle approach (Vorburg). The residential building has some fine 15th- and 16th-century paintings. A special door links the Prince's quarters with the "internal" Chapel of St Elizabeth. Next to the chapel is the mid-13th-century Dürnitz, which served originally as a ballroom and banqueting hall.

The castle approach consists of five courtyards (Vorhof). In the fourth courtyard is the "external" Chapel of St Jadwiga (Aussere Burgkapelle St Hedwig) – the work of Wolfgang Wiesinger, a native of Salzburg (1489). This has numerous original buildings, including the town hall, which was created by combining three burgher houses dating from the 14th–15th centuries The parish church of St Jakob (1353-1513) in Burghausen is a three-nave basilica.

🏰 Burg
Tel *(08677) 887 140.*

🏛 Stadtmuseum
◯ *May–Sep: 9am–6pm daily; Nov–Apr & Oct: 10am–4pm daily.*

Panoramic view of Burghausen, with its vast castle complex on the hill

Bayerischer Wald ③

The Bavarian forest stretches north to the rive Danube, between Regensburg and Passau. It is part of Central Europe's largest woodland and provides idyllic grounds for a variety of outdoor pursuits. The local rocks contain large quantities of quartz, which contributed to the early development of the glass industry here. To this day, the region produces some fine, blown-glass artifacts. The region also hosts a number of popular festivals throughout the year.

Spiegelau ❸
Spiegelau is one of the most popular starting points for tourists planning hiking trips into the mountains.

Zwiesel ❶
In the old glassworks, which survive to this day, you can watch workers using blow irons to produce vases, jugs and other objects made of glass.

Grafenau ❹
The main attractions of this small town are its snuff and furniture museums and the old town hall.

Frauenau ❷
Along with Zwiesel, this is the oldest centre of glass production in the area. The local museum illustrates the town's history.

Freyung ❺
The main attraction of the town is the Schloss (Castle) Wolfstein, which now houses a museum of hunting and fishing.

0 km	8
0 miles	8

Finsterau ❻
Situated close to a vast artificial lake, Finsterau has an interesting open-air museum that displays examples of the local building trade.

KEY

▅▅	Suggested route
═	Other road
▬	Scenic route
☀	Viewpoint

TIPS FOR WALKERS

Starting point: Zwiesel.
Distance: 82 km (51 miles).
Getting there: train to Frauenau, on the Zwiesel-Granau line, or Bodenmais, terminus of another branch line from Zwiesel.

Street-by-Street: Passau ☜

Passau, whose long history goes back to Roman times, lies on a peninsula between the rivers Danube and Inn, near the Austrian border. During the second half of the 5th century, St Severinus established a monastery in Passau as well as several more nearby. In 739, an Irish monk called Boniface, known as "Germany's Apostle", founded a bishopric here and for many years this was the largest diocese of the Holy Roman Empire. Large parts of the town were destroyed by fires in 1662 and 1680. Reconstruction was carried out by Italian artists, who gave the town its Baroque, Rococo and Neo-Classical façades. However Passau retains a medieval feel in its narrow alleys and archways.

Passauer Glasmuseum
Opposite the old town hall is the beautiful patrician Hotel Wilder Mann, which now houses the Glasmuseum. The museum's vast collection includes valuable examples of Bohemian, Austrian and Bavarian glasswork.

Deggendorf

ANGER ST

GROSSE MESSERGASSE

SCHROTT...

★ Dom St Stephan
St Stephan's Cathedral is a true masterpiece of Italian Baroque, built by Italian architect Carlo Lurago to replace the original Gothic structure, which was largely destroyed by fire in the 17th century.

Passau-Hauptbahnhof

DOMPLATZ

University

INNKAI

MARIEN-BRÜCKE

★ Altes Rathaus
Dating from the 14th–15th century, the old town hall was created by combining eight patrician houses. The structure features a Neo-Gothic tower.

Neue Bischofsresidenz
Built by Domenico d'Angeli and Antonio Beduzzi in 1713–30, the Neue Residenz has a pilaster façade with protruding balconies and roof balustrade.

★ Veste Oberhaus
This former castle of the prince-bishops now houses the Oberhaus-Museum, with displays on local and regional history and the work of local artists.

VISITORS' CHECKLIST

🏛 50,000. 🚉 🛈 Rathausplatz 3 & Bahnhofstr. 28, 94032 Passau (0851 95 59 80). 🎭 Festival Europäische Wochen (Jun–Jul) – music and theatre events, plus exhibitions by European artists; Ilzer Haferlfest (Jul); Europäisches Jugend-Musik-Festival (Oct).
www.passau.de

Schaiblingsturm
On the bank of the river Inn are the remains of Passau's Gothic town walls. They include this tower, built in 1250.

★ Wallfahrtskirche Mariahilf
High above the banks of the river Inn stands this early-Baroque abbey complex dating from 1627–30. It includes a pretty twin-towered pilgrimage church.

STAR SIGHTS

★ Altes Rathaus

★ Dom St Stephan

★ Veste Oberhaus

★ Wallfahrtskirche Mariahilf

KEY

– – – Suggested route

| 0 metres | 100 |
| 0 yards | 100 |

Berchtesgadener Land ⓷

Berchtesgadener Land is one of the most beautiful regions, not just in Germany, but in the whole of Europe. It occupies the area of the Berchtesgadener Alps whose boundaries are defined by the river Saalach to the west, the river Salzach to the east, the "Stony Sea" *(Steinernes Meer)* to the south and, to the north, Untersberg, which is 1,972 m (7,500 ft) above sea level. To the south of Berchtesgaden village lies the National Park (Nationalpark Berchtesgaden).

★ Ramsau an der Ache
Set in an enchanting location in the Ramsau Valley, this village is a popular base for visitors to the area. Spectacular views of the mountains can be enjoyed from the small parish church.

Hintersee
This scenic lake has given its name to a picturesque hamlet nearby. A walk around the lake takes about one hour.

LATTE
GEBIR

REITER
ALPE

HINTERSEE   Ramsau
Wimbachk

NATIONAL-
PARK
BERCHTESGADEN

KEHLSTEINHAUS

Standing on the summit of Kehlstein, this stone building resembling a mountain shelter is known as the Adlerhorst (Eagle's Nest). It was given to Hitler as a birthday present in 1939 by one of his closest allies, Martin Bormann, and it became one of the Führer's favourite residences. The approach to the building is a true engineering masterpiece: the initial section, the Kehlsteinstrasse, is a scenic mountain road, which passes through five tunnels and offers some breathtaking views. The final ascent is via a lift. The whole project took 13 months to complete. After the war, the Eagle's Nest fell into the hands of the Americans, then, in 1960, it passed into private hands. The building now houses a restaurant that is very popular with tourists, not only because of its history but also for the spectacular views that it provides over part of the Alps.

Nationalpark Berchtesgaden
This magnificent national park, which is home to many rare species of plants and animals, can be visited by joining organized tours between May and October.

Berchtesgaden
The capital of the region features many historic buildings. The Schloss, originally an Augustinian priory, now houses the art treasures collected by Crown Prince Ruprecht. The local salt mine has been a source of wealth since the 16th century.

VISITORS' CHECKLIST

Road map E7. 🏃 8,500. 🚉 Berchtesgaden. ℹ️ Königsseer Str. 2, 83471 Berchtesgaden (08652-96 70).

Wallfahrtskirche Maria Gern
One of the loveliest Baroque buildings in the region, the pilgrimage church of Maria Gern was built in 1709 in this idyllic location.

KEY

▬	Major road
═	Minor road
─	River
☆	Viewpoint

STAR SIGHTS

★ Königssee

★ Ramsau an der Ache

★ Königssee
Germany's highest lake, Königssee is the focal point of Berchtesgadener Land. Lying 600 m (2,000 ft) above sea level, it covers an area of 5.5 sq km (1,360 acres) and reaches a depth of 188 m (616 ft).

Touring Chiemsee 🄴

Bavaria's largest lake, Chiemsee is a real paradise for watersports enthusiasts, with sailors, water-skiers, swimmers and divers all enjoying the opportunities it offers. The lake is set amidst magnificent Alpine scenery in the region known as the Chiemgau, which stretches eastwards from Rosenheim to the border with Austria along the river Salzach. Chiemsee is surrounded by numerous small towns and villages and dotted with islands, some of which feature fascinating historic buildings. Excellent land, water and rail transport facilities ensure trouble-free travel to all destinations in the area.

Fraueninsel
Like its neighbour Herreninsel, this island is rich in art treasures. Its abbey (Klosterkirche) was founded in 766 and taken over by Benedictine nuns in the mid-9th century.

Stock
The harbour town of Stock is connected by narrow-gauge steam railway to the Chiemsee's main resort of Prien. The railway, the Chiemseebahn, is over one hundred years old.

Urschalling
The 12th-century church of St Jakobus features magnificent wall paintings dating from the 13th and 14th centuries.

Herrenchiemsee Palace
In 1873, King Ludwig II bought Herreninsel, with the intention of building a replica of the Palace of Versailles here. Funds ran out and the project was not completed, but the magnificent central section and park are well worth visiting.

KEY

▬	Motorway
▬	Major road
═	Minor road
═	River
☀	Viewpoint

Map labels: Obing, Hinzing, Halfing, HARTSEE, Eggstätt, Bad Endorf, LANGBÜRGNER SEE, SIMSSEE, Stock, Prien, Hakras, Urschalling, Bernau

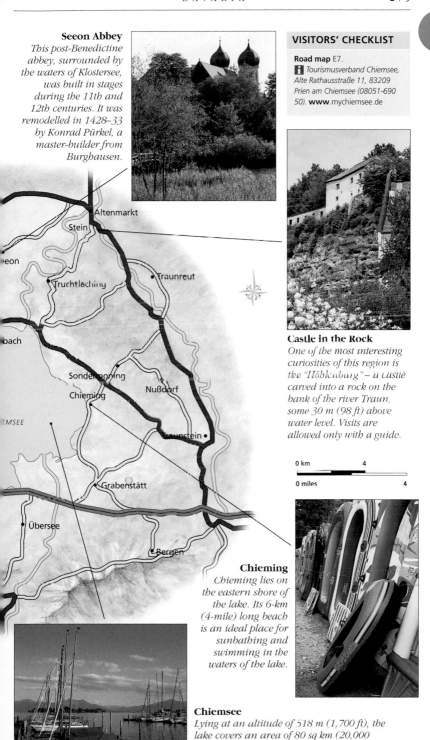

Seeon Abbey

This post-Benedictine abbey, surrounded by the waters of Klostersee, was built in stages during the 11th and 12th centuries. It was remodelled in 1428–33 by Konrad Pürkel, a master-builder from Burghausen.

VISITORS' CHECKLIST

Road map E7.
🛈 *Tourismusverband Chiemsee, Alte Rathausstraße 11, 83209 Prien am Chiemsee (08051-690 50).* **www**.mychiemsee.de

Castle in the Rock

One of the most interesting curiosities of this region is the "Höhlenburg" – a castle carved into a rock on the bank of the river Traun, some 30 m (98 ft) above water level. Visits are allowed only with a guide.

Chieming

Chieming lies on the eastern shore of the lake. Its 6-km (4-mile) long beach is an ideal place for sunbathing and swimming in the waters of the lake.

Chiemsee

Lying at an altitude of 518 m (1,700 ft), the lake covers an area of 80 sq km (20,000 acres) with a depth of 70 m (230 ft). Its size makes it popular with sailing enthusiasts.

Colourful Alpine inn, dating from 1612, in Oberammergau

Garmisch-Partenkirchen ㉟

Road map D7. 🏃 27,000. 🚉
🚆 Richard-Strauss-Platz 2 (08821-18
07 00). 🎿 Neujahrs-Springen (1 Jan);
Hornschlitten-Rennen (6 Jan); Ski World
Cup Races; Richard-Strauss-Tage (Jun).
www.gapa.de

Lying in the valley of the river
Loisach, Garmisch-Parten-
kirchen is the best-known
resort in the Bavarian Alps.
To say that it offers ideal
skiing conditions would
be to state the obvi-
ous. In 1936, it
hosted the Winter
Olympic Games
and, in 1978, the
World Skiing Cham-
pionships. From
Garmisch-Parten-
kirchen, Germany's
highest peak, Zugs-
pitze (2964 m/9,720
ft), can be reached
by taking the nar-
row-gauge railway
to Zugspitzblatt and
from there a cable
car, which reaches
the summit in a few
minutes. Garmisch
Partenkirchen's parish church
of St Martin (Alte Pfarrkirche
St Martin) is worth a visit. It
was built in the 13th century
and extended in the 15th
century and features some
well-preserved Gothic wall
paintings and net vaulting.
The **Werdenfels Museum**
shows how people in this
region lived in the past, with
a collection of furniture, clothing and room reconstructions.

🏛 **Werdenfels Museum**
Ludwigstraße 47.
Tel (08821) 21 34. ⬜ Dec–Oct:
10am–5pm Tue–Sun. 🈂

**Oriel window in
Garmisch-
Partenkirchen**

Oberammergau ㊱

Road map D7. 🏃 4,700. 🚆 Eugen-
Papst-Straße 9A (08822-923 10).
🎿 König-Ludwig-Lauf (Feb);
Oberammergauer Passionsspiele May–
Oct, every ten years: 2020); König-
Ludwig-Feiern (24 Aug).

Situated some 20 km (12
miles) north of Garmisch-
Partenkirchen, and standing on
the site of a 9th-century Welfs'
fort, Oberammergau is world
famous for its folk art
and passion plays. The
Thirty Years' War
(1618–48) and the
plague of 1632
came close to
wiping out the entire
population of the
village. Its surviving
inhabitants pledged
that if they were
saved from
extinction they
would stage for
ever more a play
about Christ's
Passion. No further
deaths occurred and,
to this day, the
villagers have kept
their pledge. Every ten years
(the next is in 2020), some
2,000 people take part in the
six-hour-long spectacle, in

which they transform themselves from Bavarians into
Jews and Romans from the
time of Christ. About one
hundred performances are
staged between mid-May and
mid-October in the huge
Passionsspielhaus.
  Among the buildings worth
seeing in Oberammergau are
the Rococo church of Saint
Peter and Saint Paul
(1735–40) and the famous
Pilatushaus, with its illusion-
ist painting of Christ before
Pilate on the façade. The
Heimatmuseum has a notable
collection of wooden cribs.

🏛 **Heimatmuseum**
Dorfstraße 8. **Tel** (08822) 941 36.
⬜ 10am–5pm Tue–Sun. ⬤ Feb,
Mar, Nov. 🈂

Ettal ㊲

Road map D7. 🏃 974.

About 4 km (2.5 miles) from
Oberammergau is the tiny
resort of Ettal, which is best
known for its Benedictine
abbey, founded by Emperor
Ludwig IV of Bavaria. The
abbey's foundation stone was
laid in 1330, while the Church
of the Virgin Mary and the
convent were consecrated in
1370. The church building
is a Gothic structure but, in
1710–52, Josef Enrico Zuccalli
and Franz Schmuzer carried
out major remodelling work
in the Baroque style. The
church interior is decorated
with rich Rococo stuccowork
by Johann Baptist and Johann
Georg Ubelhör, and wall
paintings by Martin Knoller.
  The monastery produces
some fine fruit liqueurs,
flavoured brandies and beer.

The Baroque Benedictine abbey in Ettal

For hotels and restaurants in this region see pp499–503 and pp538–42

Linderhof ㊳

In the early 1850s, Linderhof was bought by the
Bavarian King Maximilian II. This remote mountain
district had great appeal to the young heir to the throne,
Ludwig, later to become the eccentric King Ludwig II.
In 1874, work started on remodelling the existing
Königshäuschen (royal cottage) in the Neo-Rococo
style. The palace is surrounded by a delightful garden,
which is dotted with romantic little buildings, including
Schwanenweiher (Swan Lake), *Venusgrotte* (Venus grotto)
and the *Marokkanisches Haus* (Moroccan house).

VISITORS' CHECKLIST

Road map D7. **Schloss
Linderhof**. *Tel* (08822) 920 30.
☐ *Apr–15 Oct: 9am–6pm daily;
16 Oct–Mar: 10am–4pm daily.* 🎫

Tapestry Room
The walls of this room are
painted in a style that is reminiscent of tapestry work, with
depictions of pastoral scenes.

Reception Room
Although the palace was
intended as a private
residence, King Ludwig II
insisted on the provision
of a suitably ornate and
regal reception room.

Dining Room
Designed by Christian Jank,
the dining room was
completed in 1872. It features
gilded panelling by Phillip
Perron and stuccowork by
Theobald Behler.

Mirror Hall
The design of Linderhof's Mirror
Hall was based on the Mirror
Room of the royal residence in
Munich *(pp216–17)*.

Terraces
Terraces in front of the palace
are adorned with sculptures and
include a pool with a fountain.

Schloss Neuschwanstein ③

Set amidst magnificent mountain scenery high above Forggensee, Alpsee and Schwansee, this fairy-tale castle was built in 1869–86 for the eccentric Bavarian King Ludwig II, to a design by the theatre designer Christian Jank. When deciding to build this imposing residence, the king was undoubtedly inspired by Wartburg Castle in Thuringia *(see pp186–7)*, which he visited in 1867. The pale grey limestone castle, which draws on a variety of historical styles, is a steep 30-minute walk from the nearby village of Hohenschwangau and offers spectacular views of the surrounding scenery.

★ **Singers' Hall**
The Sängersaal was modelled on the singing room of the Wartburg castle in Eisenach.

Study

Vestibule
The walls of the vestibule and of other rooms in the castle are lavishly covered with paintings depicting scenes from old German myths and legends.

★ **Throne Room**
The gilded interior of the throne room reminds one of Byzantine temples and the palace church of All Saints (Hofkirche) in the Residenz (see pp216–17) in Munich.

Dining Room
Like other rooms in the palace, the dining room includes fabulous pictures, intricately carved panels and beautifully decorated furniture, all bearing witness to the skill and artistry of the 19th-century craftsmen.

★ Castle Building
Schloss Neuschwanstein is the archetypal fairy tale castle and has provided the inspiration for countless toy models, book illustrations and film sets.

Two storey arcades
surround the castle courtyard

Courtyard
The heart of the castle was supposed to have been a mighty 90-m (295-ft) high tower with a Gothic castle church. It was never built, but in 1988 its planned position was marked in white stone.

Main entrance

Gatehouse
During construction, temporary accommodation was built for the king on the second floor of the gatehouse, completed in 1872.

VISITORS' CHECKLIST

Road map D7. Neuschwansteinstrasse 20. **Tel** (08362) 93 98 80. ☐ daily. 🅿 ✆ ♿ (limited access). 🍴 🛍 ♿ 🅸 Tickets only available from ticket centre in Hohenschwangau.

STAR FEATURES

★ Castle Building

★ Singers' Hall

★ Throne Room

Hohen-schwangau ㊵

Road map D7. 🚇 Schwangau 3,818. 🅸 Schwangau, Münchenerstr. 2 (08362-819 80). Ticket service: Hohenschwangau Alpseestr. 12 (08362-930 830).

The skyline of Schwangau is dominated by two castles, Schloss Neuschwanstein (left) and the majestic **Schloss Hohenschwangau**. The fortified castle that occupied this site in the Middle Ages was remodelled in 1538–47 and, in 1567, it passed into the hands of the Wittelsbach family. It was destroyed during the Tyrolean War but in 1832 the heir to the throne (later Maximilian II) ordered the ruins to be rebuilt in Neo-Gothic style. The plans were prepared by the painter Domenico Quaglio; after his death, work on the castle was continued by the architects Georg Friedrich Ziebland and Joseph Daniel Ohlmüller.

This four storey building, standing on medieval foundations, is flanked by angular towers. The wall paintings that decorate the rooms of the castle date from 1835–36. Their iconographic content, which is based on old Germanic sagas, is the work of Moritz von Schwind. A walk around the castle provides an excellent opportunity to study the Wittelsbach family history and to see the mid-19th century furnishings. There are magnificent views of the surroundings from the castle's lovely terraced gardens.

♣ Schloss Hohenschwangau
Tel (08362) 930 830.
☐ Apr–Sep: 9am–6pm daily; Oct–Mar: 10am–4pm.
🚫 24 Dec. 🅿

Neo-Gothic castle of Maximilian II in Hohenschwangau

The Rococo Throne Room in the Kempten Residenz.

Kempten 🄌

Road map C7. 🏔 68,000. 🚉
ℹ Rathausplatz 24 (0831-252 52 37).
📷 Allgäuer Festwochen (Aug).
www.kempten.de

Kempten lies at the centre
of one of Germany's most
attractive tourist regions, the
Allgäu, which stretches from
Bodensee lake to the west
and the river Lech to the east.
The town, which boasts a
history of over 2,000 years,
was first mentioned by the
Greek geographer and
historian Strabon as a Celtic
settlement, Kambodounon.
Later, the Romans established
Cambodunum on the right
bank of the river Iller. Along
with Augusta Vindelicorum
(Augsburg) and Castra Regina
(Regensburg), this was one of
the most important towns in
the Roman province of Raetia.

Medieval Kempten grew
around a Benedictine Abbey,
founded in 752. In the northwestern part of town, near
the former abbots' residence,
is the church of St Lorenz. A
triple-nave, galleried basilica
with an octagonal cupola and
a twin-tower façade, this is
the work of Michael Beer and
Johann Serro. The town's parish
church of St Mang dates from
the 15th century. In the
Rathausplatz is an attractive
town hall dating from 1474 and
other historic buildings, including the Londoner Hof with its
Rococo façade (1764). The
Allgäu-Museum details the
history of Kempten. On the
right bank of the river Iller,
is the **Archäologischer Park**,
with excavated remains of
Roman Cambodunum.

🏛 **Allgäu-Museum**
Kornhaus, Großer Kornhausplatz 1.
Tel (0831) 540 21 20.
⬜ 10am–4pm Tue–Sun. 📷

�857 **Archäologischer Park
Cambodunum**
Cambodunumweg 3. **Tel** (0831)
797 31. ⬜ May–Oct: 10am–5pm
Tue–Sun; Nov–Apr: 10am–4:30pm
Tue–Sun. ⬤ mid-Dec–mid-Mar.

Lindau 🄂

Road map C7. 🏔 24,000. 🚉 ℹ
Ludwigstraße 68 (08382-26 00 30 or
19 433). 📷 Lindauer Kinderfest (Jul).

In Roman times Lindau was a
fishing settlement, which used
to lie over three islands. The
first historic records of the
town date from 882. On the
south side of the old-town
island lies the harbour with
its 13th-century lighthouse
(Mangturm). The new lighthouse (Neuer Leuchtturm),
built in 1856, stands on the
neighbouring pier and offers
a splendid view over the lake
and the Alps. The marble
Lion of Bavaria opposite is
the symbol of Lindau.

The old town features many
historic buildings, such as the
Gothic-Renaissance town hall
in Reichsplatz, which was
built in 1422–36 and later
remodelled in 1578. The
picturesque Maximilianstrasse
is lined with the houses of
rich patricians; their shady
arcades (Brodlauben) are
typical of Lindau architecture.

In Schrannenplatz, in the
northwest area of the town,
stands the church of St Peter.
Since 1928 this has been the
war memorial chapel for
World War I victims. Its
eastern section dates from the
mid-12th century while the
bigger, western section was
built between 1425 and 1480.
The interior contains many
wall paintings, including
some by Hans Holbein the
Elder dating from 1485–90.
Nearby stands the Diebsturm
(Thief's Tower) of 1380. The
Stadtmuseum (town museum)
is housed in Haus zum
Cavazzen (1729) in Markt-
platz, which also features a
lovely Neptune fountain.

On the south side of the
Market Square stands the
Protestant Church of St
Stephen, which dates from
the 12th century and was
remodelled in Baroque style
in 1782. The Catholic Church
of St Mary, built in 1748–52,
has a lovely Rococo interior.

🏛 **Stadtmuseum Lindau**
Marktplatz 6. **Tel** (08382) 94 40 73.
⬜ Apr–Oct: 11am–5pm Tue–Fri,
Sun, 2pm–5pm Sat. ⬤ Nov–Mar.

Epitaph of the family of Andreas Bertsch, in the Stadtmuseum Lindau

For hotels and restaurants in this region see pp499–503 and pp538–42

Oberstdorf ㊸

Road map C7. 🏠 *11,000.* 🚉
🛈 *Verkehrsamt, Marktplatz 7
(08322-70 00).*

Oberstdorf lies in the valley
of the River Iller. The ideal
skiing conditions and the
mild all-year-round climate
make this one of the most
popular health resorts and
winter sports centres in
Germany. Nearby is
the skiing stadium
(Schattenberg-
Skistadion) with its
famous ski-jump,
where the annual
"four ski-jump"
tournament starts
each year.

Although the fire
of 1865 destroyed
large sections of the
settlement here,
some of the most
important historic
buildings escaped.
These include See-
lenkapelle, whose
façade is decorated
with a 16th-century
wall painting typical
of the region, and
two chapels, Loret-
tokapelle and Josephskapelle,
which were joined together in
1707. Just to the east of Oberstdorf is the 2,224-m (7,300-ft)
Mount Nebelhorn, whose
summit can be reached in a
few minutes by cable car.
This offers a spectacular view
over the majestic Allgäuer
Alps as well as providing an
excellent starting point for
mountain hiking.

Ski-jump complex in Oberstdorf

Füssen ㊹

Road map D7. 🏠 *16,000.* 🚉 🛈
*Kurverwaltung, Kaiser-Maximilian-
Platz 1 (08362-938 50).*

Situated conveniently on an
important trade route, Füssen
experienced its most rapid
growth in the late Middle
Ages, as witnessed by many
of the buildings in Reichen-
strasse and the remains of the
town fortifications, which
include Sebastiantor
and sections of the
walls with five
turrets. Perched on
a rock, high
above the town,
stands the palace
of the Augsburg
prince bishops.
Started in 1291 by
the Bavarian Prince
Ludwig II the
Severe, construction
was continued in
1490–1503 by the
Augsburg bishops.
The residential
buildings of the
palace range
around a courtyard
whose walls are
decorated with
trompe l'oeil door and
window frames.

**Madonna in the
Church of St Mang,
in Füssen**

At the foot of the castle
stands the former Benedictine
Abbey (Kloster St Mang),
which was erected in the 9th
century at the burial site of St
Magnus, the "Apostle of the
Allgäu". The only surviving
part of the abbey is the late
10th-century crypt with the
remains of wall paintings.

**Late-Baroque interior of the Abbey
Library, in Ottobeuren**

Ottobeuren ㊺

Road map D7. 🏠 *7,500.* 🛈
Marktplatz 14 (08332-92 19 50).

Situated 8 km (5 miles) from
Memmingen, the small health
resort of Ottobeuren is the
site of one of Germany's most
famous Benedictine abbeys.
Founded in 764, the abbey
is still a place of prayer and
work for the monks who live
here, having withstood even
the radical secularization of
1803. In the 18th century the
abbey was remodelled by
the Abbot Rupert II. The
foundation stone for the
building complex was laid in
1717 and work began under
the direction of Simpert
Kraemer. The new buildings
were completed in 1731. The
richly decorated interiors, with
stuccoes by Andrea Maini, still
survive. A new abbey church
was built between 1737 and
1766 with construction supervised initially by Simpert
Kramer. In 1748, this was
taken over by Johann Michael
Fischer, who was responsible
for its final appearance.

The interior of the church
has a magnificent unity of
style: Rococo stuccoes by
Johann Michael Feuchtmayr
are in perfect harmony with
the vault frescos by Johann
Jakob Zeiller as well as the
splendid altars and stalls by
Martin Hörmann and Johann
Zeiller's brother Franz Anton
Zeiller. The abbey's three
organs, which are particularly
beautiful, can be heard at
regularly held recitals.

Augsburg ㊻

Situated at the confluence of the Lech and
Wertach rivers, Augsburg is the third largest
town in Bavaria and one of the oldest in
Germany. As early as 15 BC this was the
site of a Roman camp, which later became
a town known as Augusta Vindelicorum.
Until the end of the 13th century, the town
was ruled by powerful bishops. From 1316,
as a Free Imperial City of the Holy Roman
Empire, Augsburg grew to become one
of the richest and most powerful cities in
Germany. The Thirty Years' War (1618–48),
however, put an end to the town's prosperity.

Augustusbrunnen
*Incorporating a
statue of the Emperor
Augustus, the
fountain was created
in the workshop of
Dutchman Hubert
Gerhard in 1594.*

Dom

Church of St Anna
*The star attraction of
this unassuming ex-
Carmelite church is the
Renaissance memorial
chapel endowed by the
brothers Ulrich and
Jacob Fugger in 1509.*

PHIL.-WELSER-STRASSE

St Moritz
Kirche

ANNASTRASSE

BGM.-FISCHER-STRASSE

**Maximilian-
museum**
*Set in a Renaissance patrician
mansion, the museum has a
splendid collection of work by
local gold- and silversmiths.*

Zeughaus
*A bronze group by
Hans Reichle,
St Michael Over-
coming Satan
(1607), adorns the
façade of the former
arsenal building by
Elias Holl, the most
important early
Baroque architect.*

KÖNIGS-
PLATZ

WALLSTRASSE

For hotels and restaurants in this region see pp499–503 and pp538–42

VISITORS' CHECKLIST

Road map D6. 🏙 265,000. ✈
5 km (3 miles) to the north. 🚉
🛈 Am Rathausplatz (0821-50
20 70). 🎭 Frühjahrsplärrer
(week following Easter), Mozart-
sommer (Jul), Friedenfest
(8 Aug), Herbstplärrer (Aug/Sep).
www.augsburg.de

★ Rathaus
*The magnificent town hall,
built by Elias Holl in 1615–20,
is generally regarded as
Germany's finest example
of Mannerist architecture.*

★ Maximilianstraße
*Augsburg's main thoroughfare is the most
beautiful street in southern Germany, with
notable fountains by Adrian de Vries.*

★ Fuggerhäuser
*Commissioned by Jacob II
Fugger (1459–1525) for
himself and his family,
this Italian-style
building, with
two arcaded
courtyards,
was built in
1512–15.*

St Ulrich-
und-Afra

KEY

– – – Suggested route

STAR SIGHTS

★ Fuggerhäuser

★ Maximilianstraße

★ Rathaus

**View of the monumental Gothic
Dom of the Holy Virgin**

🔒 Dom of the Holy Virgin (Dom Unserer Lieben Frau)
Frauentorstr. 1. ⏰ 9am–5:30pm.
Originally a Romanesque
twin-choir, pillared basilica
with crypt, western transept
and two towers, dating from
994–1065, the structure was
remodelled between 1331 and
1431 along Gothic lines. The
church was given two further
side aisles, a choir with an
ambulatory and a French-style
ring of chapels. Original
features include the richly
carved portals and the famous
Romanesque bronze door
with 35 panels depicting
allegorical figures. There are
some unique stained-glass
windows, dating from 1140.

🏛 Fuggerei
Fuggerei-Museum, Mittlere Gasse 14.
Tel (0821) 319 88 10. ⏰ Apr–Oct:
8am–8pm daily; Nov–Mar: 9am–6pm
daily. 🔒 24 Dec–28 Feb. 🎫
The Fuggerei, in Augsburg's
Jakobervorstadt (Jacob's
Suburb), is Europe's oldest
social housing estate. It was
founded in 1516 by Jacob
Fugger, a member of what
was then the richest family in
Europe. The intention was to
provide homes for the town's
poorest citizens, particularly
families with children. Today,
however, it has evolved into
a home for retired citizens.

The 52 houses in Fuggerei
were built in 1516–25 and line
six streets. They are surrounded by gardens. One of the
buildings houses the **Fuggerei-
Museum,** which is devoted to
the history of the estate and
has a fascinating shop, the
Himmlisches Fuggerelädle.

BADEN-WURTTEMBERG

This German state, which includes territories of the former Grand Duchy of Baden, is one of the country's most popular tourist destinations. Its charming old university towns, such as Tübingen and Heidelberg, historic castles, luxurious resorts and the magnificent recreation areas of the Schwarzwald (Black Forest) and Bodensee (Lake Constance) guarantee enjoyable and memorable holidays.

This region's turbulent history, which has been ruled over the years by Palatinate electors, counts and finally kings of Wurttemberg, as well as by margraves and Grand Dukes of Baden, has given the province its cultural and religious diversity.

This southwestern area of Germany was the cradle of two great dynasties that played a significant part in German and European history and culture. The Hohenstaufen family – which originated from Swabia – produced kings and emperors who ruled during the most magnificent period of the German Middle Ages (1138–1254). These included Frederick I Barbarossa and Frederick II. The Hohenzollern family, also from Swabia, produced Brandenburg dukes, Prussian kings including Frederick the Great and German emperors from 1871–1918.

In Heidelberg the enlightened elector Ruprecht I founded the first university in Germany in 1386 and shortly after this epoch-making event, further universities were established in Tübingen and Freiburg im Breisgau. Many towns and villages in the region can boast a history going back to Roman times. The Romans used to grow vines in the area of Baden-Wurttemberg and now wines from the region are renowned worldwide for their high quality.

Baden-Wurttemberg, however, does not only represent an illustrious past, but also an impressive present. Unemployment figures for the region are the lowest in Germany, and many companies that are known and respected throughout the world – such as Bosch, Daimler, Porsche and the software company SAP – have their production plants here.

Magnificent French-style garden in front of the palace in Ludwigsburg

◁ Bodensee (Lake Constance) and the island of Lindau, in the foothills of the Alps

Baden-Wurttemberg

With its magnificent castles, luxurious resorts and the beautiful recreation areas of the Black Forest, Baden-Wurttemberg is one of Germany's most popular tourist destinations. In addition, the region's long and turbulent history has given it a rich cultural and religious diversity. The southwest region of Germany was the cradle of two dynasties that played important roles in German and European history and culture – the Hohenstaufen and Hohenzollern families. The great number of urban centres in the state is due to the influence of these two families. Baden-Wurttemberg also has more universities than any other state in Germany, the oldest being located at Heidelberg, Tübingen and Freiburg im Breisgau.

The picturesque castle in Sigmaringen, in the region of Schwäbische Alb

KEY

▬▬	Motorway
▬▬	Major road
▭▭	Minor road
▬▭	Main railway
—	Minor railway
▬▬	International border
▬▬	County border
△	Summit

The Gothic town hall in Ulm

Weinheim

A67

⑥ MANN

SCHWETZINGEN ⑦

HEIDELBE

36   A5

9

BRUCHSAL ⑧

35

MAULBR

KARLSRUHE ⑩

Ettlingen

36

Rastatt   Pforzheim

Gaggenau

BADEN-BADEN ⑪

462

294

A5

Hornisgrinde
1164m   BADE

Strasbourg   28

Offenburg   28

36   33   Freudenstad

Kinzig   294

Lahr   Neckar

A8

294   Gutach

294

ROTTWEIL ㉓

Emmendingen   33   *Lent*
        Villingen-   *10*
Kandel   Schwenningen   Tros
1241m   Furtwangen   Tuttlin
FREIBURG ㉙   Donaueschingen
IM BREISGAU ㉚
        Feldberg   31
Bad   *1495m*
Krozingen   315
        Blumberg
A5   Müllheim
        Todtmoos   St Blasien
3   317
        Schopfheim   314
Lörrach   Waldshut-
        Tiengen
34
Basel

SEE ALSO

• *Where to Stay* pp503–6

• *Where to Eat* pp542–5

GETTING AROUND

The main communication centres of the area are Stuttgart, which has an international airport, and Mannheim. Main motorways include the A5 from Frankfurt to Basle, via Heidelberg, Karlsruhe, Baden-Baden and Freiburg; the A81 from Würzburg to Constance, via Tauberbischofsheim, Heilbronn, Stuttgart and Schwäbische Alb; the A6 from Mannheim to Ansbach, via Heilbronn and Crailsheim; and the A8 from Karlsruhe to Ulm, via Stuttgart.

SIGHTS AT A GLANCE

Palace façade in Bruchsal

0 km   20

0 miles   20

Wertheim ❶

Road map C5. 👥 *24,500.* 🚆 ℹ️
Am Spitzen Turm (09342-1066). 🎭
Altstadtfest (Jul), Burgweinfest (Aug).

Standing at the point where the rivers Tauber and Main meet is the town of Wertheim, whose earliest historic records date from 1183. A gunpowder explosion in 1619 plus the destruction caused by the Thirty Years' War turned the **Wertheimer Burg**, the von Wertheim family castle, into a romantic ruin. Its tall watch-tower offers panoramic views.

Wertheim's market square is lined with half-timbered hou-ses, while the Baroque Protes-tant church nearby, dating from the 15th–18th centuries, has tombs of members of the von Wertheim family. The most spectacular is the tomb of Count Ludwig II von Löwen-stein-Wertheim and his wife, Anna von Stolberg. This is the work of Michael Kern (1618). Also worth visiting are the **Glasmuseum** and the **Graf-schaftsmuseum Wertheim**, with collections of Frankish costumes, paintings and coins and displays on wine-making.

🏛 **Glasmuseum**
Mühlenstraße 24.
Tel *(09342) 68 66.*
⭕ *Apr–Oct: 10am–noon & 2–5pm Tue–Thu, 1–7pm Fri & Sat, 1–5pm Sun.* ⬤ *6 Jan–Easter.*

🏛 **Grafschaftsmuseum Wertheim**
Rathausgasse 6–10. ***Tel*** *(09342) 30 15 11.* ⭕ *10am–noon, 2:30pm–4:30pm Tue–Fri, 2:30pm–4:30pm Sat, 2pm–5pm Sun.* 🎭

Half-timbered houses and tower, Tauberbischofsheim

Tauberbischofs-heim ❷

Road map C5. 👥 *13,000.* 🚆
ℹ️ *Marktplatz 8 (09341-803 33).*

Boniface, the Anglo-Saxon missionary to the German tribes, established Germany's first nunnery in AD 735. Its first prioress, Lioba, who was related to Boniface, gave her name to the Baroque church that stands in Tauberbischofs-heim's market square.

The town, which enjoys a picturesque location in the valley of the river Tauber, still has a group of original half-timbered houses. On the market square is the Baroque Rehhof (1702) and the old "Star Pharmacy" in a

house once occupied by Georg Michael Franck, grand-father of the Romantic poets Clemens and Bettina Brentano.

In the eastern section of Hauptstraße stands Haus Mackert – a Baroque mansion built in 1744 for a wealthy wine merchant. In Schloss-platz is the Kurmainzisches Schloss, an imposing edifice built in the 15th–16th centuries, that now houses the **Landschaftsmuseum**.

🏛 **Landschaftsmuseum Kurmainzisches Schloss**
Tel *(09341) 37 60.* ⭕ *Palm Sunday–Oct: 2–4:30pm Tue–Sat, 10am–noon & 2–4:30pm Sun.* 🎭

Bad Mergentheim ❸

Road map C5. 👥 *25,000.* 🚆
ℹ️ *Marktplatz 3 (07931-5 71 31).*
🎭 *Markelsheimer Weinfest (after Whitsun).*

Lying in a charming spot on the river Tauber, Bad Mergentheim was, from 1525 until 1809, the seat of the Grand Masters of the religious order of the "House of the Hospitallers of Saint Mary of the Teutons in Jerusalem", more commonly known as the Teutonic Knights. When three Hohenlohe brothers entered the Order in 1220, they contributed to it their share of their father's estate. This laid the foundations for one of the most powerful Teutonic commands at the heart of the Holy Roman Empire. From 1244 until 1250 Heinrich von Hohenlohe held the office of Grand Master.

The former Hohenlohe's castle, built in the 12th–13th centuries, was remodelled in Renaissance style in 1565–74 by Michael Bronner and Blasius Berwart. They gave the castle its winding stairs and the opulent decor of the staircase. The Baroque-Rococo Schlosskirche dominates the complex. Its interior was designed by François Cuvilliés, while the ceiling

Heraldic crest from the castle in Bad Mergentheim

Scenic castle ruins in Wertheim

fresco *(The Victorious Cross)* is the work of Nicolaus Stuber. The castle is now the home of a very interesting museum, the **Deutschordensmuseum**.

Many of the town's historic buildings survive to this day, including the 13th-century Church of the Knights of St John of Jerusalem and the Dominican church containing the epitaph of the Grand Master Walther von Cronberg. The **Pfarrkirche** (Parish church) in the Stuppach district contains a masterpiece by Grünewald (1519), known as the *Madonna of Stuppach*.

⛪ Pfarrkirche in Stuppach
Kapellenpflege.
Tel (07931) 26 05. ⬜ May–Oct:
8.30am–6.30pm daily; Mar, Apr
& Nov: 11am–4pm. 🈂

🏛 Deutschordensmuseum
Schloss.
Tel (07931) 522 12. ⬜ Apr–Oct:
10:30am–5pm Tue–Sun; Nov–Mar:
2–5pm Tue–Sat, 10:30am–5pm Sun.
🈂

Weikersheim ❹

Road map C5. 🏠 8,000. 🛈 *Am
Marktplatz 7 (07934-102 55).*

Eleven kilometres (7 miles) east of Bad Mergentheim is the picturesque little town of Weikersheim. A Rococo fountain from 1768 is at the centre of the market square while the late-Gothic parish church is on the north side. The latter is a triple-nave hall-church with a single-tower western façade and two towers by the choir. Inside are many tombs of the von Hohenlohe family. Also on the market square stands the **Tauberländer Dorfmuseum**, which charts the history of rural life in Franconia. In the western part of town stands the very well preserved **Schloss Weikersheim**, the palace complex

of the Counts von Hohenlohe, which dates from the 16th–18th centuries. Its highlight is undoubtedly the vast Rittersaal, a sumptuous banqueting hall that measures 35 m (115 ft) long x 12 m (39 ft) wide x 9 m (29 ft) high. The counts and their aristocratic guests used to enter this room on horseback. Its very rare, original furnishings include paintings and reliefs depicting hunting scenes.

A true rarity is the original Baroque Hofgarten (palace garden), designed by Daniel Matthieu and built in 1709.

⛲ Schloss Weikersheim
Tel (07934) 8364. ⬜ Apr–Oct:
9am–6pm daily; Nov–Mar: 10am–
noon & 1:30–4:30pm daily. 🈂

🏛 Tauberländer Dorfmuseum
Marktplatz **Tel** (07934) 12 09. ⬜
Apr–Oct: 2–5pm Wed, Fri, Sat, Sun. 🈂

Creglingen ❺

Road map C5. 🏠 5,000. 🚃 🛈
Romantische Straße 14 (07933-6 31).

Upstream from Weikersheim, on the Bavarian border, is the small town of Creglingen. Here, sometime in the distant past, a ploughman found a luminous holy wafer in a clod of earth and several hundred years, the **Herrgottskirche** was built, where the host was put on display for visiting pilgrims. Between 1502 and 1506 Tilman Riemenschneider

Altar by Tilman Riemenschneider, in Creglingen's Herrgottskirche

carved an altar for the church. The main theme of the polyptych is the *Assumption of the Virgin Mary*, considered to be the artist's masterpiece.

The town is also home to the esoteric collection of the famous **Fingerhutmuseum** (Thimble Museum).

⛪ Herrgottskirche
Kohlersmühle. **Tel** (07933) 338 or
508. ⬜ Feb–Mar & Nov–Dec:
1–4pm Tue–Sun; Apr–Oct:
9:15am–6pm daily.

🏛 Fingerhutmuseum
Kohlersmühle. **Tel** (07933) 370.
⬜ Apr–Oct: 10am–12:30pm & 2–
5pm Tue–Sun; Nov–Mar: 1–4pm
Tue–Sun. ⬤ Jan. 🈂

TEUTONIC ORDER

The Order of the Hospital of St Mary of the German House in Jerusalem was officially founded in Acre (Akkon) in 1190. Its aim was to care for sick pilgrims or Crusaders wounded in fights with the Saracens. In 1231–83, the Teutonic Knights took over all of Prussia and, in 1308–09 all Eastern Pomerania around Danzig, and they moved their headquarters from Venice to Marienburg on the river Nogat. In 1525 the Grand Master, Albrecht von Hohenzollern-Ansbach, converted to Lutheranism and secularized Teutonic Prussia. However, the Order remained in existence in the Holy Roman Empire: its German Master, Walter von Cronberg, who had his residence in Mergentheim, became *de facto* Grand Master. Napoleon abolished the Order in 1809, but it still exists today, with its headquarters based in Vienna since 1848.

The Wasserturm (Water Tower) in Friedrichsplatz, Mannheim

Mannheim ⑥

Road map B5. 👥 *326,000.* 🚉
ℹ️ *Willy-Brandt-Platz 3 (0621-29 38 700).* 🎬 *Mannheim-Heidelberger Filmfestival (mid-Oct).*
www.mannheim.de

Mannheim existed as a fishing hamlet as far back as 766. In 1606, Elector Frederick IV the Righteous ordered a fortress to be built on the site, at the junction of the rivers Rhine and Neckar. A trading settlement sprang up nearby and was soon granted town status. Having been repeatedly destroyed through the years, the town was finally rebuilt in Baroque style during the reign of the Elector Johann Wilhelm.

The town-centre layout follows the regular Baroque pattern of the early 18th century, when the town was divided into 136 regular squares. In 1720, when Elector Charles III Philip decided to move his residence from Heidelberg to Mannheim, the foundation stone for a Baroque palace was laid in the grounds of a former citadel.

Statue of Elector Karl Theodor in Mannheim's Jesuitenkirche

With over 400 rooms, this became one of the largest and most opulent of all German palaces. Like the residences of many European rulers at that time, it was modelled on Versailles. The main palace has a horseshoe layout, and its symmetry is emphasized by a central projecting entrance. Building work was done by Johann Clemens Froimont, Alessandro Galli da Bibiena, Nicolas de Pigage and Guillaume d'Hauberat.

The second largest town of the region, Mannheim boasts many other historic buildings, including the post-Jesuit Church of St Ignatius and St Francis Xavier, designed by Alessandro Galli da Bibiena and built in 1733–60. Original wall-paintings by Egid Quirin Asam no longer exist, but the altars have survived to this day. These include JI Saler's *Silver Madonna in Radiant Glory* (1747). Also worth visiting are the Baroque Altes Rathaus (1701–23) and Secessionist buildings in Friedrichsplatz such as the Kunsthalle and Wasserturm – the symbol of Mannheim.

The town has several interesting museums: the **Kunsthalle Mannheim** has a large collection of 19th- and 20th-century art, including Francis Bacon's *Study After Velasquez's Portrait of Pope Innocent X.* The museum is renowned for its major temporary exhibitions. The **Reiss-Engelhorn-Museen** has a fine collection of 18th-century Dutch paintings and sections devoted to early history and ethnography.

Another big attraction in Mannheim is the **TECHNOSEUM** (Museum of Technology and Labour). Opened in 1990, this houses a collection of historic machinery. Mannheim saw the first official

demonstration of many inventions that have now become part of everyday life. In 1817, Baron Karl Friedrich von Sauerbronn demonstrated his first bicycle in the town and, in 1886, Carl Friedrich Benz unveiled his first automobile, produced at the nearby factory.

🏛 **Kunsthalle Mannheim**
Friedrichsplatz 4.
Tel *(0621) 293 64 52.* ⏰ *11am–6pm Tue–Sun (to 8pm Wed).*
🔴 *Carnival, 1 May, 24, 31 Dec.*
📷

🏛 **TECHNOSEUM**
Museumsstraße 1.
Tel *(0621) 429 89.* ⏰ *9am–5pm daily.* 🔴 *Good Friday, 24, 31 Dec.*
📷

🏛 **Reiss-Engelhorn-Museen**
Quadrat D5 and C5.
Tel *(0621) 293 31 51.*
⏰ *11am–6pm Tue–Sun.* 📷
www.rem-mannheim.de

Paul Cézanne's *Pipe Smoker* (c.1890), in the Städtische Kunsthalle, Mannheim

Schwetzingen ⑦

Road map B5. 👥 *21,500.* ℹ️
Dreikönigstr. 3 (06202-94 58 75).
🎬 *Schwetzinger Festspiele (May), Mozartkonzerte (Sept).*

Schwetzingen's Baroque-Renaissance palace was built during the reign of the Electors Johann Wilhelm, Charles II Philip and Karl Theodor as their summer residence. Erected on the site of a medieval castle that was later converted into a hunting lodge, it is one of the best known palace complexes of

Baroque Schwetzingen Palace, set amid beautiful gardens

18th-century Europe. The conversion of the 16th-century hunting lodge was carried out by J A Breuning and the side wings were built by Alessandro Galli da Bibiena. The magnificent Rococo theatre, designed by Nicolas de Pigage, was built in 1752, while the palace garden is the work of Johann Ludwig Petri, who designed it in the French style. The garden includes a mosque with two minarets and a bathhouse. In 1776 Friedrich Ludwig von Sckell converted it into an English-style garden.

Heraldic insignia from Bruchsal Palace

Speyer to Bruchsal. He not only initiated the town's development but, most importantly, ordered a palace to be built for himself and his court. The foundation stone of **Schloss Bruchsal** was laid in 1720 and the building works were carried out by Maximilian von Welsch, who was responsible for the right wing, and Michael Rohrer, who built the left wing between 1723 and 1728. The main body, preceded by a ceremonial courtyard, was designed by Baron Anselm von Grünstein. The central part of the palace is occupied by a magnificent staircase built by the great Balthasar Neumann, with stuccowork by Johann Michael Feuchtmayer and paintings by Johann and Januarius Zick. The palace suffered severe bomb damage in 1945, but its major part was reconstructed between 1952 and 1977.

St Peter's church was built in 1740–49 by Michael Rohrer to Balthasar Neumann's 1736 design. The church features magnificent Baroque tombs of Schönborn and his successor Cardinal Franz Christoph von Hutten. The palace garden was designed in the French style by Johann Scheer.

This former residence of prince-bishops now houses a section of the Karlsruhe Museum, which features the largest collection of Flemish and French tapestries in Germany. It is also home to the **Deutsches Musik-automaten Museum**, which includes 200 mechanical musical instruments. Short demonstrations are given on these throughout the day.

🏛 **Schloss Bruchsal**
Tel (07251) 74 26 61. ◯ 10am–5pm Tue–Sun. ⏰ hourly.
◉ 25, 31 Dec. 📷
Deutsches Musikautomaten Museum ◯ 10am–5pm Tue–Sun. ⏰ 11am, 2pm, 3:30pm. ◉ Shrove Tuesday, 24, 25, 31 Dec. 📷

🏛 **Schloss Schwetzingen**
Tel (06202) 12 88 28.
Schloss ◯ Apr–Oct: 11am–4pm Tue–Sun; Nov–Mar: 2pm Fri, 11am, 2pm, 3pm Sat & Sun.
⏰ obligatory.
Garden ◯ Apr–Sep: 8am–8pm daily; Oct & Mar: 9am–6pm daily; Nov–Feb: 9am–5pm daily.

Bruchsal ❽

Road map B6. 🚶 40,000. 🚉 ℹ
Am Alten Schloss 2 (07251-505 94 60).

Bruchsal belonged to the Bishops of Speyer from 1056 until 1806, since when it has been part of Baden. The town rose to prominence in the 17th century, when the Prince-Bishop of Speyer, Damian Hugo von Schönborn moved his residence from

Central façade of the Baroque Schloss Bruchsal

Street-by-Street: Heidelberg 9

Situated on the banks of the river Neckar, Heidelberg is one of Germany's most beautiful towns. For centuries it was a centre of political power, with a lively and influential cultural life. In 1386, Germany's first university was established here by the Elector Ruprecht I. Building of the palace began during his reign, continuing until the mid-17th century. However, in the late-17th century, French incursions totally destroyed medieval Heidelberg, including the castle. The town was subsequently rebuilt in the early 18th-century in Baroque style.

Marktplatz
Now adorned with the Neptune Fountain, the market square was, in the past, the site of executions and the burning of witches and heretics.

HAUPTSTRASSE

HEILIGGEISTSTRASSE

FISCH

OBERE NECKARSTRASSE

STEINGASSE

LAUERSTRASS

NECKARSTADEN

★ Heiliggeistkirche
Built in 1400–41 on the site of a late-Romanesque basilica, the Church of the Holy Spirit is the town's oldest sanctuary.

| 0 metres | 60 |
| 0 yards | 60 |

Philosophenweg
Built in 1817 on the slopes of Heiligenberg, at an altitude of 200 m (650 ft), the "Philosophers' Walk" offers magnificent views of Heidelberg and its castle.

★ Alte Brücke
This imposing, nine-span bridge over the river Neckar was built in 1786–88 by Mathias Maier. In the background is the Heidelberger Schloss.

★ **Haus zum Ritter**
Built in 1592 for the family of a rich cloth merchant, the Haus zum Ritter is a fine example of German Mannerist style. It now houses a luxury hotel and restaurant.

VISITORS' CHECKLIST

Road map C6. 139,000. Hauptbahnhof (06221-194 33). Mannheim-Heidelberger Film-festival (mid-Oct), Schlossfestspiele (Jul & Aug), Weindorf (Sep), Heidel-berger Herbst (Sep), Schlossbeleuchtung (early Jun, mid-Jul, early Sep).

Hexenturm
The tower was once part of the 13th-century Medieval town fortifications.

MERIANSTRASSE

HEUGASSE

UNIVERSITÄTS PLATZ

HAUPTSTRASSE

UNTERE STRASSE

BUSEMERGASSE

LAUERSTRASSE

Universitäts-bibliothek

Alte Universität
The old university building, designed by local architect Johann Adam Breuning, was built in 1712–35.

Jesuitenkirche
This church was built in 1712–51 for the Jesuits, who arrived in Heidelberg in 1698. The ornaments on the monumental façade were carved by Paul Egell.

STAR SIGHTS

★ Alte Brücke

★ Haus zum Ritter

★ Heiliggeistkirche

KEY

— — — Suggested route

Heidelberg Castle

Detail from Ruprechtsbau

Towering over the town, the majestic castle is really a vast residential complex that was built and repeatedly extended between the 13th and 17th centuries. Originally a supremely well-fortified Gothic castle, but now mostly in ruins, this was the seat of the House of Wittelsbach palatines. After remodelling in the 16th century, the castle became one of Germany's most beautiful Renaissance residences. However, its splendour was extinguished by the Thirty Years' War and the 1689 war with France, during which most of the structure was destroyed.

★ Ottheinrichsbau
The Deutsches Apotheken-museum is housed within the shell of this Renaissance building. It features Baroque and Rococo workshops and a travelling pharmacy.

The bell tower, which was erected in the early 15th century, was remodelled frequently in subsequent years.

★ Friedrichsbau
One of the latest parts of the castle is Friedrich's Palace, which dates from 1601–07. On the façade are statues of of the Wittelsbach dynasty, including Charles the Great.

Castle moat

Englischer Bau
These imposing ruins in the castle complex are the remains of a 17th-century building that Friedrich V built for his wife Elizabeth Stuart.

STAR SIGHTS

★ Friedrichsbau

★ Ottheinrichsbau

★ Ruprechtsbau

For hotels and restaurants in this region see pp503–6 and pp542–5

Pulverturm
*Built during the reign of the
Elector Ruprecht, this 14th-
century tower once formed
part of the castle defences.*

Brunnenhalle
This Gothic loggia features early-
Romanesque columns taken from the
palace of Charles the Great in Ingelheim.

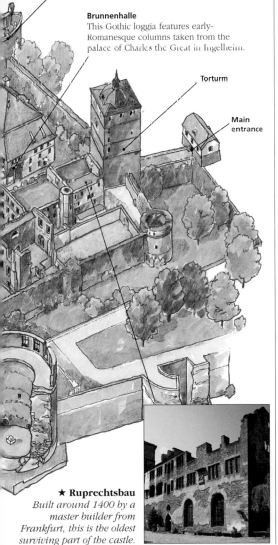

Torturm

Main
entrance

★ **Ruprechtsbau**
*Built around 1400 by a
master builder from
Frankfurt, this is the oldest
surviving part of the castle.*

🏛️ Alte Universität
Grabengasse 1. **Tel** *(06221) 54 21
52.* **Universitätsmuseum**
⬜ *Apr–Sep: 10am–6pm Tue–Sun;
Oct: 10am–4pm Tue–Sun; Nov–Mar:
10am–4pm Tue–Sat.* 🖱️
Designed by Mainz architect
Johann Adam Breuning,
the university was built in
1712–35. On the north wall
and ceiling are allegorical
paintings by Ferdinand Keller.
In front of the building is a
fountain crowned by a
sculpture in the form of the
heraldic Palatinate lion.

🏛️ Universitätsbibliothek
Plöck 107–109. **Tel** *(06221) 54 23
80.* **Ausstellungsraum**
⬜ *10am–6pm Mon–Sat*
The monumental building of
the university library, designed
by Joseph Durm of Karlsruhe,
was erected in 1901–05 near
the church of St Peter. The
Heidelberg library, with over
2 million volumes, is one of
the largest in Germany. The
exhibition rooms hold many
precious manuscripts and old
prints, including the famous
Codex Manesse, illustrated
with 137 beautiful miniatures.

🏛️ Kurpfälzisches Museum
Hauptstraße 97. **Tel** *(06221) 58 34
020.* ⬜ *10am–6pm Tue–Sun.* 🖱️
The French Count Charles de
Graimberg spent the bulk of
his considerable fortune on
building up an extensive
collection of fine drawings,
paintings, arms and various
curios associated with the
history of the Palatinate and
the castle of Heidelberg. In
1879, his collection became
the property of the town and
forms the core of this very
interesting museum, which
also includes a fascinating
archaeology section.

🔒 Heiliggeistkirche
Hauptstraße.
This collegiate church, whose
Baroque dome is one of the
city's landmarks, was built in
1400–41. The canons of the
college were also university
scholars and therefore the
church aisle features special
galleries for the extensive
collections of library books –
Bibliotheca Palatina. The
choir features a tombstone of
Ruprecht III and his wife,
Elisabeth von Hohenzollern.

Karlsruhe ❿

Road map B6. 🏛 *269,000.*
🚉 **ℹ** *Bahnhofsplatz 6 (0721)
194 33; www.karlsruhe.de*
🎭 *Internationales Trachten-und-
Folklorefest (Jun).* **www**.karlsruhe.de

Karlsruhe, which is one of
the "youngest" towns in
Germany, flourished during
the 19th century as a centre
for science and art. In 1945,
it lost its status as a regional
capital, but is now the seat of
the Bundesverfassungsgericht
– the highest courts of the
Federal Republic.

The town originated in 1715
when the margrave of Baden,
Karl Wilhelm von Baden-
Durlach, ordered a lodge to
be built in the middle of his
favourite hunting grounds.
Karl liked the area and the
lodge so much that he decided to move his residence
here and live the remainder
of his days in peace – hence
the town's name, meaning
"Karl's rest". The original
Baroque-style design was
expanded during the reign of
his successor, Karl Friedrich.

The palace, which forms
the hub of 32 streets, was
designed by Leopoldo Retti,
Mauritio Pedetti, Balthasar
Neumann, Philippe de la
Gaupière and others, and
built in 1749–81. The town is
based on a fan-like plan,
spreading from a base formed
by the open-sided wings of
the palace. The rest of the
circle, whose centre is
marked by the octagonal
palace tower (1715), is filled
with green areas, including
the palace garden.

A pyramid containing the tomb of Karl Wilhelm
von Baden-Durlach in Karlsruhe

In the early 19th century, the
town was remodelled along
Neo-Classical lines. The main
architect of this large-scale
project was Friedrich Weinbrenner, who created this
masterpiece of urban design.
The equilateral market square
is positioned along the palace
axis. It is filled with similar
but not identical buildings
and features a central pyramid
containing Karl Wilhelm's
tomb. South of Marktplatz is
the circular Rondellplatz.
Weinbrenner's other works
include the monumental town
hall (1811–25), the Protestant
town church and the Catholic
parish church of St Stephen.

Karlsruhe has some very
interesting museums. The
Badisches Landesmuseum in
the castle features a large
collection of antiquities,
decorative arts, sculpture,
porcelain and furniture, from
the Middle Ages to the

present day. In a
Neo-Renaissance
building (1843–46)
is the **Staatliche
Kunsthalle**, with its
large collection of
mainly German and
Dutch paintings
from the 16th–19th
centuries. These
include the famous
Crucifixion by
Grünewald (1523).

Entirely different
in character are the
collections of the
Zentrum für Kunst
und Medientech-
nologie (ZKM) – an
establishment that
has combined the
role of art college
and museum since 1997. It
occupies a former ammuni-
tions factory in the western
part of the town. Its core is
the **Museum für Neue Kunst**,
featuring installations, computer art and videos and
other work by contemporary
artists. The **Stadtmuseum
im Prinz-Max-Palais**, based in
a mansion named after
the last chancellor of the
Kaiserreich, contains the
local history museum.

🏛 **Staatliche Kunsthalle**
Hans-Thoma-Straße 2–6. **Tel** *(0721)
9 26 33 59.* ⬜ *10am–5pm Tue–Fri,
10am–6pm Sat & Sun.* 🖼

🏛 **Museum für Neue Kunst**
Lorenzstraße 19. **Tel** *(0721) 81 000.*
⬜ *10am–6pm Wed–Fri, 11am–6pm
Sat & Sun.* 🖼

🏛 **Stadtmuseum im Prinz-
Max-Palais**
Karlstraße 10. **Tel** *(0721) 1 33 42 31.*
⬜ *10am–6pm Tue, Fri & Sun,
10am–7pm Thu, 2–6pm Sat.*

The Baroque residence of the Dukes of Baden in Karlsruhe

For hotels and restaurants in this region see pp503–6 and pp542–5

Baden-Baden ⓫

Road map B6. 👥 *50,000.*
✈ *Baden Airport (5 km/3 miles
northwest of town).* �';'
*Schwarzwaldstraße 52 & i-Punkt in
der Trinkhalle (07221-27 52 00).*
www.baden-baden.de

Baden-Baden's casino, set in the elegant Kurhaus

Known as the "summer
capital of Europe", this
elegant spa resort is one of
the oldest towns in Germany
and was once the favourite
destination of European
aristocracy from Russia to
Portugal. Even before the
Romans built their camp here
around AD 80, the site was
occupied by a Celtic settlement of the Latenian period.

In the early years of the
modern era, *Civitas Aurelia
Aquensis* – known simply as
Aquae – was already known
in Italy for the therapeutic
properties of its waters. In the
3rd century AD, Aquae was
conquered by the Germanic
tribe of Alamains and in the
6th century AD by the Francs,
who built a fortress in the
town. The Margrave Hermann
II, known as "Marchio de
Baduon", was the first
important ruler of Baden.

During the horrific Black
Death, the qualities of the
local waters were once again
recognized as beneficial to
health. During the Palatinate
War of Succession, Baden-
Baden was almost totally destroyed but, by the end of the
18th century, it had become
one of Europe's most
fashionable resorts.

The old town of
Baden-Baden lies at
the foot of the
Schlossberg (castle
hill). The oldest
surviving building in
the town is the Gothic
collegiate church, built
during the 13th–15th
centuries and then
remodelled in the 18th
century. It contains
several valuable epi-
taphs. To the south of
the church is the bath-
ing hall – Friedrichs-
bad – which was built
in Neo-Renaissance
style in 1877. Nearby
stands the magnificent
New Palace, which was

The Neo-Renaissance Trinkhalle (pump
room) in Baden-Baden

the residence of margraves
from the 15th century
onwards. It was remodelled
along German Renaissance
lines in the 16th century by
Kaspar Weinhart. The interiors
are decorated with paintings
by Tobias Stimmer.

Most of the spa buildings
are the work of Friedrich
Weinbrenner. His elegant
Kurhaus in Werderstraße has
been used as a casino since
1838. The most famous
gamester at the casino was
Fyodor Dostoevsky, who was
not always lucky at roulette.
His novel *The Gambler* (1866)
is supposedly set in Baden-
Baden. Nearby is the Trinkhalle (pump room), with its
mineral water fountains. Built
in 1839–42, it is decorated
with wall paintings illustrating
Black Forest legends.

Rising behind the spa area
is the last project completed
by Leo von Klenze before
his death – the Orthodox

burial chapel of a Romanian
aristocratic family, the Stourd-
za Mausoleum. In Schillerstraße is the villa built in 1867
for the Russian writer, Ivan
Turgenev, who lived here
until 1874.

🎵 Brahmshaus

Maximilianstraße 85. **Tel** *(07221)
99872.* ⏰ *3–5pm Mon, Wed, Fri,
10am–1pm Sun.* 🚫
The exhibition displayed in
this house is devoted to the
life and works of the German
composer Johannes Brahms
who lived here from 1865
until 1874.

⛪ Kloster Lichtenthal

Hauptstraße 40.
Tel *(07221) 50 49 10.* ⏰ *3pm Sun,
Wed, Sat.* 🚫 *Group tours (minimum
7 persons), advance telephone
booking required* 🚫
This Cistercian nuns' abbey,
situated on the outskirts of
town, has a church dating
from the 14th–15th centuries.
Its ducal chapel contains
many epitaphs of the Baden
margraves. The abbey also
has an interesting museum.

🏛 Staatliche Kunsthalle Baden-Baden

Lichtentaler Allee 8a. **Tel** *(07221)
300 763.* ⏰ *11am–6pm Tue–Sun,
11am–8pm Wed (to 7pm Thu).*
The Staatliche Kunsthalle
Baden-Baden is an exhibition
venue that specializes in
modern and contemporary art.

🏛 Stadtmuseum

Lichtentaler Allee 10. **Tel** *(07221) 93
22 72.* ⏰ *11am–6pm Tue–Sun,
10am–8pm Wed.*
The Stadtmuseum includes
sections on glass, porcelain
and paintings, as well as some
old gambling equipment.

Maulbronn ⑫

Situated on the edge of the Stromberg region, Maulbronn grew up around a Cistercian monastery, which was founded in 1147 in the valley of the river Salzach by monks who came here from Alsace. The church, built in 1147–78, is an elongated, triple-nave basilica with a transept and a chancel. The early Gothic porch in front of the church was added in 1220. Outside the enclosure are domestic buildings, such as a former mill, a forge, a bakery and a guest house. Defence walls with turrets and a gate tower encircle the entire complex, which was designated a UNESCO World Heritage Site in 1993.

Cloisters
In the Middle Ages, monks meditated as they walked around the cloisters, which gave them protection from bad weather. Talking was strictly forbidden.

★ Brunnenkapelle
Built opposite the entrance to the refectory, the Well Chapel, with its intricate Gothic forms, is where the monks used to wash their hands before meals.

Inner Courtyard
Once a garden, the monastery's inner courtyard is surrounded by cloisters. It is a place that inspires contemplation.

Cloisters

STAR FEATURES

- ★ Brunnenkapelle
- ★ Chapter House
- ★ Mourning
- ★ Stalls

The Porch
The porch, also known as "Paradise", was built onto the church façade in the early 13th century.

★ Chapter House
The monks assembled in this Gothic hall to discuss their private and public affairs. The hall has two naves, which are supported by three pillars.

VISITORS' CHECKLIST

Road map C6. 🏠 *6,400.*
🛈 *Stadtverwaltung Maulbronn, Klosterhof 31 (07043-10 30).*
www.maulbronn.de
Info-Zentrum *Klosterhof.*
Tel *(07043) 92 66 10.*
⭕ *Mar–Oct: 9am–5:30pm daily; Nov–Feb: 9:30am–5pm Tue–Sun.*
🕒 *11:15am, 3pm.* 🎫

Church Interior
Originally the church had a wooden ceiling. In 1424 it was replaced with a network vault, which stands in stark contrast to the plain walls.

★ Mourning
This Gothic relief, made in around 1390 in the Purler family work shop, was part of an altar, which no longer exists. Today, it can be seen on the altar in the monastery's choir.

★ Stalls
Richly decorated with carved ornaments, the late-Gothic stalls date from around 1450.

Heilbronn ⑬

Road map C6. 🏠 119,000. 🚉
ℹ️ *Kaiserstraße 17 (07131-
56 22 70).* 🎪 *Pferdemarkt (Feb),
Neckarfest (Jun), Stadtfest (Jun),
Heilbronner Herbst (Sep).*

Heilbronn's earliest records
date from the 8th century,
when the town was known
as "Helibrunna". By the late
19th century, Heilbronn had
become Wurttemberg's main
industrial centre, with a large
port on the river Neckar.

Having suffered major destruction during World War II,
the town's surviving buildings
include the church of St Kilian,
a Gothic basilica from the
second half of the 13th century, with a triple-nave hall-
choir flanked by two towers.
The western tower was built
in 1508–29. The magnificent
altarpiece is an original late-
Gothic polyptych, the work
of Hans Seyffer (1498).

Near the 15th–16th-century
Rathaus (town hall) is a house
reputed to have been the
home of Käthchen, a char-
acter in Heinrich von Kleist's
play *Das Käthchen von Heilbronn*. Near the rebuilt
church of St Peter and St Paul
(originally the church of the
Teutonic Order) stands the
former Teutonic convent –
the Deutschhof.

**Isaak Habrecht's astronomical
clock on Heilbronn town hall**

**Half-timbered houses on the bank of the river
Kocher, in Schwäbisch Hall**

Schwäbisch Hall ⑭

Road map C6. 🏠 35,000. 🚉
ℹ️ *Am Markt 9 (0791-75 12 46).*
🎪 *Kuchen-und Brunnenfest der
Haller Salzsieder (Whitsun).*

Archaeological
excavations in 1939
proved the existence
of a Celtic settlement
on this site as early as
500 BC. The town fea-
tures a great number
of historic buildings
from various periods,
including many half-
timbered 15th–16th-
century houses,
Baroque town houses,
and a Rococo town
hall and town palace
(Keckenburg). The
most interesting
building is the hall-
church of St Michael,
whose Gothic main
body was built in
1427–56. The Romanesque
tower on the western façade,
however, dates from the 12th
century. The late-Gothic hall-
choir (1495–1527) is famous
for its decorative network
vaults. Original furnishings
include the main altar, the
stalls and the Holy Sepulchre.

Schwäbisch Gmünd ⑮

Road map C6. 🏠 63,400. 🚉
ℹ️ *Marktplatz 37/1 (07171-60 34
250).* 🎪 *Internationales Schatten-
theater Festival (Jun), European
Church Music (Jul).*

This town – the birthplace of
the architect Peter Parler and
painters Hans Baldung Grien

**Madonna with Child,
in Marktplatz,
Schwäbisch Gmünd**

and Jörg Ratgeb –
was once renowned
throughout Europe
for the magnificent
goods produced by
its goldsmiths. It
has many great
historic buildings,
mainly churches,
such as the late-
Romanesque
church of St John,
which dates from
around 1220, but
was subsequently
remodelled. The
church of St Cross
is famous not only for being
the first Gothic hall-church in
southern Germany, but also
the first major work of the
famous family of architects –
the Parlers. This triple-nave
hall with a hall-choir,
featuring an ambulatory
and a ring of side
chapels, was built in
several stages, between
1320 and 1521. Its
western façade has
a high triangular
top with blind
windows.

Inside the church
are many valuable
historic relics, such
as the Holy Sepulchre
(1400), the stalls,
which date from
around 1550, and
the organ gallery
(1688). Other
interesting structures
in the town include
the town fortifica-
tions and several half-timbered houses.

Bad Wimpfen ⑯

Road map C6. 🏠 6,676. 🚉 ℹ️
Carl-Ulrich-Straße 1 (07063-9 72 00).
🎪 *Talmarkt (Jun/Jul), Zunftmarkt
(Aug), Weihnachtsmarkt (Dec).*

The town of Bad Wimpfen
was created out of two
settlements, Bad Wimpfen am
Berg and Bad Wimpfen im
Tal, which remain distinct to
this day. The settlement on
top of the hill grew around
the Hohenstauf family palace,
whose chapel and well-
preserved arcade windows,
resting on pairs of decorated
columns, can still be seen.

Built at the order of Frederick I Barbarossa in 1165–75, this was the main and the biggest imperial palace (Kaiserpfalz) of the Holy Roman Empire. One of the surviving towers offers a spectacular view over the Neckar valley.

Set in a picturesque location, Bad Wimpfen features many half-timbered houses dating from the 16th–18th centuries.

Bad Wimpfen im Tal is built around the former collegiate church of St Peter and St Paul. This is a triple-nave basilica with transept, two eastern towers and cloister, dating from the 13th–15th centuries. The south façade of the transept and the portal are richly decorated with carvings, which are probably the work of Erwin von Steinbach, one of the builders of Strasbourg Cathedral. The church interior features many original carved statues and stalls.

Marbach ⑰

Road map C6. 🏠 1,450. 🚉
ℹ️ Marktstraße 23 (07144-10 20).

This small town would probably never merit an entry in any guidebook were it not for the fact that the great writer Friedrich Schiller was born here in 1759. The modest, half-timbered house, in which the famous poet spent his childhood, has survived to this day and is now a small museum – the **Schiller-Geburtshaus**. The town also possesses a vast museum of literature (**Schiller-National-museum**), which is housed in a Neo-Baroque palace. Its collection is not limited to the life and work of Schiller, but also includes many documents relating to German literature.

Other attractions in Marbach include some of the original half-timbered houses and the remains of the town walls and town gates in the old town. The late-Gothic Alexan-derkirche is also worth a visit. Built in the second half of the 12th century by Aber-lin Jörg, it features interesting network vaulting covered with ornamental paintings.

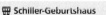

Friedrich Schiller statue in Marbach

🏠 **Schiller-Geburtshaus**
Niklastorstraße 31. **Tel** (07144) 175 67. ◯ 9am–5pm daily. ⬤ 24, 25, 26, 31 Dec. 🔲

🏛 **Schiller-Nationalmuseum**
Schillerhöhe 8–10. **Tel** (07144) 84 80 10. ◯ 10am–6pm Tue–Sun. ⬤ 24, 25, 26, 31 Dec. 🔲

Esslingen ⑱

Road map C6. 🏠 92,000.
ℹ️ Marktplatz 2 (0711 39 69 39 69).

Set among vineyards on the banks of the river Neckar, the beautiful town of Esslingen is famous for its sparkling wines. The town's historic buildings were fortunate in surviving intact the ravages of World War II. A walk through the winding streets and narrow alleys of the old centre will yield many interesting sights, while a climb to the top of the hill affords a splendid view of the town and the Neckar valley, as well as the amazing **Innere Brücke**, a 14th-century bridge. From there visitors can descend towards the market square, stopping on the way to visit Frauenkirche, a Gothic hall-church dating from the 14th century. Its front tower, the work of Ulrich and Matthäus von Ensingen, was added later. In the market square is the Stadtkirche St Diony-sius, the oldest church in town, built in the 13th century on the site of an earlier, 8th-century building. Inside are magnificent early-Gothic stained-glass windows and late 15th century Gothic furnishings, including the choir partition, the sacrarium and the font. The nearby church of St Paul, built in the mid-13th century for the Dominicans, is the oldest surviving Dominican church in Germany. In neighbouring Rathausplatz stands the half-timbered old town hall, Altes Rathaus, with its beautiful Renaissance façade, and the Baroque new town hall. Designed as a palace for Gottlieb von Palm by Gottlieb David Kandlers, the Neues Rathaus was built between 1748 and 1751.

The picturesque houses and chapel of Esslingen's 14th-century Innere Brücke

Ludwigsburg ⑲

Palace crest

Situated near Stuttgart and known as the "Versailles of Swabia", Ludwigsburg was founded in 1704 on the initiative of Eberhard Ludwig, Duke of Wurttemberg. At the heart of the town is the vast palace complex, which the Duke ordered to be built for his mistress, Countess Wilhelmina von Graevenitz. The construction of the palace, which was carried out between 1704 and 1733, involved many outstanding architects and interior decorators, including Philipp Jenisch, Johann Nette, Donato Frisoni and Diego Carlone.

Northern Garden
This magnificent Baroque park is the venue for a flower show ("Blooming Baroque") that is held here during the summer.

★ Western Gallery
The gallery features opulent stucco ornaments by Ricardo Retti and Diego Carlone (1712–15).

★ Marble Hall
This vast hall in the new wing of the palace was remodelled in 1816, but still retains some of its Baroque interior decor.

★ Queen's Library
The library is housed in the east wing of the palace, in the apartments arranged for Queen Charlotte Mathilde.

The new wing of the palace houses a museum devoted to court art of the Neo-Classical period.

★ Schloss Favorite
The "Favorite" hunting lodge was built between 1716 and 1723, but its interior has been remodelled in Neo-Classical style.

The old wing
contains the palace's oldest apartments

VISITORS' CHECKLIST

Road map C6. 80,000. *Marktplatz 6 (07141-910 22 52).* **Residenzschloss** *Schlossstraße 30.* **Tel** *(07141) 18 20 04. 10am–5pm (75 mins). In English: mid-Mar–Nov: 1:30pm Mon–Fri, 11am, 1:30pm, 3:15pm Sat & Sun. Dec–mid-Mar: 1:30pm.* **Mode-, Keramik-museums, Barock-galerie** *10am–5pm daily.*

Märchengarten
The landscaped section of the park includes the "Fairy-tale Garden", which contains figures and models from German fairy-tales.

The upper fruit garden attracts visitors with its picturesque paths, which are lined with apple trees and grapevines.

Restaurant and café

Emichsburg
This romantic castle, built in 1798–1802, was named after the founder of the Wurttemberg dynasty.

STAR SIGHTS

★ Marble Hall

★ Queen's Library

★ Schloss Favorite

★ Western Gallery

Stuttgart ⑳

The capital of Baden-Wurttemberg, Stuttgart is one of the largest and most important towns of the Federal Republic. It grew from a 10th-century stud farm, known as Stutengarten, to become the ducal (1321) and later the royal (1806) capital of Wurttemberg. Beautifully situated among picturesque hills, the town is a major industrial centre with many important manufacturing plants. It is also a well-known publishing and cultural centre, with a world-famous ballet company, chamber orchestra and splendid art collections.

Exploring Stuttgart
Start your tour of Stuttgart at Schlossplatz, continuing along Königstraße towards the Palace Gardens, with their many interesting buildings, and stopping to pay a visit to the Staatsgalerie, whose extension was designed by the British architect James Stirling. From there you can return via Konrad-Adenauer-Strasse, heading towards Karlsplatz, then to Schillerplatz and Marktplatz with its magnificent town hall, finally ending the walk at Hegelhaus museum.

🏛 Schlossplatz
At the centre of the square stands the **Jubiläumssäule** – a column erected in 1842–46 to celebrate the 25-year reign of Wilhelm I. The square also features sculptures by many famous artists, including Alexander Calder and Alfred Hrdlicka. The east side of the square features a huge palace complex, **Neues Schloss**, built in 1746–1807, while on the opposite side stands **Königs-bau**, a Neo-Classical structure erected in 1856–60.

Neo-Classical façade of Stuttgart's Staatstheater

🏛 Kunstmuseum Stuttgart
Kleiner Schlossplatz 1. *Tel* (0711) 216 21 88. ⏱ 10am–6pm Tue–Sun, 10am–9pm Wed & Fri. **www**.kunstmuseum-stuttgart.de 🖼 🍴 📷
The spectacular glass cube of the Kunstmuseum Stuttgart was designed by the Berlin architects Hascher & Jehle. It houses the Municipal Art Collection, which includes works by such artists as Adolf Hölzel, Joseph Kosuth, Dieter Krieg, Dieter Roth, the Swabian Impressionists and has an outstanding collection of Otto Dix's work.

🌿 Schlossgarten
The magnificent gardens stretching north of the Neues

Schloss were established in the early 19th century. They have maintained, to this day, much of their original charm, with neat avenues and interesting sculptures. The attractions include the **Carl-Zeiss-Planetarium**, which runs an excellent science programme, using equipment made by the famous optics company.

On the edge of the park stands a vast Neo-Classical theatre building, the **Württembergisches Staatstheater**, built in 1909–12 by Max Littmann. In 1982–3 it was given a new, dome-covered wing, the Theaterpavilion, designed by Gottfried Böhm.

🏛 Staatsgalerie
See pp312–13.

♣ Altes Schloss
Württembergisches Landesmuseum Schillerplatz 6. *Tel* (0 711) 895 3511. ⏱ 10am–5pm Tue–Sun. 📷
When Wurttemberg castle burned down in 1311, it was decided to move the family seat to Stuttgart. In 1325, the existing small castle was extended, creating Dütnitzbau. This wing has survived and can be seen from Karlsplatz. A large-scale Renaissance remodelling project, designed by Aberlin Tresch and carried out in 1553–78, gave the castle its square layout, with three-storey arcaded cloisters encircling the inner courtyard. The southwestern wing contains the Schlosskapelle (chapel), the first sacral building in Stuttgart built especially for the Protestants. The castle now houses the **Württembergisches Landesmuseum**,

The façade of Stuttgart's Neues Schloss, combining Baroque and Neo-Classical elements

Cloistered courtyard of the Renaissance Altes Schloss

which includes vast collections of decorative art, including those displaying the ducal and royal insignia of Wurttemberg. The prehistory section includes jewellery from the Frankish period and the preserved tomb of a Celtic nobleman from Hochdorf.

⊞ Schillerplatz

This is undoubtedly one of Stuttgart's most beautiful areas. It is here that the stud farm that gave Stuttgart its name is said to have stood. Today, a pensive statue of Friedrich Schiller, the work of the Danish sculptor Bertel Thorwaldsen (1839), occupies the centre of the square.

Schillerplatz is surrounded by historic buildings: the **Old Chancellery**, built in 1542–44 and extended upwards in 1566,

now houses a restaurant, the Prinzenbau (1605–78), and the Stiftsfruchtkasten, an attractive gabled granary (1578), now home to a museum of musical instruments.

⊡ Stiftskirche (Hl. Kreuz)

Stiftstraße 12.

From the south side of Schillerplatz there is a view of the presbytery of the collegiate church of the Holy Cross. This Gothic church, the work of Hänslin and Aberlin Jörg, was built in the 15th century and incorporated the walls of the previous, early-Gothic church. Despite World War II damage, this newly renovated church still has the original stone gallery of the dukes of Wurttemberg, built in 1576–84 by Simon Schlör to a design by Johann Steiner, as well as Gothic furnishings.

VISITORS' CHECKLIST

Road map C6. 🏠 586,000. ✈ south of town. 🚉 🛈 Königstraße 1A (0711-22 280). 🎪 Frühlingsfest (Apr/May), Stuttgarter Weindorf (Aug/Sep, Oct/Nov), Fellbacher Herbst (Oct), Weihnachtsmarkt (Dec). www.stuttgart-tourist.de

⊞ Hegelhaus

Eberhardstraße 53. **Tel** (0711) 216 67 33. ☐ 10am–5:30pm Mon–Fri, 10am–6.30pm Thu, 10am–4pm Sat. 🎟

Georg Wilhelm Friedrich Hegel – the creator of one of the most important modern philosophical systems – was born in this house on 27 August 1770. The house is now a museum, which houses an exhibition devoted to the life and work of the famous philosopher.

Figures of saints adorning the façade of the Stiftskirche

0 metres 300
0 yards 300

Key to Symbols see back flap

🏛 Linden-Museum/ Staatl. Museum für Völkerkunde

Hegelplatz 1. *Tel (0711) 2 02 23.*
⭕ *10am–5pm Tue, Thu–Sat, 10am–8pm Wed, 10am–6pm Sun.* 🖼

The Linden Museum is one of Germany's finest ethnology museums. It was founded by Count Karl von Linden, who was also its director from 1889 until 1910. The museum contains many fascinating exhibits from all over the world, including figures from the Indonesian theatre of shadows, a Tibetan sand mandala, a 6th–8th-century mask from Peru in South America and a full-size reproduction of an Islamic bazaar.

Peruvian mask in the Linden-Museum

🏛 Weißenhofsiedlung

Weissenhofmuseum im Haus Le Corbusier, Rathenaustr. 1–3
Tel (0711) 2 57 91 87. ⭕ *11am–6pm Tue–Fri, 10am–6pm Sat & Sun.*
Architektur-Galerie *Tel (0711) 257 14 34.* ⭕ *2–6pm Tue–Sat, noon–5pm Sun.*

A building exhibition held in 1927 in Stuttgart had housing as its main theme. It left behind an estate that still exists today, although it was badly bombed during World War II. Most of the houses represent functionalism, which was being promoted at the time by the Bauhaus. The estate, which was to serve as an example to others, has some interesting houses,

including works by Mies van der Rohe (Am Weißenhof 14–29), Le Corbusier (Rathenaustraße 1–3), Peter Behrens (Hölzelweg 3–5) and Hans Scharoun (Hölzelweg 1).

🏛 Liederhalle

Berliner Platz 1.

A must for all lovers of modern architecture, Liederhalle, in the centre of Stuttgart, is a successful synthesis of tradition and modernism. Built in 1955–56 by Adolf Abel and Rolf Gutbrod, this fine cultural and congress centre, with three concert halls clustered around an irregular hall, is still impressive today.

🏛 Mercedes-Benz-Museum

Mercedesstraße 100. *Tel (0711) 173 00 00.* ⭕ *9am–6pm Tue–Sun.* 🔴 *public holidays.*

To the east of the town centre, in the Obertürkheim district, is the famous Mercedes-Benz-Museum. Its splendid collection illustrates the development of motorcar production, from the earliest models to today's state-of-the-art, computerized products. Set up to celebrate the centenary of their inventions, the museum features over 70 historic vehicles, all in immaculate condition. The collection includes the world's two oldest automobiles, Gottlieb Daimler's horseless carriage and Carl

Some of the models on display in the Mercedes-Benz-Museum

Benz's three-wheeled automobile from 1886. Also on display is a hand-made limousine that was built in the 1930s for the Emperor of Japan and the first "Popemobile", which was built for Pope Paul VI.

Another interesting exhibit is the famous 1950s racing car, *Silberpfeil* (Silver Arrow), as well as models that were built for attempts on world speed records. Also on display are scores of the latest models that have been produced by the company.

The visitor can also learn the history of Daimler-Benz AG, which was created by the merger in 1926 of Daimler-Motoren-Gesellschaft and Benz & Cie., Rhein. The company's subsequent 1999 merger with Chrysler created one of the world's largest car manufacturing concerns, DaimlerChrysler.

🏛 Fernsehturm

⭕ *9am–10:30pm daily.*

Built between 1954 and 1956 this television tower was the world's first to be built entirely from ferro-concrete. It is 217 m (712 ft) high and stands on top of a wooded hill, Hoher Bopser. Its observation platform provides splendid views over Schwäbische Alb, Schwarzwald and, on a clear day, even the Alps.

🏛 Porsche-Museum

Porscheplatz 1. *Tel (01805) 356 911.*
⭕ *9am–6pm Tue–Sun.*

The Porsche museum was revamped and reopened in 2008. The exhibition area is

House designed by Le Corbusier in Weißenhofsiedlung

For hotels and restaurants in this region see pp503–6 and pp542–5

made up of a steel structure resting on just three concrete cores, giving it the appearance of hovering in space. More than 80 cars are on display, ranging from the Lohner-Porsche, the world's first hybrid automobile built in 1900, to the latest generation of the Porsche 911. There are also historical archives, an open workshop, a restaurant and café.

🏛 Markthalle
Dorotheenstraße 4, ☐ 7am–6:30pm Mon–Fri, 7am–4pm Sat.
Stuttgart's market hall, built in 1912–14 in Art Nouveau style on the site of an earlier vegetable market, is one of the finest in Europe. Built as a food exchange, it has magnificent frescos. Today it still sells fresh fruit and vegetables to the general public, and also houses a small restaurant and café.

⛪ Schloss Solitude
Solitude 1. **Tel** (0711) 69 66 99.
☐ Apr–Oct: 10am–noon, 1:30–5pm Tue–Sat, 10am–5pm Sun; Nov–Mar: 1.30–4pm Tue–Sat, 10am–4pm Sun.
🔲 obligatory. 🌳 garden free.
This exquisite small palace, standing on the slopes of a hill, was built for Prince Karl Eugene in 1763–67. The Prince not only commissioned the residence, but also took an active part in its design, which is the work of Pierre Louis Philippe de la Guêplère, who introduced the Louis XVI-style to Germany. Many consider this palace to be his masterpiece.

Following its full restoration in 1990, and the provision of 45 residential studio apartments, the palace now serves art students on scholarships from all over the world. A 15-km (9-mile) long, straight road connects Schloss Solitude with Ludwigsburg.

🏛 Bad Cannstatt
Once an independent health resort, Bad Cannstatt is now a district of Stuttgart. Set in a beautiful park, it has a late-Gothic parish hall-church, a Neo-Classical town hall and a Kursaal (spa-house), built in 1825–42. One of its attractions is the Neo-Classical Schloss Rosenstein, built in 1824–29 at the request of King Wilhelm I, based on amended designs by John Papworth. The King was also the initiator of the beautiful "Wilhelm's complex". This includes a Moorish-style villa located in a symmetrically laid-out park, with many Oriental-style pavilions and other decorative elements. Completed in the 1840s, its main designer was Karl Ludwig Wilhelm von Zanth. The park has now been transformed into a botanical-zoological garden.

Environs
Stuttgart provides a convenient base for exploring the surroundings. In **Sindelfingen**, 15 km (9 miles) southwest, it

is worth visiting the Romanesque Church of St Martin Canons, which was founded in 1083. While you are there, take a stroll along Lange Straße to the old town hall, which dates from 1478 and is joined with the Salt House (1592). The two buildings, both half-timbered in their upper sections, now house the town museum.

A little further to the west, **Weil der Stadt** is the birthplace of the astronomer Johannes Kepler and the reformer Johannes Brenz. The town's late-Gothic church of St Peter and St Paul was completed in 1492 by Aberlin Jörg. Inside is a beautiful Renaissance sacrarium, dating from 1611. The Marktplatz, with a statue of Kepler at its centre, has a Renaissance town hall (1582). Nearby, at Keplergasse 2, stands the house in which the famous astronomer was born and which now houses a small museum, the Kepler-Museum.

Another place worthy of a visit is **Waiblingen**, 10 km (6 miles) to the northeast of Stuttgart. It features a Romanesque church, the vaults of which are decorated with some splendid wall paintings dating from 1515.

The façade of the Schloss Solitude, in the hills to the west of Stuttgart's centre

Staatsgalerie

The Staatsgalerie grew from the museum of fine arts founded in 1843 by King Wilhelm I and containing the king's private collection. Now it ranks among the finest of German galleries. As well as its own magnificent collection of old masters and modern artists, the gallery has an extensive collection of graphics. In 1984 the art gallery acquired an extension designed by James Stirling.

The Mourning of Christ (c.1490)
This subtle depiction of Christ is the work of the Venetian artist Giovanni Bellini.

Spring Fields (1887)
One of the leading members of the French Impressionist movement, Claude Monet was unsurpassed in his rendition of iridescent light.

Mother and Child (1905)
This painting by Pablo Picasso represents his "pink period", which preceded the famous Cubist experiments of this great Spanish artist.

Entrance
to Alte
Staatsgalerie

Entrance
to Neue
Staatsgalerie

KEY

☐	14th–19th-century Art
☐	19th-century Art
☐	20th-century Art
☐	Contemporary Art
☐	Temporary exhibitions
☐	Non-exhibition rooms

Female Nude Reclining on a White Pillow (1917)
Amadeo Modigliani became famous for his idiosyncratic portraits and female nudes.

★ Iphigenie (1871)
Anselm Feuerbach's painting was inspired by a play by Goethe, Iphigenie on Tauris.

VISITORS' CHECKLIST

Konrad-Adenauer-Straße 30–32.
Tel (0711) 47 04 00.
⬜ 10am–6pm Wed, Fri–Sun,
10am–8pm Tue, Thu. 🚹
www.staatsgalerie.de

Crossing of the Rhine near Rhenen (1642)
The Dutch painter Jan van Goyen became famous for his evocative landscapes, which were often executed in uniform tones of lead-grey or brown-green.

★ St Paul in Prison (1627)
In this, one of his earliest works, Rembrandt depicted the Apostle Paul awaiting death in a humble cell.

Bathsheba at her Toilet (c.1485)
In this painting, which is a fragment of a lost triptych illustrating Justice, Hans Memling uses the Old Testament story of Bathsheba to exemplify the abuse of power, intervention by God and the reformation of a sinner.

First floor

Ground floor

GALLERY GUIDE
Permanent exhibitions are located over the first floor of the two buildings. In the Neue Staatsgalerie are works by the old masters and from the 19th-century. The Alte Staatsgalerie holds 20th-century art.

STAR EXHIBITS

★ Iphigenie

★ St Paul in Prison

Schwäbische Alb ㉑

The mountain range of Schwäbische Alb (the Swabian Jura) extends like an arc, 220 km (137 miles) long and 40 km (25 miles) wide, from the Upper Rhine around Schaffhausen, in Switzerland, to Nördlinger Ries, at the border between the federal counties of Baden-Wurttemberg and Bavaria. The highest peak in the range is Lemberg (1,015 m/3,330 ft). Beech woods and scented juniper shrubs dominate the mellow landscape, whose whole system of interconnected stalagmitic caves was carved from the sedimentary limestone rocks.

Hechingen
On the outskirts of Hechingen, the remains of a 1st–3rd-century AD Roman villa are open to the public.

Haigerloch
In the vaults of this castle is a vast bunker that was used as an atomic research laboratory towards the end of World War II.

★ Burg Hohenzollern
The ancestral seat of the Hohenzollern family was remodelled in 1850-67. Only the 15th-century St Michaelkapelle survives from the original fortress.

★ Beuron
Beuron's magnificent Benedictine Abbey was founded in the 11th century. Its subsequent remodelling resulted in a Baroque structure, which survives to this day.

Böblin
Herrenberg
Tübingen
Neckar
Rottenburg
Mössinge
Haigerloch
Hechingen
Burg Hohenzollern
Burlading
Balingen
Albsta
Dor
Messki

STAR SIGHTS

★ Burg Hohenzollern

★ Sigmaringen

★ Beuron

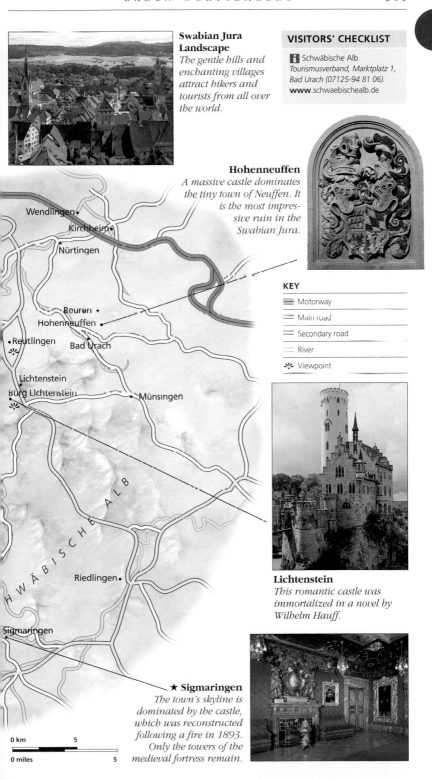

Swabian Jura Landscape
The gentle hills and enchanting villages attract hikers and tourists from all over the world.

Hohenneuffen
A massive castle dominates the tiny town of Neuffen. It is the most impressive ruin in the Swabian Jura.

KEY

▬▬	Motorway
═══	Main road
═══	Secondary road
───	River
☼	Viewpoint

Lichtenstein
This romantic castle was immortalized in a novel by Wilhelm Hauff.

★ **Sigmaringen**
The town's skyline is dominated by the castle, which was reconstructed following a fire in 1893. Only the towers of the medieval fortress remain.

0 km   5
0 miles   5

Tübingen ㉒

Road map C6. 🏛 85,000. 🚉
ℹ️ *An der Neckarbrücke 1
(07071-913 60).* 🚢 *Mon, Wed, Fri.*
www.tuebingen.de

Along with Heidelberg and
Freiburg im Breisgau,
Tübingen is the home of one
of southern Germany's three
most famous universities. It
was founded in 1477 by
Count Eberhard the Bearded.

The first records of the
fortress that later gave rise to
a settlement on this site date
from 1078. By around 1231,
the settlement had become a
town. In 1342, Tübingen passed
to the counts of Wurttemberg,
having previously belonged
to the counts Palatinate.

Schloss Hohentübingen,
which towers over the town,
has a magnificent gateway
(Unteres Tor). Built in 1606,
it is richly adorned with the
coat of arms of the House of
Wurttemberg. The walled
castle complex, with its central
courtyard and long approach,
was built in stages during
1507–15, 1534–42 and 1606.

A walk along the Burgsteige
will bring you to the picturesque old town. Here, at the
centre of Marktplatz, is the
Neptune Fountain, the work
of Heinrich Schickhard, dating
from 1617. In the western
corner of the square is a
lovely Renaissance town hall,
built in 1435 and
extended in the

Tübingen's Gothic-Renaissance town hall

16th century. It features an
astronomical clock, which
dates from 1511. *Sgraffiti* on
the western façade dates from
1876; those on the elevations
facing Haaggasse date from
the 16th century.

The collegiate church of
St George (**Stiftskirche St
Georg**), built in 1440–1529, is
a triple-nave hall with rows of
side chapels, galleries and a
single tower. Of particular
note are the ducal tombs, the
late-Gothic reading-room and
the stained-glass windows of
the choir, dating from 1475.
Magnificent stalls, adorned
with carved figures of the
Prophets, date from the late
15th century.

The bookstore in Holzmarkt
(*Buchhandlung Heckenbauer*)
is where Hermann
Hesse

once served as an
apprentice bookseller.
On the banks of the
Neckar stands the
Hölderlinturm, in
which the German
poet Hölderlin lived
from 1807 until his
death. Not far from
here stands the large
building of the Alte
Burse, which was built
in 1478–80 and later
remodelled in 1803-
1805. The building
was once used to
accommodate students
and as a lecture hall.
Martin Luther's close
associate, Philipp
Melanchthon, lectured here
between 1514 and 1518.

The Protestant seminary in
Neckarhalde was founded by
Prince Ulrich in 1536. Its
graduates include the poets
Hölderlin, Mörike and Schiller
and the philosophers Hegel
and Schelling.

The **Kunsthalle** is famous
throughout Germany not
only for its temporary
exhibitions, but also for its
fine collection of modern art.
Other popular attractions in
Tübingen include the **Stadtmuseum**, which is devoted to
the town's history, and the
Auto-und Spielzeug-museum.

🏛 **Museum Schloss
Hohentübingen**
Burgsteige 11. **Tel** *(07071) 297 73 84.*
⬭ *May–Sep: 10am–6pm Wed–Sun
(noon–8pm Thu), Oct–Apr: 10am–
5pm Wed–Sun (noon–7pm Thu).* 📷

🏛 **Stiftskirche St Georg**
Tel *(07071) 525 83.* ⬭ *Apr–Sep:
9am–5pm daily, Oct–Mar:
9am–4pm daily.* 📷

🏛 **Hölderlinturm**
Bursagasse 6. **Tel** *(07071) 220 40.*
⬭ *10am–noon, 3–5pm Tue–Fri, 2–
5pm Sat & Sun, public holidays.* 📷

🏛 **Kunsthalle**
Philosophenweg 76. **Tel** *(07071)
969 10.* ⬭ *11am–6pm Wed–Sun,
11am–7pm Tue (during exhibitions).*

🏛 **Statdtmuseum**
Kornhausstraße 10. **Tel** *(07071)
204 17 11 or 94 54 60.*
⬭ *11am–5pm Tue–Sun.* 📷

🏛 **Auto- und Spielzeug-
museum**
Brunnenstraße 18. **Tel** *(07071) 55
11 22.* ⬭ *Jan–Oct: 10am–noon,
2–5pm Wed–Fri, 10am–5pm Sun;
Nov–Dec: hours vary.* 📷

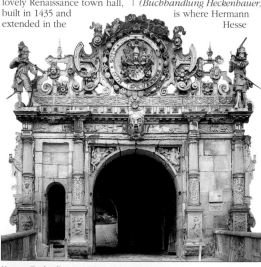

Unteres Tor leading to Schloss Hohentübingen

Rottweil 🅭

Road map C7. 🏙 24,000. 🚉 🅸
Hauptstraße 21–23 (0741-49 42 80).
🎭 *Fasnet (last Mon of Carnival),
Jazzfest (May), Klassikfestival (Jun),
Ferienzauber (Aug).*

Situated on the banks of the river Neckar, Rottweil is one of the oldest towns in Baden-Wurttemberg. It grew from a Roman settlement that was established on a hilltop here in AD 73. In 1234 Rottweil was granted town status and, by 1401, it had become a free town of the Holy Roman Empire. Between 1463 and 1802 it belonged to the Swiss Confederation, which was founded in 1291 by the cantons of Uri, Schwyz and Unterwalden. In 1802, the town passed into the rule of the dukes of Wurttemberg.

Rottweil has many historic remains, including sections of the fortified city walls, with several well-preserved turrets.

The parish church of St Cross (Heilig-Kreuz-Münster), built in 1230–1534, has a triple-nave basilica with stellar and network vaults. Late-Gothic altars, including St Bartholomew's, by Michael Wolgemut and a crucifix attributed to Veit Stoss, are among its features.

To the south of the church stands the late-Gothic town hall (1521). On the opposite side of the street, at Hauptstraße 20, the **Stadtmuseum** has an outstanding collection

Crucifixion attributed to Veit Stoss in Heilig-Kreuz-Münster, Rottweil

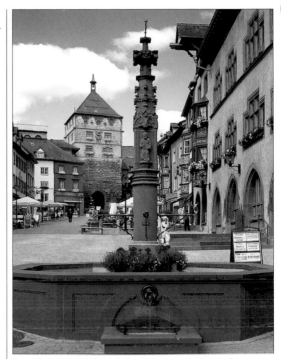

Fountain and "Black Gate" in Rottweil's main street, Hauptstraße

of prehistoric remains. The **Dominikanermuseum** has an interesting exhibition of Roman relics. These include the famous Orpheus mosaic, dating from the 2nd century AD, and an outstanding collection of late-Gothic sculpture, including the statue of St Barbara by Multscher (c 1450).

The Hauptstraße is lined with burghers' houses, displaying characteristic oriel windows. One of the most beautiful historic buildings in Rottweil is the Kapellenkirche, built in 1330–1478. Its 70-metre (230-ft) tower and three portals are adorned with carved ornaments reminiscent of the French Gothic style. The Baroque interior features frescos by Josef Fiertmayer, who was a pupil of renowned painter and architect Cosmas Damian Asam. The Gothic Dominican church, built in 1266–82 and remodelled in the 18th century, has some frescos by Joseph Wannen-

Kapellenturm, Rottweil

macher (1755). Roman baths dating from the 2nd century AD have been excavated at the corner of what is now the cemetery.

Rottweil is famous for its carnival processions *(Fasnet)*, a tradition that goes back to the Middle Ages. A collection of carnival costumes can be seen in the Stadtmuseum.

The **Puppen- und Spielzeugmuseum** has a fine collection of historic dolls and toys which is perfect for keeping the children entertained.

🏛 **Stadtmuseum**
Hauptstraße 20. **Tel** (0741) 494 330. 🕙 10am–noon, 2–4pm Tue–Sun. 🎫

🏛 **Dominikanermuseum**
Am Kriegsdamm. **Tel** (0741) 7662. 🕙 10am–5pm Tue–Sun. ● public holidays. 🎫

🏛 **Puppen- und Spielzeugmuseum**
Hauptstraße 49. **Tel** (0741) 942 21 77. 🕙 10am–12:30pm, 2pm–5:30pm Wed–Fri, 10am–12:30pm Sat, 2–5pm Sun. 🎫

Ulm ㉔

Road map B6. 🏔 115,000. 🚊
ℹ️ *Münsterplatz 50 (0731-161 28 30.*
📷 *Fischerstechen (every 4th year in Jul,*
next is 2013), Schwörmontag (3rd Mon
in Jul), Stadtfest (Jun). **www**.ulm.de

Lying on the river Danube,
Ulm dates back to 854. It
became a town in 1165 then,
in 1274, a free town of the
Holy Roman Empire. During
the 15th century Ulm was one
of the richest towns in Europe
but the Thirty Years' War put
an end to its rapid development. In 1810 Ulm came
under the rule of the Wurttemberg kings. The town is
renowned as the
birthplace of Albert
Einstein. During
World War II, most
of the old town was
destroyed during
bombing raids.

The Münster is a
true masterpiece of
European Gothic
architecture. A vast,
five-nave basilica, its
161-m (530-ft) high
west tower is the
highest church
tower in the
world. The
cathedral's
construction, from
1377 until 1545,

**Gothic font in Ulm
Cathedral**

was overseen by the greatest
builders of the German
Gothic – Heinrich and
Michael Parler, Urlich von
Ensingen, Hans Kun and
Matthäus Böblinger. The
unfinished cathedral was
extended in 1844–90, based
on the original medieval
design. The interior contains
many outstanding features,

**Astronomical clock on Ulm's
Gothic-Renaissance town hall**

including the altar by
Hans Multscher (1443),
the famous stalls with
figures of philosophers,
poets, prophets and
apostles carved by
Jörg Syrlin the Elder,
15th-century stained-
glass windows, and
the font, by Jörg Syrlin
the Younger.

The town has many fine
historic buildings, including
the Gothic-Renaissance town
hall, which is decorated with
brightly coloured frescos and
features an astronomical
clock. Other features of
Marktplatz include the Gothic
fountain *Fischkasten* (Fish
Crate), dating from
1482, and the
Reichenauer Hof,
which dates from
1370–1535.

The **Ulmer
Museum**, which is
housed in a number
of historic 16th-
and 17th-century
buildings, has a col-
lection of art span-
ning a period from
the Middle Ages up
to the present day.
The collection
includes the work
of local artists,
such as Hans
Multscher. The

Deutsches Brotmuseum
specializes in artifacts
related to bread and bread-
making, including items
depicting bread in art and
graphic designs.

🏛 **Ulmer Museum**
Marktplatz 9. **Tel** (0731) 161
43 12. 🕐 11am–5pm Tue–Sun,
11am–8pm Thu (during
exhibitions). 📷

🏛 **Museum der Brotkultur**
Salzstadelgasse 10. **Tel** (0731) 699
55. 🕐 10am–5pm daily. 📷

Ravensburg ㉕

Road map C7. 🏔 45,000. 🚊
ℹ️ *Kirchstraße 16 (0751-828 00).*
📷 *Fasnet (Feb), Rutenfest (Jul).*

The first historic records of
the "Ravespurc" fortress date
from 1088, when it was one
of the seats of the Welf
family. It is believed to be the

**Main altar by Hans Multscher in
Ravensburg's Liebfrauenkirche**

birthplace of Henry the Lion,
the powerful Duke of Saxony
and Bavaria, born in 1129.
The settlement that sprang up
at the foot of the castle was
granted town status in 1251.
From 1395, paper was
produced here and, during
the 15th century, the town
became one of the richest in
Germany from its involve-
ment in the linen trade.

Standing in Kirchstraße is
the 14th-century parish church
of Liebfrauenkirche, which
retains original 15th-century
features, including the main
altar and some fine stained-
glass windows.

In Marienplatz stands the
late-Gothic town hall (14th–
15th century), with its lovely
Renaissance bay window.
Also in Marienplatz is the
Waaghaus (1498), which
housed the weigh-house and
mint on the ground floor,
with a trading hall upstairs,
when Ravensburg was
engaged in coin production.
The watchtower *(Blaserturm)*
is crowned by a Renaissance
octagon that has become the
symbol of the town. Another
attractive building here is the
Lederhaus, which dates from
1513–14. Near the town hall is
the old 14th–15th century
granary *(Kornhaus)*.

Marktstraße features many
old burgher houses. No. 59,
the oldest house in town, dates
from 1179. The neighbouring
house was built in 1446. The
tall white cylindrical tower
that can be seen from here is
known as the "sack of flour"
(Mehlsack). It was erected in
the 16th century. A magnificent
view of the town can
be obtained from Veitsburg,
which occupies the site of
the original Welf castle.

For hotels and restaurants in this region see pp503–6 and pp542–5

Former Cistercian abbey complex in Salem, now a secular building

Weingarten ㉖

Road map C7. 👥 22,500. 🚂
ℹ️ *Münsterplatz 1 (0751 40 51 25).*
🎏 *Blutritt (day after Ascension).*

Count Henry of the House of Welf founded a Benedictine abbey in Weingarten in 1056. During the Romanesque period, around 1190, the monks of the abbey produced a chronicle of the House of Welfs, known as the *Welfenchronik*.

Ambitious plans, drawn up in the 18th century at the initiative of Abbot Sebastian Hyller, provided for an extension of the abbey and the construction of another vast complex of buildings. Two side courtyards and four external courtyards, encircled with curved galleries with smaller pavilions, were planned to be grouped around the church. These were designed by Casper Moosbrugger, Franz Beer, Enrico Zucalli and others, and built in 1715–24.

The church is reminiscent of the Basilica of St Peter's in Rome. Although it is half the size of the latter, it is nevertheless an immense structure. Inside are some magnificent ceiling frescos by Cosmas Damian Asam, while the carved and inlaid choir stalls are the work of Joseph Anton Feuchtmayer. Also of note is the organ by Josef Gabler. In an ingenious design, the organ pipes are concealed within a series of towers to avoid obscuring the windows of the façade.

The **Alamannenmuseum** has a fascinating exhibition of relicts that have been found in graves dating from the Merovingian period.

🏛 **Alamannenmuseum**
Karlstr. 28. **Tel** (0751) 405 125
⏰ 2–5pm Tue–Sun, 2–6pm Thu 🖼

Salem ㉗

Road map C7. 👥 8,500.

The first Cistercian monks arrived in Salmansweiler (now known as Salem) in 1134. Between 1299 and 1414 they built a church according to the rules of their order, which espoused poverty and banned any decoration of the monastic buildings

The abbey is a triple-nave basilica with transept and straight-end choir. Its austere façade is relieved by blind windows, some of which have attractive traceries. In later years the restraints of poverty were relaxed to the extent that the abbey now has an interesting tabernacle (1500), stalls (1594) and early-Renaissance altars (dating from the 18th century).

The new abbey buildings were built between 1700 and 1710 and constitute **Schloss Salem**. The buildings include some richly decorated abbot's apartments and the extremely impressive Emperor's room (*Kaisersaal*), which was built between 1708 and 1710.

Since its secularization in 1802, the abbey has been the private property of the Baden margraves who keep some of their art collection here. The west wing houses a private boarding school founded by Kurt Hahn, who also founded Gordonstoun in Scotland.

⛪ **Schloss Salem**
Tel (07553) 814 37. ⏰ Apr–Oct:
9:30am–6pm Mon–Sat,
10:30am–6pm Sun. 🖼

Ceiling fresco in Weingarten's abbey

The Bodensee 28

Sometimes known as Lake Constance, the Bodensee lies on the border of Germany, Switzerland and Austria. The area surrounding the lake is one of the most attractive in Germany, in terms of both natural beauty and cultural heritage. Towns and villages around the shores feature countless reminders of past times and cultures. The best time for a visit is summer, when local fishermen stage colourful fairs and water sports are possible.

The Bodensee
The lake is 15 km (9 miles) across at its widest point and 74 km (46 miles) long. It lies at an altitude of 395 m (1,295 ft) and reaches 252 m (826 ft) in depth.

Reichenau
The greatest attraction of this island is the Bene-dictine abbey, which was famed during the era of Otto the Great (10th century) for its illumi-nated manuscripts. It has a beautiful Romanesque-Gothic church and an intoxicating herb garden.

Stockach

Ludwigshafen

ÜBERLINGER SE

Über

Singen

Radolfzell

Gottmadingen

ZELLERSEE

Reichenau

M

Konsta

UNTERSEE

Kreuzlingen

★ Mainau
Mainau is known as the "Island of Flowers". The most beautiful displays are in the park surrounding the Baroque palace, which was built in 1739–46. It is currently owned by the Lennart Bernadotte family.

STAR SIGHTS

★ Konstanz

★ Mainau

★ Wasserburg

★ Konstanz (Constance)
The largest town in the region, its main attraction is the magnificent 11th-century Romanesque cathedral. The vaults over the central aisle were built between 1679 and 1683.

Meersburg
The exquisite Baroque town of Meersburg has two residences – the Baroque Neues Schloss and the Altes Schloss. The latter is a 16th-century structure built on top of a hill. It contains within its walls an old Carolingian palace.

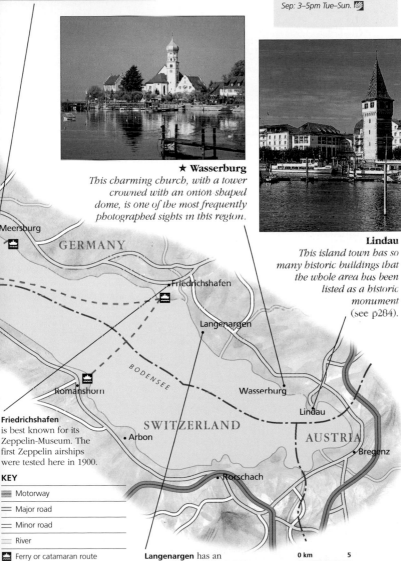

★ Wasserburg
This charming church, with a tower crowned with an onion shaped dome, is one of the most frequently photographed sights in this region.

Lindau
This island town has so many historic buildings that the whole area has been listed as a historic monument (see p284).

Meersburg

GERMANY

Friedrichshafen

Langenargen

Romanshorn

BODENSEE

Wasserburg

Lindau

Friedrichshafen
is best known for its
Zeppelin-Museum. The
first Zeppelin airships
were tested here in 1900.

SWITZERLAND
• **Arbon**

AUSTRIA

• **Bregenz**

• **Rorschach**

KEY

▦	Motorway
▭	Major road
—	Minor road
—	River
⚓	Ferry or catamaran route
– –	International border

Langenargen has an
enchanting, small Moorish-
style palace named Montfort.

| 0 km | 5 |
| 0 miles | 5 |

Freiburg im Breisgau 29

The counts von Zähringen first established Freiburg in 1120. The town, which later belonged to the counts von Urach, became so rich over the years that, in 1368, it bought its freedom and voluntarily placed itself under the protection of the Habsburgs. Marshal Vauban fortified the town in the 17th century, when Freiburg briefly belonged to France. Since 1805 it has been part of Baden. Situated between Kaiserstuhl and Feldberg, it is a natural gateway to the southern Black Forest.

Freiburg University
Freiburg University occupies a Baroque post-Jesuit complex. In the main entrance stands this statue of the pensive Aristotle.

This former Jesuit church belongs to the university complex.

Tourist information

RATHAUS–PLATZ

RATHAUSGASSE

Railway station

BERTOLDSTRASSE

Fischerau
Fischerau and, parallel to it, Gerberau are picturesque streets in the old town, running along the Gewerbebach stream.

Bertoldsbrunnen (Bertold's fountain) stands at the intersection of Bertoldstraße and Kaiser-Joseph-Straße, known as "Kajo".

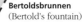

0 metres	50
0 yards	50

Martinstor
St Martin's Gate was part of the 13th-century town fortifications. Its present appearance is the result of work carried out in 1900.

STAR SIGHTS

★ Bächle

★ Münster – the Main Altar

★ Kaufhaus

KEY

– – – Suggested route

◁ **Picturesque scene with fruit trees in blossom in the Schwarzwald (Black Forest)**

Haus zum Walfisch
The façade of the Whale House in Franziskanergasse, with its lovely bay window, is a magnificent example of late-Gothic style.

VISITORS' CHECKLIST

Road map B7. 197,000. Rathausplatz 2–4 (0761-388 18 80). Fasnet (end of carnival), Frühlingsmesse (May), Internationales Zeltmusikfest (Jun), Weintage (Jun), Weinkost (Jun), Herbstmesse (Oct), Umwelt-Film-Festival (Oct). **www**.freiburg.de

Münsterplatz
The picturesque square at the foot of the cathedral, lined by houses of various periods, from Gothic to Rococo, is still used for markets.

★ Bächle
From the Middle Ages, fast flowing canals have been running along the streets, draining excess surface waters, and providing the water needed to extinguish the frequent fires.

★ Münster – the Main Altar
The cathedral, which started in c.1200 as a Romanesque basilica, was completed by 1513 in the French Gothic style. Inside is the original main altar by Hans Baldung Grien.

★ Kaufhaus
Completed in 1520, with ground-floor arcades and richly adorned gables, the Kaufhaus (literally buying house) was used by local merchants for meetings, conferences and lively festivities.

Schwarzwald (Black Forest) ③⓪

Covered with tall fir trees and spruces, the Schwarzwald is one of Germany's most picturesque regions. The area is famous not just for its cuckoo clocks, *Kirschwasser* (schnaps) and *Schwarzwälder Kirschtorte* (Black Forest Gâteau); in the past, Celts and later the Romans came to appreciate the therapeutic qualities of the local spring waters. (The sources of the rivers Donau and Neckar are here.) The area is also a paradise for skiers, climbers, ramblers, hang-glider pilots and sailors.

★ Staufen im Breisgau
The town is also known as Faust-stadt: Dr Faustus, who had resided here, died in 1539 – he is variously reputed to have blown himself up, to have been strangled or to have had his neck broken.

Todtnau
Todtnau is not only a sports centre and a base for hikers and cyclists: it also has a fantastic annual festival devoted entirely to Schwarzwälder Kirschtorte (Black Forest Gateau).

Todtmoos
The heart of this resort is the Baroque pilgrimage church, which dates from the 17th–18th centuries. Popular dog-sleigh races are held annually in the town.

For hotels and restaurants in this region see pp503–6 and pp542–5

VISITORS' CHECKLIST

Road map 7 B, C. 🛈 *Wehratal-
str. 19, Todtmoos (07674-906 00;
www.todtmoos.de).* 🔿 *Offen-
burger Weinmarkt, Weihnachtsmarkt.* 🎟 *Dog-sleigh races in
Todtmoos (Jan) and Bernau (Feb),
Schlosskonzerte in Rastatt (July).*

Gutach

*In the open-air museum near
the small town of Gutach
visitors can see the Schwarzwald's oldest house – the
Vogtsbauernhof – which
dates from the 16th century.*

★ Furtwangen
*The main attraction
of Furtwangen is its
clock museum
(Uhrenmuseum),
which houses a
collection of more
than 8,000 varied
chronometers.*

0 km   10

0 miles   10

Hangloch-Wasserfall
*This magnificent
mountain waterfall near
Todtnau is one of the
most beautiful in the
Black Forest.*

KEY

▬	Motorway
═	Main road
══	Secondary road
⋯	River
✳	Viewpoint

★ St Blasien
*In the beautiful health
resort of St Blasien is a
Benedictine Abbey,
founded in the 9th
century. Crowned with a
vast dome, its church
(1783) is an excellent
example of early
Neo-Classical style.*

STAR SIGHTS

★ Furtwangen

★ St Blasien

★ Staufen im Breisgau

WESTERN GERMANY

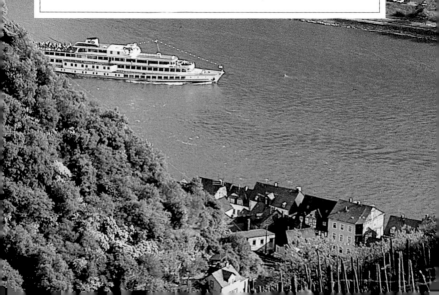

Western Germany at a Glance

Famed for its excellent wines and the festivities of
Cologne's annual carnival, Western Germany is the
country's wealthiest and most heavily industrialized
region. The Ruhr district still harbours enormous
industrial potential, while Frankfurt am Main is
Germany's largest financial centre. The region is
also rich in tourist attractions – visitors are drawn to
the romantic castles which line the Rhine and Mosel
valleys, to Cologne with its majestic twin-towered
cathedral, the spa town of Aachen, the museums of
Frankfurt and Kassel and the imposing
Romanesque cathedrals of Speyer,
Worms and Mainz.

**NORTH RHINE-
WESTPHALIA**
See pp382–415

Cologne Cathedral (see pp402–3),
*which was not completed until the
19th century, is generally considered
one of the most outstanding Gothic
buildings in Germany.*

```
0 kilometres        100
0 miles             100
```

**RHINELAND-
PALATINATE &
SAARLAND**
See pp336–59

Maria Laach
(see pp358–9) *is a
charming, beautifully
preserved Roman-
esque abbey in a
tranquil, isolated
setting on the shores
of the Laacher See.*

◁ **Burg Katz, St Goarhausen, Rhineland Palatinate**

Detmold *is best known for its magnificent castle (see p415) – one of the most beautiful examples of the "Weser Renaissance" style of architecture.*

The Museum Fridericianum in Kassel (see pp564–5), *originally built to house Friedrich II's art collection, has hosted the* documenta, *an exhibition of contemporary art that has achieved international acclaim, every four to five years since 1955.*

HESSE
See pp360–81

Fulda Cathedral (see p368) *is one of the finest Baroque churches in Hesse. It was built on the site of the previous Romanesque church and follows the original layout.*

The old town in Frankfurt am Main (see p375) *is centred around the Römerberg – a square surrounded by attractive half-timbered houses, with the Fountain of Justice as a focal point.*

Wine in Western Germany

Of the great European vineyards, Germany's are the farthest north. There are 13 wine-growing regions in Germany, but the most famous German vineyards are those in the western part of the country, especially the Rheingau, Pfalz, Rheinhessen and Mosel-Saar-Ruwer regions. The most widely drunk alcoholic beverage in Germany is beer – unlike in France, Italy or Spain – and therefore the wines produced here are mainly high-quality wines of named vineyards, with a relatively low production of table wine.

Vineyards in Edenkoben, in the southern part of the Weinstraße (see p347), in the Palatinate

The Mosel-Saar-Ruwer *region produces superb white wines from the Riesling grape. The highest quality wines are those marked with the letters QmP.*

IMPORTANT FACTS ABOUT GERMAN WINE

Region and climate

Gentle, rocky hills stretching along the river bends – perfect for Rieslings – are typical of the Mosel-Saar-Ruwer and Rheingau regions. Clay and limestone soil, appropriate for the Müller-Thurgau variety, are found in Hesse on the Rhine. The German climate is considerably more severe than that of southern countries, which gives the wines a slightly sharp, refreshing taste.

Typical grape varieties

The red grape is not cultivated in great quantities. The most popular red variety is the Spätburgunder, known in France as Pinot Noir, which produces a heavy wine with a strong flavour. White grapes are much more popular, especially the famous Rieslings, from which the best white wines are produced, the Müller-Thurgau, which gives a light wine with a fruity bouquet, the Grauburgunder (Pinot Grigio) and the Weißburgunder (Pinot Blanc). Less well-known are: Silvaner, Gewürztraminer, Grüner Veltliner and Gutedel. Rosé wines are produced from the Portugieser variety, cultivated in the Rhineland–Palatinate (Pfalz) and Rheinhessen.

Famous wine producers

Mosel-Saar-Ruwer: Fritz Haag, Heymann-Löwenstein, Karthäuserhof, Dr. Loosen, Egon Müller, J.J. Prüm, C. von Schubert, Willi Schaefer; Rheingau: Georg Breuer, Robert Weil; Rheinhessen: Gunderloch, Keller; Pfalz: Müller-Catoir, Georg Mosbacher, Dr. Bürklin-Wolf, Reichsrat von Buhl.

The Nahe *is famous for its white wines, produced from Silvaner as well as Riesling and Müller-Thurgau grapes.*

The Rheingau, *where the "Rhine" wines are made, is well known for its Rieslings, particularly the Johannisberger Riesling. A famous vineyard is Prinz von Hessen.*

The fountain of the "Wine Witch" in the small town of Winningen, in the Mosel-Saar-Ruwer region

Wine cellars in the former Cistercian monastery at Eberbach in the Rheingau region

WINE REGIONS

The two best-known wine regions are Mosel-Saar-Ruwer and Rheingau. Mosel, Saar and Ruwer are the three rivers whose names have been combined to give the region its name. Exceptional Rieslings are produced here as well as smaller amounts of other wines. The Rheingau produces a full-bodied red wine in addition to the dominant Rieslings. Rheinhessen produces not only several types of white and red wines, but also a rosé, as does the Palatinate.

Liebfrauenmilch *has been produced in the Rheinhessen region for over 40 years. Mainly designed for export, it is a sweetish, medium-class of wine, a blend of several grape varieties.*

| | | 0 km | 70 |
| 0 miles | | | 70 |

KEY

☐	Mosel–Saar–Ruwer
☐	Rheinhessen
☐	Mittelrhein
☐	Pfalz
☐	Nahe
☐	Rheingau
☐	Ahr
☐	Hessische Bergstraße

Romanesque Architecture

Western Germany boasts some of the most interesting examples of Romanesque architecture in the whole of Europe. Charlemagne's famous chapel in Aachen was erected as early as the Carolingian period. The cathedral in Trier and the church of St Maria im Kapitol in Cologne are among the most outstanding creations of early-Romanesque architecture of the Frankish dynasty. In the 12th century, the most important German centres of art were Cologne and the towns of the central Rhineland, with three magnificent cathedrals in Speyer, Mainz and Worms, and the monastery in Maria Laach, preserved to this day.

The choir of St Martin in the Dom in Mainz *is an example of the spaciousness that is typical of the late-Romanesque style.*

The front elevation of the St Gotthard-Kapelle in Mainz *has upper galleries with arcades decorated with friezes – a common feature of Romanesque architecture.*

Twin western towers

Gallery above the vestibule

Lavishly decorated main portal

The northern portal of the Dom in Worms *is framed by an offset architrave and flanked by pairs of columns, as are the portals of many other Romanesque cathedrals.*

The monastery in Maria Laach *has many capitals with intricate decorations, such as these carvings with human faces.*

Cross-vaulting (or cross-ribbed vaulting)

Tower at the intersection of the nave and transept

The system of vaults also acts as support.

Twin eastern towers

The portal of the Dom in Trier *has a magnificent tympanum, depicting Christ with the Virgin Mary and St Peter.*

ROMANESQUE CATHEDRALS

Cathedrals of the type shown here were built with a basilica-type internal arrangement, including a transept and presbytery, and a double choir usually ending in a semicircular apse. The Dom in Speyer has a massive twin-towered west front, as shown here. The other pair of towers rises above the presbytery, and the intersection of the nave and transept has a lower, broad fifth tower.

ROMANESQUE CAPITALS

Romanesque churches in the Rhine Valley feature exquisite stone sculptures. The capitals, with their extraordinary variety of form, ranging from simple blocks to fine figurative or animal-decorated compositions, are of particular interest.

Water-leaf capital of a bonded column

Simplified Corinthian capital

Cushion (or block or cube) capital

Zoömorphic (animal-decorated) capital

The St Gotthard-Kapelle in Mainz, *next to the Dom, was the archbishop's personal chapel for private prayer. It is comparable to similar private buildings in secular palaces.*

RHINELAND–PALATINATE AND SAARLAND

The Rhineland-Palatinate is one of Germany's most romantic regions, attracting visitors with its vineyards, gentle hills and fairy-tale castles along the Rhine and Mosel valleys. Several towns, such as Trier, have kept reminders of their Roman heritage.

These two states, which border France in the west, did not emerge in their present form until after World War II. The Rhineland-Palatinate was created from the previously independent Bavarian Palatinate and the southern part of the Central Rhineland, making it a true jigsaw-puzzle of territories without a coherent history. The Saarland was under French rule until 1956. Today, it forms a bridge between France and Germany, the two driving forces of European unity.

The turbulent history of the region has left many traces. The picturesque Mosel Valley is lined with grand Medieval fortresses, such as Burg Eltz, while Worms on the Rhine is the setting for most of the Nibelungen legend as well as the residence of the mythical king of Burgundy, Gunther.

The Nibelung treasure is still said to lie at the bottom of the Rhine. The impressive cathedral in Worms, along with the Romanesque cathedrals of Speyer and Mainz, is a fascinating example of Medieval sacral architecture.

The "Deutsches Eck" in Koblenz is the strategic spot where the Mosel flows into the Rhine, and Koblenz also marks the beginning of the romantic Rhine Valley. A boat trip upriver, justifiably popular with visitors, will pass some spectacular rocky scenery, including the famous Lorelei Rock and countless castles set among vineyards on either side of the gorge.

The famous ironworks complex in Völklingen is a reminder of a bygone era, when most of the Saarland's inhabitants were active in mining, steelworks and other heavy industries.

Panorama of Saarbrücken, with the Saar river in the foreground

◁ The snow-covered Medieval fortress of Burg Eltz, in the Mosel Valley

Exploring Rhineland-Palatinate and Saarland

White wine enthusiasts come here, attracted by the beautiful, picturesque valleys of the Rhine and Mosel rivers, with their Medieval castles and small towns. Travelling along the Deutsche Weinstraße (German wine route), Germany's oldest tourist route, visitors can see fascinating historic buildings and taste the different types of wine made by the numerous small vineyards scattered throughout the entire region. Speyer and Mainz have monumental Romanesque cathedrals, while Trier boasts many interesting Roman relics. The huge ironworks in Völklingen is a surprising sight, transporting visitors back to a time when heavy industry ruled much of the region.

SEE ALSO

- *Where to Stay* pp506–8
- *Where to Eat* pp545–6

The imposing red-sandstone building of the Dom in Mainz

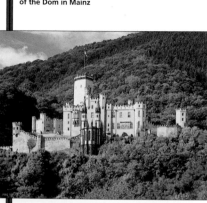

The proud complex of Schloss Stolzenfels near Koblenz, designed by Karl Friedrich Schinkel

| 0 km | | 20 |
| 0 miles | | 20 |

The interior of the Dom in Trier

SIGHTS AT A GLANCE

Koblenz pp356–7 **9**
Mainz pp348–9 **7**
Maria Laach pp358–9 **10**
Saarland p344 **2**
Speyer **4**
Trier pp340–43 **1**
Worms **5**

Suggested routes

Deutsche Weinstraße **6**
Moseltal **3**
Rheintal **8**

GETTING AROUND

The A65 motorway links Karlsruhe with Ludwigshafen, and
continues from there towards
Luxembourg or Lorraine, via
Homburg and Saarbrücken.
The A32, and later the A4, leads
from Saarbrücken to Metz or
Strasbourg. The A1 runs
northwards from Friedrichsthal
to Trier and the Mosel Valley.
Inter-City trains offer a frequent
and convenient service; Frankfurt
am Main and Köln/Bonn
(Konrad-Adenauer-Flughafen)
have international airports.

KEY

━━	Motorway
━━	Major road
━━	Minor road
═ ═	Under construction
━━	Scenic route
━━	Main railway
──	Minor railway
▬▬	International border
━━	Regional border
△	Summit

Trier ❶

One of Germany's oldest towns, Trier was founded in 16 BC as *Augusta Treverorum*, supposedly by the Emperor Augustus himself. In the 3rd and 4th centuries it was an imperial seat and the capital of the *Belgica prima* province. In the 5th century the town, which now numbered 70,000 inhabitants, was conquered and destroyed by Germanic tribes. Trier never returned to its former importance – in the 17th century it had a mere 3,600 inhabitants, and 100 years later they still numbered fewer than 4,000. The town, which is also the birthplace of Karl Marx, has a rich architectural heritage.

🚪 Porta Nigra

Tel (0651) 754 24. ⬛ *Mar: 9am–5pm daily; 1 Apr–30 Sep: 9am–6pm daily; Oct–Nov: 9am–5pm daily; Dec–Feb: 10am–4pm daily.* ✎

This town gate, named *Porta Nigra* (black gate) in the Middle Ages because of the colour of its weathered stone, was erected in the 2nd century (a similar gate would have stood at the town's southern entrance). The oldest German defensive structure, it still impresses with its colossal size: 36 m (118 ft) long, 21.5 m (70.5 ft) wide and 30 m (27 ft) high. Two gateways lead onto a small inner courtyard, and there are two tiers of defence galleries with large open windows. It is flanked by the four-storey western tower and the three-storey unfinished eastern tower.

In the 12th century, the building was transformed into the two-storey church of St Simeon and served as such until the early 19th century. Porta Nigra is a UNESCO World Heritage site.

🚪 Hauptmarkt

Trier's main market square, undoubtedly one of the most attractive in Germany, dates back to the 10th century. The Marktkreuz (market cross) erected around the same time symbolized the town's right to hold markets. Today there is a copy of the original cross mounted on a granite Roman column, with a relief of the Lamb of God. On the southeastern side of the square is the Petrusbrunnen (St Peter's fountain), from 1595, with sculptures of St Peter and the

Petrusbrunnen (fountain of St Peter) in Hauptmarkt

Four Virtues. On the southwestern side stands the 15th-century Steipe, with a steep gabled roof. Originally it was used by the town councillors as guesthouse and banqueting hall. The Baroque Rotes Haus (red house) next door dates from 1683. Löwenapotheke, in a 17th-century building on the southeastern side of the square, is Germany's oldest pharmacy, its records dating back to the 13th century.

🏛 Bischöfliches Dom- und Diözesanmuseum

Windstraße 6–8. *Tel* (0651) 710 52 55. ⬛ *9am–5pm Tue–Sat; 1–5pm Sun.* ⬤ *1 Jan, 24–26, 31 Dec.* ✎

A 19th-century building near the cathedral, once a Prussian prison, now houses the art collection of the Diocese, including early Christian works of art. Its prized possession is a 3rd-century ceiling painting from the imperial palace which once stood on the site of the cathedral. The fresco was rediscovered in 1945, and some 70,000 pieces were painstakingly reassembled over the following decades. Another exhibit is the reconstructed crypt of the Benedictine church of St Maximin, which has 9th-century Carolingian wall paintings.

⛪ Dom St Peter

Tel (0651) 979 07 90. ⬛ *Apr–Oct: 6:30am–6pm daily; Nov–Mar: 6:30am–5:30pm daily.* ✎

The present cathedral incorporates the remains of an older 4th-century church. The oldest cathedral in Germany, it was constructed in stages – in the early 11th century, late 12th century, mid-13th century and 14th century. It is a triple-nave, two-choir basilica with transept and six towers, and its furnishings include several outstanding objects, such as the tomb of the papal envoy Ivo (1144).

⛪ Liebfrauenkirche

Liebfrauenstr. *Tel* (0651) 979 07 90. ⬛ *Apr–Oct: 7:30am–6pm daily; Nov–Mar: 7:30am–5:30pm daily.* ✎

Adjoining the cathedral is the Liebfrauenkirche (Church of Our Dear Lady), built in 1235–60. Along with the

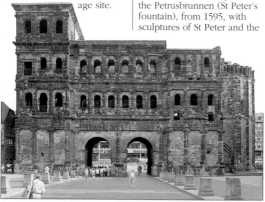

The magnificent *Porta Nigra*, gigantic Roman gateway into Trier

The Liebfrauenkirche – one of the country's earliest Gothic churches

cathedral in Marburg, this is one of the earliest examples of German Gothic architecture. Its ground plan is based on the Greek cross, and the tower above the dome accentuates the intersection of the naves. Its western portal is richly decorated with carved ornaments and iconographic symbols. The interior features many outstanding relics, including 15th-century wall paintings on twelve columns, which symbolize the 12 apostles. There are also some important tombs, including that of a local nobleman, Karl von Metternich (1636), which is in the northeast chapel.

🏛 Aula Palatina (Konstantin-Basilika)

Konstantinplatz. *Tel (0651) 42 570.* ⭘ *Apr–Oct: 10am–6pm Mon–Sat, noon–6pm Sun; Nov–Mar: 11am–noon & 3–4pm Tue–Sat, noon–1pm Sun.*

The *Aula Palatina* (Palatinate hall) dates from AD 310. An elongated, rectangular brick building 67 m (220 ft) long, 27.5 m (90 ft) wide and 30 m (98 ft) high with a vast semicircular apse, it served as the throne hall of the Roman emperor or his representative. Following the town's sacking by Germanic tribes, the building was reduced to rubble. In the 12th century the apse was converted into a tower, to

accommodate the archbishop. In the 17th century, the *Aula Palatina* was integrated into the newly-built palace and its eastern wall partly demolished. During Napoleonic and Prussian times, the hall served as army barracks. The Prussian king Friedrich Wilhelm IV eventually ordered its reconstruction. From 1856 it has served as the Protestant church of St Saviour. Restored after bombing in 1944, its giant size still seems remarkable

The monumental, austere exterior of the Aula Palatina

TRIER CITY CENTRE

0 metres 400
0 yards 400

Key to Symbols *see back flap*

Portal of the Kurfürstliches Palais

♣ Kurfürstliches Palais

Konstantinplatz. *Tel (0651) 949 42 02.* ◯ *the Palais is an administrative building and so visits that are not part of a public function are possible only by appointment.*

The Kurfürstliches Palais is considered to be one of the most beautiful Rococo palaces in the world. It has undergone several transformations over the centuries and remains of the earlier buildings can still be seen. The present building was designed by Johannes Seiz and built in 1756–62 for Archbishop Johann Philipp von Walderdorff. The sculptures were created by Ferdinand Tietz. The central tympanum shows Pomona, Venus, Apollo and a group of angels. The stairs, which lead from the garden to the inner staircase, were designed in the 18th century, but not built until 1981. They have beautiful handrails with typical Rococo motifs. The gardens are equally beautiful and include a miniature garden, a landscape garden and a mother-and-child area.

🏛 Rheinisches Landesmuseum

Weimarer Allee 1. *Tel (0651) 977 40.* ◯ *10am–5pm Tue–Sun.* ⬤ *1 Jan, 24, 25 & 26 Dec.* 📷

Only a few steps separate the electoral palace from the Rhine regional museum founded in 1877. Its collections are grouped into four sections: prehistoric, Roman, Franconian-Merovingian, and medieval to contemporary. The largest space is devoted to Roman relics. Among the star exhibits are a magnificent mosaic depicting Bacchus, from the dining room of a Roman villa, and the lovely statuette of a nymph, undoubtedly the work of a major artist. Equally impressive is a stone carving showing a ship loaded with four giant barrels, sailing on the Mosel River. Dating from AD 220, the carving decorated the tomb of a local wine-merchant.

📖 Stadtbibliothek

Weberbach 25.

The municipal library contains a number of important collections that were assembled here in the early 19th century, when many monastic libraries closed down. Among its treasures the library holds 74 full-page miniatures of the famous Trier Apocalypse (c.800), as well as one of the few surviving copies of the first Bible printed by Gutenberg.

🛡 Kaiserthermen

Weimarer Allee/Kaiserstr. *Tel (0651) 442 62.* ◯ *Apr–Sep: 9am–6pm; Oct & Mar: 9am–5pm; Nov–Feb: 9am–4pm daily.* 📷

Not far from the Rheinisches Landesmuseum are the remains of the vast imperial baths. Built in the early 4th century, during the reign of Constantine, they were the third largest bathing complex in the Roman world. The remaining sections of the walls and foundations indicate the former layout. Best preserved are the walls of the *caldarium*, the room with the hot water pool. Next to it is the round *tepidarium*, the warm baths. The spacious *frigidarium* was used for cold baths. Considerable room was given to the *palaestra*, an outdoor exercise area.

🛡 Viehmarktthermen

Viehmarktplatz.
Tel (0651) 994 10 57.
◯ *9am–5pm Tue–Sun.*

Following excavations completed in 1994, the remains of these Roman baths, along with those of medieval refuse pits and the cellars of a Capucin monastery, are now on display to the pubic under a large glass canopy.

📖 Jesuitenkirche

Jesuitenstr. 13.
◯ *7am–6pm daily.*

The Gothic Church of the Holy Trinity was built for Franciscan monks, who settled in Trier before 1238. The surviving church, from the late 13th century, went to the Jesuits in 1570. The college (1610–14) was transferred to the university following the dissolution of the Jesuit Order. It now houses a theological seminary. In the church, the tomb of Friedrich von Spee (1591–1635) is worth a visit.

Nymph in Rheinisches Landesmuseum

Vast complex of the Kaiserthermen (imperial baths)

⋔ Amphitheater

Petrisberg. *Tel* (0651) 730 10.
Apr–Sep: 9am–6pm; Oct & Mar: 9am–
5pm; Nov–Feb: 9am–4:30pm daily.
Near the imperial baths are
the ruins of the Roman amphitheatre, dating from the 1st
century AD. This was the
scene of gladiatorial fights
and animal contests. The
entire structure, consisting
of an elliptical arena and a
stepped auditorium, was
surrounded by a high wall,
divided into individual storeys
by colonnaded arcades. The
complex was designed to seat
up to 20,000 people. In the
5th century the inhabitants of
Trier used the amphitheatre
as a place of refuge from the
increasingly frequent raids by
Germanic tribes.

⛪ Heiligkreuzkapelle

Arnulfstraße/Rothachstraße.
The Chapel of the Holy Cross,
in a secluded spot, is one
of Trier's more interesting
historic buildings. Built in
the Romanesque style in the
second half of the 11th century, at the initiative of the
parson of Arnulfa Cathedral,
it is a small building with a
ground plan in the shape of
the Greek cross and an octagonal tower set within the
cross. Although it suffered
serious damage during World
War II, it was meticulously
restored to its original state in
the years 1957–8.

⛪ Basilika St Matthias

Matthiasstraße. 85. *Tel* (0651) 310
79. 8am–7pm daily.
This church's history dates
back to the 5th century, when
it became the burial place of
St Eucharius, the first bishop
of Trier. From the 8th century,
the church was run by Benedictine monks. In the 10th–
11th centuries a new church
was erected as burial site of
the relics of the apostle, St
Matthew. It was twice remodelled at the turn of the 15th
to 16th centuries, when it
acquired its rich Gothic
vaults. The present abbey
dates from the 16th century.
The shrine holding the
apostle's relics ensured that
the church became one of the
most important destinations
for pilgrims in the region.

The ruins of Barbaratherme, ancient Roman baths

⋔ Barbaratherme

Südallee. *Tel* (0651) 994 10 57.
closed until further notice
(dilapidated).
Not far from the Roman
bridge across the Mosel River
are the ruins of the Barbara
baths, dating from the 2nd
century AD. Although above
ground not much has been
preserved, the extensive
system of underground heat-
ing channels, the *hypocaus-
tum*, clearly demonstrates
the original size of this
public bath complex. In the
Middle Ages, Patrician and
aristocratic families transformed the baths into their
residences. In the 17th century Jesuit monks dismantled
the remaining structures, and
used the recovered building
materials to construct their
own college.

⋔ Kirche St Maximin

Maximinstraße. *Tel* (0651) 710 52
55. obligatory.
In the Middle Ages there were
as many as four abbeys in
Trier. St. Maximin Abbey was
founded on the burial site of
its patron saint, who died in
AD 325. The surviving church
was built in the 13th century,
on the foundations of the
previous buildings. Its
Romanesque–Gothic forms
were partly obscured by the
remodelling work carried out
in 1580–1698. The church's
most valuable historic remains
were the Carolingian wall
paintings, which originally
adorned the crypt. These
are now displayed in the
Rheinisches Landesmuseum.

⛪ Kirche St Paulin

Thebäerstraße. *Tel* (0651) 270 850.
Mar–Sep: 9am–6pm Mon, Wed–
Sat, 11am–6pm Tue, 10am–6pm Sun;
Oct–Feb: 9am–5pm Mon, Wed–Sat,
11am–5pm Tue, 10am–5pm Sun.
This church was built in the
12th century, on the foundations of an older Christian
chapel. In 1674 it was blown
up by the French army. St
Paulin, its patron saint and
bishop in Trier, was one of the
few to voice his opposition to
the Aryan credo of Emperor
Constantine II, in which he
rejected the divinity of Christ
and proclaimed himself alone
to be made in God's image.
Paulin did not meet with a
martyr's death, but was exiled
to Phrygia (now Turkey),
where he died in 358. The
present church, a true gem
of Rococo architecture, was
designed by Balthasar Neumann, who also created the
main altar.

**Baroque ceiling paintings in the
Rococo Kirche St Paulinus**

Saarland ❷

This German state, bordered by Luxembourg and France, was long disputed between France and Germany, but has now been firmly integrated into the Federal Republic. Almost forgotten are its coal and steel industries, which declined in the 1960s and 70s. The region has seen a turbulent history – it was ruled in turn by Celts, Romans and Franks. In the 17th century, on the order of Louis XIV, Vauban built the town-fortress of Saarlouis. Saarbrücken, an 18th-century town, is famous for its Baroque architecture, mostly created by Friedrich Joachim Stengel.

Von Nassau-Saarbrücken family tombs in Saarbrücken

Saarbrücken

Road map B6. 🏠 190,000. 🚉 ℹ
Rathaus St Johann, main entrance (0681-194 33 or 93 80 90). 🎭 *Max Ophüls-Preis (Jan), Perspectives du Théâtre (May), Saar Spektakel (Aug).* **www**.saarbruecken.de

The capital of Saarland, Saarbrücken was first built as the Franconian fortress of *Sarabrucca*. The town, on the Saar River, flourished in the 17th and 18th century, under the rule of Duke Wilhelm Heinrich von Nassau-Saarbrücken.

The churches and other prestigious buildings are largely the work of Friedrich Joachim Stengel, court architect to the von Nassau-Saarbrücken family. He designed the Catholic **Basilika St Johann** (1754–8) in the market square, as well as the monumental **Schloss**, the palace on the opposite bank of the Saar (1739–48). Its original, modern façade, created in 1989 after damage in World War II, is the work of the architect Gottfried Böhm.

Opposite the Schloss stands the **Altes Rathaus** (old town hall), dating from 1748–50, which today houses an interesting museum of ethnography. The Protestant **Ludwigskirche** (1762–75) is one of the last works completed by Stengel. A true architectural gem, it is laid out in the shape of a Greek cross. The **Stiftskirche St Arnual**, in the southwestern part of the town, contains the splendid Gothic and Renaissance tombs of the von Nassau-Saarbrücken family. Since 1960 it has also featured a "German–French Garden". One of the garden's entrances leads to Gulliver-Miniwelt (miniature world of Gulliver), where small versions of the world's most famous buildings are exhibited.

Völklinger Hütte, the historic steelworks in Völklingen

Völklingen

Road map B6. 🏠 43,500. ℹ *Rathausstr. 57 (06898-132 800).*

About 10 km (6 miles) west of Saarbrücken lies the small industrial town of Völklingen, which was granted town status in 1937. In 1881, Carl Röchling, a native of Saarbrücken, bought a small steel mill, the **Völklinger Hütte**, which he soon developed as the heart of his family's industrial empire. The steel mill still exists, and in 1994 it became a UNESCO World Heritage Site, listed as a historical object of international importance. Another attraction is an original, early 20th-century housing estate.

Homburg

Road map B6. 🏠 42,000. ℹ *Rathaus, Am Forum 5 (06 841-10 11 66).*

This town grew up around the Hohenburg castle, which now is just a picturesque ruin. In the Schlossberg nearby were unearthed the remains of a fortress, which was built in 1680–92 by Sébastien Le Preste Vauban on the orders of the French King Louis XIV. The greatest attraction of Homburg, however, is its Schlossberg caves, the largest man-made caves in Europe, cut into the red sandstone.

Ottweiler

Road map B5. 🏠 16,000. ℹ *Schlosshof 5 (06 824-35 11).*

The small picturesque town of Ottweiler has a beautifully preserved old town. The Alter Turm (old tower), which in the 15th century formed part of the town's fortifications, now serves as a belfry to the parish church, whose origins go back to the 15th century. Its present Baroque form was the work of Friedrich Joachim Stengel from 1756–7.

Rathausplatz is a beautifully proportioned complex of historic houses, mostly the homes of wealthy citizens, dating from the 17th and 18th centuries. Many have half-timbered upper halves. The Altes Rathaus (old town hall, 1714) combines two different building methods – the base is stone, the top half-timbered. In Schlossplatz is the Renaissance Hesse Haus (c.1590).

Moseltal ❸

The Mosel river, 545 km (338 miles) long, is one of the longest tributaries of the Rhine. The Mosel valley between Trier and Koblenz, where the Mosel flows into the Rhine, is one of the most beautiful parts of Germany. On both sides of the river, romantic castles tower over endless vineyards, where excellent white grapes are grown – both are typical features of the charming landscape.

Burg Thurant ②
Near the town of Alken stands Thurant castle, which was built in the 13th century. It is the only twin-towered castle along the Mosel.

Matthias-Kapelle ①
This late-Romanesque chapel was once used to house the remains of the Apostle Matthew. These were later transferred to the Matthiaskirche in Trier.

Burg Pyrmont ⑤
Pyrmont's grim 13th-century medieval castle was remodelled and extended several times during the Baroque era.

Cochem ⑥
The castle in Cochem, originally built in the 11th century, was completely destroyed by French soldiers in 1689. The present castle was rebuilt in the 19th century.

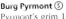

Mosel

Baybach

Dünnbach

Bremm

Ehrenburg ③
The first fortress, rising to 235 m (771 ft) above sea level, was built in 1120. It was frequently remodelled in later years.

Burg Eltz ④
The von Eltz family castle, whose history goes back to the 16th century, remains in private hands to this day, but it is open to visitors.

Burg Arras ⑦
This fortress was built around 900–950 as part of the fortifications against frequent pillaging raids by Normans.

KEY

■ Suggested route
■ Scenic route
═ Other road
═ River, lake
☼ Viewpoint

0 km _____ 5
0 miles _____ 5

TIPS FOR DRIVERS

Length of the route: about 75 km (46 miles).
Stopping-off points: there are numerous restaurants and cafes in Cochem; small pubs can be found along the entire route.
Additional attractions: a boat trip on the Mosel River, from Koblenz to Cochem or Trier.

Altar in the Dreifaltigkeitskirche, in Speyer

Speyer ❹

Road map B6. 🏛 *47,000.* 🚪 ℹ
Maximilianstraße 13 (06232-14 23 92).
🎭 *Brezelfest (Jul), Kaisertafel (Aug), Altstadtfest (Sep), Bauernmarkt (Sep).*

In the 7th century, Speyer was the seat of a diocese. As a free city of the Holy Roman Empire from 1294 until 1779, 50 sessions of the imperial parliament took place here. The most famous session was in 1529, when the Protestant states of the Holy Roman Empire lodged a protest (hence "Protestant") against the decisions of the Catholic majority.

The most important historic building in Speyer is the Romanesque **Kaiserdom** (St Maria und St Stephan), a World Heritage Site. For a time, before being superseded by the gigantic abbey of Cluny in Burgundy, this was the largest monumental Romanesque building in Europe. The Dom, built in 1025–61 on the initiative of Conrad II, is a triple-nave, cross-vaulted basilica with transept, vestibule, choir, apse and several towers. Its magnificent triple-nave crypt, the burial place of Salian emperors, has stunning stone carvings, some worked by Lombard stonemasons. **St Afra's**, dating from around 1100, has some interesting sculptures, including *Christ Bearing His Cross* and *Annunciation* (c.1470). The Domnapf, a vast stone bowl seen at the forecourt of the cathedral, dates from 1490. It was used during enthroning

ceremonies, when the newly anointed bishop would order it to be filled with wine right to the brim in order to win the hearts of his flock.

Another 11th-century interesting building is the **Mikwe** in Judenbadgasse, a ritual Jewish bath for women, and the remains of a synagogue nearby. To the west of the Dom stand the remains of the medieval fortifications including the **Altpörtel**, a 14th- to 16th-century town gate. The late-Baroque **Dreifaltigkeitskirche** (church of the Holy Trinity), built in 1701–17, is an architectural masterpiece with marvellous interiors.

Worms ❺

Road map B5. 🏛 *83,000.* 🚪
ℹ *Neumarkt 14 (06241-250 45).*

Worms is one of the oldest towns in Germany. In the Middle Ages it was the home of the Reich's Parliament, hosting more than 100 sessions. The **Dom St Peter** is one of the largest late-Romanesque cathedrals in Germany, along with the cathedrals in Mainz and Speyer. It was built in 1171–1230 as a two-choir basilica, with eastern transept, four towers and two domes. Its northern nave includes five beautiful sandstone reliefs from a Gothic cloister, which no longer exists. The interior furnishings date mainly from modern times. Particularly noteworthy is the high altar designed in the 18th century by Balthasar Neumann, and the stalls

Tombstones in the Heiliger Sand Jewish cemetery in Worms

dating from 1760. A short distance from the cathedral is the Marktplatz (market square), with the interesting **Dreifaltigkeitskirche** church of the Holy Trinity (1709–25). Northeast of the square stands the **Stiftskirche St Paul** (church of St Paul), built in the 11th–12th centuries and completed in the 18th century, with original 13th century wall paintings. Nearby is the only surviving Renaissance residential building in Worms, the **Rotes Haus** (red house).

In the western part of the old town is the **Heiliger Sand** (holy sands), the oldest Jewish cemetery in Europe, where the earliest tombstones date from the 11th and 12th centuries. Also worth a visit is the 14th-century **Liebfrauenkirche** (Church of Our Dear Lady). The most noteworthy feature of the **Magnuskirche** (11th–12th centuries) is its crypt, from around AD 800, while the **Stiftskirche St Martin** (late 11th century) has some interesting portals.

The vast Romanesque Dom St. Peter in Worms

A relief from 1488, in the Dom in Worms

Deutsche Weinstraße ⑥

The "German Wine Route" starts in Bockenheim and ends in Schweigen, near the Alsatian town of Weißenburg. The tour suggested here includes the most interesting sections of this route. This is one of the most beautiful parts of Germany, where visitors will encounter aspects of German and European historical and cultural heritage at every step, set among the picturesque scenery of the endless vineyards covering the sun-drenched slopes of the Pfälzer Wald.

Bad Dürkheim ⑧
This famous resort is best known for its annual Wurstmarkt, held in September. Despite its name, it celebrates the wine harvest, and sausages take second place.

St Martin ⑥
Not much remains of the Romanesque church of St Martin, but the 16–18th-century buildings surviving in the town continue to enchant visitors.

Hambacher Schloss ⑦
The castle's fame is based on the Hambacher Fest when, on 27 May 1832, students protested against the fragmentation of Germany. It was restored and is now a national monument and museum.

Landau ⑤
This little town has the remains of the fortress built by Vauban, and an extraordinarily beautiful post-Augustinian church.

Trifels ④
This grim, ruined castle once served as a prison for many important people, including the King of England, Richard the Lionheart.

NATURPARK PFÄLZER WALD

0 km 5
0 miles 5

Leinsweiler ③
Hilltop Hof Neukastel was once the home of the German impressionist artist Max Slevogt, and to this day, wall paintings by the artist can be seen here.

Klingbach

Bad Bergzabern ②
This town has some interesting Renaissance remains, including the Gasthaus zum Engel (Angel's Inn) and a royal castle.

TIPS FOR DRIVERS

Length: 83 km (51 miles).
Stopping-off points: Landau has many cafés and restaurants. The spa town of Bad Dürkheim, with its cafés and wine bars, is also a good place to stop.
Signs: Look for signposts showing a bunch of grapes or a wine jug.

Dörrenbach ①
The star attractions in this small town are the half-timbered town hall and the Gothic church surrounded by fortifications.

KEY

▬ Suggested route

▬ Scenic route

═ Other road

≈ River, lake

☀ Viewpoint

Mainz **❼**

The town, which grew out of the Roman military camp *Moguntiacum* established in 39 BC, is today the capital of the Rhineland-Palatinate. Mainz is the home of an important German television station (ZDF). It is also the main centre of trade for the popular Rhine wines. Its splendid late-Romanesque cathedral symbolizes the power of the Kurfürsten, the prince-electors, who used to crown German kings. Indisputably the town's most famous son is Johannes Gutenberg – the inventor of printing.

🏛 Kurfürstliches Schloss

Peter-Altmeier-Allee.
Römisch-Germanisches Zentralmuseum
Tel (06131) 91 240.
⭕ 10am–6pm Tue–Sun.
Construction of the Baroque electoral palace, which began in 1627 during the rule of Archbishop Georg von Greifenclau, was completed more than a century later, in 1775–6, under Johann Friedrich Carl Joseph von Erthal. Today the palace houses the fascinating museum of Roman and Germanic history.

🏛 Gutenberg-Museum

Liebfrauenplatz 5. *Tel* (06131) 12 26 40. ⭕ 9am–5pm Tue–Sat, 11am–3pm Sun. ⭘ public holidays. 🖼
Johannes Gensfleisch zum Gutenberg became famous as the inventor of the printing process using movable metal type. The letters were cast in a special apparatus and set in

Statue of Gutenberg in Gutenbergplatz

columns. Gutenberg himself prepared the Bible for printing and publication in 1454–5. From the original 200 copies, only 46 have survived to this day.
The museum, which opened in 1900, shows a reconstruction of the master's workshop from 1450. The collection comprises priceless early books, including the Gutenberg Bible and the Psalter published in 1457 by Fust & Schöffer, Gutenberg's erstwhile partners and latterday creditors. The Psalter was the first work to be printed using three different colours of inks.

🏛 Kaiserdom

See pp350–51.

🏛 Gutenbergplatz

A short distance from the Protestant parish church of St John is Gutenbergplatz, a pleasant square with a statue of the inventor. Set in its

Historic half-timbered houses in Kirschgarten

paving stones is a line marking the 50th parallel. The Staatstheater (state theatre) in the square is an interesting late Neo-Classical building from 1829–33.

🏛 Kirschgarten

Near the Baroque hospital of St Roch, built in 1721 and now an old people's home, runs a street called Kirschgarten (cherry orchard). This is one of the loveliest parts of old Mainz, which suffered serious damage in World War II. The well-preserved complex of historic half-timbered houses, dating from the 16th–18th centuries, makes this district worth visiting and a pleasant place for a stroll.

⛪ Kirche St Stephan

Kleine Weißgasse 12. *Tel* (06131) 23 16 40. ⭕ Mar–Oct: 10am–5pm Mon–Sat, noon–4:30pm Sun. Nov–Feb: 10am–4:30pm Mon–Sat, noon–4:30pm Sun.
A short distance from Kirschgarten stands the Gothic parish church of St Stephen. It was built in stages, on the site of an older building dating from the 10th century. Construction began in the mid-13th century and continued until the end of the 15th century. The resulting church is a triple-nave hall with eastern transept and a single-nave choir. The adjacent late-15th century cloisters are a true gem of late-Gothic design. The original stained-glass windows in the presbytery, destroyed during World War II, were replaced by six new ones in 1978–81, designed and partly made by Marc Chagall. Set

The Baroque Kurfürstliches Schloss and museum

Landing stage for boats on the Rhine

against a beautiful blue background, they depict biblical
scenes, including Abraham
with the three travellers, the
Patriarch pleading to God to
spare the righteous in Sodom
and Gomorrah, Jacob's dream,
and Moses with the Tablets of
the Ten Commandments.

The church interior contains
many other interesting
original features. The four
large brass candelabra were
cast in Mainz in 1509. The
small polyptych depicting the
Crucifixion dates from around
1400, while its movable wings

were made some 100 years
later. The niche below the
tower contains the Holy
Tomb (c.1450).

↑ Römersteine
Southeast of the University
campus are the impressive
remains of the Roman
aqueduct, dating from the 1st
century AD. The Zahlbach
valley was a vantage point for
the southwestern flank of the
Roman camp, *Castrum
Moguntiacum,* but it presented a major technical problem
of supplying the camp with

drinking water. The aqueduct
was built by Roman engin-
eers. Although some of its
pillars were 25 m (75 ft) high,
the present remains only
reach up to 10 m (32 ft).

Environs
It is also worth making an
excursion to **Oppenheim**, a
centre of the wine trade 20 km
(12 miles) to the south. The
pride of this town is its Gothic
Katharinenkirche, a church
built of red sandstone in the
13th–14th centuries. The
neighbouring hill and the ruins
of Landskron castle provide the
most spectacular view over the
Rhine valley. The Weinbau-
museum, museum of viti-
culture, is also worth visiting.

MAINZ CITY CENTRE

Gutenberg-Museum ②
Gutenbergplatz ④
Kaiserdom ③
Kirche St Stephan ⑥
Kirschgarten ⑤
Kurfürstliches Schloss ①

0 metres 250

0 yards 250

Key to Symbols *see back flap*

Kaiserdom

Crucifix in the St Gotthard-Kapelle

The greatest attraction of Mainz is its superb cathedral, gleaming red in the sunshine. Together with those of Speyer and Worms it is one of the only three Romanesque imperial cathedrals to have survived almost intact to this day. Its basic framework was laid out in 1081–1137 and 1183–1239, but its oldest parts date from the early 11th century, with the rows of Gothic side chapels added during the 13th and 14th centuries. Although neither the Gothic altars nor the magnificent choir screen have survived to this day, it is still possible to see the large group of bishops' monuments from the 13th to the 19th century.

Two large and two small towers are symmetrically positioned on the ends of the cathedral.

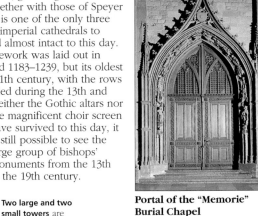

Portal of the "Memorie" Burial Chapel
The late-Gothic portal, leading to the Romanesque burial chapel of the cathedral canons, was made by Madern Gerthener, after 1425.

Pulpit
This Neo-Gothic pulpit was made in 1834 by Joseph Scholl.

St Stephen's Choir
The Romanesque eastern choir, one of the first parts to be built, is simpler in style than other parts of the cathedral.

Round staircase towers are from the previous building, built in the early 11th century.

★ Monument of Heinrich Ferdinand von der Leyen

This Baroque monument of the Dom rector, the work of Johann Mauritz Gröninger, was erected during his lifetime, in 1706.

St Martin's Choir

The late-Romanesque western choir with its trefoil closing is an early 13th-century addition.

★ Stalls

These superb Rococo oak stalls encircle almost the entire presbytery. They were created by Franz Anton Hermann, who completed them in 1767.

Main entrance

Tomb of Jakob von Liebenstein

The late-Gothic tomb of the archbishop von Liebenstein, who died in 1508, is the work of an unknown artist. It depicts the deceased in draped robes, lying under an ornate canopy.

STAR SIGHTS

- ★ Monument of Heinrich Ferdinand von der Leyen
- ★ Stalls

Rhine Valley (Rheintal) ⑧

The Celts called it *Renos*, the Romans *Rhenus*, while to Germanic tribes it was the Rhein, or *Vater Rhein* ("Father Rhine"), as it is known today. The source of this mighty, 1320-km (825-mile) long river is in Switzerland, from where it flows through Liechtenstein, Germany, Luxembourg and Holland, yet the Germans regard it as "their" river. The Rhine is steeped in many legends – it was into this river that Hagen von Tronje, faithful follower of King Gunther and slayer of Siegfried, threw the treasure of the Nibelungs, and Lohengrin's swan is said to appear near the town of Kleve *(see p388)* to this day.

Bonn
Bendorf
Rhein
Siegen
Kol
Trier
Saarbrücken
①

Stolzenfels ①
The existing castle complex has little in common with the original 13th-century fortress, which burned down in 1688. In the early 19th century, the ruins were bought by the future king Friedrich Wilhelm IV. The castle, designed by the famous Prussian architect Karl Friedrich Schinkel, was built in 1833–45.

②

0 kilometres   5

0 miles   5

Saarbrücken

Boppard ②
Boppard's most famous sights are the remains of the Roman military camp of Bodobrica, the church of St Severus (12th–13th centuries), famous for its wall paintings, and the Medieval market square, built on the site of Roman hot baths. Michael Thonet, the creator of famous chairs made from bent wood, was born here in 1796.

TIPS FOR WALKERS

Length of the route: *about 125 km (78 miles).*
Stopping-off points: *the best places to stop are Boppard or Bacharach, offering the widest choice of bars and restaurants.*
Further attractions: *a boat trip on the Rhine river, from Koblenz to Mainz.*

Burg Rheinfels ③
This castle ruin was begun in 1245 by Count Diether V of Katzenelnbogen, and was partially destroyed by French Revolutionary army troops in 1797. Some of the outer buildings are a luxury hotel, wellness centre and restaurant.

◁ **The Mosel River near Trittenheim at Rhineland-Palatinate**

Marksburg ⑧

From 1117 this castle, which towers over the Rhine and the small town of Braubach, has been owned at different times by the von Braubachs and the powerful Epstein family. The Marksburg is the only castle along this stretch of the Rhine which has never been damaged.

Loreley ⑦

The Loreley Rock, onto which many boats have been smashed by the strong currents, has been a source of inspiration for many poets. A 19th-century legend tells of a beautiful blonde combing her hair and luring unlucky sailors to their deaths with her song.

Pfalzgrafenstein ④

In the middle of the Rhine River stands the proud and mighty fortress of Pfalzgrafenstein – one of the most beautifully situated castles in the Rhineland. Its origins date back to 1326, but its present shape is the result of Baroque refurbishments in the 17th–18th centuries.

Bacharach ⑤

The town has a unique complex of historic buildings, with fortified town walls, the church of St Peter, the ruins of the Gothic chapel of St Werner, and Burg Stahleck – the castle towering over the town which today houses a youth hostel.

Burg Sooneck ⑥

In the 13th century, Sooneck castle was the home of various robber knights. The fortress fell into ruin in the late 17th century, due to frequent raids by the French. In the 19th century it was bought by the Hohenzollerns, who rebuilt the castle in its original form.

Limburg

wesel   *Kaub*

Lorch

Rüdesheim

Bingen

Kaiserslautern   *Mannheim*

KEY

▰▰	Motorway
▰	Key text
▰	Scenic route
=	River
☀	Viewpoint

Koblenz ❾

The name which the Romans gave to their camp in 9 BC – *castrum ad confluentas,* meaning the "camp at the confluence" – reflects the town's strategic importance, for it is here that the Mosel flows into the Rhine. From the Middle Ages until the 19th century, Koblenz was the seat of the powerful archbishop–electors of Trier. It was also the birthplace of Prince von Metternich, the 19th-century Austrian statesman. Today it is a modern metropolis which attracts many visitors, and is the main centre of the region's cultural life.

Romanesque twin-tower façade of the Basilika St Castor

🏛 Deutsches Eck

Ludwig-Museum im Deutschherrenhaus. Danziger Freiheit 1. *Tel (0261) 30 40 40.*
🕐 *9am–6pm daily.*
The "German corner" is the place where the Mosel flows into the Rhine. Here stands the enormous equestrian statue of Emperor Wilhelm I. Designed by Bruno Schmitz, it was erected in 1897, destroyed in World War II and replaced with a copy in 1993. The name refers to the complex of buildings known as Deutschherrenhaus belonging to the Order of Teutonic Knights. Only part of the three-wing residence of the Order's Commander, built in the early 14th century, has survived to this day. Following its refurbishment in 1992 the building now houses the Ludwig-Museum, with a collection of modern art (mainly German and French post-1945 artists) donated by Peter and Irene Ludwig.

🛕 Basilika St Castor

Kastorstraße 7.
The collegial church of St Castor was built in 817–36 on the initiative of the archbishop of Trier, on a site previously occupied by an early Christian church. The treaty of Verdun, which divided the Carolingian Empire between the three sons of Ludwig I the Pious, was signed here in 843. The present appearance of the church is the result of extensions from the 11th–13th centuries. Inside are beautiful wall epitaphs of the Trier archbishops Kuno von Falkenstein (1388) and Werner von Königstein (1418). Also noteworthy is the pulpit dating from 1625.

🏛 Florinsmarkt

Mittelrhein-Museum Florinsmarkt 15–17. *Tel (0261) 129 25 20.*
🕐 *10:30am–5pm Tue–Sat, 11am–6pm Sun.*
This square takes its name from the Romanesque-Gothic church of St Florin, dating from the 12th and 14th centuries. The Mittelrheinisches Museum with its collection of archaeology and medieval art of the Central Rhine region occupies three historic buildings. The Kaufhaus, in the centre, dates from 1419–25 and 1724. The image of a horse-rider shows the robber baron Johann von Kobem, beheaded in 1536, who now sticks his tongue out at passers-by every half hour. To its right stands the late-Gothic Schöffenhaus, and to its left is the Baroque Bürresheimer Hof, from 1659–60.

The Renaissance Alte Burg, now housing archives and a library

⛪ Alte Burg

Burgstraße 1.
In the Middle Ages, the powerful von Arken family had a fortified residence built for themselves in the northwestern section of the Roman fortifications. In 1277 it was taken over by Heinrich von Finstingen, the archbishop of Trier, who ordered its extension. The fortress was to protect him from the citizens of Koblenz who were striving for independence. Successive archbishops continued with the conversion of the building, which acquired its final shape in the 17th century. The eastern Renaissance façade of the complex is particularly attractive. Today it houses the municipal archives and parts of the library.

The spur between the Mosel and the Rhine, called Deutsches Eck

For hotels and restaurants in this region see pp506–8 and pp545–6

🛈 Liebfrauenkirche

Florinspfaffengasse 14.
Tel (0261) 315 50.
🕐 8am–6pm Mon–Sat,
9am–12:30pm Sun.

At the highest point in the old town stands the Romanesque church of Our Dear Lady. Its history dates back to early Christian times, but its present form is the result of remodelling work carried out in 1182–1250. A triple-nave basilica with galleries, it has a twin-tower western façade. The beautiful, elongated Gothic choir was added in 1404–30.

Statue of the Madonna in Liebfrauenkirche

♨ Kurfürstliches Schloss

Neustadt.

Not far from the bridge across the Rhine stands the electoral palace, an example of the Rhineland's early Neo-Classical architecture. It was built, and for a short time occupied, by Clemens Wenzeslaus von Sachsen, the last of Trier's electors. Construction of the castle began in 1777, to a design prepared by Michael d'Ixnard, and continued until

1786, overseen by Antoine François Peyère the Younger.

🏛 Festung Ehrenbreitstein

Landesmuseum Koblenz
Tel (0261) 66 75 40 00.
🕐 15 Mar–mid-Nov:
9:30am–5pm daily.

On the opposite side of the Rhine stands the mighty fortress of Ehrenbreitstein, one of the largest in the world. A smaller fortress was erected on this site in 1000, and extended in subsequent years by the archbishops and electors of Trier, who lived in this indomitable fortress from 1648 to 1786. Trier's holiest relic, the Rock Christi (vestments of Christ) was kept here. The appearance of the fortress has not changed much since

VISITORS' CHECKLIST

Road map B5. 🚶 109,300. 🚆
🛈 Bahnhofplatz 17 (0261-313 04); Jesuitenplatz (0261-13 09 20).
🎭 Internationale Musiktage (Mar/ Apr), Altstadtfest mit dem Fest der Stadtteile (Jun/Jul), Koblenzer Gauklerfest (Jul), Rhein in Flammen (Aug), Schängelmarkt (Sep), Koblenzer Mendelssohn-Tage (autumn). **www**.koblenz.de

Prussian days. It offers splendid views over Koblenz, the Rhine and the Mosel. Today, it is home to the **Landesmuseum Koblenz** (regional museum) with an interesting collection on the development of technology, and to the **Rhein Museum** with hydrological collections. At Wambachstraße 204, in the same district, is the house of Beethoven's mother.

The Classical façade of the Kurfürstliches Schloss

KOBLENZ CITY CENTRE

Alte Burg ④
Basilika St Castor ②
Deutsches Eck ①
Festung
 Ehrenbreitstein ⑦
Florinsmarkt ③
Kurfürstliches
 Schloss ⑥
Liebfrauenkirche ⑤

0 metres   250

0 yards   250

Key to Symbols see back flap

Maria Laach ⑩

Capital of a vestibule column

A true masterpiece of German and European Romanesque architecture, the Maria Laach Abbey stands next to the Laacher See, a lake formed in the crater of an extinct volcano. Its construction started in 1093 at the behest of Heinrich II, who also lies buried here. Building continued from 1093 until 1220. Until secularization in 1802, the Abbey was the home of the Benedictines. Since 1892 the church has once again been resounding with Gregorian chants, which are sung here several times a day.

View from the West
The monumental western façade of the abbey consists of a semicircular apse, a massive, square 43-m (141-ft) tall central tower, and two slim 35-m (115-ft) tall flanking towers.

★ Tomb of Heinrich II
The tomb of the Count Palatine Heinrich II, who died in 1095, dates from about 1280. His effigy has been reproduced in a magnificent walnut wood block, which to this day has kept its original colours.

Löwenbrunnen
The lion fountain, which adorns the atrium, was made in 1928. It was modelled on the famous Alhambra fountain in Granada, Spain.

Main entrance

Detail from a Column Capital
The western entrance is surrounded by columns with interesting capitals. Carved figures can be seen, including that of a devil recording the sins of each entrant and others which are pulling each other's hair out.

The "Paradise", the courtyard, is meant to symbolize the Garden of Eden.

Church entrance

Mosaics
The interior is decorated with paintings and mosaics created over centuries by artists of the Beuronese School. In the main eastern apse is a mosaic of Christ the Ruler dating from 1911.

VISITORS' CHECKLIST

Road map B5. 6032 from Niedermendig, 6031 from Andernach. **Tel** (02652) 59350. ◯ Easter–Oct: 9:30–11:15am, 1:15–4:45pm Mon–Sat, 1:45–4:45pm Sun & hols. Nov–Easter: 2:30–4:45pm Mon–Sat, Sun as above. **Crypt** video show. 🍴 🖳 📷

The church towers have arcaded galleries, typical of Romanesque style.

Stained-glass Windows
Three vast stained-glass windows in the main eastern apse were made by a contemporary artist, W. Rupprecht, in 1956.

★ High Altar
Among the most precious works preserved in the church is the late-Romanesque canopy of 1220–50, rising above the high altar.

★ Crypt
The vaults of the exquisite early-Romanesque crypt are supported by austere square capitals. This is also the resting-place of Gilbert, the first abbot at Maria Laach.

STAR SIGHTS

★ Tomb of Heinrich II

★ High Altar

★ Crypt

HESSE

esse lies in the very heart of present-day Germany. Scattered over the region are reminders of its former glory: Roman camps, Carolingian buildings, Romanesque churches and Gothic cathedrals with lofty spires. Territorial partitions, so typical of the former German Reich, brought about the blossoming of art and architecture during the Renaissance and the Baroque eras.

A post-World War II creation, the borders of this federal state roughly approximate those of its 13th-century forerunner. For most of its history, Hesse was divided between Hesse-Darmstadt and Hesse-Kassel.

Today, when admiring the distinctive panorama of Frankfurt am Main – its towering banks and skyscrapers more reminiscent of New York's Manhattan than of a European metropolis – it is hard to believe that this was the birthplace of Goethe. The importance of this city extends far beyond Hesse: it is the financial centre of the European Union, and its annual Book Fair is the largest event of its kind in the world.

Darmstadt became famous as a centre for Jugendstil (Art Nouveau) early in the 20th century. Wiesbaden is the seat of Hesse's state government, and Marburg is one of the best-known university towns. In the 16th century, at the times of fierce religious feuds, the first Protestant university was built here. The Church of St Elizabeth is one of the earliest examples of Gothic architecture in the region. Lovers of modern art will know of Kassel – every five years it hosts the *documenta*, an exciting exhibition of artistic developments.

Hesse has much more to offer. The Waldecker Land, near Kassel, boasts the Eder lake and attractive health resorts. Eberbach in the picturesque Rheingau, the wine-growing area around Eltville, has a well-preserved former Cistercian abbey, which has been used as a film setting.

Park and Baroque Orangery of the palace complex in Fulda

◁ Frankfurt's skyscraper district, nicknamed "Mainhattan"

Exploring Hesse

Eltville, situated in the Rheingau, one of Germany's most important wine-producing regions, is famous for its Riesling wine. Frankfurt am Main, known around the world as a great financial and commercial centre, also has fantastic museums, drawing visitors with their out-standing art collections, while the International Book Fair is a true paradise for readers and bookworms. In the 19th century, wealthy socialites chose Bad Homburg as their favourite spa, while the romantic town of Marburg still has the lively atmosphere of a university town.

The Dom in Limburg, overlooking the Lahn river

The giant Niederwalddenkmal near Rüdesheim

SIGHTS AT A GLANCE

SEE ALSO

- *Where to Stay* pp508–10.

- *Where to Eat* pp546–8.

The Messeturm in the Frankfurt fairgrounds, designed by Helmut Jahn

GETTING AROUND

The A7 motorway, cutting across Hesse in a north–south direction, provides a fast transport link. Starting from Hannover, it runs through Göttingen, Kassel and Fulda to Würzburg in Bavaria. The A4 runs from Dresden, via Weimar, to Bad Hersfeld. From there visitors can take the A7 or the A5, towards Gießen, Bad Homburg, Frankfurt am Main and onwards to Darmstadt and Heidelberg. The fast ICE railway connects Kassel and Frankfurt am Main with Basel (in Switzerland), Stuttgart, Berlin and Munich. Frankfurt am Main has one of Europe's largest airports.

KEY

▬▬	Motorway
▬	Main road
▭▭	Minor road
▬ ▬	Under construction
▬▬▬	Main railway
───	Minor railway
▬▬	International border
△	Summit

Statue of the Brothers Grimm in Hanau

Kassel ❶

The cultural, scientific and commercial centre of northern Hesse, Kassel suffered severe damage during World War II due to the armaments industries based here, and much of the town has been rebuilt in functional 1950s style. Today, Kassel has become synonymous with one of the most important shows of contemporary art – *documenta* – held here every five years (the 13th documenta is scheduled for 2017). The town is equally famous for its outstanding collection of European art, housed in the splendid Schloss Wilhelmshöhe, as well as for its parks and gardens, especially the large forest-park adjoining the castle.

17th-century cameo-decorated tureen in the Landesmuseum

🏛 Hessisches Landesmuseum

Brüder-Grimm-Platz 5. *Tel (0561) 316 800.* ◐ *closed for renovation until 2013.*

Outstanding items in the Neo-Baroque Hesse Regional Museum, built in 1910–13, are the astronomical instruments, originally installed in 1560 in a landgrave's castle, which no longer exists. The ethnographic section has displays of Hessian folk costumes and regional craft items.

The Landesmuseum also houses the fascinating Tapetenmuseum (wallpaper museum). Established in 1923,

Wallpaper (1670–80), in the Tapetenmuseum

the museum presents the history of wallpaper and the methods of its production around the world. The collection includes examples of leather wall coverings (cordovans) and wallpapers representing Secession and Art-Deco styles. *Vues de Suisse* (views of Switzerland), dating from 1802, is one of the earliest examples of scenic wallpaper. It was printed using 95 different inks and 1,024 wooden blocks. Equally famous is the panoramic *Rénaud et Armide*, from the workshop of Joseph Dufours, printed in 1828 using 2,386 wooden blocks.

During renovation, some displays are held in the nearby Torwache building.

🏛 Neue Galerie

Schöne Aussicht 1. *Tel (0561) 316 80 400.* ◐ *10am–5pm Tue–Sun.*

The New Gallery, founded in 1976 and devoted to 19th- and 20th-century art, occupies a Neo-Classicist building from 1871–74. The gallery's collection includes a number of canvases by artists such as Carl Schuch, Max Slevogt and Lovis Corinth.

The splendid collection of 20th-century paintings focuses on German Expressionism. An entire room is also devoted to the installations of the controversial sculptor and performance artist Joseph Beuys.

🏛 Brüder-Grimm-Museum

Schöne Aussicht 2. *Tel (0561) 787 20 33.* ◐ *10am–5pm daily (until 8pm Wed).* ● *1 Jan, Good Friday, 24, 25, 31 Dec.*

Next to the New Gallery is the small Schloss Bellevue, built in 1714 by Paul du Ry. Although brothers Jacob and Wilhelm Grimm were born in Hanau, they lived in Kassel from 1798 until 1830, and in 1960 a museum devoted to the lives and work of the famous fairy-tale tellers and philologers was opened, containing many first editions.

An illustration for Cinderella, one of the Grimm fairy-tales

🏛 Kunsthalle Fridericianum

Friedrichsplatz 18. *Tel (0561) 707 27 86.* ◐ *11am–6pm Wed–Sun.* ● *Mon–Tue.*

Königsplatz and Friedrichsplatz were designed by the court architect, Simon Louis du Ry. The northwestern side of the latter is occupied by the Neo-Classical Fridericianum, built by du Ry in 1769–76. Its founder, Landgrave Friedrich II, had always intended it to be a museum, and it became the second public museum (after the British Museum in London) to be built in Europe, and the first one on the European mainland. Since 1955, the Fridricianum has been the main venue for Kassel's multimedia contemporary art show – the *documenta*, which every five years takes over the entire city. An additional exhibition hall, the Documentahalle, was opened in 1992, in the nearby Staatstheater.

The Ottoneum, home of the first permanent theatre in Germany

🔲 Ottoneum
Steinweg 2. **Naturkundemuseum**
Tel (0561) 787 40 66. ◯ 10am–5pm Tue–Sun (until 8pm Wed, 6pm Sun). 🔲
The Ottoneum (1604–5), built for Landgrave Maurice the Learned, was Germany's first permanent theatre. Designed by Wilhelm Vernukken and remodelled in the late 17th century by Paul du Ry, it was converted into a natural history museum in 1885.

♣ Orangerie
An der Karlsaue 20c. **Tel** (0561) 316 80 500. **Museum für Astronomie und Technikgeschichte** ◯ 10am–5pm Tue–Sun (until 8pm Thu). ● 24, 25, 31 Dec. **Zeiss-Planetarium** 🎦 2pm Tue, Sat, 2 & 7pm Thu, 3pm Wed, Fri, Sun. 🔲 (free Fri.)
The southern part of Kassel is

home to Karlsaue, a vast palace and garden complex named after its founder, Landgrave Karl. The site was earlier occupied by a small Renaissance Schloss (1568), surrounded by a garden. In 1702–10 Pierre-Etienne Monnot built the large Orangery, which now houses a museum of astronomy and technology. Monnot is also the creator of Marmorbad, a bath pavilion from 1722, while the kitchen pavilion was designed by Simon Louis du Ry in 1765.

🏛 Wilhelmshöhe
Gemäldegalerie Alter Meister.
Schloss Wilhelmshöhe. **Tel** (0561) 31 68 00. ◯ 10am–5pm Tue–Sun (until 8pm Thu). ● 1 May, 24, 25, 31 Dec. 🔲
At the top of Wilhelmshöher Allee, designed in 1781, stands Wilhelmshöhe, a magnificent palace and park. The palace is situated along the axis of the avenue that runs up the hill, through a long forest glade. The original intention was to fill it with a series of cascades, but only a few of these were ever built. At the top of the hill is the Octogon, crowned with the statue of Hercules, the symbol of the town. The palace was designed by Simon Louis du Ry and

VISITORS' CHECKLIST

Road map C4. 🏠 195,000. 🚉 Hauptbahnhof, Bahnhof Wilhelmshöhe. 🛈 Obere Königsstraße 8 (0561-707 71 64). 🎭 documenta (every 5 years, next to be held in 2017), Zissel (Aug), Museumsnacht (Sep), Kasseler Musiktage (Nov). **www**.kassel.de

Heinrich Christoph Jussow and built in 1793–1801 for the Elector Wilhelm. Now it houses the Gemäldegalerie Alte Meister with its outstanding collection of European masters including paintings by Rubens, Titian, Rembrandt, Dürer and Poussin. There is a large and attractive park.

Cascades, with Octogon and Hercules statue, in Wilhelmshöhe

Fritzlar ❷

Road map C4. 🏠 15,500. 🚊 🚌
Kasseler Straße. 🏛 *Rathaus,
Zwischen den Krämen 5 (05622-98
86 43).* 🎪 *Pferdemarkt (Jul),
Stadtfest (Aug).*

The beautiful town of Fritzlar
has preserved its original,
nearly complete ring of medieval walls with watchtowers,
bastions and over 450 half-
timbered houses from various
periods. In the early 8th century, St Boniface, the apostle
of Germany, had the holy oak
of the Germanic god Donar,
which grew here, cut down to
build a Christian chapel. In
724 he founded the Benedictine **Dom** (abbey of St Peter).
In 1118 the original church
was replaced by a cruciform,
vaulted basilica with a triple-
nave crypt, and this was
remodelled in the 13th and
14th centuries. Adjacent to the
church is a lovely 14th-cen-
tury ambulatory. The church
interior is rich in historic
treasures. The east wall of the
transept is decorated with
wall paintings from c.1320,
and the south nave includes a
Pietà (1300). The 14th-century
parish church of the Franciscan Order nearby has a lovely
painting of the Madonna, on
the northern wall of the choir.

In Fritzlar's picturesque old
town stands the **Rathaus**
(town hall), whose lower
floors date from the 12th
century, while the upper ones
were added in the 15th century. The exquisite **Hochzeitshaus** (wedding house), in the
street of the same name, is a
Renaissance half-timbered
house, built in 1580–90,
which now houses a
museum. Another interesting
sight is the **Alte Brücke**, a
13th-century stone bridge
spanning the Eder River.

**Relief of St Martin, on the walls of
the Rathaus in Fritzlar**

Waldecker Land ❸

The Waldecker land, situated west of Kassel, was
once an independent county and later, until 1929,
a free state within the German Reich. Today this
region, with its Eder-Stausee (reservoir), is one
of the most attractive tourist regions in Germany. The wooded hills provide a perfect
setting for long rambles, the roads and tracks
are ideally suited for cycling tours and the
rivers and lakes permit visitors to practise
a wide variety of watersports.

Korbach ②
Korbach is a beautiful
old town with many
half-timbered houses.
Worth seeing are the
Gothic church of St
Kilian with its inter-
esting 14th-century
pulpit, and the
church of St Nicho-
las, with the
Baroque tomb of
Georg Friedrich
von Waldeck
(1692).

Frankenberg ⑤
This small town is brimming
with half-timbered houses.
The town hall (1509), also
half-timbered, has humorous
polychrome wood-carvings.
The Gothic Marienkirche with
its 15th-century wall paintings
is also worth visiting.

0 km   10

0 miles   10

KEY

▬	Motorway
▬	Suggested route
▬	Scenic road
═	Other road
═	River, lake
☀	Viewpoint

Bad Arolsen ①

Both the sculptor Christian Daniel Rauch and the painter Wilhelm von Kaulbach were born in this spa town, and they are commemorated in two museums. The star attraction, however, is the Baroque castle (1713–28) of the von Waldeck family, designed by Julius Ludwig Rothweil.

Waldeck ③

The old fortress of Waldeck is now a hotel. It offers superb views over the Eder-Stausee reservoir and the small town of Waldeck with its 18th-century half-timbered houses. The Gothic town church has a high altar (c.1500), devoted to the Virgin Mary.

Bad Wildungen ④

This popular spa town has many charming half-timbered houses. The church has a priceless altar painted with scenes of the Passion by Konrad von Soest (1403).

TIPS FOR VISITORS

Length of route: 110 km (68 miles).

Stopping-off points: There are many good cafés and restaurants in every town along the route.

Further attractions: Cruises and ferries run on the Edersee. A viewing platform on top of the Peterskopf hill, near Hemfurth, can be reached by electric train.

For additional map symbols *see back flap*

Projecting gate of the Baroque
Stadtschloss in Fulda

Fulda ❹

Road map C5. 🏛 *60,000.* 🚐 🛈
Bonifatiusplatz 1 (0661-1 02 18 12).

Fulda's history began in
March 744, when Sturmius, a
pupil of St Boniface, laid the
foundation stone for the
Benedictine abbey. Ten years
later the body of St Boniface,
who had been murdered by
Frisian pagans, was laid to
rest here. The town, which
grew around the abbey,
experienced its heyday during
the Baroque period, and a
new Baroque building,
designed by Johann Dientzenhofer, was built in 1704–12
on the foundations of the old
abbey. The **Dom St Salvator
und Bonifatius** is a triple-nave
basilica with a dome above
the nave intersection, a
monumental eastern façade
and a shrine with the saint's
relics under the high altar, in
the western section.

Opposite the cathedral
stands the **Stadtschloss**
(former episcopal palace), a
shoe-shaped edifice, built by
Johann Dientzenhofer and
Andreas Gallasini, with richly
decorated Baroque and
Rococo interiors. Particularly
noteworthy are the Kaisersaal
(imperial hall) on the ground
floor, the magnificent Mond-
saal (moon chamber, formerly
the ballroom) and the charming Rococo-style Spiegelsaal
(chamber of mirrors) on the
first floor. Today, some of the
palace chambers hold an
impressive collection of porcelain. The palace complex
includes a large landscaped
garden and an orangery,
which houses a café.

THE BROTHERS GRIMM

The two brothers are known
around the world as collectors of
German folk-tales, which were
first published in 1812 and subsequently translated into most
languages. Fairy-tales such as
Hänsel and Gretel, Cinderella and
Little Red Riding Hood have been
favourites for generations of
children. Above all, however,
the brothers were scholars. In his
German Grammar, published in
1819, Jacob Grimm proved that all German dialects sprang
from a common origin, and thus laid the foundations of
German philology. The Grimm Brothers also initiated the
publication of the *Dictionary of the German Language.*

To the north of the Dom
stands the round **Michaelskirche**, a Carolingian chapel
dating from 822, one of the
oldest church buildings in
Germany. Inside the church
has a ring of eight columns
and a crypt supported by a
single column. The circular
gallery, the long side nave
and the western tower are
11th-century additions.

Other interesting sights in
Fulda are the Baroque **Heilig-
Geist-Kirche** (church of the
Holy Spirit), built in 1729–33
by Andreas Gallasini, and the
late-18th century parish
church of St Blasius. In the
8th century, five abbeys were
established on the four hills
surrounding the town. On
Petersberg stands the former
Benedictine **Peterskirche**,
from the 9th–15th centuries,
with a Carolingian crypt.

Inside the church is one of
Germany's oldest wall paintings, dating from 836–47.

Alsfeld ❺

Road map C4. 🏛 *18,000.* 🚐 🛈
Am Markt 12 (06631-9 11 02 43).
🎭 *Pfingstfest (Whitsun),
Akademischer Marktfrühschoppen
(May), Stadt- und Heimatfest (Aug),
Historischer Markt (Sep).*

The first historic records of
Alsfeld date from the late 9th
century. Today the town
attracts visitors with its pretty
old town with numerous
16th–17th century half-timbered houses. On the eastern
side of the town square stands
a grand late-Gothic **Rathaus**
(town hall), built in 1512–16,
and one of the finest examples
of half-timbered structures

Half-timbered houses in Alsfeld

anywhere in Germany. Other interesting features in the market square are the stone **Weinhaus**, with its distinctive stepped gable (1538), and the Renaissance **Hochzeitshaus** (wedding house), dating from 1565. Opposite the town hall stands the **Stumpfhaus** (1609), its façade beautifully decorated with wood carvings and paintings. From the town hall runs the picturesque Fulder Gasse, with the Gothic parish church **Walpurgiskirche** (13th–15th centuries), which has 15th-century wall paintings. In Rossmarkt stands the former Augustian **Dreifaltigkeitskirche** (church of the Holy Trinity), from the 13th–15th centuries. It was from here that in 1522 the monk Tilemann Schnabel began to spread the Reformation in Alsfeld. The 18th-century **castle** in Altenburg, 2 km (1 mile) from Alsfeld, enjoys a hilltop position.

Detail on the Rathaus, in Marburg

Marburg ❻

Road map C4. 🏛 80,000. 🚉
🛈 Pilgrimstein 26 (06421 991 20).
🚌 Maieinsingen (30 Apr),
3-Tage Marburg (Jul), Elisabethmarkt (Oct), Weihnachtsmarkt (Dec).
www.marburg.de

When in 1248 the county of Hesse broke away from Thuringia, Marburg became one of the most important seats of the landgraves. The first landgrave, Heinrich II, lived in the castle that towers over the town. The town's history is inseparably linked with the 13th-century figure of Elisabeth of Thuringia, wife of Ludwig IV, who devoted her life to the poor and died here. In 1527, Philipp the Magnanimous founded the first Protestant university in the Reich at Marburg. He also instigated the first Marburg Colloquy in 1529, to unify the Protestant faith. The "articles" presented by Martin Luther to Melanchthon and Zwingli later formed the basis for the Augsburg Creed. Today, Marburg is a picturesque university town. A tour of the town should start from the **Elisabethkirche**, at the bottom of the hill. Built in 1235–83, it is (after Trier) Germany's second purely Gothic church. There is a large set of Gothic altars from the early 16th century, including the altars of St Elisabeth (1513) and of the Holy Family (1511). Next to the north choir entrance stands the statue of St Elisabeth with a model of the church (1480). The choir contains the tomb of the Saint, positioned under the baldachin (c.1280). The vestry houses the greatest treasure, the reliquary of St Elisabeth (1235–49). In the south choir is an interesting group of monuments to the Hessian landgraves, from the 13th–16th centuries.

The **Universitätsmuseum für Bildende Kunst** holds a collection of paintings produced after 1500, with a predominance of 19th- and 20th-century German artists. Around the market square stands a group of historic, half-timbered houses from the 14th–17th centuries. Particularly pretty are the Sonne (sun, No. 14), the Stiefel (boot, No. 17) and the house at No. 19. The Steinhaus (stone house, No. 18), built in 1318, is the oldest in Marburg, along with that at No. 13 Hirschgasse. At No. 16 Markt is the Renaissance Künstlerhaus (artists' house). High

The Gothic portal of the Elisabethkirche in Marburg

above the town (287 m/942 ft above the sea) towers the **Landgrafenschloss**, the landgraves' castle dating from the 10th–16th centuries. The two storey Fürstenbau (dukes' building) has a large ducal chamber, dating from 1330. The Wilhelmsbau was built in 1492–8. It houses a museum of sacral art with mementoes of the debate between Luther, Zwingli and Melanchthon.

🔒 **Elisabethkirche**
Elisabethstraße. **Tel** (06421) 655 73. ⬜ Apr–Sep: 9am–6pm; Oct: 10am–5pm; Nov–Mar: 10am–4pm.

🏛 **Universitätsmuseum für Bildende Kunst**
Biegenstraße 11. **Tel** (06421) 282 21 66. ⬜ 11am–1pm & 2–5pm Tue–Sun.

⚜ **Landgrafenschloss und Universitätsmuseum für Kulturgeschichte im Wilhelmsbau**
Schloss 1. **Tel** (06421) 282 21 66.
⬜ Apr–Oct: 10am–6pm Tue–Sun; Nov–Mar: 10am–4pm Tue–Sun.

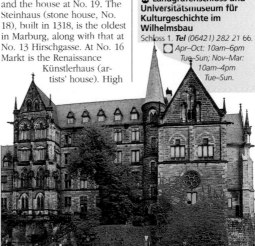

The Alte Universität (old university) in Marburg

Gießen ❼

Road map C4. 🏚 *72,000.* 🚉 ℹ️
Berliner Platz 2 (0641-194 33).

Giessen was granted town
status in 1248, and in 1607
it acquired its university. In
Brandplatz stands the partially
reconstructed **Altes Schloss**
(old palace), dating from the
14th–15th centuries. Now the
home of the Oberhessisches
Museum, it holds a large
collection of art dating from
the Gothic period to today.

The **Botanischer Garten** is
one of Germany's oldest botanical gardens, established in
1609 for the purposes of
scientific research. To the
north of it stands the **Neues
Schloss** (new palace), built in
1533–9 for Landgrave Philipp
the Magnanimous. It miraculously escaped damage when
the town was bombed in
1944. The Wallenfelssches
Haus nearby houses inter-
esting ethnological collections. The only remaining part
of the Gothic **Pfarrkirche St
Pankratius**, which was almost
completely destroyed in 1944,
is its tower, dating from 1500.

At No. 2 Georg-Schlosser-
Straße is the **Burgmannen-
haus**, an attractive half-timbered mansion
dating from
the 14th
century.

Portal of the Altes Schloss in Gießen

Along with the old stable
block in Dammstraße, it is the
only half-timbered building
that has survived to this day.

Wetzlar ❽

Road map C5. 🏚 *54,000.* 🚉
ℹ️ *Domplatz 8 (06441-997 750).*

Occupying a picturesque
spot on the banks of the
Lahn river, Wetzlar is overlooked by the ruins of the
12th-century **Kalsmunt** fortress. It was built for the
Emperor Friedrich I Barbarossa (1122–90). Only parts of
the tower remain intact. The
Dom (Collegiate Church of St
Mary) was begun in 897 but
by the late 15th century had
only been partly completed.
The splendid western double
portal has remained unusable
for the last 500 years –
although the iconography of
the tympanum was finished,
the stairs leading to the
entrance were never built. If
they had been built, they
would have led not to the
church's nave, but to a courtyard. Wetzlar's Dom is a rare,
perhaps even unique surviving example of the typical appearance of most European
churches in the mid-15th century. Inside the church are
several interesting historic
artifacts, including the statue
of the *Madonna on the Moon
Crescent* (mid-15th century)
and a late-Renaissance
Crucifixion.

In 1772, the young
Johann Wolfgang
von Goethe spent
three months in
Wetzlar working as
an apprentice at
the court of appeal.
During this time
he fell in love with
Charlotte Buff, called
Lotte, who was
engaged to one of
Goethe's friends.
The **Lottehaus**, her
former home, has a
collection of items
relating to Goethe
and Lotte. It was
the suicide of a
friend, Karl Wil-
helm Jerusalem,
who lived in the

18th-century **Jerusalemhaus**
at No. 5 Schillerplatz, that
inspired Goethe to write his
tragic novel, *The Sorrows of
Young Werther* (1774). Jerusalem had suffered unrequited
love, just like Goethe. The
novel, which was published
two years later, made Goethe
famous around Europe, but it
also unwittingly led many
young men to commit suicide.

**The Gothic south tower of the
Dom in Wetzlar**

Weilburg ❾

Road map B5. 🏚 *13,500.* 🚉
ℹ️ *Mauerstraße 6 (06471-76 71).*

Weilburg enjoys a parti-
cularly scenic location in
a bend of the Lahn River. The
town is dominated by the
majestic Renaissance–Baroque
Schloss of the Nassau-Weil-
burg family. The monumental
castle complex was created in
stages. Its main section dates
from the Renaissance era; the
east wing was built in 1533–9;
the south and west wings in
1540–48 and the west tower
in 1567. The northern part of
the palace was completed in
1570–73. In the late-17th
century, various Baroque
additions were made, mainly
to the interior of the castle.
The 16th-century furnishings
show the rich ornamentation
typical of the German Renaissance. The **Obere Orangerie**
(upper orangery), built in
1703–5 and today used for
temporary exhibitions, and
the **Hofkirche** (castle church),
dating from 1707–13, are the
work of Ludwig Rothweil.
Terraces lead from the castle

to the Lahn river, which is crossed by an 18th-century stone bridge. In Frankfurt-straße stands the **Heiliggrab-kapelle** (Chapel of the Holy Sepulchre), dating from 1505.

Limburg

Road map B5. 🏛 *31,000.* 🚉
🛈 *Bahnhofsplatz 2 (06431-61 66).*

Limburg's history dates back to the 8th century. In 1821, the town became the see of a newly created diocese.

The **Dom** (collegiate cathedral church of St George) towers high above the Lahn river. This monumental building, whose style combines late-Romanesque and early French Gothic, was erected in 1190–1250. Its well-proportioned interior contains a rich variety of historic artifacts, including some 13th-century wall paintings in the presbytery and the transept, a font dating from the same period and the tombstone of Konrad Kurzbold, who founded the first church on this site.

To the south of the Dom stands the **Burg** (castle), an irregular structure built in the 13th–16th centuries. It houses the interesting **Diözesan-museum** (Diocese museum).

Limburg has many original examples of beautiful half-timbered buildings. The houses at No. 1 Römerstraße, No. 6 Kolpingstraße, No. 4 Kleine Rütsche and No. 11

Romanesque–Gothic wall paintings in the Dom in Limburg

Kornmarkt date from the last decade of the 13th century. Near the 14th-century **Alte Lahnbrücke** (old Lahn bridge), with its defensive towers, stands a mansion belonging to the Cistercians of Eberbach. The post-Franciscan Sebastiankirche (church of St Sebastian) dates from the 14th and 18th centuries.

Bad Homburg ⑪

Road map C5. 🏛 *52,000.* 🚉
🛈 *Kurhaus, Louisenstraße 58 (06172-178 37 10).* 🎭 *Tugato (Sep every two years – 2012, 2014), Laternenfest (Sep yearly).*

Bad Homburg grew up around a fortress whose earliest records date back to 1180. Friedrich II von Hessen-Homburg initiated the conversion of the medieval castle into the **Schloss**, a Baroque palace built in 1678–86. It features a magnificent Festsaal (ballroom) and Spiegelkabinett (hall of mirrors). The only part of the former complex remaining today is the 14th-century Weißer Turm (white tower). Following the annexation of Hesse-Homburg by Prussia in 1866, the palace became the favourite summer residence of the royal then (from 1871) imperial family.

Along with Baden-Baden and Wiesbaden, Homburg was one of Germany's most fashionable spas, and today the town reflects its former splendour. The **Kurpark**, a landscaped park established in 1854–67, was designed by Peter Joseph Lenné.

The **Spielbank** (1030), in Brunnenallee claims to be the oldest casino in the world. Built in 1887–90, the **Kaiser-Wilhelm-Bad** is still used as the main bath complex for therapeutic treatments. An Orthodox chapel, designed by Leonti Nikolayevich Benois for the Russian Orthodox nobility, was finished in 1899.

Environs
Saalburg, 7 km (4 miles) to the northwest, has a Roman fortress, which was completely reconstructed in 1898–1901. The fortress formed part of the *limes*, the fortified border that separated the Roman Empire from its Germanic neighbours in the 1st to 3rd century AD.

The grand edifice of the Kaiser-Wilhelm-Bad in the Kurpark, Bad Homburg

Eltville

Road map B5. 🏰 *17,000.* 🚇 ℹ️
Rheingauer Str. 28 (06123-90 98 0).
🎭 *Biedermeier- und Sektfest (Jul).*

In the 2nd century, the area
that is now the old town was
a Roman *latifundium,* a large
agricultural estate. In 1332,
Eltville was granted town
status. Part of the Mainz
diocese, it is today known for
its excellent sparkling wine.

In 1337–45 the **Burg**
(castle) was extended at the
request of Archbishop Heinrich von Virneburg. The east
wing of the castle was added
in 1682–3 by Giovanni Angelo
Barell. The only part of it
remaining today is the five-
storey residential tower; the
rest of the building is a picturesque ruin. In the tower
are original 14th-century wall
paintings and friezes.

The twin-naved **Pfarrkirche
St Peter und St Paul** (parish
church) was built in
1350–1430. The vestibule has
well-preserved wall
paintings (1405)
showing scenes
from the Last
Judgement. The
town boasts
several attractive
mansions,
including Hof
Langenwerth
von Simmern
(1773), Stock-
heimer Hof (1550) and
Gräflich-Eltzscher Hof
(16th–17th century).

The Baroque Biebrich Palace,
south of Wiesbaden

growth of the town as a spa
resort in the 19th century, laid
the foundations for its lasting
prosperity. Today, the town is
still dominated by large-scale
developments carried out in
the spirit and style of Classi-
cism and Historicism.

The **Stadtschloss** (municipal
castle), today the seat of the
state parliament, was built in
1835–41. In Schlossplatz the
Neo-Renaissance **Markt-
kirche,** built in 1853–62, soars
above the town's other
buildings.

In front of the
church stands a
statue of Wilhelm
I the Great von
Nassau-Oranien.
The oldest
building in the
town is the
Altes Rathaus
(old town hall),
dating from 1610. In Wilhelmstraße is the imposing Neo-
Renaissance and Neo-Baroque
Hessisches Staatstheater
(state theatre). It was built in
1892–4 for Kaiser Wilhelm II
to the designs of the theatre

Crest of the Hessische Staats-
weingüter-Vinothek, in Eltville

Wiesbaden

Road map C5. 🏰 *270,000.* 🚇
ℹ️ *Marktplatz. 6 (0611-172 99 30).*
🎭 *Internationale Maifestspiele (May),
Theatrium (Jun).*

Wiesbaden is the modern
capital of Hesse. Highly
valued as a spa by the
Romans, who exploited the
healing properties of its
waters, the town grew from
a small settlement known as
aquae mattiacorum after the
Germanic tribe of the Mattiacs.
In 1774 the Nassau-Usingen
family chose Wiesbaden as
their residence. This, as well
as the subsequent rapid

architects Fellner and Helmer.
Adjacent to the Marktkirche is
the attractive Kurhauskolon-
nade (spa house colonnade).
It was erected in 1825 and is
the longest colonnade in
Europe. The early 20th-century
Kurhaus (spa house) itself,
with its grand façade and
portico, is the work of Friedrich Thiersch. Inside is the
original **Spielbank** (casino),
where Fyodor Dostoyevsky
and Richard Wagner tried
their luck at the tables.

To the south of the town
centre stands **Schloss Biebrich**, where the counts von
Nassau-Usingen resided until
the early 19th century, when
they moved to the newly built
palace in the town centre.
The Schloss was built in
stages during the 18th century. The north pavilion was
built first, in 1700, followed
nine years later by the south
pavilion. The wings, which
join the two pavilions, and
the central rotunda were
added during the first two
decades of the 18th century.
Finally, the two external
wings were added in 1734–44,
creating an overall horseshoe
layout. The interior is richly
furnished, predominantly in
Baroque-Rococo style.

On the northern outskirts of
the town is a large hill, the
Neroberg, whose summit can
be reached by funicular railway. At the top is the so-
called **Griechische Kapelle**
(Greek chapel). Built in 1847–
55 by Philipp Hoffmann, it
served as a mausoleum for
Princess Elisabeth von Nassau,
the niece of Alexander I Tsar of
Russia, who died young.

The attractive façade of Hessisches Staatstheater in Wiesbaden

For hotels and restaurants in this region see pp508–10 and pp546–8

The ornate Gothic portal of Pfarrkirche St Valentin, in Kiedrich

Kiedrich ⑭

Road map B5. 🚶 3,400. 🚐
🛈 Markstr. 27 (06123-90 50 10).

The earliest recorded mention of Kiedrich was in the mid-10th century, in a document produced by the Archbishop Friedrich of Mainz. One of the town's main attractions is the **Pfarrkirche St Valentin**, a gem of Gothic architecture. The church was built in stages, beginning with the main hall (1380–90). The west tower was added in the early 15th century and the light, lofty choir in 1451–81. Some time later the central nave was raised to the level of the choir, creating a row of galleries above the aisles, and at the same time the magnificent star vaults were created. The whole project was financed from donations made by countless pilgrims who came to pray to the relics of St Valentine, kept here since 1454. A statue of the saint adorns the western portal. The early 15th-century tympanum depicts the *Annunciation* (on the left) and the *Coronation of the Virgin Mary* (on the right); above is an image of *God the Father giving His Blessing*, with two archangels playing musical instruments. Inside, the church harbours an incredible wealth of ancient art treasures. The high altar and St Catherine's altar in the south aisle date from the late-Renaissance period. The magnificent Gothic stalls were created in 1510, while the church organ is one of the oldest in Germany, with pipes made in 1310. Next to the parish church stands a late Gothic, two-storey funeral chapel built in 1445.

Kiedrich has several interesting old mansion houses, such as the Schwalbacher Hof (1732). The **Rathaus** (town hall) is evocative of the late-Gothic style, although it was built much later (1585–6).

Environs
Five km (3 miles) west of Kiedrich, in Oestrich, is **Kloster Eberbach**, a former Cistercian abbey. This vast complex, built between the 12th and 14th centuries, was once home to nearly 300 monks and is one of the best-preserved medieval monasteries in Germany. The church interior provided the setting for some of the scenes in the film *The Name of the Rose*, based on the novel by Umberto Eco. The Cistercians used to have their own vineyards here, and today the abbey buildings are used by the Hessian Wine Co-operative to press, ferment, store and sell Eberbacher Steinberg, a famous white Rheingau wine.

A short way to the west, in **Winkel**, stands the Baroque castle of Reichardshausen, which in the early 19th century was the home of Princess Luise von Nassau.

🏰 Kloster Eberbach
Tel (06723) 91 78 115. ⏰ Apr–Oct: 10am–6pm daily; Nov–Mar: 11am–5pm daily. 🚫 24, 25, 31 December, Carnival Mon. 📷

Rüdesheim ⑮

Road map B5. 🚶 10,000. 🚐
🛈 Geisenheimer Str. 22 (06722-194 33). 🎆 Fireworks (Jul), Weinfest (Aug).

Rüdesheim, enjoying a picturesque location on the banks of the Rhine, has a long history going back to Roman times. The town is famous for its main street, the **Drosselgasse**, which is lined with countless wine bars and shops. There are also the remains of three castles: the **Boosenburg**, the **Vorderburg** and the 12th-century **Brömserburg**, which also houses a wine museum.

Rüdesheim also has several historic mansions, including the half-timbered Brömserhof (1559) with a collection of musical instruments, and the early 16th century Klunkhardshof. Above the town towers the **Niederwalddenkmal**, a statue of Germania, 10.5 m (34 ft) high, built to commemorate victory in the Franco-Prussian War of 1870–71, which resulted in German unification. The monument affords excellent views of Bingen and the Rhine valley.

Gabled and half-timbered houses in Drosselgasse, in Rüdesheim

Frankfurt am Main 🔞

Frankfurt, nicknamed "Mainhattan" and "Chicago am Main" because of its skyscrapers, is one of the main economic and cultural centres of both Germany and Europe. The headquarters of many major banks and newspaper publishers are based here, including those of the *Frankfurter Allgemeine Zeitung*, one of Europe's most influential newspapers. The city's International Book Fair is the world's largest event of its kind. Goethe was born in Frankfurt, and the Johann-Wolfgang-Goethe-Universität is one of Germany's most famous universities. The city also boasts magnificent art collections.

The Neo-Renaissance façade of the Alte Oper

🎵 Alte Oper

Opernplatz 8. *Tel* (069) 134 00.
The monumental old opera house stands near the Stock Exchange. Built in 1872–80, it was completely burned down during World War II. Subsequently rebuilt, it is today used as a conference centre. Its façade and decorations are a fine imitation of the Italian Renaissance style.

🏛 Eschenheimer Turm

Große Eschenheimer Straße
The Eschenheimer Turm, at the corner of Hochstraße, presents a silhouette typical of old Frankfurt. A relic of the medieval town's fortifications, it was designed by Klaus Mengoz; construction began in 1400 and was completed in 1428 by Madern Gerthener. The façade of the tower features

many attractive bay windows; it also has two reliefs depicting eagles, the symbol of the German empire and the city of Frankfurt.

🏛 Börse

Börsenplatz.
According to historical records, local merchants founded the town's first Stock Exchange in 1558. The new building, designed by Heinrich Burnitz and Oskar Sommer, was erected in 1864–79. It has been used again by stockbrokers since 1957, and is open to the public. Like the old opera house, the stock exchange is designed in Neo-Renaissance style.

Putti with model ship, at the front of the Börse

🏛 Hauptwache

An der Hauptwache.
Built in 1730, the Hauptwache was originally a guardhouse. Later it was turned into a

prison. Dismantled stone by stone during the construction of the town's underground system, it was reassembled in its original form following the completion of the project. Since 1904 the Hauptwache has been a chic café and a popular meeting place.

🏛 Goethehaus

Großer Hirschgraben 23.
Tel (069) 13 88 00. 🕐 10am–6pm Mon–Sat, 10am–5:30pm Sun. 📷
www.goethehaus-frankfurt.de
Southwest of the Hauptwache is Johann Wolfgang Goethe's family home. The great German poet, novelist and dramatist was born here on 28 August 1749. The house, along with many other buildings in Frankfurt, was totally destroyed in World War II, but later lovingly restored. Its interior was reconstructed to represent the style typical of the mid- to late- 18th century. Goethe lived in this house until 1775, when he moved to Weimar. The desk at which he wrote his early works, including the first versions of *Götz von Berlichingen* (1771) and *Egmont* (1774), has been preserved.

The adjacent building now houses the Goethemuseum. Opened in 1997, the museum recreates the atmosphere of the 1750–1830 period, and holds a collection of items related to the writer. There is an excellent library, which contains some of his writings.

The distinctive Neo-Classical rotunda of the Paulskirche

For hotels and restaurants in this region see pp508–10 and pp546–8

Portal of the Goethehaus, with the ancestral family crest

⚓ Paulskirche

Paulsplatz. **Tel** (069) 28 10 98.
⬜ 10am–5pm daily.

The distinctive Neo-Classical rotunda of the church was begun in 1786 but not completed until 1833, due to continuous hostilities with France. Today, however, this building is no longer thought of, or indeed used as, a church. After the first, albeit ill-fated, German National Assembly met here following the revolutionary upheavals of 1848–9, the church became a symbol of republican and liberal Germany. The Paulskirche now serves as a venue for many important events. Each year the awards ceremony for the prestigious German Publishers' Peace Prize takes place here.

🏛 Römerberg

Located in the centre of Frankfurt's old town, this square contains the Gerechtigkeitsbrunnen (fountain of justice). Its highlight, however, is the **Römer** (literally the Roman). So-called after the remains of ancient settlements, it is a complex of 15th- to 18th-century houses, including the Altes Rathaus (old town hall), which were rebuilt after World War II. Opposite is a group of half-timbered houses, commonly referred to as Ostzeile. The Steinernes Haus (stone house) was originally built in 1464 for a Cologne silk merchant. It has been reconstructed and is now the home of the Frankfurter Kunstverein (artists' league).

VISITORS' CHECKLIST

Road map C5. 🚶 660,000. ℹ️
Hauptbahnhof (069-21 23 88 00);
Römerberg 27 (069-21 23 88 00).
🎭 *Dippemesse (spring, autumn),*
Wäldchestag (Whitsun), Kunsthand-
werk Heute (May/Jun), Mainfest
(Aug), Book Fair (Oct), Christkindl-
markt (Dec). **www**.frankfurt.de

The Ostzeile on the Römerberg, one of the symbols of Frankfurt

FRANKFURT CITY CENTRE

0 metres   400

0 yards   400

Key to Symbols *see back flap*

🏛 Jüdisches Museum

Untermainkai 14–15. *Tel (069) 21 23 50 00.* ⏰ *10am–5pm Tue–Sun, 10am–8pm Wed.* 📷

The Jewish community of Frankfurt was the second largest in Germany, after that of Berlin. This museum, in the former Rothschild Palace, documents the rich cultural heritage of Frankfurt's Jews.

ⓘ St Leonhardskirche

Alte Mainzer Gasse.

Close to the banks of the Main stands the church of St Leonhard, a fine example of Gothic and Romanesque architecture. A five-naved hall-church with an elongated choir, it was built in stages in the 13th and 15th centuries. Inside are many treasures, including at the front of the main nave a copy of Leonardo da Vinci's *Last Supper* by Hans Holbein the Elder, from 1501. Next to it is St Mary's altar, created by master craftsmen from Antwerp in 1515–20. On the north wall of the choir visitors can see a fresco depicting the *Tree of Life and the Apostles* (1536) by Hans Dietz.

🏛 Historisches Museum

Saalgasse 19. *Tel (069) 21 23 55 99.* ⏰ *10am–6pm Tue, Thu–Sun, 10am–9pm Wed.* 📷

The new building housing the history museum was finished in 1972. The museum has an interesting display of items relating to Frankfurt's history, including a fascinating model of the medieval town, a collection of local prehistoric finds and several decorative

The early-Gothic Alte Nikolaikirche, in Frankfurt's Römerberg

architectural fragments from buildings that were destroyed during World War II.

The adjacent building is the Saalhof, which dates back to the time of the Emperor Friedrich I Barbarossa (1122–90). In 1333, the building passed into private hands and from then on it frequently changed its appearance.

ⓘ Alte Nikolaikirche

Römerberg.

The twin-naved church of St Nicholas, also known as Alte Nikolaikirche, was consecrated in 1290. Used as a court church until the late 15th century, it now serves a Lutheran congregation. Popular attractions are its many statues of St Nicholas (Santa Claus) and the 40-bell carillon, which twice a day plays German folk songs.

🏛 Kunsthalle Schirn

Römerberg 6. *Tel (069) 299 88 20.* ⏰ *10am–7pm Fri–Sun & Tue, 10am–10pm Wed & Thu.* 📷

One of Europe's most prestigious exhibition buildings, the Kunsthalle opened in 1986. It hosts temporary art exhibitions featuring archaeological themes and the work of old masters and contemporary artists.

ⓘ Kaiserdom

Domplatz 14. *Tel (069) 297 03 20.* ⏰ *8am–noon, 2:30–6pm daily (except Fri am).* **Dommuseum** *Tel (069) 13 37 61 84.* ⏰ *10am–5pm Tue–Fri, 11am–5pm Sat & Sun.*

Near the archaeological park, where the ruins of a Carolingian fortress have been unearthed, stands the imperial cathedral, used for the coronation of German kings from 1356, and of Holy Roman Emperors from 1562. The cathedral, dedicated to St Bartholomew and Charlemagne, was built during the 13th, 14th and 15th centuries, on the site of a Carolingian chapel. It has several priceless masterpieces of Gothic art, including the magnificent 15th-century Maria-Schlaf-Altar and a high altar dating from the second half of the 15th century. The choir has original 14th-century stalls; above these there is a fresco painted in 1427 which depicts scenes from the life of the cathedral's patron saint, Bartholomew.

The Dom's huge tower affords some magnificent views of the town. While in the cloisters is the Dommuseum which has an interesting collection of liturgical objects, sacred art and precious artifacts.

🏛 Museum für Moderne Kunst (MMK)

Domstraße 10. *Tel (069) 21 23 04 47.* ⏰ *10am–6pm Tue & Thu–Sun, 10am–8pm Wed.* 📷

The modern art museum occupies a building that looks like a slice of cake. It was designed by Hans Hollein in 1989–92. The museum's collection represents all the major artistic trends from the 1960s until the present day, and includes works by Roy Lichtenstein, Andy Warhol

The magnificent late-Gothic high altar in the Kaiserdom

Hollein's modern design, housing the Museum für Moderne Kunst

and Claes Oldenburg. Temporary exhibitions held here focus on multimedia shows, incorporating photography and video art.

🏯 Ikonen-Museum
Brückenstraße 3–7. **Tel** (069) 21 23 62 62. ◯ 10am–5pm Tue–Sun, 10am–8pm Wed. 🈳

The museum of icons holds an extensive collection of Russian Orthodox icons from the 16th–19th centuries. It is housed in the Deutschordenshaus, originally built in 1709–15 by Maximilian von Welsch for the Order of the Teutonic Knights. The present building is a faithful copy of the earlier Baroque three-wing structure destroyed in World War II. Inside is the 14th-century Teutonic Church of St Mary, with original altars and 14th- to 17th-century wall paintings.

🏛 Museum für Angewandte Kunst
Schaumainkai 17. **Tel** (069) 21 23 40 37. ◯ 10am–5pm Tue–Sun, 10am–9pm Wed.

The Museum of Applied Arts was opened in 1983, in a building designed by Richard Meier. He used a Biedermeier house, the Villa Metzler, and added a modern wing. The museum has a collection of some 30,000 objects of applied art from Europe and Asia.

Nearby, in a villa with a large garden in Schaumainkai, is the small but fascinating Museum der Weltkulturen (ethnography museum), which is well worth a visit.

🏛 Deutsches Architekturmuseum
Schaumainkai 43. **Tel** (069) 21 23 88 44. ◯ 11am–6pm Tue–Sun (to 8pm Wed and to 7pm Sun). 🈳

One of the most interesting museums in the Schaumainkai complex is undoubtedly the museum of architecture, opened in 1984 in an avant-garde building designed by Oswald Mathias Ungers. The museum has a permanent collection as well as temporary exhibitions concentrating mainly on developments in 20th-century architecture.

Nearby, at No 41 Schaumainkai, is the Deutsches Filmmuseum, which holds documents and objects relating to the art of film making and the development of film technology. The museum has its own cinema, which shows old and often long-forgotten films.

🏯 Liebieghaus
Schaumainkai 71. **Tel** (069) 650 04 90. ◯ 10am–6pm Tue–Sun, 10am–9pm Wed & Thu. 🈳

The Liebieghaus was built in 1896 for the Czech industrialist Baron Heinrich Liebig. Today it houses a museum of sculpture, with works ranging from antiquity through to Mannerism, Baroque and Rococo. The museum also has superb examples of ancient Egyptian and Far Eastern art, as well as works from the Middle Ages and the Renaissance. Its highlights are the works of Neo-Classical masters such as Antonio Canova, Bertel Thorwaldsen and Johann Heinrich Dannecker.

The Liebieghaus, home of the museum of sculpture

🏛 Naturmuseum Senckenberg
Senckenberganlage 25. **Tel** (069) 754 20. ◯ 9am–5pm Mon, Tue, Thu & Fri, 9am–8pm Wed, 9am–6pm Sat & Sun. 🈳

This museum, near the university, is one of the best natural history museums in Germany. Besides a vast collection of plants and animals, including dinosaur skeletons, it contains human and animal mummies from Egypt.

Environs
Hanau, 30 km (19 miles) east of Frankfurt, is the birthplace of the Grimm brothers. An exhibition devoted to their lives and work is held at the local history museum, in Philippsruhe, a Baroque palace.

The Deutsches Architekturmuseum, in Schaumainkai

Frankfurt – Städelsches Kunstinstitut

The founder of this excellent museum, banker Johann Friedrich Städel, left his art collection to the town in 1815. Since then, the museum has grown through acquisitions and donations, and now contains many masterpieces from seven centuries of European art. It moved to a Neo-Renaissance building in 1878, on the picturesque "museum embankment" by the Main. In the 1920s it acquired the Hohenzollern collection from Sigmaringen. The museum is undergoing renovation and new buildings are under construction, including a subterranean exhibition hall for contemporary art.

Ideal Portrait of a Woman (c.1480)
Simonetta Vespucci, mistress of Giuliano Medici, is the subject of this painting by Sandro Botticelli. Her pendant belonged at the time to the Medici collection.

Ecce Homo
Members of the family who commissioned this painting from Hieronymus Bosch also originally figured in it, but they were later painted over and now only a few figures are partially visible.

First floor

★ Lucca Madonna
This small painting by Jan van Eyck, which evokes an intimate and intensely private atmosphere, takes its name from its former owner, Charles Ludwig de Bourbon, Duke of Lucca.

KEY

- 19th-century paintings
- 20th-century paintings
- German, Dutch and Flemish 17th- and 18th-century paintings
- Italian, French and Spanish 17th- and 18th-century paintings
- German and Dutch 14th–16th-century paintings
- Italian 14th–16th-century paintings

Around 100,000 prints and drawings, dating from the 14th century to the present day and making up one of Germany's most valuable collections, are exhibited in this exhibition hall.

Main entrance

Library

★ **The Geographer** (1669)
Although the signature on the painting is not genuine, there is no doubt that this picture, depicting a scholar at work, is the work of Jan Vermeer van Delft.

VISITORS' CHECKLIST

Schaumainkai 63.
Tel *(069) 605 09 80.*
☐ *10am–6pm Tue–Sun,*
10am–9pm Wed & Thu.
📷 *(free Tue.)* 🔗 🖼 📷 📷 📷
www.staedelmuseum.de

★ **Blinding of Samson** (1636)
Rembrandt's dramatic painting depicts the violent blinding of Samson by the Philistines after Delilah cut off his hair.

Second floor

GALLERY GUIDE

The ground floor is used for changing exhibitions of prints and drawings, as well as a book store and a museum shop The first floor is devoted to 19th- and 20th-century art and the second floor to the Old Masters. The floorplan may change when new buildings open in 2012.

Pilgrimage to the Isle of Cythera (c.1710)
Jean-Antoine Watteau painted three pictures on this theme, inspired by Dancourt's play The Three Sisters. The museum holds the earliest of the three, which shows a Flemish influence.

Ground floor

Orchestra Players (1870–74)
Edgar Degas, not completely satisfied with his painting, retrieved it from its owner. In 1874, he cropped it on three sides, added a bit at the top and repainted the entire painting.

STAR EXHIBITS

★ Lucca Madonna

★ Blinding of Samson

★ The Geographer

Darmstadt ⑰

Road map C5. 🏛 138,000. 🚆
ℹ️ *Luisencenter, Luisenplatz 5
(06151-134 513); for tickets only
(06151-279 99 99).* 🎭 *Frühlingsfest
(Mar/Apr), Schlossgrabenfest (May),
Heinerfest (early Jul), Herbstfest (Oct).*
www.darmstadt.de

The earliest historical records
of Darmstadt, which was
probably named after Dari-
mund, a Frankonian settler,
date from the 12th century.
Until 1479, the castle and the
town belonged to the Counts
von Katzenelnbogen, and
later to Hessian landgraves.
In 1567, the Landgraves von
Hessen-Darmstadt chose
Darmstadt as their residence,
and they continued to live
here until 1918.

To the north of the old
town stands the **Residenzschloss**, initially a ducal
palace, and from 1806 residence of the Landgraves von
Hessen-Darmstadt. The Re-
naissance-Baroque complex is
centred around three courtyards. The earlier medieval
castle, which stood on the
same site, burned down in
1546. The present palace was
created in stages, with its
earliest parts, the Renaissance
wings, dating from 1567–97.
The Glockenbau has a 35-bell
carillon which can be heard
every half hour; it was completed in 1663. Further modifications, planned in 1715–30,
were never completed. Two

Baroque wings, the so-called
Neubau or Neuschloss (new
castle), surround older buildings to the south and west.
The Schloss was bombed in
World War II and subsequently rebuilt. Today it houses the
provincial and university
library, while the Glockenbau
is home to the fascinating
Schlossmuseum (castle
museum). As well as a
splendid collection of
coaches and furniture,
it contains the famous
Darmstädter Madonna
(1526), by Holbein.

Also worth seeing,
the late-Renaissance
Rathaus (town hall),
built in 1588–90, sur-
vived World War II.
The 15th-century choir
of the **Stadtkirche** has
an enormous monu-
ment (1587) to Magda-
lena zur Lippe, first
wife of Landgrave
Georg I the Pious. To
the southwest of the
Stadtkirche stands the
Altes Pädagog, built
in 1629 as an educa-
tional establishment.

To the north of the Schloss
is the **Hessisches Landesmuseum** (regional museum of
Hesse), erected in 1892–
1905. Its collection includes
artifacts dating from the Roman era to the 20th century.
The museum also has an
excellent natural history section, whose exhibits include
the impressive skeleton of a

**Statue on the door
of the Behrens-
Haus in Darmstadt**

mammoth as well as birds of
every species native to
southern Hesse. Set in the park
behind the museum is the
Baroque Prinz-Georg-Palais
(1710), which houses the
**Großherzoglich-Hessische
Porzellansammlung**, an
extensive porcelain collection.

The last Grand Duke of
Hesse, Ernst Ludwig, was
an important patron of the
Jugendstil, the German
Art Nouveau movement.
He initiated the build-
ing of an exhibition
and residential com-
plex, the **Mathilden-
höhe**, which was
established in 1901 in
the grounds of the
former ducal park, to
serve the existing
artists' colony led by
Joseph Maria Olbrich.
Olbrich designed the
Ernst-Ludwig-Haus,
which now houses
the **Museum Küns-
tlerkolonie**, an exhi-
bition space for the
colony's artists, as
well as the famous
Hochzeitsturm
(wedding tower), erected in
1907–8 to celebrate the Grand
Duke's wedding. The
Behrens-Haus, designed by
the Hamburg architect Peter
Behrens, is sober in contrast.
The Orthodox church of **St
Mary Magdalene** was built in
1897–9 by the Russian architect Leonti Nikolayevich
Benois, in honour of Alice,
wife of the last tsar of Russia
and sister of Ernst Ludwig.

🏛 **Schlossmuseum**
Residenzschloss, Marktplatz 15.
Tel (06151) 240 35. 🕐 10am–5pm
Fri–Sun. 📷 obligatory.

🏛 **Hessisches
Landesmuseum**
Friedensplatz 1. **Tel** (06151) 16 57
03. 🕐 10am–5pm Tue & Thu–Sat,
10am–8pm Wed, 11am–5pm Sun.
📷 ⬤ closed for renovation
until 2012.

🏛 **Museum Künstlerkolonie**
Alexandraweg 26/Mathildenhöhe.
Tel (06151) 13 33 85. 🕐 10am–5pm
Tue–Sun. 📷

🏛 **Großherzoglich-Hessische
Porzellansammlung**
Schlossgartenstr. 10.
Tel (06151) 71 32 33.
🕐 10am–5pm Fri–Sun.

Hochzeitsturm and Orthodox Church in Mathildenhöhe, Darmstadt

For hotels and restaurants in this region see pp508–10 and pp546–8

The Carolingian Torhalle (gate-house) of the Kloster (abbey) in Lorsch

Lorsch ⑱

Road map B5. 🏠 10,700. ℹ️
Marktplatz 1 (06251-175 26 0).

This small town is mainly known for the **Kloster**, a Benedictine abbey first founded in 764 by Chrodegang of Metz and one of the most important cultural and intellectual centres in Europe in the Carolingian era. It reached the peak of its power in the 8th–13th centuries, before being sold to the Archbishop of Mainz in 1232. The Benedictines were forced to leave, and in their place the Cistercians arrived. The monastery was dissolved during the Reformation, and in 1621 the Spanish Army destroyed and plundered the greater part of the complex.

Fragments of the 13th-century nave, the towers and the gate-house, dating from c.790, are all that has survived. The original 8th-century church, a basilica without transept, burned down in 1090 and was rebuilt in the 12th century. The original crypt is the burial place of Ludwig II the German, the first ruler of the Eastern Franks. The **Torhalle** (gate-house) is one of the most important architectural remains of the Carolingian period, and it was listed as a UNESCO World Heritage Site in 1991. Its lower section is made up of three arcades, equal in height and width, modelled on Roman triumphal arches. The first-floor

quarters above were probably used as a guest room or courtroom, and from the 14th century they served as a chapel. Remains of the original wall paintings are still visible here. The façade is decorated with red and white stone mosaics, which were inspired by Franco-Merovingian art. The vertical divides, created by pilasters and entablature, are copies of ancient designs – an architectural feature typical of the Carolingian Renaissance. The chapel's high roof and vaults date from the 14th century.

Michelstadt ⑲

Road map B5. 🏠 16,000.
ℹ️ *Marktplatz 1 (06061-194 33).*
🏠 *Bienenmarkt (Whitsun).*

Michelstadt, set among the hills of the Odenwald, is first mentioned in historical records in 741. From the 13th century the town belonged to the von Erbach family (the future Counts von Erbach).

The town has preserved many historic half-timbered houses and presents a typical image of medieval Germany. The 16th-century **Kellerei** is built around the remains of an earlier castle dating from 970. It now houses a regional museum. The sight most popular with photographers is the half-timbered **Rathaus** (town hall), dating from 1484, with its three towers and an

open ground-floor gallery. Nearby stands the late-Gothic, 15th-century **Pfarrkirche St Michael** (parish church of St Michael). Inside are some interesting epitaphs including the double tombstone of Philipp I and Georg I, dating from the late 15th century. A true rarity is the 18th-century **synagogue**, which escaped being burned by the National Socialists in 1938.

In the Steinbach district of Michelstadt stands the **Einhardsbasilika**, a church dating from around 821. The first church built on this site, at the initiative of Einhard, a courtier of Charlemagne, was a small, pillared and vaulted basilica with a short choir ending with a rounded apse. Under the eastern section is a crypt. The parts which remain to this day include the main nave, the north aisle with an apse and the crypt which holds precious religious relics.

Environs
In **Fürstenau**, situated about 1 km (0.6 mile) northwest of Michelstadt, is a beautiful complex including the Altschloss (old palace), remodelled from a medieval castle, the Neuschloss (new palace), dating from 1810, the park and its garden pavilions.

Erbach, 5 km (3 miles) south of Michelstadt, became famous as a centre for the art of ivory carving. In No. 1 Otto-Glenz-Straße is the Deutsches Elfenbeinmuseum (German ivory museum), which is devoted to this craft. Other attractions in this town include the overbearing Baroque Schloss (castle) and its interesting art collection.

The Carolingian Einhardsbasilika in Michelstadt-Steinbach

NORTH RHINE–WESTPHALIA

O *riginally consisting of two distinct provinces with somewhat diverging histories, the region of North Rhine-Westphalia today has its own strong identity. It encompasses the vast valley of the Ruhr river, rich in mineral deposits, where over the past 200 years huge conurbations have developed, comprising dozens of industrial cities that are gradually merging into one another.*

As a province, the North Rhineland, situated along the lower Rhine valley, goes back to Roman times. In the Middle Ages most of this area was ruled by the Bishops of Köln. The North Rhineland cities grew and prospered thanks to their trade links, and in the 19th century they became major centres of mining and heavy industry.

Westphalia forms the eastern part of the land. Once a Saxon territory, its history was often intertwined with that of the Rhineland. Only its western end has been heavily industrialized.

North Rhine-Westphalia is not the largest of the German regions, but with a population of nearly 18 million it is the most heavily populated one. It is often thought that the region, and in particular the heavily industrialized Ruhr valley, has little to offer to its visitors, but this is a mistaken belief. Its splendid past has left many priceless historic monuments and more recently, thanks to great investment, its industrial cities have transformed themselves into attractive cultural centres. The history of towns such as Bonn, Aachen, Cologne (Köln) and Xanten goes back to Roman times, and they have preserved much of their ancient heritage to this day. Evidence of Romanesque art, which flourished in the Rhineland, is today apparent in numerous impressive abbeys dotted throughout the region and in the churches of Cologne, which also boasts the colossal Gothic Dom.

Much of North Rhine-Westphalia is rural, and the region offers thousands of kilometres of tracks for walking in the Teutoburg Forest and in the Northern Eifel mountains, as well as splendid conditions for watersports and fishing in the Sauerland. It also has surprisingly good ski slopes, such as in the Rothaar Mountains.

A typical lowland landscape near Xanten, in the Rhineland

◁ The imposing Gothic Kölner Dom (Cologne cathedral), lit up at night

Exploring North Rhine-Westphalia

Despite being heavily industrialized, the land of
North Rhine-Westphalia has many attractions for
visitors. At least two days should be set aside to
admire the historic treasures in Cologne, while those
who prefer museums – or shopping – might allocate
more time for Düsseldorf. The towns of Bonn, Aachen
and Münster should also feature on every visitor's
schedule. The best areas for rest and relaxation are the
mountain ranges of the Eifel and the Teutoburg Forest,
ideally suited for walking and cycling holidays.

SEE ALSO

• *Where to Stay* pp511–13
• *Where to Eat* pp549–51

Burg Altena in the Sauerland

SIGHTS AT A GLANCE

GETTING AROUND

There are international airports at Düsseldorf, Köln–Bonn
(Konrad-Adenauer-Flughafen) and at Münster–Osnabrück.
North Rhine-Westphalia has the highest density of motorways anywhere in Germany, making it easy to travel
between cities, and providing links with other German
regions, Belgium and the Netherlands.

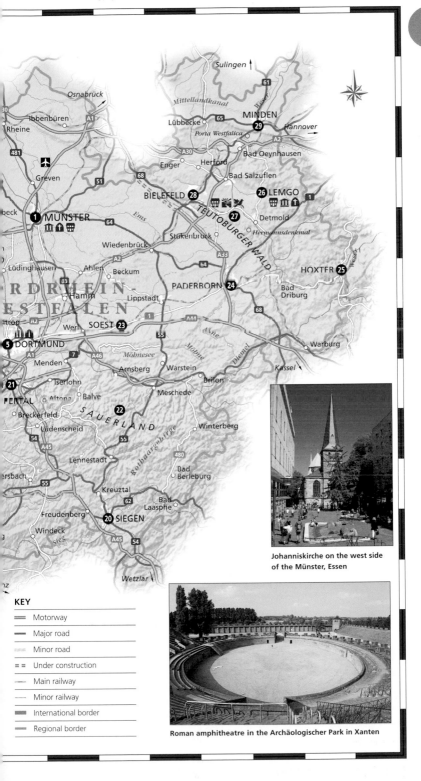

Johanniskirche on the west side
of the Münster, Essen

Roman amphitheatre in the Archäologischer Park in Xanten

KEY

▬▬	Motorway
▬	Major road
▬ ▬	Minor road
═ ═	Under construction
⊶⊶	Main railway
─ ─	Minor railway
▬▬	International border
▬	Regional border

Münster ●

Münster and its surroundings were already inhabited in Roman times, but its history proper started in the 9th century, with the establishment of a bishopric. Town status was granted in 1137, and in the 13th century Münster joined the Hanseatic League. In 1648 the Westphalian Peace Treaty was signed here, ending the Thirty Years' War. Münster's Westfälische Wilhelms-Universität (1773) is one of Germany's largest universities. World War II saw 90 percent of the old town laid to ruins, but most of it has now been rebuilt.

🏛 Erbdrostenhof

Salzstraße 38. ● *Closed to the public.*
This beautiful mansion was skilfully positioned diagonally across a corner site. Designed by Johann Conrad Schlaun, it was built in 1753–7, and despite destruction in World War II it still enchants with its "wavy", late-Baroque façade.

🏛 Rathaus

Prinzipalmarkt. **Friedenssaal**
Tel *(0251) 492 27 24.*
◯ *10am–5pm Tue–Fri, 10am–4pm Sat & Sun.* ● *25 Dec.* 🖼
The imposing Gothic town hall, the pride of Münster, was almost completely destroyed during World War II. After its splendid reconstruction, it is again a major draw for visitors. The only parts that had escaped destruction were the furnishings of the main council chamber, which have been returned to their rightful place after the rebuilding work. It

Houses on Prinzipalmarkt, reconstructed in the medieval style

was here that on 15 May 1648 part of the Westphalian Treaty was signed, ending the Thirty Years' War.

🛡 Lambertikirche

Prinzipalmarkt.
St Lamberti is an excellent example of the hall-churches characteristic of Westphalia. It was built in 1375–1450, but the openwork finial of the tower dates from 1887. The cages hanging on the tower held the bodies of the leading Anabaptists, following the crushing of their commune in 1536. It is also worth taking a look at the relief depicting the *Tree of Jesse*, above the southwest entrance, and the figures of the apostles (c.1600) by Johann Koess.

🏛 Dom St Paulus

Domkammer Domplatz.
Tel *(0251) 495 333.*
◯ *11am–4pm Tue–Sun.* 🖼
The most precious historic relic in Münster

is undeniably its massive St Paulus' cathedral, built in 1225–65 and representing a transitional style between late Romanesque and early-Gothic. The vast basilica has two transepts, two choirs and two massive towers. The northern cloister was added in the 14th century, and in the 16th–17th centuries the passage that runs around the presbytery acquired a ring of chapels. In the vestibule stands a group of 13th-century sculptures. Especially worth seeing are the two altars by Gerhard Gröninger (1st half of the 17th century), the early 16th-century stained-glass windows brought here from Marienfeldand monuments of many bishops. The cathedral's best-known treasure is the astronomical clock (1540), with paintings by Ludger tom Ring the Elder and sculptures by Johann Brabender. At noon, figures show the Magi paying tribute to the infant Jesus to the sounds of the carillon.

🏛 Westfälisches Landesmuseum für Kunst und Kulturgeschichte

Domplatz 10. **Tel** *(0251) 590 701.*
◯ *10am–6pm Tue–Sun (to 9pm Thu).*
The Westphalian regional museum specializes mainly in Gothic art, with a large collection of sculptures and altars rescued in World War II. Its most noteworthy exhibits include the works by Heinrich and Johann Brabender. The upstairs galleries show works by Conrad von Soest and the tom Ring family. Contemporary art is represented by, among others, August Macke's work. The museum is moving to a new building in 2012, and until then there is a reduced exhibition in the present venue.

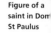
Figure of a saint in Dom St Paulus

🛡 Überwasserkirche

Überwasserkirchplatz.
The Liebfrauenkirche (Church of Our Lady) is popularly named Überwasserkirche (church above the water), after

The beautifully restored façade of the late-Gothic Rathaus

The Baroque-Classical Schloss, residence of Münster's prince-bishops

the district on the banks of the tiny Aa river. This Gothic edifice was built in c.1340–46, on the site of a Romanesque Benedictine church. Inside are 16th-century votive paintings by Ludger and Hermann tom Ring

⚜ Residenzschloss

Schlossplatz 2.
This beautiful Baroque residence was built in 1767–87 by Prince-Bishop Maximilian Friedrich. It was designed by Johann Conrad Schlaun, a local master of Baroque architecture. Maximilian Friedrich started the redevelopment of Münster in the northern Baroque style. On his initiative the town acquired a large park, part of which was transformed into a botanical garden in 1803. After World War II, the castle was rebuilt and became the headquarters of Münster university.

⛬ Museum für Lackkunst

Windthorststraße 26. **Tel** (0251) 41 85 10. noon–8pm Tue, noon–6pm Wed–Sun & public holidays.
This unique museum, devoted to lacquer ware, has a good collection with items from around the world and from different periods, making a visit to the museum a treat for those interested in this craft.

Watermill in the open-air museum in Mühlenhof

⛨ Mühlenhof

Theo-Breider-Weg 1. **Tel** (0251) 98 12 00. Apr–Sep: 10am–6pm daily, Mar, Oct: 11am–4pm daily; Nov–Feb: 11am–4pm Sun–Fri.
This small but interesting open-air museum is situated on the banks of the pictur-esque Aasee, Münster's lake and main recreation area. Displayed are a number of rural dwellings with authentic furnishings and two mills (17th and 18th centuries).

⚜ Drostenhof

Wolbeck, Am Steintor 5.
Southeast of the town, in Wol-beck (now part of the city), is an original Renaissance mansion from the mid-16th century. Its exquisite gate-house leads into the court-yard of the mansion, which has original fireplaces, doors and ceiling paintings.

MUNSTER CITY CENTRE

Dom St Paulus ④
Erbdrostenhof ①
Lambertikirche ③
Museum für Lackkunst ⑦
Rathaus ②
Überwasserkirche ⑥
Westfälisches Landesmuseum für Kunst und Kultur-geschichte ⑤

0 metres 100
0 yards 100

Key to Symbols see back flap

VOSSGASSE
SPIEKERHOF
Überwasser-kirche ⑥
TIMPEN
Residenzschloss
ROGGEN MARKT
ALTER FISCHMARKT
BÜLT
Krameramtshaus
Dom St Paulus ④
Lamberti-kirche ③
ALTER STEINWEG
SALZSTRASSE
MAURITZSTR.
DOMPLATZ
MICHAELISPLATZ
Westfälisches Landesmuseum ⑤
PRINZIPALMARKT
Rathaus ②
Erbdrostenhof ①
EISENBAHNSTR.
KRUMMER TIMPEN
BISPINGHOF
KLEMENS-STRASSE
ROTHENBURG
Clemenskirche
Graphikmuseum Pablo Picasso
Flughafen 20km (12 miles)
WOLBECK
AM STADTGRABEN
AEGIDIISTRASSE
AEGIDIIKIRCH-PLATZ
BREITE GASSE
GRÜNE GASSE
KÖNIGSTRASSE
LUDGERISTRASSE
KLOSTERSTRASSE
VON-VINCKE-STRASSE
BAHNHOFSTR.
SCHÜTZENSTRASSE
Museum für Lackkunst ⑦
Mühlenhof
KANONENGRABEN
LUDGERIPLATZ
VERSPOEL
WINDTHORSTSTRASSE
SCHOLEMERSTRASSE
ENGELSTRASSE
Haupt-bahnhof

Münsterland ❷

The region stretching in a narrow strip to the
north of Münster is the land of horses and
Wasserburgen (moated castles). The castles
were surrounded by moats or built on islands
to give their owners protection in the surrounding lowlands. Almost 50 Wasserburgen have
survived, some converted into residences. Not
all are open to visitors as most remain to this
day in the hands of the family of the original
owners. The best way to tour the flat Münsterland region is by car or bicycle.

Vischering ②
The magnificent Burg Vischering is
one of the oldest and best-preserved castles in Westphalia.
Founded in 1270, it was extended
in the 16th and 17th centuries.

Schloss Raesfeld ⑤
The beautiful 17th-
century castle has
some original 14th-
century elements.
Particularly worth
seeing is the castle
chapel with its
Baroque altar.

Havixbeck ①
Two interesting castles are near this
small town: the Renaissance Haus
Havixbeck and the Renaissance-
Baroque Burg Hülshoff, birthplace
of and museum to the 19th-century
writer Annette von Droste-Hülshoff.

Enschede
Osnabrück
Coesfeld
Nottuln
Münster
Borken
Haltern
Lüdinghausen
Hamm
Dorsten
Marl
Hamm

**Schloss
Nordkirchen** ③
This vast moated castle,
nicknamed the "Westphalian
Versailles", was designed by
Gottfried Laurenz Pictorius and
built in 1703–34 for the
Plettenberg family.

Schloss Lembeck ④
In its present shape, the
Lembeck castle complex
is the result of Baroque
remodelling, under the
direction of Johann
Conrad Schlaun. Nearby
is a nature reserve.

| 0 km | | 16 |
| 0 miles | | 16 |

KEY

▬ Suggested route

▬ Scenic route

═ Other road

═ River, lake

❀ Viewpoint

TIPS FOR DRIVERS

Length of route: 97 km
(58 miles).
Stopping-off points: Every
town has inns, and there is a
hotel in Schloss Lembeck.
Suggestions: All castles are open
to visitors Tuesday to Sunday, with
the exception of Nordkirchen,
which opens only at weekends.

Kleve (Cleves) ❸

Road map A3. 🏛 *50,000.* 🚗 �'
ℹ️ *Werftstr. 1 (02821-89 50 90).*

The town of Kleve is named after the high cliff, on which a castle was built in the 10th century. Around it a settlement developed, which became a town in 1242. It was ruled by the dukes of Kleve, whose ambitions were far greater than the size of their dominions and reached their peak in 1539, when Anne of Cleves married the English King Henry VIII.

During World War II Kleve lost most of its historic buildings. One that has survived to this day is the imposing Gothic church of the Assumption of the Virgin Mary, **St Maria Himmelfahrt** (1341–1426). It has remains of the high altar, dating from 1510–13, with reliefs by Henrik Douvermann and Jakob Dericks, as well as beautiful monuments and epitaphs to the von Kleve dukes. Equally worth seeing is the former Franciscan **St Mariä Empfängnis**, a Gothic twin-nave hall-church from the first half of the 15th century. Its noteworthy features include the Gothic stalls (1474) and a magnificent Baroque pulpit (1698). The well-preserved ducal castle of **Schwanenburg** was remodelled twice: in Gothic style in the late 15th century, and in Baroque style in 1636–66. Testifying to former splendour are the parks established in the mid-17th century by Johann Moritz von Nassau. The most beautiful of these is the **Tiergarten** (animal garden). **Haus Koekkoek**, located nearby, once belonged to the Romantic painter, Barend Cornalis Koekkoek, after whom it was named.

🏛 **Schwanenburg**
Am Schlossberg. **Tel** *(02821) 22 884.* ⬜ *Apr–Oct: 11am–5pm Mon–Fri, 10am–5pm Sat & Sun; Nov–Mar: 11am–5pm Sat & Sun.* 📷

Environs
The suspension bridge across the Rhine – at 1,228 m (4,028 ft) the longest such structure in Germany – connects Kleve with **Emmerich**. Worth a visit here is the Martinskirche, with its exquisite, late-10th-century shrine of St Willibrod.

Twelve km (7 miles) to the southeast of Kleve lies the charming town of **Kalkar** which, in around 1500, was home to the famous Kalkar School specializing in wood-carving. The church of St Nicolai has superb furnishings dating from the same period.

Six km (4 miles) southeast stands **Moyland**, a moated castle. It houses a modern art collection, which belongs to the brothers von der Grinten and includes over 4,000 works by the artist Joseph Beuys.

Xanten ❹

Road map B4. 🏛 *19,500.* 🚗 �'
ℹ️ *Kurfürstenstr. 9 (02801-983 00).*

The history of Xanten goes back to the Romans, who founded the settlement of *Colonia Ulpia Traiana* near the local garrison. The present town, however, did not rise out of the ruins of the Roman town. It was established nearby, around the memorial church built on top of the grave

The Hafentempel in the Archäologischer Park in Xanten

of the martyr St Viktor. It was named *ad sanctos* (by the saints), soon to be shortened to Xanten. A powerful town in the Middle Ages, Xanten also features in the Nibelung myth, and was said to be the birthplace of Siegfried.

Undoubtedly the most important historic building in the town is the **Dom St Viktor**, built on the graves of St Viktor and members of the Thebian Legion. The surviving Gothic cathedral dates from 1263–1517. It is worth taking a look at the Gothic sculptures standing by the pillars of the main nave, the shrine of St Victor (1129), the early-Gothic stalls (c.1240) and, above all, the exquisite Marienaltar by Henrik Douvermann. Equally fascinating are the collegial buildings and the cloister holding the tombs and epitaphs of the canons.

Xanten also has many pretty old houses, mainly clustered around the central market square. Another sight worth visiting is the **Klever Tor**, a magnificent double town-gate, dating from the late 14th century, in the northwest of the town. The **Archäologischer Park**, on the site of the Roman town, and the **Römer Museum** display many reconstructed Roman public buildings including the impressive Hafentempel (harbour temple).

🏛 **Archäologischer Park & Römer Museum**
Wardter Str. **Tel** *(02801) 29 99.* ⬜ *Mar–Oct: 9am–6pm daily; Nov: 9am–5pm daily; Dec–Feb: 10am–4pm daily.* 📷

The Gothic Dom St Victor in Xanten

The Young Horses by Emil Nolde, in the Museum am Ostwall

Dortmund **5**

Road map B4. 🏙 *600,000.* 🚊 🚌
ℹ *Königswall 18A (0231-18999222).*
🎭 *Dortmund à la carte (Jun), Dortmund aller art (Aug), Hansetage (Nov).*

The large city of Dortmund is famous not only for its excellent beer and highly developed industry, but also for its more than 1,000 years of history. In the Middle Ages, the town grew rich through trade and joined the Hanseatic League; after a period of decline it flourished again in the 19th century.

A walk through the small old town will take visitors to the **Museum für Kunst-und Kulturgeschichte** (museum for art and cultural history) with displays of interiors from various periods, including Secessionist designs by Joseph Maria Olbrich. A short distance from here is the **Petrikirche**, a Gothic 14th-century hall-church, whose greatest attraction is its high altar (1521), the work of Gilles, a master from Antwerp. Also noteworthy is the former Dominican **Propsteikirche**, with its exquisite late-Gothic main altar. A shortcut across the market square and along Ostenhellweg takes the visitor to two more churches: the **Reinoldikirche** and the **Marienkirche**. The former,

Statue on Alter Markt, in Dortmund

dedicated to St Reinold, the patron saint of Dortmund, has an early-Gothic 13th-century main body and a late-Gothic, 15th-century presbytery. It includes many Gothic sculptures and furnishings. The second one, the church of St Mary, is a 12th-century Romanesque structure. It has a magnificent main altar, by Conrad von Soest (1415–20) and a statue of the Madonna (c.1230). The **Museum am Ostwall** has an excellent modern art collection.

🏛 **Museum für Kunst-und Kulturgeschichte**
Hansastr. 3. **Tel** (0231) 502 55 22.
🕙 *10am–5pm Tue, Wed, Fri, Sun, 10am–8pm Thu, noon–5pm Sat.* 🎫

🏛 **Museum am Ostwall**
Ostwall 7. **Tel** (0231) 502 32 47.
🕙 *10am–6pm Tue, Wed; 10am–8pm Thu, Fri; 11am–6pm Sat & Sun.*

Environs
10 km (6 miles) northwest, in Waltrop, on the Dortmund-Ems Canal, is the Schiffshebewerk Henrichenburg, a hoist built in 1899 to lift ships.

Essen **6**

Road map B4. 🏙 *600,000.* 🚊
🚌 *Im Handelshof (am Hauptbahnhof 2) (0201-194 33).*
🎭 *Essen Original (Aug).*

It is hard to believe that this vast industrial metropolis has grown from a monastery, established in 852. The town owes its growth and promi-

nence to the Krupp family, who, over several generations from the mid-19th century, created the powerful German steel and arms industry.

The most important historic building in the town is the **Münster**, the former collegiate church of the canonesses. This unusual edifice consists of the 15th-century Gothic church of St John, an 11th-century atrium and the main church, which in turn has a Romanesque 11th-century frontage and a Gothic 14th– century main body. Without doubt the most precious object held by the church is the *Goldene Madonna*, a statue of the Virgin Mary with the Infant, made from sheet gold, probably c.980. The treasury has an outstanding collection of gold items from the Ottonian period.

Another important sight in Essen is the **Synagogue** built by Edmund Kömer in 1911–13. The largest synagogue in Germany, it managed to outlast the Third Reich and is now a place of commemoration.

Visitors who are interested in 20th-century architecture should see the church of **St Engelbert** in Fischerstraße, designed by Dominikus Metzendorf (1934–6), the town-garden in **Margarethenhöhe** built from 1909 to a design by Georg Metzendorf, and the opera house designed by the Finnish architect, Alvar Aalto.

Essen has much to offer to modern art enthusiasts. The **Museum Folkwang** boasts an excellent collection of 20th-century paintings, mainly German Expressionists. It also has a graphic arts section.

The **Grugapark** is a large green area with botanical gardens, zoo and the Gruga-halle, where major concerts are held. To the south of the centre, on the banks of the Baldeneysee, stands **Villa Hügel**, which belonged to the Krupp family until 1945. Today interesting art exhibitions are frequently hosted here. Further south, in **Werden**, is the former Benedictine church of St Ludger, consisting of a 13th-century body preceded by a 10th-century imperial frontage. The treasury holds many precious

The grand Villa Hügel, former home of the Krupp family in Essen

objects including a bronze crucifix from around 1060.

🏛 Museum Folkwang
Goethestr. 41. *Tel* (0201) 884 53 14. ◯ 10am–6pm Tue–Thu, Sat & Sun, 10am–10:30pm Fri. ● 1 Jan, Easter, 1 May, 24 & 31 Dec. 🏛

Environs
Visitors interested in technology should visit **Bochum**, which is also the seat of the excellent Ruhr-Universität. There are two excellent museums: the **Deutsches Bergbau-Museum** devoted to mining, and the **Eisenbahnmuseum** (railway museum) in Dahlhausen. Both have world-class exhibits.

Duisburg 🌐

Road map B4. 🏙 540,000. 🚆 🚌
🛈 Königstr. 86 (0203-285 44 11).

Duisburg, on the edge of the Ruhr region, underwent a period of rapid development in the 19th and 20th centuries. Once a small town, it became the world's largest inland harbour thanks to its location at the spot where the Ruhr flows into the Rhine.

The small old town was almost totally destroyed in World War II, but the 15th–century Gothic **Salvatorkirche** (church of St Saviour) has been rebuilt. Some of the town's greatest attractions are its museums. The **Wilhelm-Lehmbruck-Museum** focuses on the work of the sculptor Lehmbruck, who was born in Duisburg. The museum has an interesting collection of 20th–century sculptures, including works by famous

artists such as Salvador Dalí, Henry Moore, Max Ernst, Emil Nolde and Joseph Beuys. Also worth visiting is the **Museum der Deutschen Binnen-schifffahrt** with its collection of barges and inland waterway vessels. In the 16th century, Duisburg was the home of the famous geographer and cartographer Gerhard Mercator, whose collection of globes, maps and charts can now be seen in the **Kulture- und Stadthistorisches Museum**.

🏛 Wilhelm-Lehmbruck-Museum
Friedrich-Wilhelm-Str. 40. *Tel* (0203) 283 26 30. ◯ noon–7pm Wed, Fri, Sat; noon–9pm Thu; 11am–7pm Sun. 🏛

Environs
CentrO in **Oberhausen**, 14 km (9 miles) north of Duisburg, is the largest shopping and leisure complex in Europe.

Krefeld, 6 km (4 miles) southwest of Duisburg, has been a centre of silk fabric production from the 17th century, and the Deutsches Textilmuseum has over 20,000 exhibits, ranging from antiquity to the present day.

Wuppertal 🌐

Road map B4. 🏙 380,000. 🚆
🛈 Elberfeld, Informationszentrum am Döppersberg (0202-194 33); Rathaus Barmen (0202-563 66 88).

Wuppertal, capital of the Bergisches Land area, was created in 1929 by combining six towns strung along a 20-km (12 mile) stretch of the Wupper river. The towns are joined by the **Schwebebahn**, a monorail constructed in 1900. Carriages are suspended from a single rail, which rests on tall pillars.

The most interesting of the former towns is Elberfeld, with a museum of clocks, and the **Von-der-Heydt–Museum** of 19th- and 20th-century German art. The museum in the Friedrich-Engels-Haus in Barmen (Engelsstr. 10) is worth seeing, and Neviges has a Baroque pilgrimage church, with a much-visited miraculous picture of the Virgin Mary.

🏛 Von-der-Heydt-Museum
Elberfeld, Turmhof 8. *Tel* (0202) 563 62 31. ◯ 11am–6pm Tue, Wed, Fri–Sun, 11am–8pm Thu. 🏛 🏛 🏛

The unusual monorail, linking Wuppertal's six constituent towns

Düsseldorf 🟢

Düsseldorf, the administrative capital of North Rhine-Westphalia, received its municipal rights in 1288. From the late 14th century it was the capital of the Duchy of Berg, and from 1614 that of the Palatine. The town owes much to Duke Johann Wilhelm (called Jan Wellem), who lived here in 1690–1716. One of the most important industrial and cultural centres in the Rhine Valley, this European metropolis has a renowned university, superb museums and theatres and, as the German capital of fashion, many excellent shops.

🏛 Museum Kunst Palast

Ehrenhof 4–5. *Tel (0211) 899 02 00.* ⭘ *11am–6pm Tue–Sun (until 9pm Thu).* 🖼 📷 ✅ 🖥

This art museum is one of the most interesting in Germany, with a collection of paintings dating from the 16th to the 20th centuries, including works by Rubens, Cranach and Dutch masters of the 17th century. It also holds a large collection of paintings by the Düsseldorf Academy, active in the first half of the 19th century, whose best known artists were Peter von Cornelius and Friedrich Wilhelm Schadow.

🏯 Altstadt

The small old town area suffered severe damage during World War II. Among the surviving monuments it is worth seeing some of the beautiful town houses and the late-Gothic **Rathaus** (town hall), built in the years 1570–73. In

front of it stands a famous equestrian statue of the Elector Jan Wellem, built in 1703–11 by Gabriel Grupello. The Düsseldorf castle, burned down in 1872, only has the **Schlossturm** (castle tower) remaining, which now houses a museum of navigation. Another building worth visiting is the Baroque, post-Jesuit **Pfarrkirche St Andreas** (parish church of St Andrew), from the years 1622–9. It has a central ducal mausoleum complex situated behind the presbytery, where the remains of Jan Wellem and others are kept. The **Lambertuskirche**, the former collegiate church of St Lambertus, is a Gothic hall-church with a tall front tower, built in 1288–1394. Some valuable furnishings have survived, including the Gothic sacramentarium and important Gothic ducal tombs, such as that of Duke Wilhelm V, from 1595–9.

Detail from the façade of the Lambertuskirche

🏛 Kunstsammlung Nordrhein-Westfalen

K20: Grabbeplatz 5. *Tel (0211) 838 11 30.* ⭘ *10am–6pm Tue–Fri, 11am–6pm Sat & Sun. 10am–10pm 1st Wed of the month.* **K21:** Ständehausstr. 1. *Tel (0211) 838 18 30.* ⭘ *As for K20.* ⚫ *24, 25 & 31 Dec.* 🖼 📷 📷 ✅

The art collection of the state of North Rhine-Westphalia is enormous, featuring

mainly the work of 20th-century artists. Particularly valuable are 88 paintings by Paul Klee, which were acquired in 1960. There are also works by Wassily Kandinsky, Marcel Duchamp, Piet Mondrian and Pablo Picasso. The gallery at Grabbeplatz is known as K20, and a second building at Ständehäusstr. 1, where contemporary art is exhibited, is known as K21. Temporary exhibitions are held nearby, at Kunsthalle Düsseldorf, which is at No. 4 Grabbeplatz.

🏛 Hetjens-Museum

Schulstraße 4. *Tel (0211) 899 42 10.* ⭘ *11am–5pm Tue & Thu–Sun, 11am–9pm Wed.* 🖼

This museum, in the Nesselrode Palace, is the oldest German museum devoted to ceramics. Visitors can learn about techniques for producing faïence and porcelain, and see global exhibits from prehistory to the present day.

🏯 Königsallee

The "kings' avenue", often just referred to as Kö, was laid out at the beginning of the 19th century, along the edge of the old city moat. The Kö is lined with expensive shops. Luxurious galleries, exclusive boutiques, department stores, fashion houses and shopping malls are interspersed with bars and restaurants. Particularly noteworthy is the Art Nouveau Warenhaus Tietz (now housing the Kaufhof-Galleria department store), which was built in 1907–9, to a design by Joseph Maria Olbrich.

🍀 Hofgarten

Schloss Jägerhof. **Goethemuseum**: Jacobistraße 2. *Tel (0211) 899 62 62.* ⭘ *11am–5pm Tue–Fri & Sun, 1–5pm Sat.* 🖼

This charming park, originally laid out in 1769 for Elector Karl Theodor, was recreated in the English style at the beginning of the 19th century. The park is a marvellous setting for Schloss Jägerhof, a Baroque hunting lodge dating from the years 1752–63 and built according to a design by

Interior of the Pfarrkirche St Andreas

The late-Baroque Schloss Benrath

VISITORS' CHECKLIST

Road map B4. 🚄 *600,000.* 🚉 *Konrad-Adenauer-Platz.* ✈ *north of the centre (0211 42 10).* ⓘ *Immermannstr. 65B (am Hauptbahnhof), Marktstraße (0211 1720 2844).* 🎭 🎉 *Bootsausstellung (Jan), Rosenmontagsumzug (Carnival Mon), Größte Kirmes am Rhein (end Jul).* **www**.duesseldorf.de

Johann Josef Couven and Nicolas de Pigage. The castle was rebuilt after World War II. It now houses the Goethe-Museum, holding memorabilia and documents related to the writer's life, and a collection of 18th-century art, funded by Ernst Schneider.

🏛 Heinrich-Heine-Institut

Bilker Su. 12–14. **Tel** *(0211) 099 55 71.* ◻ *11am–5pm Tue–Fri & Sun, 1–5pm Sat.* 🈂
The celebrated German poet Heinrich Heine was born in Düsseldorf in 1797. This institute was established to preserve his legacy, to conduct research into his work and to organize exhibitions. Düsseldorf's university and a number of streets have also been named after Heine.

⛰ Schloss Benrath

Benrather Schlossallee. **Tel** *(0211) 899 38 32.* ◻ *11am–5pm Tue–Sun.* 🈂🈲
Benrath, part of Düsseldorf since 1929, is home to this beautiful Neo-Classical hunting palace, built for the electors of the Palatine in 1755–73 by Nicolas de Pigage. Decor, beautiful furnishings and an extensive park and gardens have survived.

The former city moat which runs alongside Königsallee

Kaiserswerth

Today a part of Düsseldorf, this area prides itself on a history dating back to the 8th century. Its Pfarrkirche St Suitbertus, a Romanesque basilica from the 12th century, has the magnificent 13th-century golden relic of its patron saint. There are also the ruins of a palace, built in the 12th century for Friedrich I Barbarossa.

Environs

The "Neanderthal" part of the Düssel valley was originally named after the poet Joachim Neander. It became famous in 1856, when the remains of apelike creatures were uncovered in a cave. A museum dedicated to these "Neanderthal Men" is located in Mettman, 17 km (11 miles) east of Düsseldorf.

DUSSELDORF CITY CENTRE

0 metres   500

0 yards   500

Key to Symbols *see back flap*

Neuss ⑩

Road map B4. 👤 150,000. 🚉 🚌
ℹ️ *Rathausarkaden, Büchel 6
(02131-403 77 95).*

The history of Neuss goes
back to Roman days. The
town developed around a
Bernhardine monastery, which
became a girls' boarding school
in the 12th century. The most
famous building is the magnificent 13th-century Romanesque
Münster St Quirinus. After a
fire in 1741, a Baroque dome
with a statue of St Quirin, the
patron saint, was added to the
eastern tower of the church.
Also worth seeing is the
Obertor (upper gate), built in
1200, one of the mightiest
gates in the Rhineland.

Dormagen ⑪

Road map B4. 👤 62,000. 🚉 🚌
ℹ️ *Dormagen, Schlossstraße 2–4
(02133-276 28 15).* 🎭 *Freilichtspiele
in Zons (Jun–Sep).*

This medium-sized town,
which principally relies on its
chemical industry, would not
be found in a guide book
were it not for two remarkable historic monuments
within the city limits. On the
banks of the Rhine lies the
fortified customs town of
Zons, established around
1373–1400 at the instigation
of archbishop Friedrich von
Saarwerden. This small regular, four-sided fortress has
survived in excellent condition. The buildings in the
settlement are mainly from a
later time, but the walls and
gates, as well as the ruined
castle **Schloss Friedestrom** are
among the most fascinating
examples of Medieval for-
tifications in the Rhine Valley.
Equally interesting is an excursion to **Knechtsteden**,
west of Dormagen, where an
amazing monastery was built
for the Norbertines in the
12th century. Set amid woods
and orchards, the vast twin-
choired basilica has mighty
towers in the eastern section.
There are impressive murals,
including a 12th-century mural
of Christ in the western apsis,
as well as attractive cloisters.

The Gothic post-Cistercian Bergischer Dom in Altenberg

Solingen ⑫

Road map B4. 👤 165,000. 🚉 🚌 ℹ️
*Clemens-Galerien Mummstr. 10 (0212-
290 36 01).* 🎭 *Frühjahrskirmes (Mar).*

Solingen is almost synonymous with its famous factory,
where quality scissors and
knives are produced. The
main attraction in town is the
Klingenmuseum, which
shows cutting tools from the
Stone Age to the present day.

Environs
Remscheid, 7 km (4 miles) east
of Solingen has the Röntgen-
museum, dedicated to the
German Nobel Prize winner
Wilhelm Röntgen, who was
born here and discovered the

Baroque façade of the local
Heimatmuseum in Remscheid

X-ray. One of the most beautiful buildings is the Heimatmuseum with displays of
typical regional interiors.
Schloss Burg, on the Wupper river, is the 12th-century
fortress of the von Berg family. Many times rebuilt, it now
houses a museum.

Altenberg ⑬

Road map B4. 👤 5,745. 🚉 🚌
ℹ️ *Bergisch-Gladbacher-Str. 2, 51519
Odenthal (02202-71 01 31).*

Altenberg near Odenthal has
preserved its **Bergischer
Dom**, a former Cistercian
cathedral and one of the most
important destinations for pilgrims. Built in 1259–1379, it is
also one of the most beautiful
Gothic buildings in Germany.
In accordance with their
rules, the Cistercians built the
church without a tower. The
interior is furnished with
Gothic works of art and has
stunningly beautiful stained-
glass windows, the altar of
the *Coronation of the Blessed
Virgin Mary* from the late
15th century, a beautiful 14th-
century *Annunciation* and a
sacrarium (1490). After the
dissolution of the Order in

1803, the cathedral suffered a turbulent history. It now serves as a church for both Catholics and Protestants.

Children also enjoy a visit to Altenberg because of its **Märchenwald** (fairy-tale wood), an enchanted forest, with interactive scenes and statues representing all the most popular fairy-tales.

Köln (Cologne) ⑭

See pp398–9.

Aachen ⑮

Road map A4. 🏘 ⸝254,000. 🚂 ⛴
ℹ️ *Elisenbrunnen (0241-180 29 60).*
📅 *Frühjahrstheil (Apr), horse-riding competitions CHIO (Jul), Europamarkt des Kunsthandwerks (Sep).*

Aachen owes its fame to its hot springs, whose healing powers were already highly rated by the Romans when they established baths here in the 1st–2nd centuries AD. The name of the town, *aquae grani* or Aquisgrani also relates to the source.

The settlement grew mainly in the 8th century, when Charlemagne chose it as his principal residence in 768. He built a huge palace complex with chapel, cloistered courtyard and hall for himself.

When Charlemagne was crowned emperor in 800, Aachen became the capital of the Holy Roman Empire. Although the town soon lost this title, it remained an important destination for pilgrims because of the valuable relics brought here by Charlemagne. From the 10th to the 14th centuries, all German kings were crowned in the palace chapel.

In the 18th and 19th centuries, Aachen gained great importance as a spa. Many magnificent buildings dating from this splendid era have long since vanished. Further destruction was inflicted by World War II, yet some historic monuments have survived. The most

important of these, in the centre of the old town, is the **Pfalz** *(see pp396–7)*, a complex of buildings belonging to Charlemagne's former palace. They include a cathedral with a palace chapel and a hall which was rebuilt as the **Rathaus**.

In the old town, not far from the cathedral complex, is the church of St Folian, where a Gothic Madonna dating from 1411 has survived. A short distance south from here stands the Elisenbrunnen (fountain of St Elizabeth), an exceptionally beautiful building where mineral water can be taken. It was built in 1822–7 according to designs by Johann Peter Cremer and Karl Friedrich Schinkel.

After admiring the attractive houses around the central market square visitors can enjoy the **Couven-Museum**. Based in an historic middle-class town house, it has an interesting collection dedicated to the life of the bourgeoisie in the 18th and 19th centuries. There is also a collection of ceramic tiles from the 17th–19th centuries.

The house where Israel Berr Josaphat Reuter established the first-ever news agency in 1850 (transferred to London a year later) now houses the **Internationales Zeitungsmuseum**, devoted to the history of the

The Neo-Classical building which houses the casino in Aachen's spa park

Statue of David Hansemann

press, with over 100,000 newspapers from the 17th century to today. The building has undergone an extensive renovation to accomodate temporary exhibition space and lecture halls. It is also worth visiting the **Suermondt-Ludwig-Museum**, a short distance beyond the town centre, which has a great collection of art from the Middle Ages until the present day, including some beautiful sculptures and paintings from the 17th century.

To the northeast of the old town extends the spa district of Aachen. Here, visitors can stroll through the spa park or spend an evening at the casino. Aachen also has much to offer lovers of modern art: the Ludwig-Forum für Internationale Kunst hosts interesting exhibitions.

🏛 **Internationales Zeitungsmuseum**
Markt 39/Haus Löwenstein.
Tel (0241) 432 49 10.
🕙 10am–6pm Tue–Sun.

🏛 **Suermondt-Ludwig-Museum**
Wilhelmstr. 18.
Tel (0241) 47 98 00.
🕙 noon–6pm Tue–Sun (to 9pm Wed).
📶 ▢ 📶 ▢

🏛 **Couven-Museum**
Hühnermarkt 17.
Tel (0241) 432 44 21.
🕙 10am–6pm Tue–Sun.
⬤ public holidays. 📶

Environs
Kornelimünster, 6 km (4 miles) southeast of the centre, is a beautiful place with a well-preserved old town and churches. The most important of these is the Pfarrkirche St Kornelius, a former Benedictine monastery which dates from the early 9th century. The surviving building is a 14th-century Gothic basilica, extended by the early 16th century to an imposing five-nave structure. In the 18th century the octagonal chapel of St Kornelius was added at the axis of the presbytery.

The Pfalz in Aachen

The original palace of Charlemagne in Aachen did not survive; of his vast construction only the Pfalzkapelle (palatine chapel) remains. Modelled on the church of San Vitale in Ravenna, Italy, it was built by Odo von Metz in 786–800. In the mid-14th century a front tower was added, and in the years 1355–1414 a new presbytery was built. Side chapels were added later, and in the 17th century the central section was covered by a dome.

Charlemagne, effigy on his shrine

Antique Columns
The arcaded ambulatory is divided by beautiful columns, made from red marble and porphyry which had been brought from Ravenna and Rome.

Hubertus- and Karls- kapelle

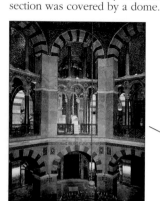

Charlemagne's Throne
This modest throne, fashioned from marbled tiles, served as the coronation throne for successive German leaders.

Candelabra
This copper candelabra, a masterpiece of Roman-esque craftsmanship, was a gift from Emperor Friedrich I Barbarossa.

Main entrance

Ungarn- kapelle

STAR SIGHTS

- ★ The Shrine of Charlemagne
- ★ Lotharkreuz
- ★ Pala d'Oro

Bronze doors
The doors, dating from the time of Charlemagne, are the oldest historic monument of their kind in Germany.

★ Lotharkreuz
This magnificent cross (c.1000), decorated with a cameo showing a portrait of Emperor Augustus, is one of the most valuable exhibits in the Schatzkammer.

The Gothic presbytery was modelled on Sainte-Chapelle in Paris.

VISITORS' CHECKLIST

Cathedral Münsterplatz. **Tel** (0241) 47 70 90. ☐ 7am–7pm (6pm winter). ☐ from 10:45am Mon–Fri, from 1pm Sat & Sun. **Treasury** Klosterplatz 2. **Tel** (0241) 47 70 91 27. ☐ 10am–1pm Mon, 10am–5pm Tue–Sun (6pm Apr–Dec), 10am–9pm first Thu of month. ☐

⋏ The Shrine of Charlemagne
The Emperor Charlemagne was canonized as a saint in 1165 and in 1215 his remains were placed in this gold and silver casket by Friedrich II. It is on display in the presbytery.

★ Pala d'Oro
The front of the main altar is adorned with valuable gold sheets from c.1020, which were funded by Heinrich II.

Matthiaskapelle

Annakapelle

Ambo
The ambo, a pulpit fashioned from gold-plated copper and inlaid with precious stones and ivories, was donated by Heinrich II in 1014.

Proserpina's Sarcophagus
This sarcophagus, in the Schatzkammer (treasury), is a beautiful example of early 3rd-century Roman sculpture. It is thought that the body of Charlemagne rested in this coffin until he was canonized.

Köln (Cologne) ⑭

Originally founded by the Romans, Köln is one of the oldest towns in Germany. The Franks ruled the town from the end of the 5th century, and Charlemagne raised its status to that of an archbishopric. Köln has remained a powerful ecclesiastical centre – it boasts 12 Romanesque churches as well as the famous Gothic cathedral. In the Middle Ages the city also played a significant role in the Hanseatic League. Present-day Köln is known for its trade fairs and as an important centre for art and culture, with excellent museums, historic buildings and art galleries. The highest number of visitors today come for the five days preceding Ash Wednesday, to watch the grand carnival processions.

⛪ St Andreas

Komödienstraße 4–8.
This late-Romanesque basilica was founded c.1200, with a presbytery added in 1414–20. Particularly noteworthy are the beautiful capitals, which link the pillars between the naves, and the stalls (c.1420–30).

⛪ Pfarrkirche St Mariä Himmelfahrt

Marzellenstraße 32–40.
The parish church of the Assumption of Mary is one of the few Baroque buildings in Köln. It was built for the Jesuit Order in 1618–89. It is easy to discover Romanesque and Gothic elements, although these are not surviving parts of an earlier building, but the result of a consciously created link with earlier styles.

⛪ Dom St Peter und Santa Maria

See pp402–3.

Picturesque houses on Fischmarkt

🏛 Römisch-Germanisches Museum

Roncalliplatz 4. *Tel (0221) 22 12 45 90.* 🕐 *10am–5pm Tue–Sun (until 10pm first Thu of month).*
This building houses Roman and pre-Roman archaeological finds from Köln and the Rhine Valley. On display are weapons, ornamental and artistic objects, the superb Dionysus mosaic and the monument to Poblicius.

🏛 Museum Ludwig

Bischofsgartenstraße 1. *Tel (0221) 22 12 61 65.* 🕐 *10am–6pm Tue–Sun, 10am–10pm first Thu of month.*
This museum has one of Europe's best collections of modern art. There are paintings by Picasso, German Expressionists, Surrealists, American Pop Artists and the Russian Avantgarde as well as many sculptures.

⛪ Groß St Martin

An Groß St Martin 9. *Tel (0221) 16 42 56 50.* 🕐 *8:30am–7.30pm Tue–Sat, 1–7:15pm Sun.*
This church, with its attractive triangular presbytery and vast tower dominating Fischmarkt, was founded for the Benedictine Order in the late 12th century. The Romans built a sports arena on this site with a swimming pool, remains of which have been uncovered under the crypt. The houses in the surrounding Martinsviertel are post-World War II, however they were built to historic designs with a medieval street layout.

🏛 Farina Haus

Obenmarspforten 21.
Tel (0221) 399 89 94. 🕐 *10am–6pm Mon–Sat, 11am–4pm Sun.*
Farina Haus traces the history of fragrance. Tours lead to the 300-year-old cellar where the Italian perfumier Johann Maria Farina first began producing Eau de Cologne, now a generic brand recognised world-wide.

Panorama with the Rathaus, Groß St Martin and the Dom, with the Rhine in the foreground

For hotels and restaurants in this region see pp511–13 and pp549–51

A detail of the Gothic section of the Rathaus façade

🏛 Rathaus

Alter Markt. ☎ (0221) 22 10.
◯ 9am–3pm Mon–Thu, 9am–noon Fri. **Jewish Baths** ◯ 10am–5pm Tue–Sun (keys available from ticket counter). **Praetorium** Kleine Budengasse. ◯ 10am–5pm Tue–Sun.
The town hall is an irregular shape created by successive modifications. In the first phase, around 1330, a wing with a Hanseatic Hall was built, decorated with Gothic sculptures of heroes and prophets. In 1407–14 a vast Gothic tower was added, and in the 16th century the arcaded Renaissance Lions Courtyard and a magnificent front lodge were built. In front of the town hall, under a glass pyramid, are the remains of 12th-century ritual Jewish baths that were destroyed after the expulsion of the Jews in 1424. From Kleine Budengasse an entrance leads to the *Praetorium*, the remains of a Roman town hall.

🏛 Wallraf-Richartz-Museum – Fondation Corboud

See pp404–5.

🏛 Gürzenich

Gürzenichstraße
This Gothic building has a huge celebration hall (1437–44), which occupies the entire first floor. Next to it are the ruins of the Romanesque church Alt St Alban. It has a copy of the sculpture *Parents* by Käthe Kollwitz.

⛪ Minoritenkirche Mariä Empfängnis

Minoritenstraße
This modest Gothic Franciscan church was established in the 13th–14th centuries. It is an elegant three-naved basilica without a tower, modelled on the Elisabethkirche in Marburg. There are historic furnishings and a 14th-century shrine with the remains of Johannes Duns Scotus, a Scottish Minorite.

VISITORS' CHECKLIST

Road map B4. 🏙 *1,005,000.*
🚉 *Hauptbahnhof.* 🚌 *ZOB Breslauer Platz.* ✈ *Konrad-Adenauer Flughafen (02203-404 001).* 🛈 *Kardinal-Höffnerplatz 1 (0221-22 13 04 00).* 🛒 *Markt bei der Apostelkirche 7am–noon Tue & Fri.* 🎭 *Rosenmontagsumzug (Carnival Rose Mon, Jan/Feb), Bierbörse (Aug/Sep).*
www.koelntourismus.de

Place of remembrance, in Alt St Alban, near the Gürzenich

KÖLN CITY CENTRE

0 metres 400
0 yards 400

Key to Symbols see back flap

Exploring Köln (Cologne)

🏛 Kolumba Museum

Kolumbastraße 4. **Tel** *(0221) 933 19 30.* ◯ *noon–5pm Wed–Mon.* 🖼
Designed by Swiss architect Peter Zumthor to much critical acclaim, this museum houses the archbishopric of Köln's collection of religious art. The building, which opened in 2007, accommodates the ruins of the late Gothic church St Kolumba; a chapel built in the 1950s to house a statue of the Madonna which miraculously escaped bombing during World War II; and a unique archaelogical excavation that was made in the 1970s.

🏛 Schnütgen-Museum

Cäcilienstraße 29. **Tel** *(0221) 22 12 23 10.* ◯ *10am–6pm Tue–Sun (to 8pm Thu).* 🖼
The Romanesque church of St Cecilia, built in 1130–60 as a nunnery, was taken over in 1479 by the Augustinian Sisters; today it houses the

The Romanesque church of St Gereon, with its vast dome

Schnütgen-Museum. Destroyed during World War II and subsequently rebuilt, this museum specializes in religious art, mainly from the Middle Ages. Its collection includes magnificient sculptures, gold and ivory items and sacral objects.

🔒 St Peter

Leonhard-Tietz-Straße 6.
The late-Gothic church of St Peter is a galleried basilica, built in 1515–39. Following its destruction in World War II, the former vaulting was replaced by a ceiling. The church's greatest attractions include its Renaissance stained-glass windows (1528–30) and the magnificient *Crucifixion of St Peter*, painted after 1637 by Peter Paul Rubens, who spent his childhood here and whose father lies buried in the church.

Detail from Stadtmuseum

🔒 St Maria im Kapitol

Marienplatz 19.
Originally built in the early part of the 11th century, as a convent, the church's extension and remodelling took until the early 13th century. Noteworthy among the furnishings are its extensive crypt and the mid-11th-century wooden door in the west closure, richly carved with reliefs depicting scenes from the life of Christ. It also has a superb Renaissance rood screen, and is the only church in Köln with cloisters.

🏢 Overstolzenhaus

Rheingasse 8.
World War II deprived Köln of many of its historic residential buildings, but this one has been lovingly restored. Built for a prosperous patrician family in the 13th century, it is regarded as one of the town's finest Gothic houses.

🔒 St Maria Lyskirchen

An Lyskirchen 12.
This, the smallest Romanesque church in Köln, was built around 1220 and slightly remodelled in the 17th century. Its greatest attractions are magnificient frescos depicting scenes from the Bible and the lives of the saints, which adorn the vaults (c.1250), as well as the *Schöne Madonna*, a huge statue of the Virgin with Infant Christ (c.1420).

🏛 Imhoff-Stollwerck-Museum (Schokoladen Museum)

Rheinauhafen 1a. **Tel** *(0221) 931 88 80.* ◯ *10am–6pm Tue–Fri, 11am–7pm Sat & Sun.* 🖼
This fantastic museum of chocolate explains the history of cocoa bean cultivation as well as the cultural significance, use and marketing of chocolate. It also shows the production process, and lets visitors sample the product.

🔒 St Georg

Georgsplatz 17.
This church was built around the middle of the 11th century, originally as a transept basilica with two choirs. In

---

ROMANESQUE CHURCHES

Köln has 12 surviving Romanesque churches, bearing testimony to the importance of the Church in the town's development. Built on the graves of martyrs and early bishops of Köln, the forms of the churches influenced the development of Romanesque architecture well beyond the Rhineland. Almost all the churches were damaged in World War II. Some, such as the church of St Kolumba, have not been restored, but most were returned to their former glory.

Towerless westwork

Tower at the junction of the naves

St Andreas

Front tower

Trefoil eastern closure

St Aposteln

For hotels and restaurants in this region see pp511–13 and pp549–51

The attractive Romanesque church of St Kunibert, seen from the Rhine

the mid-12th century the west choir was replaced by a massive frontage (westwork), but the towers were never added.

St Pantaleon
Am Pantaleonsberg 2.

A little way from the centre is this exquisite church, a former Benedictine monastery founded c.950 by Archbishop Bruno, brother of Emperor Otto I. The archbishop and the Empress Theophanu, who completed the building, are both buried here. The church has a superb late-Gothic choir screen with richly carved ornamentation. From the crypt, the remains of a Roman villa are accessible.

Severinsviertel

The Severin Quarter, a district on the southern edge of the old town, owes its name to the 13th-century Romanesque church of St Severinus. The church, largely remodelled in the Gothic style in the 15th and 16th centuries, features rich original furnishings and has a mid-10th-century crypt.

St Aposteln
Neumarkt 30.

This enormous 12th-century church of the Apostles, which towers over Neumarkt, a central square in Köln, is one of the most interesting Romanesque churches in the Rhineland. The original basilica has a trefoil eastern closure, a low tower at the junction of the naves and a tall front tower. It was given two further slim turrets flanking the apse of the presbytery.

From Neumarkt, Hahnenstrasse leads to Rudolfplatz and the Hahnentor, perhaps the most beautiful of all surviving medieval gates.

St Gereon
Gereonsdriesch 2–4.

This church must be the most unusual edifice not only in the Rhineland, but in all of Germany. Its oldest part, an oval building surrounded by small conchas, was built in the late 4th century on the graves of martyrs and – according to legend – founded by St Helen. The Romanesque

presbytery is an 11th-century addition and, in 1219–27, the oval was encircled with a ten-sided, four-storey structure in early-Gothic style. This is topped with a massive dome, 48 m (157 ft) in diameter, with ribbed vault.

St Ursula
Ursulaplatz 24.

This church was built in the 12th century, on the site of an earlier church probably dating from c.400. In the late 13th century the presbytery was rebuilt in Gothic style. The Baroque golden chamber at the southern end, added in the 17th century, is lined with many shrines. According to legend, these hold the remains of St Ursula and 11,000 virgins, all of whom were reputedly killed at the hands of the Huns. The town insignia of Köln also testify to the veneration of the virgins.

St Kunibert
Kunibertskloster 2.

Bishop Kunibert was buried in a church on this site in 663. The present Romanesque church (1215–47) has precious Romanesque stained-glass windows (c.1220–30).

The medieval Hahnentor, exit from Köln towards Aachen

Groß St Martin

Tower at the junction of the naves

Biforium

Trefoil eastern closure

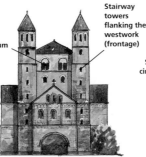

Stairway towers flanking the westwork (frontage)

St Pantaleon

Pair of front towers

Semi-circular apse

St Kunibert

Cologne Cathedral (Kölner Dom)

10th-century Gero Cross

The most famous Gothic structure in Germany, the Kölner Dom is also unusually complex, whether in terms of its splendour, its size or even simply the date of its construction. The foundation stone was laid on 15th August 1248, the presbytery consecrated in 1322. The cathedral was built gradually until c.1520. It then remained unfinished until the 19th century, when Romanticists revived interest in it. The building was finally completed in 1842–80, according to the rediscovered, original Gothic designs.

Pinnacles
Elaborately decorated pinnacles top the supporting pillars.

Cathedral Interior
The presbytery, the ambulatory and the chapels retain a large number of Gothic, mainly early-14th-century, stained-glass windows.

Engelbert Reliquary (c.1630)
The cathedral treasury is famous for its large collection of golden objects, vestments and the fine ornamentation of its liturgical books.

Main entrance

Petrusportal, or the portal of St Peter, the only one built in the second half of the 14th century, has five Gothic figures.

Buttresses support the entire bulk of the cathedral.

STAR SIGHTS

★ Gothic Stalls

★ Shrine of the Three Kings

★ Altar of the Magi

For hotels and restaurants in this region see pp511–13 and pp549–51

★ Gothic Stalls
The massive oak stalls, built in 1308–11, were the largest that have ever been made in Germany.

The contemporary German artist Gerhard Richter created an abstract stained-glass collage in 2007.

Semicircular arches transfer the thrust of the vaults onto the buttresses.

VISITORS' CHECKLIST

Cathedral ⬜ 6am–7:30pm daily. **Treasury** Domkloster 4. **Tel** (0221) 17 94 05 55. ⬜ 10am–6pm daily. 🅿 📷 **Viewing platform** ⬜ Jan/Feb & Nov/Dec: 9am–4pm; Mar/Apr & Oct: 9am–5pm; May–Sep: 9am–6pm. 📷 **Organ recitals** Jun–Aug: 8pm Tue. **Exhibition of Rubens tapestries** Whit Sunday until Corpus Christi.

High Altar
The Gothic altar slab, which dates back to the consecration of the presbytery, depicts the Coronation of the Virgin Mary, flanked by the twelve apostles.

★ Shrine of the Three Kings
This huge Romanesque reliquary was made by Nikolaus von Verdun in 1190–1220, to hold the relics of the Three Kings. These relics were brought to Köln in 1164 for Emperor Friedrich I Barbarossa.

★ Altar of the Magi
This splendid altar (c.1442), the work of Stephan Lochner, is dedicated to the Three Kings, the patrons of Köln.

Mailänder Madonna
This fine early-Gothic carving of the Milan Madonna and Child dates from around 1290. It is currently displayed in the Marienkapelle.

Wallraf-Richartz-Museum – Fondation Corboud

This museum was named after Ferdinand Franz Wallraf, who bequeathed his art collection to the city in 1824, and Johann Heinrich Richartz, who funded the first building. Medieval and early modern paintings (1250 to 1550) form the core of the collection. There are also works by Rubens and Rembrandt, as well as examples from Impressionism, Realism and Symbolism. In 2001 the Wallraf-Richartz-Museum moved to a brand-new building, incorporting many new works from the collection of Gérard Corboud.

Bleaching the Linen (1882)
Max Liebermann created this painting in the early stages of his career, when his work was largely concerned with Realism.

★ **Stigmatization of St Francis** (c.1616)
This dark and mysterious painting, originally created by Peter Paul Rubens for the Capuchin church in Köln, is untypical of the artist's work.

Third floor

Reclining Girl (1751)
This young nude, arranged on her bed in a provocative pose, is an example of the light-hearted works of so-called "boudoir art" that François Boucher specialized in.

Ground floor

★ **Fifer and Drummer** (1502–4)
This subtle painting, the wing of an altarpiece, is the work of Albrecht Dürer, who included himself in the scene – the drummer is a self-portrait of Dürer himself.

Main entrance

Girls on a Bridge
(1905)
*Edvard Munch covered
the same subject several
times (see p437). The version
held in Köln is one of the
earliest, and features an
urbanized landscape.*

Fifth floor

VISITORS' CHECKLIST

**Wallraf-Richartz-Museum –
Fondation Corboud** Ober-
marspforten. **Tel** (0221) 22 12 11
19. ☐ 10am–6pm Tue, Wed, Fri,
10am–9pm Thu, 11am–6pm Sat
& Sun. ✈ 🏧 📷 🎞 📷

GALLERY GUIDE
*Each floor in the museum
displays paintings belonging
to one era. On the second
floor, the exhibition begins
with the collection of 13th-
century art; the third floor
holds 16th–18th century
art, and on the fifth floor
works of art from the 19th
century are displayed,
organized by the schools of
art they represent.*

**Jacob accuses
Laban of giving him
Lai instead of
Rachel as a wife**
(1628)
*This biblical scene
was painted by one of
the most outstanding
Dutch masters,
Hendrick ter
Brugghen*

Second
floor

**Old Woman
and Boy**
(c.1650–60)
*This scene was
painted by Bartolome
Esteban Murillo. The
artist excelled not
only as the master of
charmingly senti-
mental depictions of
the Madonna, but
was also an excellent
observer of every-
day life in 17th-
century Spain.*

Madonna and Child
(1325–30)
*This central panel of a
polyptych by Simone Martini
is thought to have originated
from the San Agostino
church in San Giminiano.*

KEY

☐ Medieval paintings

☐ 17th- and 18th-century paintings

☐ 19th-century paintings

☐ Non-exhibition space

STAR EXHIBITS

★ Fifer and Drummer

★ Stigmatization of
St Francis

One of the artificial reservoirs in the northern Eifel

Northern Eifel ⑯

Road map A4. ⓘ *Kalvarienbergstr.*
1, 54595 Prüm (0180) 500 22 83.
🎭 *Bad Münstereifel: Burg in*
Flammen (Jul).

Barely 20 per cent of the
Eifel mountain range is in
North Rhine-Westphalia. Low,
forested mountains line the
valley of the Rur river, which
has been dammed in several
places. The resulting artificial
lakes provide a perfect opportunity for relaxation and
sporting activities. There are
also many attractive towns
and fascinating monuments.

Blankenheim is famed for
its picturesque half-timbered
houses, the late-Gothic church
and the frequently modified
12th-century castle of the
counts von Manderscheid-
Blankenheim, which today is
a youth hostel. The source of
the Ahr river can also be seen
here – a house was built over
the top of it in 1726.

In **Schleiden**, the castle,
built in the 12th century and
frequently rebuilt up until the
18th century, is worth visiting.
There is also a late-Gothic
church with valuable stained-
glass windows and an impressive organ dating from 1770.

Probably the most beautiful
town in this region is **Monschau**, which until 1919 was
called Montjoie. It is known
also for the Montjoier Dütt-
chen (croissants) and an excellent mustard. The ruin of a
13th-century castle towers on
a hill. At its foot, the Rur river
runs through a narrow valley,
with attractive small towns,
narrow, steep streets and
timber-frame houses from
various eras. In Hasenfeld

visitors can see a dam dating
from 1904, and an amazing
hydro-electric building, decorated in a way that reflects its
purpose. One of the most
interesting monuments of this
region is the Steinfeld monastery, with a history dating from
the 10th century. In 1121 the
Augustinians settled here, and
in 1126 they accepted the rule
of St Norbert of Xanten, and
this became the first monastery on German territory. A
beautiful Romanesque basilica
was built in the second half
of the 12th century. It has
retained wall paintings from
the 12th and 14th centuries,
and vaulted ceilings from the
16th century. The
Rheinisches
Freilichtmuseum
Kommern is an
open-air museum
with examples of
the building styles
typical of the
Northern Eifel. It
is also worth visit-
ing the town of **Euskirchen**,
which has an attractive Gothic
church with superb furnishings, and the moated castle of
Veynau (14–15th centuries).

Picturesque half-timbered
houses in Monschau

The spa town of **Bad Münstereifel** dates back to 830,
when a Benedictine monas-
tery was established here. The
present church is a 12th-cen-
tury Romanesque basilica
with impressive 11th-century
frontage. Also worth seeing
are the Gothic town hall and
a Romanesque house, now
housing a museum.

🏛 **Rheinisches Freilicht-
museum Kommern**
Auf dem Kahlenbusch. Mechernich-
Kommern. **Tel** (02443) 998 00.
⦿ Apr–Oct: 9am–6pm; Nov–Mar:
10am–4pm. 🖾

Brühl ⑰

Road map B4. 🏛 42,000. 🚗 🚆
ⓘ *Uhlstr. 1 (02232-793 45).*
🎭 *Hubertusmarkt (Oct).*

The small town of Brühl has
one of the most beautiful
residential complexes, since
1984 a UNESCO World Heri-
tage Site. As early as the 13th
century, a palace was established here for the archbishops of nearby Köln, but this
was destroyed in 1689. A
Baroque palace, **Augustusburg**, was built on
its foundations in
1725–8, according
to a design by
Johann Conrad
Schlaun. It was
named after the
instigator of the
building, Elector
Klemens August.
The building was almost immediately refurbished, with a
new façade and furnishings,
the work of François Cuvilliés, and in the 1940s a new
staircase was completed to a
design by Balthasar Neu-
mann. After devastation in
World War II, the palace was
carefully restored, and the
magnificently furnished late-
Baroque and Rococo interior,
especially a stunning dining
room designed by Cuvilliés,
can now be seen again. A
path leads from the orangery
to a Gothic church built for
the Franciscans in the 15th
century. The *Annunciation*
on the high altar is the work
of Johann Wolfgang van der
Auwer, while the magnificent

Merry-go-round at the
Phantasialand in Brühl

Phantasialand, the largest theme park in Germany, near Brühl

canopy above was designed by Balthasar Neumann. The castle is surrounded by a Baroque park, designed by Dominique Girard.

About 2 km (1 mile) east of the main residence is another castle, **Falkenlust**, built in 1729–40, to a design by Cuvilliés. Its captivating interior includes a lacquered and a mirror cabinet. Nearby stands an octagonal chapel, its interior decoration modelled on a secluded grotto.

It is also worth visiting the small villa near Augustusburg where the great Surrealist artist Max Ernst was born. It now houses a small display commemorating his work.

Another attraction, which draws a large number of visitors is **Phantasialand**, Germany's largest theme park. Visitors will need several days to see all the attractions of this vast fairground with its roller-coaster, water rides and numerous merry-go-rounds.

⛪ Augustusburg
Tel (02232) 440 00. ☐ Feb–Nov: 9am–noon & 1:30–4pm Tue–Fri, 10am–5pm Sat & Sun.

☐ Falkenlust
Tel (02232) 440 00. ☐ Feb–Nov: 9am–noon & 1:30–4pm Tue–Fri, 10am–5pm Sat & Sun.

☐ Phantasialand
Berggeiststr. 31–41. **Tel** (02232) 362 00. ☐ Apr–Oct: 9am–6pm daily, later in summer. ☐

Environs
Two moated houses await the visitor at **Kerpen**, 27 km (17 miles) to the north: the small 16th-century castle of Lörsfeld, and the Baroque palace of Türnich, built in 1756–66.

In **Pulheim-Brauweiler**, 30 km (19 miles) to the north, is an extremely beautiful Benedictine monastery, founded in 1024. Building began in 1048, funded by Rycheza, the wife of the Polish King Boleslav Chrobry.

From here it is worth travelling another 23 km (14 miles) west to **Bedburg**, where the

moated castle is worth seeing. This is a vast brick structure with four wings, which was established in stages over 300 years, starting in around 1300.

Bonn ⑱

See p408.

Königswinter ⑲

Road map B4. 🏃 35,000. 🚌 🚊
ℹ️ Drachenfelsstr. 51 (02223-91 77 11).

Königswinter lies in the centre of the Siebengebirge, an attractive range of small, wooded mountains (the "seven mountains"), excellently suited for walking. The most popular mountain is the Drachenfels (dragon's rock). The oldest mountain railway in Germany, built in 1883, takes visitors to the top (321 m/1,053 ft). During the ascent visitors can see the Neo Gothic Drachenburg, a palace dating from 1879–84, and on the top are the ruins of the Gothic Drachenburg, dating from the 12th century. The "dragon" in the name relates to the myth of the Nibelungs – the dragon slain by Siegfried was supposed to have lived here.

The little town of Königswinter, at the foot of the mountains, has picturesque 17th-century half-timbered houses, town houses and late 19th-century hotels.

Environs
Bad Honnef, 6 km (4 miles) to the south, is a charming spa town known as "Nice on the Rhine", where the former chancellor Konrad Adenauer lived until his death. A museum commemorates this great politician.

Situated 15 km (9 miles) to the north is **Siegburg**, where a Benedictine monastery (1064) is worth visiting. The walls of the crypt are from the 11th century, but the present church is a 17th-century building, rebuilt after World War II. The Anno-Schrein is a magnificent Romanesque reliquary box dating from 1183.

The Baroque Schloss Augustusburg in Brühl

Bonn ⑱

Bonn was founded by the Romans in 11 BC, and flourished thanks to the archbishops of Cologne. It gained fame because of Ludwig van Beethoven, who was born here in 1770, and Robert Schumann, who spent the final years of his life here. The world heard of Bonn when, on 10 May 1949, it was elevated to the status of capital of the Federal Republic of Germany. When parliament decided in 1991 to make Berlin the capital of the newly unified country, Bonn was deprived of its role, although six ministries stayed on.

The Baroque portal of the Beethovenhaus in Bonn

🏛 Beethovenhaus
Bonngasse 20. *Tel (0228) 981 75 25.* ◯ *Apr–Oct: 10am–6pm Mon–Sat, 11am–6pm Sun; Nov–Mar: 10am–5pm Mon–Sat, 11am–7pm Sun.* 🖺
The museum is housed in the Baroque 18th-century house where the composer Ludwig van Beethoven was born and lived until the age of 22. He never returned to his home town, but there is a large and impressive collection of memorabilia from his entire life.

🏛 Markt
The central market square in Bonn, shaped like a triangle, owes its present appearance to a mixture of modern and Baroque architecture. Its most outstanding feature is the late-Baroque **Rathaus** (town hall), built in 1737–8, to a design by Michel Leveilly. The centre of the market square is decorated with the Marktbrunnen, a fountain in the shape of an obelisk, erected in 1777 in honour of the Elector Maximilian Friedrich.

Not far from the Markt are some churches worth seeing. The first is the Gothic **Remigius-kirche**, built for the Franciscans in the years 1274–1317, and the second is the Baroque **Namen-Jesu-Kirche** built for the Jesuits according to a design by Jacob de Candreal in the years 1686–1717.

🏛 Rheinufer
The Rhine embankment, which changes its name several times along its course, runs along the western bank of the Rhine. Many of Bonn's attractions are grouped along this street. To the north of Kennedybrücke (Kennedy bridge) lies the Beethovenhalle, a vast concert and congress hall, and to the south of the bridge is the Bonn opera house.

Next to the opera is the Alter Zoll, the former customs house, which is based in one of the bastions that was part of the 17th-century city defences.

🏛 Universität
Am Hofgarten.
Founded in 1818, Bonn University is based in what is probably the most beautiful home for an educational institution anywhere in Germany. The stunningly attractive Baroque castle was built for the Elector Joseph Klemens in 1607–1705, to a design by Enrico Zuccalli, and extended after 1715 by Robert de Cotte.

�ᴨ Münster St Martin
Münsterplatz.
Bonn's cathedral is a magnificent example of Romanesque architecture in the Rhine Valley. The church was built in around 1150–1230, on the site of an earlier 11th-century cathedral, of which a three-naved crypt has survived. South of it, the romantic 12th-century Romanesque cloister is also worth seeing.

Gold clasps in the Rheinisches Landesmuseum

🏛 Rheinisches Landesmuseum
Colmantstraße 14–16. *Tel (0228) 20 700.* ◯ *10am–6pm Tue–Sun, 10am–9pm Wed.* **www**.rlmb.lvr.de
This interesting regional museum has a vast collection of excavated items dating back to Roman times, as well as medieval and modern art. The skull of a Neanderthal Man is also exhibited here.

The Baroque Elector's palace, housing Bonn University

🏛 Regierungsviertel

Until 1999 this was the central authority of one of the most powerful countries in Europe. Now it creates a somewhat desolate impression. Some ministries and offices have remained in Bonn, and the transfer to Berlin is under discussion, but the town is definitely changing.

The former Bundestag building, in the Regierungsviertel

🏛 Haus der Geschichte der BR Deutschland

Willy-Brandt-Allee 14. **Tel** (0228) 916 50. ☐ 9am–7pm Tue–Fri, 10am–6pm Sat & Sun.

This excellent museum details the history of Germany after World War II, with fascinating multi-media displays. It is one of the architecturally impressive buildings which form Bonn's "Museums Mile".

🏛 Kunstmuseum Bonn

Friedrich-Ebert-Allee 2. **Tel** (0228) 77 62 60. ☐ 11am–6pm Tue–Sun, 11am–9pm Wed. ● 24, 25 & 31 Dec; Sat, Sun & Mon in carnival.

This superb museum of 20th-century art, in an interesting building designed by Axel Schultes, has a great collection of Expressionist paintings, including many works by August Macke. Next to the museum is the Kunst- und Ausstellungshalle, which opened in 1992 as a venue for temporary exhibitions.

🎭 Bad Godesberg

The small spa town of Bad Godesberg was incorporated into Bonn in 1969. An elegant neighbourhood, its villas line the spa park. On top of the hill is the Godesburg, a ruined 13th-century castle.

♣ Poppelsdorf

In this leafy southwestern suburb, the Baroque Schloss Clemensruhe (1715–18) is well worth visiting. Both the castle and its extensive park with an attractive botanical garden belong to the university. It is also worth making a detour to the Baroque pilgrimage church on the Kreuzberg, a low hill. The church houses the chapel of the Holy Steps, attributed to Balthasar Neumann.

The Baroque Schloss Clemensruhe, in Poppelsdorf

BONN CITY CENTRE

Beethovenhaus ①
Markt ②
Münster St Martin ⑤
Rheinufer ③
Universität ④

0 metres   300
0 yards   300

Key to Symbols see back flap

The medieval Oberes Schloss in Siegen

Siegen ❷⓪

Road map B4. 🏙 *100,000.* 🚉 🚌
ℹ️ *Markt 2 (0271-404 13 16).*
🎭 *Kultur Pur (May/Jun), Rubensfest (Jun/Jul), Weihnachtsmarkt (Dec).*

Beautifully located amidst the hills on the high banks of the Sieg river, Siegen is the largest town in the Siegerland region. For centuries the city was the residence of the dukes of Nassau. Religious divisions in the family resulted in two castles being built in Siegen. The **Oberes Schloss** (upper castle) is a medieval building, frequently refurbished in the 16th, 17th and 18th centuries. The museum, which has been opened inside the castle, has some paintings by Peter Paul Rubens, who was born in Siegen. The lower **Unteres Schloss** is a Baroque palace, which replaced an earlier building. In the centre of Siegen it is also worth visiting the **Nicolaikirche**, a 13th-century hexagonal church with a presbytery and tower, which served as the ducal family mausoleum.

Environs
In **Freudenberg**, 10 km (6 miles) northwest of Siegen, is the small settlement of Alter Flecken, which is reproduced in virtually all German guidebooks. Founded in 1666 at the instigation of Duke Johann Moritz von Nassau, the village consists of identical half-timbered houses.

Hagen ❷①

Road map B4. 🏙 *210,950.* 🚉 🚌
ℹ️ *Rathausstr. 13 (02331-207 58 94).* 🎭 *Marktschreiertage (Jan).*

Hagen would probably not feature in the guidebooks, were it not for Karl Ernst Ost-haus, who created an artists' colony here at the beginning of the 20th century, inviting Art Nouveau designers such as Peter Behrens and Henry van de Velde. The magnificent **Hohenhof**, Osthaus' home, was created by van de Velde. It houses the **Karl-Ernst-Osthaus-Museum**, with a collection of modern art. Behrens designed the crematorium in the suburb of Delstern and the beautiful villas **Haus Cuno** (Haßleyer Str. 35) and **Haus Goedeke** (Amselgasse). In the south of the town is the Westfälisches Freilichtmuseum, a popular open-air museum, which displays many historic workshops and factories with reconstructed equipment.

Sauerland ❷②

Road map B4. ℹ️ *Sauerland-Touristik, Johannes-Hummel-Weg 1, 57392 Schmallenberg (02974-96 980).*

The Sauerland is the region to the south and east of the Ruhr coalfields, making an obvious holiday destination for the inhabitants of this large, industrialized conurbation. Embracing the northern part of the Rhenish slate massif, its densely wooded mountains are not high – the highest peak is Hegekopf at 843 m (2,766 ft). Crossed by rivers teeming with fish and full of artificial lakes, the area is perfect for walking, cycling and fishing.

Enjoyable days can be had on an excursion to one of the caves such as **Attahöhle, Dechenhöhle** and **Heinrichs-höhle** near Iserlohn. There are charming towns, too, and in **Breckerfeld**, the Gothic parish church has preserved a superb altar, from around 1520. The main attraction in **Altena** is the superb, gigantic Burg (castle), built in the 12th century and restored in the early 20th century. In 1910 the world's first youth hostel for tourists

One of the charming villages, nestling in the hilly landscape of the Sauerland

Timber-frame house, typical of the Sauerland landscape

was created here. The 14th century Schloss Wocklum in **Balve** was rebuilt in the 18th century. One of the greatest tourist draws in the Sauerland is the **Möhnesee**, a lake with a huge dam, built in 1908–12 and bombed by Allied "dambusters" in 1943 with catastrophic consequences. **Arnsberg** has a regional museum and the lovely Neo-Gothic moated castle Herdringen with assorted furnishings from other castles.

In the south extend the Rothaargebirge (red-haired mountains). Their most beautiful town is the spa resort of Bad Berleburg, while the Kahler Asten mountain and the town of Winterberg are popular winter sports areas.

Soest ❷❸

Road map B4. 👥 50,000. 🚊 🚌
🛈 Teichsmühlengasse 3 (02921-66 35 00 50). 🎭 Bördetag (May), Gauklertag (Sep), Jahrmarkt Allerheiligenkirmes (Nov).

The Westphalian town of Soest made its mark in history when, in about 1100, the town's civic rights were formulated and subsequently adopted by 65 other towns. Today the town captivates visitors with its well-preserved old town, its historic churches, and the almost completely intact walls which surround the town. The focus of the old town is the Romanesque **Propsteikirche St Patrokli**, founded in 965 by Bruno, archbishop of Cologne, and built in stages until the 13th century. Further historic buildings are grouped around the church: the 18th-century,

Baroque **Rathaus** (town hall), the 12th-century Romanesque **Petrikirche** with its Gothic presbytery, and the 12th-century **Nicolaikapelle**, a chapel with 13th-century wall paintings and an altar painted by Konrad von Soest.

In the northern part of the old town, two churches are worth seeing: the **Hohne-kirche** with beautiful Gothic and early Baroque furnishings, and the **Wiesenkirche** with a magnificent group of stained-glass windows from the 14th and 15th centuries. The window above the northern portal shows the so-called Westphalian Last Supper, depicting a table laden with plentiful Westphalian smoked ham and local pumpernickel bread.

A 'Three Hares' window, an emblem of Paderborn

Environ

In **Lippstadt**, 23 km (14 miles) east of Soest, it is worth visiting the Gothic Marienkirche. In the suburb of Bökenförde is the 18th-century Baroque moated palace Schwarzenraben, and there is an early-Baroque castle in Overhagen.

Paderborn ❷❹

Road map C3. 👥 140,000. 🚊 🚌
🛈 Marienplatz 2 (05251 88 29 80). 🎭 Puppenfestspiele (Feb), Schützenfest (Jul), Liborifest (Jul–Aug), Liborikirmes (Oct).

Paderborn has featured on the historical map for over 1,000 years. In the 8th century Charlemagne built a palace here, and in about AD 800, a bishopric was established. The town's most important monument is the beautiful **Dom St Maria, St Kilian und St Liborius**, a Romanesque-Gothic cathedral. This enormous hall-church with two transepts and tall front tower suffered greatly during World War II, but it continues to captivate visitors with its magnificent decor on the richly carved portal, the great Romanesque

crypt, interesting plaques and richly decorated bishops' tombs and epitaphs. The diocesan museum holds the Imad-Madonna, funded by Bishop Imad, an outstanding figure of the Madonna and Child dating from 1051–8. On the northern side of the cathedral a section of the foundations of the emperor's palace can be seen, together with the **Bartholomäuskapelle** (chapel of St Bartholomew), the oldest hall-church in Germany, completed in 1017.

To the south of the cathedral complex, on Rathausplatz, is the exceptionally beautiful **Rathaus** (town hall) dating from 1613–20. An example of the Weser-Renaissance style, it is crowned with richly ornamented gables. The **Heinz-Nixdorf-Museumsforum** provides a pleasant break from the past – this museum is dedicated to the history of computers.

Environs

Near **Stukenbrock**, 15 km (9 miles) north of Paderborn, is the theme park Hollywood-Park and the fascinating Safariland, where more than 500 African animals roam freely.

Tower of the Romanesque-Gothic Dom in Paderborn

Front of the early-Romanesque Abtei Corvey in Höxter

Höxter ㉕

Road map C3. 🏘 *35,000.* 🚉 🚌
ℹ️ *Weserstraße 11 (05271-194 33).*
🎷 *Corveyer Musikwochen (May–Jun), Huxorimarkt (Sep), Kirchenmusiktage (Nov–Dec).*

In a picturesque spot on the Weser river, Höxter can pride itself on its beautiful old town with many timber-frame houses, fragments of the city walls, a Renaissance **Rathaus** (town hall) from 1610, and important churches. The history of **Kilianikirche**, in the centre of the old town, goes back to the late 8th century, although in its present form it is a Romanesque building from the 11th–12th centuries. Also in

the centre of Höxter is a Gothic church built for the Franciscans in 1248–1320.

The city's greatest attraction, however, is the magnificent **Abtei Corvey**, a monastery founded in 822. It was originally built as the church of St Stephen and St Vitus, but only the grandiose two-storey frontage completed in 885 survived. It became the model for several other churches built in Westphalia, while the main body of the church was rebuilt in the 17th century.

Lemgo ㉖

Road map C3. 🏘 *42,000.* 🚉 🚌
ℹ️ *Kramerstr 1. (05261-988 70).*

This exceptionally pretty town was founded in 1190 by Bernhard II von Lippe. It was a member of the Hanseatic League, and had its heyday during the witch hunts of the 17th century. Today, Lemgo has numerous Renaissance monuments – it was spared during World War II, and the Gothic Nicolaikirche and Marienkirche, with Gothic wall paintings and a Renaissance organ by Georg Slegel, have survived. The pearl of the city is the beautiful **Rathaus** (town hall), built in the 15th–17th centuries. It contains an original pharmacy that is still in use. Many timber-frame houses have also survived, the best ones in Papen-, Mittel- and Echternstraße. The most beautiful house in

Façade of a Renaissance pharmacy inside the Rathaus in Lemgo

Lemgo is the **Hexenbürgermeisterhaus**. This "witches' mayor's house" (1571), an excellent example of Weser Renaissance, belonged to the mayor, Hermann Cothmann, who started the witch hunt. It now houses a town museum. Also worth visiting are the **Junkerhaus** (1891), the architect's home, and **Schloss Brake** (13th-16th centuries), a castle which now houses the **Weserrenaissance-Museum**.

🏛 **Weserrenaissance-Museum**
Schloss Brake. *Tel (05261) 945 00.* ⬜ *10am–6pm Tue–Sun.*

Teutoburger Wald (Teutoburg Forest) ㉗

Road map C3. ℹ️ *Detmold, Rathaus Am Markt 5 (05231-97 73 28).*
🎷 *Andreas-Messe in Detmold (Nov).*

A range of low mountains extending from Osnabrück through Bielefeld right up to Paderborn, the Teutoburg Forest is one of the most attractive tourist regions in Westphalia. The best base for walking and cycling holidays is **Detmold**, which has a very attractive old town with well-preserved timber-frame buildings from various periods, and the elegant Residenzschloss, the castle of the zur Lippe family. Originally medieval, the palace was rebuilt in the 16th century in the

The picturesque Renaissance Rathaus in Höxter

◁ **Königsallee in Autumn, Düsseldorf**

Weser-Renaissance style. The interior is composed of 17th and 19th century furnishings. The star feature is a set of eight gobelins crafted in a Brussels workshop around 1670, showing scenes of Alexander the Great's triumphs. Furnishings from the 19th century include designs by Charles Le Brun.

Three km (2 miles) south of Detmold is the spot where in the year AD 9 Cherusko Arminius, known as Hermann, leader of the Germanic tribes, triumphed against the Roman army led by Varus. At the top of the mountain, the **Hermannsdenkmal**, a huge monument designed by Ernst von Bandel, was erected in 1838–75. It was supposed to symbolize the German struggle for unification.

Two fascinating attractions near Detmold are the **Adlerwarte Berlebeck**, an ornithological research station, where eagles and many other birds of prey can be observed, and the **Vogelpark Heiligenkirchen**, a bird park with over 2,000 varieties of birds in all shapes and sizes from around the world.

Bielefeld ❷❽

Road map C3. 🏘 325,000. 🚆
🚌 🖩 *Niederwall 23 (0521-51 69 99).* 🎭 *Hermannslauf (Apr), Leinenweber-Markt (May), Bielefelder Kultur-Sommer (May–Sep), Sparrenburgfest (Jul), Weinmarkt (Sep), Weihnachtsmarkt (Dec).*

On the edge of the Teutoburg Forest, Bielefeld owes its evolution to the production of and trading in linen. The old town is dominated by the **Sparrenburg** castle, built in the 13th century for the von Ravensberg family. In the 16th century the castle was surrounded by new fortifications including new bastions, and in the 19th century the residential part of the city was greatly extended.

The central feature of the old town is Alter Markt (old market), on which stands the **Nicolaikirche**. This Gothic church suffered heavily in World War II, although the marvellous Antwerp altar (c.1520) was preserved. Nearby, on Obernstraße, stands the **Crüwell-Haus**, an interesting late-Gothic town house from the early 16th century. The street leads to **St Jodokus-Kirche**, a late-Gothic church, whose greatest treasure is the amazing figure of the Black Madonna (c.1220). Further south is the **Kunsthalle**, a modern building with a significant collection of 20th-century art. It is also worth visiting the **Marienkirche** in the new town. Built in 1280–1330, this Gothic church holds the tomb of one of the von Ravensberg dukes (c.1320) and a high altar (c.1400) with a central Gothic section.

Environs
Picturesque **Herford**, 17 km (11 miles) north of Bielefeld, has timber-frame houses, beautiful Gothic churches and **MARTa Herford**, an art and design museum by Frank O. Gehry. In **Enger**, 21 km (13 miles) to the north, in the former church of the canons, a tomb dating from 1100 holds the remains of the Saxon Duke Widukind, buried in 807.

The spa town of **Bad Salzuflen**, with its pretty old town and spa, is ideal for relaxation.

An observation tower in the Sparrenburg complex in Bielefeld

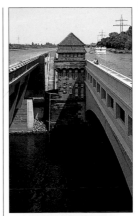
The Wasserstraßenkreuzung (waterway junction) in Minden

Minden ❷❾

Road map C3. 🏘 85,000. 🚆 🚌
🖩 *Domstraße 2 (0571-829 06 59).* 🎭 *Klassik-Open-Air (Jul/Aug).*

Charlemagne created a bishopric here as early as 798. The town evolved thanks to its strategic location on the Weser river. The city's most important monument is the cathedral, **Dompfarrkirche St Petrus und St Gorgonius**. It has a Romanesque presbytery, transept and monumental frontage built in the 11th–12th centuries, although the body of the church is an example of early-Gothic style from the 13th century. It is worth visiting the church treasury with its 11th-century crucifix.

The **Rathaus** (town hall), with 13th-century lower sections, is worth seeing, as are Minden's many charming houses around the market square. A great attraction is the **Wasserstraßenkreuz** (waterway junction), where a 375-m (1,230-ft) long bridge takes the Mittellandkanal across the Weser river.

Environs
On top of a hill in **Porta Westfalica**, 6 km (4 miles) south of Minden, is a giant monument to Kaiser Wilhelm (1892–6) by Bruno Schmitz. The **Westfälische Mühlenstraße**, (Westphalian mill route), signposted around Minden, takes visitors past 42 different mills and windmills.

Hermannsdenkmal, near Detmold

NORTHERN GERMANY

Northern Germany at a Glance

Northern Germany has very varied landscapes,
ranging from the sandy beaches on the Baltic and
North Sea coasts to the moraine hills of Schleswig-
Holstein and the moorlands of the Lüneburger
Heide. Nature-lovers are enchanted by the countless
lakes in Mecklenburg and the Harz mountains, while
those interested in history or architecture enjoy the
Renaissance castles along the Weser River and the
Gothic brick architecture in former Hanseatic towns.
Historic buildings in Goslar and Hildesheim testify
to the importance of these two towns.

Helgoland *is a popular tourist
destination. Red cliffs as high
as skyscrapers, a picturesque
town and the
sea aquarium are the star
attractions of this island.*

**SCHLESWIG-
HOLSTEIN**
(see pp454–65)

**LOWER SAXONY,
HAMBURG AND
BREMEN**
(see pp424–53)

Oldenburg, *symbolized
by its heraldic shield,
is famous for
its large collection of
paintings and interiors
in its Kunstmuseum
(art museum).*

Bremen, *a historic
harbour town, draws visi-
tors with its many historic
buildings and monuments,
including a Renaissance-
Gothic town hall.*

Fehmarn, *one of the largest of the German islands, is linked with the German mainland by a railway bridge constructed in 1963.*

Rügen *enchants visitors with its chalky white cliffs, which contrast starkly with the deep blues and greens of the surrounding Baltic Sea.*

MECKLENBURG
LOWER POMERANIA
(see pp406–81)

Lübeck *suffered massive damage in World War II, but its Gothic town hall survived the attacks and the city's beautiful old town has been rebuilt.*

| 0 km | 50 |
| 0 miles | 50 |

Hamburg *not only has attractive museums and valuable monuments, but also such lively and bustling places as the Fischmarkt, a huge market held every Sunday morning where it is possible to purchase virtually anything.*

Gothic Brick Architecture

Terracotta decoration

Brick was used as a building material in many parts of medieval Europe, but in Northern Germany it gave rise to the distinctive style of *Backsteingotik* (brick Gothic). Brick technology was introduced in the mid-12th century by Norbertine monks arriving from Lombardy. The style is characterized by a rich variety of vaults, the use of buttresses instead of supporting arches, and colourful designs achieved by using glazed bricks. Through trade and the activities of religious orders these forms spread throughout the Baltic region.

The storeys are divided by friezes.

MARIENKIRCHE IN LÜBECK
Considered the crowning achievement of Backsteingotik, this church, built from around 1260, became the model for countless others, including the cathedral in Schwerin. It is a triple-naved basilica, with a twin-towered façade, braced with buttresses.

The eastern façade *of many churches, such as the Marienkirche in Prenzlau* (above) *was often crowned by an elaborate, ornamental gable.*

A pointed arched portal, *decorated with ceramic borders, was a typical feature of many village churches.*

Main portal

Gables with tiled decorations *and intricate openwork, such as this gable of the south chapel of the Nikolai-kirche in Wismar, are a feature of many Lower Pomeranian churches.*

The vast twin-towered façade symbolizes the power of its founders – wealthy Lübeck patricians.

Terracotta tiles *with raised decorative motifs were used in brick architecture in place of stone bas-reliefs.*

Turret for smallest church bell

The arcades between the naves are tall and narrow, culminating in acutely pointed arches.

Complex star vaulting *with intricate ribbing replaced the earlier cross-ribbed vaulting.*

Flying buttresses are rare in brick-built churches.

Stepped walls were used to dress the façades of the church. They were an important element in the construction.

Beam openings *indicate that a robust type of scaffolding was used in the course of construction. The ends of the beams are incorporated in the walls.*

Friezes on the arcades, *such as this interlaced motif made from brick, are frequently used as a decorative element, even in village churches.*

SECULAR BRICK ARCHITECTURE

Backsteingotik was not confined to churches – this style was used in magnificent town halls, weigh-houses, gateways and houses, mostly on narrow plots, with elaborate gables decorated with glazed bricks and white plasterwork.

Gothic house on the market square in Greifswald

The German Coastline

The waters of two seas – the North Sea and the Baltic Sea – lap on northern Germany's shores, linked by the Kiel Canal, which cuts across the base of the Jutland peninsula. The cool climate on the coast makes for short summers yet, on a sunny day, the beaches are packed with holidaymakers, and a holiday here can have a lot to offer. Heiligendamm was the first seaside resort to be established in Germany, in 1783 by a duke of Mecklenburg. By the end of the 19th century, spas with elegant villas, promenades and piers were springing up everywhere. A popular attraction are the *Strandkörbe* – huge wickerwork beach chairs.

The sand dunes *form part of a nature reserve in the northern part of Sylt, the largest of the North Frisian islands.*

The Cliffs of Helgoland *have a characteristic reddish hue indicating the red sandstone from which they are composed.*

NORDFRIESISCHE INSELN

NORDFRIESLAND

Sylt

Flensburg

Schleswig

Rendsburg

Kiel

Neumüns

Helgoland

NORDSEE (NORTH SEA)

Itzehoe

Elmshorn

Pinneberg

Hambu

OSTFRIESLAND

Wilhelmshaven

Bremerhaven

Reinbek

Emden

Oldenburg

The Kiel Canal, *known in Germany as the Nord-Ostsee-Kanal, was constructed in 1887–95. Around 40,000 vessels pass through the canal every year.*

Borkum, *one of the East Frisian islands, was once inhabited by whalers. Garden fences were often constructed from whale bones, and some have survived to the present day.*

Bremerhaven *is a vast port at the mouth of the Weser river. It was constructed from 1827 to support the port of Bremen, which is located farther inland, away from the sea.*

Stralsund, *a Hanseatic harbour town with a medieval layout, has a large number of well-preserved historic monuments.*

On the small, flat island of Hiddensee *all car traffic is banned. The island was much loved by the writer Gerhart Hauptmann, who lies buried here in the local cemetery.*

THE COASTLINE

The hinterland of the Baltic region is generally flat and sandy, but in some areas it is steep and rocky. For visitors the greatest draw are the islands: Rügen with its steep chalky cliffs, Usedom with its wide, sandy beaches and Hiddensee. Off the lowlands and the marshy coastal region in the hinterland of the North Sea coast extends the chain of Frisian islands.

The beach at Ahlbeck *and the pier with its restaurant are the greatest attractions on the island of Usedom, at the mouth of the Oder river.*

OSTSEE (BALTIC SEA)

207

LÜBECKER BUCHT

105

20

Wismar

103

Güstrow

104

Schwerin

Rostock

Ribnitz-Damgarten

Stralsund

96

Bergen
RÜGEN

ODERBUCHT

Greifswald

E251/96

109

Anklam

Ueckermünde

0 km   60

0 miles   60

Rügen, *famous for its unusual chalky cliff formations, was immortalized by Caspar David Friedrich and continues to inspire artists.*

CROSS-SECTION OF WATT (NORTH SEA)

The Watt is a flat, boggy stretch of coastline, up to several kilometres wide, which is covered by the sea as the tide comes in, and laid bare as it goes out again. The Watt landscape is fairly monotonous, but it is fascinating to observe the rich flora and fauna, which has adapted to cope with life both underwater and exposed to the air.

Winkles and other small snails live in the coastal zone by the sea.

Starfish

Lugworm and sand cast

Sand gaper (mussel)

LOWER SAXONY, HAMBURG AND BREMEN

hree federal states – Lower Saxony and the independent city states of Hamburg and Bremen – cover an enormous terrain, embracing the whole of northwestern Germany. For the visitor they provide a series of memorable snapshots: the mighty cosmopolitan port of Hamburg, enchanting towns and villages with half-timbered houses and the blooming heather of the Lüneburger Heide.

Lower Saxony was formed in the 19th century through the merging of the kingdom of Hannover with the duchy of Brunswick, Oldenburg and Schaumburg-Lippe and other parts of northern Germany. The second-largest German state after Bavaria, it only ranks fourth in terms of the number of its inhabitants, being less densely populated than other states.

Lower Saxony is characterized by lowlands that become hillier in the south, culminating in the Harz Mountains. The only large cities are Hannover, a modern centre renowned for its trade fairs and for hosting Expo 2000, and Braunschweig, a venerable town that cherishes its link with the Saxon king Heinrich der Löwe, its first important ruler. The Romanesque splendour of Hildesheim is a magnet for visitors, as are the Renaissance centres along the Weser River including Hameln, the charming towns of Celle, Lüneburg and Einbeck, and Wolfenbüttel, Stadthagen and Bückeburg which contain some remarkable Mannerist works of art.

Nature lovers will enjoy excursions to the Lüneburger Heide or paddling in the endless expanses of mud-flats in the North Sea. Tourists are also attracted by the sandy beaches of the East Frisian islands, as well as the solitary rock of the island of Helgoland.

The "free and Hanseatic" towns of Hamburg and Bremen rejoice in a different atmosphere, urban and urbane, tolerant and multicultural, based on centuries of trade with the world.

The glorious moorlands of the Lüneburger Heide, with tall juniper bushes and flowering heathers

◁ The charming Gänselieselbrunnen (goose girl fountain) in the market square in Göttingen

Exploring Lower Saxony, Hamburg and Bremen

Hamburg and Bremen, the region's largest cities, are also the most convenient bases for tourists, offering accommodation in every price category. The most attractive area in this region is the south-eastern section, extending to the foothills of the Harz Mountains with picturesque towns, such as the university town of Göttingen, Romanesque Hildesheim or the stunningly beautiful merchant town of Goslar. A visit to the seaside and an excursion to the islands are also enjoyable.

SEE ALSO

• *Where to Stay* pp513–16
• *Where to Eat* pp552–4

The crowning feature of the bay window of the Dempterhaus in Hameln

The massive edifice of the Neues Rathaus in Hannover

KEY

▬▬	Motorway
▬▬	Main road
═══	Minor road
┄╾┄	Main railway
────	Minor railway
▬▬	National border
▬▬	Regional border

GETTING AROUND

There are international airports in Hamburg, Bremen and Hannover. A network of motorways links Lower Saxony with Scandinavia (via Schleswig-Holstein), and with the rest of western Europe (via the Netherlands or southern Germany). An extensive rail network makes the entire state accessible, although bus connections are limited.

The Grosse Wallanlagen Park in Hamburg, laid out along the city's former fortifications

0 km   40

0 miles   40

Ostfriesische Inseln (East Frisian Islands) ❶

Road map B2. 🚢 Emden-Borkum, Norden-Norddeich to Juist and Norderney, Nessmersiel-Baltrum, Bensersiel-Langeoog, Neuharlingersiel-Spiekeroog, Harlesiel-Wangerooge.
🏠 Leer, Ledastr. 10. (0491) 91 96 96 60.
www.ostfriesland.de

Moormuseum in Elisabethfehn, Ostfriesland

Along the North Sea Coast extends the belt of East Frisian Islands consisting of, from west to east: Borkum, Juist, Norderney, Baltrum, Langeoog, Spiekeroog and Wangerooge. All around them is the **Nationalpark Niedersächsisches Wattenmeer**, a large national park established to protect the unique ecosystem of the shallow seas. At low tide it turns into vast mud-flats, extending to the horizon. This is the time to tour the Watt, as it is known locally, either by horse-drawn carriage or barefoot – always making sure to return before the tide comes in!

The islands themselves, with their beautiful sandy beaches, sand dunes and healthy climate, are among the most popular holiday destinations in Germany.

The car-free island Juist, a 17-km (11-mile) strip of land less than 500 m (1,640 ft) wide, and Norderney with its main town of the same name are the most interesting islands. Neo-Classical villas recall the days when such figures as Heinrich Heine and Otto von Bismarck spent their holidays here. It is also worth

visiting Wangerooge, another island where cars are banned. Three lighthouses – Westturm, Alter Leuchtturm and Neuer Leuchtturm – indicate the island's role in the navigation of the Weser River estuary.

Ostfriesland (East Frisia) ❷

Road map B2. 🚂 Emden, Leer, Norden. 🏠 (0491) 91 96 96 60.
www.ostfriesland.de
🎪 Kiewittmarkt (Jever, end Mar); Altstadtfest (Jever, Aug).

East Frisia is a peninsula near the border with the Netherlands and the Jadebusen bay, at Wilhelmshaven. This is a land of flat meadows, grazing cows and windmills.

Emden, the region's capital, has an attractive town hall resembling that in Antwerp, and a town centre crossed by many canals. The **Kunsthalle Emden**, founded in the early 1990s by Henri Nannen, publisher of the magazine *Stern*, holds a remarkable collection of 19th-century paintings, including the works of many German Expressionists such as Emil Nolde, Max Beckmann and Oskar Kokoschka.

Another attraction is the **Moor- und Fehnmuseum** (moor and fen museum) in Elisabethfehn, which is dedicated to the extraction of peat. Its exhibits include the world's largest plough, as well as the story of Jever, the local beer. Also worth visiting are the Renaissance palace whose reception hall has a ceiling with sunken panels, and next

to the parish church the wood and stone tomb of the Frisian leader Edo Wiemken, made in 1561–4 by master craftsmen from Antwerp.

🏛 **Kunsthalle Emden**
Hinter dem Rahmen 13.
Tel (04921) 975 00. ⬜ 10am–5pm Tue–Fri, 11am–5pm Sat & Sun; 10am–9pm first Tue of month. 📷

🏛 **Moor- und Fehnmuseum**
Oldenburger-Str. 1.
Tel (04499) 22 22. ⬜ Apr–Oct: 10am–5pm Tue–Sun.

Clemenswerth ❸

Road map B3. 🚂 Sögel or Lathen. 🏠 Papenburg, Rathausstr. 2 (04961-839 60). **Schloss Tel** 05952-93 23 25. ⬜ Apr–Oct: 10am–6pm Tue–Sun. ⬤ winter.

Emsland, to the south of East Frisia, extends along the Dutch border, a poor area since time immemorial, with moors and boglands. Only the discovery of oil in the 20th century engineered its progress. Sögel, 33 km (21 miles) south of Greater Papenburg, has the region's greatest attraction, the palatial hunting lodge or Schloss Clemenswerth, built from 1737–49. In search of solitude, the elector and archbishop of Cologne Clemens August commissioned the lodge from Johan Conrad Schlaun. The design was modelled on the pavilion-pagoda of Nymphenburg in Munich. Altogether it comprises seven pavilions with mansard roofs and a chapel. All the brick buildings were laid out on a green lawn, creating a star shape around the palace. Inside there is a museum of the region.

Nationalpark Niedersächsisches Wattenmeer in the Greefsiel area

Oldenburg ❹

Road map B2. ♦ *160,000.* ▦
ℹ *Kleine Kirchenstr. 10 (0441 36 16 13 66).* ♦ *Hafenfest (7 days after Whitsun); Altstadtfest (end Aug); Kramermarkt (Sep/Oct).*
www.oldenburg.de

A thousand years old, and once part of Denmark, this town remained the seat of a duchy until 1918.

The **Lambertikirche**, in the central market square, is a late-Gothic hall-church with a Neo-Classical rotunda added in 1797. The **Schloss**, the ducal residence, displays a similar marriage of styles, particularly Baroque and Neo-Classical. The **Landesmuseum für Kunst und Kulturgeschichte** (state museum of art and culture), based in the castle, is known mainly for its collection of paintings assembled by Wilhelm Tischbein, who lived here for 25 years. The affiliated **Augusteum**, a Neo-Renaissance building in a picturesque spot, holds the museum's modern collection.

⛪ Landesmuseum für Kunst und Kulturgeschichte
Damm 1.
Tel *(0441) 220 73 00.*
◯ *10am–6pm Tue–Sun.*
◯ *1 Jan, Good Friday, Easter, 1 May, 24, 25 & 31 Dec.* ▦

Environs
The town of **Bad Zwischenahn** is worth a visit. Its star attraction is the Gothic St Johanniskirche with frescoes from 1512.

A windmill in the open-air museum in Cloppenburg

Cloppenburg ❺

Road map B2. ♦ *29,000.* ▦
ℹ *Eschstr. 29 (04471-152 56).* ♦ *Mariä Geburtsmarkt (Sep).*

The small market town of Cloppenburg boasts the **Museumsdorf**, the oldest open air museum in Germany, established in 1934. On a vast site, 50 architectural monuments from all over Lower Saxony have been assembled. There are houses, including charming examples of the half-timbered style of Wehlburg, windmills and a small 17th-century church from Klein-Escherde near Hildesheim.

To the east of Cloppenburg lies Visbek. Here the visitor is taken back to the Stone Age, with megalithic graves from 3,500 to 1,800 BC, including the 80-m (262-ft) long grave known as "Visbeker Bräutigam" (bridegroom) and the even larger, 100-m (321-ft) long "Visbeker Braut" (bride).

⛪ Museumsdorf Cloppenburg
Bether Straße 6. **Tel** *(04471) 948 40.* ◯ *Mar–Oct: 9am–6pm daily, Nov–Feb: 9am–4:30pm daily.* ▦

Osnabrück ❻

Road map B3. ♦ *157,000.* ▦
ℹ *Bierstr. 22–23 (0541-32 32 202).* ♦ *Herbstjahrmarkt (early Nov).*
www.osnabrueck.de

This Westphalian town has been a bishop's see since the time of Charlemagne. In 1648, negotiations took place here between representatives of Sweden and the Protestant duchies of the Reich. The signing of the Peace of Westphalia in 1648, which ended the Thirty Years' War, was announced from the town hall steps. It was also the birthplace of the writer Erich Maria Remarque in 1899.

Despite damage in World War II, **Dom St Peter**, Osnabrück's 13th-century cathedral, is worth visiting. It has a bronze baptismal font and enormous triumphal cross, and the late-Gothic Snetlage-Altar of the Crucifixion. From here a short walk takes the visitor to the market square, Marienkirche and the Gothic **Rathaus** (town hall), with a sculpture of Charlemagne.

Epitaph for Albert von Bevessen in the Dom in Osnabrück

Environs South of Osnabrück is the western part of the Teutoburger Wald (Teutoburg Forest). The spa town of **Bad Iburg**, 12 km (8 miles) to the south of Osnabrück, has a monumental Benedictine monastery and bishop's palace. The Rittersaal (knights' hall) has a giant ceiling fresco depicting an architectural fantasy of foreshortened perspectives.

The Schloss in Oldenburg, featuring Baroque and Neo-Classical styles

Bremen ❼

Bremen, together with its deep-water port Bremer-haven, constitutes a separate town state. Not so much a bustling modern metropolis as a peaceful country town, it is conscious of its historical origins dating back to Charlemagne. The townscape is not dominated by the port as in Hamburg, but by the old town with its magnificent cathedral and town hall. Bremen enjoyed prosperity from 1358 when it joined the Hanseatic League, its wealth based on the coffee and wool trade. Today, Bremen still benefits from its port, which ships around 700,000 cars a year.

Statue of the Bremen Town Musicians, by Gerhard Marcks

Gabled houses and the statue of Roland in the Marktplatz

Exploring Bremen
Most of Bremen's tourist attractions are in the old town, on the east bank of the Weser River. The area is easy to pick out on a map as it is surrounded by a green belt, established when the town's fortifications were demolished. The Überseemuseum (eth-nography museum) is close to the old town, and trams run to Schwachhausen, where the Focke-Museum is based.

🏛 Marktplatz
On the main square of Medieval Bremen stand the town hall and the cathedral, and, on the west side, several gabled houses. This lovely view is slightly marred by the unattractive 1960s Haus der Bürgerschaft, the state parliament building.

In front of the town hall stands a 10-m (32-ft) statue of Roland, dating from 1404. It is the largest of many similar statues in German towns, and the prototype for others. A nephew of Charlemagne, Roland symbolizes a town's independence. His gaze is directed toward the cathedral, the residence of the bishop, who frequently sought to restrict Bremen's autonomy. Roland's sword of justice symbolizes the judiciary's independence, and the engraved motto confirms the emperor's edict, conferring town rights onto Bremen.

The second, more recent (1953) monument in the square is dedicated to the Bremen Town Musicians – a donkey, dog, cat and cockerel,

who according to the Grimm fairy tale trekked to Bremen.

🏛 Rathaus
Marktplatz. **Tel** *(0421) 30 80 00.*
⏰ *11am, noon, 3pm, 4pm Mon–Sat, 11am–noon Sun.* 🅿
The original Gothic building dating from the years 1405–10 was clad with a magnificent Renaissance façade, one of the finest examples of Weser Renaissance architecture in northern Germany, designed by Lüder von Bentheim. He masterfully incorporated the Gothic figures of Charle-magne and seven Electors, as well as four prophets and four wise men. In the 40-m (131-ft) Große Halle (great hall) new laws were passed, as symbolized by the fresco (1932) of Solomon's court. Among its many other treasures is the meticulously crafted Renaissance spiral staircase. On the western side of the town hall is the entrance to the "Ratskeller" where you can sample 600 different wines, and delight in the murals from 1927, by the Impressionist Max Slevogt.

The late-Renaissance façade of Bremen's Rathaus

🏚 Schütting

Marktplatz.

On the southwestern side of Marktplatz stands this mansion used by the Merchants' Guild for their conventions. It was built in 1537–9 by the Antwerp architect Johann der Buschener in Dutch Mannerist style. The eastern gable, more classically Renaissance in style, is the work of the local builder Carsten Husmann.

🏛 Dom

Tower and "Bleikeller":
Tel (0421) 36 50 40. ⬜ Easter– 1 Nov: 10am–5pm Mon–Fri, 10am–2pm Sat, 2–5pm Sun.

This magnificent Romanesque cathedral, with its vast twin-towered façade, dates from the 11th century and has been extensively refurbished.

The Mannerist Schütting, a meeting place for merchants

At the end of the 19th century, while the southern tower was rebuilt, the façade was also reconstructed and a tower was added. Inside, it is worth looking at the sandstone bas-reliefs which divide the western choir stalls as well as fragments of Gothic stalls that were destroyed in the 19th century, with scenes of the Passion and the battle

VISITORS' CHECKLIST

Road map C2. 🏘 556,000. 🚉
ℹ Hauptbahnhof & Obernstraße (01805 10 10 30). 🚢 Port tours (0421-33 89 89). **Cruises:** May– Sep: 10 & 11:30am, 1:30 & 3:15pm daily. 🏇 🚢 Sat & Sun. 🏇 6 Tage Rennen (Jan); Osterwiese (Apr); Vegesack Harbour Festival (Jun); Bremer Freimarkt (late Oct/early Nov); Christmas market (1–23 Dec). www.bremen-turismus.de

of Judas Machabeus. There is also a Baroque pulpit paid for by Christina the Queen of Sweden in 1638, and numerous multi-coloured memorials, including one to Segebad Clüver by the entrance to the north tower (1457). The larger eastern crypt has interesting Romanesque capitals, while in the second eastern crypt visitors can admire the oldest Bremen sculpture of Christ the Omnipotent (1050) as well as the baptismal font. The latter has 38 bas-reliefs, and a bowl supported by four lions with riders. In the so-called "Bleikeller" (lead cellar) underneath the former church cloisters, eight perfectly preserved mummies are on show.

Bas-reliefs on the western choir stalls in the Dom

BREMEN TOWN CENTRE

0 metres   500
0 yards   500

Key to Symbols *see back flap*

⚏ Kunstsammlungen Böttcherstraße
Paula-Modersohn-Becker-Museum and **Roseliushaus**
Böttcherstr. 6–10. *Tel (0421) 338 8222.* ☐ *11am–6pm Tue–Sun.* **www.pmbm.de**

This once insignificant lane where coopers lived was transformed into Art Deco style in 1926–30 by Ludwig Roselius, a wealthy coffee merchant. The National Socialists preserved the street as an example of degenerate art. At the entrance to the street is a bas-relief by Bernhard Hoetger from 1920, of the Archangel Michael fighting a dragon.

The **Paula-Modersohn-Becker-Museum**, built in the Expressionist style, contains an art museum, while in the neighbouring 16th-century **Roseliushaus** the original period interiors can be admired. The street's other attraction is a carillon which chimes tuneful melodies every day at noon, 3pm and 6pm.

Archangel Michael fighting a dragon, on a bas-relief in Böttcherstrasse

⚏ Schnoorviertel
Spielzeugmuseum im Schnoor
Schnoor 24. *Tel (0421) 32 03 82.* ☐ *10am–6pm daily.*

The Schnoorviertel is a historic district of small houses dating from the 15th–18th centuries. One of Bremen's poorest areas before World War II, it miraculously escaped destruction. It has been restored gradually since 1958 and now teems with restaurants, cafés, souvenir shops and tourists. In the centre of the district is the Gothic **Johanniskirche**, which once belonged to the Franciscans. In accordance with the order's rules it has no tower, although this is compensated for by a decorative gable on the western façade, and three levels of arched alcoves and herringbone brickwork. The **Spielzeugmuseum** (toy museum) nearby is also worth visiting.

⛫ Kunsthalle
Am Wall 207. *Tel (0421) 32 90 80.* ☐ *10am–9pm Tue, 10am–6pm Wed–Sun.*

On the edge of the old town is this art gallery, which actually lost most of its collection to Russia during World War II. The pieces that remained, as well as works subsequently acquired, make the collection of great importance. There are works by Dürer, Altdorfer, Rubens, Jan Breughel, van Dyck and Rembrandt. There is also an excellent French section, with works by Delacroix, Denis, Monet and Manet, as well as 19th- and 20th-century German painters such as Beckmann and Kirchner. At the heart of the collection are about 40 paintings by Paula Modersohn-Becker.

⛫ Übersee-Museum
Bahnhofplatz 13. *Tel (0421) 160 38 101.* ☐ *9am–6pm Tue–Fri, 10am–6pm Sat & Sun.* 🅿

This museum of overseas countries transports the visitor to faraway destinations. Founded in 1891, it was originally a museum of German colonialism and is now dedicated to the culture of non-European nations. Of special interest are exhibits on Pacific cultures, with life-sized models of houses and boats from the Solomon Islands.

⛫ Focke-Museum
Schwachhauser-Heerstr. 240. *Tel (0421) 699 60 00.* ☐ *10am–9pm Tue, 10am–5pm Wed–Sun.* 🅿

The excellent collections of this museum compensate for its distant location. Founded in 1918, when the history museum was amalgamated with the decorative arts museum, it presents Bremen's art and culture from the Middle Ages to the present day. Exhibits from patrician houses and original sculptures from the façade of the town hall testify to the wealth of the Hanseatic town. Other sections are devoted to the archaeology of the region as well as whaling and emigration to the US in the 19th and 20th centuries.

The nearby Rhododendronpark offers a pleasant respite from the museums. It includes 1,600 varieties of rhododendron which become a sea of flowers from late April to June.

Environs
Three places in the Bremen area are particularly worth a detour. About 50 km (31 miles) to the north lies Bremen's deep-sea harbour **Bremerhaven**, with the

Camille Pissarro, *Girl lying on a grassy slope*, Kunsthalle

PAULA MODERSOHN-BECKER (1876–1907)

A pupil of Fritz Mackensen and wife of Otto Modersohn, Paula Modersohn-Becker was the most significant artistic figure in Worpswede. She learned about the Impressionist use of colour during visits to Paris, and her own unique sensibility made her a precursor of Expressionism. She became famous for her naturalistic paintings of poor, starving and even dying country folk. She died in childbirth, aged only 31, and this is how she was commemorated on her tombstone, in the peaceful village cemetery in Worpswede, by the sculptor Bernhard Hoetger.

Girl playing a flute in birch woods (1905)

Exhibits in the Große Kunstschau in Worpswede near Bremen

Deutsches Schifffahrts-museum. This wonderful, marine museum, designed by the renowned architect Hans Scharoun, displays both originals and models of a wide range of ships, dating from the Roman Empire to the present day. A special hall displays the *Hanse Kogge,* a merchant ship dredged from the bottom of the Weser River in 1962. Displayed outside, in the open-air part of the museum, are the last great German sailing boat *Seute Deern,* the polar ship *Grönland* and *Wilhelm Bauer,* a U-boat from World War II.

The small village of **Worps-wede**, northeast of Bremen, takes the visitor into the world of art. From 1889 until the end of World War II it was a famous artists' colony, situated in the middle of peat bogs. Apart from poets, such as Rainer Maria Rilke, and such architects as Bernhard Hoetger, the fame of this village rested principally on the painters: Fritz Mackensen, Otto Modersohn, Hans am Ende, Fritz Overbeck and Heinrich Vogeler. Unquestionably the greatest artist in Worpswede was Paula Modersohn-Becker, whose sad fairy tale world of rustic subjects cannot be defined within one style. Work by the founding members is on display in the **Große Kunstschau and the Worpsweder Kunsthalle**.

Verden an der Aller, the picturesque bishops' residence and once a free town of the Reich, is known to sports enthusiasts thanks to its horse racing tracks, training centres and stadiums, and the **Deutsches Pferdemuseum** (horse museum), with a large collection of equestrian artifacts.

Seven horse auctions are held in the town each year, and the most important are in April and October.

Above the town rises the Dom with a large, steep roof. The hall of this cathedral, a modification of earlier basilicas, is architecturally interesting, with a multi-sided presbytery, a passageway dating from 1268–1311 and Romanesque cloisters and a tower. North of the cathedral is the Domherrenhaus, housing the Historisches Museum, with exhibits on regional history and archaeological and ethnographic departments.

The **Deutsches Auswandererhaus Bremerhaven** traces the history of more than 7 million Germans who emigrated via Bremerhaven, especially to the United States. A database of records is available.

🏛 **Deutsches Schifffahrts-museum**
Bremerhaven, Hans-Scharoun-Platz 1. *Tel* (0471) 482 070. ⬜ *Apr–Oct: 10am– 6pm daily; Nov–Feb: 10am–6pm Tue–Sun.*

🏛 **Große Kunstschau**
Worpswede. Lindenallee 3 & 5. *Tel* (04792) 13 02. ⬜ *10am–6pm daily (closed Mon in Nov–Mar).*

🏛 **Worpsweder Kunsthalle**
Bergstr. 17. *Tel* (04792) 12 77. ⬜ *Apr–Oct: 10am–6pm daily; Nov–Mar: 11am–6pm daily.*

🏛 **Deutsches Pferdemuseum**
Holzmarkt 9. *Tel* (04231) 80 71 40. ⬜ *10am–5pm Tue–Sun.*

🏛 **Deutsches Auswanderer-haus Bremerhaven**
Columbusstr. 65. *Tel* (0471) 90220-0. ⬜ *Mar–Oct: 10am–6pm daily; Nov–Feb: 10am–5pm daily.*
www.dah-bremerhaven.de

The Dom in Verden an der Aller, with its unusually large roof

Hamburg ❽

Crest on the town hall

Germany's second largest city, Hamburg has an openness to the world and a variety of architectural styles in its districts, making it a fascinating place to visit. For many years, Hamburg was a leading member of the Hanseatic League and an independent trading town, and in 1945 it became a city-state of the Federal Republic. Visitors are attracted by Hamburg's enormous port, situated right in the centre of the city, colourful entertainments in the red-light district St Pauli, many attractive parks and lakes as well as the warm welcome extended by the locals who, on first encounter, may seem a little cool.

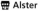

A fountain in the Neo-Renaissance Rathausmarkt

Exploring Hamburg

The best way to get around Hamburg is by metro (U-Bahn and S-Bahn), using an all-day ticket (Tageskarte) since parking space is scarce. The city centre can be explored on foot, including the area between the main railway station and the lake, along with the rest of the old town, the port and Hamburg's two largest museums.

🚏 Rathausmarkt

The symbol of Hamburg is the enormous Neo-Renaissance town hall, the fifth in the city's history. Previous town halls were destroyed by wars as well as a catastrophic fire in 1842. Little remains of the old town. The city's current appearance is characterized by 19th-century style as well as Modernism. The town hall itself, with its ornamental halls, is worth visiting.

The town hall square is enclosed on one side by Alsterfleet. Originally a small river, it is today one of numerous canals which have given Hamburg the name "Venice

of the North". A monument in memory of the victims of World War I is the work of the artist Ernst Barlach. Between Rathausmarkt and Gänsemarkt runs a network of elegantly roofed shopping arcades. These were built in the 19th century, and have since been continually extended.

🚏 Alster

Elegant arcades lead from the Rathausmarkt to Binnenalster, a large lake in the middle of the city. Like the much larger Außenalster lake further north, it was created by damming the Alster River. On a sunny day, the Jungfernstieg, an elegant boulevard running the length of the Alster, is a pleasant place for a walk. Great views of the city can be had from the café in the Alsterpavilion. There is a small quay from which boats depart for the "Alster-rundfahrt", an excursion which takes the visitor all the way to the Außenalster and to smaller canals with views of the villas in the north of Hamburg and the cityscape of the centre with its five main towers.

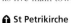

Door knocker on St Petrikirche

🔒 St Petrikirche

Mönckebergstr. **Tel** *(040) 325 74 00.* ☐ *10am–6:30pm Mon, Tues, Thu, Fri, 10am–7pm Wed, 10am–5pm Sat, 9am–9pm Sun.*
The church of St Petri, originally Gothic, was extensively rebuilt in the Neo-Gothic style after the Great Fire of 1842. The Grabower Altar that once belonged to the church has been transferred to the Kunsthalle *(see pp436–7)*. Tourists can still admire the Gothic sculpture of the Madonna, dating from 1470.

🚏 Jakobikirche

Jakobikirchhof 22. **Tel** *(040) 303 73 70.* ☐ *Oct–Mar: 11am–5pm Mon–Sat; Apr–Sep 10am–5pm Mon–Sat.*
The church of St Jacobi, from 1340, was bombed during World War II, and subsequently rebuilt in its original style. Its captivating interior includes the largest Baroque

The main altar in Jakobikirche

organ in northern Germany, the work of Arp Schnitger. The triptych of St Luke in the presbytery of the southern nave, a magnificent example of late-Gothic art, was originally created in 1499 for Hamburg's cathedral, which was pulled down in 1804.

🏛 Kontorhausviertel

Deichtorhallen Deichtorstr. 1–2. **Tel** (040) 32 10 30. ◯ 11am–6pm Tue–Sun (during exhibitions).

After World War I a district of commercial offices known as Kontorhausviertel was built between Steinstraße and Messberg. The **Chilehaus**, built by Fritz Höger in 1922–4, was an experiment in creating a traditional brick building with a Modernist design. This ten-storey building, with its pointed eastern façade resembling a ship's bow, became internationally famous as a symbol of Expressionist architecture.

Nearby are the enormous **Deichtorhallen**, market halls of the port built in 1911–12. Turned into dramatic exhibition halls in 1997, they are now used for major art exhibitions.

The Expressionist Chilehaus in Kontorhausviertel

🏛 Speicherstadt

Deutsches Zollmuseum

Alter Wandrahm 16a. **Tel** (040) 30 08 76 11. ◯ 10am–5pm Tue–Sun.

The atmosphere of the giant warehouse district by the port will seem depressing to some, charming to others. Located within the toll-free area of the port, this district is reached after crossing the customs post. It is the largest complex of warehouses in the world. The Neo-Gothic buildings, dating from the end of the 19th century, are separated by canals. They still

serve as storerooms for coffee, tea and carpets. Listed as one of the city's historic monuments, Speicherstadt now houses the Speicherstadt Museum and is part of Hafen City, a residential and office development. The **Deutsches Zollmuseum** (German customs museum) located by Kornhausbrücke, (corn house bridge), tells the story of customs and excise over the past hundred years.

HAMBURG CITY CENTRE

Alster ②
Altstadt (Old Town) ⑧
Jakobikirche ④
Kontorhausviertel ⑤
Kunsthalle ⑦
Rathausmarkt ①
St Petrikirche ③
Speicherstadt ⑥

Key to Symbols see back flap

0 metres 250
0 yards 250

Kunsthalle

The most interesting art gallery in northern Germany, the Kunsthalle in Hamburg has a tradition dating back to 1817, when the Kunstverein (friends of the fine arts), proud of its middle-class, non-aristocratic background, was established. The museum opened to the public in 1869. The collection has a standard chronological review of European art movements, with an emphasis on 19th-century German Romantics, with works by Caspar David Friedrich and Philipp Otto Runge. A four-storey extension, the Galerie der Gegenwart (contemporary gallery), was built in 1996 to a design by the architect O M Ungers. The building is reached by an underground link from the basement of the main gallery.

The Polar Sea (1823–4)
Caspar David Friedrich's dramatic seascape, with a sinking ship in the background behind the rising flow, is loaded with symbolism.

★ Hannah and Simeon in the Temple (c.1627) *Thanks to his mastery of a sense of drama, Rembrandt succeeded in depicting the psychological make-up of his elderly subjects, who have recognized the Saviour in an unspoken message conveyed to the temple by Mary and Joseph.*

High Altar of St Peter in Hamburg (1383) *This panelled painting, displaying a stunning wealth of detail, was produced by Master Bertram of Minden, the first artist in Germany to be identified by his name.*

Main entrance

Ground floor

★ Morning (1808) *This painting by Philipp Otto Runge centres around Aurora, goddess of dawn, and was intended to be part of a series called "Times of the Day". The other works were never completed due to the artist's untimely death aged 33.*

For hotels and restaurants in this region see pp513–16 and pp552–4

Self-Portrait with Model (1910 and 1926) *Sixteen years after first painting this picture, Ernst Ludwig Kirchner repainted areas, in order to emphasize the distance between model and artist.*

VISITORS' CHECKLIST

Glockengießerwall. **Tel** (040) 428 131 200. ☐ 10am–6pm Tue–Sun, 10am–9pm Thu. 📷 **Library** ☐ 11am–5pm Tue–Sat. **Café** ☐ 10am–6pm Tue–Sun, 10am–9pm Thu. www.hamburger-kunsthalle.de

GALLERY GUIDE

On the ground floor, Rooms 2–10 and 16–19 contain works of art from the first half of the 20th century. On the first floor, Rooms 101–116 display the works of old masters. In Rooms 117–136 paintings from the 19th century are exhibited, and more works from the first half of the 20th century are shown in Rooms 137–148.

First floor

★ Girls on the Pier
(c 1900) This painting is one of six variations on the same theme painted by Edvard Munch. The painter omitted the landscape, concentrating on the relationship and tensions between the girls.

Stairs down to underground link to Galerie der Gegenwart

KEY

- ☐ Gallery of old masters
- ☐ 19th-century paintings
- ☐ 20th-century paintings (first half)
- ☐ Gallery of drawings
- ☐ Non-exhibition space

Stairs to basement and Hubertus-Wald-Forum with temporary exhibitions

STAR EXHIBITS

- ★ Girls on the Pier
- ★ Morning
- ★ Hannah and Simeon in the Temple

Nana (1877) *The subject of Édouard Manet's painting was the heroine of a Zola novel. Manet was not allowed to exhibit the painting in the Paris Salon because Nana was known as a Parisian courtesan.*

🏛 Altstadt (Old Town)

Hamburg's old town extends to the south of the Rathaus (town hall) but, following the Great Fire of 1842 and bombing during World War II, only a few original buildings remain. **Katharinenkirche** (St Catherine's), with its characteristic tower, was begun in the 13th century and completed in the 17th century. It has been restored after damage in World War II. Of the neighbouring Neo-Gothic **Nikolaikirche** only a single tower remained after 1945, the Nikolaiturm, which is the third tallest in Germany. It serves as a monument to the tragic consequences of war.

Deichstrasse is one of a few surviving streets in the old town, with the original façades visible from both the road and the canal (the best view is from Hohe Brücke, a bridge). One of the many famous restaurants is at No. 25, "Zum Brandanfang", where The Great Fire of 1842 was said to have broken out, which eventually destroyed most of the city.

Ornate Baroque pulpit in Hamburg's Michaeliskirche

🏛 Michaeliskirche

Observation tower
Tel (040) 37 67 80.
⬜ *May–Oct: 9am–7:30pm daily, Nov–Apr: 10am–5:30pm daily.*

The massive Baroque church of St Michaelis, visible from afar with its 132-m (433-ft) tower (the "Michel"), is the main symbol of Hamburg. The interior is preserved in a white, grey and gold colour scheme, and some of the

The neon-lit Reeperbahn in St Pauli

fittings are made from tropical wood. The observation platform gives some splendid views of the city and its extensive harbour.

🏛 Krameramtswohnungen

Krayenkamp 10. *Tel (040) 37 50 19 88.* ⬜ *31 Mar–29 Nov: 10am–5pm Tue–Sun; 30 Nov–30 Mar: 10am–5pm Sat & Sun.*

Near the Michaeliskirche, a section of the old town, the Krameramtswohnungen, has miraculously survived. These half-timbered houses were funded by the merchants' guild and built to house the widows of shopkeepers. Today they are occupied by tourist shops, cafés and restaurants.

⚓ The Port

Cap San Diego *Tel (040) 36 42 09.*
⬜ *10am–6pm daily.* **Rickmer Rickmers** *Tel (040) 319 59 59.*
⬜ *10am–8pm daily.*

Situated 104 km (62 miles) inland along the Elbe River, Hamburg is Europe's second

largest port after Rotterdam, and the port dominates the panorama. Every year 12,000 ships dock here from 90 countries. From the U3 Baumwall metro station it is best to walk to **Landungsbrücken**, past the museum ships moored here: the freighter *Cap San Diego* and the sailing boat *Rickmer Rickmers* (1896). Landungsbrücken is a 200-m (656-ft) long building from where the passenger ferries depart. A tour of the harbour is highly recommended. Near Landungsbrücken, in a copper-domed building, is the entrance to Alter Elbtunnel (the old tunnel under the Elbe) where people and cars are lowered in a giant lift.

🏛 St Pauli

Infamous around the world, this area is also known as **Reeperbahn**, after the main street. It is a world of nightclubs and bars, pubs and theatres, sex clubs and brothels. It is here, in Hamburg's red-light district, that some teenage seasonal workers from Liverpool, the Beatles, started their careers. On Herbertstrasse, scantily clad women offer their services behind a metal barrier – women and those under 18 are forbidden entrance. St Pauli

---

FISCHMARKT – A MARKET FOR EVERYTHING

This is an attraction for early risers or for those who never get to bed at all. From 5am (7am in winter) on Sundays the Auktionshalle (auction hall) and the nearby waterside turn into a colourful market place. Fishermen returning from the sea with their freshly caught fish compete with noisy greengrocers offering their wares and bric-à-brac merchants setting out stalls. Thousands of tourists mingle with sailors and ladies of the night relaxing with a cup of steaming mulled wine after a hard night's work in St Pauli. Here and there you can hear Plattdeutsch being spoken, the northern patois. Morning mass at 10am used to mark the end of this colourful spectacle, but today's public lingers on and then hurries off to bed instead of church.

Bric-à-brac on sale at a market stall in Fischmarkt

---

even has an Erotic-Museum, where next to the exhibits are reproductions of works by artists from Rembrandt to Picasso, which are said to "prove" that everything revolves around the female posterior.

Environs
The magnificent palace in **Ahrensburg** (1595), 23 km (14 miles) to the northeast, has Baroque and Rococo interiors open to visitors.

Façade of Schloss Ahrensburg, flanked by towers

Altes Land ❾

Road map C2.

On the flood plains stretching for more than 30 km (19 miles) between Hamburg and Stade, along the Lower Elbe River, is the Altes Land (old land). This area is fertile and has the largest number

of orchards in Germany. Many visitors come here in May, when cherry and apple tree blossom turns everything into a sea of white and pink. In this riot of colour stand sturdy red-brick houses with white half-timbered panels, thatched roofs and carved gates. The most beautiful villages are **Neuenfelde**, **Jork**, **Borstel**, **Steinkirchen** and **Hollern**, with their richly furnished Baroque churches.

Stade ❿

Road map C2. ⛨ 47,000.
🚆 U3 to Neugraben, then by train or catamaran from Landungs-brücken. 🛈 Hansestrasse 16 (04141-40 91 70) www.stade-tourismus.de

This medieval Hanseatic town has retained most of its half-timbered buildings, with the most attractive in the **Alter Hafen** (old harbour). There is a also a quaint crane and the **Schwedenspeicher** (Swedish granary) dating from the Swedish occupation during the Thirty Years' War (1692–1705). It is now home to the **Schwedenspeicher-Museum**, Stade's regional museum with exhibits on the town's history and defence system, including wheels from 700 BC, which were part of a Bronze-Age cart. Nearby, an interesting building at Am Wasser West 7 houses the **Kaufmann Collection**, with works by Worps-wede artists. The entire old

The Baroque portal of the Dutch-influenced Rathaus in Stade

town is surrounded by preserved modern fortifications. Other attractions are the **Bürgermeister-Hintze-Haus** at Am Wasser West 23, a house built for the mayor, Hintze, in 1617–46, and the exquisite Baroque **Rathaus** (town hall) from 1667, its design revealing Dutch influence.

It is also worth visiting two Gothic churches: **St Wilhadi** from the 14th century which boasts an interesting Gothic hall and a leaning tower, and **St Cosmas and Damiani**, founded after the Great Fire of 1659, with marvellous Baroque furnishings.

🏛 **Schwedenspeicher-Museum**
Am Wasser West 39. **Tel** (04141) 79 77 30. ◯ 10am–5pm Tue–Fri, 10am–6pm Sat & Sun. 📷

The half-timbered houses along the waterside of Alter Hafen in Stade

Lüneburg ⓫

Road map D2. 🏘 *70,000.*
🚃 ℹ *Rathaus, Am Markt (04131-207 66 20).* **www.**lueneburg.de

It is hard to believe that this small, former Hanseatic town was once one of the wealthiest in Germany. Its prosperity was founded on salt mines. Opened in 956, they provided work for more than 2,000 people by the late Middle Ages and were the largest industry in Europe.

Lüneburg's most important monument is the **Rathaus** (town hall). The interior is even more intriguing than the frequently rebuilt façade, in particular the Großer Ratssaal (the main hall) with its Gothic stained-glass windows and 16th-century frescoes of the Last Judgement, as well as the Große Ratsstube (council chamber) with Renaissance woodwork by Albert von Soest. A remarkable collection of municipal silverware can be found in Ostpreußisches Landesmuseum.

Johnniskirche, one of Lüneburg's three Gothic churches, stands on Am Sande. It has a 108-m (354-ft) west tower, which leans more than 2 m (6 ft) from the perpendicular. In one of its five naves there is a panelled painting dating from 1482–5, the masterful work of the German painter Hinrik Funhof. Also interesting is the soaring basilica of **Michaeliskirche**, consecrated in 1409.

Not far from here is the old port on the Ilmenau River. On Lüner Straße stands the **Altes Kaufhaus**, a former herring warehouse with a Baroque façade. The 14th-century wooden crane was rebuilt in the 18th century. It was used to load salt onto ships. The decorative wavy brick lines *(Taustäbe)* on many of the old buildings are characteristic of the town.

🏛 **Rathaus**
Am Markt. **Tel** *(04131) 30 92 30.*
📷 *11am, 12:30pm, 2:30pm, 4pm Tue–Sat; 11am, 2pm Sun.*

A typical farmstead in Lüneburger Heide

Lüneburger Heide ⓬

Road map D2. ℹ *Wallstr. 4, Lüneburg (04131-30 99 60).* **www.**lueneburger-heide.de

South of Hamburg, between the rivers Elbe and Aller, is a sprawling area of heathland, grazed by heifers and sheep and buzzing with bees in the heathers and pine forests. Until the Middle Ages, this area was covered by dense mixed forests, but these were felled to satisfy demand for wood in

the saltworks of Lüneburg. The half-stepped terrain provides grazing land for Heidschnucken, the local breed of sheep. The heather moors are best seen at the **Naturschutzpark Lüneburger Heide**, a large area of nature reserve founded in 1921. From the village of Undeloh it is best to continue by foot, bike or carriage to the traditional village of Wilsede. From Wilsede it is not far to Wilseder Berg, the highest peak of this moraine region. The view of the surrounding countryside is particularly beautiful at the end of August, when the purple heather is blooming.

Soltau ⓭

Road map C3. 🏘 *23,000.* ℹ *Am Alten Stadtgraben 3 (05191-82 82 82).* **www.**soltau.de

The main attraction of the town of Soltau is **Heidepark Soltau**, a vast funfair with trains, water rides and a genuine Mississippi steamboat. For nature lovers, there is the **Vogelpark Walsrode**, 20 km (12 miles) southwest of Soltau. It holds about 1,000 species of birds, from penguins to birds of paradise. Aviaries, some 12-m (40-ft) tall, simulate the birds' natural environment.

🌿 **Heidepark Soltau**
Tel *(01805) 92 91 01.* ⏰ *Apr–Oct: 9am–6pm daily (admission till 4pm).*

🌿 **Vogelpark Walsrode**
Tel *(05161) 604 40.* ⏰ *Apr–Oct: 9am–7pm daily, Nov–Mar 10am–4pm daily.* **www.**weltvogelpark.de

Environs:
In grim contrast to both parks stands **Bergen-Belsen**, a concentration camp built in the moorland of Osterheide, about 30 km (19 miles) south of Soltau. A monument and small museum commemorate the place where 50,000 people were murdered, among them Anne Frank.

🏛 **Gedenkstätte Bergen-Belsen**
Lohheide. **Tel** *(05051) 47 59 200.*
⏰ *Apr–Sep: 10am–6pm, Oct–Mar: 10am–5pm daily.*

Eighteenth-century wooden crane in Lüneburg

For hotels and restaurants in this region see pp513–16 and pp552–4

Vogelpark Walsrode – a paradise with 1,000 different bird species

Kloster (monastery) with a beautiful 13th–14th century church. Worth seeing are its Gothic frescoes, the presbytery vaults and the 14th- and 15th-century tapestries.

🏛 **Deutsches Erdölmuseum**
Schwarzer Weg 7–9. *Tel* (05146) 92 340. ◻ Mar–Nov: 10am–5pm Tue–Sun; Jun–Aug: 10am–6pm Tue–Sun. 🖼

⛪ **Kloster Wienhausen**
Tel (05149) 18 660. ◻ Apr–Oct: 10 & 11am, 2–5pm Tue–Sat, noon–5pm Sun. 🖼

Celle ⑭

Road map C3. 🏘 74,000.
🚉 Schlossplatz. 🚌 Markt 14–16 (05141-12 12). ◻ Kunsthandwerkermarkt (Whitsun).
www.celle-tourismus.de

Between 1378 and 1705, Celle was the seat of distant relations of the Welf family, the reigning dynasty in the Duchy of Brunswick-Lüneburg. The **Schloss** (castle), rebuilt in Renaissance style after 1533, has a façade with octagonal towers, gables and bay windows. It is one of the most important early-Renaissance buildings in Germany. The Gothic chapel was rebuilt in a Mannerist style to a design by Martin de Vos, who painted 76 of its paintings, including the famous *Crucifixion* (end of the 16th century).

Celle prides itself on 500 half-timbered houses, with the most interesting ones in picturesque Kalandgasse and Zöllnerstrasse. **Hoppner Haus**, at Poststrasse 8, is richly decorated with reliefs of mythological beasts.

Equally interesting is the painted decoration of the **Rathaus** (town hall), a great example of Weser Renaissance (*see p453*) from 1579. From the **Stadtkirche** church tower great views unfold. The Baroque **Synagoge**, beyond the old town, is the only one surviving in northern Germany.

🏰 **Schloss**
Tel (05141) 12 454. ◻ Apr–Oct: 11am, noon, 1, 2 & 3pm Tue–Sun; Nov–Mar: 11am & 3pm Tue–Sun. 🖼

⛪ **Stadtkirche**
Tel (05141) 7735. ◻ 10am–6pm Tue–Sat. **Tower:** Apr–Oct: 10–11:45am 2–4:45pm Tue–Sat.

✡ **Synagoge**
Im Kreise 24. *Tel* (05141) 12 12. ◻ noon–5pm Mon–Thu, Sun; 10am–3pm Fri.

Environs:
The town of **Wietze**, 11 km (7 miles) west of Celle, has been a centre of petroleum since 1858. The **Deutsches Erdölmuseum Wietze** provides a very interesting overview on the history of oil extraction. The neighbouring village of **Wienhausen** has a Cistercian

Wolfsburg ⑮

Road map D3. 🏘 123,000. 🚉
🚌 Willy-Brandt-Platz 3 (05361-89 99 30). **www.**wolfsburg.de

During the 1930s, this small village began to develop into a sizeable town, based around the Volkswagen car works. Production of the "people's car" was conceived by Hitler – every German was to be able to afford this inexpensive car, designed by Ferdinand Porsche. The model reached its peak during the post-war economic boom years. The **Volkswagenwerk** factory is open to visitors.

Wolfsburg also has some outstanding examples of modern architecture: a cultural centre designed by Alvara Aalto, a city theatre designed by Hans Scharoun and a planetarium.

🏭 **Volkswagenwerk Autostadt**
Stadtbrücke. *Tel* (0800) 28 86 78 238. ◻ 9am–6pm daily. 🚌 every 30 mins. **www.**autostadt.de

The façade of the Schloss with octagonal towers at the corners, in Celle

The Renaissance Schloss in Stadthagen

Stadthagen ⑯

Road map C3. 🏛 *23,800.* 🚇
ℹ️ *Am Markt 1 (05721-92 50 65).*
www.stadthagen.de

The counts of Schaumburg-Lippe used the Renaissance **Schloss** (castle) as their private residence. Apart from this and the town hall, the main attraction is the church of **St Martini**, with an early Baroque mausoleum, and a masterful bronze monument by Adrian de Vries, court artist to Rudolf II in Prague.

🏛 St Martini
Schulstr.18. **Tel** *(05721) 78 070.*
⬜ *9am–noon, 2–4pm Mon–Thu,
9am–noon Fri.*

Environs
A gem of Romanesque architecture can be found at **Idensen** near Wunsdorf, 22 km (14 miles) from Stadthagen. The church interior of Alte Kirche (1120) is entirely painted with scenes from the Old and New testaments, and there is a vast Byzantine-style image of Christ's Enthronement on a vaulted ceiling.

Bückeburg ⑰

Road map C3. 🏛 *21,000.* 🚇
ℹ️ *Schlossplatz 5 (05722-89 31 81).*

In the 16th century this town became the capital of the principality of Schaumburg-Lippe. The philosopher Johann Gottfried von Herder was the preacher here. The **Stadtkirche** (town church), one of the first Protestant churches in Germany, is a pinnacle of

Mannerism with its fantasy façade. Another attraction is the **Schloss** with its enchanting chapel. The Goldener Saal (golden hall), from 1605, has a Götterpforte (portal of the divinities) and a beautiful panelled ceiling.

🏛 Stadtkirche
Lange Str. **Tel** *(05722) 957 70.*
⬜ *15 Apr–14 Oct: 10:30am–noon Tue–Fri, 2:30–4:30pm Tue–Sun, 15 Oct–14 Apr: 2:30–4:30pm Fri–Sun.*

⛪ Schloss
Tel *(05722) 50 39.* ⬜ *Apr–Sep: 9:30am–6pm; Oct–Mar: 9:30am–5pm.*

The opulent Goldener Saal in Schloss Bückeburg

Braunschweig (Brunswick) ⑱

Road map E3. 🏛 *240,000.* 🚇
ℹ️ *Vor der Burg 1 (0531-470 20 40).* 🎭 *Festival of Chamber Music (May); Medieval Fair (May/Jun).*

An important commercial and political centre from the early Middle Ages, Braunschweig was chosen as town of residence by Heinrich der Löwe (Henry the Lion), ruler of Saxony

and Bavaria. A member of the Welf family, he eventually lost in his struggle against the German emperor.

Very different in character but equally famous was Till Eulenspiegel, an ordinary man who poked fun at dim-witted citizens, the aristocracy and the clergy. His exploits were fictionalized in the 16th century, and he was immortalized with a fountain on Bäckerklint Square.

Braunschweig's continued decline culminated in the almost total destruction of the town in 1944. During reconstruction, the concept of the "Traditionsinsel" was developed: small islands of reconstructed historic monuments adrift in a sea of modernism.

A tour of the town is best started from Burgplatz (castle square). Here is the **Burglöwe**, the monument of a lion funded by Heinrich in 1166 (the original is in a museum). Symbolizing Heinrich's rule, it was the first such sculpture to be erected since Roman days. The **Dom** (cathedral) is well worth seeing. In the north nave, an extension, are unusual turned pillars, and in the transept and presbytery are 13th-century frescoes. Its marvellous treasures include a gigantic seven-armed bronze candlestick, the tomb of Heinrich and his wife Mathilde, the Crucifix of Imerward and a wooden cross with the figure of Christ modelled on the sculpture of *Voltosanto* in Lucca. Visitors can also see the column of the Passion with the figure of Christ, the work of Hans Witten.

To the west of the cathedral lies the **Altstadtmarkt** (old town market). Here are the L-shaped **Rathaus** (town hall), with a cloister, and the Gothic church of **St Martini**. The beautiful

The Burglöwe, Heinrich der Löwe's monument in Braunschweig

Gewandhaus (cloth hall) is also worth seeing.

East of the cathedral is the **Herzog-Anton-Ulrich-Museum**, the oldest in Germany. It was opened to the public as a gallery by Duke Anton Ulrich and holds a variety of gems such as Rembrandt's *Family Portrait*, a Giorgioni self-portrait and Vermeer van Delft's *Girl with a Glass of Wine*.

🏛 **Dom**
Burgplatz. **Tel** *(0531) 24 33 50.*
⬜ *10am–5pm daily.*

🏛 **St Martini**
Altstadtmarkt. **Tel** *(0531) 161 21.*
⬜ *Jan–Apr: 10am–1:30pm Tue–Sat, May–Dec: 10am–1pm, 3–5pm Tue–Fri, 10am–5pm Sat, 10am–noon, 3–5pm Sun.*

🏛 **Herzog-Anton-Ulrich-Museum**
Museumstr. 1. **Tel** *(0531) 122 50.*
⬤ *closed for renovation until end of 2012.*

The richly decorated portal of the Gewandhaus in Braunschweig

Environs
In **Königslutter**, 35 km (22 miles) east of Braunschweig, Emperor Lothar initiated the building of the Benedictine **Kaiserdom**, a monastery church and later his burial place. The portal with figures of lions, a frieze with figures of fishermen, and the cloisters reflect the taste of the times and the northern Italian origin of architects and sculptors; only the frescoes are late 19th-century additions.

Helmstedt, 45 km (28 miles) to the east, is unjustifiably only associated with the former border crossing between East

The Marienbrunnen fountain on Altstadtmarkt in Braunschweig

and West Germany. In 1576, Duke Julius of Brunswick founded the Julius Academy, one of Germany's most popular Protestant universities, where the Italian philosopher Giordano Bruno taught. Juleum (1592–7), the main building, has a central tower and two decorative gables. It is now home to the **Kreis- und Universitäts-museum**, a regional museum and library.

🏛 **Kaiserdom**
Königslutter. **Tel** *(05353) 91 21 29.*
⬜ *9am–6pm daily, in winter to 5pm.*

🏛 **Kreis- und Universitäts-museum**
Collegienplatz 1. **Tel** *(05351) 121 11 32.* ⬜ *10am–noon, 3–5pm Tue–Fri, 3–5pm Sat & Sun.*

Wolfenbüttel ⑲

Road map E3. 🏘 *53,000.* 🚌 🚆 ℹ️
Stadtmarkt 7 (05331-86 280). 🗓
Ostereiermark (Easter); Altstadtfest (Aug).

This small town has a turbulent past. From 1432 until 1753 the Welf dukes moved their seat here from Braunschweig. In the 16th century, innovative town design introduced wide avenues and spacious squares. Largely unscathed by World War II, the town has 500 historic half-timbered houses, and a magnificent library. The **Herzog-August-Bibliothek** holds 130,000 volumes, including the most valuable

book in the world, Heinrich der Löwe's Gospel book. Associated with the town are the philosopher Gottfried Wilhelm Leibniz and writer Gotthold Ephraim Lessing. The **Lessinghaus** houses a literature museum.

The centre of the town is dominated by the **Schloss**, the largest castle in Lower Saxony, refurbished in the Baroque style in 1714–16. It houses the **Schlossmuseum** with regional items such as furniture and tapestries. The Venussaal (hall of Venus) has beautiful Baroque ceiling frescoes. Opposite the castle is the **Zeughaus** (armoury), built in 1613–19 to a design by Paul Francke.

Continuing eastwards the visitor will get to the **Hauptkirche**, the 16th century church dedicated to *Beatae Mariae Virginis*, the ducal pantheon and the leading example of Protestant Mannerist architecture. Begun in 1608, the church's façade has delicate reliefs, while the interior reveals an unusual combination of styles.

♣ **Schloss and Schloss-museum**
Schlossplatz 13. **Tel** *(05331) 924 60.* ⬜ *10am–5pm Tue–Sun.*
Lessinghaus, Museum & Zeughaus Tel *(05331) 80 82 14.*
⬜ *11am–5pm Tue–Sun.* **Herzog-August-Bibliothek** ⬜ *10am–5pm Tue–Sun.*

🏛 **Hauptkirche**
Michael-Praetorius-Platz 9.
Tel *(05331) 72 055.*
⬜ *10am–noon, 2–4pm Tue–Sat.*

Baroque façade of Schloss Wolfenbüttel

Hannover (Hanover) ⑳

The capital of Lower Saxony, Hannover does not at first glance seem particularly exciting, but appearances can be deceptive: the town boasts interesting architecture in the historic centre, magnificent Baroque gardens and one of Europe's most important museums of modern art. Hannover's past was marked by its dynastic links with England, sharing the same ruler during the years 1714–1837. Annual industrial trade fairs have earned the town an international reputation, and in 2000 Hannover hosted the international exhibition Expo 2000 which attracted 18 million visitors.

Exploring Hannover

After the near-total destruction of the old town in 1944, many historic monuments have been rebuilt, and large green spaces encourage the visitor to explore the town on foot. It is best to follow an extensive circuit, starting from and returning to the railway station. The Baroque gardens at Herrenhausen in the northwest of the town are reached by metro (U-Bahn 4, 5).

🎭 Opernhaus

Opernplatz 1. *Tel (0511) 99 99 11 11.*
The opera house was built in 1845–57 by George Ludwig Friedrich Laves, Hannover's most important architect, to a fine Neo-Classical design. Particularly charming is the façade with portico columns.

🏛 Niedersächsisches Landesmuseum

Willy-Brandt-Allee 5. *Tel (0511) 980 76 86.* ◯ *10am–5pm Tue–Sun, 10am–7pm Thu.* 🈂️
The most interesting part of the state museum of Lower Saxony is the picture gallery, which holds excellent German medieval and Renaissance paintings (Dürer, Spranger, Cranach), a good section with Dutch and Flemish paintings (Rubens, Rembrandt, van Dyck) as well as German paintings of the 19th and 20th centuries, with fine examples of Romanticism and Impressionism (Friedrich, Corinth, Liebermann).

🏛 Sprengel Museum

Kurt-Schwitters-Platz 1. *Tel (0511) 16 84 38 75.* ◯ *10am–8pm Tue, 10am–6pm Wed–Sun.* 🈂️
One of Europe's finest museums of modern art, the Sprengel-Museum reflects the city's role as an artists' mecca in the 1920s, before the National Socialists destroyed works of art that they designated as "degenerate". Hannover's controversial artist Kurt Schwitters worked here, as did El Lissitzky, whose *Kabinett der Abstrakten* (school of abstraction, 1928, reconstructed) is worth seeing. Funded by Bernhard Sprengel, a chocolate magnate,

the museum was built in 1979, and holds works by Munch, Chagall and Picasso, as well as many more recent artists, including Christo.

The museum is located by Maschsee, a large artifical lake created in the centre of the city in 1936. During the summer it teems with motor and sailing boats, while Hanoverians stroll around its banks.

Mueller's *The Lovers* (1920), in the Sprengel-Museum

🏛 Neues Rathaus

Trammplatz 2. *Tel (0511) 168 45 333.* **Dome** ◯ *9:30am– 6pm Mon–Fri; 10am–6pm Sat & Sun.*
The gigantic town hall symbolizes the lofty ambitions of the wealthier citizens at the beginning of the 20th century. It was built from 1901–13, on more than 6,000 beech pillars, modelled on a Baroque palace with a central dome, and decorated with Neo-Gothic and Secessionist detail. The Swiss artist Ferdinand Hodler created a vast painting entitled *Einigkeit* (unity) for the Debating Hall, which depicts the arrival of Protestantism in the town in 1533. A unique oblique lift takes you up to the dome from where there are wonderful views.

♣ Leineschloss

Hinrich-Wilhelm-Kopf-Platz.
In the historic city centre by the Leine River stands the Leineschloss, a 17th-century palace completely rebuilt by the local architect Laves between 1817 and 1842. It had to be rebuilt again after destruction in World War II, and now serves as headquarters for the Niedersächsischer

Façade of the vast Neues Rathaus, with its central dome

For hotels and restaurants in this region see pp513–16 and pp552–4

Interior of the church of St Georg und St Jacobus, in Marktplatz

Landtag (Lower Saxony state parliament). The porticos on the façade were modelled on ancient Greek temples.

🏛 Marktplatz

Although the houses on this square had to be almost completely rebuilt after World War II, this is one of the best examples of 15th-century red-brick architecture, with amazing gables with projections as well as figurative friezes of glazed terracotta. Nearby, the Marktkirche St Georg und St

Jacobus (church of St George and St Jacob) features a 14th-century nave with a characteristic four-pinnacled tower. The most valuable object among its furnishings is the Gothic altar, with scenes of the Passion and copper engravings by the renowned artist Martin Schongauer.

🌸 Herrenhäuser Gärten

Despite having been razed to the ground during World War II, the gardens in Hannover's Herrenhausen district are among the most beautiful Baroque gardens in Germany. They were established by Duchess Sophie von der Pfalz, daughter of Elizabeth Stuart and mother of England's

VISITORS' CHECKLIST

Road map C3. 🏘 *522,000.* 🚉 *Ernst-August-Platz.* 🛈 *Ernst-August-Platz 8 (0511-123 45-111).* 🚌 *Sat.* 🎪 *Schützenfest (Jun/Jul), Maschsee-fest (Jul/Aug).* **www**.hannover.de

George I. The Großer Garten, the most important of the four gardens, has a formal layout modelled on 17th- and 18th-century Dutch parks. It is a botanical garden with fountains, including the Große Fontäne, the tallest in Europe with a 82-m (269-ft) water spout. There are grottoes, mazes, sculptures and decorative urns, and the hedges are some 21 km (13 miles) long.

The stunningly beautiful Baroque gardens in Herrenhausen

HANNOVER CITY CENTRE

0 metres   300

0 yards   300

Key to Symbols *see back flap*

Hildesheim ㉑

The undisputed capital of Romanesque culture, the old town of Hildesheim was transformed into a heap of rubble by heavy bombing on 22 March 1945. The most important monuments have now been recreated, with mixed results, surrounded by modern developments. Two churches, the Michaeliskirche and the Dom St. Mariä, are UNESCO World Heritage sites, and the Roemer-Pelizaeus-Museum of Egyptian Culture also makes a visit to Hildesheim worthwhile.

Wedekindhaus, a beautiful half-timbered house on Marktplatz

Exploring Hildesheim

Contrary to received wisdom, the city is best visited on foot. Visitors can park in the centre, for example near the church of St Michael, and then explore the main sights from here. A round tour, including the museums, should not take longer than around 4–5 hours. It is also possible to follow the Rosenroute (rose trail) around town which is marked on the pavements by white roses.

🏛 Marktplatz

Since gaining civic rights in the 11th century, the heart of the bishopric town has been its market square. Every detail has now been faithfully reconstructed, and it is easy to forget that the square looked totally different only a few years ago. In 1987, the Knochen-haueramtshaus (butchers' guild hall) was rebuilt, the largest and most famous half-timbered house in Germany, dating from 1529. Opposite are the Gothic town hall and the Tempel-haus, an original 15th-century building with round turrets and a half-timbered annexe, added in 1591. Reliefs depict the story of the Prodigal Son.

🔒 Andreaskirche

Andreasplatz. ⬜ Apr–Sep: 9am–6pm Mon–Fri, 9am–4pm Sat, 11:30am–4pm Sun; Oct–Mar: 10am–4pm Mon–Sat, 11:30–4pm Sun. **Tower** May–Oct: 11am–4pm Mon–Sat, noon–4pm Sun. ⬛ Nov–Apr.

The reconstructed Gothic church of St Andrew is notable for the brightness and the quality of the light that passes through its vast windows, as well as its soaring proportions. The 115-m (377-ft) tower was added in the 19th century.

🔒 Michaeliskirche

Michaelisplatz. **Tel** (05121) 34 410. ⬜ Apr–Oct: 8am–6pm daily; Nov–Mar: 9am–4pm daily.

Built on the instructions of Bishop Bernward, the church is a textbook example of what became known as the Ottonian style, the early Romanesque culture of the Otto dynasty. Its characteristic feature is the streamlined simplicity of interior and exterior, with square pillars intersecting with the naves. The sarcophagus of the founder, St Bernward, is in the crypt in the western part of the church.

Luckily, a rare painted 12th-century ceiling was removed during World War II and thus largely survived. It depicts the story of Redemption, from Adam and Eve through to Mary and the Saviour.

🏛 Roemer-Pelizaeus Museum

Am Steine 1. **Tel** (05121) 93 690. ⬜ 10am–6pm Tue–Sun.

The pride of this museum is the Ancient Egyptian collection, one of the best in Europe, which includes the burial figures of Hem Om and the writer Heti from the Old Kingdom (c.2600 BC). It also has fine collections of Chinese porcelain and Inca artefacts, and it is famed for its temporary exhibitions on ancient cultures.

Bas-relief on the façade of Andreaskirche

🔒 Dom St Mariä

Domhof. **Tel** (05121) 179 17 60. 🔧 for renovation; scheduled to reopen in Aug 2014.

During a hunting expedition in 815, Ludwig der Fromme (the devout), son of Charlemagne, allegedly hung relics of the Virgin Mary on a tree. When he tried to remove them they would not budge – which he took to be a heavenly sign that a church should be founded on this site and a town alongside it. The Tausendjähriger Rosenstock (1,000-year-old rose) of this legend grows to this day in the cathedral's

Presbytery of Michaeliskirche

◁ **View over Hann's rooftops, Münden**

The Bernwardsäule in the Dom St. Mariä – a huge bronze column

apse, and even survived bombing. The cathedral was reconstructed after World War II, using a model of the church's 11th-century appearance.

Original works of art bear witness to the cathedral's foundry which flourished under bishop Bernward. Bronze double doors depict the Old Testament version of the Creation on one side, and the life of Christ according to the New Testament on the other.

The Bernwardsäule, a huge bronze column from 1022, was once topped by a crucifix. The column, with scenes from the life of Christ arranged as a spiralling picture story, recalls the column of Emperor Trajan in Rome. Two further important works of art are a chandelier from 1060, with a diameter of 3 m (10 ft), and a baptismal font (c.1225) based on the personifications of the four rivers of the Garden of Eden.

🔒 Godehardkirche

Godehardsplatz. **Tel** (05121) 34578. ◯ 9am–6pm daily.
This church is dedicated to Bernward's successor, bishop Godehard, who like him has been included in the canon of saints. Built in 1133–72, it is typical of local architecture, and also recalls the earlier church of St Michaelis. It has interesting carved capitals as well as a northern doorway with the Blessed Jesus Christ accompanied by St Godehard and St Epiphany.

🔒 Mauritiuskirche

Moritzberg.
Another Romanesque church worth visiting in Hildesheim

is the church of St Maurice, west of the centre. Founded by bishop Hezilo and built in the years 1058–68, the church has enchanting cloisters, dating from the 12th century, and the sarcophagus of the founder of the church.

Presbytery of the massive Gode-hardkirche, flanked by towers

HILDESHEIM CITY CENTRE

Andreaskirche ②
Dom St. Maria ⑤
Godehardkirche ⑥
Marktplatz ①
Michaeliskirche ③
Roemer-Pelizaeus-
  Museum ④

0 metres   300
0 yards   300

Key to Symbols see back flap

Street-by-Street: Goslar ㉔

Goslar, at the foot of the Harz mountains, is a captivating
town with 1,500 charming, half-timbered houses, the largest
number in Germany. For 300 years the Holy Roman
Emperors of Germany resided in Goslar, a member
of the Hanseatic League also known as "the
treasure chest of the North". Goslar's main
source of wealth was the nearby mine in
Rammelsberg, where zinc, copper and
especially silver were mined. The
townscape has remained largely
unchanged, making it a great
tourist attraction as well as a
UNESCO world heritage site.

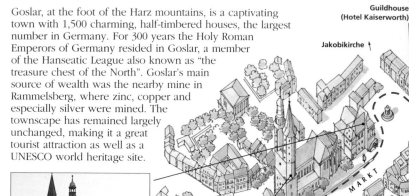

Guildhouse
(Hotel Kaiserworth)

Jakobikirche

MARKT

HOHER WEG

**Siemens-
haus**

DOM
PLATZ

★ Rathaus
*On the western side of the
market square stands the 15th-
century town hall. Its beautiful
Huldigungssaal (hall of
homage) has a ceiling and
walls with Gothic frescos.*

★ Marktkirche
*The Gothic Church of Saints
Cosmas and Damian has
Romanesque stained-glass
windows and a bronze
Renaissance baptismal font.*

**Statue of the
Emperor
Barbarossa**

KEY

— — — Suggested route

The Kaiserpfalz
*The Emperors' palace is a stone building
(1005–15), largely rebuilt in the 19th century. The chapel and the Emperors' hall
with its superb paintings are worth seeing.*

For hotels and restaurants in this region see pp513–16 and pp552–4

★ Historic Half-Timbered Houses

Many charming half-timbered buildings from various periods have survived in Goslar, creating compact rows of houses in the streets of the city centre.

```
0 metres        50
0 yards         50
```

St Annen
Stift

STAR SIGHTS

★ Rathaus

★ Marktkirche

★ Historic Half-Timbered
  Houses

🏛 Siemenshaus
Schreiberstraße 12. **Tel** *(05321) 780
620.* ⚫ *closed to the public; call for
a tour.*
This half-timbered house, one
of the most attractive, was once
owned by the Siemens family
who have their roots in Goslar.
Hans Siemens built it in 1693.

🔒 St Peter and Paul
Frankenberger Platz.
Located in the Frankenberg
neighbourhood, this was one
of 47 churches which once
stood in the town. It was built
in the 12th century, and the
tympanum of the south portal
dates from this period. Extensively refurbished, the church
prides itself on its magnificent
Baroque furnishings.

🔒 St Jakobi
Jakobi-Kirchhof. **Tel** *(05321) 303
672.* ⬜ *9:30am–4pm daily.*
The present appearance of
this church, the only Catholic
one in Goslar, is the result of
Gothic additions, although the
structure of the walls remains
Romanesque. The famous
work of art in the church is
the *Pietà* by Hans von Witten,
but it is also worth looking at
the wall paintings, the organ
and the baptismal font.

🔒 Neuwerkkirche
Rosentorstraße 27a. **Tel** *(05321) 228
39.* ⬜ *Mar–Oct: 10am–noon & 2:30–
4:30pm Mon–Sat; 2:30–4:30pm Sun.*
This impressive late-Romanesque church was built in the
12th–13th centuries for the
Cistercian Order, although the
surviving monastic buildings
date from the early 18th century. Inside, the wall paintings
and the choir partition are of
interest. The church is surrounded by a peaceful garden.

The train in the Bergbaumuseum in
Rammelsberg

🏛 Breites Tor
Breite Straße.
Some parts of the defensive
system, dating mainly from
c.1500, are well preserved.
This "wide gate", which can
be seen on the eastern
approach of the town, is the
most imposing part.

🏛 St Annen-Stift
Glockengießerstraße 65. **Tel** *(05321)
398 700.* ⬜ *10am–noon Mon, Thu, Fri.*
The hospice of St Anna for
orphans, the elderly and infirm was founded in 1494 and
is the oldest preserved half-
timbered house in Germany.
Behind its picturesque façade
is a beautiful small chapel
with superb paintings on a
wooden ceiling.

🏛 Bergbaumuseum
Rammelsberg
Bergtal 19. **Tel** *(05321) 750 122.*
⬜ *9am–6pm daily*
Goslar's mining museum is
based in the 10th-century
silver mine. One of the oldest
industrial structures in the
world, it is a UNESCO World
Heritage site. On display are
mining tools and utensils
used in various periods.
Visitors can take a train ride
through the mine and learn
about the history of mining.

The above-ground buildings of the silver mine in Rammelsberg

Einbeck 23

Road map C3. 🏛 *29,400.* 🚉
ℹ️ *Rathaus, Markt Str. 13 (05561-313 19 10).* **www**.einbeck.de

In the Middle Ages, this town had 600 breweries – more than houses – and today it is still known for its beers; Bockbier, the famous German strong beer, was invented here. Burned down in 1540 and 1549, the town was subsequently rebuilt in a uniformly Renaissance style. The historic town centre is enclosed by the city walls. More than 100 half-timbered houses have survived to this day. **Eickesches Haus** (Marktstraße 13) is particularly eye-catching, with a sculpted façade based on biblical and Classical stories. Other picturesque houses can be found in Tiedexer Straße and in **Markt-platz**. The latter boasts the **Rathaus** (town hall) and the **Rats-waage** (municipal weigh house) and **Ratsapotheke** (chemist). The tower of the neighbouring **Pfarrkirche St Jakobi** (parish church) leans 1.5 m (5 ft) from the perpendicular. In 1741, a Baroque façade was added to hide this.

Stone crest on Göttingen's Rathaus

Environs

15 km (9 miles) from Einbeck is the spa town of **Bad Gandersheim**. It grew up around a Benedictine monastery established here in 852, which in the 10th century was the home of Roswitha von Gandersheim, the first known German dramatist.

Göttingen 24

Road map C4. 🏛 *129,000.* 🚉
ℹ️ *Altes Rathaus, Markt 9 (0551-499 800).* 🎭 *Händel-Festspiele (Jun); Literaturherbst (Oct), Jazzfestival (Nov); student festivals, such as Stiftungsfest.* **www**.goettingen.de

Along with Tübingen, Marburg and Heidelberg, Göttingen is one of the most renowned German university towns. Established in 1737 by the English King George II, who was also the ruler of Hannover, the university taught the sons of wealthy German, English and Russian aristocrats. Important cultural figures worked here, including the writer Heinrich Heine, the brothers Grimm and the explorer Alexander von Humboldt. Göttingen's reputation as an educational centre continues today, partly due to the establishment of the Max Planck Institute, named after the scientist who was born in the city and developed the quantum theory.

Göttingen is a lively town thanks to its student population, with dozens of cafés, cosmopolitan restaurants and bars. University buildings are scattered all over town, and the **Aula**, a Neo-Classical Assembly Hall, is worth a visit. On the Marktplatz in the town centre stands the **Rathaus** (town hall) with a Gothic stone façade. The **Gänseliesel-brunnen**, the goose girl fountain, in front dates from 1901. It is kissed by students who have passed their exams, and much loved by tourists.

From the southeastern end of the market square, Göttingen's four main churches can be seen: St Michael to the south, St Johannis to the west, St Albani to the east and St Jakobi to the north. The latter two boast late-Gothic altars worth visiting. Together, they testify to Göttingen's early importance in the Middle Ages.

The twin-towered Gothic façade of St Cyriakus in Duderstadt

Duderstadt 25

Road map C4. 🏛 *24,500.* 🚉
ℹ️ *Marktstr. 66 (05527-84 12 00).*

To the south of the Harz mountains, not far from the former border with East Germany, lies this often overlooked gem. A walk around the medieval town is best started on **Obermarkt** (upper market). Here stands the half-timbered **Rathaus** (town hall), with an interesting façade and spiky towers. Inside it has exhibition halls and a cultural centre. East of the town hall rises the Catholic **Probsteikirche St Cyriakus** with its rich interior of altars and 15 Baroque statues. **St Servatius**, its Protestant counterpart, combines Gothic architecture with a Secessionist interior. Nearby is the **Westertorturm**, the only surviving town gate. Its strangely spiralling finial is not a decorative feature, but the consequence of a weakness in its design.

The Gothic Rathaus on Marktplatz in Göttingen

For hotels and restaurants in this region see pp513–16 and pp552–4

The Weser Renaissance Trail 26

The Weser Renaissance is an architectural and decorative style of northern Germany, dating from the mid-16th to the mid-17th century. Its tall roofs and gables were inspired by Dutch architecture, although it has many original features: the *Zwerchhäuser* (bay windows, one or more storeys high), the *Utlucht* (protruding sections of the façade), lavish decorations and multi-wing castles, some with spiral staircases in their towers.

WESERGEBIRGE

Hameln ①
Rattenfängerhaus (rat cat-cher's house), Hochzeit-shaus (wedding house) and Dempsterches Haus (Dempsters' house) are good examples of the Weser Renaissance style. The Romanesque-Gothic Münster (collegiate church) is also worth seeing.

Bevern ③
Another gem of the Weser Renaissance style, the castle in Bevern, near Holzminden, was built from Prussian stone in the years 1602–12. It has four wings as well as two towers in the corners of its courtyard.

Hämelschenburg ②
The castle, built in 1588–1612, is a three-winged building, surrounded by a moat. It has an impressive exterior with towers and decorative gables; its original interiors are also preserved.

Münden ④
The principal buildings that exemplify the Weser Renaissance style are the town hall and the castle, now a regional museum with a collection of ceramics. Fragments of a Renaissance fresco of Duke Eryk II of Calenberg can also be admired here.

0 km   20

0 miles   20

TIPS FOR DRIVERS

Starting point: Hameln.
Length: 112 km (70 miles).
Stopping-off places: good restaurants and bistros can be found in all the towns and villages along the route.

SCHLESWIG-HOLSTEIN

*S*chleswig-Holstein is the northernmost German state, situated between the Baltic and the North Sea and bordered by the Elbe River and Denmark. Weather-beaten by the unstable marine climate, the Gothic brick buildings of Lübeck, queen of the Baltic coast, testify equally to the turbulent history of this region. Today, tourists visit Schleswig-Holstein for its wide sandy beaches and impressive lakes.

Originally, this state comprised two territories: Schleswig in the north, which was inhabited by Germanic tribes (Angles, Saxons, Vikings and Danes) in the Middle Ages, and Holstein in the south, mainly populated by Slavs, who converted to Christianity as late as the 12th century. Its more recent history was characterized by struggles between the Hanseatic towns and the rulers of Denmark. In the 18th century, the entire region, from Altona in the south (now part of Hamburg) to Kolding in the north, belonged to Denmark, but in 1866 it was annexed to Bismarck's Prussia. In 1920, the political borders that exist today were established when Denmark regained the northern part of Schleswig after a plebiscite, leaving a significant Danish minority on the German side.

Schleswig-Holstein is principally an agricultural region, and less densely populated than any other state in Germany. Art lovers are mainly drawn to Lübeck, the most powerful Hanseatic town in the Baltic during the Middle Ages. Lübeck's old town, an architectural gem, has now been listed as a world heritage site by UNESCO. Other places offer surprises aplenty – the visitor will be captivated by the Romanesque churches around Flensburg, while the magnificent countryside more than compensates for the lack of major cultural monuments. A walk through the national park of Schleswig-Holsteinisches Wattenmeer, the moving sand dunes of the elegant island of Sylt, or a romantic sunset on the lake shores in Plön will leave lasting impressions.

The moated Renaissance Wasserschloss in Glücksburg

◁ **Idyllic landscape with a lighthouse on Sylt island**

Exploring Schleswig-Holstein

Undoubtedly the greatest attraction in this two-part state is Lübeck, and at least one day should be set aside to visit this town. Kiel is a popular destination during the annual Kieler Woche, the world's largest sailing festival. The sun-kissed island of Sylt invites the visitor to linger for a few days, while the stunning scenery of Helgoland is best explored in a one-day trip from Cuxhaven or Büsum. Hotels in the larger towns, such as Schleswig, Kiel or Flensburg, and many provincial boarding houses, provide a good base for excursions.

Buildings in Plön, in the Holstein Switzerland Nature Reserve

GETTING AROUND

The nearest international airport is Hamburg. Two motorways bisect Schleswig-Holstein: leaving Hamburg and the long queues for the Elbe Tunnel behind, the E47 (No 7) takes the visitor to Kiel and via Flensburg on to the Danish peninsula of Jutland, while the E22 (turning off the E47) leads via Lübeck to the Danish capital, Copenhagen.

The lake at Westensee Nature Reserve, where visitors can experience the captivating nature and wildlife close up

SIGHTS AT A GLANCE

KEY

▬▬ Motorway

━━ Main road

══ Minor road

┅┅ Main railway

── Minor railway

▬▬ National border

▬▬ Regional border

Ferries departing for excursions from the harbour in Kiel

5 FLENSBURG
o Glücksburg

Kappeln

A7
201 Schlei

6 SCHLESWIG

Owschlag o   Eckernförde **76** Gettorf

Rendsburg   Altenholz

A210 **7** KIEL   *Selenter See*

Nord-Ostee-Kanal **A7** **A215** **404** Preetz

astedt   **205**   Nortorf **76**

Bordesholm   **202**

Nortorf   Plön Eutin

Neumünster   *Grosser Plöner See* **8**   HOLSTEINISCHE

Bosau   SCHWEIZ

**SCHLESWIG-
HOLSTEIN**

Kieler Bucht

Puttgarden   *Fehmarn*

Burg

Heiligenhafen

207

Oldenburg

A1

Neustadt

Lübecker Bucht

Itzehoe **206**   Bad Segeberg   Bad Schwartau

10 LÜBECK

Kaltenkirchen   Bad Oldesloe

2 GLÜCKSTADT   **4**   **A21**

Elmshorn   *Ratzeburger See*

A23 Norderstedt   RATZEBURG **9**

Pinneberg   Ahrensburg

A7 **A1** *Schaalsee*

Wedel ✈ *Hamburg* Trittau

Reinbek   **A24**   *Berlin →*

Schwarzenbek

Geesthacht

Lüneburg   Boizenburg

SEE ALSO

• **Where to Stay** pp516–17

• **Where to Eat** pp555–6

Helgoland ●

For lovers of spices in Germany, it may have seemed a bad deal when in 1890 Germany received Helgoland from Britain in return for Zanzibar, but the island is nevertheless worth a visit. Farthest out in the open sea (50 km/31 miles from the mainland), the island always had great strategic importance, and after 1945, Britain used it as a bombing target before it was returned to Germany in 1952. Today its fresh air and spectacular red cliffs attract thousands of tourists.

VISITORS' CHECKLIST

Road map B1. 🚶 *1,900.* 🚢 *Hamburg and Büsum.* 🏠 *Lung Wai 28 (04725-20 67 99).* www.helgoland.de

Port ①
On the flat part of the island is Unterland, a small town with 1,300 inhabitants and a port. Fishermen store their nets in the colourful little houses, referred to as Hummerbuden (lobster huts).

Lange Anna ③
Tall Anna, measuring about 40 m (131ft) high, is the best known red sandstone cliff. Nearby is the Lummenfelsen, which is the smallest nature reserve in Germany.

0 metres   100

0 yards   100

Oberland ②
In the upper part of the island stands the Nikolai-kirche, dating from 1959. Close by, and worth a visit, are 16th-century tombs.

KEY

– – – Suggested route

TIPS FOR TOURISTS

Starting point: *the port of Helgoland*
Length: *1.7 km (1.1 miles).*
Stopping places: *there are numerous restaurants, bars and cafés all over the island.*

Glückstadt

Road map C2. 🏛 *12,000.* 🚉 🚌
*Große Nübelstraße 31 (04124-93 75
85).* www.glueckstadt-tourismus.de

The Danish king, Christian
IV, founded this little town
in 1617 and although less
impressive than Hamburg, the
town is worth a visit for its
layout – roads radiate out
from the hexagonal market
square, once surrounded by
fortifications. On the square
stands the reconstructed 17th-
century town hall as well as
the Baroque Stadtkirche
(town church). In 1648, parts
of the duchy of Holstein were
transferred to Glückstadt. Most
of the palaces built to house
the Dukes survived, for
example the Palais Wener
with its amazing ballroom.
The regional **museum** is now
in Brockdorff-Palais, another
palace from 1632.

🏛 **Detlefsen-Museum**
Am Fleth 43. **Tel** *(04124) 93 76
30.* ⬜ *2–5pm Wed (to 6pm Jun–
Aug), 2–6pm Thu–Sat, 2–5pm Sun.*

Meldorf ❸

Road map C1. 🏛 *7,500.* 🚉
🚌 *Nordermarkt 10 (04832-97 800).*
www.meldorf-nordsee.de

Meldorf has preserved the
Dithmarscher Dom, its
cathedral, a 13th-century
basilica with an exterior
rebuilt in the 19th century.
The vaulting in the transept is
decorated with Gothic frescos, depicting the legends of
saints Catherine, Christopher
and Nicholas. There is a richly
decorated dividing wall
(1603) and a grand triptych of
the Crucifixion (c.1520).

The port and waterfront of Flensburg

Sylt ❹

Road map B1. 🏛 *50,000.* 🚉 *in
Westerland.* 🚌 *Westerland,
Stephanstraße 6 (04651-820 20).*
www.sylt.de

The island of Sylt, the largest
of the North Frisian islands,
has long attracted wealthy
German visitors. The 50-km
(31-mile) long island offers a
rich variety of landscapes:
white, sandy beaches, shifting
sand dunes near List, towering up to 25 m (82ft) high,
steep shorelines, the Rotes
Kliff (red cliff) near Kampen
and the Watt, the endless
expanse of mudflats in the
national park, Schleswig-Holsteinisches Wattenmeer. **Westerland** is Sylt's main town,
and its promenade, Friedrichstraße, is "the" place to be
seen. There is also an interesting casino in a former
Secessionist spa building.

Flensburg ❺

Road map C1. 🏛 *84,500.* 🚉
🚌 *Rathausstraße 1 (0461-909 09
20).* ⛵ *Rum-Regatta in Flensburger
Förde (May/Jun).*

The most northerly town in
Germany, Flensburg was an
important trading centre in
the 16th century with 200

ships, although at times it
belonged to Denmark. The
Nordertor (northern gate),
dating from 1595, is an emblem of the city. The shipping
museum is fascinating while
the Marienkirche has a
Renaissance altar, sculptures
and the painting *The Last
Supper* (1598). Nearby is the
Heilig-Geist-Kirche (church of
the Holy Ghost), which has
belonged to the town's
Danish community since
1588. Other interesting
churches are **Nikolaikirche**
which boasts a magnificent
Renaissance organ, and Johanniskirche with a vaulted
ceiling dating from around
1500. Its painted scenes show
people disguised as animals,
which was a covert way of
criticizing the church and the
system of indulgences.

Environs
Schloss Glücksburg, 9 km (6
miles) northeast of Flensburg,
a square castle with massive
corner towers on a granite
base, was built from 1582–7.
Visit its captivating castle
chapel, the Roter Saal (red hall)
with its low vaulting, and the
valuable collection of 18th-
century tapestries from
Brussels. The artist Emil Nolde
lived and worked in **Seebüll**,
west of Flensburg, from the age
of 20 until his death in 1956.

The sandy beaches of the North Frisian island of Sylt, extending far to the horizon

For hotels and restaurants in this region see pp516–17 and pp555–6

The inner courtyard of Schloss Gottorf in Schleswig

Schleswig ❻

Road map C1. 🏛 *27,000.* ☐
ℹ *Plessenstr. 7 (04621-85 00 56).*
🎭 *Schleswig-Holstein Musik Festival
throughout the region (Jul/Aug);
Wikinger-Tage (Aug every other year).*
www.schleswig.de

The main seat of the Vikings,
Schleswig became a bishop's
see as early as 947, and from
1544 to 1713 it was the
residence of the dukes of
Schleswig-Holstein-Gottorf,
once related to the rulers of
Denmark and Russia. They
resided in **Schloss Gottorf**, a
castle, which now houses the
**Schleswig-Holsteinisches Landes-
museum** (regional museum)
as well as northern Germany's
most famous archaeological
museum, the **Archäologi-
sches Landesmuseum**,

exhibiting the *Moorleichen*,
prehistoric corpses preserved
in peat. It is also worth seeing
the two-storey chapel (1590).

The **Dom** (cathedral) was
built in stages between the
12th and 15th centuries. Its
largest treasure is the Bordes-
holmer Altar, a triptych altar
carved by Hans Brüggemann
in 1514–21. A masterpiece of
Gothic carving, it is 12 m
(39 ft) high and comprises
392 figures; the only one to
look straight at the visitor is
the sculptor himself, bearded
and hat askew (in the house
of Abraham and Melchisede).

Visitors can also walk around
the historic fishermen's district
of **Holm**, and visit the
Wikinger-Museum Haithabu,
about 4 km (2 miles) from the
town centre. The fortifications
have survived in the grounds

of this historic Viking settlement. The museum is housed
in a modern building, which
looks like an upturned boat.
Exhibits include the depiction
of Viking life, models of boats,
jewellery and everyday items.

🏛 **Schloss Gottorf/
Schleswig-Holsteinisches
Landesmuseum/Archäologi-
sches Landesmuseum**
***Tel** (04621) 81 30.* ☐ *Apr–Oct:
10am–6pm daily; Nov–Mar: 10am–
4pm Tue–Fri (to 5pm Sat & Sun).*

🏛 **Wikinger-Museum
Haithabu**
***Tel** (04621) 81 32 22.* ☐ *Apr–Oct:
9am–5pm daily; Nov–Mar:
10am–4pm Tue–Sun.*

Kiel ❼

Road map C1. 🏛 *245,000.* ☐
ℹ *Andreas-Gayk-Straße 31 (0431-
67 91 00).* **Town hall** ☐ *9am–6pm
Mon–Fri, 9am–1pm Sat.* 🎭 🎭
🎭 *Kieler Woche (end Jun).*

Located at the end of the
Kieler Förde inlet, Kiel marks
the beginning of the Nord-
Ostsee-Kanal (Kiel Canal), in
service since 1895, with two
giant locks. Ferries depart
from Kiel for Scandinavia, and
in the summer the "Kieler
Woche" turns the town into a
mecca for yachtsmen from
around the world.

A walk along the Schweden-
Kai (embankment) and sur-
roundings will take visitors to
the vast **Rathaus** (town hall),
dating from the beginning of
the 20th century, and the
Nikolaikirche (church of St
Nicholas) which was rebuilt
after the devastation of World
War II, with its baptismal font
and Gothic altar. Ernst Barlach created *Geistkämpfer*, the
sculpture outside the church,
which symbolizes the triumph

ROMANESQUE BAPTISMAL FONTS

There are few places in the world where visitors can see as
many Romanesque baptismal fonts as in Angeln. Generally
fashioned from granite, they have been preserved in
enchanting 12th-century churches, which can be visited by
following a 63-km (39-mile) route along the roads linking
Flensburg and Schleswig, Munkbrarup, Sörup, Norder-
brarup, Süderbrarup and finally Ulsnis.

Font in the church
in Borbry

Font in the church
in Munkbrarup

Font in the church
in Sörup

A house in Kiel's Schleswig-
Holsteinisches Freilichtmuseum

of mind over matter. Pieces of the sculpture, which had been cut up by the National Socialists, were found and reassembled after the war.

The most interesting of Kiel's many museums is the **Schleswig-Holsteinisches Freilichtmuseum**, an open-air museum in Molfsee, 6 km (4 miles) from the centre of Kiel, where German rural architecture from the 16th–19th centuries is on show. Pottery, basket-making and baking are demonstrated, and the products are sold here.

🏛 **Schleswig-Holsteinisches Freilichtmuseum**
Hamburger Landstraße 97.
Tel *(0431) 65 96 60.* ⬜ *Apr–Oct: 9am–6pm daily; Nov–Mar: 11am–4pm Sun.* 🖼

Holsteinische Schweiz (Holstein's Switzerland) ❽

Road map D1. 🚉 🛈 *Bahnhofstr. 3, Malente (0800 20 20 080).* 🎷 *Jazz-Festival in Plön (May); open-air opera during Sommerspiele in Eutin.*

The moraine hills, which reach a height of 164 m (538 ft), and 140 lakes are the reasons why this area is known as Holstein's Switzerland. The best means of transport here is the bicycle, allowing visitors to appreciate the beauty of nature and the wealth of fauna – ornithologists have counted 200 species of birds. The main centre of this holiday area is **Plön** on the Großer Plöner

EMIL NOLDE (1867–1956)

Born Emil Hansen, this great artist later adopted the name of the town in which he was born. After studying art in Copenhagen, Munich and Paris, Nolde devoted himself to painting, and was also successful in the graphic arts. From 1906–7 he belonged to the Expressionist group *Die Brücke*. He is known particularly for his use of vivid colours and highly expressive features, embuing his subjects with great emotion. Rejected and forbidden to paint by the National Socialists as an exponent of "degenerate art", Nolde settled and continued to paint in Seebüll, where a house was built for him to his own designs.

See (large Plön lake). Nearby is **Preetz**, an old shoemakers' town, which has a towerless Gothic church that belonged to a former Benedictine monastery. Older still is the Romanesque church in **Bosau**, a small town in a picturesque location on the Großer Plöner See. It was the first bishopric in this area, and home to Vizelin – the apostle of the Slavs.

It is also worth visiting **Eutin**, a small town full of picturesque buildings, which is sometimes referred to as the "Weimar of the north". The original Schloss, a brick structure with four wings, was built in the Middle Ages as the residence of the Lübeck bishops, but it was substantially altered in the years 1716–27. Worth seeing inside are the palace chapel, the Blauer Salon (blue salon) with Rococo stucco work, as well as paintings by Johann Heinrich Wilhelm Tischbein, which were inspired by the *Iliad* and the *Odyssey*, epic poems written by Homer.

The Dom in Ratzeburg

Ratzeburg ❾

Road map D2. 🏘 *12,500.* 🚉 🛈 *Unter den Linden 1 (04541-80 00 886).* 🎏 *Drachenbootfest (Jun).*

Ratzeburg, situated on an island in the Großer Ratzeburger See, is linked with the mainland by three causeways. The town was named after Ratibor, the duke of the Elbe River area. Henry the Lion established a missionary bishopric here in 1154, and later it became the residence of the Lauenburg dukes.

The **Dom** (cathedral) is one of the earliest examples of brick architecture, a style that was imported from Lombardy. The southern vestibule of the Romanesque basilica is particularly impressive – with herringbone-pattern brickwork and lines of black tiles as interior decoration. The Romanesque stalls, a 13th-century crucifix in a rainbow arch, the ducal gallery above the nave and the Baroque altar in the southern transept are some of its treasures.

The 17th-century Schloss in Plön, in Holstein's Switzerland

Street-by-Street: Lübeck ⑩

This "specific nest", as Lübeck was described by its most famous resident, Thomas Mann, is well worth a visit. The most important town in the Baltic basin by the end of the Middle Ages, it is now a magnet for fans of Backsteingotik, Gothic brick architecture which has been elevated to a national style. In Lübeck it is easy to see why: church interiors, the façades of buildings, the city gates, the unique town hall and even the Medieval hospital resemble pictures from an illustrated history of architecture brought to life. Despite a few blunders, the city has been beautifully rebuilt after World War II and enjoys a positive revival.

Buddenbrookhaus
This beautiful Gothic building was once the home of Nobel-prize-winning author Thomas Mann's grand-parents. It is now a muse-um dedicated to the Mann family.

Rathaus
Germany's most famous brick town hall, dating from 1226, has unusual walls and turrets.

Heiligen-Geist-Hospital

★ Marienkirche
St Mary's Church, larger than the cathedral and situated behind the town hall, holds great art treasures.

Holstentor
This gate, once the only entrance into Lübeck, was built by Hinrich Helmstede in the years 1466–78, based on Flemish designs. It has become the emblem of the town.

Petrikirche
The church of St Peter, from the first half of the 14th century, is Lübeck's only five-naved church.

KEY

– – – Suggested route

View of the Town
Lübeck and its seven towers can be seen from afar. Virtually all the tourist attractions are in the old town, which is enclosed by the river Trave and its channels.

| 0 metres | 150 |
| 0 yards | 150 |

St Anne's Museum
This museum, housed inside an Augustinian convent, portrays life and culture in 13th–18th-century Lübeck.

Freilicht-bühne

Herz-Jesu-Kirche
This 19th-century Catholic church houses a memorial to four clergymen who were executed during the Third Reich for their opposition to the war.

ST ANNEN-STRASSE

MÜHLENSTRASSE

STRASSE

PFERDEMARKT

PARADE

MARLESGRUBE

DANKWARTSGRUBE

STAR SIGHTS

★ Marienkirche

★ Dom

★ Dom
The cathedral, begun in 1173 at the time of Henry the Lion and completed in 1230, is 130 m (426 ft) long.

MARZIPAN FROM LÜBECK

A favourite present from Lübeck is marzipan, which has been popular throughout Europe since the 19th century. The sweets are made from two-thirds sweet almonds imported from Venice and one-third sugar and aromatic oils. The Persians referred to it as *marsaban*, and in 1530 its name was recorded for the first time in Lübeck as *Martzapaen*. From 1806, the Niederegger patisserie perfected the recipe; they established a patisserie on Breite Strasse which operates to this day.

Exploring Lübeck

All the most important monuments, with the exception of the Holstentor, are situated within the old town, which is best explored on foot.

🔒 Marienkirche

Schüsselbuden 13. *Tel* (0451) 88 99 700.
⏲ 9am–5pm daily, in winter to 4pm.
St Mary's church was constructed by the Lübeckers as a monument to themselves. The twin-towered basilica with transept and a passageway around the polygon-shaped presbytery is the brick modification of a Neo-Classical French cathedral.

Its vast interior boasts the highest vaulted brick ceiling in the world (40 m/131 ft) which dominates the other interior features. These include a 10 m (32 ft) bronze Holy Sacrament (1476–9); a baptismal font in the main nave dating from 1337; the altar dedicated to the Virgin Mary in the Sängerkapelle (singers' chapel) made in Antwerp in 1518; and the main, late-Gothic Swarte-Altar with the Madonna. The

Briefkapelle, the southwestern side chapel built around 1310, is one of the earliest examples of star vaulting in Europe.

In one of the towers, the shattered fragments of the church bells have been left embedded in the floor where they fell during the bombing in 1942; the present bells are from St Catherine's in Gdansk.

🏛 Buddenbrook-Haus

Heinrich-und Thomas-Mann-Zentrum, Mengstr. 4. *Tel* (0451) 122 42 43. ⏲ Jan–Mar: 11am–5pm daily; Apr–Dec: 10am–6pm daily. ⬤ 24, 25, 31 Dec.
Literature lovers will wish to visit the Buddenbrook house. Behind its Rococo façade from 1758 is a museum devoted to the Mann family, the great writers who lived here in 1841–91. It is here that Thomas Mann wrote the family saga of the Buddenbrooks, after whom the house is named, and for which he was awarded the Nobel Prize in 1929. The centre exhibits

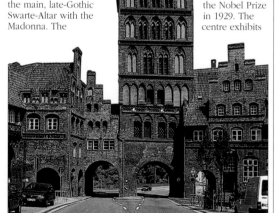

The multi-storey Burgtor, crowned by a Baroque cupola

documents relating to this famous family, in particular to Thomas and Heinrich Mann, concentrating on their time in Lübeck and their emigration and exile after 1933.

🏛 Schabbelhaus

Mengstraße 48 & 52.
Originally the western, wealthier half of Lübeck had many patrician houses, facing the streets with their ornate brick gables. Many of these were damaged in the bombing raids of March 1942, but after World War II they were carefully restored. The most interesting buildings survived in Mengstrasse, in particular the famous Schabbelhaus at No. 48. Built in 1558, this house gained a magnificent Baroque hall in the 18th century. Today it is an attraction in its own right as well as a restaurant.

Stepped gables of the Haus der Schiffergesellschaft

🏛 Haus der Schiffergesellschaft

Breite Straße 2.
The house of the Marine Guild, which dates from 1535, has a splendid interior and now houses one of the city's most elegant restaurants. The façade has stepped gables and terraces/forecourts, typical of Lübeck.

🏛 Füchtingshof

Glockengießerstr. 23.
The eastern part of the town is of an entirely different character: narrow streets link charming Höfe (courtyards) and small, modest houses. The most interesting Höfe can be

For hotels and restaurants in this region see pp516–17 and pp555–6

The façade of the Gothic Heiliger-Geist-Hospital, with its spiky towers

found at numbers 23 and 39. The Baroque portal of the Füchtingshof, at No. 23, leads to houses which, from 1639, were built for the widows of merchants and captains.

⚑ Burgtor

On the northern limits of the old town stands the castle gate, a second surviving gate of the historic fortifications. A Baroque finial was added to the gate in 1685. The five storeys of the tower are decorated with uniform rows of windows and windbreaks.

✚ Heiligen-Geist-Hospital

Große Burgstr. *Tel (0451) 79 07-841.* ◯ *Apr–Sep: 10am–5pm Tue–Sun; Oct–Mar: 10am–4pm Tue–Sun.* The Holy Ghost hospital is the best preserved Medieval building of its type in central Europe. Built in the shape of the letter T, it has a shorter western section with a twin-aisled hall-church (c. 1286), containing frescos of *Christ and the Madonna on Solomon's Throne* and *Majestas Domini*. The second section contains the actual hospice. In 1820, small cubicles were created for the elderly, who lived here until 1970.

⛪ Jakobikirche

This 15th-century church, which suffered only insignificant damage during World War II, has preserved its original, mainly Baroque features. Of particular note are the main altar as well as the side altar in the south chapel. The latter was established around 1500 by the mayor, Heinrich Brömbse,

and depicts a scene of the Crucifixion carved in sandstone. Both the small and the large organ originate from the 15th century.

⛪ Katharinenkirche

Königstraße. **Museumskirche St. Katharinen** *Tel (0451) 122 41 37.* ◯ *15 Apr–30 Sep: 10am–5pm Fri–Sun.* St Catherine's, the only surviving monastic church, was built by the Franciscans, as is apparent from the absence of a tower and its monastic gallery in the presbytery of the main nave. The western façade, with its glazed brickwork, is of a high artistic quality. In the 20th century, sculptures carved by Ernst Barlach were added *(Woman in the Wind, Beggar on Crutches* and *The Singing Novitiate)*. On the western side hangs the painting of *The*

The bright interior of the Gothic Dom

Resurrection of Lazarus by Jacopo Tintoretto, bought by a wealthy patrician; the sculpture of St George and the dragon is a copy of the famous original by the Lübeck artist Bernt Notke, which is now in Stockholm.

🏛 St Annen-Museum

St-Annen-str. 15. *Tel (0451) 122 41 37.* ◯ *Jan–May: 11am–5pm Tue–Sun, Apr–Dec: 10am–5pm Tue–Sun.* ◓ *Easter, 24, 25, 31 Dec.* The Augustinian convent houses unusual Lübeck art treasures. There is an impressive number of wooden Gothic altars, commissioned by wealthy families for their private chapels in one of the five churches. The altars were supposed to bring them eternal salvation after death, and to symbolize the wealth and prestige of the family during their lifetime. Gems of the collection are the Hans Memling altar with Christ's Passion, and the external side wings of the Schonenfahrer Altar by Bernt Notke.

⛪ Dom

Tel (0451) 747 04. ◯ *Apr–Oct: 10am–6pm daily; Nov–Mar: 10am–4pm daily.* The cathedral, completed in 1341, takes the form of a Gothic hall-church. Its most precious possession is the Triumphal Cross sculpted from a 17-m (55-ft) oak tree by Bernt Notke, a celebrated local artist. The giant figures, resplendent with emotion, include Adam and Eve, as well as the founder, bishop Albert Krummedick. Among numerous memorials, that dedicated to bishop Heinrich Bocholt, made from bronze, stands out. Additionally, two valuable sculptures can be seen; *Holy Mary Mother of God* with a crown composed of stars, as well as the *Beautiful Madonna* in the southern nave (1509). Note the bronze baptismal font by Lorenz Grove from 1455, with its three kneeling angels.

MECKLENBURG-LOWER POMERANIA

The medieval towns of Schwerin, Wismar, Rostock and Stralsund, as well as several magnificent architectural monuments, provide reason enough to visit this part of Germany, yet it also offers a largely untouched landscape of forests and lakes. Along the Baltic coastline, tourists delight in the beautiful sandy beaches of Darß or Usedom, but above all they head for the island of Rügen, with its famous white cliffs.

Mecklenburg-Vorpommern (Lower Pomerania), a mosaic of regions, can look back on an eventful history. In the 12th century, indigenous Slav tribes were colonized and converted to Christianity. The region became part of the Holy Roman Empire and German colonialism resulted in the Slavs' rapid assimilation. In the Middle Ages, several towns became rich trading centres and joined the Hanseatic League. From the 18th century, the Swedish Empire was the most powerful political force in this part of Europe. It ruled Wismar, Rügen and Stralsund until 1803 and 1815 respectively, when the territories became part of Prussia, and later the German Reich. During World War II the Baltic towns suffered terrible destruction and then from neglect under the German Democratic Republic: in 1953 all the hotels were nationalized and the unique buildings in the Hanseatic towns were left to decay or were destroyed.

After reunification, although still one of the poorest states in Germany, Mecklenburg-Lower Pomerania today has become an idyllic holiday destination. Improvements in the infrastructure, new hotels and restaurants have brought positive change, and it has much to offer. Nature lovers, walkers and cyclists, for example, can enjoy the Mecklenburg lake district and the island of Rügen. Fans of architecture will find a wealth of interest in the palace in Ludwigslust and the castle of Güstrow, as well as the Gothic brick architecture in town halls, churches and smaller buildings.

The beautiful white chalk cliffs on the island of Rügen sweep down to the blue Baltic Sea

◁ The superb Schloss of Schwerin, on an island in the middle of Schwerin lake

Exploring Mecklenburg-Lower Pomerania

This is a large region with mostly minor roads so visitors are well advised to allow extra time to explore it. The area can be divided into three: the west, stopping off in pretty Wismar or charming Schwerin with its fairy-tale castle; the centre, with the major port of Rostock as a base, and the east, which can be explored from Stralsund or Greifswald. In the central Mecklenburger Seenplatte is Müritz National Park, a vast area of lakes and forests that is ideal for camping, walking and sailing. It is also a good plan to set aside a few days for relaxation on the sandy beaches of Darß, Zingst, Usedom or Rügen.

Mecklenburg's glorious beaches

SIGHTS AT A GLANCE

SEE ALSO

Neuer Markt, surrounded by charming gabled buildings, Rostock

0 km 30

0 miles

GETTING AROUND
International flights land at Hamburg and Berlin, domestic flights at Rostock and Heringsdorf on Usedom. Ferries go from Denmark, Sweden and Lithuania to Sassnitz and Rostock, and the E55/A19 motorway runs from the south to Schwerin and Rostock.

Rügen, lit by dawn sunlight

Kap Arkona

Hiddensee

Sassnitz

Prerow

Zingst   Waase   **11**

Darss   R Ü G E N   Bergen

Ahrenshoop   Barth   Putbus

105   **10** STRALSUND

Ribnitz-   Putbus
Damgarten   **194**

Greifswalder Bodden

96   Grimmen   Wieck   **16** PEENEMÜNDE

Recknitz   **A20**   **12**   **13** WOLGAST

Gnoien   GREIFSWALD   **109**

ECKLENBURG-   Demmin   *Peene*   U S E D O M   Heringsdorf
VORPOMMERN   **111**   Ahlbeck

Teterow   *Kummerower See*   **110**   **15**

Malchin   ANKLAM **14**   Usedom   *Oderhaff*

Malchiner See   Reuterstadt   **96**   *Zarow*   **197**   Ueckermünde

108   Basedow   **104**   Friedland

Recknitz

NATIONALPARK   NEUBRANDENBURG   **7**

Waren   **192**   *Tollensee*   *Ucker*   *Randow*

Malchow   **0**   Stargard   **A20**   Pasewalk

Müritzsee   **198**

198   Neustrelitz   **109**   **104**

Mirow   **96**   **198**   Szczecin

Wittstock   ↗ Berlin   **A11**

Berlin

KEY

▬	Motorway
▬	Main road
═	Minor road
─	Main railway
─	Minor railway
▬	National border
▬	Regional border

The attractive cloisters of Schloss Güstrow

Schwerin ●

Despite protests from Rostock, the smaller town of
Schwerin was chosen as the capital of the newly united
state of Mecklenburg-Lower Pomerania. This was an
inspired choice as the town is picturesquely situated
amid several lakes, with a fairy-tale castle on an island,
and an enchanting old town with many Neo-Classical
and historic buildings that survived World War II largely
unscathed. Apart from a brief spell, the Mecklenburg
dukes resided in Schwerin from 1318–1918. Intellectual
life flourished here in the 16th century and
so the city is known as "Florence
of the North".

The Neo-Renaissance Schloss on an island in Schweriner See

Exploring Schwerin

The old town of Schwerin is
situated between Pfaffenteich
railway station and Schweriner See, a vast 65-sq km
(25-sq mile) lake. All the
town's most important tourist
attractions can easily be visited on foot. Close by to the
north is Schelf, which was
once a separate town.

♣ Schloss

Schlossinsel. **Tel** (0385) 52 52 920.
☐ 15 Apr–14 Oct: 10am–6pm
daily; 15 Oct–14 Apr: 10am–5pm
Tue–Sun.
Situated on Burg Island, this
castle is often referred to as
the "Neuschwanstein of
Mecklenburg", after the
famous Bavarian castle. The
Schweriner Schloss was in
fact largely built in 1843–57 to
an eclectic design by Georg
Adolph Demmler and Fried-
rich August Stüler, who were
inspired by the turrets of
Château Chambord in France.
Major refurbishment tried to
recreate some of the castle's
original Renaissance features,

of which only the ceramic
decorations have remained.
Inside, the castle chapel built
by Johan Batista Parra in
1560–63 has survived. The
elegant rooms in the castle –
Thronsaal (throne chamber),
Ahnengalerie (ancestral gallery), Rote Audienz (red auditorium), Speisesaal (dining
chamber) – are decorated
with gilded stucco work. Despite the proliferation of their
styles these rooms delight
visitors, transporting them
back to the 19th century.

♣ Burg-und Schlossgarten

The remaining part of the
island is occupied by the
Burggarten (fortress garden),
which has an orangery and
an artificial grotto, built from
granite around 1850. A bridge
leads to the larger Schlossgarten (castle garden) which
is a favourite place for the
town's inhabitants to relax.
The Kreuzkanal, a canal
built in 1748–56, one of the
garden's axes, is lined with
copies of Baroque statues

including the *Four Seasons*,
created by the renowned
sculptor of the Dresden
Zwinger, Balthasar Permoser.

🏛 Staatliches Museum

Am Alten Garten 3. **Tel** (0385) 595
80. ☐ Apr–Oct: 10am–8pm Tue,
10am–6pm Wed–Sun; Oct–Apr:
10am–5pm Tue–Sun. 🎫
The state art museum stands in
Alter Garten, one of the most
attractive squares in Germany,
where the waters reflect the
castle and Neo-Renaissance
theatre. The museum, which
features lions on its façade and
a portico with Ionic columns,
houses an art collection based
on that of Duke Christian
Ludwig II, a testimony to his
taste and erudition. As well as
works by German artists such
as Cranach, Liebermann and
Corinth, and the Dutch painters Hals and Fabritius, it holds
works by many French artists.
This includes 34 paintings by
Jean-Baptiste Oudry, who was
court painter to Ludwig XIV, as
well as paintings by Dadaist
artist Marcel Duchamp and
sculptures by expressionist
artist Ernst Barlach.

🏛 Marktplatz

The town hall square is
surrounded by the homes of
wealthy citizens, often with
19th-century façades conceal-
ing older walls. This is true of
the Gothic town hall, which is
hidden under an English
mock-Tudor-style façade.
Demmler was the architect
who is responsible for
numerous Neo-Renaissance

***Venus and Amor* (1527) by Lucas
Cranach in the Staatliches Museum**

The Dom and houses in Schwerin

and Neo-Gothic buildings, the showpieces of Schwerin. One of the outstanding buildings in the market square is Neues Gebäude on the north side. This "new building" is a covered market from 1783–5, with a showpiece façade comprising 12 Doric columns

🛈 Dom St Maria und St Johannes

Am Dom 4. *Tel* (0385) 56 50 14 **Tower** ⬚ Apr–Oct: 10am–5pm Mon–Sat, noon–5pm Sun; Nov–Mar: 11am–2pm Mon–Fri, 11am–4pm Sat, noon–3pm Sun. 🖼

This cathedral is regarded as the most important work of Gothic brick architecture in the Baltic region, in spite of its Neo-Gothic tower, which affords a marvellous view of the entire town. The basilica, dating from 1240–1416, with its

wide transept and passageway around the presbytery and its wreath of chapels, is reminiscent of the design of French cathedrals. A number of outstanding original features compare well with the finest works from Antwerp during this time. They include the wooden late-Gothic multi-panelled Crucifixion worked in sandstone, the 14th-century baptismal font, a memorial to Duchess Helen of Mecklenburg created by the Vischer workshop in Nuremberg and the tombstones of Duke Christopher and his wife (1595)

🏛 Freilichtmuseum Schwerin-Mueß

Alte Crivitzer Landstraße 13. *Tel* (0385) 208 41-0. ⬚ *late Apr–late Sep: 10am–6pm Tue–Sun; late Sep–Oct: 10am–5pm Tue–Sun.* 🖼

The museum contains a collection of Mecklenburg folk architecture, including 17 houses of the 17th–19th centuries, which strive to recreate the look of an original village. Combine a visit with a leisurely day on the beach in Zippendorf.

Houses of an earlier era in open-air Freilichtmuseum in Schwerin-Mueß

SCHWERIN CITY CENTRE

Hauptbahnhof
500 m (550 yards)

Dom St Maria & St Johannes ⑤

Neues Gebäude

RATHAUS PLATZ ④ Rathaus

Mecklenburgisches Staatstheater

ALTER GARTEN

③ Staatliches Museum

Schloss ①

Schweriner See

Burgsee

Burggarten

Freilichtmuseum

Schlossgarten ②

0 metres 300

0 yards 300

Key to Symbols see back flap

One of 24 waterfalls in Ludwigslust Park

Ludwigslust ❷

Road map D2. 🚂 12,600.
🚉 north of centre, 15 min. walk.
ℹ️ Schlossstr. 36 (03874-52 62 51).
www.stadtludwigslust.de

At the beginning of the 18th century, the small village of Klenow was founded here; from 1765 it grew into a town. The town was laid out around the **Schloss**, residence of the dukes of Mecklenburg-Schwerin until 1837. The "Versailles of Mecklenburg" is quite different from its French namesake. The Baroque palace was built entirely in brick, concealed beneath sandstone from the Ruda hills. The ornate interior, particularly the elegant Goldener Saal (gold hall), was decorated in Ludwigsluster Carton, a type of papiermâché, in order to cut costs.

In the mid-19th century, the vast **Schlosspark** was redesigned by Peter Joseph Lenné as an English-style landscaped garden. On a scenic walk round the garden, the visitor can discover some 24 waterfalls, a canal, artificial ruins, a stone bridge and the mausoleum of Helena Pavlovna, daughter of Tsar Peter I,

who died tragically young. In the town you will find the Protestant **Stadtkirche**, built in 1765–70 to look like an antique temple. In the presbytery is a giant mural, *The Adoration of the Shepherds*.

⛪ **Schloss**
Tel (03874) 57 19 0.
🕐 15 Apr–14 Oct: 10am–6pm daily; 15 Oct–14 Apr: 10am–5pm Tue–Sun. 🔴 24, 31 Dec. ♿

🔒 **Stadtkirche**
Tel (03874) 21 968. 🕐 varies, call ahead.

Gadebusch ❸

Road map D2. 🚂 6,600. 🚉 ℹ️
Mühlenstr. 19 (03886-21 21 10).
www.gadebusch.de

This small town, next to the former East–West border, has two interesting historic monuments. The **Stadtkirche**, which dates from 1220, is the oldest brick church in Mecklenburg. Its cross vaulting, chunky pillars and goblet-shaped capitals are Romanesque in style. One of its most precious pieces is the bronze baptismal font (1450). Angels hold the bowl, on which 22 scenes of the Passion were sculpted by an unknown artist.

In the 16th and 17th centuries, the **Schloss** was the

Baptismal font in the Stadtkirche in Gadebusch

residence of distant relations of the dukes of Mecklenburg. Resembling the castle in Wismar, it is decorated with glazed reliefs and pilasters. It is not open to visitors.

Wismar ❹

Road map D2. 🚂 55,000. 🚉
ℹ️ Am Markt 11 (03841-19 433).

Wismar is undoubtedly one of the most attractive towns in Mecklenburg. During the Middle Ages, it was an important Hanseatic centre, as evidenced by the monumental brick church, which is completely out of proportion with the provincial town of today. After the Thirty Years' War, in 1648, the Swedes were established in the town, and rebuilt it as the strongest fortress in Europe. In 1803 they leased Wismar to Mecklenburg, but never claimed it back.

The town centre has a grand market square measuring 100 x 100 m (328 x 328 ft), with **Wasserspiele** (well-house), a Dutch-Renaissance pavilion from 1602 in the centre. Water was piped here from a source 4 km (2 miles) away, until 1897, to supply 220 private and 16 public buildings. The most beautiful house on the square is the **Alter Schwede** (old Swede), built about 1380, with a protruding Gothic

The Baroque residence of the dukes of Mecklenburg-Schwerin in Ludwigslust

For hotels and restaurants in this region see pp518–19 and pp556–7

Alter Schwede and Wasserspiele in the market square in Wismar

brick gable. To the west of the market there are two churches, which act as sad examples of the GDR's neglect of its historical legacy. The reconstruction of the **Georgenkirche**, badly damaged in World War II, was begun in 1989, and it will soon be returned to its former glory. The **Marienkirche** has only one surviving tower – the ruined nave was blown up in 1960. Nearby lies the **Fürstenhof**, residence of the dukes of Wismar. The north wing is the most interesting – its Mannerist style was inspired by the Italian town of Ferrari and northern European ceramic traditions (such as Lübeck workshop). The magnificent sandstone portal is flanked by pairs of intertwined fauns. **Nikolaikirche** is a gem of Wismar architecture. Spared in World War II, the façade of this late-Gothic basilica from the 14th and 15th centuries is decorated with glazed friezes of mythological creatures, saints and, at the peak of the transept, a huge rose window. The proportions of the interior and the height of the vaulted main

A pair of fauns from the portal of Fürstenhof in Wismar

nave measuring 37 m (121 ft) are captivating. Some of the interior fixtures and fittings came from other churches in the city, which were either ruined or no longer exist, including the so-called Krämeraltar with a sculpture of the *Beautiful Madonna and Child* (c.1420). The room by the tower has the most complete cycle of frescos in the region (c.1450).

Bad Doberan ⑤

Road map D1. 🚉 11,900. 🚌
ℹ *Severinstr 6 (038203-621 54).*

When Duke Henry Borwin was hunting deer, a passing swan reportedly shouted *"Dobr Dobr"* (a good location) as the deer fell. Borwin duly founded the most important Cistercian monastery in the Baltic region here. The **Münster** was built in 1295–1368, with a severe interior and a small bell, in accordance with the order's rules which stipulate that no tower should be built. The interior is fascinating, its walls surfaced in red, with white plasterwork and colourful ribbing. Most of the original fixtures and fittings have survived almost intact. Among the treasures are a vast, gilded panelled painting, produced in Lübeck in 1310, a 12-m (39 ft) Holy Sacrament made from oak, a small cupboard holding the chalice and relics from an earlier Romanesque

building, as well as a statue of the Virgin Mary. Beautiful tombs mark the resting places of the rulers of Mecklenburg, of the Danish Queen Margaret, and Albrecht, King of Sweden, who died in 1412. Visitors can walk around the outside of the church which has a pleasant lawn. Beyond you can find a small octagonal building, beautifully decorated with glazed brickwork – this lovely piece of 13th-century architecture is the morgue.

A stroll around the health spa is also recommended. Right in its centre it has two early 19th-century pavilions with Chinese features – an ideal place for a coffee break.

Environs

Another adventure the visitor could try is a trip on the "Molli", a narrow-gauge railway that links Bad Doberan with Heiligendamm and Kühlungsborn, where there is a 4-km (2-mile) long beach. On the way, a little gem of 13th-century country architecture, the church in **Stefenshagen**, calls for a visit. On its south portal, see the terracotta figures of the Apostles. Across the presbytery runs a brickwork relief with mythological creatures.

🏛 **Doberaner Münster**
Klosterstraße 2. **Tel** (038203) 627 16. ☐ *May–Sep: 9am–6pm Mon–Sat, 11am–6pm Sun, Mar, Apr, Oct: 10am–5pm Mon–Sat, 11am–5pm Sun; Nov–Feb: 10am–4pm Mon–Sat; 11am 4pm Sun.* 🚶 *daily.*

The monumental Cistercian Münster in Bad Doberan

The imposing Schloss, dominating the skyline of Güstrow

Güstrow **6**

Road map D2. 32,500. ![icon] ![icon]
Franz-Parr-Platz 10 (03843-68 10 23).
www.guestrow.de

Güstrow is one of the most harmonious towns of the former German Democratic Republic, with an attractive old town, unmarred by prefabricated tower blocks. All the most important monuments are within easy reach. The town is dominated by the **Schloss**, built from 1558 by Franz Parr, a member of a renowned family of sculptors and architects from northern Italy. German, Italian and Dutch elements come together here, including fantastical chimneys and two-storey arcades in the courtyards. The architect's brother decorated the Festsaal (ballroom) with a hunting frieze – the stucco heads of the deer have real antlers.

In the nearby **Dom**, a brick cathedral of the 13th and 14th centuries, there is a fascinating Gothic altar (c.1500). Look for the vast figures of the Apostles on the pillars of the nave and the 16th-century tomb of Duke Ulrich and his two wives, with a large genealogical family tree of all three of them. In the north nave hangs the burly *Schwebende* (Hovering Angel), a remarkable work by Ernst Barlach, who lived here from 1910 until his death in 1938. He described his works to Bertolt Brecht as: "beautiful without beautifying, sizeable without enlarging, harmon-

ious without smoothness, and full of vitality without brutality". Barlach's work bore the brunt of National Socialist condemnation – the original *Schwebende* was melted down and made into cannons but the copy that replaced it was made from the original plaster cast. Other works by Barlach can be seen in the museum dedicated to him.

It is worth concluding a visit to this town in the market, near which rises the **Pfarrkirche St Marien**. This church has a magnificent high altar, a panelled work of art with painted wings by Belgian artists (c.1522).

Environs
The open-air museum in **Groß-Raden**, near Sternberg, is popular with tourists as well as archaeology students. A village has been re-created with houses, workshops and a system of fortifications.

🏛 Archäologisches Freilichtmuseum
Groß-Raden. **Tel** (03847) 22 52.
⬤ Apr–Oct: 10am–5:30pm daily; Nov–Mar: 10am–4:30pm Tue–Sun. ⬤ 24 Dec, 31 Dec.

Neubrandenburg **7**

Road map E2. ![icon] 75 000. ![icon] ![icon]
Stargader Str. 17 (01805-17 03 30).
www.neubrandenburg.de

Founded in 1248 as a sister town to Brandenburg on the Havel, the town was laid out in the form of a regular oval. It prospered as a trading centre until the Thirty Years' War, after which it fell into disrepair. As a result it now has what is probably the only example of post-World War II concrete tower blocks surrounded by medieval town walls, which have survived virtually intact. The walls extend for 2.3 km (2515 yds), originally with a keep open to the interior, and subsequently interspersed with half-timbered houses, known as **Wiekhäuser** (there were once 58, of which 24 survive). Of the four city gates the most interesting are **Friedländer Tor** (begun in 1300), with inner and outer gateways and a tower, as well as Neues and Stargarder Tor, decorated on the town side with mysterious terracotta figures of women with raised hands (c.1350).

In the town centre stands the Medieval **Marienkirche**, which was damaged during World War II and is now restored as a concert hall.

Environs
The castle in **Stargard**, some 10 km (6 miles) to the south, is the oldest secular building in Mecklenburg. Its 4 m (13 ft) walls were begun in 1200; the residence in 1236. Today it houses a youth hostel.

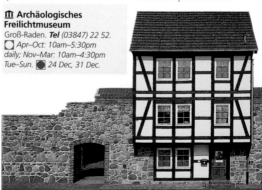

A typical half-timbered Wiekhaus in the town wall in Neubrandenburg

Nationalpark Müritz ⓼

There are about a thousand lakes between Schwerin and Neubrandenburg; the largest of these is Müritzsee, to the east of which a national park was established in 1990. A particularly attractive part of the lake district is the so-called Mecklenburgische Schweiz (Swiss Mecklenburg), with its hilly moraines, such as Ostberg, 115 m (377 ft) above sea level. Tourists are attracted by the breathtaking scenery, perfect conditions for water sports and fascinating castles and palaces.

VISITORS' CHECKLIST

Road map E2. ⓘ Waren, Neuer Markt 21. (03991-66 61 83); Neustrelitz, Strelizerstr. 1 (03981-25 31 19).

Schlitz ②
This palace is the most important Neo-Classical monument in Mecklenburg (1800–1823). In its beautiful landscaped park stands the Nymphenbrunnen, the famous fountain of nymphs. Cast in 1903 in Secessionist style for the Berlin department store Wertheim, it was transferred to this site in 1930.

Basedow ①
For 600 years Basedow was in the hands of the von Hahn family, who built this irregular three-winged palace.

Malchiner See

108

Kölpinsee

192

192

3

Müritz

192

198

Woterfitzsee

Jäthensee

Zierker See

96

5

Grosse Labussee

Woblitz- see

198

4

Müritz ④
Müritz (meaning "small sea") is, at 115 sq km (44 sq miles), the second largest lake in Germany after Lake Constance.

KEY

▬	Tour route
▬	Scenic route
=	Minor road
=	River, lake
☀	Viewpoint

Neustrelitz ⑤
The palace (1712) was the seat of distant relations of the Mecklenburg-Strelitz dukes who established the town and its church, and after 1733 resided here.

0 km   15

0 miles   15

Waren ③
Waren, an ideal base for tourists, is close to Binnen-müritz with its beaches and shops with watersports equipment for sale or hire.

Rostock 🎇

The history of the most important German port in the Baltic has been turbulent. This prosperous Hanseatic town had established trade links with distant ports such as Bergen (Norway), Riga (Latvia) and Bruges (Belgium) as early as the 15th century. In 1419 the first university in northern Europe was founded here, and it flourished again in the 19th century. After it suffered heavy damage in the Allied air raids of 1942, Rostock was rebuilt on a grand scale as the GDR's showpiece.

Kröpelinerstraße – a promenade with 17th century houses

Exploring Rostock

A visit to the town is best started from the Neuer Markt (new market), from where the most important monuments can easily be reached on foot.

🏛 Rathaus

The town hall, on Neuer Markt, has a Baroque façade (added in 1727–9), from which seven Gothic towers of the original building emerge. At the rear of the building, in Große Wasserstraße, it is worth seeking out Kerkoffhaus, the best preserved Gothic house in Rostock with a splendidly ornate façade featuring glazed brickwork, dating from 1470.

🏛 Steintor

A few minutes south of Neuer Markt is the Steintor, the best known of the gates in the old city wall. One of only three surviving gates of the original fortifications (at one time with 22 gates), it received its characteristic crowning feature during the Renaissance.

🏛 Marienkirche

Am Ziegenmarkt 4. *Tel (0381) 492 33 96.* ⏰ *phone to check times.* 📷

This church, meant to exceed the height of its Lübeck counterpart, was completed in the mid-15th century, after almost 250 years of construction. The nave, built after the original roof had collapsed, has an untypical, short body, while the massive western tower is as wide as three naves. Interconnected swathes of glazing decorate the exterior of the church, while much of the whitewashed interior features star vaulting. The main attraction is the astronomical clock, constructed in 1472 by maestro Düringer of

Baptismal font in the Marienkirche

Nuremberg. Its mechanism will show the correct time and date until 2017. Every afternoon its clockwork apostles parade before the tourists.

🏛 Kröpelinerstraße

The most popular street in the city is lined by houses from the 17th to the 19th centuries. In summer students congregate around the "Brunnen der Lebensfreude" (fountain of happiness) on the Universitätsplatz (university square). The main university building was built in the years 1867–70 in Neo-Renaissance style. The southern part of the square is occupied by a palace with a beautiful Baroque hall where concerts are performed. A Neo-Classical annexe with a Doric colonnade (1823) stands nearby. A statue on the square commemorates the town's most famous resident, Field Marshal Blücher, who helped defeat Napoleon at Waterloo.

Environs

Between Rostock and Stralsund lies a delightful coastal area. The peninsula, with the three former islands of **Fischland**, **Darß** and **Zingst**, attracts visitors to its quiet, beautiful beaches and splendid natural scenery. Particularly attractive are the villages of **Ahrenshoop**, which was originally an artists' colony, **Prerow**, which has traditional fishermen's houses and churches, and **Wieck**, with its charming thatched houses. A national park has been established here, and includes Darß and its magnificent forest, Zingst, the west coast of Rügen and the island of Hiddensee.

The richly decorated pulpit in the Marienkirche

Stralsund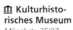

After Lübeck, Stralsund is the most interesting Hanseatic town in northern Germany. During its history, it has had to defend its independence against Lübeck, Denmark, Holland and Sweden. In the Thirty Years' War, General Wallenstein vowed that he would take the town even if it was chained to heaven – but he failed. Subsequently, Lower Pomerania stayed under Swedish rule for 200 years until 1815, when it became Prussian. Despite its turbulent history, 811 protected buildings survived in the old town, among them some truly remarkable examples of architecture.

The Rathaus with its small turrets

Exploring Stralsund

The town centre of Stralsund is surrounded by water on all sides – in the north by the Strelasund bay, and on the other sides by lakes formed in the moats of the former bastions, Knieperteich and Frankenteich. All the most interesting historic monuments are easily accessible on foot from here.

🏯 Alter Markt

The old market square affords the best view of the filigree façade of the town hall, beyond which stands the vast edifice of St Michael's church. It is surrounded by houses from various eras, of which the two most important are the Gothic Wulflamhaus, and the Commandantenhaus, Baroque headquarters of the town's former Swedish commandant. The Rathaus dates from the 13th century with a 14th-century façade and ground-floor arcades, and resembles the one in Lübeck. In 1370 the Hanseatic League

and the defeated Danish king signed a peace treaty here.

The Nikolaikirche, built from 1270–1360, was inspired by French Gothic cathedrals as well as the Marienkirche in Lübeck. It has rare free-standing flying buttresses in brick, which are much more unusual than in stone. Inside there are several intriguing furnishings, for example, the statue of St Anna (c.1290), an astronomical clock (1394), as well as fragments of the Novgorod stall with various fascinating scenes including one of hunting for sables. The Baroque main altar was designed in 1798 by renowned Berlin architect and sculptor Andreas Schlüter.

Portal of the Nikolaikirche

🏛 Kulturhistorisches Museum

Mönchstr. 25/27. **Tel** (0381) 12 87 90. ⬜ Feb–Nov: 10am–5pm daily. 🎟

The Katharinenkloster, a former 15th-century Dominican abbey, now houses two museums. Its abbey rooms provide an appropriate setting for historic exhibitions – the refectory has vaults supported by stylish columns – including copies of the famous Viking treasure from Hiddensee and a collection of 18th- and 19th-century toys and dolls' houses. A branch of the Museum, in Böttcherstraße, has a collection devoted to village life, folklore and costumes of the Baltic region.

VISITORS' CHECKLIST

Road map E1. 🚏 62,000. 🚉
🛈 Alter Markt 9 (03831-246 90). www.stralsund.de
🎭 Sundschwimmen (Jul); Wallenstein-Tage (Jul); Stralsunder Segelwoche (Jun).

🏛 Deutsches Meeresmuseum

Katharinenberg 14. **Tel** (03831) 265 0210. ⬜ Oct–May: 10am–5pm daily; Jun–Sep: 10am–6pm daily. ⬛ 24, 31 Dec. 🎟

Highlights of this museum of the sea, based in a former Dominican convent and the Ozeanum building, include almost 100 aquariums stocked with sharks, seahorses, coral fish and giant turtles, and a 16-m (52-ft) long skeleton of a fin whale. It is also a scientific establishment researching the life of sea organisms.

🏰 Marienkirche

Tower ⬜ 10am noon, 2–4pm Mon–Fri, 10am–noon Sat. **Organ concerts:** summer: 11am Mon–Wed, Fri Sun. 🎟

Dominating the Neuer Markt is the town's largest church, St Mary's, built in 1383–1473, with an octagonal tower (with good views of Stralsund). Star vaulting lightens the impact of the monumental 99-m (325-ft) high interior. Main attractions are Gothic frescos, carved wooden figures of saints and a late Gothic baptismal font. The huge Baroque organ is used for concerts in summer.

Marienkirche with its dominant, octagonal tower

Rügen ⓫

The largest of Germany's islands at 926 sq km (357 sq miles), Rügen is also the most beautiful and diverse, boasting steep cliffs next to sandy beaches and a hilly hinterland with forests and peat bogs. The island is only 50 km (31 miles) across, yet its rugged coastline extends for hundreds of miles. The Huns once ruled here, and their tombs can still be seen. It was fortified by the Slavs, then ruled by Danes and Swedes. In 1815 Rügen came under Prussian rule, and in 1936 it was linked to the mainland by the 1 km- (0.6 mile-) long Rügendamm.

Kap Arkona
There are two lighthouses on Kap Arkona. The smaller was built in 1827 and is now a museum. The larger was built in 1902 and is still in use.

Hiddensee
This small island is accessible from Stralsund or Schaprode on Rügen. Horse-drawn carts and bikes replace cars in this oasis of tranquillity.

KEY

▅	Motorway
═	Main road
⛴	Ferry crossing
☀	Viewpoint

★ **Waase**
At this typical fishing village on the island of Ummanz, an unusual work of art has survived: an altarpiece from Antwerp, from around 1520.

STAR SIGHTS

★ Nationalpark Jasmund

★ Putbus

★ Waase

Altenkirchen
Dranske
Wiek
Breege
Nobb
A
WITTOW
Grieben
BUG
Hiddensee
Lebt Boo
HIDDENSEE
Schaprode
Trent
UMMANZ
Gingst
Kubitzer Bodden
Samtens
Stralsund
Poseritz
Brandshagen

Jasmund Peninsula
The northeast of the peninsula is occupied by the Stubnitz forest of beech trees, which continues down to the sea, interrupted by dazzling white chalk cliffs. The symbol of Rügen, they inspired artists like Caspar David Friedrich.

VISITORS' CHECKLIST

Road map E1. 🚃 ℹ️ Bergen, Markt 23 (03838-811 206). Binz, Heinrich-Heine-Str. 7 (038393-148 148); Hiddensee, Norderende 162, Vitte (038300-642 26); Putbus, Alleestr. 35 (038301-4 31). 🎭 In Ralswiek (near Bergen) open-air performances take place under the title of "Festival of Klaus Störtebeker" (Jun–Sep). www.ruegen.de

★ Nationalpark Jasmund
An attractive walk starts at the viewpoint of Königsstuhl (king's seat; 119 m/390 ft), continues along the Hochuferweg (cliff-top walk), past Victoriasicht and Wissower Klinken viewpoints, to end at Sassnitz.

Ostseebad Binz
Rügen's largest and most popular seaside resort, Binz has a beautiful white beach, grand early 20th-century villas and a pier.

(Map labels: Lohme, NATIONAL PARK JASMUND, Sagard, Sassnitz, JASMUND, Kleiner Jasmunder Bodden, Prorer Wiek, Ostseebad Binz, Ostseebad Sellin, Ostseebad Baabe, Putbus, Ostseebad Göhren, Rügischer Bodden, Greifswalder Bodden)

0 km   5
0 miles   5

★ Putbus
This elegant late Neo-Classical town was planned after 1807 on the model of Bad Doberan. Its centrepiece is the theatre, which was built in 1819 to a design by Wilhelm Steinbach.

Greifswald ⑫

Road map E1. 🏠 *54,000.* 🚌 🛈
Rathaus Am Markt (03834-52 13 80).
🎭 *Musical concerts "Greifswalder
Bachwochen" (Jun); Jazz Evenings in
Eldena (Jul); Fischerfest (Jul).*
www.greifswald.de

This former Hanseatic town is
situated 5 km (3 miles) from
the Bay of Greifswald. From
afar the picturesque silhouette
of the town with its three
church towers, nicknamed Fat
Mary, Little Jakob and Long
Michael, appears like a
painting by Caspar David
Friedrich – the town's most
famous resident – come to life.
Charm pervades the old town,
its architectural mix resulting
from 40 years of East German
rule. Greifswald, an important
academic centre and market
town, has geared up more for
tourism since 1989. It is certainly worth a visit – a short
walk from east to west will
enable the visitor to see all
the most important
monuments in town.

The 14th-century **Marienkirche** has a vast square tower,
giving it a rather squat appearance and its nickname, Fat
Mary. Inside, the church
contains the remains of frescos
and an amazing Renaissance
pulpit depicting the Reformation figures of Luther, Bugenhagen and Melanchthon. The
Gemäldegalerie has a collection
of paintings by Caspar David
Friedrich, including his famous
landscapes of the ruined
monastery of Eldena, *Ruined
Eldena in the Riesengebirge,*
which he transposed to the
mountains of present-day
Poland and Czech Republic.

The market square with its
Baroque town hall is surrounded by patrician houses, with
exemplary rich brickwork
façades (particularly numbers
11 and 13). Nearby rises the
vast **Dom St Nikolai**. The cathedral's octagonal tower, topped
with a Baroque helm, affords
extensive views of the town.
The Rubenow-Bild (1460), one
of the paintings inside, depicts
the founding professor of
Greifswald's university in front
of Mary, Mother of God.

Environs
Wieck, an attractive working
fishing village, is now
incorporated into Greifswald. It
has a drawbridge dating from
1887, reminiscent of typical
Dutch bridges. The Cistercian
monastery of **Eldena**, just 1
km (0.6 mile) south of Wieck
district, was made famous by
the Romantic paintings of
Caspar David Friedrich. The
monastery was founded in
1199 and plundered by the
Swedes in 1637. Its ruined red
walls amid the green grass and
trees look wildly romantic.

Alter Speicher – the half-timbered
granary in Wolgast

Wolgast ⑬

Road map E1. 🏠 *15,000.* 🚌
🛈 *Rathausplatz 10 (03836-60 01 18).*
🎭 *Hafenfest (Jul).*
www.stadt-wolgast.de

From 1295 the seat of the
Pomeranian-Wolgast dukes,
Wolgast castle was destroyed
in 1713, when Peter the Great
ordered the town to be burned.
A notable surviving building is
the 12-sided cemetery chapel
with star vaulting, supported
by a single column. The most
valuable work of art can now
be seen in **Pfarrkirche St Petri**,
a 14th-century parish church.

Renovated houses around the Fischmarkt in Greifswald

Dating from the turn of the 17th to the 18th century, the *Totentanz* frieze is an imitation of the famous *Dance of Death* by Hans Holbein in Basle. Another notable artifact is the epitaph of Duke Philip I, crafted in 1560 by the Saxon artist Wolf Hilinger.

Other attractions in the town are the **Alter Speicher**, an 80 m- (262 ft-) long half-timbered granary (Burgstraße, 1836), and the family home of Philipp Otto Runge, famous romantic painter and adopted son of Hamburg.

Fishing boat on the beach at Usedom

🏠 **Philipp-Otto-Runge-Gedenkstätte**
Kronwieckstraße 45.
Tel (03836) 20 30 41.
🕐 May–Oct: 11am–6pm Tue–Fri,
11am–4pm Sat & Sun.

One of the models in the Otto Lilienthal-Museum in Anklam

Anklam ⑭

Road map E2. 🏘 16,400. 🚉
🛈 Markt 3, Rathaus (03971-835 154). **www**.anklam.de

A former Hanseatic town, Anklam's erstwhile importance is revealed by its vast defensive walls, in which is set the mid-15th century city gate, **Steintor**. It is worth visiting the Gothic **Marienkirche**. Inside, the church's octagonal pillars and the arches of its arcades are painted with graceful figures, which reveal a Lübeck influence. A museum recalls the life and inventions of Otto Lilienthal, born here in 1848. After observing storks, he built a flying machine and completed his first flight in 1891. In total he created 2000 machines, none of which flew further than 350 m (1148 ft).

🏛 **Otto-Lilienthal-Museum**
Ellbogenstraße 1. **Tel** (03971) 24 55 00. 🕐 Jun–Sep: 10am–5pm daily; Oct & May: 10am–5pm Tue–Fri, 1pm–5pm Sat & Sun; Nov–Apr: 11am–3:30pm Wed–Fri, 1pm–3:30pm Sun.

Usedom ⑮

Road map E1. 🚉 🛈 Heringsdorf, Kurverwaltung, Waldstr. 1 (038378-477 10), Ahlbeck, Kurverwaltung, Dünenstr. 45 (038378-244 14).

The island, named after the village of Usedom and separated from the mainland by the Peenestrom, is the second largest in Germany at 445 sq km (172 sq miles). A small corner in the east was incorporated into Poland after 1945. Usedom is almost as attractive as Rügen, possessing white beaches, forests, peat bogs and bays overgrown with rushes in the south. It is linked with the mainland by two drawbridges (near Anklam and Wolgast). The resorts follow one another like pearls on a string: Bansin, Heringsdorf and Ahlbeck, known as the "three sisters", are connected by a wide beach. At the beginning of the 20th century they evolved into elegant holiday resorts, with white villas, hotels and boarding houses, as typical of seaside resorts. Worth a visit is the industrialist Oechler's house in Heringsdorf

(Delbrückstr. 5), which has an antique appearance with mosaics on its façade. During the past few years, the early 20th-century piers in all three spas have been rebuilt and restored. The longest, in Heringsdorf, is also the second largest in Europe, after one in Poland. The Marienkirche, one of the island's main attractions, was erected in the 19th century.

Peenemünde ⑯

Road map E1. 🏘 650.

Historically the most interesting spot on the island of Usedom is the **museum** at Peenemünde, based on military territory. It demonstrates the evolution of space travel, pioneered at this research station since 1936. During World War II, long-distance rockets, powered by liquid fuel and known as V-2 (*Vergeltungswaffe;* retaliatory weapon), were produced here, which inflicted heavy damage on London and Antwerp in 1944. After the war, the chief engineer, Wernher von Braun, worked for NASA and helped develop the Apollo rockets.

🏛 **Historisch-technisches Museum**
Im Kraftwerk.
Tel (038371) 50 50.
🕐 Apr–Sep: 10am–6pm; Oct–Mar: 10am–4pm.
🔒 Mon (Nov–Mar).
www.peenemuende.de

V-2 rocket in Peenemünde

TRAVELLERS' NEEDS

WHERE TO STAY

It is relatively easy to find a room in a hotel or pension in Germany, even in small towns or large villages. The range of prices for a night's accommodation is wide, depending on the standard of services offered and the location of the establishment. In smaller towns located in attractive tourist areas, you can also find rooms to rent at a reasonable rate in private homes. In large towns and cities it is harder to find inexpensive accommodation.

Hotel porter

If cost is a consideration, it may be necessary to take a room in a hotel that is some distance from the city centre. Within the list of hotels provided on pages 488–519 there is a choice of around 250 hotels and pensions, which represent various price categories and a high standard of services. Tourist offices supply lists of accommodation and may be able to find a room for you. Information on other accommodation options can be found on pages 486–7.

The spacious lobby of the Hotel Palace, Berlin

THE RANGE OF HOTELS

German hotels are awarded stars following the same system that is used in other countries, with the number of stars awarded depending on the facilities offered by the hotel rather than the standard of service. This means that it may be possible to enjoy a more pleasant stay in a small hotel that has only a single star than in a three-star hotel that offers lifts, a swimming pool, restaurant and business centre, but where refurbishment is long overdue.

If the name of the hotel includes the appellation *"Garni"*, this indicates that there is not a restaurant on the premises, but only a dining room where breakfast is served. *"Apartmenthotel"* means that the establishment is comprised of suites that include equipped kitchens or a kitchen annexe. The price of suites is such that it is not worth booking them for just one night, although a booking of several days for a family or group of friends can turn out to be very economical.

Standards vary enormously between hotels. In large cities there will be no difficulty in finding a deluxe (and, of course, expensive) hotel, which typically will be part of an international chain. The choice of less expensive accommodation usually, though not necessarily always, entails accepting a lower standard of service or a less convenient location.

Away from cities, high prices generally apply to rooms in comfortable hotels in particularly peaceful and beautiful locations, or to those provided within historic palaces or villas. Smaller hotels in such areas usually offer good accommodation at very affordable prices, where visitors can enjoy their stay in small, but cosy and comfortable rooms.

HOW TO BOOK

As in other countries, hotel accommodation can be booked directly by telephone, letter or fax, as well as by e-mail or through the Internet. Reservations can be made directly with the hotel or through a local tourist office. They may request written confirmation of the booking, and will almost certainly ask for a credit card number. Tell the owners what time you will be turning up, and let them know if you are delayed, in order not to lose the room.

For those who have not pre-booked, the local tourist office can usually find a hotel room or provide information about rooms in private homes. They are also a good source of advice about the availability of other accommodation options in the area.

Entrance of Opéra Hotel, Munich

◁ **The Hotel Alte Post in Oberammergau**

The deluxe Hotel Vier Jahreszeiten in Hamburg *(see p515)*

INTERNATIONAL AND GERMAN CHAIN HOTELS

Throughout Germany there are hotels belonging to virtually all the well-known international chains, as well as to German national chains. Many places in Germany have an IBIS, which can be relied on to provide inexpensive, usually two-star accommodation. In season, they offer a double room for little more than €100.

Somewhat more expensive, and of a higher standard, are hotels belonging to the Best Western chain. Their excellent standard of service, combined with an affordable price, ensures their popularity with tourists. Hotels belonging to the Sorat group are also recommended. Their standard is similar to that of Best Western establishments and can be two-, three- or even four-star, but their premises always have interesting interiors, designed by renowned architects. Many hotels belonging to chains are, in fact, four- or deluxe five-star. Among the finest are the Kempinski and Vier Jahreszeiten hotels. In addition to these, there is no shortage of hotels belonging to chains such as Hilton, Holiday Inn, Inter-Continental, Mercure, Ramada and Hyatt Regency.

HOTELS IN HISTORIC BUILDINGS

Germany, like many other countries, has numerous palaces, castles and other historic buildings that have been converted into hotels. Often the name *Schlosshotel* is used to indicate that an establishment is a hotel within a palace. Many of these hotels are members of international organizations, such as **European Castle Hotels and Restaurants** or **Romantik Hotels und Restaurants**, who can provide further information.

HOTEL PRICES

In Germany, a complicated hotel categorization system operates, with a diverse range of prices depending on the season, as well as on various events that are taking place. In summer resort areas, it is obviously most expensive during the summer, while in large cities visited frequently for business the most expensive seasons are spring and autumn. In cities where commercial fairs are held, prices may double during the most popular fairs – for example, in Berlin during the tourist fair ITB, in Hanover during the information-computer fair CeBIT and in Frankfurt during the car and publishing fairs. It is the same, of course, in Munich during the October beer festival.

Many hotels offer significant reductions at weekends, and often there is the opportunity for a discount for those who turn up without a reservation. Prices can also sometimes be negotiated for longer bookings, especially during periods when business is slack.

ADDITIONAL COSTS

Tax is included in the basic price of a hotel room, but tips should be given for additional services such as having your baggage taken to your room or having theatre tickets reserved for you. Additional costs can come as a surprise when you settle your bill. In the most expensive hotels, for example, breakfast is not included in the cost of the room. Most hotels have their own parking facilities, but the cost may be unacceptably high. Check in advance the cost of making direct-dialled telephone calls from the hotel room, as well as the commission charged by the hotel for cashing traveller's cheques and the rate offered when exchanging currency. Using the mini-bar and pay-to-view TV channels in your room can also prove to be expensive.

The elegant spa in the Hotel de Rome, Berlin *(see p488)*

The picturesque Alter Wirt Hotel in Bernau

PENSIONEN AND GASTHOFE

A *Gasthof* is a traditional inn with a restaurant on the ground floor and rooms to rent on the upper floor. A wide range of establishments is covered by this simple description, however, from small, inexpensive, family-run hotels, with modestly equipped rooms, to the most luxurious and elegant accommodation in an exquisitely restored country inn.

Pensionen are less formal establishments than hotels and are typically run by a family. They usually provide modest accommodation, breakfast and a pleasant family atmosphere. They are always comfortable and very clean, at affordable prices.

INEXPENSIVE ACCOMMODATION

Germany has a very widely developed chain of youth hostels (*Jugendherberge*) and these provide the cheapest option for an overnight stay. A youth hostel can be found in every large town, as well as in small holiday centres. The most attractive are those that are located in old castles, beautiful villas or other historic buildings. Most hostels are of a high standard. Accommodation may be provided in double and triple rooms, as well as in dormitories. In order to be eligible to use youth hostels, you must carry a valid membership card of the Youth Hostels

Association. Membership is available from the YHA of your own country. The fee for overnight accommodation with breakfast is around €13.50–25. Unless you are carrying a sheet sleeping bag with you, you must hire one at the hostel, for which an additional charge will be made. The hostels are usually closed during the day, so you must ensure that all arrangements connected with your stay are arranged before 9am or after 4–4:30pm. In large cities during the high season, when demand for beds is particularly heavy, your stay may be limited to 2–3 days. Apart from in Bavaria, overnight accommodation is open to everyone who is in possession of a valid membership card. In Bavaria, however, young people are given priority, but older people can stay too (although for an additional charge), as can families with young children.

Guesthouse near Neuschwanstein

Private accommodation offers another inexpensive option. In attractive tourist areas, it is common for owners of larger villas and private houses to rent rooms to tourists, often offering breakfast as well. Houses with rooms available to rent are indicated by the sign *Fremdenzimmer* or *Zimmer frei*. Details of such accommodation can be obtained and booked in tourist information offices.

During the summer months, students may also benefit from acommodation in student hotels that otherwise house university students during term times in German university towns. Again, information about such accommodation may be obtained from tourist offices.

Mountain hut at Feldberg, Black Forest

AGROTOURISM

Agrotourism is very popular in Germany, as an attractive, low-cost and eco-friendly holiday-choice, particularly for families with children. The rooms that are available are of a perfectly acceptable standard and meals can often also be provided by the farmers.

For younger children, and especially those from towns and cities, it is a great thrill to observe the daily work on a farm and to have contact with farm animals. Often, farmers who take holidaymakers keep a number of different animals on the farm. They may also offer the possibility of horse-riding, or hiring bicycles, a boat or fishing tackle. Agro-tourist holidays can be booked through **Zentrale für den Landurlaub Landschriften** and by **AG Urlaub & Freizeit auf dem Lande**. For more information on eco-friendly accomodation *see p569.*

MOUNTAIN HOSTELS

Mountainous regions of Germany are generally well prepared to accommodate walkers. Shelters, hostels and mountain hotels can be found not only along Alpine trails, but also in the Thuringian Forest, the Black Forest and the Harz Mountains. Details about such accommodation can be obtained from local tourist information bureaux.

CAMPING

Travelling with a camping trailer, camper van or just a tent continues to be very popular in Germany, with a highly developed network of more than 2,000 camping sites throughout the country. Of a generally high standard, sites are equipped with washrooms and kitchens. There is usually a shop and café and some have swimming pools.

DISABLED TRAVELLERS

Virtually all hotels of a higher standard are equipped to accommodate disabled guests. At least one entrance will have ramp access, and a few rooms will have bathrooms adapted to the needs of those who are confined to a wheelchair. Facilities for the disabled are worse in lower-category hotels, where specially adapted fixtures and fittings are rarer. In such hotels, you may have to negotiate steep stairs, as many rooms are located on the upper floors of buildings.

In order to receive additional help and advice during a journey, a disabled person can contact the **Bundesarbeits-gemeinschaft Selbsthilfe e.V.**, or the **Bundesverband Selbsthilfe Körperbehinderter e.V.**

TRAVELLING WITH CHILDREN

Travelling with children through Germany should not present any problems. In most hotels, facilities such as cots and high chairs can be

A mountain shelter in Oybin, Saxony

obtained and there is often no additional accommodation charge for a young child. In better hotels, a few hours of babysitting for the children can usually be booked. Few hotels, however, provide children's playrooms. The standard equipment in every restaurant includes a high chair for toddlers, while menus always include the option of children's portions.

DIRECTORY

Choosing a Hotel

Hotels have been selected across a wide price range for facilities, good value and location. All rooms have private bath, TV, air conditioning and are wheelchair accessible unless otherwise indicated. Most have internet access, and, in some cases, fitness facilities may be offsite. The hotels are listed by area. For map references, *See pp114–15*.

PRICE CATEGORIES
Price categories are for a standard double room for one night in peak season, including tax, service charges and breakfast:
€ under €75
€€ €75–€125
€€€ €125–€175
€€€€ €175–€225
€€€€€ over €225

BERLIN

EASTERN CENTRE Alexander Plaza Berlin
€€€
Rosenstraße 1, 10178 **Tel** *(030) 240 010* **Fax** *(030) 240 017 77* **Rooms** *92*   **Map** *5 D1*

This top-quality hotel, opened in 1997, is located near the S-Bahn station Hackescher Markt. Rooms in the late 19th-century building, an intriguing mixture of stucco ceilings, glass and steel, are large, comfortable and full of light, with soundproof windows. There is a nice lobby bar and café. **www.alexander-plaza.de**

EASTERN CENTRE ARCOTEL John F
€€€
Werderscher Markt 11, 10117 **Tel** *(0)30 4050 460* **Fax** *(0)30 4050 46100* **Rooms** *190*   **Map** *5 D2*

This simple boutique hotel at the outer brink of the Mitte district is far enough from the centre for a quiet stay, but close enough to see all the sights and nightlife. The décor is cool and modern and rooms are furnished with custom-made furniture. The restaurant serves regional cuisine. **www.arcotelhotels.com/en/johnf_hotel_berlin/**

EASTERN CENTRE Art'otel Berlin Mitte
€€€
Wallstraße 70–73, 10179 **Tel** *(030) 240 620* **Fax** *(030) 240 622 22* **Rooms** *109*   **Map** *5 E3*

Overlooking the Spree river, this upmarket hotel is well priced and features original Georg Baselitz art. Inside, it is modern with simple and elegant furniture. In summer there is a café on a riverboat tied to the riverbank. The hotel is popular with young, culture-oriented guests. **www.artotel.de**

EASTERN CENTRE Derag Residenz Hotel Henriette
€€€
Neue Rossstraße 13, 10179 **Tel** *(030) 246 009 00* **Fax** *(030) 246 009 40* **Rooms** *54*   **Map** *5 E3*

The small and intimate Henriette is the nicest – and the most unknown – of the many Derag hotels in town. Despite the relatively modern building, Hotel Henriette exudes an incredibly elegant, historic flair, with oak furniture, precious carpets and beds. The hotel provides excellent service. **www.deraghotels.de**

EASTERN CENTRE Hotel Gendarm
€€€
Charlottenstraße 61, 10117 **Tel** *(030) 206 06 60* **Fax** *(030) 206 066 66* **Rooms** *27*   **Map** *4 C3*

The Gendarm has a reputation as one of the best and most popular smaller hotels in Berlin, however reports suggest that quality may be slipping. Nevertheless, a great location off Gendarmenmarkt and traditional, elegantly furnished rooms make this a serious competitor of the big five-star hotels nearby. **www.hotel-gendarm-berlin.de**

EASTERN CENTRE Mövenpick Hotel Berlin
€€€
Schöneberger Straße 3, 10963 **Tel** *(030) 230 060* **Fax** *(030) 230 061 99* **Rooms** *243*   **Map** *4 B4*

The Mövenpick is a surprisingly nice hotel in the rough, but fascinating, neighbourhood of Kreuzberg. The spacious designer rooms all have modern office and entertainment amenities. The deluxe rooms under the roof are particularly cosy. **www.moevenpick-berlin.com**

EASTERN CENTRE The Regent Berlin
€€€€
Charlottenstraße 49, 10117 **Tel** *(0)30 2033 8* **Fax** *(0)30 2033 6119* **Rooms** *195*   **Map** *4 C2*

A discreet and quiet luxury hotel off Gendarmenmarkt. The convenient location and classical decor attract a celebrity crowd. Service is impeccable and the rooms have impressive views, though some can be a little dark. The Michelin-starred restaurant Fischer's Fritz is a must for seafood lovers. **www.regenthotels.com/berlin-hotel-de-10117/berre**

EASTERN CENTRE Sofitel am Gendarmenmarkt
€€€€
Charlottenstraße 50–52, 10117 **Tel** *(030) 203 750* **Fax** *(030) 203 751 00* **Rooms** *92*   **Map** *4 C3*

This luxury hotel offers well-furnished rooms and excellent service. It is conveniently located near the Gendarmenmarkt, not far from Unter den Linden and sights such as the Brandenburg Gate and the Reichstag. The Aigner restaurant downstairs specializes in good Austrian food. **www.sofitel.com**

EASTERN CENTRE Hotel de Rome
€€€€€
Behrenstraße 37, 10117 **Tel** *(030) 460 60 90* **Fax** *(030) 460 60 92 000* **Rooms** *146*   **Map** *5 C2*

Hidden behind the classicist façade of a former 19th-century bank, this is a shining star among the city's first-class hotels. The interior design is very modern, with subdued colours complementing the historic setting. The service is impeccable and the fairly large rooms offer wonderful views of Opernplatz. **www.hotelderome.com**

Key to Symbols *see back cover flap*

WESTERN CENTRE Arte Luise Kunsthotel
Luisenstraße 19, 10117 **Tel** *(030) 284 480* **Fax** *(030) 284 484 48* **Rooms** *50*   **Map** *1 E3*

An authentic Berlin artist's hotel, the Künstlerheim (literally "home for artists") welcomes the artsy crowd into individually designed rooms, created by various German artists, in an early 19th-century house. It is steps away from the Scheunenviertel and offers great service. **www.arte-luise.com**

WESTERN CENTRE Hotel Astoria
Fasanenstraße 2, 10623 **Tel** *(030) 312 40 67* **Fax** *(030) 312 50 27* **Rooms** *32*   **Map** *2 A4*

Managed by the same family for three generations, this intimate hotel occupies a 19th-century building and is considered to be one of the best of its kind in town. The rooms are comfortable and the lack of a restaurant is made up for by the hotel's proximity to Savignyplatz. **www.hotelastoria.de**

WESTERN CENTRE Berlin Marriott Hotel
Inge-Beisheim-Platz 1, 10785 **Tel** *(030) 220 000* **Fax** *(030) 220 001 000* **Rooms** *379*   **Map** *4 A3*

The Marriott at the Beisheim-Center near Potsdamer Platz is an elegant four-star hotel with a towering entrance atrium. Its spacious rooms offer lovely views of the green Tiergarten and the government district. You get the same facilities for less than half the rate of the adjacent Ritz-Carlton. **www.marriott.de**

WESTERN CENTRE Ellington Hotel
Nürnberger Straße 50–55, 10789 **Tel** *(030) 683 150* **Fax** *(030) 683 55 555* **Rooms** *285*   **Map** *2 C5*

An oasis of modern design behind the stunning façade of a 1920s Bauhaus-style office building, the Ellington is an affordable stylish alternative to other central hotels. The bright colours, perfect service and great location more than make up for the small rooms, with many thoughtful touches ensuring a comfortable stay. **www.ellingtonhotel.de**

WESTERN CENTRE Hotel Brandenburger Hof
Eislebener Straße 14, 10789 **Tel** *(030) 214 050* **Fax** *(030) 214 051 00* **Rooms** *72*   **Map** *2 B5*

An intimate family atmosphere, impeccable service and quiet luxurious rooms make this one of the most desirable top-notch hotels in Berlin. The enchanting building has been restored and rooms feature Bauhaus furniture. The award-winning restaurant, Die Quadriga is a must *(see p527)*. **www.brandenburger-hof.com**

WESTERN CENTRE Hotel Concorde Berlin
Augsburger Straße 41, 10789 **Tel** *(030) 800 999 0* **Fax** *(030) 800 999 99* **Rooms** *311*   **Map** *2 B4*

Offering sophisticated charm, this modern hotel is decorated in minimalist style, with a lot of glass, warm lights and wooden panelling. The large comfortable rooms, impeccable service and French restaurant, Faubourg, all contribute to its appeal, as do the views of bustling street life on Kurfürstendamm. **www.hotelconcordeberlin.com**

FURTHER AFIELD Die Fabrik
Schlesische Str. 18, 10997 **Tel** *(0)30 611 7116* **Fax** *(0)30 618 2974* **Rooms** *30*

Situated in a factory building from the turn of the 20th century, in an up-and-coming Berlin neighbourhood, this hostel features simple, alternative design and high ceilings. The Fabrik offers spotless single and multi-bed rooms at unbeatable prices. The downstairs bar is a hotspot for backpackers from around the world. **www.diefabrik.com**

FURTHER AFIELD Eastern Comfort
Mühlenstraße 77, 10243 **Tel** *(030) 667 638 06* **Fax** *(030) 667 638 05* **Rooms** *24*

Set on a historic and meticulously restored wooden houseboat on the Spree river, in the up-and-coming district of Friedrichshain, the Eastern Comfort may well be Berlin's most unusual hotel. There are three different types of room – all small – but most offer a good view of the Warschauer Brücke. **www.eastern-comfort.de**

FURTHER AFIELD Michelberger Hotel
Warschauer Str. 39/40, 10243 **Tel** *(0)30 2977 8590* **Fax** *(0)30 2977 85929* **Rooms** *119*

Those looking to get a real taste of the artsy side of Berlin should look no further than the Michelberger. With authentic Berlin art and an industrial feel, this hotel suits young travellers well. Open lounge areas are inviting for making new friends in the heart of one of Berlin's hippest districts. **www.michelbergerhotel.com**

FURTHER AFIELD Art Hotel Charlottenburger Hof
Stuttgarter Platz 14, 10627 **Tel** *(030) 329 070* **Fax** *(030) 323 37 23* **Rooms** *46*

A must for any traveller looking for a real Berlin experience, the Charlottenburger Hof is a successful version of a traditional *Hotelpension* for young tourists. The individually designed rooms are decorated with art by Mondrian and equipped with computers and free Internet. The staff are very helpful. **www.charlottenburger-hof.de**

FURTHER AFIELD Hotel Müggelsee Berlin
Müggelheimer Damm 145, 12559 **Tel** *(030) 658 820* **Fax** *(030) 658 822 63* **Rooms** *176*

This is an excellent hotel, far from the hustle and bustle of the city. Tucked away in the greenery of the Müggelsee in Köpenick, it is perfect for a relaxed stay. Rooms are fairly spacious, and all of the three guest floors are decorated differently in Italian, Asian and German styles. **www.hotel-mueggelsee-berlin.de**

FURTHER AFIELD Hotel Otto
Knesebeckstraße 10, 10623 **Tel** *(0)30 5471 0080* **Fax** *(0)305471 00888* **Rooms** *46*   **Map** *2 A3*

Offering a minimalist gray-and-white design with homely colourful touches, this hotel offers simple rooms at reasonable prices in the western town centre. In summer, guests can enjoy an organic breakfast on the sun terrace. Service is warm, and staff are friendly and knowledgeable. **www.hotelotto.com**

FURTHER AFIELD Hotel-Pension Kastanienhof

Kastanienallee 65, 10119 **Tel** *(030) 44 30 50* **Fax** *(030) 443 051 11* **Rooms** *35*

The Kastanienhof is a budget *Pension* hidden in a fully restored, typical Berlin tenement house. Its location is perfect for exploring the clubbing scene in Prenzlauer Berg. The rooms are surprisingly nice and come equipped with a hairdryer, mini bar and safe. **www.kastanienhof.biz**

FURTHER AFIELD Ku' Damm 101

Kurfürstendamm 101, 10711 **Tel** *(0)30 5200 550* **Fax** *(0)30 5200 55555* **Rooms** *170*

An archetypal design hotel at the western end of the Kurfürstendamm. The Ku' Damm 101 is stylishly decorated with quiet and cosy rooms that will suit families and business travellers alike. There is a nice bar and restaurant. Breakfast is served in a 7th-floor breakfast room with panoramic views over the city. **www.kudamm101.com**

FURTHER AFIELD Meininger City Hostel

Schönhauser Allee 19, 10435 **Tel** *(0)3098321074* **Fax** *030 66636222* **Rooms** *712*

A great budget option located in one of Berlin's most interesting districts, Prenzlauer Berg. Calling itself "an urban traveller's home", this hostel-style hotel is youth- and familiy-oriented. Despite the bright and slightly garish decor - wooden beds and bright red red walls - rooms are clean and comfortable. **www.meininger-hotels.com**

FURTHER AFIELD Pension Dittberner

Wielandstraße 26, 10707 **Tel** *(0)30 881 6485* **Fax** *(0)30 885 4046* **Rooms**

This hotel offers a traditional, old-style Berlin *Pensionen* experience. Located in quiet side street of the Kurfürstend-amm, Pension Dittberner is a homely, family-run hotel with the cosy atmosphere of a bed and breakfast. Comfortable rooms are situated in an authentic old-style Berlin apartment. **hotel-dittberner.de**

FURTHER AFIELD Honigmond

Tieckstraße 11, 10115 **Tel** *(030) 284 45 50* **Fax** *(030) 284 455 11* **Rooms** *60*

Map *1 F2*

The Honigmond is great for exploring the Mitte and Prenzlauer Berg arts scenes. Originally a traditional 19th-century tenement house with a courtyard, it has individuallly designed rooms, some of which feature four-poster beds and parquet floors, while other rooms entice you with their summerhouse feel. **www.honigmond.de**

FURTHER AFIELD Schlossparkhotel

Heubnerweg 2a, 14059 **Tel** *(030) 326 90 30* **Fax** *(030) 326 903 600* **Rooms** *39*

The modern Schlossparkhotel is part of a private clinic and is known as a very pleasant and small, but top-class, hotel near the beautiful gardens of Schlosspark Charlottenburg, making this the only downtown hotel in a green setting. Request a room with a balcony overlooking the gardens. The S-Bahn Westend is nearby. **www.schlossparkhotel.de**

FURTHER AFIELD Soho House Berlin

Torstraße 1, 10119 **Tel** *(0)30 4050 440* **Fax** *(0)30 4050 44109* **Rooms** *40*

Conveniently located in Mitte, this stylish hotel is situated in a restored Bauhaus building that used to be the Socialist party headquarters. Amenities include a rooftop pool, a spa and a nightclub. The vibrant atmosphere and British-influenced, quirky decor attracts an über-cool crowd. **www.sohohouseberlin.com**

FURTHER AFIELD Schlosshotel in Grunewald

Brahmsstraße 10, 14193 **Tel** *(030) 895 840* **Fax** *(030) 895 848 00* **Rooms** *53*

This exclusive hotel was formerly a palace, built in 1912 for Walter von Pannwitz, the Kaiser's personal lawyer. The contemporary interiors were created by Karl Lagerfeld. and the lobby's magnificent coffered ceiling is breathtaking. The hotel's restaurant, the Vivaldi *(see p528)*, is very popular. **www.schlosshotelberlin.com**

BRANDENBURG

BRANDENBURG Kurth's Landgasthaus und Hotel

Dorfstraße 3–4, 14778 **Tel** *(033836) 40 24 5* **Fax** *(033836) 49 71 2* **Rooms** *14*

The vines spilling out of the upstairs windows are somehow very inviting, especially in this lovely lakeside hotel, situated in Radewege, outside the town of Brandenburg. Inside, light bright decoration and furniture counteracts cramped rooms, and the dark exposed beams in the attic are charming. **www.kurths-landgasthaus.de**

BRANDENBURG Villa Lindenhof

Chausseestraße 21, 14774 **Tel** *(03381) 40 43 0* **Fax** *(03 381) 40 43 33* **Rooms** *16*

This is a very traditional establishment with old-fashioned wooden furniture and chiffon curtains. It is a more homely experience than the larger, chain hotels would offer. They also have a restaurant that has tables in the garden in the summer months. **www.lindenhof-plaue.de**

BRANDENBURG Axxon Hotel

Magdeburger Landstraße 228, 14770 **Tel** *(03381) 32 10* **Fax** *(03381) 32 11 11* **Rooms** *119*

Not too far from the lake, though the hotel's location is not so picturesque. The rooms are comfortable, if a little small, but the fitness area is vast and well equipped. They have four apartments, which have a cosy quality and are well suited to families. **www.axxon-hotel.de**

Key to Price Guide *see p.488* **Key to Symbols** *see back cover flap*

CHORIN Waldseehotel Frenz
Neue Klosterallee 12, 16230 **Tel** *(033366) 53 10* **Fax** *(033366) 53 14 1* **Rooms** *14*

A hilltop rural setting offers wonderful views over the tops of trees and across a lake, and as you would expect in such a setting, the outside is more important and impressive than the inside. The slightly unimpressive façade disguises a comfortable but not overly fashionable interior. **www.neue-klosterschaenke.de/**

COTTBUS Ahorn Hotel & Restaurant
Bautzener Str. 134 / 135, 03050 **Tel** *(0355) 47 80 00* **Fax** *(0355) 47 80 04 0* **Rooms** *21*

This is a well-run hotel and restaurant. The guest rooms are decorated in an uncluttered and smart manner, and have the usual amenities you would expect. There is also an added attraction of a pleasant beer garden in which to relax after a day's sightseeing. **www.ahorn-hotel.com**

COTTBUS Radisson SAS Hotel Cottbus
Vetschauerstr. 12, 03048 **Tel** *(0355) 47 61 0* **Fax** *(0355) 47 61 90 0* **Rooms** *241*

This hotel offers stylish and well-appointed wood-panelled rooms, and as you would expect from this global hotel chain, there is a full range of facilities, amenities and services, including free Internet throughout the hotel. All expectations will be met willingly by the courteous and helpful staff. **www.radissonblu.de**

COTTBUS Sorat Hotel
Schlosskirchplatz 2, 03046 **Tel** *(0355) 78 44 0* **Fax** *(0355) 78 44 24 4* **Rooms** *101*

Whoever designed the interior of this place managed to achieve a style that is very modern, but not overly trendy or at all aloof. As such it is all very welcoming, tidy and pleasant, and replete with comforts and all the usual amenities found in these larger chain hotels. **www.sorat-hotels.com/hotel/cottbus.html**

JÜTERBOG Zum Goldenen Stern
Markt 14, 11913 **Tel** *(03372) 40 14 76* **Fax** *(03372) 40 16 14* **Rooms** *29*

The rooms here are fresh, breezy and fun, and the garden style furniture scattered about makes you feel as though you are outside. They will even serve your breakfast in a glass-encased winter garden. A pleasant change from more formal hotels. They also rent in-line skates. **www.hotel-goldener-stern.de**

LEHNIN Hotel Restaurant Markgraf Lehnin
Friedenstr. 13, 14797 **Tel** *(03382) 76 50* **Fax** *(03382) 76 54 30* **Rooms** *40*

A comfortable, rambling and family-friendly hotel that should appeal to pretty much everyone. Rooms are simple and comfortable. Sauna, solarium, spa and other well-being and beauty services are offered, as is a large conference hall. Overall, it is a pleasant and welcoming place. **www.hotel-markgraf.de**

NEURUPPIN Altes Kasino
An der Seepromenade 11, 16816 **Tel** *(03391) 3059* **Rooms** *21*

Rooms are a little spartan and basic, but they have made an effort to brighten the place up with contemporary and colourful decor and furnishings. They have a good restaurant and there is a pleasant outdoor eating area. Simple, but pleasant and good value. **www.hotel-altes-casino.de**

NEURUPPIN Am Alten Rhin
Friedrich-Engels-Straße 12, 16827 **Tel** *(03391) 76 50* **Fax** *(03391) 76 51 5* **Rooms** *33*

Here you will find sturdy, wooden, cottage-like furniture in clean bright rooms. It all adds up to simple, honest comfort. The hotel is located only a short distance from a river and lake, which encourages the guests to get out and enjoy the surroundings. **www.hotel-am-alten-rhin.de**

NEURUPPIN Seehotel Fontane
Seeufer 20, 16816 **Tel** *(03391) 40 35 0* **Fax** *(03391) 40 35 24 59* **Rooms** *140*

Nestled on the edge of Ruppiner See, this hotel could almost be classed as a resort, especially with the addition of a sauna facility that appears to hover over the lake. Rooms are classy and have the standard conveniences expected in a resort-style hotel, and most overlook the lake. **www.seehotel-fontane.de**

POTSDAM Arcona Hotel am Havelufer
Zeppelinstraße 136, 14471 **Tel** *(0331) 98 15 0* **Fax** *(0331) 98 15 55 5* **Rooms** *123*

This hotel is just a stone's throw from Sanssouci, and is a palace packed with art in its own right. Although the hotel is very bright and modern, it still has a natural feel with exposed wooden beams here and there. Abstract art features quite extensively in the decoration. **http://potsdam.arcona.de**

POTSDAM Mercure Potsdam
Lange Bruecke, 14467 **Tel** *(0331) 27 22* **Fax** *(0331) 27 20 23 3* **Rooms** *210*

This chain hotel is conveniently located near the train station. Inside, it sticks to the international Accor hotels recipe of maximum comfort from pleasingly minimalist design. Everything is neat, tidy and smartly tucked away, and all the amenities you would expect are provided. **www.mercure.com**

POTSDAM NH Voltaire Hotel
Friedrich-Ebert Straße 88, 14467 **Tel** *(0331) 23 17 0* **Fax** *(0331) 23 17 10 0* **Rooms** *156*

A grand and gracious façade hides rooms that have a modern style and all the usual modern amenities such as cable television, mini bar, wireless internet and an in-room safe. Other facilities include a sauna, solarium and spa, as well as on-site parking. **www.nh-hotels.com**

POTSDAM Relexa Schlosshotel Cecilienhof   €€€
Neuer Garten, 14469 **Tel** *(0331) 37 05 0* **Fax** *(0331) 29 24 98* **Rooms** *41*

This is an extraordinary place that retains the atmosphere of a lordly manor rather than a hotel. Thankfully, if the luxury is all too much, you can head to the courtyard (in summer, at least) where there are normal chairs, without padding, rather than the luxurious thrones scattered throughout the rest of the hotel. **www.relexa-hotels.de**

WITTSTOCK Scharfenberger Krug   €
Scharfenberg 28, 16909 **Tel** *(03394) 71 24 17* **Fax** *(03394) 44 37 15* **Rooms** *10*

Located on the Scharfenberg hill, which was the site of the bloodiest battle of the Thirty Years' War (1618–48), this hotel's accommodation is a little cramped, especially in the attic rooms, but it is also home to all manner of medieval memorabilia. **www.scharfenberger-krug.de**

WITTSTOCK Seehotel Ichlim   €
Am Nebelsee 1, 17248 **Tel** *(039827) 30 26 4* **Fax** *(033966) 60 25 3* **Rooms** *29*

This is an enormous barn-shaped building on the side of a lake with large, pleasantly decorated, comfortable rooms, plenty of health and beauty services, and all manner of water sports on offer. There is even a jetty and a small private beach. **www.seehotel-ichlim.de**

SAXONY-ANHALT

BERNBURG Parkhotel Bernburg   €€
Aderstedter Str. 1, 06406 **Tel** *(03471) 362-0* **Fax** *(03471) 362-111* **Rooms** *111*

This hotel, partly housed in a 17th-century inn, represents a clever and competent compromise between a business-class and a tourist-style hotel. Everything is very smart and comfortable, but there is still a very welcoming sense of homely warmth that makes it a nice place to stay. **www.parkhotel-bernburg.de**

DESSAU Kleinring 5   €
Kleinring 14, 6849 **Tel** *(0)340 858 2136* **Rooms** *1*

This comfortable and charming bed & breakfast situated in the Bauhaus neighborhood is perfect if you are looking for a relaxing stay with good service at a reasonable price. A generous breakfast is included in the price. The staff are friendly and knowledgeable about the area. **www.bauhaus-erleben.de**

DESSAU NH Hotel   €€
Zerbster Straße 29, 06844 **Tel** *(034) 02 51 40* **Fax** *(034) 02 51 41 00* **Rooms** *152*

Like all the hotels in this trendy global chain, the NH here is clean, smart and very stylish. Space tends to be used very well, and even though some rooms are not large, they do not feel cramped. The hotel also features a classy restaurant, casual-style bar and sauna. **www.nh-hotels.com**

DESSAU Radisson Blu Fürst Leopold   €€
Friedensplatz, 06844 **Tel** *(0340) 25 15 0* **Fax** *(0340) 25 15 17 7* **Rooms** *204*

This hotel's design is heavily influenced by Bauhaus, with rooms that are similarly unfussy and functional. Anything that will not enhance your productivity or comfort has been left out, but earthy-toned walls and plants add a restful and natural touch. There is also a vast sauna and spa area. **www.hotel-dessau-city.de**

FREYBURG Berghotel Zum Edelacker   €€
Schloss. 25, 06632 **Tel** *(0344) 64 35 0* **Fax** *(0344) 64 35 33 3* **Rooms** *83*

The Edelacker is an inviting country hotel overlooking vineyards and the surrounding hills. A short walk from the medieval Schloss Neuenburg and downtown Freyburg, the hotel offers standard rooms with good views. In summer, the restaurant, serving local dishes and wines, invites diners onto a shady terrace. **www.edelacker.de**

HALBERSTADT Parkhotel Unter den Linden   €€
Klamrothstr. 2, 38820 **Tel** *(03941) 62 54 0* **Fax** *(03941) 62 54 44 4* **Rooms** *43*

Every room in this hotel is unique, some with bay windows, some with balconies and others with interior arches. It gives a sense of history and character to the building that adds a nice touch to your stay. They even have a sauna in the attic. It also has an excellent restaurant of the same name *(see p531)*. **www.pudl.de**

HALLE Hotel Rotes Ross   €€€
Leipziger Straße 76, 06108 **Tel** *(0345) 23 34 30* **Fax** *(0345) 23 34 36 99* **Rooms** *88*

Style and elegance are the hallmarks of this historic hotel located in the heart of Halle. The guest rooms are replete with luxury and also have a lovely and unique charm. Other highlights include an excellent restaurant and superb fitness and spa area. **www.dormero-hotel-rotes-ross.de**

ILSENBURG Zu Den Rothen Forellen   €€€
Marktplatz 2, 38871 **Tel** *(039452) 93 93* **Fax** *(039452) 93 99* **Rooms** *52*

A stunning hotel located in a lovely setting right beside a lake. The guest rooms have a rich, warm and elegant cottage charm, the pool and spa area is sparkling, and the restaurant is an attraction it its own right *(see p531)*. Overall, this hotel is a delightful discovery. **www.rotheforelle.de**

Key to Price Guide *see p.488* **Key to Symbols** *see back cover flap*

MAGDEBURG Classik Hotel Magdeburg

*Leipziger Chaussee 141, 39120 **Tel** (0391) 62 90 0 **Fax** (0391) 62 90 51 9 **Rooms** 109*

There is a fresh and friendly appeal about this big yellow building. Rooms are by no means large, but are brightly furnished and have a spacious and airy feel thanks to lots of colourful touches. The restaurant is smart without being stifling, and there is a pleasant lobby area with an open fire. **www.classik-hotel.de**

MAGDEBURG Hotel in der grünen Zitadelle

*Breiter Weg 9, 39104 **Tel** (0)391 620780 **Fax** (0)391 62078199 **Rooms** 42*

It's difficult to miss this South Beach–inspired hotel with its unusual architecture and pink façade, designed by Austrian artist Friedensreich Hundertwasser. Guests can enjoy the eclectic decor and the unusual art that is featured throughout the hotel. Basic but cosy rooms have small balconies and interesting views. **www.hotel-zitadelle.de**

MAGDEBURG Hotel Residenz Joop

*Jean-Burger-Straße 16, 39112 **Tel** (0)39162620 **Fax** (0)3916262100 **Rooms** 25*

Quaint and intimate, this simply designed bed-and-breakfast-style hotel offers friendly service and a relaxing yet romantic atmosphere, with lace curtains and creamy colours. The surrounding garden, a sun terrace and the lovely A-frame-style building add to the delightful ambience. **www.residenzjoop.de**

MAGDEBURG Herrenkrug Parkhotel

*Herrenkrug 3, 39114 **Tel** (0391) 85 080 **Fax** (0391) 85 08 50 1 **Rooms** 147*

This attractive hotel provides a very tidy arrangement of cosy rooms in a lovely Art Nouveau house situated in the middle of a sprawling park. All the expected comforts and a full range of amenities are offered in a happy marriage of old and new styles. **www.herrenkrug.de**

MAGDEBURG Maritim Hotel

*87 Otto-Von-Guericke Straße, 39104 **Tel** (0391) 59 49 0 **Fax** (0391) 59 49 99 0 **Rooms** 514*

This hotel has a striking, ultra-modern exterior with a distinctive glass cylinder entrance. The central hall is breathtaking and the suites are amazing. It has a choice of restaurants, one with a summer terrace and a piano bar. There is also a pool, sauna and fitness area. **www.maritim.de**

MERSEBURG Radisson Blu Hotel

*Oberaltenburg 4, 06217 **Tel** (03461) 45 20 0 **Fax** (03461) 45 21 00 **Rooms** 132*

As you would expect from a top hotel chain, this establishment has all the amenities (including a solarium) and is superbly run. It is well worth asking for a room with a view of the palace and gardens. The Belle Époque restaurant is highly recommended (see p531). **www.merseburg-radissonblu.com**

NAUMBURG Stadt Aachen

*Markt 11, 06618 **Tel** (03445) 26 10 60 **Fax** (03445) 26 106 130 **Rooms** 39*

This hotel is in an excellent location close to the market square. The building itself looks rather historic but has been renovated to meet modern hospitality standards. The rooms are large and bright and scattered with pleasant furniture. **www.hotel-stadt-aachen.de**

NAUMBURG Zur alten Schmiede

*Lindenring 36/37, 06618 **Tel** (03445) 24 36 0 **Fax** (03445) 24 36 66 **Rooms** 42*

What was an 18th-century blacksmith's workshop has been knocked down and replaced with a hotel and restaurant, both of which have been designed to retain the historic feel combined with modern convenience and quality. Accommodation is pleasantly simple with touches of rustic charm. **www.hotel-zur-alten-schmiede.de**

QUEDLINBURG Hotel Domschatz

*Mühlenstraße 20, 06484 **Tel** (03946) 70 52 70 **Fax** (03946) 70 52 71 **Rooms** 15*

This is a distinctive lime-green Fachwerk building – a rescued timber frame historic house – which is now home to 15 modern and warmly decorated guest rooms. The staff also arrange some interesting special offers, packages and tours. **www.quedlinburg-hoteldomschatz.de**

STENDAL Altstadt-Hotel

*Breite Straße 60, 39576 **Tel** (03931) 69 89 0 **Fax** (03931) 69 89 39 **Rooms** 28*

This mid-range family-run hotel is centrally located. It has themed decor – plenty of wood panelling and pastel-patterned furniture – which makes you feel that you could be on a boat at sea. The guest rooms come with safes and cable television. Parking is also available. **www.altstadthotelstendal.de**

TANGERMUNDE Ringhotel Schwarzer Adler

*Lange Straße 52, 39590 **Tel** (039322) 96 0 **Fax** (039322) 36 42 **Rooms** 56*

The guest rooms here are filled with comforts encased in floral wallpaper and furnishings. Other facilities at the hotel are a bit more practical but no less pleasing, with the attractive glass-roofed dining room being of particular note. **www.adler-tgm.de**

WERNIGERODE Ringhotel Weisser Hirsch

*Marktplatz 5, 38855 **Tel** (03943) 26 71 10 **Fax** (03943) 26 711 199 **Rooms** 54*

While the smart reception suggests that this is a business-class hotel, the rooms are more homely than you might expect, although not at all short on luxury. Merely staying in such a grand Fachwerk building in this great location would be pleasant enough, but the hotel's comforts are also very appealing. **www.hotel-weisser-hirsch.de**

WITTENBERG Stadthotel Wittenberg   €

Schloßstraße 2, 06886 **Tel** *(03491) 42 04 34 4* **Fax** *(03491) 42 04 34 5* **Rooms** *20*

The location is a big plus here, as you can walk to most of the interesting sights and attractions from the hotel. The rooms themselves have a very warm appearance and are fitted with the standard conveniences such as Internet access and satellite television. The staff are very helpful. **www.stadthotel-wittenberg.de**

WÖRLITZ Wörlitzer Hof   €€

Markt 96, 06786 **Tel** *(034905) 41 10* **Fax** *(034905) 41 122* **Rooms** *50*

Located adjacent to a pleasant square with trees and a little fountain, this hotel has a calm and welcoming feel. This cosy feel continues in the rooms, which, though a little plain, are not short on the standard comforts. The beer garden under the lime trees is its most attractive feature. **www.woerlitzer-hof.de**

SAXONY

BAUTZEN Goldener Adler   €€

Hauptmarkt 4, 02625 **Tel** *(03591) 48 66 0* **Fax** *(03591) 48 66 20* **Rooms** *30*

Ideal for those who like light and space as the rooms have high ceilings and simple, smart furnishings. It is a nice contrast to the cosy feeling of its adjoining wine cellar and curved-roofed beer hall and restaurant. The historic charm of the original 1540s building has been retained. **www.goldeneradler.de**

BAUTZEN Villa Antonia   €€

Lessingstraße 1, 02625 **Tel** *(03591) 50 10 20* **Fax** *(03591) 50 10 44* **Rooms** *16*

This late 1890s villa, located in a quiet and up-market part of town, is a historic monument that was once owned by a concert pianist. It has since been refreshed and renovated and is now this small hotel which is straightforward but pleasant and comfortable. **www.hotel-villa-antonia.de**

CHEMNITZ Günnewig Hotel Chemnitzer Hof   €€

Theaterplatz 4, 09111 **Tel** *(0371) 68 40* **Fax** *(0371) 67 62 58 7* **Rooms** *98*

This late-1920s building has been renovated to its former glory. The foyer is gleaming and grand, although the period charm is lost in the rooms themselves which are merely tidy and stylish. All rooms have wireless Internet, safes and satellite television. **www.guennewig.de**

CHEMNITZ Mercure Hotel Kongress Chemnitz   €€

Brueckenstraße 19, 09111 **Tel** *(0371) 68 30* **Fax** *(0371) 68 35 05* **Rooms** *386*

This hotel is located in a striking glass tower and has rooms which are simple and have all the amenities you would expect from a hotel that is owned by an international chain. Hotel facilities include meeting rooms, conference rooms, a fitness room and a sauna. An airport shuttle is also available. **www.mercure.com**

CHEMNITZ Ringhotel Schlosshotel Klaffenbach   €€

Wasserschloßweg 6, 09123 **Tel** *(0371) 26 11 0* **Fax** *(0371) 26 11 10 0* **Rooms** *49*

A turreted fairy-tale hotel flanked by two wings of more modest buildings. The rooms vary from simple standards to some very interesting options. Easily the most attractive aspect of the hotel is the location as a moated castle right in the historic centre of Chemnitz. **www.schlosshotel-klaffenbach.de**

DRESDEN Hotel und Restaurant Klosterhof   €€

Alteubnitz 12, (0)1219 **Tel** *(0)35132016500* **Fax** *(0)35132016667* **Rooms** *24*

This small and charming hotel in the outskirts of Dresden is the perfect location for those looking for a relaxing stay outside of the city centre. While rooms are basic with few amenities, the historic buildings and very hospitable service make this a good alternative to hotels in the city. **www.dresden-klosterhof.de**

DRESDEN Innside by Melia   €€€

Salzgasse 4, 1067 **Tel** *(0)351795150* **Fax** *(0)351795154099* **Rooms** *180*

This modern hotel with a chic design boasts a central location, just steps away from historic attractions. The Innside Dresden offers stylish and comfortable accommodation complete with a restaurant, a spa and two bars to choose from. The rooms are impeccably decorated and all have king-size beds. **www.innside.de**

DRESDEN Romantik Hotel Pattis   €€€

Merbitzer Straße 53, 01157 **Tel** *(0351) 42 55 0* **Fax** *(0351) 42 55 25 5* **Rooms** *46*

This is very much a family-run hotel (pictures, birth dates and other family information are given on the website) and offers a mix of business-class standards and personal touches that will make you feel both important and relaxed at the same time. The charming old building is set in a park minutes from the city centre. **www.pattis.de**

DRESDEN Steigenberger Hotel de Saxe   €€€

Neumarkt 9, 01067 **Tel** *(0351) 43 86 0* **Fax** *(0351) 43 86 88 8* **Rooms** *185*

Even the simple rooms are vast and elegant and offer Internet, satellite television, safes and the usual list of comforts and conveniences. There is a definite sense of sparkle and fresh opulence in the dining areas. This is a very refined establishment with a stylish spa. **www.steigenberger.com/dresden**

Key to Price Guide *see p.488* **Key to Symbols** *see back cover flap*

DRESDEN Hotel Taschenbergpalais Kempinski

Taschenberg 3, (0)1067 **Tel** *(0)3514912636* **Fax** *(0)3514912812* **Rooms** *182*

Situated in the heart of historic Dresden, the Hotel Taschenbergpalais offers elegant luxury accommodation and excellent, unobtrusive service. Rooms are comfortable and spotlessly clean with high ceilings and river views. The hotel features a spa and wellness centre, two bars and three restaurants. **www.kempinski.com**

FREIBERG Silberhof

Silberhofstraße 1, 09599 **Tel** *(03731) 26 88 0* **Fax** *(03731) 26 88 78* **Rooms** *30*

The rooms in this interesting-looking building are decorated in a distinctive style somewhat influenced by rococo themes with lots of gleaming satin and white-painted wood. All the usual modern amenities are on offer as well, such as satellite television, Internet access and mini bars in all rooms. **www.silberhof.de**

GÖRLITZ Romantik Tuchmacher Hotel

Peterstraße 8, (0)2826 **Tel** *(0)358147310* **Fax** *(0)3581473179* **Rooms** *60*

Dating back to the Renaissance and located in the old quarter of the city, the Romantik is one of the top-rated hotels in Görlitz. The excellent service, friendly ambience and comfortable, individually decorated medieval-style rooms make a stay here a real experience. The restaurant focuses on hearty local dishes. **www.tuchmacher.de**

KAMENZ Goldner Hirsch

Markt 10, 01917 **Tel** *(03578) 78 35 0* **Fax** *(03578) 78 35 59 9* **Rooms** *30*

Established in 1550 and one of the few buildings in the city that was not destroyed in the 1842 fires, there is a successful mixture of old and new in this hotel. The rooms are simple but classy and comfortable, and there are two restaurants and a beer garden. **www.hotel-goldner-hirsch.de**

LEIPZIG Alt-Connewitz Hotel - Restaurant

Meusdorfer Straße 47a, 04277 **Tel** *(0341) 30 13 77 0* **Fax** *(0341) 30 13 80 0* **Rooms** *33*

A simple and straightforward hotel with very reasonable prices. The comfortable guest rooms have a fresh, clean decor and include Internet access and TV. The hotel also has a good restaurant offering hearty regional cuisine. **www.alt-connewitz.de**

LEIPZIG Leipzig Marriott Hotel

Am Hallischen Tor 1, 04109 **Tel** *(0341) 96 53 0* **Fax** *(0341) 96 53 99 9* **Rooms** *231*

Dark wood and richly patterned carpets and furnishings create an environment in which you can nestle in warmth and comfort. It can feel a bit old fashioned, but services such as Internet access and air conditioning ensure that it is not. The hotel is well located in the historic part of town and just across from the train station. **www.marriott.com**

LEIPZIG SAS Radisson Blu Hotel Leipzig

Augustusplatz 5-6, 4109 **Tel** *(0)34121460* **Fax** *(0)3412146815* **Rooms** *214*

This city centre hotel is ideally located, right across the street from the Opera house. The hotel is beautifully decorated and the tastefully furnished rooms come complete with rainfall showers and comfortable beds. The staff are pleasant and accommodating. The restaurant, Spagos, serves international cuisine. **www.radissonblu.com**

LEIPZIG Westin Leipzig

15 Gerber Straße, 04105 **Tel** *(0341) 98 80* **Fax** *(0341) 98 81 22 9* **Rooms** *436*

The beds are the big attraction here. They have what is called a Heavenly Bed which features a special mattress and four layers of covers. The guest rooms are richly and tastefully decorated. An equally stylish "fitness" bar and pool are also available. **www.westin.com/leipzig**

MEISSEN Hotel Andree

Ferdinandstraße 2, 01662 **Tel** *(03521) 75 50* **Fax** *(03521) 75 51 30* **Rooms** *85*

This hotel is in the centre of town but in a quiet location. The guest rooms are decorated and furnished in a simple and uncomplicated style. The excellent restaurant is certainly worth a visit because it serves a good variety of local cuisine. **www.hotel-andree.de**

MORITZBURG Landhaus Moritzburg

Schlossallee 37, 01468 **Tel** *(035207) 89 69 0* **Fax** *(035207) 89 69 19* **Rooms** *17*

A good away-from-it-all option, where you can stay in an attic-style room and look out over meadows. The rooms range from cosy to spacious, and have an almost Scandinavian feel to them. There is a decent restaurant, including terrace dining in the pleasant garden in warmer months. **www.landhaus-moritzburg.de**

PIRNA Romantik Hotel Deutsches Haus

Niedere Burgstraße 1, 01796 **Tel** *(03501) 46 88 0* **Fax** *(03501) 46 88 20* **Rooms** *40*

A charming, historic place occupying three Renaissance houses. There is also a lovely, atmospheric brick vault cellar and highly recommended restaurant, Deutsches Haus *(see p534)*. There are beautiful riverside walks nearby along the banks of the Elbe. **www.romantikhotel-pirna.de**

ZITTAU Schwarzer Bär

Ottokarplatz 12, 02763 **Tel** *(03583) 55 10* **Fax** *(03583) 55 11 11* **Rooms** *19*

The Black Bear is so named because the landlord in 1694 was expelled for keeping a black bear. This is a homely and very pleasant place with attractive, simply decorated guest rooms and a reputable restaurant. **www.hotel-schwarzer-baer.de**

ZWICKAU Achat Hotel €€

Leipziger Straße 180, 08058 **Tel** *(0375) 87 20* **Fax** *(0375) 87 29 99* **Rooms** *204*

A full range of all the services and facilities you would expect in a smart, modern hotel. The rooms are simple, clean and comfortable, with just a subtle sprinkling of charm. An ideal place to stay if you are not interested in splashing out on luxuries but appreciate friendly service. **www.achat-hotel.de**

THURINGIA

ALTENBURG Hotel Engel €

Johannis Str. 27, 4600 **Tel** *(03447) 56 510* **Fax** *(03447) 56 51 14* **Rooms** *12*

This small, family-run hotel is located in the heart of the old city, just a short walk from the central market square. It has a homely feel, with individually decorated rooms and hand-crafted fittings. The restaurant serves hearty meals, and the cellar bar reaches down into the historic tunnels that run beneath the city. **www.hotel-engel-altenburg.de**

ALTENBURG Altenburger Hof €€

Schmöllnsche Landstraße 8, 4600 **Tel** *(03447) 58 40* **Fax** *(03447) 58 44 99* **Rooms** *140*

The guest rooms are decorated in a straightforward, clean, modern style, with long vertical striped curtains, neutral tones and simple furniture. All rooms have desks and Internet connections. The hotel has a good restaurant and cocktail bar, as well as a sauna and wellbeing area. **www.altenburger-hof.de**

EISENACH Steigenberger Hotel Thuringer Hof €€

Karlsplatz 11, 99817 **Tel** *(03691) 28 0* **Fax** *(03691) 28 19 0* **Rooms** *127*

If you want to combine art and hospitality the Steigenberger hotel is the right place. There are paintings and wooden sculptures in the lobby, and the modern rooms are just as elegant. Some have a beautiful view over the castle and surrounding area. The restaurant serves delicate fusion cuisine. **www.eisenach.steigenberger.de**

EISENACH Hotel auf der Wartburg €€€

Wartburg Castle, 99817 **Tel** *(03691) 79 70* **Fax** *(03691) 79 71 00* **Rooms** *35*

A little castle perched high on a cliff. Expect nothing but the best, and then have your expectations exceeded. The individually decorated rooms are well equipped, including wireless Internet access. Cosiness, palatial luxury and a great view are all combined here. **www.wartburghotel.de**

ERFURT Mercure Hotel Erfurt Altstadt €€

Meienbergstr. 26-27, 99084 **Tel** *(0)36159490* **Fax** *(0)3615949100* **Rooms** *141*

This 4-star Mercure hotel offers comfortable, modern accommodation in the Old Town of Erfurt. Close to the cathedral, shops and restaurants, the hotel is surrounded by charming medieval streets, perfect for an evening stroll. The restaurant serves international cuisine that can be enjoyed on a terrace in the summer. **www.mercure.com**

ERFURT Pullman Erfurt am Dom €€€

Theaterplatz 2, 99084 **Tel** *(0361) 64 45 0* **Fax** *(0361) 64 45 10 0* **Rooms** *160*

The towering glass box entrance hints at the business-class quality of the hotel. Rooms are smart and comfortable with a muted-brown and burgundy decor. All rooms have safes, mini bars, satellite and pay television and internet access. **www.accorhotels.com**

ERFURT Zumnorde €€€

Anger 50/51, 99084 **Tel** *(0361) 56 80 0* **Fax** *(0361) 56 80 40 0* **Rooms** *54*

Stately rooms with muted style and quality polished wood furniture. The hotel is located in the historic centre of town near the Mariendom and St Severi. It also offers special discounts through its website, particularly for weekend visits. **www.hotel-zumnorde.de**

GERA Pentahotel €€

Gutenbergstraße 2a, 07548 **Tel** *(0365) 29 09 0* **Fax** *(0365) 29 09 10 0* **Rooms** *165*

The rooms here are all pretty generous in terms of space, and are decorated in a mildly lively and colourful way. Wireless internet access operates throughout the hotel. The location is quiet and almost has a residential feeling about it. **www.pentahotels.com**

GOTHA Hotel am Schlosspark €€

Lindenauallee 20, 99867 **Tel** *(03621) 44 20* **Fax** *(03621) 44 24 52* **Rooms** *95*

With parts of the hotel being set in a greenhouse-style glass box, there is a summery feeling to this place at any time of year. Guest rooms have all the facilities that one would expect of a four-star hotel. The hotel's restaurant of the same name is pleasant *(see p535)*, and a spa and sauna are also available. **www.hotel-am-schlosspark.de**

GREIZ Schlossberg Hotel €

Marienstr. 1–5, 07973 **Tel** *(03661) 62 21 23* **Fax** *(03661) 62 21 66* **Rooms** *33*

Guest rooms are light and uncomplicated, and all have mini bar and television and all have free wireless Internet access. There is no restaurant onsite, but there is a restaurant offering traditional regional fare just a few minutes' stroll away. **www.schlossberghotel-greiz.de**

Key to Price Guide *see p.488* **Key to Symbols** *see back cover flap*

JENA Jembo Park
🏨 �🏨 €

Rudolstädter Str. 93, 07745 **Tel** *(03641) 68 50* **Fax** *(03641) 68 52 99* **Rooms** *48*

For accommodation that is attached to a bowling alley and pub, it looks surprisingly good. This is an easygoing kind of place that is often used for wedding receptions and parties, and offers a no-nonsense straightforward kind of comfort. **www.jembo.de**

MÜHLHAUSEN Mirage Hotel
€€

Karl-Marx-Str. 9, 99974 **Tel** *(03601) 43 90* **Fax** *(03601) 43 91 50* **Rooms** *77*

Things are very clean and simple here in a business-like way. The guest rooms are very stylish with muted colours and minimal furniture. All rooms have satellite television and wireless Internet access. It is situated in the perfect location for the old town and all the best sights of Mühlhausen. **www.mirage-hotel.de**

OBERHOF Treff Hotel Panorama
€€

Theodor-Neubauer-Straße 29, 98559 **Tel** *(036842) 50 0* **Fax** *(036842) 22 55 1* **Rooms** *409*

This huge hotel offers stunning architecture and a huge range of activities, especially for children. Set in parkland, it rises out of the woods like a pyramid. There are tennis, squash and badminton courts as well as an indoor climbing gym. An apartment for four is available. **www.treff-hotel-panorama.de**

WEIMAR Hotel Anna Amalia
€€

Geleistrasse. 8-12, 99423 **Tel** *(03643) 49 56 0* **Fax** *(036430) 49 56 99* **Rooms** *51*

Conveniently located within strolling distance of all of the things you may wish to see while in town. The interior is supposed to follow the theme of Goethe's Italian travels, but this does not really extend beyond naming the rooms after Italian cities. The rooms and apartments are comfortably furnished. **www.hotel-anna-amalia.de**

WEIMAR Ringhotel Kaiserin Augusta
€€

Carl-August-Allee 17, 99423 **Tel** *(03643) 23 40* **Fax** *(03643) 23 44 44* **Rooms** *134*

An elegant-looking old building that has guest rooms that either look out across the old part of town or onto a courtyard. All rooms are decorated in light colours and feel spacious and airy, and are tidy and comfortable without feeling too stiff or formal. **www.hotel-kaiserin-augusta.de**

WEIMAR Dorint am Goethepark
€€

Beethovenplatz 1-2, 99423 **Tel** *(03643) 87 20* **Fax** *(03643) 87 21 00* **Rooms** *143*

A three-minute walk to the historic town centre, this rather interesting building offers a good mix of comfort and convenience, and also combines the old and the new in a surprising but effective way. The building itself consists of a new, modern style construction that sits between two classical mansions. **www.dorint.com**

WEIMAR Hotel Elephant
€€

Markt 19, 99423 **Tel** *(03643) 80 20* **Fax** *(03643) 80 26 10* **Rooms** *99*

Despite the hotel's name, the style here is very refined and stately. Everything is squared-off, neat, respectable and comfortable. All rooms also have original artworks, and the hotel has a tradition of being a meeting place for artists, poets and intellectuals. **www.hotelelephantweimar.com**

WEIMAR Grand Hotel Russischer Hof zu Weimar
€€€

Goetheplatz 2, 99423 **Tel** *(03643) 77 40* **Fax** *(03643) 77 48 40* **Rooms** *126*

A place of tradition and time-honoured luxury, this hotel has gleaming floors, an astrological grandfather clock, polished wood, heavy curtains tied back with tasselled golden ropes, textured walls and ceilings, and a range of fine dining options. It is really rather grand. **www.russischerhof.com**

MUNICH

Vi Vadi Hotel
€

Marsstraße 6-10, 80335 **Tel** *(089) 545190* **Fax** *(089) 54519100* **Rooms** *145*   **Map** *Map 1 E3*

A stone's throw from the train station, this gem of a hotel offers sound proofed rooms with kitchenettes, an Italian restaurant, sleek flat-screen TVs and free Wi-Fi. High quality materials and design touches create an atmosphere of luxury. Rooms are spacious by European standards and some have a balcony. **www.vivadihotel.de**

Am Siegestor
€€

Akademienstraße 5, 80799 **Tel** *(089) 399550* **Rooms** *20*

The building where the hotel stands became a hotel in 1950 and still houses the original lift, one of Munich's oldest hotel lifts, dating back to the late 1800s. It is situated close to the lively Schwabing scene with good shops, bars and restaurants. Guest rooms are simple but adequate. **www.hotel-siegestor.de**

Gästehaus Englischer Garten
€€

Liebergesellstraße 8, 80802 **Tel** *(089) 3839410* **Fax** *(089) 38394-133* **Rooms** *25*

A cosy little guesthouse with pleasant, if small rooms. The hotel is quiet and family run. Longer-stay apartments are also available, offering more space and a balcony. Once a watermill, the now listed building has a lovely garden where you can sit out and enjoy breakfast. **www.hotelenglischergarten.de**

Hotel am Nockherberg
€€

Nockherstraße 38a, 81541 **Tel** *(089) 6230010* **Fax** *(089) 623 00129* **Rooms** *38*

Modern, small, neat and clean sums up this hotel. What it lacks in stylish design it makes up for in convenient location, being close to the river Isar, Deutsches Museum and Gasteig cultural centre. The decor is simple but comfortable in neutral tones. A welcoming and friendly place. **www.nockherberg.de**

Hotel Eder
€€

Zweigstraße 8, 80336 **Tel** *(089) 554660* **Fax** *(089) 5503675* **Rooms** *25*   **Map** *1 E4*

This small hotel has been run by the same Bavarian family since 1947. Antique furniture and warm wood provide atmosphere, but it's the personal touches that make this place. The hospitable owners are a goldmine of tourist tips and go to great lengths to accommodate individual wishes. Near the main train station. **www.hotel-eder.de**

Jedermann Hotel
€€

Bayerstraße 95, 80335 **Tel** *(089) 543240* **Fax** *(089) 54324111* **Rooms** *55*

An excellent base during Oktoberfest, this affordable hotel charms guests with generous breakfast buffets and attentive service. In the evening you can relax with a Bavarian brew in the bar. The rooms themselves are spartan but well-kept. Book quarters facing the inner courtyard for a quiet night. **www.hotel-jedermann.de**

Motel One
€€

Herzog-Wilhelm-Straße 28, 80331 **Tel** *(089) 51777250* **Fax** *(089) 517772510* **Rooms** *241*   **Map** *1 F5*

Few cut-rate design hotels in Germany have been as successful as Motel One. Dark hardwoods, polished granite and leather sofas give an air of luxury. Rooms are on the snug side but great value in this location: Munich's old town is on your doorstep. **www.motel-one.com**

Wombat's
€€

Senefelderstraße 1, 80336 **Tel** *(089) 59989180* **Fax** *(089) 599891810* **Rooms** *65*   **Map** *1 E4*

Munich's new generation of hostel-hotels is led by Wombat's. In the Australian spirit of easy hospitality, staff serve a welcome drink and chit-chat with obvious pleasure. The double rooms have IKEA-style beds and private bathrooms. Ideal for sociable, young-minded guests seeking affordable comfort. **www.wombats-hostels.com**

Advokat
€€€

Baaderstraße 1, 80469 **Tel** *(089) 216310* **Fax** *(089) 2163190* **Rooms** *50*

Advokat is the designer sister hotel of the Admiral. It is situated right in the trendy artistic quarter where you can find nice boutiques and great cafés. The decor throughout is in an elegant, classic style, with lots of paintings, flowers, sculptures and contemporary design. Minimal but stylish. There is a small roof terrace. **www.hotel-advokat.de**

Cosmopolitan Hotel
€€€

Hohenzollernstraße 5, 80801 **Tel** *(089) 383810* **Fax** *(089) 38381-111* **Rooms** *71*   **Map** *2 C1*

A contemporary hotel in a quieter side street in the fashionable Schwabing district. There is a modern design feel throughout and rooms have Ligne Roset furniture. Enjoy breakfast on the outdoor terrace in warmer weather. It is located just a short walk from the English Garden. **www.geisel-privathotels.de**

Insel Mühle
€€€

Von-Kahr-Straße 87, 80999 **Tel** *(089) 81010* **Fax** *(089) 812 0571* **Rooms** *38*

This hotel has a dreamy romantic setting in an old mill in beautiful gardens by a small river. The style is simple, country and comfortable. There is also an excellent restaurant, beer garden, wine cellar and bar. Choose tables in shady spots, under trees, or simply relax and wander around the grounds. **www.insel-muehle.com**

Novotel Muenchen City
€€€

Hochstraße 11, 81669 **Tel** *(089) 661070* **Fax** *(089) 66107 999* **Rooms** *307*

A very contemporary four-star hotel with simple, sleek, bright decor. The welcoming breakfast room has large floral photographs. There is also a spacious pool and relaxation room plus fitness area. Its central location means that you can walk to Marienplatz, the Gasteig cultural centre or museums. **www.novotel.com**

Olympic
€€€

Hans-Sachs-Straße 4, 80469 **Tel** *(089) 231890* **Fax** *(089) 23189199* **Rooms** *38*

A small hotel with neo-Baroque appeal and stylish, arty charm in the heart of the creative area. It is favoured by artists, photographers and fashion designers. The decor is Italian modern classic with an art gallery lobby. Most rooms look out onto an inner courtyard, offering a peaceful atmosphere. **www.hotel-olympic.de**

Admiral
€€€€

Kohlstraße 9, 80469 **Tel** *(089) 216350* **Fax** *(089) 293674* **Rooms** *33*

Situated just around the corner from the Deutsches Museum this small four-star hotel offers traditional style, efficient staff, a wonderful breakfast buffet, some rooms with balconies overlooking the garden and a bar for evening drinks. Caters for families too. Tranquil location not far from the river Isar. **www.hotel-admiral.de**

Anna
€€€€

Schützenstraße 1, 80335 **Tel** *(089) 599940* **Fax** *(089) 599 94333* **Rooms** *73*   **Map** *1 F4*

A very design-conscious hotel in the heart of Munich with a gold-coloured reception desk, designer seating in the café, bar and restaurant, and pillars, a wonderful chandelier and purple sofas in the lounge. Try the innovative cuisine with Euro-Asian inspiration. It is located just ten minutes by foot from Marienplatz. **www.geisel-privathotels.de**

Key to Price Guide *see p.488* **Key to Symbols** *see back cover flap*

Asam Hotel ⬚ €€€€

Josephspitalstraße 3, 80331 **Tel** *(089) 2309700* **Fax** *(089) 2309/097* **Rooms** *24* **Map** *1 F5*

A popular hotel among celebrities, it offers good service and a certain level of style. Guest rooms have marble bathrooms and you can choose from international cuisine in the hotel's own Speisekammer restaurant and enjoy cocktails in the bar. The surrounding streets are quiet at night. **www.hotel-asam.de**

Cortiina ⬚ ▤ €€€€

Ledererstraße 8, 80331 **Tel** *(089) 2422490* **Fax** *(089) 2422 49100* **Rooms** *39* **Map** *2 C4*

You might be forgiven for thinking the hotel lobby is an art gallery. A favourite among the fashionable and design set, there is a stylish bar and oak panelling in the rooms, and it is located right in the heart of the city. They can provide a babysitter and daily newspapers are complimentary. **www.cortiina.com**

Opera ⬚ ♟ €€€€

St-Anna-Straße 10, 80538 **Tel** *(089) 2104940* **Fax** *(089) 21049477* **Rooms** *25* **Map** *3 D4*

Tucked in a side street close to the designer shops is Hotel Opera in a smart town house. It has a beautiful façade and Italian Renaissance courtyard. Enjoy the peace and quiet in the lovely garden or try some of the French, German or Italian specialities in the fine restaurant Gandl *(see p536)*. The guest rooms are all different. **www.hotel-opera.de**

Splendid-Dollmann ⬚ €€€€

Thierschstraße 49, 80538 **Tel** *(089) 238080* **Fax** *(089) 23808 365* **Rooms** *36* **Map** *3 D4*

The Splendid has an English town house feel to it. Expect a traditional and charming hotel in quiet Lehel, an old quarter of the town rich in tradition. It offers a restaurant, babysitting service and a lovely small garden, library and bar. The guest rooms are elegant and have antique furniture. **www.hotel-splendid-dollmann.de**

Bayerischer Hof ⬚ ▥ ▨ ♟ ▤ ▤ €€€€€

Promenadeplatz 2–6, 80333 **Tel** *(089) 21200* **Fax** *(089) 2120906* **Rooms** *395* **Map** *2 A3*

A large luxurious hotel in a prominent central location near the best shops, museums, opera house, theatres and restaurants. Elegant rooms with swathes of fabrics mixing plaids and florals in a country-house style. It also has a spa, three restaurants, including the Garden Restaurant *(see p537)*, and a great bar. **www.bayerischerhof.de**

Hotel Königshof ⬚ ▥ ♟ ▨ ▤ €€€€€

Karlsplatz 25, 80335 **Tel** *(089) 551360* **Fax** *(089) 55136113* **Rooms** *87* **Map** *1 F3*

A renowned hotel with classical elegance, first-class service, comfort and an internationally acclaimed cuisine in its Michelin-starred restaurant of the same name *(see p537)*. This is top class luxury in a central location, close to the shops and museums. Make use of the fitness, sauna and wellbeing area. **www.geisel-privathotels.de**

Kempinski Hotel Vier Jahreszeiten ⬚ ▥ ▨ ♟ ▨ ▤ €€€€€

Maximilianstraße 17, 80539 **Tel** *(089) 21250* **Fax** *(089) 2125 2000* **Rooms** *308* **Map** *2 C4*

The top address in Munich (built for King Maximilian II in 1858) nestled among the designer stores on Maximilianstraße. Excellent service, gastronomy and bars. A stunning entrance hall in rich gold and reds sets the tone. The pool and wellness floor was completely revamped in 2006. **www.kempinski-vierjahreszeiten.de**

Mandarin Oriental ⬚ ▥ ▨ ♟ ▨ ▤ €€€€€

Neuturmstraße 1, 80331 **Tel** *(089) 290980* **Fax** *(089) 222539* **Rooms** *73* **Map** *2 C4*

This centrally located, luxury Munich property offers spacious rooms, marble bathrooms with separate bath and shower and panoramic views of the city from the rooftop terrace's heated swimming pool. Dine in the fine Mark's restaurant with its Michelin star, or alfresco on the terrace. **www.mandarinoriental.com/munich**

BAVARIA

ALTÖTTING Zur Post ⬚ ▥ ▨ ▨ €€

Kapellplatz 2, 84503 **Tel** *(08671) 5040* **Fax** *(08671) 6214* **Rooms** *93*

Located in the heart of a charming small town on one of Germany's oldest squares, the rooms here are classically elegant with fine wooden furniture, some with views over church spires. Guests can also enjoy several restaurants, as well as a pool with sauna and steam bath. **www.zurpostaltoetting.de**

ANSBACH Bürger-Palais ▥ €€

Neustadt 48, 91522 **Tel** *(0981) 95131* **Fax** *(08671) 95132* **Rooms** *12*

Ornate and Baroque in style with a lovely garden and terrace. The restaurant is Bavarian rustic with stained-glass windows and waitresses in traditional costume. Period furniture, chandeliers and original fireplaces enhance the ambience. Prices go up during Bach week from the end of July to early August. **www.hotel-buerger-palais.com**

ASCHAFFENBURG Wilder Mann ⬚ ▥ ▨ €€

Löherstraße 51, 63739 **Tel** *(06021) 3020* **Fax** *(06021) 302234* **Rooms** *74*

The Wilder Mann dates back to a 16th-century inn at the old bridge over the river Main. It has no-fuss, comfortable modern rooms and its restaurant of the same name *(see p538)* serves good quality regional food and you can even eat up on the roof terrace. There is also a spa area. **www.hotel-wilder-mann.de**

ASCHAU IM CHIEMGAU Residenz Heinz Winkler

Kirchplatz 1, 83229 **Tel** *(08052) 17990* **Fax** *(08052) 1799-66* **Rooms** *32*

A culinary destination for real gourmands. Masterchef Heinz Winkler took over the original Post Hotel here in 1989. The former medieval building now has luxurious rooms plus invigorating and rejuvenating spa treatments. Enjoy the great terrace and garden. **www.residenz-heinz-winkler.de**

AUGSBURG Dom Hotel

Frauentorstraße 8, 86152 **Tel** *(0821) 343930* **Fax** *(0821) 34393200* **Rooms** *52*

A recently restored historic hotel near the cathedral and within walking distance of all the sights and local restaurants. An extra plus is the pool, sauna and fitness area. The Dom has been family owned for four generations and lies in a quiet side street by the Bischofsmauer, which is the old town wall. **www.domhotel-augsburg.de**

AUGSBURG Steigenberger Drei Mohren

Maximilianstraße 40, 86150 **Tel** *(0821) 50360* **Fax** *(0821) 157864* **Rooms** *105*

In the heart of the historic old town, it is an excellent base for visiting all the sights. Well-appointed rooms contain antiques and old paintings. It also has an excellent restaurant. A short walk from the museum, theatre and palaces. Comfort and high quality service. **www.steigenberger.com**

BAMBERG Alt-Ringlein

Dominikanerstraße 9, 96049 **Tel** *(0951) 95320* **Fax** *(0951) 9532500* **Rooms** *33*

A pleasant and comfortable hotel in Bamberg's centre. Enjoy the choice of Franconian meals in its restaurant of the same name *(see p538)* and try one of several local beers, including their own home-brewed one. In the wing dating back to 1296 they have Franconian styled rooms. Make sure you spend time in the nice beer garden. **www.alt-ringlein.com**

BAMBERG Welcome Hotel Residenzschloss

Untere Sandstraße 32, 96049 **Tel** *(0951) 60910* **Fax** *(0951) 6091701* **Rooms** *184*

This hotel has classic rooms in a listed building on the banks of the river Regnitz. Now a spa and conference hotel, it began life as a hospital back in 1789. Guests can choose between two restaurants, and there is also a piano bar and small chapel, which sometimes holds classical concerts. **www.residenzschloss.com**

BAYREUTH Bayerischer Hof

Bahnhofstraße 14, 95444 **Tel** *(0921) 78600* **Fax** *(0921) 7860560* **Rooms** *50*

A luxury hotel within walking distance of the Oberfrankenhalle and Festival Hall for the famous Wagner Festspiele music festival. It offers spacious elegant rooms, a French bistro, a restaurant, a pool and sauna, garden area, sun terrace and also a roof terrace. **www.bayerischer-hof.de**

BAYREUTH Lohmühle

Badstraße 37, 95444 **Tel** *(0921) 53060* **Fax** *(0921) 5306469* **Rooms** *42*

Located on the banks of the pretty Mülbach river, this privately owned three-star hotel offers a peaceful setting and classic contemporary decor in a half-timbered house close to the pedestrianized area. Expect traditional Franconian hospitality and fresh, locally-caught fish on the restaurant menu. **www.hotel-lohmuehle.de**

BAYREUTH Ramada Hotel Residenzschloss

Erlanger Straße 37, 95444 **Tel** *(0921) 75850* **Fax** *(0921) 7585601* **Rooms** *102*

This tastefully appointed four-star hotel, located on the edge of town, has a light airy restaurant looking out onto the garden. You can sample regional and international food from the menu. Wireless Internet is available and you can make use of the hotel's own fitness club with sauna and whirlpool. **www.ramada.de**

BERCHTESGADEN Hotel Edelweiss

Maximilianstraße 2, 83471 **Tel** *(08652) 97990* **Fax** *(08652) 9799266* **Rooms** *124*

Right on the old market square, the rooms in this hotel pamper with plush linens, just-right mattresses and bathrooms the size of a small principality. A Families will appreciate the child-care and play facilities. Don't miss the rooftop restaurant's regional delicacies. **www.edelweiss-berchtesgaden.com**

BURGHAUSEN Landhotel Reisingers Bayerische Alm

Robert-Koch-Str. 211, 84489 **Tel** *(08677) 9820* **Fax** *(08677) 982200* **Rooms** *23*

A superior family-run hotel in Burghausen, overlooking Europe's longest castle and old town. Enjoy excellent food in the hotel's beautiful beer garden of the same name *(see p539)*. Amenities include Wireless Internet, free parking and anti-allergy beds, a garden of the five senses and healthy or macrobiotic menus. **www.bayerischealm.de**

COBURG Festungshof

Festungshof 1, 96450 **Tel** *(09561) 80290* **Fax** *(09561) 802933* **Rooms** *14*

The Festungshof offers simple but adequate rooms in a comfortable rustic style. Located at the foot of the Coburg fortress, it dates back to 1337 and boasts great views across the surrounding countryside. Eat traditional Franconian fare in the wood-panelled Wallensteinstube or the large beer garden. **www.hotel-festungshof.de**

DACHAU Zieglerbräu

Konrad-Adenauer-Straße 8, 85221 **Tel** *(08131) 454396* **Fax** *(08131) 4543 9898* **Rooms** *12*

In the middle of Dachau's old town, the Zieglerbräu has undergone a pleasant transformation. Major and much needed renovation has brought it into the 21st century. Rooms are bright, colourful, comfortable and fresh. As well as beer from its own brewery, it offers guests typical Bavarian and international food. **www.zieglerbraeu.com**

DINKELSBÜHL Deutsches Haus

Weinmarkt 3, 91550 **Tel** *(09851) 6058* **Fax** *(09851) 7911* **Rooms** *18*

The building dates back to 1440. Its famous half-timbered German High Renaissance façade is one of the best in the region. With classic old-style rooms, modern facilities and an excellent restaurant of the same name *(see p539)*, the town of Dinkelsbühl is a highlight on the Romantic Road from Würzburg to the Alps. **www.deutsches-haus-dkb.de**

EICHSTÄTT Adler Hotel

Marktplatz 22–24, 85072 **Tel** *(08421) 6767* **Fax** *(08421) 8283* **Rooms** *28*

Double studios overlook the Baroque market square at the front and the town wall to the rear. Centrally located but quiet nonetheless. The rooms are furnished in a rather simple style but are clean and comfortable. The listed building retains a certain traditional atmosphere. **www.adler-eichstaett.de**

FREISING Isar Hotel

Isarstraße 4, 85356 **Tel** *(08161) 8650* **Fax** *(08161) 8655 55* **Rooms** *56*

A family-owned hotel which is welcoming and centrally situated by the river Isar close to the old town. It has German country-style wooden decor and offers wireless Internet access in the lobby, as well as a bar and a restaurant specializing in Asian food. Bike hire is available plus a sauna and massage and beauty treatments. **www.isarhotel.de**

FÜSSEN Alpenblick

Uferstraße 10, 87629 **Tel** *(08362) 50570* **Fax** *(08362) 505773* **Rooms** *61*

Come to this hotel for the stunning view across the lake and Alps more than the style, which is quite cosy and chintzy. Füssen lies close to King Ludwig II's beautiful and famous castles. Opportunities for hiking, fishing, cycling or sauna, steam bath and solarium are all nearby. **www.alpenblick.de**

FÜSSEN Treff Hotel Luitpoldpark

Bahnhofstraße 1–3, 87629 **Tel** *(08362) 9040* **Fax** *(08362) 904678* **Rooms** *131*

A majestic pale pink building with modern classic decor. It is in the heart of Fussen, surrounded by Allgäu's Alps, lakes and the pretty park, the King's Nook. Choose from four top restaurants serving Bavarian cuisine *(see p540)* The hotel also boasts a large Fit and Fun athletic centre. **www.luitpoldpark-hotel.de**

GARMISCH-PARTENKIRCHEN Garmischer Hof

Chamonixstraße 10, 82467 **Tel** *(08821) 9110* **Fax** *(08821) 51440* **Rooms** *54*

Located close to the centre of town, Garmischer Hof is a traditional chalet-style hotel which is elegant, if a little dated. From the balconies of south-facing rooms you get a good view of the surrounding mountains and it is quiet at night. The hotel also boasts a garden and a restaurant with a summer terrace. **www.garmischer-hof.de**

GARMISCH-PARTENKIRCHEN Hotel Bavaria

Partnachstraße 51, 82467 **Tel** *(08821) 3466* **Fax** *(08821) 76466* **Rooms** *32*

Bavaria is a small family-run hotel near the centre of Garmisch, offering guests old-fashioned charm and hospitality. It has a wonderful garden and you can even fish in the hotel's peaceful stretch of river. The guest rooms are tastefully decorated. **www.hotel-bavaria-garmisch.com**

GARMISCH-PARTENKIRCHEN Atlas Grand Hotel

Ludwigstraße 49, 82467 **Tel** *(08821) 93630* **Fax** *(08821) 9363 2222* **Rooms** *58*

The oldest and most traditional building in town is located in the pedestrianized area. King Ludwig II housed his generals here. It has antique wooden furniture, traditional Bavarian style, rich colours, compact and cosy rooms, a lovely garden terrace with mountain views and an elegant restaurant. **www.atlas-grandhotel.com**

INGOLSTADT Ara Hotel

Schollstraße 10a, 85055 **Tel** *(0841) 95430* **Fax** *(0841) 9543444* **Rooms** *95*

The family-run Ara Hotel is near the centre of Ingolstadt. It is a large crimson-coloured hotel in a contemporary building with outdoor sun terrace and compact comfortable rooms. Also, non-smoking and disabled rooms are available. The Italian restaurant, La Tosca, is light and spacious. **www.hotel-ara.de**

KEMPTEN Bayerischer Hof

Füssener Straße 96, 87437 **Tel** *(0831) 57180* **Fax** *(0831) 5718100* **Rooms** *51*

A four-star hotel in a traditional house in the centre of Kempten. It offers rooms with views over the park or river, a complimentary bottle of mineral water, Internet access, a Bavarian restaurant and beer garden, plus a small fitness area. The hotel also has a pretty garden and terrace for use in summer. **www.bayerischerhof-kempten.de**

LANDSHUT Romantik Hotel Fürstenhof

Stethaimer Straße 3, 84034 **Tel** *(0871) 92550* **Fax** *(0871) 925544* **Rooms** *24*

An elegant and classic hotel with a romantic and regal aura, set in a beautiful Art Nouveau villa in the centre of Landshut. This hotel offers a sauna and a peaceful garden. The very good restaurant has one Michelin star and provides healthy cuisine using fresh local produce such as duck and venison. **www.romantikhotels.com/landshut**

LINDAU Hotel Garni Brugger

Bei der Heidenmauer 11, 88131 **Tel** *(08382) 93410* **Fax** *(08382) 4133* **Rooms** *23*

A cozy B&B with friendly owners and a superb location on the island of Lindau. Rooms are furnished in pleasant country style and the cellar houses a small but welcoming spa area. Generous breakfasts are prepared with care. Internet access is by direct cable only. **www.hotel-garni-brugger.de**

LINDAU Reutemann Seegarten

Ludwigstraße 21, 88131 **Tel** *(08382) 9150* **Tel** *(08382) 915591* **Rooms** *64*

A great setting right on the promenade of this pretty town on Lake Constance. There is a lovely view of the Austrian Alps across the lake from the balconies and terrace or bar. Fitness and wellbeing facilities plus an open-air pool can be used in the sister hotel next door. Make the most of the hotel's bikes. **www.reutemann-lindau.de**

LINDAU Bayerischer Hof

Bahnhofplatz 2, 88131 **Tel** *(08382) 9150* **Fax** *(08382) 915591* **Rooms** *97*

A luxurious Neo-Classical building dating back to 1854, located on the harbour front which has spacious rooms and suites, good service and excellent fitness, pool, sauna and wellbeing facilities. Enjoy the international cuisine in the restaurant of the same name *(see p540)* and unforgettable lake views from the bar. **www.bayerischerhof-lindau.de**

LINDAU Villino

Hoyerberg 34, 88131 **Tel** *(08382) 93450* **Fax** *(08382) 934512* **Rooms** *18*

Located behind Lindau in the bordering village of Hoyern, on the Hoyerberg hill. Culture and haute cuisine are paramount in this idyllic country residence set in a beautiful garden. Its restaurant of the same name *(see p540)* offers cuisine inspired by Asian-Italian fusion. There is a peaceful terrace, spa and wireless Internet access. **www.villino.de**

MURNAU AM STAFFELSEE Alpenhof Murnau

Ramsachstraße 8, 82418 **Tel** *(08841) 4910* **Fax** *(08841) 491100* **Rooms** *60*

A top class spa and chalet-style retreat between Garmisch and Munich, close to Oberammergau which borders the Murnauer Moos nature reserve, overlooking the majestic Alps and Lake Staffel. It is an idyllic setting. Enjoy the renowned cuisine in the Reiterzimmer restaurant. **www.alpenhof-murnau.com**

NEUBURG AN DER DONAU Neuwirt

Färberstraße 88, 86633 **Tel** *(08431) 2078* **Fax** *(08431) 38643* **Rooms** *30*

A traditional and typical small Bavarian hotel with a cosy feel. It has a *Stube* tavern and a spacious beer garden in a sunny courtyard, partly undercover. The guest rooms are simply decorated with a rustic charm and are adequate and clean. **www.neuwirt-neuburg.de**

NÜRNBERG Burghotel

Lammsgasse 3, 90403 **Tel** *(0911) 238890* **Fax** *(0911) 2388 9100* **Rooms** *58*

Charming simple rooms filled with light offer some great views over the roofs of the old town. Burghotel has traces of ancient castle life, such as armour and coats-of-arms. There is also a lounge with an open fire, rustic bar, sun terrace and sauna. **www.altstadthotels-nuernberg.de**

NÜRNBERG Romantik Hotel am Josephsplatz

Josephsplatz 30–32, 90403 **Tel** *(0911) 214470* **Fax** *(0911) 21447-200* **Rooms** *36*

A romantic hotel dating back to 1675 located within walking distance of Nürnberg's old centre. There are small apartments which would suit a family. Enjoy the good breakfast buffet, roof terrace, sauna, solarium, fitness room and winter garden. There are also several restaurants close by. **www.hotel-am-josephsplatz.de**

OBERAMMERGAU Turmwirt

Ettalerstraße 2, 82487 **Tel** *(08822) 92600* **Fax** *(08822) 1437* **Rooms** *22*

Built in the Bavarian country-house style and owned by the same family for three generations, this small hotel has a welcoming wooden reception area with antique chests and rugs. It has a sun terrace and outdoor tables under chestnut trees, an *à la carte* restaurant and a café. **www.turmwirt.de**

OBERSTDORF Kappeler Haus

Am Seeler 2, 87561 **Tel** *(08322) 96860* **Fax** *(08322) 968613* **Rooms** *45*

This chalet-style hotel in the Allgäu Alps is located in the heart of Obertsdorf, the southern-most village in Germany. An in-house beautician is on hand to pamper guests. Music recitals take place in the hotel, too. There is also a garden and pool and it is set in a quiet location. **www.kappeler-haus.de**

PASSAU Passauer Wolf

Rindermarkt 6–8, 94032 **Tel** *(0851) 931510* **Fax** *(0851) 9315150* **Rooms** *41*

This hotel is located in the old town of Passau, next to the pedestrian precinct and on the banks of the Danube. The St Stephan cathedral and several museums and unique sights are within walking distance. Choose between rooms with a view over the river, the old town or the courtyard. **www.hotel-passauer-wolf.de**

PASSAU Residenz

Fritz-Schäffer-Promenade, 94032 **Tel** *(0851) 989020* **Fax** *(0851) 98902200* **Rooms** *45*

A fabulous river setting with great views of castle, boats and the Danube plays host to this historic building offering comfort and a lovely little terrace. Built in the 15th century, it has a history of river trade and travellers. The town square is very close as are the boats for taking trips down the Danube. **www.residenz-passau.de**

REGENSBURG Bischofshof am Dom

Krauterermarkt 3, 93047 **Tel** *(0941) 5 84 60* **Fax** *(0941) 5846 146* **Rooms** *55*

Situated opposite the cathedral, this rustic-style hotel boasts an elegant, renowned restaurant, David *(see p541)*. The rooms have a romantic style with pretty country-house fabrics in florals and stripes. It has a quiet location looking out onto the side street or courtyard. All rooms are individually decorated. **www.hotel-bischofshof.de**

Key to Price Guide *see p.488* **Key to Symbols** *see back cover flap*

REGENSBURG Sorat Inselhotel €€€

Müllerstraße 7, 93059 **Tel** *(0941) 81040* **Fax** *(0941) 810 4444* **Rooms** *75*

This is a contemporary, comfortable and well-established hotel in a central location with lovely town views over the river. Enjoy the restaurant Brandner, lobby bar with full-length window and views downstream, plus spa, fitness centre and wireless Internet. **www.sorat-hotels.com**

ROTHENBURG OB DER TAUBER Gasthaus am Siebersturm €

Spitalgasse 6, 91541 **Tel** *(09861) 3355* **Fax** *(09861) 933823* **Rooms** *9*

A friendly and family-run hotel with romantic medieval charm near the old tower that serves good quality hearty Franconian meals in its own little restaurant. Some rooms look out over the famous Tauber valley. Splash out on a room with a four-poster, or stick to the more affordable standard doubles. **www.siebersturm.de**

ROTHENBURG OB DER TAUBER Prinzhotel €€

An der Hofstatt 3, 91541 **Tel** *(09861) 9750* **Fax** *(09861) 97575* **Rooms** *52*

Within the old town walls, this historic hotel is in a very quiet location surrounded by the town's medieval history. All the sights are within walking distance. The hotel's restaurant serves Franconian–Italian cuisine. Parking is available in front of the hotel. **www.prinzhotel.rothenburg.de**

WÜRZBURG/ HÖCHBERG Minotel Zum Lamm €€

Hauptstraße 76, 97204 **Tel** *(0931) 3045630* **Fax** *(0931) 408973* **Rooms** *37*

The hotel lies in Höchberg, outside the baroque centre of Würzburg and offers guests a typical Franconian hospitality and great gourmet food. It also boasts a lovely courtyard and garden. Guests are spoiled with great food and wine, and it is popular with cyclists, motorcyclists and hikers touring the area. **www.lamm-hoechberg.de**

BADEN-WURTTEMBERG

BAD MERGENTHEIM Hotel Gästehaus Alte Münze €

Münzgasse 12, 97980 **Tel** *(07931) 5660* **Fax** *(07931) 566222* **Rooms** *30*

In a quiet location near the Knight's Castle in the centre of town, this hotel has light, airy and modern, if simply decorated, guest rooms. There is also a cosy familiar breakfast room for guests with lots of plants. Discover the rich history of the area, the powers of the mineral water and enjoy walks in the surrounding countryside. **www.hotelaltemuenze.de**

BAD MERGENTHEIM Hotel Victoria €€

Poststraße 2–4, 97980 **Tel** *(07931) 5930* **Fax** *(07931) 593500* **Rooms** *78*

An intimate and highly-regarded spa hotel located in the centre close to the Kurpark thermal baths. It has well-equipped rooms and wine buffs will appreciate the Vinothek restaurant and enjoy sampling some of the 400 top wines from France and Italy, which you can buy in the shop along with olive oils. **www.victoria-hotel.de**

BADEN-BADEN Tannenhof €€

Hans-Bredow-Straße 20, 76530 **Tel** *(07221) 300990* **Fax** *(07221) 3009951* **Rooms** *27*

The Tannenhof has a wonderful, peaceful and idyllic setting with panoramic views. It is a great place to relax, whether in the garden, on the sun terrace, lawn or in the sauna and solarium. The house restaurant, Piemonte *(see p542)*, specializes in Northern Italian food and wines. **www.hotel-tannenhof-baden-baden.de**

BADEN-BADEN Hotel Belle Epoque €€€€

Maria-Viktoria-Straße 2c, 76530 **Tel** *(07221) 300660* **Fax** *(07221) 300666* **Rooms** *16*

Housed in a beautiful Neo-Renaissance villa surrounded by its own verdant park, all the rooms and suites in this hotel are decorated with original furniture from the Belle Epoque period. An elegant hotel with excellent service. **www.hotel-belle-epoque.de**

BADEN-BADEN Radisson Blu Badischer Hof €€€€

Lange Straße 47, 76530 **Tel** *(0800) 10 10 880* **Fax** *(07221) 934470* **Rooms** *139*

Baden-Baden's oldest hotel offering palatial grandeur with palms, pillars and plants. Some of the guest rooms have balconies, while others have thermal water pumped into the bathrooms. There are also indoor and outdoor thermal pools, plus a medical spa. **www.hotel-badischerhof-badenbaden.de**

ESSLINGEN Am Schelztor €€

Schelztorstraße 5, 73728 **Tel** *(0711) 39 69 640* **Fax** *(0711) 359887* **Rooms** *33*

A small, personal, family-run hotel with a historic touch, this hotel boasts a panoramic view of the vineyards of Esslingen and the castle. Close to the station and large cinema complex. Relax in the Finnish sauna or use the fitness room. There is a good restaurant nearby in a converted stable. Families are welcome. **www.hotel-am-schelztor.de**

FREIBURG IM BREISGAU Zum Roten Bären €€€

Oberlinden 12, 79098 **Tel** *(0761) 387 870* **Fax** *(0761) 3878717* **Rooms** *25*

Situated in a building that dates back to the 12th century, just minutes form the centre of Freiburg, this hotel also has a lovely traditional *Stube*, a tavern-style restaurant serving regional seasonal food. The guest rooms are comfortable and there is also a peaceful courtyard. **www.roter-baeren.de**

FREIBURG IM BREISGAU Colombi Hotel
Rotteckring 16, Am Colombi Park, 79098 **Tel** *(0761) 21060* **Fax** *(0761) 31410* **Rooms** *117*

This is a hotel offering elegant luxury and style, excellent service and a quiet, central location. It faces a park with a small castle and is not far from the Freiburg monuments. In addition to an award-winning gourmet restaurant, café, bar and tavern, the hotel has a pool, sauna and beauty spa, and other sports facilities nearby. **www.colombi.de**

FRIEDRICHSHAFEN Buchhorner Hof
Friedrichstraße 33, 88045 **Tel** *(07541) 2050* **Fax** *(07541) 32663* **Rooms** *96*

Located between Lake Constance and the main train station, this bright lakeside hotel blends the best of a luxury resort and a family inn. The bar is a lively meeting point for both locals and visitors. The halls are studded with hunting trophies, although this town is better known for the Zeppelin Museum not far from the hotel. **www.buchhorn.de**

HEIDELBERG Guest House Heidelberg
Bergheimer Straße 24, 69115 **Tel** *(06221) 872710* **Fax** *(06221) 8727170* **Rooms** *40*

This guest house combines the intimacy of a B&B with the freedom of a studio apartment. Rooms are spacious, and each has its own kitchenette. While breakfast is not provided, you can pick up freshly-made sandwiches and coffee in the foyer. Conveniently located near the old town, university and train station. **www.guesthouse-hd.de**

HEIDELBERG Holländer Hof
Neckarstaden 66, 69117 **Tel** *(06221) 60500* **Fax** *(06221) 605060* **Rooms** *39*

An old house in the centre of town with a pretty façade and classic, elegant rooms, this hotel is within easy reach of the famous castle and not far from the shops, restaurants, churches and pedestrianized area of Heidelberg. It is also close to where boat rides are run up and down the Neckar. **www.hollaender-hof.de**

HEIDELBERG Die Hirschgasse
Hirschgasse 3, 69120 **Tel** *(06221) 4540* **Fax** *(06221) 454111* **Rooms** *20*

First mentioned in 1472, Hirschgasse has a sense of history. The hotel boasts innovative chefs in its non-smoking restaurants, the very smart Le Gourmet and the Mensurstube, and a tavern, which has been the meeting place for Heidelberg's student fraternities for centuries. **www.hirschgasse.de**

HEIDELBERG Europäischer Hof Hotel Europa
Friedrich-Ebert-Anlage 1, 69117 **Tel** *(06221) 5150* **Fax** *(06221) 515506* **Rooms** *118*

The best in the area this hotel has luxurious suites, high quality rooms, courteous and helpful staff, *à la carte* dinners in the Kurfürstenstube, a terrace overlooking a garden, a shopping arcade and the Panorama spa and fitness club. There is everything you could possibly want to make it a memorable stay. **www.europaeischerhof.com**

HEILBRONN Ringhotel
Lohtorstraße 7, 74072 **Tel** *(07131) 62240* **Fax** *(07131) 627828* **Rooms** *80*

A modern concrete, steel and glass building, convenient for the romantic old centre of town. The rooms are comfortable and clean and the design is contemporary throughout. Very close to the public swimming baths with saunas. The hotel's restaurant, Vinopolitan, serves typical Swabian fare. **www.ringhotel-heilbronn.de**

KARLSRUHE Alfa Garni
Bürgerstraße 4, 76133 **Tel** *(0721) 29926* **Fax** *(0721) 29929* **Rooms** *36*

This small city hotel is right on Ludwigsplatz in the heart of Karlsruhe. The modern, light-filled building has comfortable rooms and art prints in the hallways. Enjoy the local cafés and restaurants with Mediterranean flair in the town centre, a few minutes by foot from the hotel. **www.alfa-karlsruhe.com**

KARLSRUHE Renaissance
Mendelssohnplatz, 76131 **Tel** *(0721) 37170* **Fax** *(0721) 377156* **Rooms** *215*

This is a recently renovated building with good location and facilities. It is not ideal for families as it has quite a business-like atmosphere. The Baroque castle, botanic gardens and zoo are close. Baden-Baden's casino and health spa are also not far away. Rooms are modern and functional. **www.renaissancehotels.com**

KONSTANZ Barbarrossa
Obermarkt 8–12, 78462 **Tel** *(07531) 128990* **Fax** *(07531) 12899700* **Rooms** *50*

Centrally located in the heart of the old town, this is where in 1183, Emperor Friedrich I, known as Barbarossa (Red Beard) signed a peace treaty with Lombardy. It has a very old painted façade, terrace seating at the front, stylish modern rooms and bright décor with red accents. **www.barbarossa-hotel.com**

KONSTANZ Hotel Sonnenhof
Otto Raggenbass Straße 3, 78462 **Tel** *(07531) 22257* **Fax** *(07531) 20358* **Rooms** *11*

This family-friendly hotel enjoys a central location in a historic neighbourhood. Guest rooms are simple but well-kept, and quarters to the rear have balconies. The friendly owners cater to your individual wishes with a smile. Enjoy views of the orchard from the breakfast room or the sunny terrace. No Internet access. **www.hotel-sonnenhof-konstanz.de**

KONSTANZ Villa Barleben am See
Seestraße 15, 78464 **Tel** *(07531) 942330* **Fax** *(07531) 9423328* **Rooms** *8*

Set in a wonderful spot right by the lake, this hotel is housed in a beautiful villa with antique furniture and ornaments, a cultivated atmosphere and a lovely terrace restaurant on summer evenings for hotel and outside guests. The guest rooms with a lake view are more expensive but worth the cost. **www.hotel-barleben.de**

Key to Price Guide *see p.488* **Key to Symbols** *see back cover flap*

LUDWIGSBURG Nestor 　　　　　　　　　　€€

Stuttgarter Straße 35/2, 71638 **Tel** *(0/141) 9670* **Fax** *(07141) 967113* **Rooms** *179*

This listed building in central Ludwigsburg, not far from the Baroque castle, the Friedenskirche church and market square, used to be a bakery. The guest rooms are modern; suites and executive doubles are also available. The hotel also has a sauna, solarium and fitness area. **www.nestor-hotels.de**

LUDWIGSBURG Schlosshotel Monrepos 　　　　　　　　€€€

Domäne Monrepos 22, 71634 **Tel** *(07141) 3020* **Fax** *(07141) 302200* **Rooms** *80*

Whether you want to laze on the pretty garden terrace under the chestnut trees, take a stroll around the Monrepos castle grounds, swim in the hotel's pool, have a massage or enjoy the culinary delights in one of the three restaurants, Monrepos is a peaceful and beautiful place to relax. **www.schlosshotel-monrepos.de**

MANNHEIM Maritim Parkhotel 　　　　　　　　€€€€

Friedrichsplatz 2, 68165 **Tel** *(0621) 15880* **Fax** *(0621) 1588800* **Rooms** *173*

A traditional hotel with an impressive façade situated on Friedrichsplatz with its historical buildings dating back to the Art Nouveau era. This elegant hotel has a palatial foyer, a fine vaulted restaurant, spacious rooms, an indoor swimming pool and marbled bathrooms, all set in wonderful parkland. **www.maritim.de**

MARBACH Parkhotel 　　　　　　　　€€

Schillerhöhe 14, 71672 **Tel** *(07144) 9050* **Fax** *(07144) 90588* **Rooms** *56*

Set in lush parkland with great views overlooking the Neckar valley and close to the Schiller Museum and the German literature archive, this hotel is ideally located and its lovely restaurant Schillerhöhe *(see p544)* allows you to dine out on the terrace in warmer weather to watch the beautiful sunset. **www.parkhotel-schillerhoehe.de**

RAVENSBURG Romantik Hotel Waldhorn 　　　　　　　　€€€

Marienplatz 15, 88212 **Tel** *(0/51) 36120* **Fax** *(0751) 3612100* **Rooms** *30*

A family-run hotel (five generations) in Ravensburg's pedestrianized area. The hotel has a fine gourmet restaurant serving delicious game and fish dishes. Its stylish, modern rooms are comfortable and classic with contemporary touches. Romantic, old and full of tradition but with all the comforts you would expect. **www.waldhorn.de**

ROTTWEIL Hotel Haus zum Sternen 　　　　　　　　€€

Hauptstraße 60, 78628 **Tel** *(0741) 53300* **Fax** *(0741) 533030* **Rooms** *11*

One of Rottweil's oldest stone houses, dating from 1278, this hotel is located in the heart of the historic town. It has many historic features, including an old wine cellar, which can be seen from the basement Platinum Bar. The rooms are a mix of old charm and modern comfort. It has an excellent restaurant of the same name *(see p544)*. **www.haus-zum-sternen.de**

SALEM Reck's Hotel Restaurant 　　　　　　　　€€

Bahnhofstraße 111, 88682 **Tel** *(07553) 201* **Fax** *(07553) 202* **Rooms** *20*

A high class hotel with the famous Reck's restaurant *(see p544)*, close to Lake Constance in beautiful countryside, this hotel has pleasant, comfortable rooms with period furniture and views out over the orchard. The fine restaurant offers a renowned cuisine of fresh, regional and seasonal food, including fish from the lake. **www.recks-hotel.de**

SCHWÄBISCH GMÜND Hotel Einhorn 　　　　　　　　€€

Rinderbachergasse 10, 73525 **Tel** *(07171) 1046990* **Fax** *(0/141) 61680* **Rooms** *18*

This Baroque hotel is bright, elegant and modern, it is housed in an old building with a Roman entrance and modern facilities, such as wireless Internet access. It also boasts the Barbarossa jazz bar and the brick-vaulted Barbarossakeller restaurant, plus a separate summer café, Einhorn, in the old town. **www.hotel-einhorn-centre.com**

SCHWÄBISCH HALL Hotel Hohenlohe 　　　　　　　　€€€

Weilertor 14, 74523 **Tel** *(0791) 75870* **Fax** *(0791) 758784* **Rooms** *114*

A dreamy location on the banks of the Kocher River, with the charms of the historic old town opposite. The rooms are compact but cheerful and hold all the amenities you'd expect from a four-star establishment. The spa has a huge salt-water whirlpool that will bring out the playful side of any guest. **www.hotel-hohenlohe.de**

SIGMARINGEN Hotel Fürstenhof 　　　　　　　　€

Zeppelinstraße 14, 72488 **Tel** *(07571) 72060* **Fax** *(07571) 720644* **Rooms** *34*

Smart business hotel strategically placed between the Danube and the town centre. Rooms are decorated in an appealing pastoral style, and those facing south have a terrace or balcony. Spend the day in the nearby Upper Danube Valley Nature Park before ordering delicious regional cuisine in the house restaurant. **www.fuerstenhof-sig.de**

ST BLASIEN Dom Hotel 　　　　　　　　€€€

Hauptstraße 4, 79837 **Tel** *(07672) 924690* **Fax** *(07672) 9246999* **Rooms** *9*

This country-style hotel sits in the shadow of St Blasien cathedral. The friendly owners take pride in their service and the quality of the in-house restaurant. Tastefully appointed rooms are an oasis of calm with a creek gurgling outside your window. A perfect base for exploring the Black Forest. No internet access. **www.dom-hotel-st-blasien.de**

STUTTGART Hansa Hotel 　　　　　　　　€

Silberburgstraße 114–116, 70176 **Tel** *(0711) 6567800* **Fax** *(0711) 617349* **Rooms** *80*

This is located near the pedestrianized area, so it is a good central base for exploring the Swabian capital of Stuttgart. It is also close to shops, restaurants, the station and museums. There is Internet access, bike hire, a restaurant, Petrarca, offering Mediterranean specials, and a beer garden. **www.hansa-stuttgart.de**

STUTTGART Kronen Hotel
Kronenstraße 48, 70174 **Tel** *(0711) 22510* **Fax** *(0711) 2251404* **Rooms** *80*

Located in a quiet spot, but still with easy access to the railway station, this hotel has a nice garden with terrace. Enjoy the great breakfast buffet in the modern breakfast room, looking out onto a palmed terrace. Guests can also take drinks at the little lobby bar or use the hotel sauna. **www.kronenhotel-stuttgart.de**

STUTTGART Hotel am Schlossgarten
Schillerstraße 23, 70173 **Tel** *(0711) 20260* **Fax** *(0711) 2026888* **Rooms** *116*

A modern hotel in the extensive Schlossgarten parklands. It has luxurious rooms and suites with elegant floral furnishings. There are several dining options, such as the gourmet French restaurant, the Zirbelstube, or classic, light modern and regional food in the hotel restaurant. **www.hotelschlossgarten.com**

TÜBINGEN Krone
Uhlandstraße 1, 72072 **Tel** *(07071) 13310* **Fax** *(07071) 133132* **Rooms** *48*

A good place to stay to capture the romance and medieval feel of Tübingen's past, Krone has elegant, comfortable rooms and a refined restaurant, and has been in the same family for over a century. Sample typical regional dishes in the fine Uhlandstube restaurant or try the less formal Ludwig's for coffees and light meals. **www.krone-tuebingen.de**

ULM Hotel Anker
Rabengasse 2, 89073 **Tel** *(0731) 63297* **Fax** *(0731) 1611641* **Rooms** *10*

This lively hotel close to Ulm's towering Dom is an unexpected delight. Housed above a Spanish wine restaurant, the rooms are on the tight side but smartly designed with large bathrooms. Guests rave about the attentive service, and the restaurant has a reputation for working wonders with fish. No internet access. **www.tourismus.ulm.de**

ULM-LEHR Engel
Loherstraße 35, 89081 **Tel** *(0731) 140400* **Fax** *(0731) 14040-300* **Rooms** *46*

A modern hotel located outside the centre of Ulm in the quieter suburb of Lehr, the rooms are clean and comfortable with simple decor. There is also a sauna and solarium, a bar and a restaurant. The owners also took over a local fish farm, so the fish dishes on the menu come highly recommended. **www.hotel-engel-ulm.de**

WEINGARTEN Walk'sches Haus
Marktplatz 7, 76356 **Tel** *(07244) 70370* **Fax** *(07244) 703740* **Rooms** *26*

This hotel is in a 16th-century half-timbered house. The original walls dated back to 1509, but it was rebuilt after damage in the Thirty Years' War (1618–48). It also has a wonderful little French restaurant with tables in the garden. The cuisine is light, contemporary and original. Internet access is available in the rooms. **www.walksches-haus.de**

WORMS Weingut Sandwiese
Fahrweg 19, 67550 **Tel** *(06241) 95610* **Fax** *(06241) 956111* **Rooms** *26*

Each room in this historic 18th-century manor is named after a grape variety. Guests will appreciate the large, airy and stylishly decorated rooms as well as the location not far from Worms' Cathedral. The restaurant serves regional fare and will arrange wine tastings on request. The breakfast buffet is excellent. **www.weingut-sandwiese.com**

RHINELAND-PALATINATE AND SAARLAND

BAD DÜRKHEIM Hotel an den Salinen
Salinenstraße 40, 67098 **Tel** *(06322) 94040* **Fax** *(06322) 940343* **Rooms** *12*

This comfortable hotel on the German Wine Road exudes peace and tranquillity. Rooms are nicely appointed, with romantic views of the surrounding vineyards and St Michael's chapel. Close by you'll find the therapeutic saltworks and a famously oversized wine barrel, the Dürkheimer Riesenfass. **www.hotel-an-den-salinen.de**

BAD HONNEF Avendi Hotel
Hauptstraße 22, 53604 **Tel** *(02224) 1890* **Fax** *(02224) 189189* **Rooms** *101*

This hotel sits regally overlooking the Rhine. There is a large fitness and wellbeing area, including an indoor pool. Creatively decorated and comfortable rooms have all the modern trappings. There is a restaurant as well as a bistro, which specializes more in drinks and small snacks than main meals. **www.avendi.de**

BAD NEUENAHR Steigenberger Hotel
Kurgartenstraße 1, 53474 **Tel** *(02641) 9410* **Fax** *(02641) 941410* **Rooms** *224*

Architecturally impressive and very comfortable, the genteel rooms here are spacious and furnished with antiques. There is a restaurant, café, cocktail lounge and beer garden. There is also a golf course 2.5 km away, and the hotel has lockers for stowing golf bags and has the facility to book tee-times. **www.steigenberger.com**

BOPPARD Weinhaus Ohm Patt
Steinstraße 30, 56154 **Tel** *(06742) 2366* **Fax** *(06742) 81280* **Rooms** *13*

"Come as a guest, leave as a friend" is the motto of this congenial hotel run by an English couple. Rooms are plain but clean and quiet. You can enjoy a beer or local wine in the downstairs pub. The hotel is conveniently located close to restaurants, although dinner is offered by prior arrangement. **www.hotelweinhauspatt.de**

Key to Price Guide *see p.488* **Key to Symbols** *see back cover flap*

COCHEM Haus Schwarzenberg

Moselstraße 24, 56814 **Tel** *(02671) 915699* **Fax** *(02671) 915698* **Rooms** *7*

Overlooking the Moselle River, this family-run hotel is located in Ernst, 5 km from Cochem. Sport-minded guests can go hiking, cycling or canoeing nearby. The wine tavern offers scrumptious regional dishes and wine tastings. Rooms have views of the river or the surrounding vineyards. No Internet access. **www.haus-schwarzenberg-mosel.de**

KOBLENZ Diehl's Hotel

Rheinsteigufer 1, 56077 **Tel** *(0261) 97070* **Fax** *(0261) 9707213* **Rooms** *57*

Located on the banks of the Rhine and opposite where the Rhine and the Mosel rivers meet, this hotel has a terrace overlooking this beautiful area, and all guest rooms have a similar view. There is restaurant serving creative international cuisine, as well as banquet facilities for large functions such as weddings. **www.diehls-hotel.de**

KOBLENZ Hotel Scholz

Moselweißer Straße 121, 56073 **Tel** *(0261) 94260* **Fax** *(0261) 942626* **Rooms** *67*

The oldest family-run hotel in Koblenz, it has been in the family for three generations. The present generation conducted extensive renovations and modernization. The small rooms are comfortable and well equipped. There is a rustic restaurant serving traditional German cuisine in an unmistakably German setting. **www.hotelscholz.de**

KOBLENZ Top Hotel Krämer Garni

Kardinal-Krementz-Straße 12, 56073 **Tel** *(0261) 406200* **Fax** *(0261) 41340* **Rooms** *25*

A comfortable and new hotel, with a touch of the traditional German style. The rooms have a 1990s feel about them, and fresh flowers are a colourful touch which contrast well with the somewhat minimalist decor. The service is friendly and enhances the personal atmosphere of the hotel. **www.tophotel-k.de**

LAHNSTEIN Best Western Hotel Koblenz Lahnstein

Rhein-Höhen Weg/Zu den Thermen 1, 56112 **Tel** *(02621) 9120* **Fax** *(02621) 912101* **Rooms** *227*

Located in a park which has beautiful footpaths. There are tennis courts nearby, and tennis lessons can be arranged for guests. The hotel has two restaurants with stunning views over the city, as well as a café and comfortable lounge bar. Their pool and wellness area has been renovated. **www.hotel-lahnstein.bestwestern.de**

MAINZ Favorite Parkhotel

Karl-Weiser-Straße 1, 55131 **Tel** *(06131) 80150* **Fax** *(06131) 8015420* **Rooms** *122*

There is a pleasant surprise around every door here. Apart from the ultra-comfortable rooms and suites, there is a greenhouse with different varieties of palms, a gourmet restaurant and a beer garden that is a favourite meeting place for locals as well as guests. **www.favorite-mainz.de**

MAINZ Novotel Mainz

Augustusstraße 6, 55131 **Tel** *(06131) 9540* **Fax** *(06131) 954100* **Rooms** *217*

The bright and well-equipped rooms are very comfortable, and there is a spacious and relaxing pool area. Their restaurant offers elegant dining and a must-see wine bar, Kasematten, which is situated in a 17th-century vaulted cellar, providing a distinctive atmosphere for wine tastings. **www.novotel.com**

MARIA LAACH SeeHotel Maria Laach

Ortsteil Maria Laach, 56653 **Tel** *(02652) 5840* **Fax** *(02652) 584522* **Rooms** *69*

Situated near a 900-year old monastery, this hotel scores highly for relaxation and comfort. Beautiful lake views, a pleasant café with terrace seating in their winter garden as well as a high-class restaurant of the same name *(see p546)*, serving delicate regional and seasonal dishes, make this a delightfully comfortable place to stay. **www.seehotel-maria-laach.de**

NIEDERZISSEN Hotel am Bowenberg

Auf Brohl 7, 56651 **Tel** *(02636) 6217* **Fax** *(02636) 8317* **Rooms** *9*

A quaint hotel set amidst peaceful countryside, some of the rooms here have balconies overlooking the tree tops surrounding the hotel, and there is a library with a big fireplace, which is the perfect place for contemplating the next day's activities. It is close to the city centre and nearby tennis courts. **www.hotel-am-bowenberg.de**

OTTWEILER Schafbrücker Mühle

Schafbrücker Mühle 9, 66564 **Tel** *(06824) 3237* **Fax** *(06824) 5855* **Rooms** *21*

This converted oil mill occupies a charming spot near the picturesque old town of Ottweiler. Run by the same family for decades, the hotel has traditional interiors fashioned by local craftsmen. The restaurant enjoys a fine reputation for its regional cuisine, including fish hooked from the pristine Maisbach. **www.schafbruecker-muehle.de**

RÜSSELSHEIM Columbia Hotel

Stahlstraße 2–4, 65428 **Tel** *(06142) 8760* **Fax** *(06142) 876805* **Rooms** *150*

A hotel with a high level of service and excellent facilities. A favourite with both business guests and tourists. Each room is styled with warm colours and wooden furniture. There is a well-stocked gym and a landscaped pool. The main restaurant is French in style. They also have a bistro and lounge bar. **www.columbia-hotels.com**

SAARBRÜCKEN Hotel am Triller

Trillerweg 57, 66117 **Tel** *(0681) 580000* **Fax** *(0681) 58000303* **Rooms** *110*

An artistically inclined hotel with a lot to offer, the top floor suites here are astronomically themed, and have been named after constellations. The design merely begins here. Other themes include Moulin Rouge and The Four Seasons. There is a pool and an extensive wellness area. It is a ten-minute walk to the town centre. **www.hotel-am-triller.de**

SAARBRÜCKEN Victor's Residenz-Hotel €€€
Deutschmühlental, 66117 **Tel** *(0681) 588210* **Fax** *(0681) 58821199* **Rooms** *145*

This hotel is close to the French border and reflects the French influence well. It is surrounded by a forest and next to a lake. The atrium lobby is impressive and leads into their own casino and cocktail lounge. There is a luxurious wellness area and a restaurant that serves gourmet French cuisine. **www.victors.de**

SPEYER Hotel am Wartturm €
Landwehrstraße 28, 67346 **Tel** *(06232) 64330* **Fax** *(06232) 643321* **Rooms** *17*

Named after an old defence tower that dates back to 1451, this hotel is not, however, housed in the tower. It does offer comfortable rooms, though, some of which have balconies overlooking a garden. There is also a very cheerful wine bar that oozes character, where you may also enjoy light meals. **www.hotel-amwartturm.de**

SPEYER Domhof €€
Bauhof 3, 67346 **Tel** *(06232) 13290* **Fax** *(06232) 132990* **Rooms** *49*

Here you will find very spacious rooms that have been decorated with a refined taste. The hotel is set in a quiet area that has a calm and serene atmosphere. The elegant restaurant offers creative cuisine and the beer garden is a sanctuary of traditional German beer drinking. **www.domhof.de**

SPEYER Maximilian €€
Korngasse 15, 67346 **Tel** *(06232) 1002500* **Fax** *(06232) 1002529* **Rooms** *3*

This snazzy boutique hotel stands right next to the Old Gate. The trio of guest apartments and maisonettes are thoughtfully decorated with a blend of the modern and historic. Light sleepers should note that this a lively part of town. Attached to the hotel is a popular restaurant serving light international cuisine. **www.cafe-maximilian.de**

SPEYER Lindner Hotel & Spa Binshof €€€€
Binshof 1, 67346 **Tel** *(06232) 6470* **Fax** *(06232) 647199* **Rooms** *135*

The focus of this hotel is on the wellness and spa facilities, which should not be missed. All tastes are catered for in this huge spa complex. The guest rooms are just as luxuriously furnished, and there is a restaurant that serves fantastic Mediterranean food. **www.lindner.de**

TRIER Hotel Blesius Garten €€
Olewigerstraße 135, 54295 **Tel** *(0651) 36060* **Fax** *(0651) 360633* **Rooms** *62*

This is a unique hotel with beautiful rooms. It dates back to the 18th century, although it has kept itself modern through renovations. The winter garden restaurant has an open fireplace and they operate a terrace in the summer months. They also have their own brewery. **www.blesius-garten.de**

TRIER Hotel Eurener Hof €€
Eurener-Straße 171, 54294 **Tel** *(0651) 82400* **Fax** *(0651) 800900* **Rooms** *86*

An ostentatious building, standing on the corner of the street. Many of the rooms have small balconies and the corner rooms have wonderful views. There is a delightful garden terrace where you can enjoy breakfast. Elegant and comfortable rooms and a majestic dining area, where you can sample their fine cuisine. **www.eurener-hof.de**

TRIER Römischer Kaiser €€
Porta-Nigra-Platz 6, 54292 **Tel** *(0651) 9770100* **Fax** *(0651) 97701999* **Rooms** *43*

This hotel is housed in part of a historic building in the illustrious Porta Nigra Square. First mentioned in 1885, the hotel has a great central location and offers a decadent retreat in the heart of Trier. The rooms are tastefully furnished and spacious. It has a highly recommended restaurant of the same name *(see p546)*. **www.friedrich-hotels.de**

TRIER Mercure Hotel Trier Porta Nigra €€€
Porta-Nigra-Platz 1, 54292 **Tel** *(0651) 27010* **Fax** *(0651) 2701170* **Rooms** *106*

One of the largest hotels in Trier, it is well situated and furnished with all the comforts that you could expect, including a fitness centre, wellness area and spa facilities. The surrounding area is littered with historical sights and buildings. Their restaurant is well known and there is an imaginatively decorated bar. **www.mercure.com**

VÖLKLINGEN Parkhotel Albrecht €€€
Kühlweinstraße 70, 66333 **Tel** *(06898) 914700* **Fax** *(06898) 23655* **Rooms** *13*

Surrounded by magnificent parkland, this award-winning hotel is an ideal base for exploring the Saarland. Spacious and bright, each room bears not a number but the name of a town. In fact, little is generic about this hotel and its top-notch service. The Orangerie restaurant is noted for its gourmet cuisine and wine list. **www.parkhotel-albrecht.de**

HESSE

ALSFELD Zum Schwalbennest €
Pfarrwiesenweg 12–14, 36304 **Tel** *(06631) 911440* **Fax** *(06631) 71081* **Rooms** *65*

First constructed in 1968, the "Swallow's Nest" is a serene and cheerful place to stay. It has comfortable rooms, a rustic restaurant, relaxed beer garden and is within an easy walking distance of the centre of Alsfeld. There is even a dance floor for those fond of a waltz or two. **www.hotel-schwalbennest.de**

Key to Price Guide *see p.488* **Key to Symbols** *see back cover flap*

BAD HOMBURG ParkHotel
€€€

Kaiser-Friedrich-Promenade 53–55, 61348 **Tel** *(06172) 8010* **Fax** *(06172) 801400* **Rooms** *123*

A very pleasant, privately-owned hotel, where the beds are very inviting and the rooms are decorated with a sense of colour and with an eye for comfort. The hotel offers baby beds and babysitters can be arranged at reception. There are two restaurants, one Italian and one Chinese. **www.parkhotel-bad-homburg.de**

BAD HOMBURG Maritim Kurhaushotel
€€€€

Ludwigstraße 3, 61348 **Tel** *(06172) 6600* **Fax** *(06172) 660100* **Rooms** *158*

Right next door to a peaceful park, some of the rooms here have balconies overlooking the trees, and all are impeccably decorated. There is a nice pool for laps, and golfing facilities for the enthusiasts. They have a bistro, bar and a good restaurant which caters to the vegetarian palate. **www.maritim.de**

DARMSTADT Hotel Friends Darmstadt
€€

Spessartring 53, 64287 **Tel** *(06151) 391550* **Fax** *(06151) 3915529* **Rooms** *23*

A small hotel that combines a central location with a peaceful ambience, each of the rooms here have balconies and are quite large with all the modern necessities available. This hotel is comfortable, cozy and modern, with free Wi-Fi and makes for a good weekend getaway. **www.hotel-friends-darmstadt.de**

DARMSTADT Jagdschloss Kranichstein
€€€€

Kranichsteiner Straße 261, 64289 **Tel** *(06151) 97790* **Fax** *(06151) 977920* **Rooms** *15*

Housed in one of the most beautiful Renaissance castles in the region, this hotel offers a unique experience. A perfect setting for a wedding reception, the hotel often finds all 15 of their rooms booked by wedding parties. The grounds are stunning and well kept, and there is a beautiful forest nearby. **www.hotel-jagdschloss-kranichstein.de**

ELTVILLE AM RHEIN Kronenschlösschen
€€€

Rheinallee, 65347 **Tel** *(06723) 640* **Fax** *(06723) 7663* **Rooms** *18*

The hotel fits beautifully in the little village of Eltville. The rooms are stylish and charming, each having its own individual shape and furnishings. The bathrooms are works of art. The restaurant serves very elegant cuisine, as does the bistro, which may tempt those less inclined to empty their wallet. **www.kronenschloesschen.de**

FRANKFURT AM MAIN Hotel Borger
€€

Triebstraße 51, 60388 **Tel** *(06109) 30900* **Fax** *(06109) 309030* **Rooms** *36*

A family-styled hotel with a comfortable atmosphere and a convenient location, the rooms here offer the basic amenities, and the hotel is the perfect base for exploring the city and surrounding areas. The villa has been in the family for over a hundred years and was renovated late in the 20th century. **www.hotel-borger.de**

FRANKFURT AM MAIN Hotel Cult
€€

Offenbacher Landstraße 56, 60599 **Tel** *(069) 9624460* **Fax** *(069) 962446666* **Rooms** *69*

A chic boutique hotel in the buzzing quarter of Sachsenhausen. Pop-art colours and daring floor plans confirm the owner's enthusiasm for progressive design. Staff are helpful and professional, and transport links are convenient, with a U-Bahn stop across the street. Bargain rates compared to other city-centre hotels. **www.hotelcult.de**

FRANKFURT AM MAIN Hotel Topas
€€

Niddastraße 88, 60329 **Tel** *(069) 230852* **Fax** *(069) 237228* **Rooms** *31*

A block from Frankfurt train station, this spotless, friendly city hotel is popular with both business and holiday visitors. Facilities include 24-hour reception, safes, large work desks and minibars. Laundry service is free. Guest rooms and bathrooms are unusually large for this category and quiet despite the busy location. **www.hoteltopas.de**

FRANKFURT AM MAIN Frankfurt Hotel Savoy
€€€€

Wiesenhüttenstraße 42, 60329 **Tel** *(069) 273960* **Fax** *(069) 27396795* **Rooms** *144*

This hotel has a classy attitude. Situated in a convenient location for trade fairs and with good access to the airport, guests will find the hotel itself a charming place to explore. There is a swimming pool on the top floor, which offers a rare and beautiful skyline view of Frankfurt am Main. **www.savoyhotel.de**

FRANKFURT AM MAIN Hessischer Hof
€€€€€

Friedrich Ebert Anlage 40, 60325 **Tel** *(069) 75400* **Fax** *(069) 75402924* **Rooms** *117*

An exquisitely styled hotel with a sense of class. The rooms are styled either in a modern manner or with more of an antique feel about them, with some of the suites furnished with pieces from the Prince of Hesse. The restaurant and bar compliment each other well. **www.hessischer-hof.de**

FULDA Maritim Hotel am Schlossgarten
€€€

Pauluspromenade 2, 36037 **Tel** *(0661) 2820* **Fax** *(0661) 282499* **Rooms** *112*

An ostentatious hotel with a refined atmosphere, some of the upper floors here have balconies with great views, and all the guest rooms are spacious and luxurious. There are two restaurants in unique settings: one in an intimate wine cellar; the other in a historic hall with Baroque styling. They also have a good pool area. **www.maritim.de**

GIESSEN Hotel Tandreas
€€

Licher Straße 55, 35394 **Tel** *(0641) 94070* **Fax** *(0641) 9407499* **Rooms** *34*

This family-run establishment on the outskirts of town has tastefully appointed accommodation and a Michelin-starred restaurant that draws diners from miles around. The owners do their utmost to ensure you enjoy your stay. Book a rear-facing room with balcony, as the front rooms can be noisy from the traffic. **www.tandreas.de**

KASSEL Adesso Hotel Astoria 🔲 €€

Friedrich-Ebert-Straße 135, 34119 **Tel** *(0561) 72830* **Fax** *(0561) 7283199* **Rooms** *40*

Friendly and comfortable service with bright and airy rooms, this is quite a well-located hotel that satisfies guests of all types, be it for business, visiting the many museums in the area or exploring the region. There are very good conference facilities here, with six dedicated rooms and extensive inclusive packages. **www.adesso-hotels.de**

KASSEL Hotel Residenz Domus 🔲 €€

Erzbergerstraße 1–5, 34117 **Tel** *(0561) 703330* **Fax** *(0561) 70333498* **Rooms** *55*

An intimate hotel that gives each guest a feeling of being personally looked after, the Art Nouveau design of the Domus's rooms betrays the modern comforts that are offered. In addition though, there is also an old-fashioned gambling room with a pool table. **www.hotel-domus-kassel.de**

KASSEL Schlosshotel Bad Wilhelmshöhe 🔲 🍴 🏋 📺 ▤ €€

Schlosspark 8, 34131 **Tel** *(0561) 30880* **Fax** *(0561) 3088428* **Rooms** *101*

Dating back to 1767, this hotel is situated in one of the most exclusive areas of Kassel. There are beautiful grounds to wander through and a plethora of wellness programmes to enjoy. The guest rooms are refined and relaxing, and the suites are spacious and opulent without being garish and over-exuberant. **www.schlosshotel-kassel.de**

LIMBURG Romantik Hotel Zimmermann 🍴 €€

Blumenröder Straße 1, 65549 **Tel** *(06431) 4611* **Fax** *(06431) 41314* **Rooms** *20*

Different styles in each of the rooms, ornate furnishings and a restful environment all make this hotel an ideal base for all types of guest. Each bathroom is fitted with Italian marble, and for the convenience of business guests there is wireless Internet access throughout the hotel. **www.romantikhotel-zimmermann.de**

MARBURG Waldecker Hof 🔲 🏊 🏋 📺 €€

Bahnhofstraße 23, 35037 **Tel** *(06421) 60090* **Fax** *(06421) 600959* **Rooms** *40*

A comfortable and pleasant hotel with a nice pool and fitness area, the hotel itself is still family run, and the service reflects a high level of care that has been put into creating a welcoming atmosphere for guests. The delicious buffet breakfast is great. Situated close to the main train station. **www.waldecker-hof-marburg.de**

MARBURG Vila Vita Hotel & Residenz Rosenpark 🔲 🍴 🏊 🏋 📺 ▤ €€€€

Rosenstraße 18–28, 35037 **Tel** *(06421) 60050* **Fax** *(06421) 6005100* **Rooms** *138*

Ostentatious and elegant at the same time, the glass dome in the lobby lends a palatial quality to the hotel, as does the impeccable service. There are 30 apartments also available, which is why it is also called "Residenz". There are three restaurants to choose from, as well as a wine cellar and lounge bar. **www.vilavitahotels.com**

MICHELSTADT Zum Grünen Baum 🍴 🔲 €

Große Gaße 17, 64720 **Tel** *(06061) 2409* **Fax** *(06061) 73281* **Rooms** *5*

The half-timbered façade of this centrally-located inn is typical of this charming historic town in the Odenwald forest. The prize-winning restaurant uses fresh, local ingredients such as trout, wild boar or fallow deer. Rooms ooze old-fashioned cosiness but don't skimp on modern comforts (apart from no Internet access). **www.gruenerbaum-michelstadt.com**

RÜDESHEIM AM RHEIN Jagdschloss Niederwald 🔲 🍴 🏊 🏋 €€€

Am Niederwald 1, 65385 **Tel** *(06722) 71060* **Fax** *(06722) 7106666* **Rooms** *52*

Set in a historic hunting castle, this hotel offers all that you could wish for, including a tennis court and swimming pool. Its restaurant has a terrace with a panoramic view, and the wine cellar has the best wines from the region. The cocktail bar serves a very nice Long Island Ice Tea. **www.niederwald.de**

WEILBURG Schlosshotel Weilburg 🔲 🍴 🏊 📺 €€

Langgasse 25, 35781 **Tel** *(06471) 50900* **Fax** *(06471) 5090111* **Rooms** *50*

This castle from the Renaissance period provides a luxurious place to rest one's weary head. Apart from the beautiful architecture and design of the hotel itself, the surrounding area exudes a sense of history. The rooms are tastefully decorated and spacious. It has an excellent restaurant, Alte Reitschule *(see p548).* **www.schlosshotel-weilburg.de**

WETZLAR Landhotel Naunheimer Mühle 🔲 🍴 €€

Mühle 2, 35584 **Tel** *(06441) 93530* **Fax** *(06441) 935393* **Rooms** *33*

Set in a quiet area adjacent to the Lahn, the hotel itself was once mill-powered by the flowing waters. With an intimate design mixed with a traditional slanting towards comfort, the rustic restaurant serves cuisine from the region. The terrace and outside seating area is a great place to relax. **www.naunheimer-muehle.de**

WIESBADEN Klee am Park 🔲 🍴 €€€

Parkstraße 4, 65189 **Tel** *(0611) 90010* **Fax** *(0611) 9001310* **Rooms** *60*

Most rooms at this pretty hotel have their own balcony, offering a wonderful view over Wiesbaden. The restaurant serves delicious international dishes, and the surrounding park is the perfect place to burn off some calories from over-indulging. **www.klee-am-park.de**

WIESBADEN Nassauer Hof 🔲 🍴 🏊 🏋 📺 ▤ €€€€

Kaiser-Friedrich-Platz 3, 65183 **Tel** *(0611) 1330* **Fax** *(0611) 133632* **Rooms** *139*

This exclusive hotel offers eight different grades of superb rooms, all the way up to the presidential suite. The architecture and design brings a historic sense of aristocratic opulence, and yet this marries well with the modern amenities. The wellness area and restaurant attracts many non-residential guests. **www.nassauer-hof.de**

Key to Price Guide *see p.488* **Key to Symbols** *see back cover flap*

NORTH RHINE-WESTPHALIA

AACHEN Art Hotel Aachen €
Adenauerallee 209, 52066 **Tel** *(0241) 608360* **Fax** *(0241) 60836555* **Rooms** *38*

An art-themed hotel in the leafy Burscheid district, close to the motorway and a 15-minute bus ride from Aachen train station. Rooms are individually decorated and inspired by famous European artists or celebrities. A highlight is the spa with saunas, swimming pool and steam room. Room sizes differ; check when you book. **www.art-hotel-aachen.de**

AACHEN Best Western Hotel Royal garni €€€
Jülicher Straße 1, 52070 **Tel** *(0241) 182280* **Fax** *(0241) 18228699* **Rooms** *35*

Centrally located, this hotel makes a good base for business meetings, trade fairs and sightseeing tours into the city and surrounding areas. The rooms have a minimalist style and the suites come with private terraces and kitchenettes. The Aachener Cathedral lies within half a kilometre of the front door. **www.royal.bestwestern.de**

AACHEN Pullmann Aachen Quellenhof €€€€
Monheimsallee 52, 52062 **Tel** *(0241) 91320* **Fax** *(0241) 9132100* **Rooms** *185*

A grand hotel in every sense of the word, the elegant rooms and suites here are just the tip of the iceberg. The sauna, swimming pool and fitness area are stunning, as is the restaurant which offers Mediterranean-style food and sprawls out onto a terrace with a wonderful view of the park. **www.sofitel.com**

BIELEFELD Comfort Garni Hotel Stadt Bremen €
Dahmhofstraße 32, 33602 **Tel** *(0521) 521980* **Fax** *(0521) 52198113* **Rooms** *46*

Located in the pedestrianised precinct of Bielefeld's inner city, and near the railway station and convention centre, this hotel has been completely redecorated and renovated to be modern and comfortably furnished. There is a good breakfast buffet from 6:30am to 10am, a terrace and a hotel bar. **www.comfort garni.de**

BIELEFELD Brenner Hotel Diekmann €€
Otto-Brenner-Straße 133, 33607 **Tel** *(0521) 29990* **Fax** *(0521) 299 9220* **Rooms** *65*

A quaint little hotel with a homespun charm, there is a small bowling alley here which adds to the unique character of the hotel. There is also a restaurant that caters to large groups and functions, as well as a bar with lots of traditional paraphernalia on the walls and a beer garden outside. **www.brenner-hotel.de**

BONN Schlosshotel Kommende Ramersdorf €€
Oberkasselerstraße 10, 53227 **Tel** *(0228) 440734* **Fax** *(0228) 444400* **Rooms** *18*

Situated in a fairytale castle, the rooms and hallways here are filled with antiques and works of art that help set it apart from other hotels. There is a medieval feel to the hotel, and each room is individual. The restaurant is also worth a visit. **www.schlosshotel-kommende-ramersdorf.de**

BONN Hilton Bonn €€€
Berliner Freiheit 2, 53111 **Tel** *(0228) 72690* **Fax** *(0228) 7269700* **Rooms** *252*

With spacious and classy rooms equipped with all the modern conveniences you would expect, the hotel caters well for families, as does their wellness and fitness area. They have a nice pool and gym, which is the perfect place to burn off the calories consumed in the fantastic, Mediterranean-style restaurant. **www.hilton.de/bonn**

BONN Kaiser Karl €€€
Vorgebirgsstraße 56, 53119 **Tel** *(0228) 985570* **Fax** *(0228) 9855777* **Rooms** *42*

Exquisitely decorated rooms and a keen eye for details make this hotel a welcome oasis of leisure and pleasure. All rooms cater to those with allergies. Many famous guests have passed through the doors, and more than a few have tinkled the keys of the piano in the old-fashioned and dignified bar. **www.kaiser-karl-hotel-bonn.de**

BONN Dorint Hotel Venusberg €€€€€
An der Casselsruhe 1, 53127 **Tel** *(0228) 2880* **Fax** *(0228) 288288* **Rooms** *85*

This hotel sits on the banks of the Rhine and has colourful and decadent rooms that overlook the surrounding forest. There are a number of sporting facilities in the area, such as golf and tennis, and there is a jogging track inside the hotel for fitness fans. **www.dorint.com**

DETMOLD Lippischer Hof €€
Willy-Brandt-Platz 1, 32756 **Tel** *(05231) 9360* **Fax** *(05231) 936222* **Rooms** *25*

There is an attractive view from the windows of this hotel, set in the heart of Detmold. It has a deceptive simplicity with a high level of comfort and service. The restaurant is quite romantic, and on occasion there are functions held in the larger rooms used for conferences with set menus. **www.hotellippischerhof.de**

DORTMUND Cityhotel Dortmund €€
Grafenhof/Silberstraße 37, 44137 **Tel** *(0231) 4779660* **Fax** *(0231) 47796669* **Rooms** *50*

You'll be in good hands at this clean, efficiently-run hotel just a few steps from the main train station. The comfy rooms brim with carefully-selected artworks. Perks include free Wi-Fi and parking. The excellent English-speaking staff welcome guests with a bottle of free mineral water. Terrific breakfast buffet. **www.cityhotel-dortmund.de**

DÜSSELDORF Hotel Weidenhof

Oststraße 87, 40210 **Tel** *(0211) 1306460* **Fax** *(0211) 13064619* **Rooms** *36*

A ten-minute walk from all the central sights, there is a genteel charm to the rooms here, which are tastefully decorated with subtlety. It is a relatively small hotel but one that attracts many returning guests. There are six apartments which are well suited to families and small groups. **www.hotelweidenhof.de**

DÜSSELDORF Ibis Hauptbahnhof

Konrad-Adenauer-Platz 14, 40210 **Tel** *(0211) 16720* **Fax** *(0211) 1672101* **Rooms** *166*

A hotel with all the basic comforts and necessities, this hotel has a nice little bar near the modern lobby and wireless Internet throughout. The location is one of the best in Düsseldorf for access to the train station and general sightseeing. Guaranteed to deliver exceptional value. **www.ibishotel.com**

DÜSSELDORF Madison

Graf-Adolf-Straße 94, 40210 **Tel** *(0211) 16850* **Fax** *(0211) 1685328* **Rooms** *100*

There is a sporting and fitness centre connected to the hotel, which is very extensive and well equipped. Each room is tastefully decorated with warm colours and cosy furniture. There is a bistro with a terrace for the warmer months and another restaurant in the hotel. **www.azimuthotels.de**

DÜSSELDORF Steigenberger ParkHotel

Königsallee 1a, 40212 **Tel** *(0211) 13810* **Fax** *(0211) 1381592* **Rooms** *130*

This is an elegant hotel with delicately styled rooms, some of which are furnished with antiques while retaining a high level of comfort at the same time. Well situated, close to the Altstadt and the Rhine, a highlight here is the restaurant, which has a diverse menu and an extensive wine list. **www.steigenberger.com/duesseldorf**

ESSEN Astoria Hotel

Wilhelm-Nieswandt-Allee 175, 45326 **Tel** *(0201) 83584* **Fax** *(0201) 8358040* **Rooms** *102*

With new, intimate and colourful rooms in a modern building that has been renovated and expanded, this hotel is ideally placed for sightseeing and visiting the business districts. For functions there is the facility to arrange catering for the outside areas of the hotel, which are leafy and peaceful. **www.kchhotelastoria.de**

ESSEN Hotel Bredeney

Theodor-Althoff-Straße 5, 45133 **Tel** *(0201) 7690* **Fax** *(0201) 7691143* **Rooms** *293*

Close to the fairgrounds and other central locations, this hotel has become popular among business guests. There is a colourful lounge and lobby area, and very large facilities for conferences, including a hall. They also have a pool, fitness area and indoor skittles. **www.hotel-bredeney.de**

ESSEN Welcome Hotel

Schützenbahn 58, 45127 **Tel** *(0201) 17790* **Fax** *(0201) 1779199* **Rooms** *176*

A very modern and colourful hotel, the rooms here are filled with everything you could desire, and the beds are soft and comfortable. They can cater for people suffering sensitive allergies, for whom it would be better to avoid their beautiful but pollinated garden restaurant which operates in summer. **www.welcome-to-essen.de**

HOXTER Ringhotel Niedersachsen

Grubestraße 3–7, 37671 **Tel** *(05271) 6880* **Fax** *(05271) 688444* **Rooms** *80*

Set in a beautiful area this hotel has an expansive wellness and spa area, with a sizeable swimming pool. Some of the guest rooms have an unorthodox style to them, with big wooden beams. The hotel also boasts four restaurants to keep your taste buds occupied. **www.hotelniedersachsen.de**

KÖLN Motel One

Max-Planck-Straße 46, 50858 **Tel** *(02234) 200134* **Fax** *(02234) 200135* **Rooms** *105*

Given the subtle design touches throughout, you might never guess this is a chain hotel. Lovers of natural materials will feel right at home: dark hardwoods and marble offset the cheery blue-and-white tones of the fabrics and seating ensembles. Close to the motorway on the west side of town. **www.motel-one.com**

KÖLN Leonardo Hotel

Waldecker Straße 11–15, 51065 **Tel** *(0221) 67090* **Fax** *(0221) 6709321* **Rooms** *161*

Set in an otherwise dull area this hotel is an oasis of comfort and hospitality. The air conditioned rooms are spacious and well equipped. The hotel is still family run and great care has gone into retaining its charm. They have a large pool and good fitness facilities. It attracts mostly business guests for trade fairs. **www.leonardo-hotels.com**

KÖLN NH Köln Mediapark

Im MediaPark 8b, 50670 **Tel** *(0221) 27150* **Fax** *(0221) 2715999* **Rooms** *217*

Part of an Italian chain of hotels, this one displays the subtle and refined styling that serves them well. There are luxurious and comfortable rooms and facilities, situated in the MediaPark, next to the tall tower. There are excellent fitness and wellness facilities, and guests receive discounts at the nearby Holmes gym. **www.nh-hotels.de**

KÖLN Dorint Hotel am Heumarkt

Pipinstraße 1, 50667 **Tel** *(0221) 28060* **Fax** *(0221) 28061111* **Rooms** *262*

Hotel am Heumarkt is one of the most refined hotels in the city. It is very close to the Old Town, and an easy walking distance from the trade fairs. The bars, restaurants and cocktail lounges have become famous by themselves, and the fitness/pool area is state of the art. **www.dorint.com**

Key to Price Guide *see p.488* **Key to Symbols** *see back cover flap*

KÖLN Hotel im Wasserturm

Kaygasse 2, 50676 **Tel** *(0221) 20080* **Fax** *(0221) 2008888* **Rooms** *88*

Integrated into a historic water tower in the heart of Cologne, this top class hotel is one of the most distinctive in the city. The building's shape has spawned oddly shaped rooms, some with two levels. On the 11th floor is an opulent restaurant, La Vision *(see p551)*, that has been awarded a Michelin star. **www.hotel-im-wasserturm.de**

LEMGO Im Borke

Salzufler Straße 132, 32657 **Tel** *(05266) 1691* **Fax** *(05266) 1231* **Rooms** *37*

Here you will find a peaceful atmosphere that is well-suited to families. A lot of care has been put into making this hotel a welcome and friendly place to stay, and it has paid off. There is a restaurant of the same name *(see p551)* serving international cuisine in a traditional environment, and there is also a bowling alley downstairs. **www.hotel-im-borke.de**

MÜNSTER Romantik Hotel Hof zur Linde

Handorfer Werseufer 1, 48157 **Tel** *(0251) 32750* **Fax** *(0251) 327513* **Rooms** *48*

Built on the banks of the Werse river, with magnificent views and plenty of room to stroll around, this is about as authentic as a farm cottage hotel gets. There are suites and cottages with their own fireplaces and the restaurant serves high quality dishes, seasoned with herbs fresh from the hotel's own garden. **www.hof-zur-linde.de**

MÜNSTER Schloss Wilkinghege

Steinfurter Straße 374, 48159 **Tel** *(0251) 144270* **Fax** *(0251) 212898* **Rooms** *35*

A successful blend of modern comfort and historic charm, the top suite here has been furnished with antiques, and the bathroom adorned with Philip Starck fixtures. The restaurant serves refined cuisine with a subtle French flair. Next door there is a golf course and tennis courts. **www.schloss-wilkinghege.de**

SIEGEN Best Western Parkhotel Siegen

Koblenzer Straße 135, 57072 **Tel** *(0271) 33810* **Fax** *((0271) 3381450* **Rooms** *88*

A hotspot for business guests, the area around this hotel is quiet and serene, which makes for a relaxing atmosphere. The rooms and suites are quite modern and stylishly furnished. The ideal evening involves their sauna and steam room, the cocktail lounge and a leisurely stroll to a nearby restaurant. **www.parkhotel-siegen.bestwestern.de**

WUPPERTAL Art Fabrik & Hotel

Bockmühle 16-24, 42289 **Tel** *(0202) 28370* **Fax** *(0202) 2837100* **Rooms** *149*

Set in a building that was once the home of Friedrich Engels, the Communist theorist, this hotel is packed with original works by 80 artists. Spacious rooms are flooded with natural light, and guests can enjoy quarters equipped with saunas and amenities including in-room computers and entertainment centers. **www.art-fabrik-hotel.de**

XANTEN Fürstenberger Hof

Fürstenberg 11, 46509 **Tel** *(02801) 1613* **Fax** *(02801) 900771* **Rooms** *28*

Set in a nature reserve, this castle-like hotel offers peace and quiet in classy surrounds. Each room is decked out with royal accents such as chandeliers, Louis XIV furniture and gilt-framed paintings. Book a massage by a roaring fire or on the sunny terrace. A perfect base for exploring the Roman city of Xanten. **www.fuerstenbergerhof-xanten.de**

LOWER SAXONY, HAMBURG AND BREMEN

BREMEN Landhaus Radler Garni

Kastanienweg 17, 27404 **Tel** *(04281) 98820* **Fax** *(04281) 988210* **Rooms** *16*

A family-owned and managed hotel, this place is a little distant from the centre of Bremen, but offers a peaceful atmosphere that is appreciated by families. There is a playground for children and the surrounding area is perfect for cycling and exploring on foot. Nestled in the rear is a well-maintained little garden. **www.landhaus-radler.de**

BREMEN Atlantic Grand Hotel Bremen

Bredenstraße 2, 28195 **Tel** *(0)421620620* **Fax** *(0)42162062500* **Rooms** *138*

The Atlantic Grand Hotel in the heart of the city's old town offers surprisingly stylish and modern accommodation in a historic setting. Mostly catering to business travellers, the airy rooms are decorated with dark colours, modern art and bright carpets. The rooftop lounge offers a great view of the skyline. **www.atlantic-hotels.de**

BREMEN Landhaus Höpkens Ruh

Oberneulander Landstraße 69, 28355 **Tel** *(0421) 205853* **Fax** *(0421) 2058545* **Rooms** *8*

A small, stylish hotel with decor emulating the French country style, each of the eight rooms here is individually furnished, which will be obvious when you see the level of detail that has been applied. Set in parkland with a good restaurant serving seasonal and regional cuisine. **www.hoepkens-ruh.de**

BREMEN Lichtsinn

Rembertistraße 11, 28203 **Tel** *(0421) 368070* **Fax** *(0421) 327287* **Rooms** *31*

Very spacious and genteel, with a splash of home-style comfort, this hotel is family owned and has a sedate elegance that symbolizes German hospitality. Each room is individually furnished and quite tastefully so, with some having a more modern decor than others. The river is a few minutes walk away. **www.hotel-lichtsinn.de**

BREMEN Best Western Zur Post

Bahnhofsplatz 11, 28195 **Tel** *(0421) 30590* **Fax** *(0421) 3059591* **Rooms** *170*

There is an undercurrent of understated unorthodoxy here, although it all works very well. Some of the rooms have imaginative murals and decoration, and the bar is worthy of admiration for its colour and style. The hotel is in the heart of the city, and sits right outside the central train station. **www.zurpost.bestwestern.de**

BREMEN Park Hotel

Im Bürgerpark, 28209 **Tel** *(0421) 34080* **Fax** *(0421) 3408602* **Rooms** *177*

Opulent and expansive, the Park Hotel brings to life all your dreams of luxury and comfort. The grounds are well sculpted and spectacular, as are the rooms which are guaranteed to make you feel relaxed. There are several restaurants, bars and bistros, so take your pick. **www.park-hotel-bremen.de**

CELLE Hotel am Braunen Hirsch

Münzstraße 9c, 29223 **Tel** *(05141) 93930* **Fax** *(05141) 939350* **Rooms** *24*

Primarily famous for the historic restaurant next door, this hotel has a lot to offer the weary traveller. With comfortable and spacious rooms that are sunny and cheerful, and architecture that is angular and sharp, affecting the layout of the rooms, every corner of this hotel has its own character and charm. **www.hotel-ambraunenhirsch.de**

CELLE Fürstenhof Celle

Hannoversche Straße 55–56, 29221 **Tel** *(05141) 2010* **Fax** *(05141) 201120* **Rooms** *76*

Seated amidst history in beautiful Celle, this top class hotel is a comprehensive palace of comfort. Their Michelin-starred gourmet restaurant, Endtenfang *(see p553)*, attracts guests from all over the region. Enjoy authentic Italian fare at the rustic Palio restaurant. There is also an impressive fitness area. **www.fuerstenhof-celle.de**

CLOPPENBURG Park Hotel

Burgstraße 8, 49661 **Tel** *(04471) 6614* **Fax** *(04471) 6617* **Rooms** *51*

Restful, cheerful and quiet, lying close to the Soeste river and near to the centre of Cloppenberg, this makes a good nest for fledgling explorers new to the town. There is a golf course, tennis courts and a skittle alley nearby for sportier guests, and a sauna bath for the more contemplative ones. **www.parkhotel-cloppenburg.de**

DUDERSTADT Zum Löwen

Marktstraße 30, 37115 **Tel** *(05527) 3072* **Fax** *(05527) 72630* **Rooms** *42*

Renowned also for its restaurant, this hotel provides a comfortable respite from the larger chain hotels. Some of the rooms have balconies, from which guests can view the beautiful city of Duderstadt. The restaurant serves regional German cuisine, and there is an intimate cellar bar. **www.hotelzumloewen.de**

GOSLAR Der Achtermann

Rosentorstraße 20, 38640 **Tel** *(05321) 70000* **Fax** *(05321) 7000999* **Rooms** *152*

A touch of the modern in a historic city, this hotel is decorated in an Art Deco style with an efficiency that sets a high standard. The pool and sauna area is large and well equipped, offering yoga and massages. There is a restaurant and a nice little café outside with seating in the shade of trees. **www.der-achtermann.de**

GOSLAR Treff Hotel Das Brusttuch

Hoher Weg 1, 38640 **Tel** *(05321) 34600* **Fax** *(05321) 346099* **Rooms** *13*

The building is part of the UNESCO-protected Altstadt in Goslar. Although the building itself is over 480 years old, it has been successfully renovated to provide all the modern comforts. There is a large restaurant in the hotel and a swimming pool for guests. The rooms are spacious and quaint. **www.brusttuch.de**

GÖTTINGEN Hotel Stadt Hannover

Goethe-Allee 21, 37073 **Tel** *(0)551547960* **Fax** *(0)55145470* **Rooms** *32*

Situated in a renovated 18th-century townhouse, the family-run Stadt Hannover is an elegant address for those in search of charm, tradition, smooth service and quiet rooms. The hotel is ideally located close to the city centre and within walking distance of the central train station. **www.hotelstadthannover.com**

GÖTTINGEN Romantik-Hotel Gebhard

Goetheallee 22–23, 37073 **Tel** *(0551) 49680* **Fax** *(0551) 4968110* **Rooms** *50*

Popular amongst business guests, Gebhard Hotel is also fantastically located close to both the centre of town and the main train station. Warm and luxurious rooms make for a comfortable stay, and the little restaurant provides a romantic atmosphere. There is also a sauna and whirlpool. **www.gebhardshotel.de**

HAMBURG Gastwerk Hotel Hamburg

Beim Alten Gaswerk 3, 22761 **Tel** *(0)4089062424* **Fax** *(0)40890620* **Rooms** *141*

Housed in a renovated industrial building 6 km (4 miles) away from Hamburg City centre, the Gastwerk Hotel features modern design with a industrial twist. The loft-like rooms – some of the biggest you will find in Hamburg – have exposed brick walls and minimalist furniture. Check out the exceptional spa. **www.gastwerk.com**

HAMBURG The George Hotel

Barcastraße 3, 22087 **Tel** *(0)40280030* **Fax** *(0)4028003030* **Rooms** *124*

Situated in a vibrant district Außenalster, the George is a few minutes' walk from the train station but a good distance from the city centre. Claiming to be "very British", the hotel is decorated in dark, hushed colours, modern furniture and ironic Classicist touches. The DaCaio Restaurant serves Italian cuisine. **www.thegeorge-hotel.de**

Key to Price Guide *see p.488* **Key to Symbols** *see back cover flap*

HAMBURG Side Hotel Hamburg

Drehbahn 49, 20354 **Tel** *(040) 309990* **Fax** *(040) 30999399* **Rooms** *178*

This five-star dream of a hotel is a comfortable and centrally located alternative to the more classic top hotels in the downtown area. The architecture and interior design is cutting edge; rooms are decorated in soft, shiny beige and white colours. For a little extra you can book an Executive room with a kitchenette. **www.side-hamburg.de**

HAMBURG Le Royal Meridien

An Der Auster 52–56, 20099 **Tel** *(040) 21000* **Fax** *(040) 21001111* **Rooms** *284*

Situated on the banks of Alster lake this modern, luxury hotel offers some of the best views Hamburg has to offer. Rooms are sparsely furnished but offer all the amenities of a first-class hotel. The Meridien spa and fitness club is considered to be one of the best designed in Germany. **www.leroyalmeridienhamburg.com**

HAMBURG Fairmont Hotel Vier Jahreszeiten

Neuer Jungfernstieg 9–14, 20354 **Tel** *(040) 34940* **Fax** *(040) 34942600* **Rooms** *157*

Elegance and style reign in this hotel. Many rooms overlook the Alstersee and some have a private balcony. Each room is individually furnished with both antiques and modern pieces. There are a number of bars and restaurants in the hotel, one of which has been awarded a Michelin star. **www.fairmont-hvj.com**

HAMBURG Park Hyatt

Bugenhagenstrasse 8, 20095 **Tel** *(040) 33321234* **Fax** *(040) 33321235* **Rooms** *252*

The Park Hyatt is located in the heart of historic Hamburg and off Mönckebergstrasse – the city's main shopping pedestrian zone. Rooms are modern and feature large-screen TVs and moveable bathroom doors. The breakfast buffet offers a huge range of international and German dishes. **www.hamburg.park.hyatt.com**

HANNOVER Best Western Parkhotel Kronsberg

Gut Kronsberg 1, 30539 **Tel** *(0511) 87400* **Fax** *(0511) 867112* **Rooms** *200*

Conveniently located opposite the fairground, the hotel has become a favourite with business guests. With lots of light and space, the lobby is crowned with a glass dome. There is a mixture of room styles which are all comfortable and spacious. The restaurants and bistros serve good food. Weekend discounts are offered. **www.kronsberg.bestwestern.de**

HANNOVER Kastens Hotel Luisenhof

Luisenstraße 1-3, 30159 **Tel** *(0)51130440* **Fax** *(0)5113044807* **Rooms** *139*

Located close to the main train station, this refurbished hotel housed in an elegant 19th-century mansion offers clean facilties and quiet, very large rooms. The design may be somewhat bland, but the spa and fitness facilities, the overall upmarket elegance and the warm service make this a good-value option. **www.kastens-luisenhof.de**

HANNOVER Hotel Kaiserhof

Ernst-August-Platz 4, 30159 **Tel** *(0511) 36830* **Fax** *(0511) 3683114* **Rooms** *80*

Housed in a historic building constructed in 1915, this hotel has been well preserved. There is a subtle French style to the tastefully detailed rooms. It is located opposite the main train station and close to the city centre. The restaurant is highly acclaimed, and serves trout that they raise themselves in a courtyard fountain. **www.centralhotel.de**

HILDESHEIM Parkhotel Berghölzchen

Am Berghölzchen 1, 31139 **Tel** *(05121) 9790* **Fax** *(05121) 979400* **Rooms** *80*

This hotel dates back to 1770 when it began as a restaurant, which is still the jewel in their crown, serving regional delicacies. It has spacious and well-equipped rooms. A cosy beer garden operates in the warmer months. There is also the facility for long-term renting rooms. **www.berghoelzchen.de**

HOHEGING Hotel-Restaurant Waldesruh

Am Baumweg 2, 49685 **Tel** *(04471) 94850* **Fax** *(04471) 948516* **Rooms** *22*

This peaceful little hotel is nestled amongst trees and pastures. Tennis courts are available for guest use and there is a golf course nearby. The recently refurbished rooms are cosy and offer the basic comforts. The restaurant serves regional cuisine, with a reasonable selection for vegetarians. **www.waldesruhhotel.de**

KÖNIGSLUTTER Avalon Hotelpark Königshof

Braunschweigerstraße 21a, 38154 **Tel** *(05353) 5030* **Fax** *(05353) 503244* **Rooms** *174*

This is a spread-out hotel with a lot of amenities, including tennis courts, swimming pool and bowling alley. They have 15 conference rooms, with many conference packages that include spa treatments and sporting facilities. The restaurant, Merlin *(see p554)*, serves regional cuisine, and there is also a disco. **www.hotelpark-koenigshof.de**

LÜNEBURG Bremer Hof

Lüner Straße 12, 21335 **Tel** *(04131) 2240* **Fax** *(04131) 224224* **Rooms** *53*

A family affair since 1889, the Bremer Hof has been serving up comfort and hospitality unceasingly. Individually styled, some rooms incorporate the dark wooden structural beams into their design. It stands in the shadow of St Nicolai church, and is within easy walking distance of the town centre. **www.bremer-hof.de**

OLDENBURG Best Western Hotel Heide

Melkbrink 49–51, 26121 **Tel** *(0441) 8040* **Fax** *(0441) 884060* **Rooms** *92*

Chic yet comfortable, the style of the lobby here is an insight into the design of the rooms, with a contrast of dark and light colours accentuating space. The hotel is quite modern and is popular with business guests. Their elegant restaurant serves international and seasonal dishes, and has a large wine cellar. **www.hotel-heide.de**

OSNABRÜCK Romantik Hotel Walhalla
Bierstraße 24, 49074 **Tel** *(0541) 34910* **Fax** *(0541) 3491144* **Rooms** *69*

Built in 1690 and carefully renovated, the Walhalla is almost a museum of architecture. The loft has been converted into spacious and beautiful suites and their standard rooms are also dapper and spacious. There is a peaceful beer garden and two restaurants. **www.hotel-walhalla.de**

OSNABRÜCK Steigenberger Hotel Remarque
Natruper-Tor-Wall 1, 49076 **Tel** *(0541) 60960* **Fax** *(0541) 6096600* **Rooms** *156*

The hotel is named after German author Erich Remarque (1898–1970), whose works can be found in their elegant library. The restaurant, Vila Real, is highly acclaimed and has a very comprehensive wine list. The hotel also has a wine shop where they sometimes hold wine tastings. **www.steinberger.com**

WOLFENBÜTTEL Parkhotel Altes Kaffeehaus
Harztorwall 18, 38300 **Tel** *(05331) 8880* **Fax** *(05331) 888100* **Rooms** *75*

This hotel hosts a mixture of the modern and traditional. While the rooms are a little generic, the atmosphere around the hotel is friendly. The beer garden is popular in the summer months, and the wine cellar offers an opportunity to sample local wines. The French restaurant of the same name is also worth a visit *(see p554)*. **www.parkhotel-wolfenbuettel.de**

WOLFENBÜTTEL Rilano 24/7 Hotel Wolfenbüttel
Bahnhofsstraße 9, 38300 **Tel** *(05331) 98860* **Fax** *(05331) 988611* **Rooms** *48*

Close to the centre of Wolfenbüttel. An airy lobby awaits you, as does the prompt and friendly service. Rooms are very stylish and there is a cinema and bowling alley on the premises, as well as an American-style bar. They also have a nice terrace where you may dine in the summer months. **www.rilano-wolfenbuettel.de**

WOLFSBURG Brackstedter Mühle
Zum Kühlen Grunde 2, 38448 **Tel** *(05366) 900* **Fax** *(05366) 9050* **Rooms** *50*

Set in the peaceful German countryside, each room here is unique due to the development and refurbishment of the hotel. There are banquet facilities offering delicacies such as suckling pig and other traditional dishes. It also has a beautiful winter garden with a glass roof. **www.brackstedter-muehle.de**

WOLFSBURG Tryp Hotel
Willy-Brandt-Platz 2, 38440 **Tel** *(05361) 899000* **Fax** *(05361) 899444* **Rooms** *121*

With well-designed and spacious rooms and suites that have an early 1990s colour scheme, this hotel is close to the Volkswagen plant and theme park. There is a classy restaurant with an extensive wine list. In the summer months they operate an outdoor terrace. **www.solmelia.com**

SCHLESWIG-HOLSTEIN

BAD MALENTE Gartenhotel Weisser Hof
Vossstraße 45, 23714 **Tel** *(04523) 99250* **Fax** *(04523) 6899* **Rooms** *18*

A small hotel with a big heart. Family owned and family run, there is also a high level of professionalism here. The rooms are bright and spacious, and there is an excellent restaurant of the same name *(see p555)*. They have a nice pool and wellness area and there is a nearby golf course. The garden has ample space for children to play. **www.weisserhof.de**

FLENSBURG Am Wasserturm
Blasberg 13, 24943 **Tel** *(0461) 3150600* **Fax** *(0461) 312287* **Rooms** *34*

Located in a quiet area – you are guaranteed to get a peaceful night sleep here – and furnished in a reserved and tasteful manner, this hotel caters to large groups and offers special rates for 15 people and up. The breakfast is diverse and satisfying, and you can enjoy it out on the terrace. **www.hotel-am-wasserturm.com**

HELGOLAND Atoll Ocean Resort
Lung Wai, 27498 **Tel** *(04725) 8000* **Fax** *(04725) 800444* **Rooms** *49*

This is the hotel of tomorrow, designed in a futuristic and creative manner. Each room is a work of art, with colour blending well with a minimalistic style. Situated overlooking the water, many rooms have a wonderful view. The restaurant serves fantastic fresh seafood dishes as well as international cuisine. **www.atoll.de**

KIEL Atlantic Hotel Kiel
Raiffeisenstraße 2, 24103 **Tel** *(0)431374990* **Fax** *(0)4313749950* **Rooms** *187*

The Atlantic Kiel is one of the city's biggest hotels. The knowledgable staff and a central location, close to shops and restaurants, make this a decent base for exploring the city. Rooms are airy and overlook part of the harbour, but the decor can be a little dark. The restaurant has a great wine selection and fresh local seafood. **www.atlantic-hotels.de**

KIEL Kieler Yacht-Club
Hindenburgufer 70, 24105 **Tel** *(0431) 88130* **Fax** *(0431) 8813444* **Rooms** *57*

The rooms here have picturesque sea views and some have balconies or are connected to terraces. Close to all the water-related activities and attractions. They also have quite large conference facilities and offer extensive packages. The restaurant serves some of the freshest seafood in town. **www.hotel-kyc.de**

Key to Price Guide *see p.488* **Key to Symbols** *see back cover flap*

LÜBECK Kaiserhof

Kronsforder Allee 11–13, 23560 **Tel** *(0451) 703301* **Fax** *(0451) 795083* **Rooms** *58*

Sitting in the middle of the "island", you could not ask for a better location. Close to historic attractions and museums, some guest rooms here have a balcony. Their restaurant focuses on fish and there is an elegant banquet hall which is often used for weddings and other functions. **www.kaiserhof-luebeck.de**

LÜBECK Radisson Blu Senator Hotel

Willy-Brandt-Allee 6, 23554 **Tel** *(0451) 1420* **Fax** *(0451) 1422222* **Rooms** *224*

Overlooking the river and close to the centre, the rooms here are very comfortable and bright. There are many facilities to keep children occupied and when accompanied by parents they eat in the restaurant free. Along with the restaurant, there is a cocktail bar, a café and a tavern with adjoining beer garden. **www.senatorhotel.de**

OEVERSEE Romantik Hotel Historischer Krug

Grazer Platz 1, 24988 **Tel** *(04630) 9400* **Fax** *(04630) 780* **Rooms** *60*

This hotel has been in the same family since 1815, and has a history that goes back to the 16th century. It is a sanctuary of relaxation and luxury, providing massages, beauty treatments, spas and saunas. They also have a nice restaurant and terrace. **www.historischer-krug.de**

RATZEBURG Der Seehof

Lüneburger Damm 1–3, 23909 **Tel** *(04541) 860100* **Fax** *(04541) 860102* **Rooms** *50*

This hotel is situated so close to the water it is practically floating. There are magnificent water views from the rooms, some of which have large terraces and balconies. The restaurant specializes in fish and other seafood, although their regional dishes are spectacular as well. The wellness area is quite comprehensive. **www.derseehof.de**

SCHLESWIG Waldschlösschen

Kolonnenweg 152, 24837 **Tel** *(04621) 3830* **Fax** *(04621) 383105* **Rooms** *117*

Lying a little out of town, there are many opportunities for walking, cycling and exploring. The rooms are large and tastefully furnished. Access to the wellness area and swimming pool is included in the rates. There are two restaurants and a chic lounge bar. **www.hotel-schleswig.de**

SYLT Hotel Aarnhoog

Gaat 13, Keitum, 25980 **Tel** *(0)46513990* **Fax** *(0)465139910* **Rooms** *13*

The enticing Aarnhoog may be one of the island's most traditional and beautiful hotels: Surrounded by dunes, forests and marshes, the family run hotel has cosy rooms with antique furniture and warm service. Prices may seem high, but the house, grounds and ambience are truly authentic. **www.faehrhas-hotel-collection.de**

SYLT Fährhaus Hotel Sylt

Bi Heef 1, Munkmarsch, 25980 **Tel** *(0)465193970* **Fax** *(0)465193970* **Rooms** *44*

The traditionally designed white exterior, featuring wrap-around balconies and views over the North Sea, are the hallmark of this delightful hotel. Rooms are comfortable and spacious, with an airy Scandinavian design. Dine at one of three restaurants or enjoy the luxurious spa facilities and indoor pool. **www.faehrhaus-hotel-collection.de**

SYLT Romantik-Hotel Benen-Diken-Hof

Süderstraße 3, 25980 **Tel** *(04651) 93830* **Fax** *(04651) 9383183* **Rooms** *45*

A delightful country hotel with all the amenities of an inner-city hotel. The hotel also specializes in the rental of apartments for longer stays, while it is still possible to rent their studio apartments for short stays. There is a golf course in the area and the pool is very elegant, with terrace seating outside. **www.benen-diken-hof.de**

SYLT Dorint Hotel Söl'ring Hof Sylt

Am Sandwall 1, 25980 **Tel** *(0)4651836200* **Fax** *(0)46518362020* **Rooms** *15*

The Dorint Söl'ring Hof Hotel is probably the top luxury hotel on Sylt, and the playground for Germany's rich and beautiful. The charming thatch-roofed building is idyllically set amid windswept dunes, just a few steps away from the shore. The restaurant is romantic and the spa facilities are outstanding. **http://www.soelring-hof.de/**

TIMMENDORFER STRAND Maritim Seehotel

Strandallee 73, 23669 **Tel** *(04503) 6050* **Fax** *(04503) 6052450* **Rooms** *241*

The shores of the Baltic Sea lap at the door of this magnificent hotel. All the floors have great views, with the rear-facing rooms overlooking the parklands. Some of the rooms also have amazing corner balconies. There is a huge wellness area, as well as an indoor and an outdoor pool if the sea is not enough for you. **www.maritim.de**

TRAVEMÜNDE Hotel Columbia Casino

Kaiserallee 1, 23570 **Tel** *(04502) 3080* **Fax** *(04502) 308333* **Rooms** *72*

This hotel has variously styled rooms that are all superbly furnished and detailed. Some rooms have a sea view and terrace. The conference and function facilities are stunning and there is an elegant ballroom. There is a choice of three restaurants with an emphasis on seafood, and there is a golf course nearby. **www.columbia-hotels.de**

TRAVEMÜNDE/LÜBECK Maritim Strandhotel

Trelleborgallee 2, 23570 **Tel** *(04502) 890* **Fax** *(04502) 892020* **Rooms** *240*

The hotel sits at the mouth of the estuary and enjoys superb panoramic views. Some of the guest rooms have balconies. The café on the 35th floor has an amazing view over the surrounding district and Baltic Sea and attracts guests from outside the hotel. **www.maritim.de**

MECKLENBURG-LOWER POMERANIA

GREIFSWALD Kronprinz Hotel Greifswald €€

22 Lange Straße, 17489 Tel (03834) 79 00 Fax (03834) 79 01 11 Rooms 31

Set in a good location in the town centre and close to the cathedral, the rooms here are uncluttered and clean, with simple wooden furniture and patterned bedspreads. They also have a mini bar and television. There is a German-style brasserie with live music nights. **www.hotelkronprinz.de**

Greifswald Mercure Hotel Greifswald €€

Am Gorzberg, 17489 Tel (0)38345440 Fax (0)3834544444 Rooms 113 Map

This hotel, set 2 km (1.2 miles) from the city centre, offers rooms with traditional and simple design. A quaint spa and fitness center compliment the extensive conference and business facilties. The Aquarell restaurant offers a variety of regional specialties, which can be enjoyed on the terrace in summer. **www.mercure.com**

GÜSTROW Kurhaus am Inselsee €€€

Heidburg 1, 18273 Tel (03843) 85 00 Fax (03843) 85 01 00 Rooms 39

A very relaxing hotel in a peaceful, sleepy setting. One of the more lavish hotels in the area, the wellness treatments and packages are very attractive. The rooms are comfortable and some offer a nice view of the surrounding countryside. The garden terrace has a great atmosphere, especially in the afternoons. **www.kurhaus-guestrow.de**

HEILIGENDAMM Grand Hotel Heiligendamm €€€€€

Prof.-Dr.-Vogel-Straße 16–18, 18209 Tel (038203) 74 00 Fax (038203) 74 07 47 4 Rooms 225

This is an opulent hotel with such stately buildings and a lovely seaside location that it is easy to simply relax and embrace it all. There are five big buildings, one of which is a castle, and all of which offer rooms that effortlessly combine class and comfort. This hotel is entirely unique. **www.grandhotel-heiligendamm.com**

INSEL RÜGEN Hotel am Meer & Spa €€€€

Strandpromenade 34, 18609 Tel (038393) 44 0 Fax (038393) 44 44 4 Rooms 60

A beautiful hotel in a fantastic position, just off the beach, the rooms here are stunning, offering a maritime theme. Each floor has its own theme colour, and different wood types to match. The wellness and fitness area is quite new, and expansive. You will definitely find yourself relaxing the moment you arrive. **www.hotel-am-meer.de**

MECKLENBURG Hotel Vier Jahreszeiten Binz €€€

Zeppelinstraße 8, 18609 Tel (038393) 500 Fax (038393) 50430 Rooms 76

Not far from the centre of Binz, and a short distance from the beach, the rooms here have a very bright and fresh style, while still retaining some classic, smart (almost naval) formality. This is a very polished and classy hotel in a lovely beachside town. **www.jahreszeiten-hotels.de**

MECKLENBURG Robinson Club Fleesensee €€€

Penkower Strasse 2, 17213 Tel (039932) 80200 Fax (039932) 8020100 Rooms 201

This resort in the heart of the Mecklenburg lake region is one of Germany's top wellness and sports resorts. A country-club style setting and friendly staff makes this a great base for exploring the unspoilt surroundings or for relaxing in the spa. A good restaurant serves light regional fish dishes. **www.robinson-fleesensee.de**

NEUBRANDENBURG Landhotel Broda €€

Oelmühlenstraße 29, 17033 Tel (0395) 569170 Fax (0395) 5691729 Rooms 13

There is a summery holiday atmosphere here but the standard of service and inclusion of conference facilities place it in the business-class category. All rooms have a terrace or balcony, satellite television and are wheelchair-friendly (spacious and uncluttered). **www.landhotel-broda.de**

PREROW TOP Ostseehotel Waldschloesschen €€€

Bernsteinweg 4, 18375 Tel (038233) 61 70 Fax (038233) 61 74 03 Rooms 33

You will have to walk 300 m (980 ft) if you want to stroll on sandy Baltic Sea beaches, but while in the hotel you will enjoy the luxury of what was once a lavish private residence. Rooms are scattered among three buildings and all are tastefully decorated and offer good basic facilities. **www.waldschloesschen-prerow.de**

ROSTOCK Godewind €€

Warnemünder Straße 5, 18146 Tel (0381) 60 95 70 Fax (0381) 60 95 71 11 Rooms 47

In a location that takes advantage of the landscape around the southern coast of the Baltic Sea, this family-run complex consists of a hotel, restaurant and apartments. The guest rooms have a relaxed feel about them and some have a balcony. **www.hotel-godewind.de**

ROSTOCK Pentahotel €€

Kropeliner/Schwaansche Str. 6, 18055 Tel (0381) 49 70 0 Fax (0381) 49 70 700 Rooms 150

This is really something extraordinary, combining an old-town square historic frontage with a direct link to a gleaming, modern shopping centre. It is a business-class hotel and so offers all the usual facilities for business guests, but it would also be quite a treat for tourists. **www.pentahotels.com**

Key to Price Guide *see p.488* **Key to Symbols** *see back cover flap*

ROSTOCK Trihotel am Schweizer Wald 🛂 🍴 ♨ 🏃 📺 €€

Tessiner Straße 103, 18055 **Tel** *(0381) 65 97 0* **Fax** *(0381) 65 97 60 0* **Rooms** *101*

All the rooms here are laid out and furnished a little differently, but they are all cosy, comfortable and furnished with a bit more adventure than you would expect to find in a business-class or chain hotel. There is also a full range of health and spa treatments and facilities available. **www.trihotel-rostock.de**

ROSTOCK Sonne Hotel Rostock 🛂 🍴 🏃 📺 €€€

Neuer Markt 2, 18055 **Tel** *(0381) 49 73 0* **Fax** *(0381) 49 73 35 1* **Rooms** *111*

Located on the market square, this hotel is housed in a carefully renovated 200-year-old building. All the modern conveniences are here, such as wireless Internet access, while the historic feel has been maintained with some specially designed furniture. There are a range of beauty and wellness services. **www.rostock.steigenberger.de**

ROSTOCK Neptun Hotel Rostock 🛂 🍴 ♨ 🏃 📺 🍽 €€€€

Seestraße 19, 18119 **Tel** *(0381) 77 78 71* **Fax** *(0381) 77 74 00* **Rooms** *337*

As you would expect from a luxury resort located right on the beach, every room has a balcony with a sea view. The rooms have been completely refurbished and all offer excellent facilities. The resort has a full range of health, fitness and fun services. **www.hotel-neptun.de**

ROSTOCK-WARNEMUNDE Yachthafenresidenz Hohe Düne 🛂 🍴 🏃 📺 🍽 €€€€

Am Yachthafen 1-8, 18119 **Tel** *(0381) 50 40 0* **Fax** *(0381) 50 40 63 64* **Rooms** *368*

This hotel is situated right at the harbour of Rostock-Warnemunde and is a maritime luxury – some rooms are designed as ship quarters with wooden panels and floors, and all rooms include modern amenities. As well as a seafood restaurant there are superb spa and wellness facilities on offer. **www.hohe-duene.de**

RÜGEN Landhotel Herrenhaus 🍴 🏃 📺 €€

Bohlendorf bei Wiek, 18556 **Tel** *(038391) 77 0* **Fax** *(038391) 70 28 0* **Rooms** *29*

This is not a hotel, it is a home. It looks like it has been handed down through generations. The rooms are bright and clean and have simple period-style furniture. There is a terrace, café (with home-made cakes and toffees) and a fireplace room for warming toes and reading a good book in winter. **www.bohlendorf.de**

RÜGEN Villa Sano 🛂 🍴 🏃 📺 €€

Strandstraße 12–14, 18586 **Tel** *(038303) 12 66 0* **Fax** *(038303) 12 66 99 9* **Rooms** *46*

Aimed at families and only a five-minute walk from the beach, this is a good option for those wanting to combine more than one room to form a family suite (there are interconnecting doors) without paying the high beachside prices. They also offer services such as playrooms and child-minding. **www.villasano.de**

RÜGEN Dorint Strand Hotel 🛂 🍴 ♨ 🏃 📺 🍽 €€€

Strandpromenade 58, 18609 **Tel** *(038393) 43 0* **Fax** *(038393) 43 10 0* **Rooms** *63*

With crisp linen, sparkling water, a sandy beach and high standards of service, this is a luxury treat with a nautical theme and big windows that overlook the sea. Rooms also have air conditioning and wireless Internet access. Dining options include balconies and terraces, also with sea views. **www.hotel-ruegen.dorint.com**

SCHWERIN Fritz Hotel 🍴 €€

Dorfstraße 3b, 19061 **Tel** *(0385) 64 63 70* **Fax** *(0385) 64 63 79 9* **Rooms** *22*

This is a big and welcoming building in a huge garden. There is a lot of greenery about, and the garden has a pond. The rooms are simply decorated, with pastel-pink bedding. The large park-like setting is extremely relaxing and appealing. **www.fritz-hotel.de**

Schwerin Crowne Plaza Schwerin 🛂 🍴 🏃 📺 🍽 ♿ 🖥 W €€€

Bleicher Ufer 23, 19053 **Tel** *(0)38557550* **Fax** *(0)3855755777* **Rooms** *99*

This upscale hotel offers large and very quiet rooms overlooking Ostorfer Lake. The decor is somewhat tired in some areas and the location is not very central, but service is of a high quality and the staff are pleasant and friendly. The restaurant, offering fish and game dishes, is surprisingly good for a small town. **www.crowne-plaza.m-vp.de**

Seebad Ahlbeck Romantik Seehotel Ahlbecker Hof 🛂 🍴 ♨ 📺 🍽 ♿ 🖥 W €€€€€

Dünenstraße 47, 17419 **Tel** *(0)38378620* **Fax** *(0)3837862100* **Rooms** *73*

One of the few luxury hotels in the area, the Romantik Seehotel boasts an idyllic seafront location with fantastic views of the Baltic. Rooms are on the small side, but they are comfortable and have all of the amenities you would expect from a hotel of this quality. The hotel also has an indoor pool and spa facilities. **www.romantikhotels.com**

Stralsund Radisson Blu Stralsund 🛂 🍴 ♨ 🏃 📺 ♿ 🖥 W €€

Grünhufer 18-20, 18437 **Tel** *(0)383137730* **Fax** *(0)38313773100* **Rooms** *114*

This sleek modern hotel is designed in Scandinavian style, with airy spaces, light woods and bright colours. Pride of place, however, goes to the attached spa and water park, popular with locals and tourists alike. The only drawback is the location, which is 3 km (2 miles) from the historic town centre. **www.radissonblu.com**

WARNEMUENDE KurPark Hotel 🛂 🍴 🏃 €€€

Kurhausstraße 4, 18119 **Tel** *(0381) 44 02 99 0* **Fax** *(0381) 44 02 99 9* **Rooms** *18*

This is a hotel situated in a rather lovely old house. There is a choice of "English, Mediterranean (and) Louis-Philippestyle" guest rooms, but the only real difference is the pattern on the duvet cover. The best way to choose a room is to ask for one with a balcony. **www.kurparkhotel-warnemuende.de**

WHERE TO EAT

The crest of the
Forsthaus Paulsborn
restaurant in Berlin

German cuisine does not enjoy the same reputation as that of, say, France, but nevertheless you can eat very well here. There are many establishments that specialize in regional cuisine, which, although somewhat heavy, is always very appetizing. It is also easy to find good restaurants serving ethnic cuisine, such as Italian, Greek, Indian, Chinese, Thai or Turkish. In the past few years, some fine restaurants have opened. Run by renowned master chefs, they serve excellent cuisine of the very highest European standards.

From the many thousands of restaurants throughout Germany, we have chosen the finest for inclusion in this guidebook, with a view to catering for a variety of budgets. Detailed information on the selected restaurants can be found on pp526–57.

TYPES OF RESTAURANTS

The term *Restaurant* is used to define both restaurants offering exquisite cuisine and excellent service, at steep prices, and popular local establishments with affordable prices. The word *Gasthaus* usually indicates a traditional style of inn that specializes in straightforward regional cuisine. In many towns, there is a *Ratskeller* established in the cellar of the town hall. These are usually good, not overly expensive restaurants serving dishes that represent the regional cuisine. They usually have atmospheric, stylized interiors that are well adapted to the vaulted, dark spaces of the historic cellars. A *Weinstube* is a wine bar, where good, usually local, wine is served. Often decent food is also available here. A *Bierstube* is similar in style, except that the beverage is beer. The term *Café* has a variety of connotations in Germany. This is a place that serves an excellent breakfast with various options in the mornings, while from noon they offer lunch dishes. The choice is usually somewhat heavy, though varied. In addition, at any time of the day and evening, customers can have a coffee here, eat some ice cream or a cake, drink beer or some other alcoholic beverage. In the evenings there is often music.

A typical venue in which you can spend an evening is a *Kneipe*. In terms of its atmosphere, this is somewhat reminiscent of an English pub. Patrons generally come here to have a drink, but there are usually a few hot dishes on offer to appease their hunger. Self-service venues offering snacks are known as *Imbiss*. These can have a very varied character, from a stall serving baked sausages and cans of drink, to elegant kiosks offering a large choice of salads and fast food. These kiosks are often run by immigrants. In fact in most large German towns there are numerous kiosks serving Arabic, Turkish, Chinese and American food. If shoppers feel the need for a snack, they might like to take advantage of the restaurant or cafeteria facilities in department stores. These are usually self-service establishments known as *Stehcafé*, which means "Stand Up Café".

Entrance to a *Gasthaus* near the cathedral in Cologne

WHAT AND WHEN TO EAT

Breakfast is usually a hearty affair with various types of bread accompanied by cheese, sausages and marmalade. On Sundays brunch is served in most places until 2pm: this is a combination of breakfast and lunch, in the form of a Swedish buffet. During the lunch period (between noon and 2pm) most establishments serve an excellent salad or a bowl of filling soup, while many restaurants offer a special fixed-price menu that is significantly cheaper than in the evenings. Restaurants start to fill up in the evenings between 6 and 7pm, although dinner is most usually eaten after 8pm.

Altdeutsche Weinstube in Dörrenbach

Wine festival in Alter Hof in Munich

OPENING HOURS

Cafés generally open from 9am, while restaurants are open from noon, sometimes with a break from 3 to 6pm. The most expensive places do not open until dinner time and are frequently closed for one day during the week.

A street stall serving snacks of freshly cooked sausages

MENU

In most good restaurants the menu is written in German and English, and sometimes also in French. In cafés and less expensive restaurants, the menu may be handwritten, in which case the staff may be able to help with a translation. In many of the less expensive places there is, in addition to the regular menu, a daily menu with attractive seasonal dishes. Sometimes the chef's special offers are written on a blackboard. In all restaurants and cafés, a menu showing prices will be displayed outside the establishment.

RESERVATIONS

Making a prior reservation is essential in all the best restaurants while in most good and medium standard restaurants it is advisable to do so, particularly on a Friday or Saturday night. If you have not made a reservation, try one of the popular restaurant complexes where you can usually get a table.

PRICES AND TIPS

The cost of restaurant meals in Germany is unusually diverse depending on location. A three-course meal without alcohol can be found for around €10–15, but in the centre of larger cities a minimum of €20–25 would be more usual. In a luxury restaurant, the bill for a six-course meal, without drinks, can cost in excess of €80. The price of alcoholic drinks also varies, but beer is the cheapest drink.

Prices include service and tax, but it is usual to leave a tip – generally around 10 per cent of the total bill. When paying for a meal by credit card, the tip can be added to the total. Restaurants and cafés that accept credit cards usually display the logos of acceptable cards near the entrance. Before ordering, it is best to find out whether a minimum charge is applied to customers who wish to pay their bill by credit card.

DRESS CODE

Germans usually prefer to dress comfortably, casually and practically, preferring a sporty style to more formal attire. When going out in the evenings, many women – regardless of their age – wear trousers and comfortable low-heeled shoes, though some prefer elegant dresses. Men generally wear jackets and ties only during office hours.

Going to a restaurant does not require any particular preparation unless you wish to go to a luxurious, gourmet restaurant, for which you will probably have to book up to two months in advance.

Formal interior of a restaurant in Berlin

CHILDREN

Restaurants usually provide high chairs for toddlers and, particularly during the lunch period, there will be light dishes for children – or you can order small portions.

VEGETARIANS

Increasingly, Germans are turning to vegetarianism, although the number of vegetarian restaurants is still limited. However, a few vegetarian dishes can usually be found on most menus. If necessary, choose a restaurant that serves a national cuisine in which there is no shortage of vegetarian dishes – for example Indian or Thai.

DISABLED VISITORS

If a table with wheelchair access is required, it is best to specify this when making the reservation. At the same time, check whether toilets are easily accessible.

Picnicking – a popular form of relaxation in Germany

The Flavours of Germany

Germany is famous for its hearty sausages, meats, breads, beer and wine. But German cuisine is much more regionally varied than many visitors might imagine. In addition to standard high-calorie plates, young chefs are coming up with creative new versions of German classics and old regional recipes. The key to this new trend is the fresh German produce found at colourful farmers' markets and old-world stores in quaint little towns around the country. Locally grown vegetables, pork, poultry and game, as well as freshwater and ocean fish, freshly made breads, cakes and dumplings are usually of a very high standard.

Harzer Roller and Emmentaler cheeses

Coffee and cakes at a typical city Konditorei (café)

NORTHERN AND EASTERN GERMANY

The frugality and hardships of life in the northern and East German lowlands and coast are reflected in the hearty fish- and game-based dishes found in this region. Ocean fish like halibut, sea bass, cod, herring or plaice feature in local dishes like Hamburg's *Finkenwerder*

Scholle (plaice fried with North Sea shrimps and bacon), as do freshwater fish such as pike-perch (a Berlin-Brandenburg favourite) or trout, served as *Grüne Forelle* or *Forelle Müllerin Art*, two herb-oriented recipes for roasted trout. Warming winter soups and stews such as lentil or potato soup or *Pichelsteiner Eintopf* (a one-pot dish with meat, potatoes and vegetables

cooked in broth) are omni-present – as is the famous potato salad, which is served in numerous ways. In East Germany, Thuringian and Saxonian cuisines have made a stunning comeback with *Thüringer Bratwurst* (spicy, roasted sausage served with hot mustard), *Sauerbraten* (roast beef marinated in vinegar) and some of Germany's best cakes, such as *Dresdner Christstollen*

Mehrkornbrötchen (mixed grain roll)   **Berliner Landbrot (mild rye bread)**

Laugenbrötchen (salty sourdough rolls)

Grau-oder Mischbrot (wholewheat)

Semmel (milk-dough roll)

Selection of typical German loaves and bread rolls

CLASSIC GERMAN FOOD

Many of the classic German dishes revolve around meat, particularly pork and poultry. Berliners and North Germans love *Kasseler Nacken*, a salted and dried slice of pork, served with mashed potatoes and *Sauerkraut*, while Bavarians prefer roast pork knuckle. There are delicious fish recipes, too, with Hamburg and Northern Germany leading the way. Ocean fish dishes like *Matjes* (salted herring with onions and cream served with baked potatoes) are now enjoyed throughout the country, as are freshwater fish and even sweet river crabs. German pasta and dumplings, along with soups, and a great selection of desserts and cakes round up any classic German menu.

Pork salamis

Maultaschen, *large pasta parcels, are stuffed with a meat or vegetable filling and served in soup or with butter.*

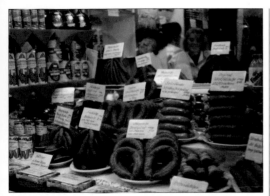

Display of traditional German sausages in a Berlin butcher's shop

(Christmas cake with raisins, nuts and marzipan) or *Baumkuchen* (a very sweet, multi-layered pyramid cake covered in chocolate glaze).

WESTERN AND SOUTHERN GERMANY

This part of Germany, and in particular the German wine regions around the rivers Rhine, Mosel and Neckar, has always had a love of superb, often French influenced, gourmet feasts. Alsace-Lorraine is a fascinating hotch-potch of French and German cooking. Regions such as the Pfalz, Schwaben, Franken, the Black Forest and many others, have also developed their own, very distinctive, delicious and often very hearty cuisines. The Pfalz, for example, is famous for its *Pfälzer*

Saumagen, a sow's stomach filled with sausage, herbs and potatoes; the Schwaben are known for their *Maultaschen* and an endless varieties of *Spätzle* (curly pasta); and the Franken for their *Nürnberger Rostbratwürstchen* (little

Fresh vegetables from the Brandenburg region

spicy roast sausages), various fish dishes, using rare types such as sheatfish, and perhaps the best gingerbread found anywhere in the country. In the far southeast, Austrian and Eastern European influences are evident in great goulash and dumpling dishes. But pride of place possibly goes to the Bavarians, whose hearty, no-nonsense dishes are what the world considers to be German cuisine. Here, *Weißwürste* (white sausages with a beer pretzel) are enjoyed in the morning, often with a beer, while dinner might be soup with liver dumplings, roast pork, *Sauerkraut* and a pile of potato dumplings.

NEW GERMAN CUISINE

In the early 1970s, chefs like Eckart Witzigmann broke free of the high-carb diet of postwar times, and cooked light, delicate "nouvelle" German dishes with superb ingredients in innovative combinations. Witzigmann, still Germany's most popular chef, won the first three German Michelin stars in 1979. A new generation of chefs calling themselves "Junge Wilde" (young wild) are still enjoying the shock waves today: healthy, international cooking is the norm in restaurants and homes, and almost no traditional recipe is sacrosanct.

Zanderfilet, *or Havel-Zander, is delicious pan-fried pike-perch served with a vegetable sauce, onions and potatoes.*

Schweinshaxe *is roast pork knuckle, best accompanied by Sauerkraut, potato dumplings and a good, strong beer.*

Rote Grütze *mixes summer berries with spices and red wine, which is set into a jelly and topped with cream.*

What to Drink

Throughout Germany, beer is undoubtedly the most popular drink, and each region has its own beer-brewing traditions. However, the country is also renowned for excellent wines, which are produced in the south. The most well known are Mosel and Rhine wines, although these are not necessarily better than Franconian wines. Stronger spirits and liqueurs are also available, as are some very pleasant non-alcoholic cold drinks.

Shop in Eberbach stocked with wine from the adjoining monastery

HOT DRINKS

Herbal infusions include mint and camomile tea

In German establishments there is no difficulty in getting a cup of tea *(Tee)*, but don't be surprised if the waiter asks whether you mean mint tea *(Pfefferminztee)* or camomile *(Kamillentee)*, since herbal infusions are popular in Germany. To be sure of being served Indian tea, it is advisable to specify *Schwarztee* when placing the order.

Coffee is another popular drink. In general, filter coffee, which is fairly mild, is served. For customers who prefer a stronger coffee, it is best to order an espresso.

NON-ALCOHOLIC COLD DRINKS

Apfelschorle

Various types of carbonated drinks and fruit juices – ubiquitous throughout Europe and the US – are popular, and an extensive choice is available in every café and restaurant in Germany. A refreshing non-alcoholic drink is *Apfelschorle*, which is apple juice mixed with equal proportions of sparkling mineral water. (The alcoholic version is *Weinschorle*, which is wine mixed with mineral water.) Another popular non-alcoholic drink is *Spezi*, which is a mixture of cola and Fanta.

Although tap water is generally safe to drink, it is not usually served with restaurant meals. To order a bottle of mineral water, ask for *Mineralwasser*, adding the phrase "*stilles Wasser*" if still water is preferred.

Mineralwasser (Mineral water)

Limonade (Lemonade)

SPIRITS AND LIQUEURS

Bitter-sweet spirit, Jägermeister

Herbal/root-flavour spirit, Kümmerling

Strong spirits are often drunk after heavy meals, particularly pork dishes. It is best to order one of the popular drinks distilled from rye or wheat, such as *Doppelkorn*. Brandy (known as *Weinbrand*) is also produced in Germany. Liqueurs are also popular, as is a spirit flavoured with herbs and roots (known as bitters). Among the most popular are *Kümmerling* and *Jägermeister* while, in Berlin, *Kaulsdorfer Kräuterlikör* is served. In many restaurants various kinds of whisky can be ordered, including well-known Scottish and Irish brands and popular American bourbons, but connoisseurs may miss their personal favourites. Italian restaurants often serve grappa, a grape spirit, after a meal, while in Greek restaurants ouzo – an aniseed spirit – may be offered.

Weizen Doppelkorn (rye spirit)

WINES

Germany is renowned for its excellent white wines, particularly those made from the Riesling grape. Among the most highly prized wines are those from the Rheingau region. Lovers of red wine might like to try Assmannshausen Spätburgunder wine, which is produced from the Pinot Noir grape.

Germany has a system of classifying wines into three groups according to their quality: the lowest quality is *Tafelwein*, then *Qualitätswein* and the highest quality *Qualitätswein mit Prädikat*. The latter includes wines produced from appropriately selected grapes, which is always confirmed on the bottle label. The term *Trocken* indicates a dry style, *Halbtrocken*, semi-dry and *Süß* means sweet. Very good sparkling wines, known as *Sekt*, are also produced in Germany.

Mainstockheimer Hofstück Spätburgunder

Spätburgunder from the Rheingau region

Riesling Schloss Vollrads

BEERS

Beermat with brewery logo

Each region of Germany has its own beer-brewing tradition: the most popular breweries in the north are Jever in Freesia and Beck's in Bremen, along with Bitburger, Warsteiner and Karlsberg. In the Rhine region, the biggest producers are DAB from Dortmund and König in Duisburg. In Berlin, Schultheiss, Berliner Kindl and Engelhardt compete for the primary position, while in Dresden the principal beers are produced by a brewery in Radeberg. However, Bavaria is by far the major brewing centre – the names of the breweries Löwenbräu, Hofbräu and Paulaner are known to every beer lover around the world. The most commonly drunk beer is Pils, a bottom-fermented lager of the pilsner type. Brown ales are also popular, particularly in the south. Schwarzbier, a bottom-fermented brown ale of over 4 per cent alcohol, is popular. Weizenbier, a bitter top-fermented beer, also has many fans, as has Bock, which is strong, at around 6 per cent alcohol.

Löwenbräu beer

König Ludwig Dunkel beer

Schultheiss beer

Wheat beer mixed with fruit juice, Berliner Weiße mit Schuss – speciality of Berlin

Franziskaner Hefe Weissbier beer

A tankard of beer with the essential head of foam

Choosing a Restaurant

The restaurants in this guide have been selected across a wide range of price categories for their good value, exceptional food and interesting location. This chart lists the restaurants by region, in chapter order. Map references for Berlin restaurants correspond with the Berlin Street Finder, *See pp114–19.*

PRICE CATEGORIES
The following price ranges are for a three-course meal for one, including a half-bottle of house wine, tax and service:
€ under €30
€€ €30–€45
€€€ €45–€60
€€€€ €60–€90
€€€€€ over €90

BERLIN

EASTERN CENTRE Brauhaus Georgbräu €€
Spreeufer 4, 10178 **Tel** *(030) 242 42 44* **Map** *5 E2*

At first sight, this restaurant looks like a typical tourist trap with large tables, big dining halls and masses of people, but you should not be fooled. If you are not a fan of sausages, try *Brauhausknüller*, a Berlin dish with pork knuckle, mashed split peas, *Sauerkraut* and potatoes with cold beer.

EASTERN CENTRE Historische Weinstuben €€
Poststraße 23, 10178 **Tel** *(030) 242 41 07* **Map** *5 E2*

This popular wine bar is housed in one of the most decorative buildings of the Nicolaiviertel. Traditional dishes from Berlin, such as *Kohl* or *Rinderrouladen* (rolled and roasted stuffed beef), can be accompanied by a drink from a small but exquisite wine list of 50 mostly German vintages.

EASTERN CENTRE Weinbar Rutz €€
Chausseestraße 8, 10115 **Tel** *(030) 24628760* **Map** *1 F2*

The Weinbar Rutz is one of the city's best venues for wine lovers. The family-owned friendly wine bar and restaurant serves traditional but light German dishes, with a Mediterranean influence. Try the "surprise" regional menu paired with wine (four, five or six courses) for a delicious culinary experience.

EASTERN CENTRE Zum Nussbaum €€
Am Nussbaum 3, 10178 **Tel** *(030) 242 30 95* **Map** *5 E2*

Situated in an alley in the Nicolaiviertel, this is a reconstruction of a 16th-century country inn. The menu offers traditional Berlin cuisine such as tender pork knuckle, rollmops or *Berliner Boulette*, a spicy hamburger pattie without a bun. In summer, the garden is a great place to dine and enjoy the various brands of local beer.

EASTERN CENTRE Borchardt Berlin €€€
Französische Straße 47, 10117 **Tel** *(030) 81886262* **Map** *4 C2*

Borchardt is the place to "see and be seen". Actors, politicians and other celebrities dine here on German and French dishes. The historic Wilhelmine-style dining hall is always packed. The food is simple, understated and good value for money, and the *Vienna Schnitzel* is definitely worth a try. In summer, ask for a table in the lovely courtyard.

EASTERN CENTRE Lutter & Wegner €€€
Charlottenstraße 56, 10117 **Tel** *(030) 202 95 40* **Map** *4 C3*

The first restaurant to start the revitalization of the gourmet scene in the historic centre of Eastern Berlin. Traditionally a fine German champagne brand, Lutter & Wegner now serves delicious German–Austrian food. The huge *Wiener Schnitzel* with potato salad, best served lukewarm, is a delight as are the duck and goose specialities in winter.

EASTERN CENTRE Oxymoron €€€
Rosenthaler Straße 40–41, 10178 **Tel** *(030) 283 918 86* **Map** *5 D1*

This fashionable restaurant, with its distinctive red-and-gold interior reminiscent of a 19th-century salon, has mainly Mediterranean and light German dishes on the menu. For lunch, dine at a table in the courtyard, which is the most beautiful inside historic Hackesche Höfe, and enjoy excellent fare at a reasonable price.

EASTERN CENTRE Sale E Tabacchi €€€
Kochstraße 18, 10969 **Tel** *(030) 252 11 55* **Map** *4 C4*

The Sale E Tabacchi offers reliable Italian food (but almost never pizza) in a dark, cosy Kreuzberg interior. In summer, the courtyard is the preferred dining area, mostly frequented by politicians and journalists from the neighbouring newspaper companies. For lunch, try one of the inexpensive three-course meals.

EASTERN CENTRE Reinstoff €€€€
Schlegelstraße 26c, 10115 **Tel** *(030) 30881214* **Map** *1 F2*

One of Berlin's top restaurants, the Reinstoff (meaning "pure things") has a Michelin star. Set in the hip Mitte district, the restaurant rediscovers traditional Berlin and German recipes, combining surprising ingredients with creative presentation. White asparagus, poultry, calf liver, game and local fish are some of the standard fare here.

Key to Symbols *see back cover flap*

EASTERN CENTRE Vau

⊞ 🍷　€€€€€

Jägerstraße 54–55, 10117 **Tel** *(030) 202 97 30* **Map** *4 B2*

This restaurant stands out with its elegant and unpretentious interior. The excellent and imaginative Austrian- and French-based dishes are created by Berlin's star chef, Kolja Kleeberg. The service is welcoming and there is a selection of good wines. The small courtyard is used during lunch. Closed Sun.

EASTERN CENTRE Facil

♿ 🧍 ⊞ 🍷　€€€€€

Potsdamer Straße 3, 10785 **Tel** *(030) 590051234* **Map** *4 A3*

A minimalist-designed, Michelin-starred restaurant at the Mandala Hotel, the Facil offers some of Berlin's most creative German cuisine with French touches. Chef Michael Kempf uses fresh local produce, mostly fish and poultry, for light five- to seven-course dinners. Lunch is an inexpensive way to sample the delicious cuisine.

WESTERN CENTRE Hot Spot

⊞ 🍷　€

Eisenzahnstraße 66, 10709 **Tel** *(030) 89006878*

Specializing in traditional cuisine from the Sichuan, Jiangsu and Shanhai provinces, Hot Spot is one of the city's best Chinese restaurants and still a well-kept secret. Owner Mr. Wu is a real wine connoisseur, offering a great range of top German wines. The decor is simple and service can be rushed, but outside tables are great for a summer lunch.

WESTERN CENTRE Nolle

€€

Georgenstraße 203, 10117 **Tel** *(030) 208 26 55* **Map** *4 C1*

The Nolle is a pleasantly decorated, 1920s-style Berlin restaurant tucked way under the S-Bahn tracks. The lush greenery around the place, the elegantly appointed tables and candlelight make a perfect setting for its international and German dishes. The *Schnitzel* selection is impressive.

WESTERN CENTRE Nu

♿ ⊞　€€

Schlüterstraße 55, 10625 **Tel** *(030) 887 098 11*

Among the locals, Nu is a very popular Asian-inspired restaurant serving fusion cuisine. Its Thai, Chinese and Vietnamese dishes are served on huge tables shared with other customers. On weekend nights, DJs play smooth lounge music that appeals to the young and very hip clientele. At lunchtime, there is an inexpensive special menu.

WESTERN CENTRE Café Einstein

🍷　€€€

Kurfürstenstraße 58, 10785 **Tel** *(030) 261 50 96* **Map** *3 D4*

This Berlin landmark is located in an elegant villa once owned by a German movie star. The old-fashioned waiters are dressed in black suits and bow ties, while the fine Viennese food has *fin de siecle* Austrian charm. All the traditional dishes are good, but the *Wiener Schnitzel* and *Gulasch* are exceptional.

WESTERN CENTRE Desbrosses

♿ 🍷　€€€

Potsdamer Platz 3, 10785 **Tel** *(030) 337 776 400* **Map** *4 A3*

Desbrosses has the most authentic French brasserie interior in all of Berlin. Dark wood-panelled walls, comfortable, plush leather bistro chairs, an open show kitchen and recordings of Piaf, all make for a real French experience. A must here is the seafood platter.

WESTERN CENTRE Francucci's

♿ 🧍 ⊞ 🍷　€€€

Kurfürstendamm 90, 10711 **Tel** *(030) 323 3318* **Map** *4 B1*

One of Berlin's best-kept secrets and a favourite among locals is this upscale neighbourhood restaurant offering hearty but supreme Tuscan country cooking. Specialities include the home-made pasta dishes and meat recipes as well as Berlin classics such as their signature pizza, served by the slice.

WESTERN CENTRE Ganymed

⊞ 🍷　€€€

Schiffbauerdamm 5, 10117 **Tel** *(030) 285 900 46* **Map** *4 B1*

A good-quality brasserie restaurant in charming surroundings with a small garden and views of the Spree river. The chef favours fish dishes, including Berlin fish specialities, but also offers traditional French fare such as steak tartare, fresh scallops sautéed in white wine, and a good cheese selection.

WESTERN CENTRE Käfer im Bundestag

🍷 🧍　€€€€

Reichstag, Platz der Republik, 10557 **Tel** *(030) 226 299 33* **Map** *4 A2*

A favourite dining place of the Mitte district, thanks to its unique location on the rooftop of the Reichstag, right next to Sir Norman Foster's cupola. The German cooking is creative and true to the owner, German catering star Käfer. Service is impeccable. Book ahead for lunch.

WESTERN CENTRE Kuchi

€€€€

Kantstraße 30, 10623 **Tel** *(030) 315 078 15* **Map** *2 A4*

Kuchi, one of the best value Japanese restaurants in Berlin, offers excellent sushi and regional dishes. A simple, unpretentious Asian interior and a welcoming service make it the ideal venue for a dinner for two. The dim sum rotation and the sampler are particularly tasty. Reservations advised.

WESTERN CENTRE Hugo's

🍷　€€€€€

Budapester Straße 2, 10787 **Tel** *(030) 260 212 63* **Map** *2 C4*

This restaurant, in the Inter-Continental Hotel, is one of the best in Berlin. Unusual French and international dishes are prepared with a German influence. The fish and seafood dishes are proof of the chef's real mastery. An attraction is the restaurant's rooftop location with great views. Reservations necessary. Closed Sun.

FURTHER AFIELD Blaues Band

Alte Schonhauser Strasse 7/8, 10119 **Tel** *(030) 283 850 99*

Despite its location in the trendy Mitte district, the Blaues Band is a secret to many Berliners. The ambience is friendly and relaxed, and the food delicious. It offers specialities from a specific country or region. German cuisine is particularly recommended. The menu has fresh asparagus in early summer and duck and goose in winter.

FURTHER AFIELD Mao Thai

Wörtherstrasse 30, 10405 **Tel** *(030) 441 92 61*

This is one of Berlin's best Thai restaurants, with an interior filled with beautiful antiques. The menu offers a full range of aromatic dishes, toned down to suit European tastes. Fresh and top-quality vegetables, carved into creative forms, are a speciality here. Reservations for dinner strongly advised.

FURTHER AFIELD Merhaba

Wissmannstraße 32, 12049 **Tel** *(030) 692 17 13*

People from all over Berlin come to this charming restaurant to join the local Turks and Germans who enjoy the food served here. Even if you are not particularly hungry, you will not be able to resist the various appetizers. There is outdoor dining in summer and belly dancing on Fridays and Saturdays. Closed at lunchtime.

FURTHER AFIELD Mutter

Hohenstaufenstraße 4, 10781 **Tel** *(030) 219 15 100*

True to its name, Mutter (German for "mother") serves generous portions to its patrons, mostly students. A fixture of the bustling Winterfeldplatz nightlife scene, it offers cool Caribbean drinks and an eclectic mix of some traditional German, Italian and Asian dishes, with an emphasis on sushi and Thai food.

FURTHER AFIELD Wirtshaus Moorlake

Moorlakeweg 1, 14109 **Tel** *(030) 805 58 09*

Situated on the secluded bank of the Havel river this historic restaurant serves German dishes. Although it is worth trying all the game dishes on its menu, the most highly recommended are game ragout with cranberries and buttered *Spätzle*, and the barbeque sampler, Moorlake with pork fillets and sauce bearnaise.

FURTHER AFIELD Grunewaldturm

Havelchaussee 61, 14193 **Tel** *(030) 417 20001*

Combining a meal in this restaurant with a trip to Grunewald Forest is a fine way to spend an afternoon. The menu mostly offers game or hearty meat dishes but also serves some local fish such as perch. Lunch or supper with wonderful views is an ideal end for this kind of outing.

FURTHER AFIELD Remise im Schloss Klein-Glienicke

Königstraße 36, 14109 **Tel** *(030) 805 40 00*

This is the ideal place for an elegant meal on the outskirts of Berlin. Now run by Franz Raneberger, one of Berlin's most prominent chefs, the restaurant offers excellent German cuisine, with perch, crayfish and game, all prepared with a dose of imagination. The restaurant is also a good choice for lunch. Closed Mon–Tue.

FURTHER AFIELD Restauration 1900

Husemannstraße 1, 10435 **Tel** *(030) 442 24 94*

One of the oldest and most traditional in this part of Berlin, this restaurant welcomes its guests into a simple dining room with an outstanding historic bar counter and other antiques. It offers light cuisine with some dishes of German origin and a large selection for vegetarians. The terrace looks over to Husemannstraße.

FURTHER AFIELD Vivaldi

Brahmsstraße 10, 14193 **Tel** *(030) 895 845 20*

A luxurious restaurant in the expensive Schlosshotel *(see p490)*. The interior, designed by Karl Lagerfeld, features panelled walls, gold leaf and chandeliers. Due to many changes in the management, the restaurant has lost its gourmet standard, but still makes for a pleasant evening with exquisite French food. Book ahead.

BRANDENBURG

BRANDENBURG Bismarck Terrassen

Bergstraße 20, 14770 **Tel** *(03381) 300 9 39*

Typical and modern Brandenburg dishes in a historic but fun setting. This restaurant is located in the oldest quarter of Brandenburg and is managed by an intriguing and passionate group. Various *flambé* dishes as well as roasted pork are favourites. Extensive wine and beer list. Enjoy traditional music during holidays and some weekends.

BRANDENBURG Sorat Hotel Brandenburg

Altstädtischer Markt 1, 14770 **Tel** *(03381) 59 70*

The intimate, yet refined setting at this efficient restaurant reminds one of an old English-style mansion. White table cloths, wooden floors and black leather seating welcome you along with the delicious smells wafting from the kitchen. Try the candlelit dinner, which changes menu seasonally.

Key to Price Guide *see p526* **Key to Symbols** *see back cover flap*

CHORIN Alte Klosterschänke ⊞ €€
Amt Chorin 9, 16230 **Tel** *(033366) 530 100*

Famed throughout the region for its highly polished service, this charming restaurant is located inside a 270-year-old half-timbered building. Surrounded by trees, the small garden is a great place to sit during the summer and enjoy the dishes from their extensive menu. Call ahead if there are more than six in your party.

CHORIN Haus Chorin ⊞ €€
Neue Klosterallee 10, 16230 **Tel** *(033366) 500*

This hotel-restaurant is based in a stylish Art Nouveau villa situated on the shores of a lake. Several regional and national specialities are on the menu, including pork fillet with honey on paprika and *Häckerle* (fish salad). Most of the vegetables on the menu come from local organic farmers and are delivered daily. Closed Wednesdays.

COTTBUS Mosquito €
Altmarkt 22, 3046 **Tel** *(0355) 2 88 90 444*

A South American twist on the café, bar and restaurant experience in Cottbus. Join the staff at Mosquito every day for happy hour or on Tuesdays for drink specials (a different one each month). Live music during the week and on special occasions. There is a lovely brunch on Sundays from 10am to 3pm. Try the chilli olive bread.

COTTBUS Cavalierhaus Branitz ▣ €€
Zum Kavalierhaus 8, 3042 **Tel** *(0355) 71 50 00*

Located in the centre of Branitzer Park, this beautiful and refined restaurant is a great place for dessert as well as dinner. Sample the delectable *Pückler torte* or wonderful *Pückler Eis* dessert for a taste of what keeps local patrons returning for more. They have wonderful wines from all over the world and the service is excellent.

COTTBUS Stadtwächter Cottbus ▮ ▦ €€
Mauerstr. 1, 3046 **Tel** *(0355) 2 36 18*

The menu at Stadtwaechter Cottbus offers a huge selection of lovingly and freshly prepared food. For a quieter or more private dinner, there are tables in the exclusive tower. The restaurant's specialty is *Schnitzel*, which can be enjoyed in a number of different variations. The kitchen stays open until 4am.

LEHNIN Markgraf ▤ ⊞ ▥ €€
Friedenstr. 13, 14797 **Tel** *(03382) 76 50*

This restaurant belongs to the Hotel Markgraf *(see p491)*. Austrian cuisine is the house standard and to a high standard by the head chef. Enjoy a glass of Austrian wine or German beer with your meal or alone after a long day. Outside tables are available during the summer when the weather is pleasant.

LEHNIN Rittergut Krahne ⊞ €€
Hauptstraße 6a, 14797 **Tel** *(033 835) 602 87*

A uniquely different eatery with a fetish for knights and swords. The extensive menu features wild boar and other local specialities, as well as dishes from assorted regions of the world. Try the baked apple with walnut ice cream for dessert. Reservations for larger groups are recommended. Parking is available for your car or horse.

LÜBBENAU Hotel Schloss Lübbenau ⊞ ▥ €€€
Schloßbezirk 6, 0-3332 **Tel** *(03542) 87 30*

An award-winning restaurant connected to a four-star hotel of the same name. The menu emphasizes fresh produce as well as delightful meat and fish dishes. Most items combine the flair of international cuisine with local ingredients. Furnishings are more old English than German. Sit on the terrace during breakfast and enjoy the view.

NEUHARDENBURG Parkhotel Schloss Wulkow ▥ €€€
Hauptstr. 24, 15320 **Tel** *(033476) 580*

This restaurant is based in the Parkhotel Schloss Wulkow, which was an imperial palace and is close to a nature preserve and natural lake. They use fresh produce and meats from local producers. The extensive wine list includes bottles from all over the world. The decor is quite elaborate, including crystal chandeliers.

NEURUPPIN Altes Kasino am See ▤ ⊞ €
Seeufer 11 / 12, 16816 **Tel** *(0339) 130 59*

Enjoy breakfast or drinks in the atrium of this cosy 100-year-old eatery. This hotel-restaurant sits directly by the water and is home to some of the most relaxing views of the area. A good selection of game and fish dishes is available. Try the fish plate for a sample of different varieties and preparation methods of the local catch.

NEURUPPIN Seeperle ▤ ▤ ⊞ ▮ €
Rutscherweg 6, 16816 **Tel** *(03391) 398291*

Dine dockside at this charming, family-run guesthouse, which is popular with boat owners who moor at the Seeperle's small pier. The menu includes home-made dishes, featuring seafood and regional specialities, with a few vegetarian options as well. Open for both lunch and dinner.

ORANIENBURG Gasthaus Charlottenhof ⊞ €
Neulöwenberger Straße 26, 16775 **Tel** *(0330) 94 50 417*

A quiet, intimate restaurant attached to the Gasthaus Charlottenhof hotel. The outdoor seating area is great in summer. Regional cuisine dominates the menu and features several pork and fish dishes. Try one of the delicious soups for something light but filling. There is bar seating for single guests or a quick drink.

ORANIENBURG Galerie   🅰   €€

André-Pican-Straße 23, 16515 **Tel** *(0330) 169 00*

This restaurant is in the excellent Stadthotel Oranienburg. Fresh flowers and interesting art help add to the welcoming ambience. It is well lit and appropriately decorated and the staff are friendly and well dressed. It is also child and family friendly. The bar is popular with business travellers, but does not stay open late.

POTSDAM Brauhaus Krongut Bornstedt   🖩   €€

Ribbeckstr. 6–7, 14469 **Tel** *(0331) 550 65 0*

Enjoy dining in this 400-year-old wine cellar, brewery and café on this former Prussian royal estate. Guests at Krongut Bornstedt can enjoy regal dishes such as "Freidrich's *Leibspeise*", potato soup with bacon. The baked apple desserts are well worth a try.

POTSDAM Restaurant Juliette   🅰 🍴   €€€

Jägerstraße 39, 14467 **Tel** *(0331) 270 17 91*

A French restaurant with all the romantic trimmings you would expect – candles, white tablecloths and a lit fireplace. French food traditionalists beware, the decorated and imaginative chef serves up both traditional and experimental cuisine. Try the ever-popular *crème brûlée* for dessert. There are vegetarian options on the menu.

POTSDAM Speckers Gaststätte zur Ratswaage   🅰 🖩 🍴   €€€

Am Neuen Markt 10, 14467 **Tel** *(0331) 280 43 11*

French-influenced cuisine reigns supreme at this restaurant located in the centre of the city. Modern decor with fresh and elegant touches produces a charming, comfortable but unpretentious dining experience. Family run and famous for its excellent service as well as exquisite menu. Produce arrives to the restaurant fresh daily from local producers.

POTSDAM Restaurant Friedrich Wilhelm, Bayrisches Haus   🖩 🍴   €€€€€

Im Wildpark 1, Potsdam (West), 14471 **Tel** *(0331) 550 50*

This restaurant is in a top class hotel of the same name. It is famed for its luxury, service and French-inspired cuisine. Extensive menu offers meals in predetermined courses, a great option for those looking for a mix of house specialities. Fresh flowers abound year round. Enjoy the terrace in summer with its great views.

WANDLITZ SeePark Wandlitz   🖩 🍴   €€

Kirchstr. 10 (Hinter der alten Dorfkirche am See), 16348 **Tel** *(0333) 977 50*

This Mediterranean-style restaurant also offers German fare. All the dishes are prepared with locally grown produce. Steak fillet with a sage, ham and almond stuffed Spanish onion is a culinary highlight. They have an extensive wine list, including superb wines that are only available by the glass. Open for lunch and dinner.

WITTSTOCK Stadt Hamburg   🍽 🖩 🧍   €€

Röbeler Str. 25, 16909 **Tel** *(03394) 404 60*

This restaurant is regarded in the region as a good eatery for travellers or those with children in tow. It is tastefully furnished and the service is good. The menu has limited options for vegetarians. Open for both lunch and dinner, it can get busy during national holidays and local events.

SAXONY-ANHALT

BAUTZEN Restaurant Burghof Bautzen   🅰 🧍 🖩 🗒 🍴   €€

Ortenburg 6, 2625 **Tel** *03591 531336*

Set in a historic courtyard of the castle, with a 1920s decor, this homely restaurant features solid seasonal cuisine. The traditional dishes on offer include suckling pig and roast vegetables, *schnitzel*, salmon and cooked ham. In late spring to summer, when it's in season, the white asparagus dishes are a must.

BERNBURG Zille Stube   🍽   €

Siedlung 37a, 0-6406 **Tel** *(03471) 33 31 90*

A very traditional, quaint and unfussy German restaurant, although more like a pub. Dark, hardwood furniture and friendly staff are standard. They specialize mostly in traditional German cuisine and beers. Look out for regional artisan crafts throughout as well as paintings by various local artists.

BLANKENBURG Hotelrestaurant Viktoria Luise   🍴   €€

Hasselfelder Str. 8, 38889 **Tel** *(03944) 91170*

Less than 20 minutes from the Harz National Park, this restaurant is a great location for health-conscious diners. All dishes are home-made regional creations centred on fresh ingredients. There are several vegetarian offerings, including many organic options. Delightful fish and duck courses. There is also a wine cellar with a lovely terrace.

DESSAU Teehäuschen   🍽 🅰 🖩   €

Im Grünen der Stadt-Im Stadt Park, 0-6844 **Tel** *(0340) 21 49 96*

A lovely garden surrounds this teahouse in the Stadtpark area. For over 30 years, patrons have enjoyed the wide variety of teas, cakes and light meals made fresh daily, though more substantial meals are also on offer. Everything is delicious. Larger parties are welcome, but call ahead for more information. Closed Mon.

DESSAU Kornhaus €€

Kornhausstr. 146, 0-6846 **Tel** *(0340) 640 41 41*

The proprietors of Kornhaus are in love with food and hope to share their passion with all their guests. Try one of the three-course meals or order *à la carte*. There are organic items on the menu and several options for vegetarians or others with dietary concerns. For dessert, try the *Rote Grütze* with vanilla sauce. Closed Thursdays.

DESSAU Restaurant Fürst Leopold €€

Friedensplatz 1, 6844 **Tel** *(0340) 2515257*

The cuisine of Saxony-Anhalt is tasty and down-to-earth, with hearty casseroles, game specialities from the Harz region and delicious egg-based dishes and pastries. The Fürst Leopold menu impresses with creative, seasonal and regional cuisine. Enjoy a glass of sparkling white burgundy or a famous Anhalt beer as an accompaniment.

DESSAU Weinstuben Paechterhaus €€

Kirchstr. 1, 0-6846 **Tel** *(0340) 650 1447*

Set in a half-timbered house over 300 years old, this wine *Stube* has much on offer for patrons. The food menu focuses on interesting flavour combinations and textures, while the wine menu offers a little something for everyone. A popular place throughout the region for its relaxed atmosphere and expert staff.

HALBERSTADT Parkhotel Unter den Linden €€€

Klamrothstr. 2, 38820 **Tel** *(03941) 625 40*

The restaurant of the Parkhotel Unter den Linden *(see p492)*. The service here is great and the staff are very friendly. They have an international menu with German influences. The wine list is extensive and there is a wine cellar on the property Try the French apple tart with home-made champagne rice for dessert.

HALLE Dorint Hotel Charlottenhof €€

Dorotheenstraße 12, 0-6108 **Tel** *(0345) 292 30*

This restaurant belongs to the Dorint Hotel Charlottenhof, which is located in the city centre. Guests can watch their food being elegantly prepared while in the restaurant dining area. The food is above average and served by friendly and knowledgeable staff. There is also a pleasant hotel bar.

HALLE Enchilada €€

Universitätsring 6, 0-6108 **Tel** *(0345) 686 77 55*

A Mexican themed bar-restaurant near the university. It is geared towards the younger crowd or those looking for a taste of something different. The focus is more on drinks than food. However, the food is good and temperature adjustable for those not so keen on spicy food. Happy hour daily from 6pm to 8pm.

ILSENBURG Landhaus "Zu den Rothen Forellen" €€€

Marktplatz 2, 38871 **Tel** *(039452) 93 93*

In a delightful setting by a lake close to the Hochharz nature preserve – come here for a relaxing dining experience. Restored in 1995, the 400-year-old structure is home to a restaurant and hotel *(see p492)*. Sit directly by the lake for dinner if you dine outside. The staff are very friendly and knowledgeable.

MAGDEBURG Amsterdam €

Olvenstedter Str. 9, 39108 **Tel** *(0391) 400 54 00*

There is a bistro-type atmosphere at this very hip address near the centre. Several beers are on offer and a smaller wine selection. Try the "Do-It-Yourself" breakfast menu where guests can mix and match items for a set price. The French cheese plate or one of the other international dishes are great for something lighter in the evening.

MAGDEBURG Le Frog €

Heinrich-Heine-Platz 1, 39114 **Tel** *(0391) 53 13 55 6*

This brasserie and lounge is a cool place to eat or sip one of the local brews. It is located in the middle of Stadtpark, which is a local hotspot catering to a fun and vibrant crowd. They have a buffet brunch on Sundays with several tasty treats and magnificent creations. The beer garden seats over 400 people and there is a large terrace as well.

MAGDEBURG Tokio Haus €

Johannes-Göderitz-Straße 27, 39130 **Tel** *(0391) 506 94 93*

A bit harder to find, but well worth the effort to locate for the delicious Japanese food at this locally-owned restaurant. There are many varieties of sushi on the menu, including *maki* and *sashimi*. The lunch menu is a good choice for those watching their budget or looking for a variety to sample. Closed Tue.

MAGDEBURG Ritters Weinstuben €€€

Große Ritterstraße 22, 06217 **Tel** *(03461) 33660*

One of the oldest gourmet restaurants in town, Ritters Weinstuben caters to many tastes. Gourmands can choose from light German dishes and an extensive wine list in the tastefully furnished dining area, while hikers and bikers will appreciate a cool beer on the terrace and one of the very affordable lunch specials.

MERSEBURG Belle Epoque €€

Oberaltenburg 4, 6217 **Tel** *(03461) 452 00*

An exquisite restaurant in the Radisson Blu Hotel Halle-Merseburg *(see p492)*, which is located on the cathedral hill. They specialize in German cuisine, as well as a few international dishes. Interesting decor and very good service. The café includes a terrace. The Raben bar is a highlight for business travellers.

NAUMBURG Zur alten Schmiede

Lindenring 36/37, 0-6618 **Tel** *(03445) 243 60*

A delightful, traditional restaurant in the wine-producing region of the Saale-Unstrut. It is located in the town centre and the current structure dates back to 1700 when it was used as a blacksmith's shop. Excellent location for sampling some of the local wines and regional food specialities. There is a romantic fire on colder evenings.

QUEDLINBURG Weinkeller Theophano im Palais Salfeldt

Kornmarkt 6, 0-6484 **Tel** *(3946) 96300*

A family-owned establishment. This 400-year-old wine cellar is a restored structure with sandstone vaulted ceilings. The staff are welcoming and friendly and the lighting is soft. The menu combines German as well as international dishes and is refreshingly seasonal, with many items only offered during peak season. Very popular with the locals.

QUEDLINBURG Weinstube, Romantik Hotel am Brühl

Billungstr. 11, 0-6484 **Tel** *(03946) 961 80*

Famed for its service, menu and extensive wine list, this restaurant is a great option for those in town or staying near by. Wines available include varieties from France, Italy, California and, of course, regional favourites. A glorious inner courtyard is wonderfully relaxing on clear days, so eat outside if possible.

STENDAL Altstadt-Hotel

Breite Str. 60, 39576 **Tel** *(03931) 698 90*

A quaint but pleasant place to enjoy a meal or light snack. Open for both lunch and dinner, this hotel *(see p493)* and restaurant is located in the centre of town. Tastefully furnished and relaxing, you can sit outside in good weather. The menu offers international and German dishes, although there are few options for those with special dietary needs.

TANGERMÜENDE Kutscherstübchen

Lange Str. 52, 39590 **Tel** *(039322) 23 91*

Part of the historic Schwarzer Adler Hotel *(see p493)*, this is a nice family-friendly restaurant. Pleasantly furnished and tranquil, most meals are served in generous portions with the focus on regional fare, although some international ingredients and cooking methods influence the menu.

WERNIGERODE "Die Stuben", Gothisches Haus

Marktplatz 2, 38855 **Tel** *(03943) 67 50*

This restaurant is connected to a mid-sized four-star hotel of the same name. The main train station is approximately one kilometre away. Enjoy dining among the half-timbered houses in the centre of this wonderfully romantic town. The restaurant includes a bar, outdoor seating area and wine tavern (they have an extensive wine list).

WITTENBERG Grüne Tanne

Am Teich 1, 0-6896 **Tel** *(03491) 62 90*

Located on the outskirts of town, this former knight's manor is over 400 years old. This pleasant restaurant, based in a hotel of the same name, serves above average traditional and regional German dishes. They have a small but good wine list. Open for dinner from 5:30pm on weekdays and for lunch from 11am.

WITTENBERG Schlosskeller

Am Schlossplatz 1, 0-6886 **Tel** *(03491) 48 08 05*

Located in the rustic, vaulted basement of a 16th-century house, this place is sure to please anyone looking for something traditional and cosy with its fascinating decor. The menu includes time-honoured German and Saxonian fare. Various regional and national beers are on offer, as well as wines. The staff dress in medieval costumes.

SAXONY

AUGUSTUSBURG Café Friedrich

Hans-Planer-Str. 1, 0-9573 **Tel** *(037291) 66 66*

Over 100 years of family tradition await you at this lovely café, which is situated in a hilly, picturesque part of the town with amazing views of Castle Augustusburg. They offer both lighter and heavier dishes, and their desserts, especially cakes, are to die for. There is a play area for children in the garden.

BAD MUSKAU Am Schlossbrunnen

Köbelner Str. 68, 0-2953 **Tel** *(035771) 5230*

Operated by the Wieczorek family, this hotel and restaurant sits on the edge of town. It has a delightful interior. Both regional and international dishes are served, with a focus on fish, most of it caught locally in the heathland lakes. Also, try one of the steak dishes or the excellent *Fürst-Puckler* ice cream, which is a local speciality.

BAUTZEN Bautzener Brauhaus

Thomas-Mann-Str. 7, 0-2625 **Tel** *(03591) 49 14 56*

As the name of this eatery suggests, this is one of the local brew houses. Choose from several varieties of beer, including *Schwarzbier*, or black beer, and the original *Pilsner*. Enjoy your beer either on site, or take some home. The menu offers mostly standard German fare but at good prices. Tours of the brewery are also available.

Key to Price Guide *see p526* **Key to Symbols** *see back cover flap*

CHEMNITZ Glashaus

Salzstr. 56, 0-9113 **Tel** *(0371) 334 10*

Based in the Renaissance Hotel and surrounded by lush greenery, this restaurant offers great views of the old town and the restaurant pond. International dishes are served in this lovely, modern venue, which rivals any botanical garden. There is also an attractive terrace and various seasonal events available to guests.

CHEMNITZ Sächsischer Hof

Brühl 26, 0-9111 **Tel** *(0371) 461 480*

This restaurant is in a hotel of the same name. They offer international and regional dishes made with a creative flair. Crème sauces, salads and fish entrées dominate the menu. The service is first rate and the staff extremely friendly. Dark wood furniture and greenery greet you inside, as does a bar. Some credit cards are accepted.

DRESDEN Cuchi

Wallgäßchen 5, 0-1097 **Tel** *(0351) 862 75 80*

Chinese, Vietnamese and Japanese fusion cuisine all under one roof. The sushi menu is extensive, as are the wine and beer lists. Try one of the meals served in a wok. The Chillout Garden lives up to its name and is very relaxing and calm. Open daily at noon Monday to Thursday. Evening reservations are recommended.

DRESDEN Sophienkeller

Taschenberg 3, 0-1067 **Tel** *(0351) 49 72 60*

One of the most popular and lively restaurants in Dresden. It is one of three eateries located in the Taschenbergpalais. Come here for the re-created rustic atmosphere of an 18th-century beer cellar. They have authentic regional cuisine on the menu. The staff wear period costumes. Ask to sit at the indoor carousel table.

DRESDEN Kahnaletto

Terrassenufer / Augustusbrücke, 1067 **Tel** *(0351) 495 30 37*

Situated on a boat on the river, Kahnaletto offers charming service and an impressive view of the Old Town skyline. The menu serves up modern and light Mediterranean and international dishes. On mild summer evenings, the torch-lit terrace is the perfect place to sit back and relax while enjoying Italian seafood delicacies.

DRESDEN Das Caroussel

Röhnitzgasse 19, 0-1097 **Tel** *(0351) 000 00*

The hotel and restaurant are based within a recently restored Baroque palace in the historic city centre, dating from the 18th century. Famed in the region as one of the best restaurants in Saxony, dine on Mediterranean cuisine while sipping one of the first-class wines. Truly spectacular.

KAMENZ Goldener Hirsch Ratskeller

Markt 10, 0-1917 **Tel** *(03578) 78350*

The restaurant of the Goldener Hirsch hotel *(see p494)*, which is in the market square. This elegant establishment serves exquisite Italian dishes. The rustic Ratskeller, which serves traditional German fare, is also recommended. Reservations are not usually required, but call ahead if your party is large.

LEIPZIG Zest

Bornaische Str. 54, 0-4277 **Tel** *(0341) 2319126*

A fresh and creative take on meatless international fusion food. Try one of the wildly imaginative and intriguing vegan/vegetarian dishes, such as spinach risotto balls with a cashew nut crust and coconut crème. The rosemary lemon cake is also tempting and worth sampling. An extensive wine list. Open daily at 11am.

LEIPZIG Alte Nikolaischule Gasthaus

Nikolaikirchhof 2, 4109 **Tel** *(0341) 2118511*

Located in the heart of Leipzig next to the famous St Nikolai Church, this traditional German gastropub serves local specialities such as *Schnudendunker*, a hearty baked savoury soufflé and has a wide range of regional and international wines. For guests who prefer lighter dishes, the restaurant also offers Italian-influenced meals.

LEIPZIG Michaelis

Paul-Gruner-Str. 44, 4107 **Tel** *(0341) 26780*

This is a restaurant based in a hotel situated in a building that dates back over 100 years. Look for the usual, mostly European cuisine as well as local specialities. The well-lit dining area is intimate and nice in good weather. There is a child-friendly seating area and menu, although there are few options for those with special dietary needs. Closed Sun.

LEIPZIG Restaurant Macis

Markgrafenstr. 10, 4109 **Tel** *(0341) 22 28 75 20*

A hip, up-market restaurant located in the centre of the city. The menu focuses on the Mediterranean with fresh, high quality ingredients, especially vegetables and fish. Take your pick of lighter or heavier meals. The wine list is certainly better than average. Open daily at noon and closed between 3pm and 6pm.

MEISSEN Bauernhäusel

Oberspaarer Str. 20, 1662 **Tel** *(03521) / 73 33 17*

Join the traditional, uniform-wearing and friendly staff at this historic pub in Meissen. Wine is the top drink on offer and is very good. The menu is traditional German, with some French, Austrian, Italian, English and American influences. Open Tuesday to Sunday (brunch on some Sundays).

MEISSEN Domkeller

🏛 🔝 📋 🍷 €€

Domplatz 9, 1662 **Tel** *(03521) 457676*

Founded in 1470, Domkeller is the oldest restaurant in Meissen. Although a little non-descript from the outside, the atmosphere within is warm and very welcoming. In summer, a terrace offers lovely views over the city. The menu provides a wide range of German and international cuisine along with a broad selection of wines from local wineries.

MORITZBURG BEI DRESDEN Churfürstliche Waldschaenke

♿ 🔝

€€

Große Fasanenstr., 0-1468 **Tel** *(035207) 860-0*

This restaurant, in the Waldschänke Hotel and near a former pheasantry, serves regional German and European food. There is a good choice of game dishes on the menu. There is a large wine selection to choose from, including brands from the immediate vicinity and other parts of the region. Large parties can be accommodated, but call ahead.

PIRNA Escobar

📋 🔝 🍷

€

Obere Burgstr. 1, 0-1796 **Tel** *(03501) 582773*

Nestled in a building over 80 years old, which has been renovated. Visit this café, bar and restaurant for a decor reminiscent of 1950s South America. The South American influence continues on the menu with dishes such as fish curry with plantain fillets. Brunch buffet every Sunday beginning at 10am.

PIRNA Deutsches Haus

♿

€€

Niedere Burgstr. 1, 0-1796 **Tel** *(03501) 46 880*

This modern restaurant, part of a hotel belonging to the Romantik Hotels chain *(see p495)*, is highly rated and very popular with locals. The food is mostly German with some international influences. Reservations are rarely needed, but call ahead on extended holiday weekends or if your party has special needs.

TORGAU Central-Hotel

€

Friedrichplatz 8, 0-4860 **Tel** *(03421) 732 80*

This attractively furnished but modest restaurant is based in a hotel of the same name. It specializes in cuisine from Baden, so come here for food that is uncomplicated but delightful – the desserts are especially good. However, there are few vegetarian options. The service is courteous and attentive. Open for both lunch and dinner.

ZITTAU Riedel

🔝

€€

Friedenstr. 23, 0-2763 **Tel** *(03583) 68 60*

Serving German foods from several regions, this hotel-restaurant is a good place to sample all things German. There are several grilled and roasted pork dishes on the menu. Relax in the beautiful and comfortable beer garden in good weather or enjoy a pint of one of the many beers on offer in the Bavarian-style pub.

ZWICKAU Drei Schwaene

🔝 🍷

€€€

Tonstr. 1, 0-8058 **Tel** *(0375) 204 76 50*

A lovely French restaurant. Lots of fresh flowers on the tables make your dining experience intimate as well as first class. As expected, the wine list is phenomenal and focuses mostly on French producers. Reservations are recommended for dinner. There are very few vegetarian options on the menu, but ask your waiter for house selections.

THURINGIA

ALTENBURG Altenburger Hof

📋 ♿ 🔝 🍷

€€

Schmöllnsche Landstr. 8, 0-4600 **Tel** *(03447) 58 40*

The Altenburger Hof Hotel *(see p495)* restaurant is typical of many in the region. Expect good service and decent quality food at affordable prices. The café is also fairly standard, but charming all the same. The hotel also has a bar. As in most regions of Germany, hotel bars often close earlier than you might expect.

EISENACH Café Lackner & Julian's Restaurant

🔝

€

Johannisstr. 22, 99817 **Tel** *(03691) 78 45 50*

A family-owned (since 1929) café plus adjoining restaurant. It has a very tranquil outdoor seating area, so sit outside if the weather is nice. Service is exceptional and the staff are very knowledgeable about the menu and surrounding area. It can get busy during dinner, so call ahead if you want to guarantee a table.

EISENACH Lutherstuben, Eisenacher Hof

♿ 🔝

€€

Katharinenstr. 11–13, 99817 **Tel** *(03691) 293 90*

A historic restaurant in the Eisenacher Hof Hotel, specializing in reformer Martin Luther's favourite medieval delicacies. Try one of the many pork or fish dishes. The wine list is decent. There is also a pleasant hotel bar, a café with a terrace and an in-house disco some nights.

ERFURT Feuerkugel

🔝

€

Michaelisstr. 3-4, 99084 **Tel** *(0361) 7891256*

Located at the famous Krämerbrücke bridge in Erfurt's historic centre, this restaurant offers an authentic Thuringian dining experience at an unbeatable price. The wood-panelled interior is dark but cosy, creating a traditional pub atmosphere. The staff are very accommodating, and an inviting beer garden awaits in the summer.

Key to Price Guide *see p526* **Key to Symbols** *see back cover flap*

ERFURT Naumburgischer Keller

Michaelisstr. 49, 99084 **Tel** *(0361) 540 24 50*

A restaurant located in a half-timbered building over 300 years old. The culinary focus is on Thuringian food and local beers. Try the *Rostbrätel*, or roasted meat with braised onions, as an entrée. The special Christmas menu features typical regional Christmas fare. The wine list has an excellent selection.

ERFURT Köstritzer "Zum güldenen Rade"

Marktstr. 50, 99084 **Tel** *(0361) 5 61 35 06*

There is a little something here for everyone, especially those with discriminating tastes, with the very international menu – try something Italian or French. There are several vegetarian dishes on the menu as well as typical German and local fare. Dark woods and plush colours abound. Wheelchair accessible and family friendly.

ERFURT Zum alten Schwan

Gotthardstr. 27, 99084 **Tel** *(0361) 674 00*

Situated in the historic city centre of Erfurt, this restaurant is housed in the IBB/Sorat Hotel. The cooking is of a very high standard and there is a wide selection of dishes on offer. Choose one of the lighter dishes if you are not hungry enough for a full meal, such as fresh salads or light but filling soups.

ERFURT Alboth's Restaurant im Kaisersaal

Futterstr. 15/16, 99084 **Tel** *(0361) 568 82 07*

Very fancy and highly rated. This restaurant, located in the hotel Kaisersaal, has earned its reputation as one of the city's classiest places to dine. Top-notch wine list. The innovative head chef creates memorable meals using ultra-fresh ingredients and international food preparation techniques. Superb desserts.

GERA Cafe Haus Graf Zeppelin

Rudolf-Diener-Str. 17, 7545 **Tel** *(0365) 824260*

Dishes and wines from the Thuringer region feature strongly on the menu at Cafe Haus Graf Zeppelin. This café serves good-value meals from breakfast until dinner. Other dishes include Mediterranean specialities and children are well-catered for too

GOTHA Hotel am Schlosspark

Lindenauallee 20, 99867 **Tel** *(03621) 44 20*

A relaxing hotel *(see p496)* restaurant enhanced by the indoor foliage and sunny outdoor surroundings in good weather. Enjoy coffee or your favourite beer while sitting in the outdoor seating area. They offer both classic regional fare and international dishes. The restaurant is situated at the end of the castle park.

JENA Schwarzer Bär

Lutherplatz 2, 7743 **Tel** *(03641) 40 60*

A hotel and restaurant in a historic building near the University of Jena. Eat in the same place Martin Luther once stayed. Choose this restaurant if you are looking for simple, modern and regional food. Try the Goethe menu, which has leg of lamb, puréed potato soup with sausages and two delicious desserts.

JENA Scala

Leutragraben 1, 7743 **Tel** *(036 41) 35 66 660*

A wonderful restaurant located on the 28th floor of the former Carl Zeiss Jena tower and affording a panoramic view of the city. Try the fillet of bass on a saffron risotto with a white wine sauce. The restaurant also includes conference rooms, all named after famous cities around the world. Highly recommended.

MÜHLHAUSEN Brauhaus zum Löwen

Kornmarkt 3, 99974 **Tel** *(03601) 4710*

This local brewery serves its own beer in the restaurant and pub. Most of the food is traditional German and so there are few vegetarian options. Try one of the *bretzels* or sausages as a snack, or any of the main courses for something more substantial. The hotel is also adjacent to the dining areas.

SCHMOLLN Hotel Restaurant Bellevue

Am Pfefferberg 7, 4626 **Tel** *(034491) 70 00*

An award-winning restaurant, based in a hotel of the same name. The atmosphere is refined with crisp tablecloths, silver cutlery and nice indoor greenery. Views from the terrace are astounding. The menu focuses almost exclusively on continental cuisine, with some non-European influences. A very good wine list.

WEIMAR Zum Schwarzen Bären

Markt 20, 99423 **Tel** *(03643) 853847*

One of Weimar's oldest restaurants, Zum Schwarzen Bären offers a traditional Thuringian gastropub experience in a historic setting in the town centre. The dining rooms are simple and the tasty food is well-prepared. A great place to sample Thuringian specialities such as bratwurst or beef roulade with a draft beer.

WEIMAR joHanns Hof

Scherfgasse 1, 99423 **Tel** *(03643) 493617*

This pleasant bistro-like restaurant focuses on refined European cuisine and the excellent Saale-Unstrut wines of the region. Wood-panelled walls showcase a venerable wine collection. Service is attentive, making this an appealing place to eat in the heart of historic Weimar.

WEIMAR Wolff's Art Hotel and Restaurant

Freiherr-vom-Stein-Allee 3a/b, 99425 **Tel** *(03643) 540 60*

As you would expect with a name like Art Hotel and Restaurant, there is lots of art on display here for guests to enjoy. Both the Art Hotel and its restaurant are furnished in the style created by the Bauhaus School. The menu includes foods from all regions of the world, with an emphasis on European cuisine.

MUNICH

Alter Simpl

Türkenstraße 57, 80799 **Tel** *(089) 2723083*

Map Map 2 B1

For a traditional atmosphere, this cozy student pub in Schwabing is just the ticket. Thomas Mann, Hermann Hesse and writers of satirical magazine *Simplicissimus* used to hang out here, and that era is recalled in the faded covers on display. Expect traditional Bavarian dishes such as *Hax'n* (pork knuckle) and wallet-friendly snacks.

Hot Shot Café-Bar-Restaurant

Herzogstraße 29, 80803 **Tel** *(089) 71674063*

Perfect for a pre-clubbing pit stop in the heart of Schwabing's nightlife quarter. Cool guys and girls can be spotted here munching tapas, spare ribs and club sandwiches while plotting their weekend exploits. The leathery, bistro-style interior and relaxed terrace are great spots for people-watching or a tasty lunch.

Ignaz

Georgenstraße 67, 80799 **Tel** *(089) 2716093*

One of Munich's best vegetarian restaurants, Ignaz impresses with both the creativity of its cuisine and its mammoth portions. Great value for money makes Ignaz popular with the nearby student community. All dishes cost just €5 for takeaway. The attached café is known for drop-dead delicious cakes and pastries.

Königsquelle

Baaderplatz 2, 80469 **Tel** *(089) 220071*

A must for whisky lovers who flock here for the whisky bar. The food here ranges from homely and simple to refined high-class cooking. The veal *Wiener Schnitzel* comes highly recommended. A warm friendly atmosphere with good reliable service. The range of beers and wines is also good. It is popular so it is best to book ahead.

La Fiorentina

Goethestraße 41, 80336 **Tel** *(089) 534185*

Map 1 E5

Run by a friendly Tuscan team, this garden trattoria is renowned for authentic Florentine specialities such as farfalle with steamed clams, gorgonzola-pear risotto or shrimp linguini. Deciphering the hand-written menu and copious wine list can be a challenge, but the talkative waiters are happy to translate.

Cohen's

Theresienstraße 31, 80333 **Tel** *(089) 2809545*

Map 2, B1

This kosher Jewish restaurant with Eastern European influences is a rarity in Munich. Tucked away in a rear courtyard, its small but elegant dining room is studded with fresh flowers. The owners put an ethnic spin even on fish and schnitzel dishes, served huge and tender with a fresh side salad. The kosher wines are particularly good value.

Prinz Myshkin

Hackenstraße 2, 80331 **Tel** *(089) 265596*

Map 2 A5

You don't need to be a vegetarian to love this stylish place, consisting of a café and beer-hall-style restaurant. The large selection of classic Italian and Asian-influenced dishes include tofu stroganoff and soya medallions. There can be long waits and the occasional brusque waiter, but the quality of food more than makes up for it.

Ruffini

Orffstraße 22–24, 80637 **Tel** *(089) 161160*

With 25 years of experience behind it, Ruffini is a well-established address for good regional Italian cuisine. Try the organic roast pork with rosemary potatoes or penne with Italian smoked sausage, tomatoes and paprika. It is also popular as a bright, sleek café and patisserie. By evening the guests come for the good Italian wine and food.

Zum Franziskaner

Residenzstraße 9, Perusastraße 5, 80331 **Tel** *(089) 2318120*

Map 2 B4

Rich in tradition and one of the best places to head for typical Bavarian specials. Their home-made white sausage, *Weißwurst* is famous in Munich. Also, try the Bavarian meatloaf with mustard, fillet of ox, plus a variety of salads and vegetarian dishes. Being the brewery's restaurant, you must try the Franziskaner beer, originally brewed by monks.

Al Pino

Frans-Hals-Straße 3, 81479 **Tel** *(089) 799885*

Excellent Italian dishes mastered by chef Valerio Scopel, open for lunch (except Sunday) or dinner. It has an understated decor, where portraits reminiscent of the Medici line the walls. Try the red mullet on fennel purée, zucchini flower ravioli in saffron butter and green apple mousse on cassis cream.

Key to Price Guide *see p526* **Key to Symbols** *see back cover flap*

Dallmayr   €€€

Dienerstraße 14–15, 80331 **Tel** *(089) 2135100*   **Map** *2 B4*

Dallmayr is a Munich institution, famous for its coffee house and café. The elegant restaurant offers delicious treats such as zucchini flowers with lobster on a bed of ratatouille in curry sauce, plus a selection of superb wines. Very popular with locals and tourists for its high level of service, patisserie and cuisine.

Gandl   €€€

St-Anna-Platz 1, 80538 **Tel** *(089) 29162525*   **Map** *3 D4*

Gandl is the hotel restaurant of the attractive Opera Hotel *(see p498)*, serving light Italian cuisine at midday and a fine French cuisine in the evenings. Depending on the time of year, you can eat by the open fire or on the lovely terrace. Excellent starters, steak, lamb, fish and duck dishes followed by French cheeses are available.

Nektar   €€€

Stubenvollstraße 1, 81667 **Tel** *(089) 45911311*

A contemporary, decadent experience awaits at Nektar. A supper club atmosphere where you eat several courses while reclining, with performances in-between. Everything is white, emphasizing the futuristic lighting, design, chilled music and video projections. Daily changing menus and good Old World wines. Book ahead.

Spatenhaus   €€€

An der Oper, Residenzstraße 12, 80333 **Tel** *(089) 2907060*   **Map** *2 B4*

A classic place to sample traditional high quality Bavarian cuisine, part of the renowned Kuffler company. The First Floor is more informal, while the Second Floor is more sophisticated and has great views of the Opera House. Specials include the stuffed breast of veal or meatballs with home-made potato salad or a slow baked cabbage roll.

Acetala   €€€

Nymphenburgerstraße 215, 80639 **Tel** *(089) 13929077*

This small and narrow, friendly and stylish restaurant has a small menu based entirely around balsamic vinegar. Try the cauliflower soup and home-made ravioli filled with riccotta cheese and mushrooms or pecorino, topped with a drop of the real 25-year-old balsamic vinegar from Modena. There are seats out front in the summer.

Austernkeller   €€€€

Stollbergstraße 11, 80539 **Tel** *(089) 298787*   **Map** *2 C4*

Munich's famous seafood restaurant specializes in oysters. The cuisine is typically French and uses the freshest catch of the day. Be sure to ask for the daily specials. Well established with a great reputation for over 75 years, the scallops and French onion soup are highly recommended. There is a romantic and intimate feel.

Broeding   €€€€

Schulstraße 9, 80634 **Tel** *(089) 164238*

Broeding is a fine restaurant and also an Austrian wine importer. There is a daily changing five-course set menu (fish every first Wednesday in the month) and a list of top quality wines. Set up by a sommelier and a chef who share a passion for excellent food and wine. Small but simply the best. Book well ahead.

Dukatz   €€€

Maffeistraße 3A, 80331 **Tel** *(089) 710407373*   **Map** *2 B3*

A cultural spot in Munich's Literaturhaus ("house of literature"), this restaurant has won accolades for its food and reasonable pricing. The bistro serves an excellent choice of light Mediterranean dishes with seasonal menus, which change on a daily basis. Meat or fish with vegetables or salads are available in a mouthwatering variety of dishes.

Acquarello   €€€€€

Mühlbaurstraße 36, 81677 **Tel** *(089) 4704848*

This restaurant serves fabulous Michelin-starred Italian cuisine using fresh ingredients and special seasonings. Ask chef and owner Mario for his wine recommendations. Try the tortelli of figs and *foie gras*, squab with red wine, walnut and parsley sauce followed by lemon ricotta tart. There is typically Italian kitsch decor and excellent food

Bistro Terrine   €€€€

Amalienstraße 89, 80799 **Tel** *(089) 281780*   **Map** *2 B1*

Bistro Terrine is Tantris' younger sister and a high quality restaurant. They specialize in delicious low-calorie dishes and especially good are the lamb and fish. There is also a lovely garden terrace and children are welcome. It is light, bright and very stylish with antique beaded lamps. Located in the lively studenty area of Schwabing.

Käfer Schänke   €€€€

Prinzregentenstraße 73, 81675 **Tel** *(089) 4168247*

Michael Käfer's renowned gourmet restaurant attracts a mix of politicians and artsy and business types. Open all day from 11am for lunch and dinner whenever you want. There are cosy, intimate dining rooms in contemporary chic mixed with traditional Bavaria – hunting room, opera room and a lounge with an open fire.

Königshof   €€€€€

Karlsplatz 25, 80336 **Tel** *(089) 557360*   **Map** *1 F4*

A Michelin-starred gourmet restaurant in the hotel of the same name *(see p499)*. Chef Martin Fauster creates wonderful food such as medallion of venison with chanterelles and cabbage, fillet of sea bass with artichoke fond and ravioli or crème brûlée and liquorice ice cream with poached pear. There is a refined atmosphere.

Tantris
Johann-Fichte Straße 7, 80805 **Tel** *(089) 3619590*   🔲   €€€€€

A classic establishment and a Munich institution for over 30 years. Designed in a 1970s style it offers gourmet menus, a high standard of luxury and also has two Michelin stars, a garden and a terrace. Booking is essential. Try the specials, aubergine and sardine terrine with pesto or lukewarm salmon in leek purée and brown butter.

BAVARIA

ANSBACH Madame Thu Trang
Platenstraße 2, 91522 **Tel** *(0981) 9723399*   🎒   €

Hidden in a passage of Ansbach's shopping district, this incongruous little Asian eatery serves some of the best and most authentic sushi in the area. You can wash it down with the delicate house sake, Asian beers or one of Madame Trang's aromatic teas. Save room for a dollop of vanilla ice cream served in warm coconut milk.

ASCHAFFENBURG Schlappeseppel
Schlossgasse 28, 63739 **Tel** *(06021) 25531*   🔳🎒🔲   €

An easy walk from neighbouring Schloss Johannisberg, this earthy pub is beloved for its house-brewed pils and masterful versions of Bavarian standbys such as pork knuckle, veal sausage and liver dumpling soup. Expect old-fashioned wooden benches and regulars enjoying a roster of seasonal brews.

ASCHAU IM CHIEMGAU Heinz Winkler
Kirchplatz 1, 83229 **Tel** *(08052) 17990*   🔳🔲🔲   €€€€

Masterchef Heinz Winkler took over the original Post Hotel here in 1989 *(see p499)*. He has created a culinary destination for real gourmands with a wonderful Apline backdrop by the Chiemsee. Dine in palatial surroundings in the Venetian lounge, garden salon, winter garden or loggia terrace. Exceptional food and wine.

AUGSBURG Ratskeller
Rathausplatz 2, 86150 **Tel** *(0821) 31988238*   🔲🎒🔲🔲   €€

Ratskeller is situated in a traditional vaulted cellar in the town hall and has a cosy atmosphere. The menu is known for local specialities such as *Schweinebraten* – roasted pork with dumplings and red cabbage. There are light fish dishes and fresh salads too. Service is excellent and every Monday night there is a jazz band.

AUGSBURG Symposium
Gögginger Straße 82, 86159 **Tel** *(0821) 5976319*   🔲🎒🔲🔲   €€

With its lush green interior and bamboo tables, this Greek restaurant is anything but typical. Flavourful meat dishes include souvlaki and steaks, grilled to a tender perfection on a lava-stone grill. Vegetarians can choose from original noodle and salad recipes. Reserve ahead if you can, as it's popular, especially at weekends.

AUGSBURG Magnolia Restaurant im Glaspalast
Beim Glaspalast 1, 86153 **Tel** *(0821) 3199999*   🔲🔲🔲   €€€

Magnolia offers a refined, modern international menu. It is housed in a listed industrial glass building, alongside original works of art. The menu changes weekly. Try the tuna tartar with caviar *crème fraiche* and rocket, or Provençale fillet of beef with *foie gras*. Fish dishes are equally impressive, as are much simpler creations.

BAMBERG Schlenkerla
Dominikanerstraße 6, 96049 **Tel** *(0951) 56060*   🔳🎒🔲   €

A Bamberg institution, this historic brewpub is best known for its gorgeous *Rauchbier*, a smoky beer exported all over the world. The cuisine is straightforward Franconian: steamed sausages, *Leberkäse* (spicy meatloaf), and roast duck with *Kloss und Soss* (dumplings and savoury brown sauce). Niches and nooks abound for quiet conversations.

BAMBERG St Nepomuk
Obere Mühlbrücke 9, 96049 **Tel** *(0951) 98420*   🔲   €€

Dine in a traditional restaurant which has been a staple in the community for centuries. Good selection of game and fish dishes as well as accompanying local wines and beers. The cuisine is generally international. Part of a former mill, it has a charming atmosphere and great views across the river and the town.

BAYREUTH Kraftraum
Sophienstraße 16, 95444 **Tel** *(0921) 8002515*   🔳🎒🔲   €

Seeking a break from heavy meat dishes? If so, the "Weights Room" fits the bill. Tasty organic dishes such as vegetable noodle gratin, savoury pancakes and a dozen-odd fresh salads are ideal for health-conscious grazing. A favourite student hang-out, the restaurant is a five-minute walk from Bayreuth's renowned opera house.

BAYREUTH Restaurant Lohmühle
Badstraße 37, 95444 **Tel** *(0921) 53060*   🔲🔲🔲   €€

Freshwater fish is the speciality here, all fattened up and caught in the restaurant's own pond. Look out for trout, carp and blue wels catfish on the menu. There is also a good choice of regional Franconian wines to complement the food. Just a stroll from the town centre, it is housed in a quaint old tannery at the edge of a babbling brook.

BAYREUTH Schlossgaststätte Eremitage
Eremitage 6, 95448 **Tel** *(0921) 799970*

An incredibly beautiful setting in the castle where there is also a terrace for alfresco summer dining, an orangerie for the afternoon or aperitifs and a café. Excellent cuisine, service and international wines. Highly recommended is the fine perch, or steak in balsamic and shallott sauce with rocket roast potatoes. The desserts are also exquisite.

BAYRISCHZELL Der Alpenhof
Osterhofen 1, 83735 **Tel** *(08023) 90650*

High quality, Michelin-starred Bavarian and international specials. Fish, game, meat, vegetables and superb desserts. Situated south of Munich near the Austrian border, in an Alpine village close to the Tegernsee and with splendid Alpine views. There is a very welcoming comfortable atmosphere.

BERCHTESGADEN Bräustüberl
Bräuhausstraße 13, 83471 **Tel** *(08652) 976724*

For typical Bavarian cuisine in quaint surrounds, this venerable brewhouse and eatery with a pretty courtyard takes some beating. The menu ranges from bite-sized snacks to giant portions of *Schnitzel*, goulash, fish, pork steak and salads, and service is fast and cordial. The atmosphere is wonderfully relaxed and children have room to romp.

BURGHAUSEN Bayerische Alm
Robert-Koch-Str. 211, 84489 **Tel** *(08677) 9820*

Guests come here not only for the excellent Austrian and Mediterranean specialties, but also for the unrivalled view of Europe's longest castle with the Alps as a backdrop. Dine outdoors in the beer garden or on the terraces in warm weather. Local produce is favoured. Part of the Landhotel Reisingers Bayerische Alm *(see p500)*.

COBURG Der Kräutergarten & Die Petersilie
Rosenauer Straße 30c, 96450 **Tel** *(09561) 426080*

A fine roast lamb in herbs and garlic served with French beans and potato gratin is one of the house specials, as is the rainbow trout in Riesling sauce. A fine establishment on the edge of Coburg with an authentic, cosy and rustic interior. Herbs play the lead role in the cuisine here, hence the name Krautergarten, "herb garden".

DINKELSBÜHL Zum kleinen Obristen
Dr.Martin-Luther-Straße 1, 91550 **Tel** *(09851) 57700*

A superb restaurant located in the centre of the old town in Hotel Eisenkrug's ancient vaulted rooms. Gastronomic delights range from exotically spiced dishes to regional homely cuisine. The chef's seasonal specialities include game from September to March and asparagus in spring. There is a good selection of regional wines.

DINKELSBÜHL Deutsches Haus
Weinmarkt 3, 91550 **Tel** *(09851) 6058*

An impressive patrician's house dating back to 1440 is the setting for this hotel *(see p500)* and restaurant. Traditional German food with home-made specialities and light creative dishes are served in three different rooms, as well as outside in summer. Choose from high quality meat, fish and vegetables. The whole place is steeped in history.

EICHSTÄTT Gasthof Krone
Domplatz 3, 85072 **Tel** *(08421) 4406*

This restaurant is situated in a family-run guesthouse dating from 1670, in the centre of Eischstätt, directly opposite the Dom. The menu specialises in hearty Bavarian cuisine featuring fresh venison, delicate Juralamm (lamb from Altmuhltal), fruit and vegetables from local farmers and fresh fish.

FREISING Zur Alten Schießstätte
Dr.-v.-Daller-Straße 1-3, 85356 **Tel** *(08161) 5320*

Within the Dorint hotel in Freising, this restaurant has a good and well-deserved reputation for high quality Bavarian cuisine. Just a stroll from the historic centre of the town, which is close to Munich's airport and 30 minutes from Munich city centre. It has a 470-year-old vaulted beer cellar and a beer garden under chestnut trees.

FÜSSEN Steakhaus Füssen
Tiroler Straße 31, 87629 **Tel** *(08362) 509883*

This family eatery serves up a cross-section of the wild kingdom: ostrich, bison, and crocodile feature alongside thick juicy beef steaks that would do a Texan proud. If you're still not full, the side dishes of potato wedges, ratatouille, salads and corn on the cob will do the trick. By the Lechfall car park south of town, close to the Austrian border.

FÜSSEN Treff Hotel Luitpoldpark
Luitpoldstraße 1, 87629 **Tel** *(08362) 9040*

This magnificent hotel *(see p501)* offers various gastronomic treats, from the elegant restaurant Kurfürst von Bayern with its Bavarian specialities and international gourmet cuisine, to the cosy and traditional tavern Lautenmacher Stube, the Viennese café or even a Mexican restaurant.

GARMISCH-PARTENKIRCHEN Best Western Hotel Obermühle
Mühlstraße 22, 82467 **Tel** *(08821) 7040*

The Mühlenstube restaurant in the Best Western Hotel Obermühle is a mere five-minute stroll from the centre of Garmisch, and boasts magnificent views of Mt Zugspitz and other Alpine peaks. Open for both lunch and dinner, it offers an international menu, as well as the Mill Wheel bar (Mühlradl) where you can feast on Bavarian specialities.

GARMISCH-PARTENKIRCHEN Reindl's

Bahnhofstraße 15, 82467 **Tel** *(08821) 943870*

This top restaurant is found in the Partenkirchner Hof Hotel. With a long-standing tradition of fine cuisine, excellent service and refined atmosphere, the current chef presents a Bavarian menu with a classic French leaning. From the marinated wild salmon to veal kidneys, rack of lamb or venison, expect great quality and some wonderful wines.

GARMISCH-PARTENKIRCHEN Grand Hotel Sonnenbichl

Burgstraße 97, 82467 **Tel** *(08821) 7020*

Set in fabulous Alpine scenery, Grand Hotel Sonnenbichl's fine gourmet restaurant is called the Blue Salon. The impressive Art Nouveau building offers magnificent views of the mountains. In sunny weather guests can dine out on the terrace. The Blue Salon serves a fine variety of international dishes in classic elegant decor.

INGOLSTADT Weissbräuhaus zum Herrnbräu

Dollstraße 3, 85049 **Tel** *(0841) 32890*

Honest, hearty Bavarian fare is always served with a smile at this homely restaurant in the heart of Ingolstadt. Bright honey-coloured wood and farmhouse tablecloths set the tone for roast pig in dark beer sauce or giant potato dumplings with bacon-slaw salad. Wash it all down with a foamy Herrnbräu wheat beer.

KEMPTEN Peterhof

Salzstraße 1, 87435 **Tel** *(0831) 52440*

The Peterhof hotel is conveniently located in the heart of Kempten, next to the historical city centre and the pedestrianized area. It has a smart, modern restaurant which serves a variety of Italian dishes. It is familiar, informal and contemporary. Enjoy several light courses with Italian wine, rounded off by a great espresso.

LANDSHUT Schloss Schönbrunn

Schönbrunn 1, 84036 **Tel** *(0871) 95220*

Situated just outside Landshut in a magnificent pale pink 17th-century Bavarian castle, this classic, vaulted hotel and restaurant is the place to try some good old-fashioned Bavarian cooking. The hearty meals in traditional style form the basis of the menu, but the chef also serves international dishes. Wonderful beer garden too.

LINDAU Alte Post

Fischergasse 3, 88131 **Tel** *(08382) 93460*

This attractive family-run restaurant was built in 1700 and offers diners a roof terrace, tables alfresco in the secluded square or indoor dining in a cosy room. Located in a quiet corner of the old town on the island. Local produce is used to create a variety of simple to gourmet meals with a hint of tradition. Families with children are welcome.

LINDAU Gasthaus zum Sünfzen

Maximilianstraße 1, 88131 **Tel** *(08382) 5865*

This ancient, rustic tavern draws the locals with its Bavarian and Swabian delights, served by waiters in traditional dress. The house butcher turns dishes like pepper steak in cognac sauce, leg of wild hare or roast lamb into masterpieces. Being close to wine-growing country, it offers fine local vintages including delicate Rieslings.

LINDAU Villino

Hoyerberg 34, 88131 **Tel** *(08382) 93450*

Run by the young family Fischer, the Villino hotel and its restaurant *(see p501)* have a wonderfully warm atmosphere. Close to the lake in an idyllic garden setting, you can dine on the peaceful terrace under the shade of the trees. Enjoy the high quality dishes that combine the cuisines of Asia and Italy.

NEUBURG AN DER DONAU Zum Klosterbräu

Kirchplatz 1, 86633 **Tel** *(08431) 67750*

A well-established restaurant dating back to 1744, it is run by a young family and a creative chef. You can either dine in the slightly more private Jakobsstube for a romantic meal, or the cosy Gaststube specializing in typical high quality Bavarian cuisine and a Sunday roast. There is also a romantic garden for alfresco dining in fine weather.

NEU-ULM Landhof Meinl

Marbacher Straße 4, 89233 **Tel** *(0731) 70520*

This hotel-restaurant has a welcoming rustic feel with a touch of modern elegance. Set in quiet country surroundings (part of the so-called Silence hotel chain), the food served here is influenced by Swabian Alb cuisine. Try the lovely fresh salads with fish or chicken breast, or turkey in creamed pepper sauce with pan-fried potato *rösti*.

NÜRNBERG Sebald

Weinmarkt 14, 90403 **Tel** *(0911) 381303*

A smart contemporary restaurant in the centre of the old town. The chef combines his global experience to serve appetizing dishes with a German and Italian predominance, from *vitello tonnato* to clear oxtail soup, scallops, *Wiener Schnitzel*, fish and meat dishes. The cuisine does not disappoint. It is very popular, so be sure to book.

NÜRNBERG Wonka

Johannisstraße 38, 90419 **Tel** *(0911) 396215*

A true gem, housed in a former bakery. It offers an excellent range of tasty dishes with a slightly exotic flair, from soups to fish, seafood and desserts. Good, friendly service and a wine list with each wine offered by the glass. Moderate prices for the city and highly recommended for the atmosphere and food.

Key to Price Guide *see p526* **Key to Symbols** *see back cover flap*

NÜRNBERG Essigbrätlein €€€€€
Weinmarkt 3, 90403 Tel (0911) 225131

Just a stroll away from the main market square, this small intimate restaurant only has 20 tables so booking ahead is essential. Tightly packed, cosy and familiar, there is excellent food, staff and wines. You can choose from the daily changing menu or let the head waiter and sommelier advise you. Delicious fish dishes plus exquisite desserts.

OBERAMMERGAU Böld €€€
König-Ludwig-Straße 10, 82487 Tel (08822) 9120

The restaurant in this classic chalet-style hotel offers traditional Bavarian hospitality. Expect a warm welcome, rustic but smart decor and good quality fare based on regional recipes and fresh local produce. You can decide between the restaurant, bar or sun terrace. It has a spectacular view of the surrounding mountains.

OBERSTDORF Exquisit €€€
Prinzenstraße 17, 87561 Tel (08322) 96330

Set in an Alpine paradise with terraces overlooking sweeping lawns where guests can relax and dine in summer. A cosy country-style Bavarian restaurant, decked out in blue plaid, with very attentive, friendly but unobtrusive waiting staff. The cuisine is varied, from gourmet to low calorie, just let them know what you prefer

PASSAU Christophorus Stüberl €
Pfaffengasse 7, 94032 Tel (0851) 7568090

For hearty home cooking head to the old-fashioned Christophorus Stüberl in a narrow old street in the heart of Passau. In addition to traditional regional cuisine they offer international dishes such as steaks and fish. It is nestled in a cobbled street between the cathedral and the Danube and the owners also sell fine Italian gourmet products.

PASSAU Heilig-Geist-Stift Stiftskeller €€€
Heilig-Geist-Gasse 4, 94032 Tel (0851) 2607

Dark wood panelling throughout with a historical feel and old tiled stoves. Dinner is served in the hunting room or bishop's room, where coats of arms, hunting trophies and old prints adorn the walls. This rustic restaurant and wine bar specialize in Bavarian food. Try the freshwater fish caught in the local rivers. Closed Wednesday.

REGENSBURG Rosenpalais €€€
Minoritenweg 20, 93047 Tel (0941) 5997579

The ground floor of this beautiful palace is taken over by the restaurant. The delightful Baroque rooms on the first floor are only used for special occasions. There are high ceilings, cool simple rooms, elegant style, large windows and a rose garden. The high standard of cuisine has its roots in the local Oberpfalz cooking with game and meat dishes dominating.

REGENSBURG Restaurant Gänsbauer €€€€
Keplerstraße10, 93047 Tel (0941) 57858

A light Mediterranean cuisine is served in this historic spot with a long-standing reputation as one of the town's best restaurants. Whether you try the duck, fish, meat or seafood, it will not disappoint. There is a lovely little romantic courtyard garden too. They offer wine tastings in their wine store, Stehladl, plus cookery courses. Closed Sunday.

REGENSBURG David €€€€€
Krauterermarkt 3, 93047 Tel (0941) 561858

A lovely first-rate restaurant in the Bischofshof am Dom hotel (*see p502*) in the centre of town, it takes its name from the story of David and Goliath – murals of which, dating back to 1573, can be admired on the building's façade. They provide classic gourmet food and there are great views from the roof terrace.

ROTHENBURG OB DER TAUBER Gerberhaus Cafe €
Spitalgasse 25, 91541 Tel (09861) 94900

Try a local Franconian specialty such as *Nürnberger Bratwürstl mit Sauerkraut* (Nürnberg sausages with Sauerkraut) in the lovely beer garden of the Hotel Gerberhaus, below the city wall. The popular café offers great pastries and cappuccino. Other light meals are served accompanied by local wine from the Tauber valley.

ROTHENBURG OB DER TAUBER Eisenhut €€€€
Herrngasse 3–7, 91541 Tel (09861) 7050

A delicately pretty restaurant in the very old Eisenhut hotel. The dining room is reminiscent of an aristocratic country manor with antique furniture, rugs, paintings and elegant table decorations. It overlooks the tranquil garden at the back. Enjoy regional and international specials, local wines and music from the hotel's piano bar in the next room.

WÜRZBURG Auflauf €
Peterplatz 5, 97070 Tel (0931) 571343

This popular student bistro in the old town centre specializes in casseroles and noodle gratins. You can assemble your own creation from a country-themed list of meat and vegetarian ingredients, including cheeses and sauces. Everything is served piping hot by staff known for their friendly, easy-going manner.

WÜRZBURG Zum Lamm €€€
Hauptstraße 76, 97204 Tel (0931) 3045630

The Lamb is a well-known restaurant in the region. Established back in 1732 it used to serve crusaders. Today, the guests are both locals and tourists who come for the Franconian and international cuisine, the cosy feel and the romantic courtyard garden in summer. The emphasis is on locally farmed produce and seasonal recipes.

WÜRZBURG Schloss Steinburg
Auf dem Steinberg, 97080 **Tel** *(0931) 97020*

The romantic Steinburg castle provides the attractive setting for this hotel and restaurant. It boasts fabulous views over the town from the garden terrace in fine weather. Steeped in history the castle was first mentioned in 1236. Enjoy German gourmet specialities with excellent service. Perhaps book a romantic candlelit dinner for two.

BADEN-WURTTEMBERG

BADEN-BADEN Löwenbräu
Gernsbacher Straße 9, 76530 **Tel** *(07221) 22311*

This cavernous, non-touristy restaurant on the edge of the Black Forest serves up original Bavarian cuisine and big mugs of Löwenbräu, the legendary Munich brew. Generous portions of pork roast or *Weisswurst* (veal sausage flecked with parsley) taste wonderful in the leafy beer garden or under the vaulted ceiling of the dining hall.

BADEN-BADEN Besitos
Lange Straße 79, 76530 **Tel** *(07221) 973298*

This popular outlet of a Spanish tapas chain has a decidedly non-chain feel. A lounge atmosphere prevails as 20-somethings sip cocktails on the terrace or (in winter) on sofas next to a roaring fire. Middle Eastern tabouleh, crayfish in honey-mustard sauce and Spanish chorizo sausage are among the dozens of hot and cold tapas on offer.

BADEN-BADEN Piemonte
Hans-Bredow-Straße 20, 76530 **Tel** *(07221) 300990*

An attractive restaurant within the Tannenhof hotel *(see p503)* overlooking Baden-Baden in the foothills of the Black Forest. It is set in peaceful surroundings away from the tourist bustle and has a small stylish dining room. It was refurbished in early 2006. The chef re-creates Northern Italian cuisine with some Piedmontese specials.

BADEN-BADEN-NEUWEIER Restaurant im Schloss Neuweier
Mauerbergstraße 21, 76534 **Tel** *(07223) 800870*

In 2004 German chef, Armin Röttele, took over the Neuweier castle with his wife, where they offer rooms as well as a fantastic restaurant. Try the castle's own fine wine and gourmet delights such as roast saddle of suckling-pig in an orange cumin crust with asparagus risotto, or smoked sole on a basil purée, and some amazing cheeses.

BADEN-BADEN-NEUWEIER Zum Alde Gott
Weinstraße 10, 76534 **Tel** *(07223) 5513*

The vineyards of Neuweier are the lovely setting for this family-run, traditional German restaurant. Dishes include regional specials cooked with a light touch, such as home-made goose-liver pâté, pheasant with kale purée and chestnuts and figs in beer batter. To accompany the food ask for their great selection of Baden wines.

BRAUNSBACH Schloss Döttingen
Buchsteige 2, 74542 **Tel** *(07906) 1010*

A romantic, relaxing atmosphere reigns in this hotel-restaurant, which is part of Schloss Döttingen, a 12th-century hunting lodge. Choose between the elegant restaurant, the wine bar, café, terrace on balmy evenings or drawing rooms with open fire on cold nights. Enjoy regional Hohenlohe specialities, especially the locally farmed meat.

FREIBURG Martin's Bräu
Kaiser Joseph Straße 237, 79098 **Tel** *(0761) 387000*

Germany has oodles of microbreweries, many of them tiny affairs pumping out a few thousand hectolitres a year. Martin's Bräu is proudly small-time, and charms with a rustic cellar pub serving brews to crowds of thirsty regulars. Steaks, salads and noodle dishes, plus some tasty beer snacks keep the suds from going to your head.

FREIBURG Enoteca
Gerberau 21, 79098 **Tel** *(0761) 3899130*

With 20 years of experience, Enoteca is one of Freiburg's leading restaurants. It offers a high level of light but classic Italian cuisine, where the emphasis is on simplicity and wonderful fresh produce. There are several menus to choose from, a simple choice, the fish menu, daily menu or *à la carte*. The dining room is stylish and understated.

HEIDELBERG Schlossweinstube
Im Schlosshof, 69117 **Tel** *(06221) 8727000*

In the magnificent old Heidelberg castle, this stylish and spacious restaurant offers modern cuisine of international and regional dishes. Good choices are fish, duck or game. For a special treat book a candlelit dinner for two. There is also a lovely terrace to dine outdoors on warm evenings. There are fish and vegetarian menus.

HEIDELBERG Simplicissimus
Ingrimstraße 16, 69117 **Tel** *(06221) 183336*

Owing to the busy central location in Heidelberg's old town, booking is recommended. Tourists and locals flock here for the simple but outstanding cuisine, combining regional fresh produce, French flavours and good wines. Sit in the intimate dining room or in the flower-filled courtyard. Wine-tasting events take place every first Friday of the month.

HEILBRONN Grüner Kranz 🔥 💶💶

Lohtorstraße 9, 74072 **Tel** *(07131) 96170*

This friendly little town hotel has a lovely restaurant where you can sample some simple local Swabian specialities as well as more international gourmet dishes. Run by a young couple who welcome families and young children, there are good local beef dishes on the menu, plus salads and local *Spätzle* noodles. Be sure to try one of the region's wines.

KARLSRUHE Ketterer 💶💶💶

Bahnhofplatz 14–16, 76137 **Tel** *(0721) 3715112*

The impressive Residenz hotel with its solid pillared arcade is home to the smart Ketterer restaurant. Locally grown Wurttemberg asparagus is a house speciality, worked into a variety of dishes when in season. Other typical favourites are the pork in gravy and the doughy *Spätzle* noodles which crop up all over the region. Also has a bistro and terrace.

KARLSRUHE Oberländer Weinstube 💶💶💶💶💶

Akademiestraße 7, 76133 **Tel** *(0721) 25066*

Tradition and service rank high in this well-established family-run restaurant. The wood-panelled interior with tiled corner stoves provides a cosy atmosphere. The creative modern chef offers star-rated combinations using traditional recipes with modern flair. For example, salmon and perch roulade on pearl barley risotto with wild garlic butter.

KARLSRUHE-DURLACH Zum Ochsen 💶💶💶💶💶

Pfinzstraße 64, 76227 **Tel** *(0721) 943860*

The menu at the renowned Zum Ochsen is dominated by French dishes. The fish is delicate and the cuisine creative. Try the Breton red mullet fillets on fennel salad, glazed dove breast on chanterelle mushrooms or marinated lamb fillets on Provençale vegetable salad. The lobster salad in warm orange butter is a house special.

KONSTANZ Die Bleiche 💶💶

Bleichstraße 8, 78467 **Tel** *(07531) 9422860*

Housed in a former bleaching factory owned by the local tent company Stromeyer, this restaurant features lofty rooms, friendly service and a great beer garden in summer. You look right onto the Rhine flowing past. A variety of regional dishes are served and they also offer an affordable lunchtime buffet. Sundays is a brunch buffet and Thursdays a fish buffet.

KONSTANZ Rheinterasse 💶💶

Spanierstraße 5, 78467 **Tel** *(07531) 56093*

A wonderful setting next to the Rhine public bathing spot. Very popular in the summer especially with families as the children can play on the lawns next door. Also favoured by the fashionable who come for coffees, dinner or music in the early hours. It has the best terrace from which to watch the sunset. International cuisine and good wines.

LUDWIGSBURG Goldener Pflug 💶💶

Dorfstraße 4–6, 71636 **Tel** *(07141) 44110*

A friendly, informal little restaurant, part of the hotel of the same name. The Golden Plough serves a wide choice of familiar regional dishes with both a daily and standard menu. Try the local variety of soup with *Maultaschen* (filled noodle parcels) or the beef roasted in onions and red wine. The cheese *Spätzle* noodles are particularly good.

MANNHEIM Gasthof zum Ochsen 💶💶

Hauptstraße 70, 68259 **Tel** *(0621) 799550*

Housed in a listed building dating back to 1632, this restaurant can be found in the Freudenheim area of Mannheim. Despite its age, it offers a contemporary atmosphere, simple styling and a warm welcome. The menu changes seasonally. Excellent fish dishes, locally farmed ox and a fine mixed grill.

MANNHEIM Hahnhof 💶💶💶💶

Keplerstraße 32, 68165 **Tel** *(0621) 447455*

Conveniently located just a stroll from the Arts Centre in central Mannheim, the Hahnhof is a rustic and convivial place to eat. Expect old stained-glass windows, chequered tablecloths and geraniums in the windows. It offers friendly service, good wines and regional seasonal specials, such as Viennese cutlets, truffles, game and fresh fish.

MARBACH Schillerhöhe 💶💶

Schillerhöhe 12, 71672 **Tel** *(07144) 34081*

A timeless elegance fills the Schillerhöhe. The international gourmet cuisine makes it the best in the area. Enjoy a meal either by candlelight or on the terrace with a view across the Neckar valley. Delicious salads with barbary duck breast or scallops on a bed of fresh crisp leaves. We also recommend the various fish, from snapper to bass.

MAULBRONN Klosterschmiede 💶💶

Klosterhof, 75433 **Tel** *(07043) 1080*

Part of a sprawling monastery, this cosy eatery occupies a historic timber-framed house in the courtyard. First-time visitors should try the *Maultaschen*, the Swabian ravioli braised to perfection in numerous meat and vegetarian versions. The wine cellar is stocked with fine whites from surrounding vineyards.

MEERSBURG Gutsschänke Meersburg 💶💶

Seminarstraße 6, 88709 **Tel** *(07532) 807630*

Run by a state-owned vineyard, this classy restaurant offers sweeping views over Lake Constance and a regional wine selection that is second to none. The German-international cuisine wins rave reviews from critics without putting a serious dent in your wallet. Consider picking up a bottle of the prized local Weissherbst (a rosé) in the wine shop.

RAVENSBURG Gasthof Engel

Marienplatz 71, 88212 **Tel** *(0751) 3636130*

A traditional establishment, a favourite with visitors since 1878. In the heart of the pedestrianized area, it is a good place to stop for a meal while touring the town. Typical Swabian specials are on offer, plus regional beers and wines. Sit outdoors in front of the little guesthouse in summer. Good for either lunch or dinner.

RAVENSBURG Bärengarten

Schützenstraße 21, 88212 **Tel** *(0751) 18970720*

Conveniently located right in the town centre. It has the oldest and nicest beer garden in town plus a playground. Choose between menus with several courses or simple regional cooking, accompanied by local wines and beers. Good for the regional onion roast, *Maultaschen*, *Spätzle* noodles with cheese and sausage salad.

ROTTWEIL Haus zum Sternen

Hauptstraße 60, 78628 **Tel** *(0741) 53300*

High quality cuisine taking inspiration from traditional recipes and local home cooking is offered in this restaurant in the hotel of the same name *(see p505)*. House specials include beef consommé with herb pancake strips, Swabian onion roast beef with *Spätzle* dough noodles followed by apple pie and vanilla ice cream.

SALEM Reck's

Bahnhofstraße 111, 88682 **Tel** *(07553) 201*

This restaurant is in a hotel *(see p505)* just outside Salem in the beautiful landscape behind Lake Constance. All food is reared and grown locally, then lovingly prepared and presented. The owner-chef learned his trade in France and is now supported by his daughter, who has also trained at top places. Sophisticated dining with fresh, regional cooking.

SALEM Salmannsweiler Hof

Salmannsweilerweg 5, 88682 **Tel** *(07553) 92120*

This half-timbered house provides a relaxed rustic atmosphere, whether you dine indoors or on the terrace. Fish and the home-grown vegetables are recommended. They also have a good house schnapps. Try the large bowl of organic salad, freshly picked on the premises. They serve some good locally produced wines.

SCHWÄBISCH GMÜND Gasthaus Schwanen

Vordere Schmiedgasse 10, 73525 **Tel** *(07171) 66061*

A family-run restaurant in the old town occupying a historic, timber-framed building. Expect scrumptious local cuisine served with unforced, attentive hospitality – the kind of place where the chef comes out personally to chat with guests. The *spätzle* noodles and *Sauerbraten* (marinated pot roast) are legendary.

SCHWÄBISCH HALL Gallo Nero Ristorante

Moorstraße 2, 74523 **Tel** *(0791) 7055*

The distinguished chef runs one of the region's most discerning Italian restaurants with seating in an attractive, centuries-old courtyard. From its good-value pizzas to pricier fish and meat dishes, everything down to the classic espresso is made with loving care. The restaurant is located in Gallenkirchen, 11km (6 miles) north of Schwäbisch Hall.

STUTTGART Café Stella

Hauptstätter Straße 57, 70178 **Tel** *(0711) 6402583*

This is one of Stuttgart's most laid-back cafés, appealing in some way to just about everyone. From breakfast to lunch and afternoon coffee through to the evening hours, the clientele changes seamlessly with the time of day: students, business folk, hippies, retirees and local shop owners are all drawn to this cosy oasis.

STUTTGART Schlossgastronomie Solitude

Solitude 2, 70197 **Tel** *(0711) 4690770*

An impressive sprawling rococo castle from 1775 is the setting for this restaurant. The elegant restaurant offers dinners only. The chef concentrates on French cuisine with light dishes using fresh local produce, but also serves regional specials and international cooking. It has a lovely garden terrace. Closed Sun–Mon.

STUTTGART Trattoria da Loretta

Büchsenstraße 24, 70173 **Tel** *(0711) 2804507*

Loretta Petti opened her homely Tuscan Trattoria in 2005, after years running speciality food stores in Stuttgart. She cooks her way into the hearts of local Italophiles who love the regional cooking from her homeland. It is open, modern, laid-back and simple, in both design and cuisine.

STUTTGART Cube

Kleiner Schlossplatz 1, 70173 **Tel** *(0711) 2804441*

A gastronomic delight within Stuttgart's modern art museum. The vast glass cube houses this excellent restaurant for cultured dining on the fourth floor. Minimal, stylish and cosmopolitan, the Pacific Rim cuisine in the evenings offers fusion dishes such as honey-and-soya-glazed duck breast on chilli-vanilla cabbage.

TÜBINGEN Gasthaus Neckarmüller

Gartenstraße 4, 72074 **Tel** *(07071) 27848*

Not much to look at out front, this restaurant and brewpub is home to the town's best beer garden, with shady chestnuts and a stunning view over the Neckar River. Order a tasty house brew and a Rhineland *Flammkuchen* (thin-crust pizza), and watch the student punts drift past one of Tübingen's prettiest vistas.

Key to Price Guide *see p526* **Key to Symbols** *see back cover flap*

TÜBINGEN Carat

*Wöhrdstraße 7, 72072 **Tel** (07071) 139100*

Fine dining at the edge of the river in the heart of Tübingen. The modern hotel has floor-to-ceiling windows on the river side. It is just minutes across the bridge from the old town centre. Choose between a fine light regional cuisine or a coastal Mediterranean-style cuisine. There is a garden terrace in summer. Closed Sunday.

RHINELAND-PALATINATE AND SAARLAND

BACHARACH Bacharacher Hof

*Marktstraße 8, 55422 **Tel** (06743) 1422*

It takes some doing to stand out in a pretty wine town, and this old-world eatery does it with ease. Seasonal dishes such as venison ragout with fresh porcini or prime rump with cranberry sauce are given the chef's signature twist. The wine list is stuffed with classic vintages from the Rhine and Moselle valleys for quite reasonable prices.

BAD DÜRKHEIM Spötzl's Rebstöckel

*Lingenfelder Straße 2, 67098 **Tel** (06322) 987091*

On a sun-kissed stretch of the German Wine Road, this locale is a favourite stop of afternoon hikers, vinophiles and lovers of good food. The rump steak with braised potatoes is typical of honest Palatinate cuisine, prepared with melt-in-your mouth care. The delightful head waiter doles out good cheer along with some extraordinarily fruity wines.

DIEBLICH Halferschenke

*Hauptstraße 63, 56332 **Tel** (02607) 1008*

Located not far from the river, in a quiet area, the cuisine is international with some really fantastic Mediterranean dishes. The chef is happy to explore new tastes and has "surprise" menus for patrons, even going so far as to select accompanying wines. There is a nice terrace and beer garden.

HEIDESHEIM Crevette

*Budenheimer Weg 61, 55262 **Tel** (06132) 5270*

This is a spectacular palace of seafood. The restaurant is quite extensive, with a number of beautiful and atmospheric dining areas both inside and out. The staff are very friendly and helpful when deciding which white wine best accompanies their fantastic paella.

KOBLENZ Çafé Miljöö

*Gemüsegasse 8, 56068 **Tel** (0261) 14237*

This cosy bistro wins accolades with its friendly service, art exhibits and a mind-set that sees absolutely nothing wrong with a late afternoon breakfast. The cuisine is an eclectic mix of vegan and regional fare, with crepes, fried garlic shrimp and turkey steak all rubbing shoulders.

KOBLENZ Da Vinci

*Firmungstraße 32b, 56068 **Tel** (0261) 9215444*

An Italian restaurant with a sophisticated atmosphere and superb cuisine. There are often functions held here, such as wine tastings and fashion shows. The walls are covered with paintings and there is often soft music playing. The fresh ingredients and traditional Italian dishes have made this restaurant popular amongst the locals.

MAINZ EisGrub-Bräu

*Weißliliengasse 1a, 55116 **Tel** (06131) 221104*

Just a short distance from the Dom, this restaurant/beer hall is teeming with charm. They brew several kinds of beer, serving them to enthusiastic patrons who love the bustling ambience. Famous for their huge steaks, there is also a buffet in the cellar that is a great way to sample the various regional dishes they prepare.

MAINZ Der Halbe Mond

*In der Witz 12, 55252 **Tel** (06134) 23913*

A tiny restaurant offering some very special creations. Because there are only five tables it is a good idea to make reservations first. The dishes have a refined flavour and a French influence. The night is not complete without sampling their white and dark chocolate mousse with caramelized hazelnuts.

MARIA LAACH Seespiegel-Seehotel Maria Laach

*Orsteil Maria Laach, 56653 **Tel** (02652) 584512*

This unique and well-respected restaurant is located in a hotel *(see p507)* close to a 900-year-old monastery, which provides the kitchen with fresh produce. Seafood has a starring role on the menu, although their lamb fillet salad is tempting and seductive. The chef is sympathetic to vegetarians and provides them with fantastic fare.

NEUNKIRCHEN Hostellerie Bacher

*Limbacher Straße 2, 66539 **Tel** (06821) 31314*

Set in a stylish hotel, this is an elegant and impressive restaurant. Apart from the traditional elegance of the dining area there is also a wonderful winter garden, which has a glass roof and looks out onto the garden. The chef creates innovative cuisine that defies categorization and which is imaginatively presented.

SAARBRÜCKEN Schloss Halberg
Funkhaus Halberg, 66121 **Tel** *(0681) 63181*

Fantastically positioned in Halberg castle, the inside blends a modern design with the historic atmosphere of the castle and creates a wonderful environment. The cuisine is decidedly French in style, and the desserts are just gorgeous. Try the flambé. There is a terrace for outside dining in the warmer months.

SAARBRÜCKEN Villa Weismüller Restaurant Quack
Gersweilerstraße 43a, 66117 **Tel** *(0681) 52153*

An extensive restaurant with a number of different rooms, some of which are available for private functions. Apart from the restaurant there is a lounge, a beer garden and a brasserie. The restaurant is popular with the locals as well as travellers. The menu is quite large and comprehensive. Their salads are diverse and very filling.

SPEYER Feuerbachhaus
Allerheiligenstraße 9, 67346 **Tel** *(06232) 70448*

The birthplace of the German painter Anselm Feuerbach (1829–80). This wine bar/restaurant is part of a museum about him. Some rooms are dedicated to art. The menu is rather limited, although quite tasty, and the wine list has many good German wines, particularly whites. There is a garden area with tables.

SPEYER Zum alten Engel
Mühlturmstraße 5, 67346 **Tel** *(06232) 70914*

This innovative little cellar locale is steeped in the tradition of regional products, both from home and far-flung destinations. Whether Australian crocodile, exotic Asian fish dishes or grandma's secret *Sauerbraten* recipe, the long-serving chef prides himself on artisanal offerings. The wine list features vintages available only in the Palatinate.

SPEYER Zweierlei
Johannesstraße 1, 67346 **Tel** *(06232) 61110*

There is a calm ambience in this restaurant. The cuisine is mostly German and regional, with a few surprises thrown in. The service is great and they are very happy to help when it comes to the selection of both the dishes and the wine. The restaurant has a modern design that complements the eating experience.

ST INGBERT Die Alte Brauerei
Kaiserstraße 101, 66386 **Tel** *(06894) 92860*

Positioned in a historic building dating back to the 18th century, this restaurant has a very intimate ambience. The outside appears rustic, yet the inside reveals a modern design, which is reflected in the New German cuisine that has earned the chef a Michelin Bib Gourmand. Quite a good selection of German wines.

TRIER Römischer Kaiser-Taverne
Porta-Nigra-Platz 6, 54292 **Tel** *(0651) 97700*

This restaurant is inside the Römischer Kaiser hotel *(see p508)*, which is located at the edge of a scenic square in Trier. The specials are often interesting and tasty, especially the game dishes. There is an extensive wine list that has a number of international wines as well as a good selection of German wines. It is best to book on the weekends.

TRIER Pfeffermühle
Zurlaubener Ufer 76, 54292 **Tel** *(0651) 26133*

This restaurant overlooks the Mosel river and has a great view that can be enjoyed from their terrace in the warmer months. The building dates back to the 19th century and provides an intimate location to enjoy their international cuisine. The terrace is a little more sociable, as there are more tables outside.

WORMS La Carbonara
Adenauerring 4, 67547 **Tel** *(06241) 28220*

The occasional German celebrity notwithstanding, Worms' finest Italian eatery generally keeps a low profile. The interior is stylish and nuanced, in line with the gastronomic spirit of the place. In the chef's skilled hands, a simple buffalo mozzarella and tomato salad becomes a work of art, and *penne all'arrabiata* isn't so much pasta as poetry.

HESSE

ALSFELD Krone
Schellengasse 2, 36304 **Tel** *(06631) 4041*

Consistently great service and delicious food. The speciality would have to be the game dishes, which are always being refined and perfected. The dining area is relatively small and yet spacious at the same time, and the size ensures that the waiters and waitresses deliver a more personalized service.

BAD HOMBURG Jacobis
Louisenstraße 15, 61348 **Tel** *(06172) 269698*

In the baroque old quarter, this brasserie is the place to go for quality cocktails and honest, mouth-watering cuisine. The he-man XXL burger and chips is something like an ode to joy. Lamps and leather benches recall a train station waiting hall at the turn of the 20th century. Prices are quite fair for this swanky old-money town near Frankfurt.

BAD WILDUNGEN Wickenhof　　　　　　　　　　　　　€

Rilsteinstraße 67, 34537 **Tel** *(05621) 5190*

You know it as soon as you step in the door; you are in waffle country. Wall-to-wall waffles here, with over 100 varieties. The cuisine is not restricted to the mighty waffle, though, with many regional dishes in very generous proportions for hungry people. Along with the main restaurant there is a nice terrace and beer garden.

DARMSTADT Café Habibi　　　　　　　　　　　　　€

Landwehrstraße 13, 64293 **Tel** *(06151) 6602760*

The vegan and vegetarian creations in this old-fashioned café are nothing short of magical. Pakistani, Indian and Turkish spices seem to dance across the palate. Vegan tiramisu or the veggie gyros wraps taste just like the real thing, only better. This is a perfect spot to unwind after visiting one of Darmstadt's renowned art galleries.

EGELSBACH Schuhbeck`s Check Inn　　　　　　　　€€€

Flugplatz, 63329 **Tel** *(06103) 4859380*

Located next to a domestic airfield, with spectacular views of the runway. The restaurant itself is housed in an old hangar. The food is mostly regional, with a few hints of Asian and Mediterranean influences. There are a number of good vegetarian dishes. There is also a microbrewery and beer garden.

ELTVILLE Burg Schwarzenstein　　　　　　　　　€€€€€

Rosengasse 32, 65366 **Tel** *(06722) 99500*

This 19th-century faux Gothic castle, in Geisenheim, 12 km (7.5 miles) east of Eltville, is nestled in vineyards on the banks of the Rhine. As much care goes into the choice of ingredients (think Galloway beef or brill caught off Brittany) as their meticulous preparation. The wine list features award-winning wines from Schloss Johannesburg.

ELTVILLE AM RHEIN Alta Villa　　　　　　　　　€€

Gutenbergstraße 18, 65343 **Tel** *(06123) 705100*

This popular restaurant in the town centre matches historic charm and progressive cuisine in a seamless fashion. The menu is brief but eclectic: old friends such as cordon bleu and *Königsberger Klopse* (potato dumplings) turn up alongside such house gems as sea bass in wild garlic crust. Try to nab a table in the romantic courtyard out back.

FRANKFURT AM MAIN Malepartus　　　　　　　　　€

Bornheimer Landwehr 59, 60385 **Tel** *(069) 447910*

This earthy pub weaves a spell with its *Ebbelwoi* (apple wine) and hearty regional fare in a lively part of town. Hessian dishes such as *Grüne Sosse* (fresh herb purée with boiled eggs and potato) share the menu with the owner's Indian creations. The dark-panelled interior is stuffed to the gills with local bric-a-brac.

FRANKFURT AM MAIN Peninsula Atrium　　　　　　€€€

Konrad-Adenauer-Straße 7, 60313 **Tel** *(069) 2981-174*

Located in the Arabella Sheraton Hotel *(see p509)* this is an atmospheric, international restaurant. There are several restaurants in the hotel offering different cuisines – this one focuses on the Mediterranean. It has a high-ceiling glass cupola which adds to the elegant ambience. The chefs prepare the food in view of the diners.

FRANKFURT AM MAIN Zum Schwarzen Stern　　　　€€€

Römerberg 6, 60311 **Tel** *(069) 291279*

A restaurant serving traditional fare as well as international dishes. There is a specific menu section called "Grandmother's recipes" which caters to the taste for regional cuisine. It is located next to the cathedral in a very old building and there are references to it dating back to 1453.

FRANKFURT AM MAIN Villa Rothschild Kempinski　€€€€

Im Rothschildpark 1, 61462 **Tel** *(06174) 29080*

A must for gourmets, this elegant hotel-restaurant with two Michelin stars occupies a castle-like mansion 26 km (16 miles) to the northwest, in the town of Königstein. The award-winning team of chef Christoph Rainer specializes in a light version of high French cuisine. The sommelier will help select from hundreds of wines and champagnes.

FULDA Dachsbau　　　　　　　　　　　　　　　€€€

Pfandhausstraße 8, 36037 **Tel** *(0661) 74112*

Creative and elegant cuisine with inspired presentation is served here. Guests can feel the chef's personality in each of the dishes, which have French and regional influences. There is a large selection of wines to choose from, both German and international. The atmosphere in the restaurant is intimate and friendly, with an eclectic decor.

GIESSEN Köhler "Klemens"　　　　　　　　　　　€

Westenlage 33–35, 35390 **Tel** *(0641) 979990*

The hotel and adjoining restaurant are family owned and they take pride in the service they provide. The Klemens restaurant does not fail to deliver. Fantastic international cuisine with a French leaning is complemented by the extensive wine selection. There is also a wine bar with a huge selection of wines.

KASSEL Zum Steinernen Schweinchen　　　　　　€€€€€

Konrad-Adenauer-Straße 117, 34132 **Tel** *(0561) 940480*

The gourmet restaurant inside the Zum Steineren Schweinchen will delight and seduce you. There is a beautiful glass-enclosed dining area that offers diners views out into the garden. Their cuisine has become very highly acclaimed, and they now offer classes on how to perfect such dishes as their grilled lamb fillets on a bed of polenta.

KIEDRICH Klostermühle

Eltviller Straße 2, 65399 **Tel** *(06123) 4021*

A romantic escape well away from the tourist rabble, this former monastery serves traditional recipes and fruity Rheingau wines. A plump, rosy side of *Tafelspitz* (boiled roast beef) with a glass of Riesling is a terrific conclusion to a day's sightseeing along the Rhine. Vegetarians will enjoy the wine soup and meat-free *Flammkuchen* pizzas.

KLOSTER EBERBACH Klosterschänke

Pfortenhaus, 65346 **Tel** *(06723) 9930*

For something special, consider a romantic evening meal in this atmospheric former monastery. Scenes from the 1986 medieval thriller *The Name of the Rose* were shot here. The vaulted dining hall is a great backdrop for terrific seasonal dishes from the region. The signature house wines are made from grapes harvested on the property.

LIMBURG Wirsthaus Obermühle

Am Huttig 3, 65549 **Tel** *(06431) 5840084*

This cosy traditional restaurant is located next to an old mill dating back to the 12th century with the waters of the Lahn river flowing past. The wheel of the mill still moves on occasion, which can make the beer garden a little noisy, although the inside is peaceful. The food is excellent and reflects an ongoing evolution of German cuisine.

LORSCH Gaststätte Schillereck

Schillerstraße 27, 64653 **Tel** *(06251) 5701027*

In this sleepy riverside hamlet, Schillereck is an unexpected find for gastronomes on a budget. Fixed menus include a surprise starter (sent with the chef's personal greetings), a large fresh salad, perfectly turned main courses such as crispy roast duck or rump steak and a tasty dessert. Seasonal decor rounds out a memorable dining experience.

MARBURG Das Kleine Restaurant

Barfüssertor 25, 35037 **Tel** *(06421) 22293*

True to its name, this is a small restaurant although there is much in the way of flavour and style. There is a blend of French and German approaches to the food, with eclectic ingredients and creative presentation. The wine list extends to a very impressive, if not intimidating, 450 wines.

MICHELSTADT Drei Hasen

Braunstraße 5, 64720 **Tel** *(06061) 71017*

Its name means "three hares" and this hotel-restaurant is renowned in the area for its traditional ambience as well as its delectable regional cuisine, specifically the fish dishes. The interior has a strong rustic charm that fits the cuisine perfectly. They also have an extensive beer garden which is served by the same kitchen.

OFFENBACH Markthaus am Wilhelmsplatz

Bieberer Straße 9B, 63065 **Tel** *(06982) 80101883*

This restaurant is located in a traditional building in the Offenbach marketplace. It was originally built in 1911 as a shelter and storage for market tradesmen. Today, it is a cosy restaurant with an outside terrace, where you can watch the market. The cuisine is traditional, with dishes such as home-made wurst with black bread and potato dumplings.

RÜDESHEIM AM RHEIN Krone

Rheinuferstraße 10, 65685 **Tel** *(06722) 4030*

Situated in a hotel of the same name, Krone serves classic French and contemporary German cuisine in a traditional setting. In summer, the flower clad terrace offers scenic views over the Rhine. The extensive wine cellar includes a good range of regional wines.

WEILBURG Alte Reitschule

Langgasse 25, 35781 **Tel** *(06471) 5090 717*

This restaurant is located in the Schlosshotel Weilburg *(see p510)* and serves international and regional dishes in a picturesque setting. There is a terrace with outside seating that offers patrons a wonderful view of the castle and surrounding area. The restaurant often has offers on Sundays with reasonably priced set menus.

WETZLAR Der Postreiter

Parisergasse 20–22, 35578 **Tel** *(06441) 903444*

One of three restaurants in the Bürgerhof Hotel. This one serves international cuisine which makes the most of seasonally available produce. Their fish dishes are fresh and highly acclaimed, and there are some great vegetarian courses as well. The staff are happy to help you choose from their comprehensive wine list.

WIESBADEN Domäne Mechtildshausen

Domäne, 65205 **Tel** *(0611) 7374660*

A comfortable and relaxing restaurant with a Mediterranean style to the design and menu. The tables are decorated with fresh flowers, and there is seating in the beautiful garden. The restaurant is set in a complex comprising a bakery, guesthouse and farmlands, which provide the restaurant with most of its fresh produce.

WIESBADEN Kaefers Bistro

Kurhausplatz 1, 65189 **Tel** *(0611) 536200*

There is a busy atmosphere in this French-style bistro. The restaurant seats over 200 guests and it has no difficulty filling those seats. The food marries German portions and produce with a French subtlety, balancing the two with a good variety of wines from the region. There is often live music and they have a large terrace for outside dining.

Key to Price Guide *see p526* **Key to Symbols** *see back cover flap*

NORTH RHINE-WESTPHALIA

AACHEN Schloss Schönau €€€
Schönauer Allee 20, 52072 **Tel** *(0241) 173577*

Set in a castle dating from the 11th century, this restaurant has become well known for its set menus. The decor is stunning and opulent, rather apt for the inside of a castle. The chef likes seafood and the menu has a wide variety of different dishes. The Schloss itself is set in parkland and the restaurant has scenic views of the surrounding area.

AACHEN St. Benedikt €€€€€
Benediktusplatz 12, 52076 **Tel** *(02408) 2888*

This gourmet restaurant has a cottage feel about it, and provides an elegant atmosphere in which to enjoy the great cuisine. In spring the façade of the restaurant is covered with flowers and the inside is no less attractive, with antique chairs and oil paintings on the walls.

BIELEFELD Westfälische Hofstube €€
Niedernholz 2, 33699 **Tel** *(0521) 20900*

Located in the Oldentruper Hof Hotel, along with two other restaurants, the name suggests the cuisine, with the focus squarely on regional and traditional dishes from the Westphalia area, though there are international dishes on the menu as well. The service is warm and friendly and the atmosphere is comfortable.

BONN Zur Lindenwirtin Aennchen €€€
Aennchenplatz 2, 53173 **Tel** *(0228) 312051*

The interior is very ornate and the stylish setting creates an intimate and romantic atmosphere. The kitchen produces international dishes with a leaning towards France. Their carefully chosen wine list encompasses great wines from nine different countries. The service is impeccable and polite.

BONN-BAD GODESBERG Halbedel's Gasthaus €€€€€
Rheinallee 47, 53173 **Tel** *(0228) 354253*

A stone's throw from the Rhine in an exclusive part of town in a nondescript villa. The chef concocts fantastic and interesting international cuisine and is constantly inventing new dishes. They cater to the serious wine lover, too, with more than 700 different wines. The service is first rate.

BRÜHL Seerose €€
Römerstraße 1–7, 50321 **Tel** *(02232) 2040*

This restaurant is in the Ramada Treff hotel, which is situated between Bonn and Cologne in a forested area. They prepare international food in a modern and colourfully designed dining area. Nearby is the Schloss Brühl which often hosts outdoor concerts of classical music.

DETMOLD Strate's Brauhaus €
Lange Straße 35, 32756 **Tel** *(05231) 999945*

Until 1918 Detmold was the capital of a proud little principality, Lippe, and this beer temple smacks of feisty individuality. Strate's fruity pilsener and cloudy wheat beer can be enjoyed with specialities such as *lippischer Pickert* (crispy pan-baked potatoes with raisins). Guest areas filled with brewing paraphernalia are attractions in themselves.

DORTMUND Boomerang Australian Pub & Grill €€
Kuckelke 20, 44135 **Tel** *(0231) 2888734*

Lots of steak, lots of fried things and lots of beer. Such is the perception of Australian cuisine, and this restaurant is not bursting the bubble. The food is rigorous and heavy, and comes in impressive proportions. The atmosphere is unique and cheerful in a typically Australian manner.

DUISBURG Walsumer Hof €€
Rheinstraße 16, 47179 **Tel** *(0203) 491454*

Fish lovers will be in heaven. Start with a complimentary aperitif and salad of North Sea sprats before ordering the catch of the day, grilled, steamed or fried according to your personal order. Fried potatoes are all you can eat. The chef shows up in sailor's garb to shake your hand before you waddle home.

DÜSSELDORF Brauerei Uerige in der Altstadt €
Berger Straße 1, 40213 **Tel** *(0211) 866990*

The highlight at this legendary brewpub is *Altbier*, an amber bitter served since the dawn of time in little 0.25l glasses. The food is solid german fare (think pork leg, sausage and goulash) but the atmosphere in the half-dozen dimly-lit rooms including a knights' hall is unforgettable. The standing tables outside are popular with the regulars.

DÜSSELDORF Jimmy's Bar-Restaurant €€
Stromstraße 47, 40221 **Tel** *(0211) 30038303*

This popular and stylish restaurant is located in the harbour area of Düsseldorf, facing Frank O. Gehry's famous curved buildings. The Mediterranean-style menu features fish dishes such as gilthead and Dover sole. The basement lounge has live music on Friday and Saturday evenings.

DÜSSELDORF Libanon Restaurant

Berger Straße 19–21, 40213 **Tel** *(0211) 134917*

Guests are greeted by beautiful Middle-Eastern flair and style at this popular Lebanese restaurant. There is a large selection of authentic dishes with generous portions. The kitchen also caters for large functions of 20 or more people. There are belly-dancing shows in the evenings, adding to the already authentic atmosphere.

DÜSSELDORF Im Schiffchen

Kaiserswerther Markt 9, 40489 **Tel** *(0211) 401050*

Reservations should be made months in advance to this fabulous restaurant. It is one of only five restaurants in Germany to have been awarded three Michelin stars. The thoroughly informed staff will guide you through their extensive and creative menu, as well as their 900-strong wine list.

ESSEN Tio Pepe

Witteringstraße 92, 45130 **Tel** *(0201) 87898415*

Situated in the heart of Essen, just a few blocks from the Stadtgarten, Tio Pepe tempts diners with stylish decor and tasty Spanish dishes. Specialities are *paella valenciana* (order in advance), zarzuela and tapas. For dessert, try the delicious *crema catalana flambeada*, a caramelized custard dish similar to *crème brûlée*.

ESSEN Casino Zollverein

Gelsenkirchener Straße 181, 45309 **Tel** *(0201) 830240*

Located in an old mine, this casino and restaurant have a unique character. The styling and design is trendy, as is the food. They claim to "keep in touch" with the traditional miner's food, although the fillet of ostrich would probably not have appeared in the lunchbox of the average miner.

ESSEN Résidence

Auf der Forst 1, 45219 **Tel** *(02054) 8911*

Located in the beautiful Résidence Hotel, this restaurant attracts patrons from all over Germany. The holder of two Michelin stars, the chef produces irresistible cuisine that never fails to impress, particularly the fish dishes. The chef also gives private cooking lessons and is happy to chat with diners.

HAGEN Felsengarten

Wasserloses Tal 4, 58093 **Tel** *(02331) 3911 200*

This restaurant serves a wide variety of international dishes and caters to different tastes. The kitchen puts a lot of effort into the presentation of the food. The restaurant is located in the Mercure Hotel and there is an accompanying beer garden and terrace, which is pleasant in the summer months. It has modern, bright decor.

HÖXTER Bauernstube Schenkenküche

Kapenberg 6, 37671 **Tel** *(05278) 889*

This restaurant is idyllically set in a massive country farmhouse where rosy-cheeked kids play among the haystacks as their parents savour the remains of the day. Treat yourself to something decadent like oven-baked ham flambée with wild berry sauce. About 3 km (2 miles) northeast of Höxter. Reservations are a good idea.

KÖLN Engelbät

Engelbertstraße 7, 50674 **Tel** *(0221) 246914*

This beloved creperie lies in the heart of the trendy Belgian quarter. Prepared on a massive hotplate, the crêpes are reliably fresh, delicious and belt-buckling, stuffed with melted cheese, spinach, hamburger, fresh garlic and a range of other ingredients of your choice. Fans of gooey Nutella spread will be pleased with the desserts.

KÖLN Restaurant Pöttgen

Landmannstraße 19, 50825 **Tel** *(0221) 555246*

This traditional and cheerful restaurant has been in the Pöttgen family for four generations and is still going strong. The history of the restaurant and family can be seen in the charming decor. The food is always very tasty and is fantastic value. The chef has kept some dishes from the menus of his ancestors.

KÖLN Alcazar

Bismarckstraße 39a, 50672 **Tel** *(0221) 515733*

An institution in Cologne's humming nightlife quarter, this seductive little bar-eatery marries French and German cuisine in a pint-sized kitchen. Lunch is the best bet for a table, as evenings are often packed solid. During Carnival it's a hub of abandon with dancing and whole-hearted guzzling of Kölsch like there's no tomorrow.

KÖLN Il Carpaccio

Lindenstraße 5, 50674 **Tel** *(0221) 236487*

This is one of the best-known Italian restaurants in Cologne. One of their secrets is the top-quality ingredients they use – always fresh and authentic. Their home-made pasta is quite simply fantastic. Every Friday and Saturday there is live music. Great food, stylish design and a good wine selection.

KÖLN Landhaus Kuckuck

Olympiaweg 2, 50933 **Tel** *(0221) 485360*

This restaurant is located in a quiet part of Cologne and has a reputation for its fine cuisine as well as its very extensive wine cellar. The menu is changed frequently and the chef makes good use of seasonal produce. The outside seating area has a very pleasant ambience. They are happy to cater for large functions and groups.

Key to Price Guide *see p526* **Key to Symbols** *see back cover flap*

KÖLN L'escalier 🔲 €€€€
Brüsseler Straße 11, 50674 **Tel** *(0221) 2053998*

A French restaurant with a passion for cuisine. The elegant entrance reflects the style of the establishment, which is confirmed by the stylish dining area. Delicious food is on offer, especially the game dishes, and the service is fantastic. A special treat is their soufflé which takes 45 minutes to prepare, so be prepared for a wait.

KÖLN La Vision 🔲🔲🔲 €€€€€
Kaygasse 2, 50676 **Tel** *(0221) 20080*

Seated like a crown on the Hotel Im Wasserturm *(see p512)*, La Vision is on the top floor with a beautiful view over Cologne. The fine French cuisine is complemented by the outstanding wine list. The quality of the entire dining experience has earned the restaurant a Michelin star. There is also a terrace with panoramic views.

LEMGO Im Borke 🔲🔲 €€
Salzufler-Straße 132, 32657 **Tel** *(05266) 1691*

Housed in the Im Borke hotel *(see p512)*, this rustic little restaurant has a cosy charm. On the weekends it has a bustling and friendly atmosphere and attracts many people from the surrounding region. The menu is mainly regional cuisine with a number of international dishes as well, including some great Indian dishes.

MONSCHAU Wiesenthal 🔲🔲 €
Laufenstraße 82, 52156 **Tel** *(02472) 860*

The dining area of this restaurant is pleasant, mixing modernity with a refined style. Along with a bistro, the restaurant is located in the Carat Hotel. The cuisine is New German and the menu is changed often, with creative specials incorporating seasonal produce from the region.

MÜNSTER Alter Pulverturm 🔲 €
Breul 8, 8143 **Tel** *(0251) 45830*

This restaurant is where the old powder tower was sited, hence the name. The spot is quiet and peaceful and the adjoining beer garden is a great place to relax or meet friends before dining at the restaurant. They have an extensive menu with a variety of cuisines, including some very nice vegetarian dishes.

MÜNSTER Landhaus Eggert 🔲🔲 €€€
Zur Haskenau 81, 48157 **Tel** *(0251) 328040*

The hotel and restaurant are family owned and run, and there is a personal approach to the service. The chef produces fantastic and varied menus, exploring international cuisine while also showcasing the region's best dishes. The setting is a peaceful country area and the hotel was once a farm.

MÜNSTER Villa Medici €€€
Ostmarkstraße 15, 48145 **Tel** *(0251) 34218*

Boasting a simple design and imaginative food, this place is one of the best Italian restaurants in Germany. The dishes are wonderfully balanced and the presentation is genuinely exciting. There is a sophisticated simplicity to the cuisine, and the same can be said for the decor of the dining area, with colourful art contrasting the white walls.

PADERBORN Balthasar 🔲 €€€€
Warburger Straße 28, 33098 **Tel** *(05251) 24448*

The kitchen in this attractive and modern restaurant enthusiastically mixes art with food. The chef uses a variety of interesting ingredients to create new and imaginative dishes, and also suggests wines that would complement the food. The extensive wine list includes a 1928 Sauternes.

SIEGBURG Gaststätte zur Talsperre 🔲🔲 €
Braschosser Straße 55, 53721 **Tel** *(02241) 383988*

The experienced chef worked in a top Swiss resort before opening this charming half-timbered restaurant. Expect modern takes on classic dishes such as chanterelles in cream sauce, pangasius fillet or Holstein steak, washed down with a freshly tapped Bitburger. It's about 5 km (3 miles) east of town in the suburb of Braschoss.

TROISDORF Restaurant Forsthaus Telegraph 🔲 €€€€
Mauspfad 3, 53842 **Tel** *(02241) 76649*

This restaurant serves international dishes in a very refined setting. The sauces are rich and diverse, with the chef combining the best of all styles and cuisines. The restaurant operates a catering service as well as a food outlet. It has become extremely popular because of its ever-changing and innovative menus, so book ahead.

WUPPERTAL Scarpati 🔲 €€€€€
Scheffelstraße 41, 42327 **Tel** *(0202) 784074*

As the name suggests, this restaurant and hotel has Italian heritage and does it proud with their cuisine and service. Their pasta dishes are fresh and rich; definitely worth the calories. The ambience is relaxed and intimate, and the dining area has a pleasant view over the garden. There are rooms for private dinners and functions.

XANTEN Hotel van Bebber 🔲🔲🔲 €€€
Klever Straße 12, 46509 **Tel** *(02801) 6623*

Located in the hotel of the same name, this restaurant produces excellent traditional regional cuisine. Particular favourites among the locals are the chef's fish dishes. Apart from their traditionally styled dining area they also have a unique wine cellar with occasional live piano performances.

LOWER SAXONY, HAMBURG AND BREMEN

BAHRENFELD Graceland   €€

Stresemannstraße 374, 22761 **Tel** *(040) 89963100*

Cajun and Creole cooking, with more than a dash of an American influence, is on offer here. The food is really tasty and incorporates some spicy Central American cuisine as well. There is often live music and sometimes dancing at the restaurant, which has quite a large capacity. They do takeaway as well, if you need that fried catfish to go.

BRAUNSCHWEIG (BRUNSWICK) Herrendorf   €€

Am Magnitor 1, 38100 **Tel** *(0531) 47130*

Proclaiming itself to cater to "everybody's gums", this restaurant does a fine job living up to this proclamation. Housed in a building that dates back to 1476, it is part of the Stadthotel Magnitor, and is quite modern in design. The kitchen produces great regional fare, sometimes straying into French territory with their sauces.

BREMEN Meierei   €€

Im Bürgerpark, 28209 **Tel** *(0421) 3408619*

This restaurant was first opened in 1881. There is a Mediterranean flavour running through the menu, however, one should not overlook their fabulous rabbit *ragout*. The inside is inviting with a warm fireplace in the dining area which is dominated by earth tones. There is a large wine selection, especially Italian wines.

BREMEN Schröter's Leib und Seele   €€

Schnoor 13, 28195 **Tel** *0421 32 66 77*

Centrally located in the historic Schnoor quarter of Bremen, Schröter's Leib und Seele is a modern but homely upmarket restaurant. One of the area's best places to sample typical Bremen fare, the menu offers traditional dishes such as ox ribs or white bait with cucumber-mustard sauce. There are also a few vegetarian dishes on offer.

BREMEN Ratskeller   €€€

Am Markt, 28195 **Tel** *(0421) 3059888*

Bremen Ratskeller is housed in the oldest operating wine cellar in Germany, established over 600 years ago. There is a wine bar which offers over 600 different wines. The restaurant serves great international food in a truly magnificent dining area, complete with wood-panelled walls, chandeliers and wall paintings.

BREMEN Das Kleine Lokal   €€€€

Besselstraße 40, 28203 **Tel** *(0421) 7949084*

Each dish is a surprise at this modern restaurant. The creative presentation is reinforced by the unorthodox plate designs and perfectly suited to the stylish design of the dining area. The portions are petite and delicious. The sommelier is thoroughly knowledgeable and helpfully chatty.

BÜCKEBURG Ambiente   €€€

Herminstraße 11, 31675 **Tel** *(05722) 9670*

True to its name, the Ambiente restaurant (in the hotel of the same name) has a very serene and enjoyable dining area, with high glass ceilings and lots of indoor plants. The cuisine is mainly German and Italian, with large portions. As well as the great dining area there is a little garden where guests may dine in the warmer months.

CELLE Camelot   €€

Am Heiligen Kreuz 6, 29221 **Tel** *(05141) 6400*

Step back into the Middle Ages at Camelot, into what at first seems to be a redecorated dungeon. This restaurant creates an atmosphere emulating the days of knights and knaves, with cuisine to match. If you crave game dishes this is definitely the place for you. There are a number of shows in the evenings, fire-eating being just one example.

CELLE Endtenfang   €€€€€

Hannoversche Straße 55–56, 29221 **Tel** *(05141) 2010*

Located in the Fürstenhof Celle *(see p513)*, this is one of the most highly acclaimed restaurants in town. The chef produces fantastic French cuisine, with a number of Mediterranean influences as well. It has been awarded a Michelin star, not only for the great food but also for the outstanding service and unique location.

CLOPPENBURG Restaurant Margaux   €€€

Lange Straße 66, 49661 **Tel** *(04471) 2484*

This restaurant is located in the Hotel Schäfer. The young chef at this restaurant has a passion for cooking and it shows in the cuisine. There is a variety of different styles and ingredients to enjoy, with a special highlight being the bouillabaisse. There is a warm and friendly atmosphere.

EPPENDORF jus   €€

Lehmweg 30, 20251 **Tel** *(040) 42949654*

Seasonally influenced dishes with its finger on the pulse of modern cuisine. The chef marries traditional ingredients with subtlety and confidence. It is a small restaurant, but it is fast building a healthy reputation. Because of its size and popularity, it is becoming necessary to make reservations.

Key to Price Guide *see p526* **Key to Symbols** *see back cover flap*

GOTTINGEN Restaurant Gaudi €€€

Rote Straße 16, 37073 **Tel** *(0551) 5313001*

Dedicated to the life and works of the Spanish architect Antoni Gaudi (1852–1926), this restaurant provides some fine Spanish and Mediterranean cuisine. Apart from the exquisite fish dishes they also have a great tapas selection, which is popular at lunchtime. The design is unorthodox, just like Gaudi himself.

HAMBURG Die Bank €€

Hohe Bleichen 17, 20354 **Tel** *040 23 800 30*

Die Bank occupies a historic former bank building in the city centre. Attracting a business clientele for lunch and an arty crowd for dinner, the Bank's elegant dining hall is always buzzing. Chef Thomas Fisher creates unexpected variations of well-known local dishes with an emphasis on fresh fish and vegetables. The wine list is impressive.

HAMBURG Old Commercial Room €€

Englische Planke 10, 20459 **Tel** *040 366319*

A true Hamburg legend, the Old Commercial room offers tasty local dishes in a homely if somewhat kitsch maritime setting. It's famous for its *Labskaus* – a mix of beef and fish puree served with an egg, red beets and cucumbers. Other popular Hamburg dishes include *Scholle Finkenwerder* (plaice with bacon).

HAMBURG Calla €€€

Heiligengeistbrücke 4, 20459 **Tel** *(040) 368060*

The Calla is in the Steigenberger hotel along with a bistro and piano bar, which has live music. The high windows and open plan design create a bright atmosphere. The walls have been adorned with the designs of a Chinese restaurant. The menu has a very Asian flair to it, mixing a little European influence as well. Closed Sun & Mon.

HAMBURG Fischereihafen-Restaurant €€€

Grosse Elbstraße 143, 22767 **Tel** *(040) 381816*

This is the place to go for fresh, delicious seafood (though other dishes are offered). The large menu is changed often to suit the seasons. The terrace overlooks the water and has one of the best views in the harbour. The list of famous guests is longer than the extensive wine list and reflects the great food and outstanding service

HAMBURG Fischküche €€€

Kajen 12, 20459 **Tel** *(040) 365631*

Fresh fish and seafood are the fare in this restaurant. The decor leaves no doubt of the influence of the sea in this place, and the staff seem to know more about seafood than most fishermen. The crab dishes have earned the chef renown amongst the locals and visitors to the harbour. The wine list has been chosen with care.

HAMBURG Fischmarkt €€€

Ditmar-Koel-Straße 1, 20459 **Tel** *(040) 363809*

A bustling, friendly restaurant where they create some very exciting fish dishes. Housed inside the fish market after which it is named, the restaurant is popular among tourists who visit the area. The ambience inside is relaxed yet professional, with great staff who are very helpful when it comes to selecting dishes.

HAMBURG Henssler & Henssler €€€€

Große Elbstraße 160, 22767 **Tel** *040 38 69 90 00*

Located in the harbour dock area, this stylish and popular restaurant is set in a renovated warehouse. The restaurant, owned by renowned German TV chef Steffen Henssler and his father, serves a fusion of Californian and Japanese cuisine. The menu offers a variety of hot dishes and an impressive selection of creative sushi and sashimi.

HAMBURG Au Quai €€€€

Grosse Elbstraße 145, 22767 **Tel** *(040) 38037730*

Housed in a refurbished cold storage depot, the conversion has resulted in a fantastic place to try the best of Hamburg's seafood. Operated by a brother and sister, the kitchen reflects their heritage with great Mediterranean dishes and a subtle French influence that works well with the delicate fish-dominated menu.

HAMBURG Jacobs Restaurant €€€€€

Elbchaussee 401–403, 22609 **Tel** *(040) 822550*

This restaurant, situated in the beautiful Hotel Louis C. Jacob, is among the best in the city. The cuisine is international with a definite French infusion. There is also a wine cellar that keeps connoisseurs happily occupied for hours, with the help of the master sommelier. There is an adjacent wine bar and a terrace.

HAMBURG Tafelhaus €€€€€

Neumühlen 17, 22763 **Tel** *(040) 892760*

The chef in this elegant restaurant produces fantastic and innovative cuisine from all over the world. Of special renown are his Asiatic dishes. The terrace overlooks the harbour, although the dining area offers the more romantic atmosphere. The chef also gives cooking lessons to enthusiastic students.

HANNOVER Gallo Nero €€€

Gross-Buchholzer Kirchweg 72b, 30655 **Tel** *(0511) 5463434*

The "Black Rooster" offers top-quality Northern Italian cuisine, ranging from basic flavours and produce to more refined sauces and spices. The interior of the restaurant resembles a Tuscan art gallery, which gives a very intimate and unique atmosphere to enjoy their unpretentious food. They have a large selection of Italian wines.

HANNOVER Hindenburg Klassik

Gneisenaustraße 55, 30175 **Tel** *(0511) 858588*

This restaurant has been set-up in a way to reflect a traditional Italian eating area with long tables to accommodate the largest of families. There is a comprehensive specials menu that changes daily, and there is always their fantastic home-made pasta, which makes this place a favourite among the locals.

HANNOVER Le Chalet

Isernhagener Straße 21, 30161 **Tel** *(0511) 319588*

An intimate dining experience in an elegant part of town. The French cuisine has won popularity with its rich sauces and exquisite salads. The staff blend into the background until they are needed, at which time they seem to materialize out of thin air. This is particularly helpful when selecting wines, as they are experts. Closed Mon.

HANNOVER Restaurant Pier 51

Rudolf-von-Bennigsen-Ufer 51, 30173 **Tel** *(0511) 8071800*

This award-winning restaurant on the banks of Lake Masch is a stylish maritime hot spot for the city's party crowd who enjoy the elegant interior, the outside pier-style terrace, the exquisite cocktails and the light German and international fish, meat and pasta dishes (all of which can be ordered as half portions).

HANNOVER Clichy

Weißekreuzstraße 31, 30161 **Tel** *(0511) 312447*

The chef here conjures up some fantastic traditional German and French dishes. With rich sauces and strong flavours, the menu is forceful and entertaining. The staff are courteous and very helpful when it comes to choosing from the menu and wine list. Quite a busy restaurant, so make reservations.

HANNOVER Die Insel

Rudolf-von-Bennigsen-Ufer 81, 30519 **Tel** *(0511) 831214*

There is a picturesque view of nearby Lake Masch from the dining area. This restaurant attracts customers from the music industry to politics. The cuisine is hard to pin down, with some great regional dishes as well as some great oriental creations. The food is matched by the equally impressive wine selection.

HANNOVER Restaurant Titus

Wiehbergstraße 98, 30519 **Tel** *(0511) 835524*

This restaurant has one of the more unorthodox restaurant interiors. The fabulous creations that come out of the kitchen keep pace with the decor. The grilled venison in bitter chocolate is but one example of the innovative and experimental cuisine. They have a terrace which is open in the warmer months.

KÖNIGSLUTTER Merlin

Braunschweigerstraße 21a, 38154 **Tel** *(05353) 5030*

Part of the beautiful Königshof Hotel *(see p515)*, the Merlin is internationally recognized for its fantastic cuisine and character. During the day the high windows create a bright, open atmosphere and at night time the dark surrounds give a feeling of intimacy. The staff are generous with their time and the service is very good.

OLDENBURG Kiebitz-Stube

Europaplatz 4-6, 26123 **Tel** *(0441) 8080*

There are a few bistros and restaurants in the City Club Hotel, with the Kiebitz-Stube being the most elegant. There is a formal atmosphere in the evenings, with well-constructed set menus, but lunchtime is less formal. A terrace opens out over a peaceful garden, where it is possible to dine in the warmer months.

OSNABRÜCK Vila Real

Natruper-Tor-Wall 1, 49076 **Tel** *(0541) 60960*

An innovative restaurant that combines fresh ingredients with imagination. The chef alternates between Italian and Mediterranean cuisine and succeeds in every domain. The crayfish ravioli is just sublime. There is a large selection of wines, which is partly due to the adjoining Enoteca wine shop, which also has tapas evenings and wine tastings.

STADTHAGEN Fischhaus Blanke

Rathauspassage 5, 31655 **Tel** *(05721) 81786*

This restaurant has been serving the freshest seafood in town for over 80 years. They serve a vast variety of different fish, shellfish and everything else that lives in water. It is unpretentious and cosy, and the food speaks for itself. The owners have a seafood outlet which supplies superbly fresh produce for the restaurant.

WOLFENBÜTTEL Parkhotel Altes Kaffeehaus

Harztorwall 18, 38300 **Tel** *(05331) 8880*

Part of the Parkhotel *(see p516)*, the Altes Kaffeehaus is quite an elegant restaurant, offering good value cuisine with a number of vegetarian dishes. There is a wine grotto in the cellar which is quite attractive and has a vaulted brick roof that adds to the ambience. The overall cuisine is basic, regional fare with large portions.

WOLFSBURG La Fontaine

Gifhorner Straße 25, 38442 **Tel** *(05362) 9400*

La Fontaine serves cuisine that refuses to be categorized, combining the best of all styles and ingredients. A speciality is combining regional and international produce and ingredients to create innovative new tastes, and their venison with Shiitake mushrooms is a good example. There is a dining terrace open in the summer months.

Key to Price Guide *see p526* **Key to Symbols** *see back cover flap*

SCHLESWIG-HOLSTEIN

AHRENSBURG Berlin Milljöh
Große Straße 15, 22926 **Tel** *(04102) 52919*

This happy little restaurant is a fantastic place to enjoy local dishes at very affordable prices. More a tavern than a restaurant, the food is still satisfying and authentic. The atmosphere is a little dark because of the worn wooden furnishings, though it does have a comfortable and friendly ambience.

AHRENSBURG Le Marron
Lübecker Straße 10a, 22926 **Tel** *(04102) 2300*

Le Marron is in the Park Hotel Ahrensburg. The restaurant scores highly among international critics, especially for its fantastic and friendly service. The food is diverse with influences from all over the culinary spectrum. There is also a comfortable winter garden. They welcome families and there is a playroom for children.

BAD MALENTE Gartenhotel Weisser Hof
Vossstraße 45, 23714 **Tel** *(04523) 99250*

Set in a peaceful rural environment, this restaurant is a cosy place to sample the regional food. There is a warm and friendly atmosphere and the portions are generous. It is part of the Weisser Hof hotel *(see p510)*, which is situated in parkland. Many customers combine a trip to the relaxing wellness area in the hotel with a visit to the restaurant.

FLENSBURG Im Alten Speicher
Speicherlinie 44, 24937 **Tel** *(0461) 12018*

Generous portions and delicious seafood dishes. This is quite a large restaurant with a number of dining rooms and areas. They are well set-up for functions and large groups, and have a catering service as well. There is a somewhat understated outside terrace, which is best enjoyed in the afternoons.

HUSUM Eucken
Hotel Altes Gymnasium Söderstrasse 2-10, 25813 **Tel** *(04841) 8330*

Staged as a cosy hideaway in the romantic, red-brick Hotel Altes-Gymnasium, Eucken serves imaginative, Oriental-inspired dishes. The menu features exotic fish combined with light vegetables. A comprehensive wine list, superb service and the understated, North-German flair of Eucken adds to the overall style of this establishment.

KIEL Restaurant Bellevue
Bismarckallee 2, 24105 **Tel** *(0431) 38940*

Serving delicious seafood, the Bellevue Restaurant in Kiel also boasts an incredible vista over the Kiel fjord. You can watch the boats and ships passing by on the fjord, while dining in a grand room complete with attractive chandeliers. The restaurant offers a variety of organic dishes to suit all tastes.

LÜBECK Historischer Weinkeller
Koberg 6-8, 23552 **Tel** *(0451) 76234*

This unique restaurant is located in an 800-year-old wine cellar under a historic hospital. There is a medieval tone to the restaurant, which has retained the ambience of its heritage while at the same time creating a light and friendly atmosphere. Their fish and potato dishes have won the hearts of locals and tourists.

LÜBECK Wullenwever
Beckergrube 71, 23552 **Tel** *(0451) 704333*

A very elegant restaurant that offers a number of unique rooms and dining areas, the chef is liberal with his creations, happily giving out recipes to interested patrons. The set menus have been artfully chosen to give a perfect balance of tastes, and there are wine suggestions for each dish. It has become rather well-known, so book ahead.

RATZEBURG Hansa Hotel
Schrangenstraße 25, 23909 **Tel** *(04541) 2094*

The Hansa hotel and restaurant is in a quiet area on an island in Ratzeburg. The menu changes every fortnight and makes good use of seasonal vegetables and fish. The dining area is relatively small, which creates a mellow atmosphere and emphasizes the polite and unobtrusive service of the friendly staff.

SCHLESWIG Strandhalle
Strandweg 2, 24837 **Tel** *(04621) 9090*

This is a cheerful restaurant in a pleasant hotel. There is a definite family atmosphere and the restaurant is often booked for celebrations and functions. The restaurant and hotel are family owned and the staff are very welcoming. An open fireplace creates a cosy feeling in the wintertime and a beautiful terrace is used in the summer.

SIEK Alte Schule
Hauptstraße 44, 22962 **Tel** *(04107) 877310*

Located in an old schoolhouse, this restaurant has been going strong for over 30 years now and has been run by two successive generations. It serves mostly regional and German dishes, with some French affiliations. There are a few good vegetarian meals and a very good wine list with many German and French producers.

SYLT Sansibar
Hörnumer Straße 80, 25980 **Tel** *04651 96 46 46*

Sansibar is perhaps the most famous restaurant in Sylt and the island's most popular, often boisterous, hangout amongst German high society. The rustic, cottage-like setting, excellent service and maritime cuisine, with fresh fish and meat, and a huge wine cellar attract thousands of visitors each day. Reservations should be made well in advance.

SYLT Fährhaus
Heefwai 1, 25980 **Tel** *(04651) 93970*

This highly regarded restaurant has become one of the best on Sylt and is justifiably popular. The young chef, who has been awarded two Michelin stars, creates miracles with contrasting flavours and ingredients. The sommelier is happy to guide you through the 780 wines they have in the cellar.

SYLT Restaurant Jörg Müller
Süderstraße 8, 25980 **Tel** *(04651) 27788*

This leading restaurant is one of the most famous on the island, and attracts customers from all over Europe. The dining area is comfortable and unpretentious. The hotel is secondary in status to the restaurant and there are many packages incorporating dining. There is also cheerful and enthusiastic service.

UETERSEN La Cave
Marktstraße 2, 25436 **Tel** *(04122) 3640*

This restaurant delivers gourmet cuisine from Southern France and the Mediterranean. Of particular renown are their fish dishes, which are constantly changing in keeping with seasonal availability. The staff are helpful and friendly. As you would expect, they have a good selection of French wines.

MECKLENBURG-LOWER POMERANIA

AHLBECK Das Ahlbeck
Dünenstr. 48, 17419 **Tel** *(038378) 49940*

This restaurant, with its terrace overlooking the beach, is an excellent choice in summer, particularly for lovers of *Flammkuchen*, a kind of crispy German pizza, served here in several delicious varieties. The indoor dining area features vaulted windows and elegant classical decor. Service can be slow.

BAD DOBERAN Gourmet Restaurant Friedrich Franz
Prof.-Dr.-Vogel-Str. 16–18, Heiligendamm, 18209 **Tel** *(038203) 7400*

Friedrich Franz is a comfortable restaurant in the Grand Hotel Heiligendamm. The extensive menu includes regional and national dishes, as well as cuisine from the four corners of the globe, with an emphasis on European. The wine and beer lists are respectable. There are only ten tables so reservations are recommended. Closed Tue.

DASSOW Schlossgut Gross Schwansee
Am Park 1, 23942 **Tel** *(38827) 88480*

Located in a beautiful castle estate, this romantic, fine dining restaurant has an ancient vaulted ceiling and white interior. The menu, which focuses on Mediterranean cooking styles, changes every month. In warmer months, the terrace tables offer views of the sea. There is also a snug bar with a fireplace.

GREIFSWALD Wallensteinkeller
Markt 3, 17489 **Tel** *(03834) 855945*

This is one of two rustic restaurants in the region owned by the same proprietor. Finger foods and soups feature on the menu as well as potatoes and roasted pork entrées. Enjoy one of the many draught beers. The staff are friendly and there is an engaging atmosphere (look for the authentic suit of armour near the entrance).

GÜSTROW Marktkrug
Markt 14, 18273 **Tel** *(03843) 68 12 82*

This restaurant is situated in the centre of town and has two floors and a relaxing beer garden. The delicious food reminds you of typical Mecklenburgian home-cooked meals. Plums are very popular in regional gastronomy and you will find them here in abundance. Try the *Meckelbörger Rippenbraten*.

NEUBRANDENBURG Gasthaus "Zur Lohmühle"
Am Stargarder Tor, 17033 **Tel** *(0395) 5442843*

Set in a half-timbered water mill dating back to the 14th century, this inn offers traditional German food in a rustic atmosphere at the edge of the old town, right next to one of the ornate city gates. Home-cooked dishes include game, fish and Mecklenburg specialities.

NEUBRANDENBURG Zur Alten Münze
Burg 5, Burg Stargard, 17094 **Tel** *(039603) 274026*

A beautiful provincial estate with a wine *Stube* and restaurant on site. Step back in time and enjoy centuries-old traditions in this very uncomplicated eatery. The selection of wines is very good. The dishes on offer are typical of the region and high quality, made with the freshest of ingredients.

Key to Price Guide *see p526* **Key to Symbols** *see back cover flap*

RALSWIEK/RÜGEN Schlossrestaurant Ralswiek €€€
Parkstr. 35, 18528 **Tel** *(03838) 20 32 0*

This restaurant is in the Hotel Ralswiek, which is a former castle. Service is very attentive and the staff are warm and welcoming. The menu offers dishes based on international cuisine. Desserts include lemon panna cotta with wild berries and a wonderful tiramisu – both are very highly recommended.

ROSTOCK Zur Kogge €€
Wokrenter Str. 27, 18055 **Tel** *(0381) 4934493*

This restaurant is part of the oldest guesthouse in Rostock. The establishment's long history and resulting memorabilia decorate the walls. As you would expect, fish and seafood dominate the menu and are prepared well. Some vegetarian options can be found on the menu. There are several wines to choose from.

ROSTOCK Silo 4 €€€
Am Strande 3d, 18055 **Tel** *(0381) 458 58 00*

This restaurant is right by the water and overlooks the docks. It has a huge panoramic window offering great views. The service is courteous and they have a great wine list, including wines from Spain, Italy, Germany and South Africa. Check out the very cool bar, which radiates different colours of light during the evening.

ROSTOCK Chezann €€€€
Mühlenstr. 28, 18119 **Tel** *(0381) 5107177*

A wonderfully modern bistro near the Seepromenade. Its atmosphere is tranquil and chic. Warm lighting and fresh flowers help create a fine dining experience. Try one of the game or fish dishes, and the desserts are incredibly good. A full vegetarian menu is available. They have an extensive wine list. Highly recommended.

ROSTOCK Der Butt €€€€
Am Yachthafen 1, 18119 **Tel** *0381 5040 6520*

Part of the hotel Hohe Düne, Der Butt earned its first Michelin star just eight months after opening. Chef Tillmann Hahn uses mainly regional organic ingredients to create superb French-influenced haute cuisine. A particular treat for wine connoisseurs is a walk through the glass wine cellar.

RÜGEN Poseidon €€
Binz, Lottumstr. 1, 18609 **Tel** *(038393) 26 69*

A large and spacious fish restaurant where you can enjoy your meal in the restaurant or on the terrace in good weather. The focus is on Italian and German cooking with good quality ingredients. Advance booking is usually not required in the evenings, but it is preferred that larger parties should call in advance.

RÜGEN Orangerie €€€
Binz, Zeppelinstr. 8, 18609 **Tel** *(038393) 50444*

A small, elegant restaurant in the Hotel Vier Jahreszeiten, specializing in traditional fish dishes, served in varying styles. The menu focuses on both healthy as well as more indulgent dishes, so something is available for all tastes. Renowned locally for both its menu and clientèle, reservations are advisable, especially at the weekends.

SCHWERIN Alt Schweriner Schankstuben €
Am Schlachtermarkt 9-13, 19055 **Tel** *(0385) 5925313*

A traditional, rustic North German pub. The Alt-Schweriner Schankstuben is one of the cosiest restaurants in town, located in the heart of Schwerin and specialising in hearty regional fish and meat dishes. In summer you can eat your meal on the shady terrace or enjoy a chilled local beer or wine.

SCHWERIN Altstadtbrauhaus 'Zum Stadtkrug' €
Wismarsche Straße 126, 19053 **Tel** *(0385) 5936693*

A microbrewery built in 1936 where tradition is central – the beer is still brewed in accordance to 1516 brewery laws. The decor is rustic and antique but comfortable. Try one of the regional dishes or a huge *Schnitzel*. The restaurant also has a beer garden. Take a look at the copper brewing tanks.

SCHWERIN Weinhaus Wöhler €
Puschkinstr. 26, 19055 **Tel** *0385 5 55 83-0*

Operating since 1819, the Wöhler is a historic gastropub complete with wood-panelled walls, lead-framed windows, old paintings and a glass-covered courtyard. The food is surprisingly good and the menu offers a combination of regional meat and fish dishes along with lighter Italian fare.

STRALSUND Tafelfreuden €€
Jungfernstieg 5a, 18437 **Tel** *(03831) 29 92 60*

This modern restaurant is situated in a converted wooden house. The unpretentious decor creates a tranquil and comfortable atmosphere. The menu focuses on German and Mediterranean dishes. Try the *Zarzuela*, a Spanish fish soup, as a starter or one of the pork dishes. A children's menu is also available.

STRALSUND Valentin's am Kloster €€€
Bei der Heiligeistkirche 1, 18439 **Tel** *03831 278393*

Valentin's is one of the more stylish harbour restaurants. Located next to the Heiliggeist Church with a view of the harbour, the restaurant serves a wide range of seafood along with a few meat dishes. The Valentin specializes in dishes such as *Matjes* (pickled herring). In winter, the great tea selection make for a cosy afternoon visit.

SHOPPING IN GERMANY

Germany is known for its regional handicrafts, high quality manufacturing, good wines and beers, as well as wonderful bread, cakes and fresh produce. Make sure you sample some of the various cakes from the Konditorei. Organic food and produce is also big in Germany, more so than elsewhere in Europe. All towns have the usual international brands of clothing and accessories,

Black Forest cuckoo clock

as do German department stores. The food markets are a real treat for seasonal local produce and are a meeting place for locals once or twice a week. The pedestrian precinct is also common in German town centres where there is usually a department store, a post office, boutiques and a weekly market, as well as cosy cafés and ice-cream parlours. Often it is considered the social hub of the town.

OPENING HOURS

In 2003 the law was relaxed and shops were allowed to remain open until 8pm on weekdays and Saturdays. As a general rule, shops open between 9 and 10am and close at 8pm. Department stores are also open until 8pm. However, in smaller towns, shops will often close at lunchtime from 12:30 to 2:30pm and in the evening at 6:30pm. On the last four Sundays before Christmas, shops stay open until 6pm. The only other shops opening on Sundays are those in railway stations and some of the bakeries and cake shops (though these only open for a few hours in the morning). Everything shuts on public holidays. Outside these hours the only places open are petrol stations or railway kiosks. Dispensing chemists work on a rota so that there is always one open 24 hours in each town. Each chemist displays a sign in the window saying which one is on duty.

METHODS OF PAYMENT AND VAT REFUNDS

Cash is widely used for small items and at markets. Large department stores take credit cards, as do international chains of boutiques. Smaller shops will only accept the local E-Card or debit card and no cheques, so visitors are advised to use cash where credit cards are not taken. Cash machines are widely available, though some are inside the bank and only accessible during opening hours.

Visitors from countries outside the EU can claim a VAT refund *(Mehrwertsteuer)* in shops displaying the Tax-Free sign. Ask for a special form to be completed and, on leaving the country, all forms have to be stamped for a refund at the border, which may be given on the spot or sent to your address. Goods bought tax-free must remain unopened in the original packaging for a valid refund at the border.

SALES

End of season goods are sold off at a discounted price during the twice-yearly sales *(Schlussverkauf)* – in summer at the end of July and in winter at the end of January. Depending on trading, discounts of 30 to 70 per cent may be given.

Food market in Munich selling fresh local farmers' produce

GREEN SHOPPING

Germans are very ecologically aware when it comes to shopping and recycling. They buy locally when it comes to basics and fresh fruit and vegetables, supporting local farmers and small businesses. Shoppers can be seen all over the country with their wicker shopping baskets at markets and local stores, and any additional bags are reusable cotton totes, rather than plastic bags. Cotton bags are also available to buy at cash desks in every supermarket or department store, and you are always asked if you need a plastic bag or whether you can do without. Organic shopping has boomed. Several organic supermarkets

One of Germany's very popular organic supermarkets

have opened up in the cities, selling fresh and packaged food, cosmetics, clothing and household goods.

FASHION

What Germany does best in the way of clothing and accessories is casualwear, jeanswear, sportswear and outerwear. Typical brands originating in Germany are Esprit, S. Oliver, Hugo Boss, Bogner, Adidas and Puma. German fashion design is classic, purist and discreet.

Although it is not on a par with Italy or France, well-known names on the international scene include Jil Sander, Strenesse, Wolfgang Joop, Escada and the famous couturier Karl Lagerfeld. Classic department store chains are Karstadt and Galeria Kaufhof; there are also independent department stores such as Ludwig Beck in Munich. Speciality stores (*Fachhandel*) are still common in German towns, especially for leather goods and homeware. International chains have a high presence, though mixed brand boutiques are still thriving.

Factory outlets are another way of getting hold of German design, albeit for seconds or reduced goods. Metzingen has a high concentration – Hugo Boss was the first outlet, followed by Bogner, Jil Sander and Escada. Other stores worth trying here are Villeroy & Boch in Mettlach and Puma in Herzogenaurach.

High Fashion in KaDeWe department store, Berlin

REGIONAL PRODUCTS

There are many high quality regional products on sale throughout Germany which make ideal souvenirs. The most common are glass from Saxony and Bavaria, porcelain and ceramics from Meissen in Saxony, and gourmet products and intricate carved wooden objects, such as cuckoo clocks, from the Black Forest. Traditional toys, dolls and dolls houses are common around the Nürnberg area with its long standing reputation of toy manufacturing and traditional Christmas markets. In terms of food, marzipan is a speciality of Lübeck, gingerbread comes from Nürnberg, jams from the Black Forest, cheese from Allgäu, ham from Westphalia, and each region has its own special sausages.

MARKETS

Once or twice a week, local farmers set up their stalls in town centres in the market square or a car park. They sell farm produce from the

Gingerbread (*Lebkuchen*) on sale at a market stall

region, as well as imported goods, such as exotic fruits. It is a colourful, lively sight full of local flavour. Flea markets are also popular all over Germany.

FOOD AND DRINK

Wine and beer are readily available at supermarkets. Specialist wine stores are also common in most towns. Germans drink a lot of sparkling water at home, often mixed with the widely produced sparkling apple juice (*Apfelsaftschorle*), as well as beer, wine and other soft drinks. All these are bought at the wholesaler (*Getränkemarkt*) with a deposit on bottles and crates. Local food is best sought in the markets, though supermarkets and specialist delicatessen offer a good choice as well.

Traditonal beer tankard

SIZE CHART

Women's dresses, coats and skirts

European	36	38	40	42	44	46	48
British	10	12	14	16	18	20	22
American	8	10	12	14	16	18	20

Women's shoes

European	36	37	38	39	40	41
British	3	4	5	6	7	8
American	5	6	7	8	9	10

Men's suits

European	44	46	48	50	52	54	56	58 (size)
British	34	36	38	40	42	44	46	48 (inches)
American	34	36	38	40	42	44	46	48 (inches)

Men's shirts (collar size)

European	36	38	39	41	42	43	44	45 (cm)
British	14	15	15½	16	16½	17	17½	18 (inches)
American	14	15	15½	16	16½	17	17½	18 (inches)

Men's shoes

European	39	40	41	42	43	44	45	46
British	6	7	7½	8	9	10	11	12
American	7	7½	8	8½	9½	10½	11	11½

OUTDOOR ACTIVITIES AND SPECIALIST HOLIDAYS

Germany is home to some of the most active holiday-makers in the world, so it is certainly fitting that there is an abundance of leisure activities available throughout the country. Outdoor pursuits of every kind are readily accessible, from mountain sports, such as climbing, skiing and hiking, to water sports,

Holiday-makers on a yacht

such as sailing, water-skiing and diving. Numerous other, slightly less adventurous activities such as golf, tennis, biking and spas are available and all are thoroughly organized and regulated. Any regional tourist office can provide you with detailed information and advice about planning your outdoor activities.

Walking in the Trettachtal valley in the Bavarian Alps

GENERAL SPORTING INFORMATION

The **Deutscher Sportbund** can provide a great deal of general information about sport in Germany.

WALKING AND HIKING

Walking trails are everywhere in Germany, from the most demanding of Alpine trails to gentler excursions in the Erzgebirge of Saxony (see p166) and over the hills and mountains of the picturesque Thuringian Forest (see pp190–91) and Black Forest (see pp326–7).

Before setting off on an expedition you should get maps showing the walking trails in your chosen region. Detailed information can be obtained from the **Deutscher Volkssportverband e.V.** (German Sports Federation) or the **Deutscher Wanderverband** (German Hiking Club). Guided walking

excursions can also be organized through the local tourist offices or by contacting the **Deutscher Wanderverband**. The **DAV Summit Club** is also a very useful source of information.

CYCLING

Cycling is a great way of enjoying the German countryside. In most towns and tourist areas, bicycles can be hired for just a few days or for a week or more. A bike can easily be transported on trains and on the urban U-Bahn or S-Bahn trains for a minimal fee. You will find that most towns and cities are bike-friendly with cycle lanes and plenty of bike stands. For those interested in mountain biking and more adventurous cycling there are many great places to visit, and the **ADFC (Allgemeiner Deutscher Fahrrad-Club)** (German Cycling Federation) can supply maps, guidebooks and advice.

WATER SPORTS

Germans enjoy all kinds of water sports. Water-skiing and wake-boarding are extremely popular, especially at lakes equipped with static towing lines, where you pay an hourly fee and can take as many trips skiing around the lake as you want. The **Deutscher Wasserski- und Wakeboard Verband e.V.** can provide detailed advice on locations and prices.

There is excellent sailing in the lakeland areas of Mecklenburg (see pp468–9), the coastal regions and on Lake Constance (see pp320–21). As is the case in most countries, you must demonstrate sailing knowledge before being allowed to hire a full-sized boat or small catamaran by showing a valid sailing licence. To find out more about sailing locations, boat hires and regulations, contact the **Deutscher Segler-Verband e.V.** There are also plenty of opportunities for

Cyclists outside a tavern in Rhineland-Palatinate

scuba diving, mostly centred on the lakes or the protected coastal regions. The **Verband Deutscher Sporttaucher (VDST) e.V.** (German Divers' Association) can provide up-to-date advice.

Canoe trips can be taken on many of the country's rivers – from calm and picturesque stretches of water and the canals of the Spreewald *(see p141)*, to exhilarating adventures in rapidly flowing Alpine streams that demand professional skill.

GOLF AND TENNIS

Over the last decade or so golf has become hugely popular in Germany and the number of courses has increased. Golf is usually played at a club, however.

Golfing on the Castle Hotel course in Kronberg, Hesse

You usually need to prove a certain level of golfing proficiency before you are allowed onto the course. This can be achieved by showing a membership card from a course or club back home. Alternatively, look for one of the "Pay & Play" courses, which can be found throughout the country and usually have only six holes. For further information contact the **Deutscher Golf Verband e.V.**

Most large German towns have tennis courts that can be hired for a few hours and there is almost always a private tennis club in all the sizeable towns and cities. For more information on how to make a booking, contact the **Deutscher Tennis Bund e.V.**

Canoeing on a stretch of the River Main in Miltenberg

SKIING AND MOUNTAIN SPORTS

The most renowned centre for skiing is still Garmisch-Partenkirchen *(see p280)*. Other regions such as the Black Forest *(see pp326–7)* and the Erzgebirge *(see p166)* also offer skiing. Some of the larger cities have indoor skiing halls, though they are a poor substitute for the Alps *(see pp204–5)*. Cross-country skiing is also popular, and there are many well-prepared routes. Information can be obtained from local tourist information offices or contact the **Haus des Ski, Deutscher Skiverband DSV** (German Ski Association).

The Alps are the centre of German climbing. Here you can find sport climbers mixing with Alpinists. The Allgäu region is probably the most well-known place for climbers but challenges can also be found in the Ries basin. The **Verband Deutscher Berg- und Skiführer (VDBS)** (Association of German Mountain and Ski Guides) can help you with hiring a guide.

Interesting rock formations that provide memorable challenges are not only to be found in the Alps, but throughout Germany. Places such as the Harz Forest *(see p147)*, Fichtelgebirge and the Schwäbische Alb *(see pp300–1)* are all outstanding places for sport climbing. Also, you can find indoor climbing gyms in most cities. The **Deutscher Alpenverein (DAV) Bundesgeschäftsstelle** (German Alpine Association) can help with all your climbing requirements.

NATIONAL PARKS

Germany has a richly varied landscape, from mountains to coasts, and has many nature reserves, biosphere reserves and national parks. From the swamp-like Spreewald *(see p141)* to the lush forests and mountain peaks of the Bavarian Forest *(see p257)*, each park has its own spectacular natural characteristics and offers a range of different visitor services and facilities.

All parks have sign-posted trails and most have special maps for walking, biking or jogging tours. These are also excellent locations for observing and enjoying the flora and fauna of Germany's various regions. Many parks have notices posted to inform visitors about the animals and plants indigenous to the area. To find out more about the various locations and holidays available in Germany's national parks and nature reserves contact the **Verband Deutscher Naturparke** or **Europarc Deutschland e.V.**

Mountain sports in the Schildenstein Mangfall mountains

CAMPING AND CARAVANNING

During the months of July, August and September there are a great many foreign holiday-makers on Germany's Autobahns heading for the camping parks. The word "camping" in Germany means primarily caravanning, not pitching a tent. Most sites are privately owned and offer a lot of extras. The majority have wash facilities, snack stands or restaurants as well as small shops and playgrounds. The more upscale parks will offer electricity as well as group activities, caravans and bungalows for hire. To find out more contact the **Deutscher Camping-Club e.V.** Tent-pitching holidays are also possible and this is strongly regulated in order to avoid misuse of national parks. Tents are often allowed in the camping parks mentioned above and many national parks have places set aside for tents and campfires. **Backpacker Network Germany e.V.** is a good resource for information about camping.

Spiegelau, the well-known hiking spot in the Bavarian Forest

HISTORIC AND SCENIC ROUTES

Germany has over 50 official driving routes. These routes highlight the best features of an individual region. The following are just a few of many excellent drives. The **Burgenstraße e.V.** (Castle Road) is over 1,000 km (620 miles) long, from Mannheim *(see p294)* through Bavaria to Prague. It offers plenty of romantic castles and historical

Burgenstraße (Castle Road) scenic route following the Rhine

sites. The **Deutsche Märchenstraße** (Fairytale Route) covers more than 600 km (370 miles) from Bremen *(see pp430–33)* to Hanau *(see p377)*, linking more than 70 towns and villages associated with the Brothers Grimm and the realm of fairytales, sagas, myths and legends. The **Deutsche Weinstraße e.V.** (Wine Route) *(see p347)* is 85 km (52 miles) and runs from Bad Dürkheim to Bad Berzabern. The **Touristik Arbeitsgemeinschaft Romantische Straße** (Romantic Road) is Germany's most famous and popular tourist route. It runs for 350 km (217 miles) through a rich and varied landscape along the River Main to the Alps. The **Tourismusverband Ruppiner Land e.V. "Deutsche Tonstraße"** (Ceramics Route) is a circular route running 215 km (134 miles) through the Ruppiner Land area of northern Brandenburg *(see pp130–31)*.

SPECIALIST HOLIDAYS

Language tours offer you the chance to immerse yourself in German culture. Living arrangements range from homes to hotels and hostels, depending upon budget. The **Goethe Institut** is the best place for information on this type of holiday.

Wine holidays are becoming more commonplace because German wines are coming back into popularity. Most winemakers offer tastings and small meals, but some also

offer packaged holidays. To find out more about wine holidays contact **Deutsches Weininstitut GmbH** or **Viniversität – Die Weinschule GmbH**.

There are equestrian centres in many parts of Germany where visitors can ride under supervision or head off on their own. Specialized weekends or week-long riding vacations are available throughout Germany. More information can be obtained from the **Deutsche Reiterliche Vereinigung e. V.**

SPA VACATIONS

Germany has more than 350 health and spa resorts, as well as numerous hotels and holiday centres, where your wellbeing is the top priority. Cultural delights, culinary experiences, sights of historical importance and physical activites all form part of the German philosophy of looking after yourself, known as "Das Wellness". Health and fitness breaks are available all year round and facilities vary from the minimalist ultra-modern to marble and gold imperial luxury, with everything in between. Each region has something special to offer, though some of the most well-known spas are in the Black Forest *(see pp326–7)*, on the East Frisian Islands *(see p428)* and in Schleswig-Holstein *(see pp455–65)*. The **Deutscher Heilbäderverband e. V.** can help you find the right spa and holiday package.

Wine from the Mosel

DIRECTORY

GENERAL SPORTING INFORMATION

Deutscher Sportbund
Otto-Fleck-Schneise 12,
Frankfurt am Main.
Tel (069) 67 000.
www.dosb.de

WALKING AND HIKING

DAV Summit Club
Am Perlacher Forst 186,
81545 München.
Tel (089) 64 24 00.
www.dav-summit-club.de

Deutscher Volkssportverband e.V.
Fabrikstraße 8,
D-84503 Altötting.
Tel (08671) 96310.
www.dvv-wandern.de

Deutscher Wanderverband
Wilhelmshöher Allee
157–159, D-34121 Kassel.
Tel (0561) 938 730.
www.wanderverband.de

CYCLING

ADFC (Allgemeiner Deutscher Fahrrad-Club)
Bundesgeschäftsstelle,
Postfach 10 77 47,
28077 Bremen.
Tel (0421) 34 62 90.
www.adfc.de

WATER SPORTS

Deutscher Segler-Verband e.V.
Gründgensstr. 18,
22309 Hamburg.
Tel (040) 632 00 90.
www.dsv.org

Deutscher Wasserski- und Wakeboard Verband e.V.
Am Campingpark 10,
49597 Rieste.
Tel (5464) 969 11 66.
www.wasserski-online.de

Verband Deutscher Sporttaucher (VDST) e.V.
Bundesgeschäftsstelle,
Berliner Str. 312,
63067 Offenbach.
Tel (069) 9819025.
www.vdst.de

INLINE SKATING

Inline News
Thalkircher Str. 101,
81371 München.
Tel (089) 747 19 633.
www.inlinenews.de

GOLF AND TENNIS

Deutscher Golf Verband e.V.
Postfach 21 06,
65189 Wiesbaden.
Tel (0611) 990 200.
www.golf.de/dgv

Deutscher Tennis Bund e.V.
Hallerstraße 89,
20149 Hamburg.
Tel (040) 411780.
www.dtb-tennis.de

SKIING AND MOUNTAIN SPORTS

Deutscher Alpenverein (DAV) Bundesgeschäftsstelle
Von-Kahr-Str. 2–4,
80997 München.
Tel (089) 140030.
www.alpenverein.de

Haus des Ski, Deutscher Skiverband DSV
Am Erwin-Himmeseher-Platz Hubertusstraße 1,
D 82152 Planegg.
Tel (089) 857900.
www.deutscherskiverband.de

Verband Deutscher Berg- und Skiführer (VDBS)
Bahnhofstr. 25,
83646 Bad Tölz.
Tel (08041) 7938606.
www.bergfuehrer-verband.de

NATIONAL PARKS

Europarc Deutschland e.V.
Friedrichstraße 60,
D-10117 Berlin.
Tel (030) 28878820.
www.europarc-deutschland.de

[continued]

Verband Deutscher Naturparke
Platz der Vereinten
Nationen 9, 53113 Bonn.
Tel (0228) 9212860.
www.naturparke.de

CAMPING AND CARAVANNING

Backpacker Network Germany e.V.
Postfach 160138, 60064
Frankfurt.
Tel (040) 43 18 23 10.
www.backpacker
network.de/home/

Deutscher Camping-Club e.V.
Mandlstraße 28,
80802 München.
Tel (089) 3801420.
www.camping-club.de

HISTORIC AND SCENIC ROUTES

Burgenstraße e.V
(Castle Road)
Allee 28,
D-74072 Heilbronn.
Tel (07131) 5640 28.
www.burgenstrasse.de

Deutsche Märchenstraße
(Fairytale Route)
Kurfürstenstr. 9,
34117 Kassel.
Tel (0561) 92 04 79 10.
www.deutsche-maerchenstrasse.de

Deutsche Weinstraße e.V.
(Wine Route)
Martin-Luther-Str. 69,
67433 Neustadt an der
Weinstraße.
Tel (06321) 912333.
www.deutsche-weinstrasse.de

Tourismusverband Ruppiner Land e.V. "Deutsche Tonstraße"
(Ceramics Route)
Fischbänkenstr. 8,
16816 Neuruppin.
Tel (03391) 659630.
www.deutschetonstrasse.de

[continued]

Touristik Arbeitsgemeinschaft Romantische Straße
(Romantic Road)
Segringer Str. 19,
91550 Dinkelsbühl.
Tel (09851) 551387.
www.romantischestrasse.de

SPECIALIST HOLIDAYS

Deutsche Reiterliche Vereinigung e.V.
Freiherr von
Langen-Straße 13,
48231 Warendorf.
Tel (025 81) 63 620.
www.pferd-aktuell.de

Deutsches Weininstitut GmbH
Gutenbergplatz 3–5,
55116 Mainz.
Tel (06131) 28290.
www.deutscheweine.de

Goethe Institut
Dachauer Straße 122,
80637 München.
(Postal address: P.O. Box
19 04 19, 80604
München).
Tel (089) 159210.
www. goethe.de
50 Princes Gate,
Exhibition Road,
London SW7 2PH.
*Tel (020) 7596 4000 or
(020) 7594 0240.*

Viniversität – Die Weinschule GmbH
Bilker Allee 49, 40219
Düsseldorf.
Tel (0211) 39 002 650.
www.viniversitaet.de

SPA VACATIONS

Deutscher Heilbäderverband e. V.
Reinhardtstr. 46, 10117
Berlin.
Tel (030) 24 63 6920.
www.deutscher-heilbaederverband.de

SURVIVAL
GUIDE

PRACTICAL INFORMATION

Germany is a country that is particularly well prepared to receive visitors. Every town, large or small, has a helpful tourist information centre that can assist with finding accommodation and provide information about local restaurants, attractions and activities. Virtually all the larger cities have websites with up-to-date information on hotels, restaurants, museums and historic monuments.

Posters advertising future events

The country is served by an excellent public transport system and a first-rate network of roads and motorways, which makes getting around quick and easy. There is a plentiful supply of comfortable, affordable tourist accommodation in Germany, but it is worth bearing in mind that hotels can become booked up quickly during the festivals and fairs that occur throughout the year in different parts of the country.

WHEN TO GO

In Germany, a pleasant vacation can be enjoyed at any time of the year. If you are planning to visit cities and historic monuments, however, it is best to come in the spring or early autumn. July and August are ideal for a restful holiday by the sea, in the lake districts or in the mountains. Arriving in Bavaria in the last half of September offers the chance to take part in Oktoberfest. In December, Christmas markets all over the country enchant shoppers with their old-world charm, while later in the winter, skiing is a popular pursuit in the Black Forest, the Alps, and the Harz Mountains.

Road traffic increases during school holidays, the dates of which may vary between states. Roads can also be quite busy at the start of the "long weekends" that occur at Easter, Whitsun, and around other national holidays.

VISAS AND PASSPORTS

Citizens of EU countries, apart from the UK and Ireland, can enter Germany with a national identity card. Visitors from the UK, Ireland, the US, Canada, Australia and New Zealand will need a full passport. Non-EU citizens may visit Germany for up to 3 months without a visa, after that a residence permit *(Aufenthalt-serlaubnis)* is required. For more information and to check the visa requirements visitors should consult the website of their German embassy. Visitors from South Africa need to obtain a valid visa before entering Germany for any length of stay.

Germany is one of the 25 European countries that are part of the Schengen Agreement for shared border control. Once you enter a Schengen country, you may travel continuously between the member countries for up to 90 days. Non-EU visitors require a passport when entering the Schengen Zone and a Schengen visa is required for visitors from most Asian and African states.

CUSTOMS REGULATIONS

German regulations prohibit importation of drugs, animals and exotic plants that are under special protection. Importation of cigarettes is also regulated. An adult may bring in 200 cigarettes or 50 cigars, and 250g (9oz) of tobacco, as well as one litre of spirits and two litres of wine. You can also import up to 5kg (11lb) of food, but restrictions apply to meat and dairy products. Beyond these limits, goods must be cleared by Customs when entering the country.

TOURIST INFORMATION

Tourist information centres, can be found in all German cities and most of the larger towns. They provide information on accommodation, addresses and opening hours of historic monuments and museums, cruises, organized excursions and city tours, as well as brochures covering the most important tourist information. They sell useful guide books, maps and postcards and may be able to find and book hotel rooms.

The embassies of most countries, including the UK and US, are located in Berlin. Consulates are also based in other major German cities.

Oktoberfest celebrations at the Theresienwiese, Munich

◁ **Beer tankards from Heidelberg**

Tourist information centre in Berlin

ADMISSION PRICES

Admission to museums and monuments can be expensive and prices vary. Entry to a small regional museum, for example, may cost as little as €2–5, a large state-run museum around €5–10, while a private venue may charge up to €12. Admission to smaller churches is usually free, but a fee may be charged in some cathedrals, monastic churches and church treasuries.

In many cases, discounted tickets are available for students, seniors and families. Combination tickets, offering entry to multiple sites, are often good value *(see p568)*.

OPENING HOURS

Opening hours of shops, offices, and other businesses depend on the size of the town. In larger cities, typical opening hours are from 9am–6pm, while large stores are open until 8pm. Banks have shorter hours in smaller towns *(see p572)*. Trading is limited on Saturdays, especially in rural areas and on Sundays and public holidays, only airport and train station shops are open *(see p558–9)*.

Museums in Germany are generally open from 9am–6pm, in smaller towns from 10am to 4 or 5pm. Some museums open later, on Wednesdays or Thursdays, while on Mondays most museums tend to be closed. Larger churches in major cities are accessible to tourists throughout the day. In smaller places, visits may require prior arrangements.

LANGUAGE

Although German is spoken nationwide, many areas have dialects that are virtually incomprehensible, even to those from neighbouring regions. Travellers can usually be understood in Germany by speaking English, particularly in larger cities and in places that are frequented by tourists.

SOCIAL CUSTOMS AND ETIQUETTE

Although generally polite and friendly, Germans tend to be very honest and direct, sometimes to the point of seeming rude. However, most people, particularly the older generation, attach great importance to courteous behaviour. You constantly hear *"Guten Tag"* when entering a shop, and *"Auf Wiedersehen"* – or the more youthful *"Tschüss"* – when leaving. Germans are also very punctual and consider even a small delay to be impolite. Arriving slightly early for an engagement is regarded as courteous.

Among younger Germans, however, ideas of politeness are changing. Older people and women are shown less respect and are no longer automatically offered seats on public transport. Another change is the tolerance shown towards unruly children by parents and other adults.

The German dress code, except in a work environment and among the older generation, is rather casual. Formal dress is required in only the most upmarket restaurants. Nudity in parks and at beaches may shock some visitors.

Most traffic rules are strictly observed. Crossing the street on a red light, even if the road is deserted, is considered an offence and can result in an official reprimand.

ACCESSIBILITY OF PUBLIC CONVENIENCES

In large cities, public toilets (often automatic cubicles) can usually be found without much difficulty. Instructions on how to use these facilities are given in several languages on the doors of the cubicles. Public toilets can also be found in museums, cafés, restaurants and department stores. Men's toilets are marked *Herren* and ladies' *Damen* or *Frauen*.

TAXES AND TIPPING

There are no standard rates for tipping in Germany, but taxi drivers are usually tipped €1–2. Service and tax is generally included on restaurant bills, but it is usual to leave a tip of about 10 per cent of the bill.

Exterior of Brandhorst Museum in Munich *(see p220)*

Kids' Kingdom at the Deutsches Museum in Munich (see pp228-9)

TRAVELLERS WITH SPECIAL NEEDS

Germany is relatively well prepared to receive disabled travellers. Large museums and important historic monuments have ramps or lifts for wheelchair access and public toilet facilities are designed to accomodate disabled travellers. The majority of hotels are well equipped for disabled travellers (see p487). A large proportion of public transport vehicles have been adapted for wheelchair users. Public transport companies are also making efforts to accommodate visually impaired people.

A disabled person may, however, still have problems in gaining access to some places, such as the smaller museums, certain historic monuments, and toilets in restaurants, which are often located in the cellar.

Contact **NatKo** for detailed information on travelling with special needs in Germany. Companies such as **Directions Unlimited** (in the US) and **Holiday Care** (in the UK) also offer useful information and advice for disabled travellers.

TRAVELLING WITH CHILDREN

Families travelling in Germany benefit from a range of cost cutting discounts. The majority of hotels and guesthouses offer discounts for children (see p487). Discounts or even free travel for the youngest children are available on various forms of transport and there are similar concessions in most museums. In many German cities it is possible to purchase family tickets that provide substantial discounts on fares and admission fees.

Restaurants can usually provide a high chair for toddlers and offer a special *Kinder-menu* (children's menu) with smaller portions. Public toilets in railway stations, airports and motorway service stations, as well as in many museums and stores, usually offer a separate facility for mothers and babies.

An ISIC card (international student identity card)

GAY AND LESBIAN TRAVELLERS

Germans have a very relaxed and welcoming attitude toward gay travellers, especially in Berlin, Cologne, Hamburg, Munich, and Frankfurt, where there is a lively gay scene with a variety of hotels, clubs and bars. Gay pride is celebrated nationwide with Christopher Street Day parades and festivals throughout June and July. The **National Tourist Office** offers detailed information on gay cultural events nationwide.

TRAVELLING ON A BUDGET

You can save on airfare by travelling to Germany off-season and flying with a low-cost carrier (see p576). Cheap hostels can be found in most German cities, providing an option that is increasingly popular with families (see p486). For eating out, try one of the many cheap eateries (Imbiss), for German *wurst* or ethnic food. Some of the larger German cities sell city cards that double as public transport passes and discount cards at museums and events. City cards can be purchased at tourist offices, many hotels, and public transport ticket counters. For several cities, the cards can also be bought online before travel.

For students, an **International Student Identity Card** (ISIC) entitles the holder to a 50 per cent discount to many museums and reductions on some theatre and cinema tickets. It also allows students to get discounts on hostel prices, air tickets, rental cars and bicycles.

Christopher Street Day celebrations, Berlin

TIME

Germany uses Central European Time (GMT plus one hour). Clocks move forward one hour on the last Sunday in March and back on the last Sunday in October.

ELECTRICITY

UK 220V appliances can be used with an adaptor; US 110V appliances will also need a transformer.

RESPONSIBLE TOURISM

Germany is one of the most environmentally aware countries in Europe, with 17% of the energy used coming from renewable sources. Agrotourism is gaining popularity as a cost effective holiday option (see p486), and bicycle tours and walking holidays are increasingly common (see p583). An eco-friendly alternative to staying in a hotel is camping, there are over 2,000 camping sites throughout the Germany (see p487).

Hostels and hotels are becoming increasingly aware of environmental issues and encourage the responsible use of resources. German eco-tour operator **Viabono** offers a search engine for eco-hotels and lodges across Germany. The **Blaue Schwalbe** ("Blue Swallow") is an eco-award given to hotels meeting certain sustainability standards and offering organic local food. The **Verträglich Reisen** website provides a full list of accredited hotels. In Bavaria,

environmentally friendly hotels are awarded the *Umweltsiegel* (eco-label).

Organic and locally grown produce is clearly labelled and widely available at most shops and supermarkets. Many towns hold regular markets selling organic and traditional produce, allowing visitors to give back to the local community.

Information on local green tourism activities and initiatives can be found through tourist offices.

Stall at Oktomarkt, an organic market in Kollwitzplatz, Berlin

DIRECTORY

EMBASSIES

Australia
Wallstraße 76–79, 10179 Berlin.
Tel (030) 880 08 80.
Fax (030) 880 08 8-210.
www.germany.embassy.gov.au

Canada
Leipziger Platz 17, 10117 Berlin. *Tel* (030) 20 31 20.
Fax (030) 20 31 25 90.
www.kanada-info.de

Republic of Ireland
Jägerstr. 51, 10117 Berlin.
Tel (030) 22 07 20.
Fax (030) 22 07 22 99.
www.embassyofireland.de

New Zealand
Friedrichstraße 60, 10117 Berlin. *Tel* (030) 20 62 10.
Fax (030) 20 62 11 14.
www.nzembassy.com

South Africa
Tiergartenstraße 18, 10785 Berlin.
Tel (030) 22 07 30.
Fax (030) 22 07 31 90.
www.suedafrika.org

United Kingdom
UK Embassy:
Wilhelmstraße 70, 10117 Berlin. *Tel* (030) 20 45 70.
Fax (030) 20 45 75 49.
www.britischebotschaft.de

UK Consulate:
Harvestehuder Weg 8a, 20148 Hamburg.
Tel (040) 448 03 20.
Fax (040) 410 72 59.

United States of America
US Embassy:
Pariser Platz 2, 10117 Berlin.
Tel (030) 8 30 50.
Fax (030) 83 05 10 50.
www.usembassy.de

US Consulates:
Clayallee 170, 40191 **Berlin**
Tel (030) 8305-1200.
Königinstraße 5, 80539 **Munich.**
Tel (089) 288 80.
Fax (089) 280 99 98.
Gießener Str. 30, 60435 **Frankfurt am Main**
Tel (069) 7535-0.

TOURIST OFFICES

National Tourist Office
PO Box 2695, London, W1A 3TN, UK.
Tel (020) 731 70908
www.germany-tourism.de

Berlin Tourist Information
Tel (030) 25 00 25.
http://visitberlin.de/en

TRAVELLERS WITH SPECIAL NEEDS

Directions Unlimited
123 Green Lane, Bedford Hills, NY 10507, USA.
Tel (800) 533 53 43.

Holiday Care
Tel 0845 1249971.
www.holidaycare.org or **www**.tourismforall.org.uk

NatKo e.V. (Nationale Koordinationsstelle Tourismus für Alle)

Fleher Straße 317 a, 40223 Düsseldorf.
Tel (0211) 336 80 01.
www.natko.de

GAY AND LESBIAN TRAVELLERS

www.gay-web.de,
www.gay.de/
www.cometogermany.com

TRAVELLING ON A BUDGET

ISIC Card
www.isig.org

RESPONSIBLE TOURISM

Blaue Schwalbe
www.sanftes-reisen.org.

Viabono
Tel (02205) 9198353.
www.viabono.de

Verträglich Reisen
www.vertraeglich-reisen.de

Security and Health

Pharmacy sign

Germany is a safe place for visitors, but it is always a good idea to take sensible precautions especially in larger towns and cities. Extra caution should be taken against pickpockets – particularly on public transport or in busy tourist areas. It is worth using a money belt or other means of hiding your money and documents. Taking out medical insurance cover is always advisable when travelling abroad, but for minor health problems that do not require the services of a doctor, pharmacists are a good and easily accessible source of assistance.

Policeman and policewoman

POLICE

German police can be easily identified by their blue uniforms, except in Bavaria and the Saarland where the traditional green uniforms are still worn. Investigators of criminal offences, *Kriminalpolizei*, are generally dressed in plain clothes. They will produce their identification and badge as necessary.

Municiple officers and traffic wardens also wear the navy-blue uniforms. They are in charge of minor offences such as illegal parking, crossing at a red light, littering or riding a bicycle on the sidewalk and are entitled to check documents and issue fines.

To report a crime, it is necessary to go to a local police station (*Polizeiabschnitt*) and, in event of theft, get a *Bericht*, the report required by insurance. In the case of a traffic accident or an emergency, call 110 or 112.

WHAT TO BE AWARE OF

Violent crime is very rare in Germany and the law is enforced energetically.

The most serious threat for a tourist is always the pickpocket. These thieves tend to prowl in crowded places, such as railway platforms, train carriages and buses. They also frequent popular tourist sights and any events where large groups of people are likely to gather. It is best to leave your valuable items and documents in the hotel safe. Park your car in the hotel car park whenever possible and never leave valuable items in the vehicle, especially if it has to be left in the street overnight. Should you become the victim of a crime, the **Crime Victim Hotline** offers a councelling service.

Buying counterfeit items like cigarettes from street vendors is an offence and should be avoided.

Although alcohol is sold at every fuel station, drinking and driving is not a good idea and it is against the law to drive with a blood alcohol level over 50mg/dl, the equivalent of one beer.

It is illegal to use your mobile phone while driving or even sitting in a car with the engine running; doing so can result in a fine of €40.

Be aware of cyclists. They tend to be everywhere but the autobahn, and have right of way in dedicated bike lanes.

A woman travelling on her own will not surprise anyone in Germany and only the usual safety precautions need be taken. However, it is best to avoid certain areas in towns where there is a lively nightlife, particularly in large cities – for example, the Reeperbahn in Hamburg. Hitchhiking is quite popular in Germany, but a better option for single women may be to use the services of *Mitfahrzentrale (see p581)*.

IN AN EMERGENCY

The national emergency number for medical assistance and the fire brigade is 112. In a medical emergency, call an ambulance, which will take you to the nearest emergency room (*Rettungsstelle*). In large hotels, medical care for minor ailments can often be provided on the premises.

If a road accident or breakdown occurs call for help on your mobile phone (110 or 112 for police and ambulance). Several breakdown companies offer roadside assistance *(see p581)*. If your car breaks down in the middle of nowhere, you can call 0800 6 683 663 on your mobile phone. This automobile emergency service is equipped to track you down.

If you witness a crime on the platform of an underground or commuter railway, a designated emergency alarm button can be used to summon assistance. Special alarm buttons, within small red boxes, also provide a direct connection with the fire brigade (*Feuerwehr*). These alarm buttons are easy to find, usually located in prominent positions on the streets and in large department stores.

Alarm button for the fire brigade

In an emergency, consulate officials can help travellers with legal or other advice, locate a translator, or contact family members. In some circumstances they may be able to lend money for a ticket home *(see p569)*.

Fire engine from the Berlin fire brigade

Ambulance of the paramedic rescue services

Traditionally coloured white and green police van

LOST AND STOLEN PROPERTY

Before leaving home it is advisable to take out an insurance policy to cover property against loss or theft. Theft and burglaries must be reported to the police immediately and a certificate obtained to confirm that the loss has been reported; this is needed if an insurance claim is submitted.

If property has been lost, it is worth checking at a lost property office (*Fundbüro*). These exist in every German city. The **Deutsche Bahn** has its own lost property offices, as do transport systems in individual towns.

In the event of a lost or stolen mobile phone, inform the service provider immediately to have the account locked and avoid unwanted charges on your bill. They may also be able to trace the phone. You should also report a theft to the nearest police station. The police will need the phone's identification number (IMEI).

To replace lost or stolen passports, visit your local consulate who can issue a replacement. Keep a photocopy of your passport/ID in your luggage to reduce hassle if it gets lost or stolen.

HOSPITALS AND PHARMACIES

For a serious illness or injury, visit a hospital (*Krankenhaus*) or call an ambulance. All emergency rooms are part of the public health system, so your EHIC or supplementary insurance will cover you. The symbol for hospitals is a red cross on white background.

Pharmacies in Germany are indicated by a red stylized letter "A" for *Apotheke* and are usually open 8am–6pm; in small towns they may close 1–3pm. In larger towns there is always a rota and this is clearly displayed in the window of each pharmacy with a note of addresses. Information on rota pharmacies may also be obtained from tourist offices, local newspapers or the Internet.

MINOR HAZARDS

Germany poses few serious health hazards for travellers. Tap water is safe to drink throughout the country, there are no prevalent diseases, and the country is well served with hospitals and pharmacies. No vaccinations are required when entering Germany.

Entrance to a pharmacy in Heidelberg

However, ticks are prevalent in forests and rural areas, especially during summer, and visitors should seek medical advice if bitten.

HEALTH INSURANCE

Citizens of countries within the European Union with a European Health Insurance Card (EHIC) are entitled to free medical care in Germany. It is also advisable to take out some form of supplementary health insurance, as some services, such as repatriation costs, are not covered.

If plans include sporting activities, particularly dangerous sports, make sure the policy covers rescue services (e.g., mountain rescue). This type of insurance is usually much more expensive.

Banking and Local Currency

Logo of the ReiseBank

Debit and credit cards are widely accepeted in Germany, but it is still advisable to travel with some cash. Some of the smaller shops, cafés, and bars, do not accept credit cards. Cash can be easily obtained from automatic cash points (ATMs), and bank branches are easy to find. Exchange Bureaus are located at airports and larger railway stations.

BANKS AND BUREAUX DE CHANGE

There are no limits on the amount of foreign currency that can be brought into the country and credit and debit cards are accepted in most of the larger hotels, restaurants and shops. Foreign currency can be exchanged in a bank or exchange bureau (*Wechselstube*). Both offer a similar rate, but usually charge a commission. Be sure to check commission rates and confirm how much you will have to pay before beginning a transaction. Money can also be changed at special ATMs. Some hotel reception desks will change cash, but the exchange rate may be poor.

Most banks are open Monday–Friday 9am–5pm, with a break for lunch, and once a week they are open until 6pm. Opening hours may be a little longer in larger cities and some of the larger branches open until 1pm on Saturdays. It is often more convenient to take advantage of the services offered by branches located in airports and larger railway stations as soon as you arrive.

Cash point machine (*Geldautomat*)

Travellers' cheques are best purchased in euro denominations and can be used to pay for goods and services or hotel bills, but they are not always accepted. To avoid hassle, it is often better to pay by cash or card.

For wiring money, contact a Western Union branch in a major city. If you hold a bank-issued **Visa** or **MasterCard** credit card, you can transfer money through the **Western Union Bank** website.

Note, for all financial transactions in Germany, decimals are indicated by a comma and thousands by a point.

ATMS

The most convenient way to get cash is at an ATM (*Geldautomat*), found on main streets and in shopping centres, airports and railway stations. Most have multilingual instructions or are self-explanatory and carry logos showing which cards are accepted.

Costs for cash withdrawals vary, so contact your bank for advice before traveling, to avoid any high fees.

DEBIT AND CREDIT CARDS

In Germany, the most popular cards are **Maestro** debit cards. **Visa, MasterCard** and **American Express** are widely accepted, **Diner's Club** a little less so. Always check that credit or debit cards are an acceptable method of payment before making a purchase, and watch for minimum charges in restaurants and cafés.

Lost credit cards or travellers' cheques should be reported immediately to the issuing bank or company.

DIRECTORY

LOST CREDIT CARDS/ TRAVELLERS' CHEQUES

All Cards
Tel 116 116 (nationwide free number).

American Express
Tel (069) 97 97 10 00.

Barclaycard
Tel (040) 89 09 98 77.

Diner's Club
Tel 01805 070704.

EC/Maestro and Bank Cards
Tel 01805 021021.

MasterCard
Tel 0800 819 10 40.

VISA
Tel 0800 811 8440.

WIRING MONEY

Western Union Bank
Tel 0800 33 44 33 55 (free hotline).
Tel (0180) 18 18 123 (English).
www.westernunionbank.com

A branch of Sparkasse branch, Berlin

CURRENCY

The euro (€) is the common currency of the European Union. It went into general circulation on 1 January 2002. Germany was one of the 12 original countries taking the euro; the Deutschmark was phased out by mid-2002. EU members using the euro as sole official currency are known as the Eurozone.

Euro notes are identical throughout the Eurozone countries, each one including designs of fictional architectural structures and monuments. The coins, however, have one side identical (the value side), and one side with an image unique to each country. Both notes and coins are accepted in all of the participating EU countries (not all European nations belong to the Eurozone).

Euro Bank Notes

Euro bank notes have seven denominations. The €5 note (grey in colour) is the smallest, followed by the €10 note (pink), €20 note (blue), €50 note (orange), €100 note (green), €200 note (yellow) and €500 note (purple). All notes show the stars of the European Union.

€5 note

€10 note

€20 note

€50 note

€100 note

€200 note

€500 note

€2 coin   €1 coin   50 cents   20 cents   10 cents

Coins

The euro has eight coin denominations: €2 and €1; 50 cents, 20 cents, 10 cents, 5 cents, 2 cents and 1 cent. The €2 and €1 coins are both silver and gold in colour. The 50-, 20- and 10-cent coins are gold. The 5-, 2- and 1-cent coins are bronze.

5 cents

2 cents

1 cent

Communications and Media

Postal and telecommunications services in Germany work very efficiently. Though it may be necessary to queue for a few minutes for service, letters and post-cards are usually delivered within the country in 24 hours. Public phones are simple to use, many with foreign language instructions, but they are becoming rarer due to the popularity of mobile phones. The distinctive yellow mail-boxes are a common sight.

Telekom phones at Frankfurt Hauptbahnhof

INTERNATIONAL AND LOCAL TELEPHONE CALLS

Public telephones are serviced by **Deutsche Telekom** and can still be found in busy places like railway stations and malls. Most phones will only accept telephone cards, which can be purchased at Telekom shops, fuel stations and newsstands. Some older telephones however, are coin-operated and require a minimum deposit, which is the cost of a single local call. Travellers can also purchase an international phone card, which is valid in several countries and can be used when calling from a public telephone, a mobile or a hotel phone. The cards offer low rates on calls abroad and have a prepaid balance – ask to see call rates before purchase.

Call shops are common in all major German cities and provide an economical way to make international calls. They usually charge a small initial fee, and then offer a low rate per minute, which is paid at the end of the call. These shops also sell

international phone cards and often double as Internet cafés.

Depending on the time and day, different tariffs apply to local, intercity and international calls. The most expensive period to make a call is between 7am and 6pm. Calls cost less between 6pm and 9pm, and later in the evening they are even cheaper. Likewise, calls are cheaper on weekends than on weekdays.

MOBILE PHONES

Mobile phone coverage is generally good throughout the country, although the signal may be weaker in more remote areas. German mobile

phones use standard European frequencies, so UK phones will work provided they have a roaming facility enabled. North American phones will only operate in Germany if they are tri- or quad-band.

Making and receiving calls outside your home country can be very expensive and travellers should check roaming charges before travel. If you are planning to use your phone frequently, it may be economical to buy a local SIM card with a German telephone number from a local provider such as **Base**. Check with your service pro-vider to ensure your phone is SIM-unlocked and compatible with local technology. Anti-terrorism laws have made it more complicated for non-residents to buy a SIM card, as travellers will need a valid ID and a German address (a hotel address should work).

If your phone is Wi-Fi capable, you can save on roaming costs by locating a free Wi-Fi (wireless Internet) network and making calls with **Skype**. Bear in mind that as useful as a smartphone can be overseas, all data use will be charged at a higher rate.

It is wise to carry your mobile provider's contact details so you can deactivate your card if your phone is lost or stolen.

INTERNET AND EMAIL

Many hotels include Internet access in their room rates, but this varies, so be sure to check in advance. Some hotels have Internet terminals allowing guests to check emails and go online for free.

Internet cafés, where online access can be obtained for a small fee (typically €1–2

USEFUL TELEPHONE NUMBERS

- Directory enquiries, national numbers: 11 833 or 11 837 (English service).
- National telephone directory (White Pages): www.dastelefonbuch.de
- Directory enquiries, international numbers: 11 834.
- International calls: Dial 00, wait for dialling tone, then dial country code, area code + number, omitting first 0.
- Country codes: UK 44; Eire 353; Canada and US 1; Australia 61; South Africa 27; New Zealand 64.

per hour), can be found in most towns and cities. Usually, the higher the number of terminals, the better the rates. If you are going to be online for a while, a special multi-hour pass may be the most cost effective option.

Wi-Fi access is increasingly available in Germany. Expect to find Wi-Fi at many cafés, libraries, hostels and hotels. Most networks are password-protected and an access code is required, although it is often provided free of charge to the customer. Free Wi-Fi hotspots are located in public areas around most larger towns and cities.

A kiosk selling newspapers and cigarettes

Postbank logo

POSTAL SERVICES

Dedicated Deutsche Post offices have virtually disappeared and postal services are instead offered by **Postbank Finanzcenter**, newsstands and some other shops, including selected supermarkets. These retailers also sell phone cards, postcards and mailing supplies.

Stamps are sometimes sold with postcards, or can be bought from vending machines. It costs €0.65 to send a postcard anywhere in Europe and €1 to overseas destinations. When posting a letter in a mail-box, be aware that some boxes have two slots – one for local post only, the other for all other destinations.

Germany also has a private mail network, **PIN Mail**, which

Information plaque indicating the collection times

Opening for local letters

Opening for long-distance mail

The distinctive yellow mail-box of Germany's official postal service

offers competitive prices for mail and package delivery. For quick delivery of a package, look for one of the courier services. **DHL** is the national parcel delivery service. Packages can be sent via DHL from post offices or DHL-affiliated retailers. **Federal Express** or **UPS** are also available, but they are more business-oriented.

NEWSPAPERS AND MAGAZINES

Every city or state has its own newspapers and listings magazines. In Berlin the most widely read newspapers are *Berliner Zeitung*, *Der Tagesspiegel* and *Berliner Morgenpost*. In southern Germany it is *Süddeutsche Zeitung*. Popular national newspapers include *Frankfurter Allgemeine Zeitung* and *Bild*. *Der Spiegel*, Germany's leading news magazine, has an English-language version online. Major German cities have a listings magazine called *PRINZ* – where *PRINZ* is not available, ask for the *Stadtmagazin*.

Foreign language publications, such as the *International Herald Tribune*, the *Guardian*, *Le Monde*, *El País*, and *Corriere della Sera*, are available at kiosks, railway stations and airports, as well as in more expensive hotels.

TELEVISION AND RADIO

German television is exclusively in German – all foreign movies are dubbed rather than subtitled. Non-German broadcasts are hard to find, but hotels usually

provide a number of English-language channels, such as *BBC World*, *CNN* and *NBC Super Channel*. German sports channels often show soccer highlights and major sporting events can be watched at most sports bars. Very little English-language radio is available terrestrially, although *BBC World* and *NPR* can be picked up in most parts of Germany.

DIRECTORY

INTERNATIONAL AND LOCAL CALLS

Deutsche Telekom
www.telekom.com

MOBILE PHONES

BASE
www.base.de

Skype
www.skype.com

INTERNET AND EMAIL

Internet cafés
www.online-cafes.net

Wi-Fi hotspots
www.hotspot-locations.de

POSTAL SERVICES

DHL Express
Tel (0)1805 34 53 001 (national).
Tel (0)1805 34 53 003 (international).

FedEx
Tel (0)1803 123 800.

PIN Mail
www.pin-ag.de.

Postbank Finanzcenter
www.postbank.de

UPS
Tel (0)1805 882 663.

TRAVEL INFORMATION

Travelling in Germany is very efficient and easy. All of the big cities have airports, most of which offer international connections. The entire country is linked by a dense network of motorways with convenient facilities for travellers, while main roads are also of a high standard and are well signposted. Rail travel throughout the

Lufthansa plane

country is comfortable and reliable; for longer journeys it is worth taking advantage of the fast connections offered by InterCity Express (ICE). Buses are also comfortable and efficient and are particularly useful in rural areas not served by rail. In German cities, trams, buses and sometimes underground rail systems provide reliable services.

![The arrival hall of Dusseldorf airport]

The arrival hall of Dusseldorf airport

ARRIVING BY AIR

Germany's most important airports are Frankfurt am Main, Munich, Cologne-Bonn and Düsseldorf, from where connecting flights can be made to other German cities. Airport expansion in Berlin will create a major air hub on completion in mid-2012.

The country's national carrier, **Lufthansa**, operates regular, scheduled flights to most of the world's major destinations. **British Airways** also offers regular flights to Germany from London (Heathrow and Gatwick) as well as from several regional airports in the United Kingdom. The US is well served, with flights to German cities, particularly to Frankfurt, which is Germany's largest airport and one of the busiest in Europe. Direct flights are usually available from major US cities, including New York (JFK), Washington, DC, Boston, Chicago, San Francisco and Los Angeles. Although Canada does not

have many direct flights to Germany, **AirCanada** operates a regular flight from Toronto to Frankfurt.

Among the busiest airports are Düsseldorf, Munich, and Cologne-Bonn. In 2012, Tegal airport in Berlin will close to make way for the Berlin Brandenburg International Airport (BBI) at Schönefeld, a major new airport, which will serve the whole of the capital.

Control tower at Munich's international airport

Frankfurt am Main is the largest German airport and is comprised of two huge terminals, which are connected by a fast overground railway. The modern Munich airport is somewhat smaller but still very busy. When changing planes, transfers may take longer due to the long walk between two terminals. Düsseldorf is smaller than Frankfurt and Munich Airports and easier to navigate, with a central building connecting the three terminals. Cologne-Bonn, a smaller airport, is usually hassle-free.

TICKETS AND FARES

The cost of scheduled airfares can vary considerably, so early reservation and online price comparison is a good idea. Cheap Apex tickets work for those willing to book and pay well in advance and unlikely to change their travel plans. They are not available for one-way journeys. All Apex airfares must be booked in advance (usually a minimum of at least 14 days); some require a 28-day advance booking to qualify for the lowest airline ticket prices.

When buying a ticket it is worth finding out about any price reductions for children, young people and elderly passengers. Students and passengers under the age of 26 are often eligible for discounts. If the journey is going to be undertaken by a large group, it is worth checking whether a group discount on the fare or a free ticket for the group leader is available.

The exterior of Cologne Bonn airport

Remember that once booked, it is extremely difficult if not impossible to reschedule discount tickets, so it is wise to take out insurance to cover the loss if travel plans have to be changed.

The cheapest airfares are often those offered by low-cost, no-frills airlines such as **EasyJet** and **Ryanair**, or by discount agents. The latter offer discounted seats on charter or scheduled flights.

DOMESTIC FLIGHTS

In addition to Lufthansa, there are a number of other smaller carriers in Germany including **Air Berlin** and **German Wings**. These carriers provide air links with small airports, such as Augsburg, Dortmund and Erfurt, that would not be economically viable for Lufthansa to operate. Smaller airlines often offer cheaper fares than Lufthansa on internal routes.

ON ARRIVAL

Prior to departure, you should check with authorities or online which items cannot be brought to Germany and what the import regulations are *(see p566)*. Normally, clearing customs and immigration is fast and painless in German airports.

All major German airports are served by public transportation. Information on transport into the city centre, tickets and fares can be found in the arrival hall or the lobby. Tickets should be purchased from vending machines before boarding trains or buses. On most forms of public transport, one or two pieces of luggage may be carried at no extra cost, for two or more items you may be charged extra.

Taxis are available from all of the main city airports. It is best to pre-book a taxi or confirm the cost of the journey before travelling.

DIRECTORY

AIRLINES

Air Berlin
Tel (01805) 73 78 00.
www.airberlin.com

Air Canada
Tel (069) 27 11 51 11.
www.aircanada.com

British Airways
Tel (01805) 00 34 19.
www.britishairways.com

Continental
Tel (01803) 21 26 10.
www.continental.com

Delta Air Lines
Tel (01803) 33 78 80.
www.delta.com

Easyjet
Tel (01805) 00 02 02.
www.easyjet.com

German Wings
Tel (0871) 702 99 87.
www.germanwings.com

Lufthansa
Tel (01805) 83 84 26.
www.lufthansa.com

Qantas
Tel (01805) 25 06 20.
www.qantas.com

Ryanair
Tel (0900) 116 05 00.
www.ryanair.com

United Airlines
Tel (069) 50 07 03 87,
www.united.com

AIRPORT	INFORMATION	DISTANCE FROM CENTRE	JOURNEY TIME TO CENTRE BY TAXI	JOURNEY TIME TO CENTRE BY PUBLIC TRANSPORT
Berlin Schönefeld	(0180) 500 01 86	20 km (12 miles)	45 min	S-Bahn: 35 min
Dresden	(0351) 881 33 60	9 km (5.5miles)	25 min	Bus: 30 min
Düsseldorf	(0211) 42 10	8 km (5 miles)	25 min	S-Bahn: 13 min
Frankfurt am Main	(01805) 372 46 36	10 km (6 miles)	20 min	Train: 11 min S-Bahn: 10 min
Hamburg	(040) 50 75 25 57	13 km (8 miles)	30 min	Bus: 30 min
Hannover	(0511) 97 70	12 km (7.5 miles)	20 min	S-Bahn: 13 min
Cologne-Bonn	(02203) 40 400 1	Bonn: 28 km (17.5 miles) Cologne: 17 km (10.5 miles)	Bonn: 15 min Cologne: 20 min	Bus to Bonn: 35 min Bus to Cologne: 45 min
Munich	(089) 97 52 13 13	40 km (25 miles)	45 min	S-Bahn: 40 min Bus: 45 min
Nürnberg	(0911) 937 00	6 km (4 miles)	20 min	Bus: 45 min U-Bahn: 12 min

Travelling by Train and Ferry

Travelling around Germany by train is not the cheapest form of transport, but it is undoubtedly one of the most comfortable. German trains are renowned for their punctuality, safety and cleanliness, though in peak travel season, visitors may feel that these are a little overrated. Germany is also well served by ports to which ferries and passenger ships operate.

InterCity Express train

ARRIVING BY TRAIN

There are regular rail services into Germany from most European cities. Travelling by train from the UK usually costs more than flying. The most common routes into Germany are to travel to Brussels by **Eurostar** or take the **Eurotunnel** shuttle to France and continue your journey by road or rail.

TRAVELLING BY TRAIN

Germany's fastest trains, InterCity Express (ICE), can travel at more than 200 km/h (125 mph), which means that a journey from Hamburg to Munich takes only a few hours. *ICE* and *ICE Sprinter* trains (even faster) operate on routes linking the largest cities.

Somewhat slower and less expensive are the *InterCity (IC)* trains, which stop only at larger towns and cities. When travelling over shorter distances it is often quicker to take the *Regional Express (RE)* trains. Alternative service providers like **Interconnex** and **Metronom** often have lower fares than **Deutsche Bahn** but run less frequently.

Train aficionados can enjoy a trip on one of the steam-engine trains travelling along the Baltic coast (**Rasender Roland**) or a mountain route (**Brockenbahn**).

DB

Logo of German railways (Deutsche Bahn)

RAILWAY STATIONS

In large towns and cities, railway stations are generally located in the centre. They include dozens of shops (often open on Sundays), car rental firms, hotel reservation bureaux, and other services, such as cash points, left luggage provision and public toilets with shower facilities.

TICKETS AND FARES

Train fares are expensive in Germany and express trains have a surcharge (*Zuschlag*). For multiple train trips, buy a BahnCard, which gives a 25 or 50 per cent discount. Otherwise, discounts are available only if tickets are bought 3 or 7 days ahead and low-price seats have not sold out.

When planning a lengthy stay in Germany and travelling around the country, it is worth acquiring an Inter-Rail card, which is available to every European citizen, regardless of age. Regional tickets, offering unlimited travel within a state for a set period of time, are also available. Each year the variety of discounted fares to which this card entitles the bearer is extended, so it is worth checking out the full range. Schoolchildren and students are entitled to a reduced-rate

TRAIN ROUTES AND FERRY PORTS IN GERMANY

0 kilometres   75

0 miles   75

KEY

—— Main railway lines

⛴ Ferry port

(Map labels: Århus, Fredericia; Westerland (Sylt); Flensburg; København; Niebüll; Puttgarden; Ostseebad Binz; Stralsund; Kiel; Warnemünde; Seebad Heringsdorf; Neumünster; Rostock; Lübeck; Schwerin; Pasewalk; Norddeich Mole; Hamburg; Neustrelitz; Szczecin; Emden; Ludwigslust; Oldenburg; Bremen; Wittenberge; Emden Außenhafen; Uelzen; Stendal; Berlin; Frankfurt (Oder); Bad Bentheim; Hannover; Wolfsburg; Potsdam; Warszawa Poznán; Amsterdam Schipol; Osnabrück; Magdeburg; Amsterdam; Rheine; Braunschweig; Lutherstadt Wittenberg; Cottbus; Krakow; Recklinghausen; Münster; Bielefeld; Hildesheim; Görlitz; Gelsenkirchen; Hamm; Paderborn; Halle (Saale); Leipzig; Riesa; Oberhausen; Dortmund; Göttingen; Dresden; Wrocław; Duisburg; Bochum; Nordhausen; Weimar; Prague, Brno, Vienna, Budapest; Düsseldorf Flughafen; Essen; Hagen; Kassel; Eisenach; Düsseldorf; Wuppertal; Solingen; Bebra; Erfurt; Jena; Köln; Aachen; Montabaur; Limburg; Giessen; Fulda; Saalfeld; Bonn; Koblenz; Lichtenfels; Brussels, Paris; Frankfurt (Main); Wiesbaden; Aschaffenburg; Bamberg; Mainz; Würzburg; Erlangen; Trier; Ffm Flughafen; Darmstadt; Nürnberg; Luxembourg; Kaiserslautern; Mannheim; Saarbrücken; Heidelberg; Ansbach; Regensburg; Paris; Karlsruhe; Treuchtlingen; Plattling; Passau; Baden-Baden; Aalen; Ingolstadt; Vienna, Linz; Strasbourg, Paris; Stuttgart; Augsburg; Vienna, Budapest, Klagenfurt, Graz, Zagreb, Ljubljana; Offenburg; Ulm; München; Salzburg; Tübingen; Memmingen; Kufstein; Berchtesgaden; Freiburg; Friedrichshafen; Kempten; Singen; Lindau; Konstanz; Garmisch-Partenkirchen; Insbruck, Verona, Milan, Venice; Zürich, Interlaken, Brig, Chur; Basel; Zürich; Oberstdorf; Bregenz, Zürich, Innsbruck)

---

card. Non-European residents can buy a Eurail global, regional or country pass.

Train tickets can be bought and reservations made online, at travel agents or at the *Reisezentrum* (travel centre) at railway stations. It is simple to plan your journey yourself using this facility. Reservations cost €5 per person for a return trip if paid online with a ticket purchase, or €9 at a ticket counter.

Advance booking is necessary for the ICE Sprinter and Thalys trains (between Cologne and Aachen). The sleeper CityNightLine trains also require reservations. On all other trains, reservations are advisable when travelling at peak times or in a group.

ARRIVING BY FERRY

Visitors travelling to Germany by car from the UK will have to decide which crossing to use (unless using the Channel Tunnel). The crossings from Dover to Ostend, in Belgium, or to Calais, in France, are the shortest, while the Harwich to Hook of Holland route is useful for those travelling from further north. There are many links between German ports and other countries. The main ferry terminals are Kiel, Lübeck and Rostock on the Baltic Sea coast. **Color Lines** run a service from Oslo (Norway) to Kiel and **Scandlines** operate between Trelleborg (Sweden) to Rostock and Sassnitz. Scandlines also run ferries from Denmark.

Ship taking passengers to Helgoland

Travelling by Car and Coach

Sign for parking ticket machine

A fast and comfortable way of travelling around Germany is to use the motorways. The excellent network of toll-free routes guarantees fast progress over longer distances, while a well-maintained system of main roads enables you to reach interesting places throughout the country. Motorways have the advantage of regularly sited service stations, where travellers can stop for fuel and something to eat. On lesser roads and in remote areas, petrol stations may be few and far between.

A selection of traffic signs on German roads

ARRIVING BY CAR

With the addition of Poland and the Czech Republic to the Schengen Area, border checkpoints are now largely non-existent. Border stations do occasionally check cars, and trucks. Trains and tourist buses are sometimes stopped for passport checks.

Those wishing to drive to Germany from the UK will need to travel to France with their vehicle either by ferry or on the Eurotunnel shuttle *(see p578)*.

WHAT YOU NEED

When driving in Germany, visitors must carry a valid driving licence as well as their vehicle's registration document and a valid insurance policy. All cars must carry a plate indicating country of origin, a first-aid kit and a red warning triangle for use in case of breakdown.

If you plan to drive in large cities, check whether you need an environmental badge (*Umweltplakette, see p582*).

ROADS AND TOLLS

The German motorway network is extensive. Roads are toll-free and have regularly spaced petrol stations as well as service areas with parking areas, toilets, restaurants and motels. On the hard shoulder there are yellow poles with emergency buttons, which can be used to call for help in case of breakdown or accident. An *Autobahn* (motorway) is indicated by the letter "A" and a number – some also have a letter "E" and a number, denoting that the road crosses the German border. A *Bundesstraße* (main road) is indicated by the letter "B" and a number.

Motorway telephone

ADDITIONAL ROAD SIGNS

In addition to internationally understood road signs on German roads, there are a few other signs. On motorways, for example, a yellow triangular warning sign with a row of cars is a warning about the possibility of traffic jams,

which may be accompanied by the word *Stau*. On mountain roads, a warning sign showing a car tyre wrapped in a chain, accompanied by the word *Schnee*, warns against driving without chains when there is snow.

A diversion is indicated by the colour yellow and the word *Umleitung*, while the diversion route is indicated by the letter "U" followed by the number of the road. A sign with the word *Baustelle* always precedes a stretch that is being renovated.

A sign showing a horizontal blue arrow with the word *Einbahnstraße* indicates a one-way street.

RULES OF THE ROAD

Germans on the whole drive in accordance with the regulations. They are generally courteous, but they can be a little aggressive, particularly on motorways. German drivers hurtle along the outside lane at great speed and get very annoyed if they have to slow down because of other drivers. Visitors should be very careful if they are not used to driving on the right.

Seatbelts are compulsory and children under 12 must sit in the back, with babies and toddlers in child seats.

In the event of an accident on the motorway, or if a traffic jam necessitates an abrupt reduction in speed, drivers should turn on their flashing emergency lights to warn drivers behind of the impending danger.

Driving after drinking a glass of beer or wine (50mg/dl) is allowed, but if an accident occurs, the consequences will be more severe if alcohol is found in your blood.

Fuel station at a motorway service area

Cars in heavy traffic on the Autobahn A3 near Ratingen

In built-up areas the speed limit is 50 km/h (31 mph); beyond this it is 100 km/h (62 mph), and on motorways there is no limit. When travelling with a caravan or trailer outside built-up areas, do not exceed 70 km/h (44 mph), and on motorways 100 km/h (62 mph). Drivers will be fined for speeding, tailgating and parking offences. Note that parking meters may be quite far away from where you park.

BREAKDOWN SERVICES

In the event of a breakdown, turn on your flashing emergency lights and position a warning triangle 100 m (100 yd) behind your vehicle. Roadside assistance is offered by **ADAC** and **AVD** automobile associations – although they may insist you become a member. If you breakdown when lost, use one of the telephones set at intervals along the hard shoulder *(see p580)*. If a road accident occurs, contact the police immediately.

CAR HIRE

Car-hire firms such as **Avis**, **Hertz** and **Sixt Rent-a-Car** can be found at airports and railway stations. Drivers need to produce their passport and driving licence. Most rental agencies require drivers to be over the age of 21 and to have an international licence.

HITCHHIKING

Hitchhiking is popular among young people, but a safer method of finding a lift or a travelling companion is through **Mitfahrzentrale**, a contact agency for drivers who offer spare seats on a journey for an agreed fee. You can even catch a ride from or to other EU countries, (including the UK).

ARRIVING BY COACH

Travelling to Germany by coach from the UK is not a very attractive option, as the journey times are very long and the fares are not particularly cheap. Routes are operated by **Eurolines**, depart at Victoria Coach Station and arrive at Berlin's central coach station at the Funkturm (ZOB). Other routes, also departing from Victoria Station, terminate in Frankfurt, Duesseldorf, Cologne, Dortmund or Munich.

TRAVELLING BY COACH

There is a good network of inter-city coach services in Germany, and journeys are generally cheaper than travelling by express train. Most towns have a central station (*Zentraler Omnibus Bahnhof*) close to the train station. It is here that most bus services originate and where timetables can be obtained and tickets purchased. All national bus companies have websites, making ticket purchases easy. Many local coach services also operate from the central bus station, so it is easy to make a connection on arrival. **Reisebus 24** offers a search and reservation portal for bus tours of Germany

Comfortable, long-distance, double-decker coaches

Travelling within Cities

The S-Bahn logo

Driving around Germany's huge cities is not easy, and the historic centres are best visited on foot. Large towns often suffer from traffic congestion and parking can be hard to find. It is advisable to leave your car in a car park on the outskirts and use the city/suburban railway (S-Bahn), underground (U-Bahn), trams or city buses. The latter operate frequent services and can usually avoid traffic jams as they run in dedicated traffic lanes. All modes of public transport run less frequently on weekends.

Electric car charging station in Berlin

GREEN TRAVEL

Public transportation in Germany is extensive and reliable within urban areas and there are fast train connections between cities. There is not much need for a car unless you wish to explore the countryside extensively. Some car rental companies offer hybrid or electric cars, and many taxis run on bio fuel.

There is an emphasis on public and alternative transport in Germany. Many cities have introduced low-emission zones, which only allow vehicles with an **Umwelt Permit** (*Umweltplakette*). Tourists need to obtain this permit prior to travelling to Germany in their own car (*see p583*).

Bike rentals are everywhere, and with a good network of bike lanes and paths, Germany is a safe country to ride a bicycle. Drivers are very aware of bikes. Many tour operators offer guided bicycle tours – a good way to start and gather confidence on two wheels. **German Cycling Tours** offers guided bike tours of Germany and **Fahradreise** runs a portal with search engines for bicycle tours and accommodation, arranged by region, price and date.

Bike & Bus is an interesting concept that works like a shuttle for cyclists. You tour Europe by bus while your bike is transported in a trailer and available for use where the shuttle stops.

U-BAHN AND S-BAHN

Most big German cities have a network of fast connections by underground railway (U-Bahn) and commuter rail (S-Bahn). The U-Bahn offers frequent services – in peak hours, every 3–5 minutes – and individual stations are quite close to each other. The S-Bahn offers less frequent services, every 10–20 minutes, and connects city centres with the suburbs.

Generally, S- and U-Bahn, buses and trams within a city use the same tickets. Tickets can be bought from machines at the entrance to stations or on platforms; the tickets need to be validated in the red punching machines nearby. Railway stations have no ticket-operated barriers, but tickets are frequently checked and €40 fines are imposed on the spot for those not holding a valid ticket.

U-Bahn stations are indicated by square signs with a white "U" on a dark blue background, while S-Bahn stations have round signs with a white "S" on a green background. On maps of the network, each line of the U- and S-Bahn is marked in a different colour and has its own number. The direction of the route is indicated by the name of the terminus station. On every platform a display shows the destination of the next incoming train. A white circle or oval on the map indicates an interchange station.

Carriage doors on U- and S-Bahn trains are sometimes opened manually, but they close automatically. Passengers are not allowed to board the train after an operator's call of "*Zurückbleiben!*" (the doors are about to close).

BUSES

Bus operating hours vary from city to city and are much shorter in rural areas. Timetables can be found online or in ticket or tourist offices. Bus tickets can be purchased from the driver.

During the journey, the driver generally announces the name of the bus stop that the bus is approaching. In the centre of town, this is not so important, as in heavy traffic the bus stops at every bus stop. However, further away from the city centre or when traffic is lighter, you will need to listen for these announcements. At many bus stops, the driver will pull in only on request, so passengers must press the "Halt" button in plenty of time.

A city bus in Munich

A modern type of tram that operates in German cities

TRAMS

Trams are comfortable and do not get stuck in traffic jams. They run as frequently as buses do and have similar operating hours – check with local tourist offices or online for more information.

TICKETS

Large cities are generally divided into public transport zones, with the cost of a ticket depending on which zones are travelled through.

In addition to standard tickets (*Normaltarif*), there are also cheaper tickets (*Kurzstrecke*) that limit you to short distances. In many cities you can buy tickets in the form of a strip, which is punched according to the length of your journey.

Children under 14 travel at a reduced rate, while those under the age of six go free. Other types of tickets include a one-day ticket (*Tageskarte*), a one-day group ticket (*Gruppentageskarte*), and a weekly ticket (*7-Tage-Karte*). Some towns issue a Welcome-Card that includes travel, plus discounts at local attractions.

Most U-Bahn and S-Bahn trains permit transportation of bicycles in designated cars with a separate ticket.

DRIVING

Many cities, including Berlin, Munich and Cologne, have introduced a low-emissions zone, indicated by the word *Umwelt* in a red circle. All vehicles must carry a permit in these zones or incur a fine. Permits can be bought online (*see Directory*). Alternatively, use "Park and Ride" (P+R) facilities near S-Bahn stations.

Watch out for bus lanes marked by round blue signs, which can only be used by taxis and cyclists.

Parking in towns can be difficult, the best option is to find a car park (*Parkhaus*). Cars left in a controlled parking zone must display a ticket bought from a machine nearby. Illegally parked cars can be towed; retrieving them is expensive and difficult.

Cream coloured taxis found throughout Germany

TAXIS

Taxis are a comfortable though expensive way of getting around. If several people share a cab however, it can be cheaper than using the bus or train. All taxis are cream coloured and have a "TAXI" sign on the roof; this is illuminated if the taxi is free. Taxis can be hailed on the street or booked by telephone. They can also be picked up at taxi ranks, though these are rare.

CYCLING

Cycling is popular in Germany. There are numerous cycle lanes, making it safe, and many junctions have special lights for cyclists. Bicycles can be hired from hostels or at various hire places (*Fahrrad-verleih*). In some major cities, you can use the **Call-A-Bike** hire system. It is relatively expensive – about €15 a day, unless you hold a BahnCard.

DIRECTORY

GREEN TRAVEL

Bike and Bus
www.bike-and-bus.de

Fahrradreisen
www.fahrradreisen.de

German Cycling Tours
www.germancyclingtours.com

UMWELT Permits
www.umwelt-plakette.de

PUBLIC TRANSPORTATION NETWORKS

BVG Berlin
www.bvg.de

HVV Hamburg
www.hvv.de

MVV Munich
www.mvv-muenchen.de

VGF Frankfurt/M.0
www.vgf-ffm.de

TAXIS

Berlin
Berlin Taxi
Tel (030) 21 01 01.

Frankfurt
Taxis Frankfurt
Tel (069) 23 00 01 or
(069) 25 00 01.

Hamburg
Taxi Hamburg
Tel (040) 666 666.

Munich
Taxi Central
Tel (089) 21 610.

CYCLING

Call-A-Bike
Tel 07000 522 522.
www.callbike-interaktiv.de

Bicycles for public hire near the Hofgarten in Munich

General Index

Acknowledgments

Dorling Kindersley and Wiedza i Życie would like to thank the following people for their help in preparing this guide:

Additional Text
Michał Jaranowski, Barbara Sudnik-Wójcicka, Grażyna Winiarska, Konrad Gruda, Bożena Steinborn

Additional Photographs
Amin Akhtar, Francesca Bondy, Maciej Bronarski, Demetrio Carrasco, Witold Danilkiewicz, Claire Jones Grzegorz Kłosowski, Renata and Marek Kosińscy, Sergiusz Michalski, Nils Meyer, Ian O'Leary, Jürgen Scheunemann, Andrzej Zygmuntowicz and Ireneusz Winnicki, Władysław Wisławski

Publishing Manager
Helen Townsend

Managing Art Editor
Kate Poole

Consultant
Gerhard Bruschke

Factcheckers
Joel Dullroy, Claudia Himmelreich, Barbara Sobeck, Jürgen Scheunemann

Director of Publishing
Gillian Allan

Editorial and Design Assistance
Sam Atkinson, Claire Baranowski, Sonal Bhatt, Hilary Bird, Arwen Burnett, Susi Cheshire, Sherry Collins, Lucinda Cooke, Jo Cowen, Conrad Van Dyk, Jeremy Gray, Marcus Hardy, Lucinda Hawksley, Christine Heilman, Jacky Jackson, Claire Jones, Maite Lantaron, Carly Madden, Nicola Malone, Jeroen van Marle, Claire Marsden, Ferdie McDonald, Sam Merrell, Rebecca Milner, Kate Molan, Casper Morris, Sangita Patel, Marianne Petrou, Dave Pugh, Marisa Renzullo, Simon Ryder, Sadie Smith, Andrew Szudek, Leah Tether, Karen Villabona, Stewart J. Wild

Additional Picture Research
Rachel Barber, Marta Bescos, Rhiannon Furbear

The publisher would also like to thank all the people and institutions who allowed photographs belonging to them to be reproduced, as well as granting permission to use photographs from their archives:

Archäologische Staatssammlung in Munich; Arthothek (Jürgen Hinrichsowi); Bavaria Filmstadt; Bayerisches Nationalmuseum in Munich; Bildarchiv Preussischer Kulturbesitz in Berlin (Heidrun Klein); Bildvorlagen Römerschatz – Gäubodenmuseum Straubing (Dr. Prammer); Bischöfliches Dom- und Diözesanmuseum Mainz (Dr. Hansowi-Jurgenowi Kotzurowi); Brecht-Weigel-Gedenkstätte in Berlin (Elke Pfeil); Bridgeman Art Library; Bröhan-Museum in Berlin (Ingrid Jagr and Frau Betzker); Brücke-Museum in Berlin; Brüder-Grimm-Museum in Kassel; Corbis; Das Domkapitel (Gertraut Mockel, Büro Dr Georg Minkenberg); Deutsches Apothekenmuseum in Heidelberg; Deutsches Historisches Museum in Berlin (Kathi Rumlow); Deutsche Presse Agentur (dpa) in Berlin (Tanija Teichmann); Deutsches Museum in Munich (Sigrid Schneider and Marlene Schwarz); Deutsches Schifffahrtsmuseum in Bremerhaven (Hansowi-Walterowi Kewelohowi); Deutsches Tapetenmuseum Kassel (Sabine Thümmler); Deutsches Technikmuseum Berlin (Renate Förster); Diözesanmuseum in Bamberg (Birgit Kandora); Dombauverwaltung des Metropolitankapitels Köln (Birgit Lambert); Dresden Museum für Geschichte der Stadt Dresden (Dr. Christel Wünsch); Flash Press Media (Sylwii Wilgockiej); Forschungs- und Gedenkstätte Normannenstraße (Stasi-Museum) in Berlin (Andrei Holland-Moritz); Fürstlich Hohenzollernsche Schlossverwaltung in Sigmaringen (Heldze Boban); Gemäldegalerie Alte Meister (Steffi Reh); Gemäldegalerie Neue Meister (Gisela Mehnert); Germanisches Nationalmuseum in Nuremberg (Hermanowi Maué); Hamburger Bahnhof in Berlin; Hamburger Kunsthalle; Hessisches Landesmuseum Kassel; Käthe-Kollwitz-Museum in Berlin (A. Ingrid Findell); Komische Oper Berlin (Gaby Hofmann); Kunstmuseum Düsseldorf (Anne-Marie Katins); Kunstsammlungen Paula Modersohn in Bremen (Hubertusowi Morgenthalowi); Kunstsammlungen zu Weimar (Angelice Goder); Kunstverlag Maria Laach (Helmutowi Keipowi); Kurdirektion des Berchtesgadener Landes (Vroni Aigner, Birgit Tica); Landesmuseum Trier (Margot Redwanz); LBB Photo Archives (Dyrektorowi Christophowi Kalischowi); Linden-Museum Stuttgart, Staatliches Museum für Völkerkunde (Dr. Doris Kurelli); Lutherstube in Wittenberg (Jutcie Strehle); Markgräflisches Opernhaus in Bayreuth; Mercedes-Benz-Museum in Stuttgart; Museum am Ostwall in Dortmund; Museum der Bildenden Künste in Leipzig (Roswitha Engel); Museum Folkwang in Essen, Stadt Essen (Mr Hildebrandowi); Museum of the City of Berlin; Porzellansammlung (Ulrike Maltschew); Rheinisches Landesmuseum Bonn (Dr Gerhard Bauchhenß); Rüstkammer (Yvonne Brandt); Schlösserverwaltung in Munich (Frau Gerum); Seebul Ada and Emil Nolde (Dr Andreasowi Fluckowi); Staatliche Graphische Sammlung in Munich (Wiebke Tomaschek); Staatliche Kunstsammlungen Dresden, Albertinum,Grünes Gewölbe; Staatliche Porzellan-Manufaktur Meißen GMBH (Christine Mangold); Staatliche Schlösser und Gärten, Pforzheim (Herr Braunowi); Staatsarchiv Hamburg (Kathrin Berger); Staatsgalerie Stuttgart (Frau Fönnauer); Städelsches Kunstinstitut in Frankfurt am Main (Elisabeth Heinemann); Stadt Köln, Wallraf-Richartz-Museum in Cologne (Dr Roswitha Neu-Kock and Dr Mai); Stadtmuseum in Munich; Stiftung Luthergedenkstätten in Sachsen-Anhalt; Stiftung Preussische Schlösser und Gärten Berlin (Carli Kamarze); Superstock Polska Sp. z.o.o. (Elżbiecie Gajewskiej); Von der Heydt-Museum Wuppertal (Margarecie Janz); Wartburg-Stiftung in Eisenach (Petrze Wilke); Zefa (Ewie Kozłowskiej)

The publisher would also like to thank the following for their assistance on the guide:
Joanna Minz for coordinating information, Tamara and Jacek Draber for their help with correspondence and telephone contacts, Jürgen Christoffer of Deutscher Wetterdienst for meteorological information.

Picture Credits
a-above; b-below/bottom; c-centre; f-far; l-left; r-right; t-top

Works of art have been reproduced with the permission of the following copyright holders: DACS, London 2011: 27cl, 31cl, 59clb, 87cl, 89tl, © Munch Museum/Munch - Ellingsen Group, BONO, Oslo/DACS, London 2011 88cr, 405tc, 437cr; © Succession Picasso/DACS, 2011 96tl, 313crb

Aachener Dom (Copyright: Domkapitel Aachen – photo. Ann Münchow) 396t, 396ca, 396cb, 396t (Skarbiec), 397ca, 397cb, 397br, 397bl; **Alamy Images**: alwaysstock, LLC/Michael Hill 562tr; archivberlin Fotoagentur GmbH/J. Henkelmann 107tl; Arco Images 12tr, 558cr; Jon Arnold Images/Walter Bibikow 22t; BL Images Ltd 10cl, 231cr; Caro/Waechter 583c; David R. Frazier Photolibrary, Inc. 12bc; FAN travelstock/Sabine Lubenow 11c, 11tl, 560br, 561cl; Iconotexc/Ettore Venturini 559tr; imagebroker/ Manfred Bail 231tl, 580bl; imagebroker/Michael Fischer 561br; imagebroker/Stephan Goerlich 232tc; ImageState/ Pictor International 11br; Andre Jenny 230cr; Stan Kujawa 13tr; Yadid Levy 230bl, 522cl; Werner Otto 13br, 142; Gillian Price 560cl; John Stark 10br; Robert Stainforth 576cla; **Albertinum** (Dresden) 172t; **Allianz Arena München Stadion GmbH** 233tl; **Amt für Stadtmarketing und Touristik, Limburg** (Mr Michael Hild) 219d; **Archäologische Staatssammlung** (Munich) 219d; **Arthotek** 30t, 30b, 31cla, 31blb, 54t, 176ca, 176cb, 176b, 177t, 177ca, 177cb, 177fb, 175cb, 222cb, 261b, 436t, 436b, 437t, 437cb, 444t; Joachim Blauel 31bra, 50t, 222t, 222b, 223cb, 260t, 294cr; Blauel/Gnamm 218t, 222ca, 223t, 223ca, 259tr; Bayer d'Mitko 223c; Sophie-R. Gnamm 226; Alexander Koch 31trb; Christoph Sandig 470d; G. Westermann 432b, 437t. **Basic AG** 558bl; **Bavaria Filmstadt** 227t; **Bayerische Staatsoper** Wilfried Hösl 232bl; **Berlin Tourismus Marketing GmbH** www.berlin-tourist-information. de 97br, 569cra; visitberlin.de 556br; **BerlinerFestspiele**

Bianka Gobel 109tl; **Berliner Sparkasse** 572bl; **Brecht-Weigel-Gedenkstätte** (Berlin) 101c; **Bridgeman Art Library** 34br, 103t; **Britstock** 328–329; **Bronarski Maciej** 334t, 350t, 350c, 350b, 351t, 351ca, 351cb, 351b; **Bröhan-Museum** (Berlin) 96t; **Brüder-Grimm-Museum** (Kassel) 364tr, 368tr (© Staatliche Museum Kassel). **City of Munich – Fire Department** 571tl; **Congress-und Tourismus-Zentrale Nürnberg** 257tl; **Corbis** 28tr, 28bra, 28blb, 172c (© Jack Fields/Corbis), 446–447 (©Bob Krist/Corbis), 454 (© Nilk Wheeler/Corbis); Corbis Sygma/Annebicque Bernard 523tl; Michael S.Yamashita 523c; zefa/Wolfgang Deuter 211cr; zefa/Frank Lukasseck 182; Zefa/Herbert Spichtinger 232cr; Danilkiewicz Witold 425b, 466, 474t; **Deutsches Postbank** 575cl; **Deutsche Telekom** 574c; **Deutsches Apothekenmuseum** (Heidelberg) 298tr; **Deutsches Technikmuseum Berlin** 81b; **Deutsches Historisches Museum Berlin** (Zeughaus) 26b, 28c, 34ca, 34cla, 34clb, 34crb, 34br, 35cla, 35tlb, 35tr, 35clb, 35cb, 35cib, 35cbr (Holz & Kunststoff), 36 cla, 46, 52tl (R. Bemke), 52tr (Jurgen Liepe), 52c, 52b (A.C. Theil), 53t (R. Boemke), 54b, 55t, 55cla, 56cl, 60b, 61bl, 126tr, 126b, 127t; **Deutsches Museum** (Munich) 228–229 (all images), 568tl; **Deutsches Schiffahrtsmuseum Bremerhaven** 50d; **Diözesanmuseum** (Bamberg) 251t; **dpa** 26tra, 27tl, 27cra, 27crb, 27br, 27bl, 28tl, 28tr, 35cla, 35cra, 35bl, 46ti, 60ca, 139t, 109t, 205tl, 293t, 461t; Jens Büttner 61t; Claus Felix 43b; Matthias Hiekel 40b, Peter Förster 40t; Wulf Hirschberger 41b; Ralf Hirschberger 38b; Peer Grimm 22tr; Frank Leonhardt 39t; Wolfgang Kluge 28b; Wolfgang Kumm 61br; Kay Nietfeld 38t, 39t; Frank Mächler 41t; Carsten Rehder 38t; Wulf Pfeiffer 41d; Martin Schutt 42t, 181d, Roland Scheidemann 43t; Ingo Wagner 61t, Heinz Wieseler 42b; **DK Images** Posteritati/Judith Miller 112cl; **Dresden Museum für Geschichte der Stadt Dresden** 55crb. **Eisenach-Wartburg Stiftung** 186cla, 186cla, 186clb, 186crb, 187c. **Foto-Thueringen** Barbara Neumann 122c. **Gäubodenmuseum Straubing** 47bl. **Germanisches Nationalmuseum** (Nuremberg) 260–61 (all images); **Getty Images** AFP 556cl, 571cla, 583br; Sean Gallup 582cla; Tina & Horst Herzig 561tr; Popperfoto 27tr; Andreas Rentz 368br; Patrik Stollarz 581tl; **Grünes Gewölbe** (Dresden) 172t.**Gullivers Bus GmnH** 581bl; **Hamburger Bahnhof** (Berlin) 93bl; **Hamburger Kunsthalle** (Hamburg) 30cla, 436t; **Hessisches Landesmuseum Kassel Deutsches Tapetenmuseum**) **Hotel Palace, Berlin** 484cl. KaDeWe store, Berlin 559bl; Quelle 559bl; **Käthe-Kollwitz-Museum** (Berlin) 87t; Kłosowski Grzegorz 24cra; **Kloster Maulbronn** 302t, 302b, 303cla, 303crb, 303b; **Köln Bonn Airport** 577tl; **Kölner Dom** 402tl, 402c, 402b, 403t, 403ca, 403cb, 403bl, 403br (© Dombauarchiv Köln, Matz und Schenk); **Komische Oper** (Berlin) Monika Ritterhaus 108b, 108br; **Kosińscy, Renata and Marek** 24clb, 24bra, 24blb, 25cla, 25tlb, 25blb, 204tl, 205ca, 205tr, 205cl, 205cr, 205br; **Kunstmuseum Düsseldorf** 30clb; **Kunstsammlungen Paula Modersohn** 433tl; **Kunstverlag Maria Laach** 334b, 358tl, 358tr, 358ca, 359t, 359ca, 359cb, 359b; **Kurdirektion des Berchtesgadener Landes** Storto, Leonberg 276b. **Landesmuseum Trier** Thomas Zühmer 342t; **Linden Museum für Völkerkunde** (Stuttgart) 310tlb; **Lübeck and Travemuende Tourist-Service GmbH HLTS** 462cla; **Ludwigsburg – Schloss** 306ca, 306cb, 306b, 307t; **Lutherstube** (Wittenberg) 127t. **Mainz – Dom** 335b (© M. Hankel-Studio); **Mercedes-Benz-Museum** (Stuttgart) 310tra; **Meyer Nils** 60cb; Michalski Sergiusz 20t; **Mittelalterliches Museum** (Rothenburg ob der Tauber) 262br; **Munich Police**

570cla, 571cl; **Museum der Bildenden Künste** (Leipzig) 51t (MdbK, Gerstenberger 1994); **Museum Brandhorst** 567br; **Museum Folkwang** (Essen) 31t; **Museum für Naturkunde** (Berlin) 93br; **Museum am Ostwall** (Dortmund) 390t; **Musikinstrumenten-Museum** (Berlin) 85ca. **Nationalmuseum** (Munich) 219t. **Opernhaus** (Bayreuth) 252t. **Philharmonie** (Berlin) 85t; **Photolibrary** imagebroker.net/Martin Moxter 574cla; **Popkomm GmbH** 109bc; **Presse- und Informationsamt des Landes Berlin** BTM/Drewes 92bl; BTM/Koch 92cla; G. Schneider 43t. **Rheinisches Landesmuseum Bonn** 408t; **Robert Harding Picture Library** H P Merten 13cl; **Rocco Forte Hotel de Rome** 485br; **Rosas Dance Company, Belgium** Herman Sorgeloos 109cr. **Schauspielhaus (Konzerthaus Berlin)** 72d; **Schloss Sigmaringen** 315b; **Karsten Schirmer** 108cl; **Schlösserverwaltung** (Munich) 246ca, 247t, 247ca, 247cb, 247b, 282t, 282ca, 282cb, 282b; **Schneider Guenter** 62–3; **Sea Life München** 233cr; **Slips Fashion,** Munich 230tc; **STA Travel** 569tr; **Staatliche Museen Preußischer Kulturbesitz** (Berlin) 48c, 55br, 56–7, 57tl, 57br, 58t, 58cra, 58clb, 58b, 59t, 59bl, 59br, 60t, 64br, 65cra, 75t, 76ca, 77t, 89t, 90cb, 91clb, 98cla, 104t, 124tl, 125brb; Hans-Joachim Bartsch 49e, 49b, 55bl, Jorg P. Anders 84c, 84b, 80b, 90ca, 90d, 90ca, 90b, 91t, 91cra, 91d; Grammes 48br; Klaus Göken 56b, 59c, 76b, 77d; Erich Lessing 74clb, 76t, 77cb; Jurgen Liepe 75c, 76cb; Georg Niedermeister 77ca; Arne Psille 47br, 48tr, 48bl; Steinkopf 81tr; **Staatliche Porzellan-Manufaktur Meißen GMBH** 34cra, 124tr, 124cra, 124clb, 124b, 125t, 125bra, Klaus Tänzer 125cra; **Staatsgalerie Stuttgart** 312tra, 312tlb, 312t, 312b, 313t, 313ca, 313cb, 313b; **Städelsches Kunstinstitut** (Frankfurt am Main) 378t, 378c, 378b, 379t, 379ca, 379cb, 379b; **Stadtmuseum Berlin** 69c, 71t; Hans-Joachim Bartsch 5t; Sudnik 25crb; **Stasi-Museum** (Berlin) 102b; **Stiftung Preussische Schlösser und Gärten Berlin** 54c, 98cl, 99ca, 99b, 99crb, 135cr, 136b, 139b; **Superstock Polska Sp. zo.o.** 324t; **Tourismuszentrale Rügen GmbH** Dieter Lindemann 478tr; **Tourist Office – Altötting** 270t, 270b; **Wallraf-Richartz-Museum** (Cologne) 404t, 404ca, 404cb, 404b, 405t, 405c, 405br, 405bl (© Rheinisches Bildarchiv); **www.dresden.de** Christoph Münch 168tr; **Zefa** 25cl, 202–3c, 387b, 412–13, 422bra, 422t, 423b, 433b, 450t, 450c, 451tl, 451tr, 451b, 453b, 478t; Bloemendal 5t; Damm 21b, 398b, 288, 394b, 451tra, 467d; Eckstein 23b, 423tl, 423tr, 477b; Freytag 19b, 204tr, 327t; Haenel 1, 313cb, 456b, 469t, 481t; Kehrer 25cr; Kinne 406t, 406b; Kohlhas 409t; Leidorf 15t, 15b; Rossenbach 8 9, 322–3, 398c, 410b, 411t, 412–13, 459b, 470t; Rose 411t; Steeger 423t; Streichan 352–3, 363t, 383b; Svenja-Foto 394t, 403cra; Waldkirch 450tr; M. Winkel 402tr; **Zwinger** (Dresden) 174t, 174cb, 175b; Gemäldegalerie Alte Meister 176t.

JACKET
Front - AWL IMAGES: Danita Delimont Stock.
Back - ALAMY IMAGES: ImageState/Pictor International cla; CORBIS: Jon Hicks bl, Herbert Spichtinger tl; DORLING KINDERSLEY: Paweł Wojcik clb.
Spine - AWL IMAGES: Danita Delimont Stock.
FRONT ENDPAPER
ALAMY IMAGES: Werner Otto R tc; CORBIS: Zefa/Frank Lukasseck R clb.

All other images © Dorling Kindersley.
For further information see: www.dkimages.com

SPECIAL EDITIONS OF DK TRAVEL GUIDES

DK Travel Guides can be purchased in bulk quantities at discounted prices for use in promotions or as premiums. We are also able to offer special editions and personalized jackets, corporate imprints, and excerpts from all of our books, tailored specifically to meet your own needs.

To find out more, please contact:
(in the United States) **SpecialSales@dk.com**
(in the UK) **TravelSpecialSales@uk.dk.com**
(in Canada) DK Special Sales at **general@tourmaline.ca**
(in Australia) **business.development@pearson.com.au**

Phrasebook

In an Emergency

Where is the telephone?	Wo ist das Telefon?	voh ist duss tel-e-fone?
Help!	Hilfe!	**hilf**-uh
Please call a doctor	Bitte rufen Sie einen Arzt	**bitt**-uh **roof**'n zee ine-en artst
Please call the police	Bitte rufen Sie die Polizei	**bitt**-uh **roof**'n zee dee poli-**tsy**
Please call the fire brigade	Bitte rufen Sie die Feuerwehr	**bitt**-uh roof'n zee dee **foyer**-vayr
Stop!	Halt!	**hult**

Communication Essentials

Yes	Ja	**yah**
No	Nein	**nine**
Please	Bitte	**bitt**-uh
Thank you	Danke	dunk-uh
Excuse me	Verzeihung	fair-**tsy**-hoong
Hello (good day)	Guten Tag	**goot**-en tahk
Goodbye	Auf Wiedersehen	owf-**veed**-er-zay-ern
Good evening	Guten Abend	goot'n **ahb**'nt
Good night	Gute Nacht	goot-uh **nukht**
Until tomorrow	Bis morgen	biss **morg**'n
See you	Tschüss	chooss
What is that?	Was ist das?	voss ist duss
Why?	Warum?	var-**room**
Where?	Wo?	**voh**
When?	Wann?	**vunn**
today	heute	**hoyt**-uh
tomorrow	morgen	**morg**'n
month	Monat	**mohn**-aht
night	Nacht	**nukht**
afternoon	Nachmittag	**nahkh**-mit-tahk
morning	Morgen	**morg**'n
year	Jahr	yar
there	dort	**dort**
here	hier	**hear**
week	Woche	**vokh**-uh
yesterday	gestern	**gest**'n
evening	Abend	**ahb**'nt

Useful Phrases

How are you? (informal)	Wie geht's?	vee gayts
Fine, thanks	Danke, es geht mir gut	dunk-uh, es gayt meer goot
Until later	Bis später	biss **shpay**-ter
Where is/are?	Wo ist/sind...?	voh ist/sind
How far is it to...?	Wie weit ist es...?	vee **vite** ist ess
Do you speak English?	Sprechen Sie Englisch?	shpresh'n zee **eng**-glish
I don't understand	Ich verstehe nicht	ish fair-**shtay**-uh nisht
Could you speak more slowly?	Könnten Sie langsamer sprechen?	**kurnt**-en zee **lung**-zam-er **shpresh**'n

Useful Words

large	gross	**grohss**
small	klein	**kline**
hot	heiss	**hyce**
cold	kalt	**kult**
good	gut	**goot**
bad	böse/schlecht	**burss**-uh/**shlesht**
open	geöffnet	g'**urff**-nett
closed	geschlossen	g'**shloss**'n
left	links	**links**
right	rechts	**reshts**
straight ahead	geradeaus	g'**rah**-der-**owss**

Making a Telephone Call

I would like to make a phone call	Ich möchte telefonieren	ish mer-shtuh tel-e-fon-**eer**'n
I'll try again later	Ich versuche es später noch einmal	ish fair-zookh-uh es **shpay**-ter nokh ine-mull
Can I leave a message?	Kann ich eine Nachricht hinterlassen?	kan ish **ine**-uh nakh-risht hint-er-**lahss**-en
answer phone	Anrufbeantworter	an-roof-be-**ahnt**-vort-er
telephone card	Telefonkarte	tel-e-**fohn**-kart-uh
receiver	Hörer	**hur**-er
mobile	Handy	han-dee
engaged (busy)	besetzt	b'zetst
wrong number	Falsche Verbindung	falsh-uh fair-**bin**-doong

Sightseeing

library	Bibliothek	bib-leo-**tek**
entrance ticket	Eintrittskarte	ine-tritz-**kart**-uh
cemetery	Friedhof	**freed**-hofe
train station	Bahnhof	**barn**-hofe
gallery	Galerie	**gall**-er-ree
information	Auskunft	**owss**-koonft
church	Kirche	**keersh**-uh
garden	Garten	**gart**'n
palace/castle	Palast/Schloss	pallast/shloss
place (square)	Platz	**plats**
bus stop	Haltestelle	**hal**-te-shtel-uh
national holiday	Nationalfeiertag	nats-yon-**ahl**-fire-tahk
theatre	Theater	tay-**aht**-er
free admission	Eintritt frei	ine-tritt fry

Shopping

Do you have/ Is there...?	Gibt es...?	geept ess
How much does it cost?	Was kostet das?	voss **kost**'t duss
When do you open/ close?	Wann öffnen Sie? schließen Sie?	vunn **off**'n zee **shlees**'n zee
this	das	duss
expensive	teuer	**toy**-er
cheap	preiswert	**price**-vurt
size	Größe	**gruhs**-uh
number	Nummer	**noom**-er
colour	Farbe	**farb**-uh
brown	braun	brown
black	schwarz	**shvarts**
red	rot	**roht**
blue	blau	**blau**
green	grün	**groon**
yellow	gelb	**gelp**

Types of Shop

antique shop	Antiquariat	antik-**var**-yat
chemist (pharmacy)	Apotheke	appo-**tay**-kuh
bank	Bank	**bunk**
market	Markt	**markt**
travel agency	Reisebüro	**rye-z**er-boo-roe
department store	Warenhaus	**vahr**'n-hows
chemist's, drugstore	Drogerie	droog-er-**ree**
hairdresser	Friseur	freezz-**er**
newspaper kiosk	Zeitungskiosk	tsytoongs-kee-osk
bookshop	Buchhandlung	**bookh**-hant-loong

bakery	Bäckerei	beck-er-**eye**
post office	Post	posst
shop/store	Geschäft/Laden	gush-**eft/lard**'n
film processing shop	Photogeschäft	**fo**-to-gush-**eft**
self-service shop	Selbstbedienungsladen	selpst-bed-**ee**-nungs-lard'n
shoe shop	Schuhladen	shoo-lard'n
clothes shop	Kleiderladen, Boutique	klyder-lard'n, boo-**teek**-uh
food shop	Lebensmittelgeschäft	**lay**-bens-mittel-gush-eft
glass, porcelain	Glas, Porzellan	**glars, Port-sellahn**

Staying in a Hotel

Do you have any vacancies?	Haben Sie noch Zimmer frei?	harb'n zee nokh **tsimm**-er-fry
with twin beds?	mit zwei Betten?	mitt tsvy bett'n
with a double bed?	mit einem Doppelbett?	mitt ine'm **dopp**'l-bet
with a bath?	mit Bad?	mitt **bart**
with a shower?	mit Dusche?	mitt **doosh**-uh
I have a reservation	Ich habe eine Reservierung	ish **harb**-uh ine-uh rez-er-**veer**-oong
key	Schlüssel	shlooss'l
porter	Pförtner	**pfert**-ner

Eating Out

Do you have a table for…?	Haben Sie einen Tisch für…?	harb'n zee tish foor
I would like to reserve a table	Ich möchte eine Reservierung machen	ish **mer**-shtuh ine-uh rezer-**veer**-oong makh'n
I'm a vegetarian	Ich bin Vegetarier	ish bin vegg-er-**tah**-ree-er
Waiter!	Herr Ober!	hair **oh**-bair!
The bill (check), please	Die Rechnung, bitte	dee **resh**-noong bitt-uh
breakfast	Frühstück	**froo**-shtock
lunch	Mittagessen	**mit**-targ-ess'n
dinner	Abendessen	**arb**'nt-ess'n
bottle	Flasche	**flush**-uh
dish of the day	Tagesgericht	**tahg**-es-gur-isht
main dish	Hauptgericht	**howpt**-gur-isht
dessert	Nachtisch	**nahkh**-tish
cup	Tasse	**tass**-uh
wine list	Weinkarte	vine-kart-uh
tankard	Krug	khroog
glass	Glas	**glars**
spoon	Löffel	**lerff**'l
teaspoon	Teelöffel	tay-lerff'l
tip	Trinkgeld	**trink**-gelt
knife	Messer	**mess**-er
starter (appetizer)	Vorspeise	**for**-shpize-uh
the bill	Rechnung	**resh**-noong
plate	Teller	**tell**-er
fork	Gabel	**gahb**'l

Menu Decoder

Aal	**arl**	eel
Apfel	**upf**'l	apple
Apfelschorle	**upf**'l-shoorl-uh	apple juice with sparkling mineral water
Apfelsine	**upf**'l-seen-uh	orange
Aprikose	upri-**kawz**-uh	apricot
Artischocke	arti-**shokh**-uh	artichoke
Aubergine (eggplant)	or-ber-jeen-uh	aubergine
Banane	bar-**narn**-uh	banana
Beefsteak	**beef**-stayk	steak
Bier	beer	beer
Bockwurst	**bokh**-voorst	a type of sausage
Bohnensuppe	burn-en-zoop-uh	bean soup
Branntwein	brant-vine	spirits
Bratkartoffeln	brat-kar-toff'ln	fried potatoes
Bratwurst	brat-voorst	fried sausage
Brötchen	bret-tchen	bread roll
Brot	brot	bread
Brühe	bruh-uh	broth
Butter	**boot**-ter	butter
Champignon	**shum**-pin-yong	mushroom
Currywurst	**kha**-ree-voorst	sausage with curry sauce
Dill	**dill**	dill
Ei	**eye**	egg
Eis	**ice**	ice/ ice cream
Ente	**ent**-uh	duck
Erdbeeren	ayrt-**beer**'n	strawberries
Fisch	**fish**	fish
Forelle	for-**ell**-uh	trout
Frikadelle	Frika-dayl-uh	rissole/hamburger
Gans	ganns	goose
Garnele	**gar**-nayl-uh	prawn/shrimp
gebraten	g'**braat**'n	fried
gegrillt	g'**grilt**	grilled
gekocht	g'**kokht**	boiled
geräuchert	g'**rowk**-ert	smoked
Geflügel	g'**floog**'l	poultry
Gemüse	g'**mooz**-uh	vegetables
Grütze	**grurt**-ser	groats, gruel
Gulasch	**goo**-lush	goulash
Gurke	**goork**-uh	gherkin
Hammelbraten	hamm'l-**braat**'n	roast mutton
Hähnchen	haynsh'n	chicken
Hering	**hair**-ing	herring
Himbeeren	him-**beer**'n	raspberries
Honig	**hoe**-nikh	honey
Kaffee	kaf-**fay**	coffee
Kalbfleisch	kalp-flysh	veal
Kaninchen	ka-**neensh**'n	rabbit
Karpfen	**karpf**'n	carp
Kartoffelpüree	kar-toff'l-pooray	mashed potatoes
Käse	**kayz**-uh	cheese
Kaviar	**kar**-vee-ar	caviar
Knoblauch	k'**nob**-lowkh	garlic
Knödel	k'**nerd**'l	noodle
Kohl	**koal**	cabbage
Kopfsalat	**kopf**-zal-aat	lettuce
Krebs	**krayps**	crab
Kuchen	**kookh**'n	cake
Lachs	**lahkhs**	salmon
Leber	**lay**-ber	liver
mariniert	mari-neert	marinated
Marmelade	marmer-**lard**-uh	marmalade, jam
Meerrettich	may-re-tish	horseradish
Milch	**milsh**	milk
Mineralwasser	minn-er-**arl**-vuss-er	mineral water
Möhre	**mer**-uh	carrot
Nuss	**nooss**	nut
Öl	**erl**	oil
Olive	o-**leev**-uh	olive
Petersilie	payt-er-**zee**-li-uh	parsley
Pfeffer	**pfeff**-er	pepper
Pfirsich	**pfir**-zish	peach
Pflaumen	**pflow**-men	plum
Pommes frites	pomm-**fritt**	chips/ French fries
Quark	kvark	soft cheese
Radieschen	ra-**deesh**'n	radish
Rinderbraten	**rind**-er-brat'n	joint of beef
Rinderroulade	**rind**-er-roo-lard-uh	beef olive
Rindfleisch	**rint**-flysh	beef
Rippchen	**rip**-sh'n	cured pork rib
Rotkohl	roht-koal	red cabbage
Rüben	rhoob'n	turnip
Rührei	**rhoo**-er-eye	scrambled eggs
Saft	**zuft**	juice
Salat	zal-aat	salad
Salz	**zults**	salt

Salzkartoffeln	zults-kar-toff'l	boiled potatoes
Sauerkirschen	zow-er-**keersh**'n	cherries
Sauerkraut	zow-er-krowt	sauerkraut
Sekt	**zekt**	sparkling wine
Senf	**zenf**	mustard
scharf	sharf	spicy
Schaschlik	shash-lik	kebab
Schlagsahne	shlahgg-zarn-uh	whipped cream
Schnittlauch	shnit-lowhkh	chives
Schnitzel	**shnitz**'l	veal or pork cutlet
Schweinefleisch	**shvine**-flysh	pork
Spargel	**shparg**'l	asparagus
Spiegelei	shpeeg'l-eye	fried egg
Spinat	shpin-art	spinach
Tee	**tay**	tea
Tomate	tom-art-uh	tomato
Wassermelone	vuss-er-me-lohn-uh	watermelon
Wein	**vine**	wine
Weintrauben	vine-trowb'n	grapes
Wiener Würstchen	veen-er voorst-sh'n	frankfurter
Zander	**tsan**-der	pike-perch
Zitrone	tsi-trohn-uh	lemon
Zucker	**tsook**-er	sugar
Zwieback	tsvee-bak	rusk
Zwiebel	**tsveeb**'l	onion

Numbers

0	null	**nool**
1	eins	**eye'ns**
2	zwei	**tsvy**
3	drei	**dry**
4	vier	**feer**
5	fünf	**foonf**
6	sechs	**zex**
7	sieben	**zeeb**'n
8	acht	**uhkht**
9	neun	**noyn**
10	zehn	**tsayn**
11	elf	**elf**
12	zwölf	**tserlf**
13	dreizehn	**dry**-tsayn
14	vierzehn	**feer**-tsayn
15	fünfzehn	**foonf**-tsayn
16	sechzehn	**zex**-tsayn
17	siebzehn	**zeep**-tsayn
18	achtzehn	**uhkht**-tsayn
19	neunzehn	**noyn**-tsayn
20	zwanzig	**tsvunn**-tsig
21	einundzwanzig	**ine**-oont-tsvunn-tsig
30	dreißig	**dry**-sig
40	vierzig	**feer**-sig
50	fünfzig	**foonf**-tsig
60	sechzig	**zex**-tsig
70	siebzig	**zeep**-tsig
80	achtzig	**uhkht**-tsig
90	neunzig	**noyn**-tsig
100	hundert	**hoond**'t
1000	tausend	**towz**'nt
1 000 000	eine Million	**ine**-uh **mill**-yon

Time

one minute	eine Minute	**ine**-uh min-**oot**-uh
one hour	eine Stunde	**ine**-uh **shtoond**-uh
half an hour	eine halbe Stunde	**ine**-uh hullb-uh **shtoond**-uh
Monday	Montag	**mohn**-targ
Tuesday	Dienstag	**deens**-targ
Wednesday	Mittwoch	**mitt**-vokh
Thursday	Donnerstag	**donn**-ers-targ
Friday	Freitag	**fry**-targ
Saturday	Samstag/ Sonnabend	**zums**-targ zonn-ah-bent
Sunday	Sonntag	**zon**-targ
January	Januar	**yan**-ooar
February	Februar	**fay**-brooar
March	März	**mairts**
April	April	april
May	Mai	my
June	Juni	**yoo**-ni
July	Juli	**yoo**-lee
August	August	ow-**goost**
September	September	zep-**tem**-ber
October	Oktober	ok-toh-ber
November	November	no-**vem**-ber
December	Dezember	day-**tsem**-ber
spring	Frühling	**froo**-ling
summer	Sommer	**zomm**-er
autumn (fall)	Herbst	**hairpst**
winter	Winter	**vint**-er

Road Map of Germany